THE AMERICAN ALPINE JOURNAL
2002

Above: Descending the south ridge of Jack Tar Peak, Rigneys Bjerg, Greenland (page 283). *Jim Gregson*
Cover: Stephen Koch on Luna, Mini Moonflower, Alaska ("Light Traveler," page 86). *Marko Prezelj*

Spires upon spires. The top photo shows lenticular clouds building over the Fitz Roy group in Argentine Patagonia, while the alpenglow at left offers hope of more promising conditions during the amazingly productive winter season 2001-2002 (see pages 316-327). *Topher Donahue (2)*

Far left: The Rabbit Ears near the Mendenhall Towers in the Juneau Icefield, Alaska Coast Range (page 253). *Jacek Maselko*

Nathan Martin descending from the summit of Fitz Roy after climbing Tonta Suerte ("True Value," page 144). *Tim O'Neill*

Corporate Friends

OF THE

AMERICAN ALPINE JOURNAL

We thank the following for their generous
financial support of the 2002
American Alpine Journal

Unclimbed peaks near Bassom Tso, eastern Tibet. *John Harlin III*

Mauro "Bubu" Bole during the first ascent of Women and Chalk on Shipton Spire, Pakistan (page 369). *Fabio Dandri*

Friends
OF THE
AMERICAN ALPINE JOURNAL

WE THANK THE FOLLOWING FOR THEIR
GENEROUS FINANCIAL SUPPORT:

Ann Carter
Yvon Chouinard
Gregory Miller
Louis Reichardt

The H. Adams Carter Endowment Fund
for The American Alpine Journal

THE AMERICAN ALPINE JOURNAL
710 Tenth Street, Golden, Colorado 80401
Telephone: (303) 384-0110 Fax: (303) 384-0111
E-mail: getinfo@americanalpineclub.org

ISBN 0-930410-91-2

Unclimbed peaks near Bassom Tso, Eastern Tibet. *John Harlin III*

Rob Owens during the first ascent of Haunted by Waters, near Banff, Alberta. *Andrew Querner*

The American Alpine Journal

Volume 44   **2002**   Issue 76

CONTENTS

Alexander Huber on the sixth pitch of Bellavista on the north face of Cime Ouest, Tre Cime di Lavaredo. *Heinz Zak*

CONTENTS (cont.)

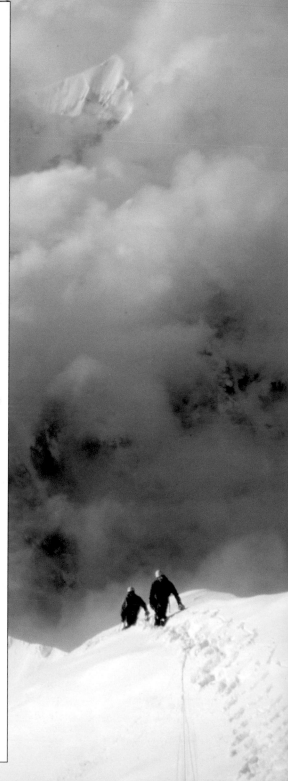

The American Alpine Journal

John Harlin III, *Editor*

Advisory Board
James Frush, *Managing Editor*
Chris Jones, Dougald MacDonald
Phil Powers, Mark Richey

Assistant Editor
Kelly Cordes

Art Director
Adele Hammond

Production & Editorial Assistants
Lisa Henzler, Joe Kelsey, Bree Loewen
Steve Roper, Kristin Skinner

Contributing Editors
Steve Hutchins, *AAC Centennial;*
Frederick O. Johnson, *Club Activities;* David Stevenson
Book Reviews; Geoffrey Tabin, M.D., *Mountain Medicine*

Cartographer
Martin Gamache, Alpine Mapping Guild

Translators
Marina Heusch & Rusty Sachs, *French;* Christiane
Leitinger & Henry Pickford, *German;* Ana Perčič,
Slovenian; Christian Santelices & Christian Oberli, *Spanish*

Indexer
Jessica Kany

Regional Contacts
Raphael Slawinski, *Canadian Rockies;* Steve Schneider,
Yosemite; Alan Bartlett, *Sierra Nevada;* Evelio Echevarría,
South America; Antonio Gomez Bohórquez, *Peru;*
Hernan Jofre, *Chilean Patagonia;* Rolando Garibotti,
Argentine Patagonia; Damien Gildea, *Antarctica;* Bill
Ruthven, *United Kingdom;* Lindsay Griffin, *United
Kingdom;* Bernard Domenech, *France;* Franci Savenc,
Slovenia; Vladimir Linek, *Slovakia;* Grzegorz Glazek,
Poland; Vladimir Shataev, *C.I.S.;* Vladimir Kopylov,
C.I.S.; Harish Kapadia, *India;* Elizabeth Hawley, *Nepal;*
Asem Mustafa Awan, *Pakistan;* Tamotsu Nakamura,
Japan; Kim Woo-Sun, *Korea*

With additional thanks to
Conny Amelunxen, Jim Earl, Sean Easton, Hans Florine
Claude Gardien, Rolando Garibotti, James Garrett
Danika Gilbert, Lindsay Griffin, Jeff Hollenbaugh
Danny Kost, Craig & Silvia Luebben, Jean-Claude
Marmier, Sue Nott, Tim O'Neill, Bart Paull, Marko
Prezelj, Joe Reichert, Mark Richey, Charlie Sassara
Marcelo Scanu, Steve Schneider, Jake Swan, Mark Synott
Mik Shain, Zack Smith, Jack Tackle, Talkeetna Air Taxi
Talkeetna Ranger Station, JuanJo Tome
Jonathan Thesenga, Fred Wilkinson

Ben Gilmore and Doug Chabot on the northeast ridge of Mt. Hunter, heading for the summit (page 108). *Kevin Mahoney*

PREFACE

Twenty years ago H. Adams Carter answered his doorbell and ushered me into his home office, where he edited the *American Alpine Journal*. The files were stacked high, boxes brimmed over with note cards and correspondence, and his well-worn typewriter looked like it had written more letters in the last year than I had in my 26-year-old life. Certainly that keyboard had processed more languages than I ever would, because the man who used it famously juggled a half-dozen tongues in the quest to gather reports on big routes from across the globe. The *AAJ* was born in 1929, when Ad was 15 years old. Its prime mission has been constant ever since: to document and communicate mountain exploration as it happens. Indeed, this mission has been at the heart of the American Alpine Club ever since its own founding in 1902, and it is enshrined in the Club's charter. But it was Ad's 35-year tenure—from 1960 to his death at age 81 (while the 1995 edition of the *AAJ* was at the printer)—that cemented this publication's reputation as the world's journal of record, *the* place to document the big mountain events of the previous year. This history, this tradition, this connection to the great expanding web of climbing and mountain exploration—these also happen to be ingrained in my own soul, and I think in the soul of the greater mountain community. Today I can pull from my filing cabinet the typewritten notes that Ad sent me in response to my own *AAJ* submissions, and I only wish I could tell him how proud I am to be picking up his reins and seeing where the journey leads.

Of all times to treasure a legacy, you can't beat a centennial. This year the American Alpine Club celebrates its 100th birthday, and as its flagship publication, the *American Alpine Journal* is delighted to take part in the festivities. The *AAJ*'s primary objective, of course, is to document the prior year's significant new mountain ventures. Still, over the years we've tried to place today's events in the historical context, the better to understand where we are and to appreciate where we've been. On the occasion of our 100th, we're devoting the front of the book to a long gaze across the horizon already traveled. We'll pause at many interesting points in the century to remember highlights from our American journey. Our opening collection, "Ten Climbs to Remember," makes one stop per decade. If this story whets your appetite, stay tuned for next year's *AAJ*, wherein 100 such fascinating highpoints will be celebrated, albeit more briefly. A working group of over 50 prominent AAC members has already generated a list of more than 200 climbs that shouldn't be forgotten. More than a dozen people are currently making the hard choices to narrow this list down to 100 climbs representing the 100 years. Our sleuthing has produced fascinating results, and we can't wait to share them with you.

In this year's *Journal*, we follow up on the Ten Climbs with a longer collection of great books from the Club's first century. Frankly, I was stunned to discover just how entertaining it is to learn history through David Stevenson's brief distillations of so many incredible stories. It's like sitting by a campfire and listening in on 100 years' worth of great storytellers who've been given one minute each to spin their finest yarns. If you agree that a minute isn't nearly long enough, there's always the full book to take you the rest of the way.

In "100 Years of Alpine Leadership" you'll hear directly from every currently living Club president, and briefly learn of those who remain with us only via their legacies. These past and current leaders will share their perspectives on the primary issues that shaped their terms of office, helping us to understand our Club and its role in sculpting history. They make great mountain companions, these presidents, and I'm sure you'll enjoy their conversation.

Of course, there's a time for remembering history, and a time for making it. Many of our presidents were at the top of the game during the storm years of their youths, to borrow Gaston Rébuffat's great phrase. But for many those years have long past, and you'll feel the tempo pick up markedly as we enter the bright light of today's remarkable climbers. As is the long-standing *AAJ* tradition, we'll hear straight from those who do the climbing that builds history year by year. These are direct connections to the deeds that will be remembered at the AAC's second centennial, in 2102. But keep this in mind when you think of the 22nd century's challenge in choosing their list of the second 100 climbs: if they pick a single ascent per year, they will have to pick just one out of each annual *AAJ*.

In my mind, though, it's Climbs and Expeditions—pages 198-439—that comprises the meat of each year's *Journal*. Sure, it's marvelous to stand back in awe of just how sharp today's cutting edge can be. And it's fascinating to put these routes into historical perspective, especially during our Club's centennial. But best of all is to be out there in the mountains, doing it for ourselves. And that's what Climbs and Expeditions is all about: documenting everything big (defined as an all-day climb or longer) that's new for the reporting year. Some of these climbs are truly state of the art; most are the stuff we all dream of doing whenever the pioneer in our soul cries out. Like so many climbers before me, and countless climbers to follow, I've marched to the library to research old *AAJ*s before heading off to distant ranges. This year, thanks to cartographer Martin Gamache, we've added locator maps for mountain ranges in most countries, the better to understand the reports. Look for more maps in the future, as well as *AAJ*s on CD-ROM and on the Web. The idea behind the *AAJ* isn't just to provide convenient documentation for historians, it's to help us realize our own dreams of high places.

Crafting the *American Alpine Journal* each year may be love, but it's not without labor. Fortunately, I early discovered how many climbers believe in the *Journal* and work tirelessly to help pull it together each year. I inherited a network of contacts and passionate *AAJ* supporters, some of whom were first brought in by Ad Carter himself, while others were added by Christian Beckwith, who took over when Ad died. Christian filled shoes that many thought unfillable, and took a venerable publication with a daunting legacy and brought it into the modern age—from an invigorated connection to modern climbing, to an updated book design and computerized networking and production. For his efforts we should all be grateful. But there's one fruit of his labor for which I'm particularly thankful, and that's his discovery of Kelly Cordes, Christian's and now my assistant editor. Kelly's passion, connections, talents, and energy were vital beyond words in making this *Journal* as rich as it is.

My personal bonds to the mountains and to the *AAJ* run deep; you could say they were bred into me. My father not only taught me to climb at age six—precisely four decades ago—but he also published annually in the *AAJ*. During those years—the early 1960s—we lived in Germany and Switzerland, and mountains ruled our lives. The Eiger finally took Dad from us in 1966, an event that has shaped my perspective in so many ways, some still to be discovered. I've carried the pride and the burden of my father's legacy wherever I've gone in the mountain world, but I have never felt it more than I do now as I craft the journal where Dad used to publish his record. Back then the *American Alpine Journal*'s editor was a man named Ad Carter. I hope you'll join me in remembering Ad and all those whose footsteps we've followed to reach our own routes ahead.

JOHN HARLIN III, *Editor*

TEN TO REMEMBER

A thousand climbs couldn't capture the richness of our last century.
So here are 10 to get us started.

While editing the stories that follow I had to start deleting the word "inspire"—it just came up too often. In fact, the I-word applies to every climb on this list, which is hardly a coincidence. The range and diversity of these first ascents is nearly as wide and complex as the century they span, though there is a huge difference. Human history during the 20th century hit as many low points as it did high points, whereas the stories that follow are nothing short of, well, inspirational.

These climbs were chosen to represent their decade not because they were necessarily the hardest of their era, but because they reveal something vital about that period in our history, something we're better off remembering than forgetting, something that reminds us of the heights we've already achieved and the wonders that, ahem, inspire us as climbers.

With that in mind, the writers of each of the following essays have a personal connection to the stories they tell. Kitty Calhoun, who led an alpine-style ascent of Makalu's west pillar, enjoys sharing stories like that of Fanny Bullock Workman on Pinnacle Peak in order to remind us that women have always been at the forefront of our sport. Dee Molenaar, whose watercolors grace this entire collection, describes the Sourdough ascent of Mt. McKinley's North Peak from his own experience with Denali, and also as one of our most valued mountain historians. When it comes to history, Chris Jones literally wrote the book—*Climbing in North America*—and would understand as well as anyone how the east ridge of the Grand Teton fits into our historical puzzle. Nick Clinch led the first American expedition to reach a higher summit than Minya Konka—some 36 years after the ascent he describes herein. While Allen Steck writes that the Lost Arrow Chimney was the first big-wall climb in America, others look admiringly to his own first ascent of the north face of Sentinel Rock three years later, also with John Salathé.

Crossing the midpoint of the century, Jim Wickwire takes the 1953 attempt on K2 as

inspiration for his own first American ascent of that mountain, 23 years after. And if anyone can understand the 1963 traverse of Mt. Everest described here, it's Ed Webster, who himself participated in one of the great climbs on that mountain, the alpine-style first ascent of the Kangchung Face, which cost him the tips of most of his fingers from frostbite. Barry Blanchard unveils the 1974 ascent of the north face of North Twin with great intimacy not only because he is one of the hard men of the Canadian Rockies, but also because he placed the only other route on the north face of that mountain. Dan Mazur's own outstanding Himalayan career includes a rare alpine-style ascent of Makalu, not unlike the earlier story he tells here from 1980. And Steve Schneider happens to be one of the fastest and most talented of the Yosemite big wall climbers; who better to understand Lynn Hill's achievement on the Nose in 1994?

What all these people have in common is a gratitude and respect for those who've climbed before. And, dare I say it, they're inspired by history—and they want to pass it on.

JOHN HARLIN III

Watercolor paintings of the 10 peaks by Dee Molenaar.

1906. PINNACLE PEAK

KITTY CALHOUN

"What do you think of the trend of todays' climbers pushing harder and harder?" The question came at a recent mountain symposium, but it could just as easily have been asked a century ago. If you consider the knowledge and equipment that climbers had back then compared to today, I would say that the old achievements are just as impressive, if not more so, than those of today.

In the early 1900s maps of the Himalaya were crude, when they existed at all. Mountains were often unnamed, and climbers could not tell which drainage would most easily lead to their chosen peak. Moreover, none of the airports and few of the roads and bridges that are commonly used today had been built back then, which meant that expeditions began in the lowlands. In those days one of the "easiest" approaches was to K2 in the Karakoram: it was only 350 miles, and took a mere month. Equipment consisted of heavy cotton tents, wool clothing, nailed boots, hemp ropes, and long wooden axes. Although climbers roped together on the glacier, they knew little about snow or ice anchors, and if one member fell on a route it could mean the death of the whole party. Avalanches were poorly understood, and nothing was known about high altitude illnesses.

Despite these challenges, climbers in the 1900s pushed hard, and Fanny and William Bullock Workman were at the forefront. When William, a surgeon, retired early because of poor health, the couple began a series of long bicycle tours across Europe, Algeria, Ceylon, and India. Their first Himalayan expedition came in 1899, when they climbed and named several peaks in Kashmir, including 21,000-foot Koser Gunge. Between 1899 and 1912, they organized seven expeditions to the Karakoram.

The high point of Fanny's expeditioning came in 1906 with the ascent of Pinnacle Peak

(22,810 feet) in the Nun Kun region of India. It was immediately recognized as one of the outstanding achievements of its time, the highest summit yet reached by a woman (and not far short of man's disputed altitude record). The couple had an unusual "avant-garde egalitarianism" in their partnership, and in fact, Fanny is credited with being the "mastermind" of their well known 1912 Siachen Glacier expedition. It was on this excursion that she climbed a smaller and more technical mountain, Hispar-Biafo (Watershed Peak), which she enjoyed as much as Pinnacle Peak: "Altho not as high, it yielded nothing in thrilling incident and arduousness of ascent, and in magnificence of panorama, to my highest Himalayan peak."

The Bullock Workmans' legacy continues not only in the inspiration they gave other climbers, but also in the maps they produced and the numerous travel accounts and magazine articles they wrote. Founding members of the American Alpine Club, their explorations were chronicled in five attractively illustrated books on the Himalaya: *In the Ice-World of Himalaya* (1900); *Ice-bound Heights of the Mustagh* (1908); *Peaks and Glaciers of Nun Kun* (1909); *The Call of the Snowy Hispar* (1910); and *Two Summers in the Ice-Wilds of Eastern Karakoram* (1917).

1910. MT. MCKINLEY'S NORTH PEAK

DEE MOLENAAR

At first the reported ascent of Mt. McKinley's North Peak by three miners from Fairbanks was dismissed as a tall tale from fertile boomtown imaginations. Eventually it was deemed one of the greatest feats in mountaineering history. The heroic ascent by the hardy "sourdoughs" is unique, even though they scaled the 19,470-foot North Peak rather than McKinley's true summit, the 20,320-foot South Peak.

The Sourdough climb was preceded by two expeditions, the first in 1903 to attempt the north wall (Wickersham Wall) by a five-man group led by Judge James Wickersham. The other, in 1906, was the infamous hoax perpetrated by Dr. Frederick Cook, who claimed to have reached the summit from the southeast. His "summit" was shortly proven to be a 5,000-foot foothill now called Fake Peak. Believing that the great McKinley should be climbed first by the territory's locals rather than by "outsiders," the Sourdough party was led by Thomas Lloyd and included miners Pete Anderson, Charlie McGonagall, and Billy Taylor, along with E.C. Davidson (a licensed surveyor) and two of his friends. But the latter three left the party after a heated argument with Tom Lloyd, and with them went the party's photographic expertise.

Departing Fairbanks in late December 1909 with two dog teams and adequate food supplies—but without a climbing rope or any knowledge of how one is used—they fought their way across swamps and muskeg and several glacier streams before reaching McGonagall Pass, which McGonagall had discovered during a solo hike years earlier. Wearing bib overalls, home-made crampons, alpenstocks, and using double-edged hatchets for ice axes, they carried a 14-foot spruce pole as an aid in crossing snow-bridged crevasses and to plant on the summit with the American flag. They then pioneered a route up the Muldrow Glacier and Karstens Ridge to the Harper Glacier above.

From their foreshortened perspective they believed the North Peak to be the true sum-

mit—and more likely to be visible from the Fairbanks saloon. So they climbed directly up from the Harper Glacier via a steep snow slope between rock ribs that dominated the south flank of the North Peak. On April 3, 1910, while McGonagall dropped back to plant the flagpole in the last rocks below the top—and to care for frost-nipped feet—Taylor and Anderson continued on the snow crest to the top of the North Peak.

The climb involved an amazing single 8000-foot push from their highest camp at 11,000 feet above the Muldrow Glacier, and the descent was made without problems. But en route home, while the others inspected mining claims in the foothills, Lloyd reached Fairbanks alone and announced they had all had reached the summit. The news was spread from the Fairbanks paper to the outside world via the *New York Times*. However, when the others arrived with the full story, which included the fact that the overweight and middle-aged Lloyd had only reached the base of the mountain, the veracity of the entire enterprise was questioned, especially since there were no photographs to support their claim. To add to the confusion, Lloyd later reported that the other three returned to the mountain and climbed to 18,200-foot Denali Pass, while another story had them returning to the flagpole. By then the claimed ascents were treated as another Alaskan tall tale.

The Sourdough Party's ascent was confirmed in 1912 when their flag-draped pole was spotted clearly against the deep-blue sky by members of the Hudson Stuck party during the first ascent of the peak's true (South) summit.

1929. East Ridge of the Grand Teton

Chris Jones

Rising dramatically from the surrounding plains, Wyoming's Tetons are a climber's paradise: beautiful, accessible, good rock, great climbs. The highest peak in the small range, the 13,767-foot Grand Teton, was climbed in 1898 via a tricky but short and barely fifth-class route. But until the 1920s, the small range was almost unknown to the few serious mountaineers in the United States. With their corps of professional guides, the European Alps and the Canadian Rockies were the place to be.

One of these dedicated climbers, Rhodes Scholar Albert Ellingwood, learned of Wyoming's great peaks and their climbing potential. He had picked up rock climbing while at England's Oxford University, and in 1923 he began a series of ascents in the Tetons. Phil Smith and Fritioff Fryxell, newly appointed rangers in the new Grand Teton National Park, were self taught but at least as eager. They climbed many new routes, but in common with others failed to get up Mt. Owen. The next team to make their mark, Eastern climbers Robert Underhill and Kenneth Henderson, were already excellent technicians schooled in the Alps. Climbing with guides, as was then still common, Underhill had been up the Brenva and Peuterey ridges of Mont Blanc, and had made the first ascent, with his future wife Miriam O'Brien and guide Armand Charlet, of the Aiguilles du Diable Ridge. This caliber of alpine climbing was quite unknown in the United States at the time. Henderson likewise had a dazzling resume of ascents in the Alps and Canadian Rockies. It was not until the 1940s that American climbers on their own turf reached comparable standards.

By 1929 the 30-year-old Owen-Spaulding Route was still the only way up the Grand Teton, while the much-longer east ridge had seen some five attempts. What an objective for Underhill and Henderson! After assessing the Molar Tooth, a tower at about mid-height that had foiled prior attempts, they traversed around it and attacked the slabs above. Rated 5.7 today, the east ridge is even today described in the guidebook as "a significant mountaineering objective." The following year these two teamed with Fryxell and Smith to finally make the first ascent of Mt. Owen. Once on top and ready to rope off, they were astonished to learn that Fryxell and Smith had never even seen or heard of a rappel. The lack of such a key technique illustrates how much a backwater the Tetons then were.

With these climbs the stage was set for a remarkable flowering of talent. The Mt. Owen companions had great climbs yet to come: the north ridge of the Grand and the complete Exum Ridge among them. In 1932 Fryxell would chronicle these climbs in a book, *The Teton Peaks and Their Ascents*. This compact range was to become, and largely remains to this day, the premier mountaineering range of the lower 48 states. It was where climbers from all over the country would go for alpine climbing. Here they would meet others of the nascent climbing fraternity. Here they would hatch plans for Alaska, the Andes, and the Himalaya. Did Underhill and Henderson have any idea what a great climbing ground the Tetons were to become as they roped up on July 22, 1929? With their already extensive knowledge of the Alps, I would like to believe that they did.

1932. MINYA KONKA (GONGGA SHAN)

NICK CLINCH

At 2:40 p.m. on October 28, 1932, Terris Moore and Richard Burdsall stood on the summit of Minya Konka. At 24,891 feet, this was the highest mountain in western China, and the highest mountain to be summited by Americans for the next 26 years. They took pictures of the American and Chinese flags as well as a complete 360-degree panorama of the view from the top before beginning their descent.

The climb was the culmination of a brilliant effort by four young Americans, Richard L. Burdsall, Arthur B. Emmons, Terris Moore, and Jack T. Young. (Young was an American of Chinese ancestry.) The mountain was high, dangerous, little known, and in remote warlord-torn China. The advantage of having American missionaries along the way was offset by violently unsettled conditions. The mountains of western China and eastern Tibet are isolated, rough country, with almost constant bad weather and significant avalanche danger. Like the Alps in the early 19th century, the countryside was well populated and traveled by locals, but the mountains themselves were completely unknown. The American climbers traveled so far back in the boonies of one of the most underrated mountain areas in the world, and were so far ahead of their time in their style, that despite writing a book (*Men Against the Clouds*, 1935), their achievement has long been under-appreciated.

The Americans went by ship to Shanghai, armored boat to Chungking, bus to Chengdu, hired porters escorted by soldiers, and finally used yaks to reach the base of the mountain. They explored and surveyed the peak, selected the most feasible route, the northwest ridge, and climbed it. Unlike previous Himalayan expeditions, they did not use porters. As Burdsall and Moore wrote, "In Alaska, where there are no native porters, American climbers ... have developed a technique

of cutting down to bare essentials, using only the lightest-weight equipment, then carrying these minimum needs on their own backs."

They had the essential ingredients for success on big mountains: skill, aggressiveness, judgment, and luck. The mountain was technically moderate but it had treacherous obstacles and considerable risk from storms and avalanches. They split the seam on the far edge of the envelope, but remained inside. They reached the summit, sustaining serious frostbite (including a loss of Emmons' toes), and returned alive. Later climbers would not be so fortunate, dying in falls and avalanches.

The next climb of Minya Konka was in 1957 by a large Chinese party. The leader questioned the lack of evidence of the American party on the summit, but in his *Alpine Journal* article graciously said the Americans made the first ascent. He must have liked the description in their book of the view from the summit, since he copied it in his article.

The Americans' lack of fuss, in a region away from the beaten mountaineering track of the Himalaya and Karakoram, in a time of depression and world war, obscured their accomplishment. But as storms and avalanches trap an increasing number of mountaineers in the wilds of the border country between China and Tibet, the reputation of the 1932 climb will grow. Their example will never fail to inspire American mountaineers.

1947. THE LOST ARROW

ALLEN STECK

When Anton Nelson and John Salathé reached the summit of the Lost Arrow via the Arrow Chimney, they had just completed the most demanding climb yet in the brief history of Yosemite climbing. The ascent took five and a half days in early September 1947, and though agile climbers with modern gear can do the climb in far less time today, it is still one of the premier routes in the Valley.

Both Nelson and Salathé had been on the route several times prior to their ascent. Some of these were multiday attempts, and they had opportunity to work out many of the major problems facing them: the amount of water required, special equipment needs including bolts and pitons, proper rations for hot, dry climbing, and more. One of the most important items of equipment—without which the climb certainly would not have succeeded—were the hard-steel pitons that Salathé had crafted. Salathé was born in Switzerland and trained early as a blacksmith. He eventually emigrated to Canada and then to California where he started his Peninsula Wrought Iron Works. He became interested in climbing sometime in 1945 on joining the Sierra Club Rock Climbing Section and soon became aware of the problems regarding soft iron pitons: they deformed easily when used on Yosemite granite and did not last long under repeated usage. He solved this problem by using steel from Model A Ford axles to make his own pitons; these could be used and reused as often as needed during an ascent. On one eight-hour pitch during his Lost Arrow climb, Salathé often had to hammer his pitons directly into rotten granite, which they penetrated without undue deformation. But this was not his only genius.

In August of 1946, with minimal climbing experience, he agreed to join some climbing friends at Yosemite Point to make an attempt on the Arrow Tip. Through a misunderstanding his friends did not arrive, and so Salathé decided to try it solo. He rappelled to the notch, and through the use of his special pitons and a bolt he succeeded in reaching a ledge some 100 feet below the top before retreating. Realizing that solo climbing is dangerous, he came back a week later with a friend, John Thune, to try again. Salathé climbed to his ledge and then Thune belayed him as he made his way up the discontinuous crack system leading to the summit. This effort took most of the day and when Salathé was just 40 feet from the top he called down to Thune to tell him he had reached the end of the crack system and that the drill was too dull to continue and besides it was getting dark. So they retreated. By virtue of his aid climbing skill Salathé had come within a few bolt holes of making the first ascent! A full year later he was back with Nelson to make the final ascent of the Lost Arrow.

Nelson's seminal article about the climb in the 1948 *Sierra Club Bulletin* was groundbreaking in many ways. Not only does he discuss the matter of equipment at some length, he ponders the question of motivation in climbing, perhaps the first American author to do so: "One cannot climb at all unless he has sufficient urge to do so. Danger must be met—indeed it must be used—to an extent beyond that incurred in normal life." In other ways, the climb was representative of a new era as it was the first big wall done with multiple bivouacs and hard steel pitons, and the first use of bolts for upward progress.

1953. K2 Expedition

Jim Wickwire

Hillary and Tenzing's climb to the top of Everest earlier in 1953 provided the world with electrifying news. But the events on K2 that year were the stuff of legends, growing even more striking with the passage of time. The American expedition's struggle with wind, storm, sickness, high altitude, and the loss of a companion seems more poignant than other expeditions that achieved success. Why? As much as anything, because they did not succeed. When a great mountain is climbed for the first time—particularly if it is an Everest or a K2—the media attention is substantial. But when the effort falls short of the goal and the climbers are faced with a situation that threatens their lives, it can be even more compelling. This seems especially true in the face of tragedy—as on K2 in 1953.

For many climbers, K2 is the ultimate mountain. At 28,262 feet (8,614 meters), it is second only to Everest, a scant 773 feet higher. With its classic pyramidal shape, K2 is the perfect embodiment of our mental image of what a mountain should be. The climber who has designs on K2's summit must not only contend with extreme altitude and difficult rock and ice, but with sudden storms that deplete strength and erode willpower. Although K2 was first climbed by a large Italian expedition in 1954 when Achille Compagnoni and Lino Lacedelli reached the summit, the American expedition's attempt of K2 the year before ranks as one of the most memorable in the

history of Himalayan mountaineering.

After two other American expeditions nearly succeeded in 1938 and 1939, the 1953 Charles Houston-led team made a valiant effort to become the first to climb the still-virgin summit. Like its forerunners, the 1953 expedition was carried off in the finest style. Lightweight by comparison with other Himalayan expeditions of the same period, these bold attempts on K2 came very close to success.

Poised for the summit at 25,000 feet in early August, the entire team of eight climbers was pinned down in their tents by an unexpected 10-day storm. Worse, they were confronted with a medical emergency so serious that it forced them to abandon their objective. Art Gilkey was stricken with blood clots in one of his legs, and Houston determined that his only chance for survival was to descend immediately. Since Gilkey was unable to walk, they wrapped him in a makeshift litter and began the almost impossible task of lowering him down the Abruzzi Ridge. But before they could reach the top of the ridge, one of the climbers slipped and almost the entire team was involved in a fall down the mountain's exposed upper slopes. Only Pete Schoening's now-legendary ice axe belay saved his teammates from certain death.

After the accident, the sick man was lashed to the slope while the climbers injured in the fall were assisted to a nearby campsite. When they returned for Gilkey 10 minutes later, to their shock and disbelief, he had been swept into the abyss. His death most certainly was due to avalanche. But it is not beyond the realm of possibility that Gilkey sacrificed himself to save the others. The answer will never be known. It took the survivors five more storm-filled days to reach the safety of base camp.

The most remarkable aspect of the 1953 expedition was the way these men stayed together through thick and thin, to the end. There was absolutely no thought of leaving Gilkey to save themselves. They would get down together or not at all. In the years that followed, most notably during that tragic summer of 1986 when 13 climbers lost their lives on K2, equally dramatic events have occurred on the mountain. But never has the 1953 expedition's unified resolve in the face of extreme peril been exceeded—or matched for that matter. It was what enabled these men to survive one of the epic experiences of Himalayan mountaineering history. It was what enabled them to maintain lifelong friendships afterward.

When my companion Louis Reichardt and I neared the summit of K2 in 1978, I recall being filled with a tremendous sense of history and admiration for what had gone on so many years before. We could look down to where Houston's team had withstood the week-long storm. The site of the accident was clearly visible. We could also see the crest of the famed Abruzzi Ridge, which dropped off steeply to the Godwin-Austen Glacier more than 12,000 feet below us. As we walked those last few steps to the summit, I could feel the presence of Charlie Houston, Bob Bates, Pete Schoening, and the others who, but for the vagaries of storm and circumstance, would have been there 25 years ahead of us. Their heroic struggle and the character they displayed is one of the greatest mountaineering stories ever.

1963. EVEREST WEST RIDGE TRAVERSE

ED WEBSTER

For Tom Hornbein and Willi Unsoeld, such a tentsite—if you could call it that—couldn't have been a more thrilling perch for the night. From 27,200 feet up this prominent couloir on Everest's north face, a glance out the tent door revealed Gyanchung Kang and Cho Oyu, proud patriarchs astride the Nepal-Tibet border. Frozen footsteps from Al Auten and their support Sherpas disappeared below and marked their tenuous link with the known world and safety. Life—exploring, achieving, the comradeship of partners, food, and a hot drink—could only be continued if Willi and Tom, somehow, managed to traverse Everest's summit and join Lute Jerstad and Barry Bishop on the South Col route.

No one had traversed the summit of Everest before; likely, no mountaineer had ever considered it a viable option. Unsoeld and Horbein did. But clearly there was now no easy seduction of "descent" or "going down." There was only the blue, nearly oxygenless sky embracing them, frost crystals tinkling into the 10,000-foot abyss beneath them, and the mountain's upper, wind-chiseled west ridge. They were scared, but not terrified. Each man was an academic and an adventurer, scholarly in his own bent. Tom and Willi were secure in what they believed in and firm in their self confidence. Together, they could think and rationalize and climb their way out of most any blind corner.

"It's like Long's Peak—just bigger," mused Tom, contemplating his summer training grounds on Colorado's most challenging 14,000-foot peak, recalling his halcyon adventures making the first ascents of Zummie's Thumb and the Hornbein Crack. And in those morning hours of May 22, 1963, as he turned another corner in the gully, Tom's partner did likewise, cocking his oxygen mask upward to see the raw limestone of the Yellow Band, a rocky headstone barring their exit onto Everest's summit ridge. "Whew, just a little bit more than the Grand Teton, isn't it?" said Willi.

Surpassing the 28,000-foot-mark, the two men severed every fiber of earthly connection

that had secured them to the rest of humanity. Now, tied to a single climbing rope, they were anchored to each other and to fate and the stars that would soon sparkle overhead if they didn't escape the confines of this rock-walled gully.

Next came the crux, moving diagonally right, crampons scraping on limestone, against the friable former ocean bed of the Tethys Sea. Welcoming terrain, easier ground but exposed—so exposed!—beckoned the pair onto the summit ridge of the world, the final pyramid-sharp crest of Everest's upper west ridge. The sun dropped into the western haze of the Himalayan horizon. The men's hearts pounded in a constant drumbeat, conversation now reduced to exclamations as their jagged ridge gradually merged with a snow arête leading to … a wind-torn flag, planted on the summit three weeks earlier by Jim Whittaker and Nawang Gombu.

A small town "can-do" attitude and that resilient American curiosity had compelled Tom and Willi to step out of the bounds of safety, to go stridently beyond reasonable risk, to grapple with fears unknown, to climb a route into the unknown on Earth's highest mountain. Out of both plan and necessity, they would make the first traverse of Everest. After photographing the sunset, the two commenced descending, following the recent footsteps of their companions Lute and Barry who'd attained the summit earlier that day.

Miles to go before these four men could sleep, a reunion high upon Everest's southeast ridge, then a stern forced bivouac above 28,000 feet—at the time, the highest ever made—that would steal some of the men's fingers and toes. But their brave footsteps, their friendship and camaraderie, would inspire every generation of mountaineers worldwide to climb into the high unknown after them.

1974. North Face of North Twin

Barry Blanchard

It is, hands down, the hardest face in the Canadian Rockies. Five thousand feet of sheer, black, and north-facing limestone, steeper than the Eiger, one and a half times as high as El Cap, a great dark cape of a peak. Hundred-foot seracs calve thunderously from its belly, wisps of water ice hang from its brow like icicles tacked to a ship's prow, and rockfall-darkened icefields foot its soaring pillars. Then there is the loose rock and the falling rock ... at times it makes the Eiger look like a child's sandbox. Climbers are familiar with almost every crack on El Cap, yet, after 30 years of attempts, just two routes have been established up the shadowland of North Twin; its mystery unmarred, its aura enhanced by each and every one of the vanquished.

In the dog days of August, 1974, George Lowe and Chris Jones venture onto the Twin in full-on *Eiger Sanction* mode: full-shanked leather boots, wool knickers, Dachstein mitts, nylon tops. They find climbing similar to the hardest ground in the Dolomites (5.10 A4) yet their situation, in what local climbers refer to as the "Black Hole" of the Canadian Rockies, is far more serious than any climb in the Dolomites. They are a full day of mountainous travel from the nearest road, and once past the first quarter of the wall, rescue—even given today's techniques—is impossible; furthermore, the wall they are on is glaciated, vertical to overhanging, and brazed with alpine ice. The *Reader's Digest* version is that there is really nothing comparable to North Twin in the Alps. George and Chris strive; wet blowing snow frequently smears slush onto the holds. On the fifth day they are battered by hail and George "goofs-up" a hop step while waiting for Chris to remove and send up a piton from the belay; George falls 30 feet and loses the critical aid placement of the pitch. They are 4,000 feet up the wall. That night, their fifth on the wall, neither man sleeps until 3 a.m. When they admit to each other that they no longer have enough gear to retreat and that there is no chance of a rescue, they agree that there are no options; if they are to survive they have to climb.

The dawn of day six brings swirling clouds and snow. George leads an improbable and time consuming traverse across a snow-peppered slab, then escapes into an ice runnel that he gains by liebacking the edge of a roof and pressing his knees into the remains of the winter's snow/ice. Falling snow matures into hail, avalanches run, George leads through the storm for 15 pitches on ice. They have all of three ice screws. Chris and George summit and set-up their small tent right there. Accumulating snow collapses the tent twice in the night.

Writing in *Ascent* Chris stated that he and George had crossed an indefinable line. On their eighth day out, searching for the descent by compass atop the Columbia Icefield, they caught a brief glimpse of a helicopter and heard warden Hans Fuhrer's words, diced by the rotor, "ARE YOU OK?" "We realized someone cared about us," wrote Jones, "that we were not alone ... tears ran down my face."

I'll suggest that, in 1974, the route that George and Chris opened on the north face of North Twin was the hardest alpine route in the world. I believe that nothing then accomplished in Patagonia, the Alps, Alaska, or the Himalaya measured up to what George and Chris accomplished with "a rope, a rack, and two packs."

1980. MAKALU WEST PILLAR

DAN MAZUR

On May 15, at 3:45 p.m., a small bold team from Spokane, Washington completed the first American ascent of Makalu and the first lightweight ascent of its difficult west pillar. This was a seminal moment in Himalayan climbing history: it symbolized the budding acceptance of the lightweight Himalayan style, it showed that American teams were attempting the most difficult objectives in the Himalaya, and it stood proud in John Roskelley's incredible two-decade-long Himalayan climbing career.

Paying homage to someone as legendary as John Roskelley is no easy task. I can only share my own feelings of what it was like to follow in his hard-to-fill footsteps to the summit of Makalu. In 1995, when three friends and I reached the summit in alpine style via the southeast ridge, I swam through deep, sugary, avalanche-prone snow and nearly fell to my death from a windblown ledge at 8370m, just below an upper plateau leading to the tiny summit pyramid. When I read Roskelley's 1981 *AAJ* account of his own battle with the same "hip-deep, bottomless powder," I was swept by a feeling of déjà vu, and I shuddered at his painful description of how "[I] front-pointed my way toward the ridge, with nothing sure for my heavily gloved hands." Roskelley paints an evocative picture of Himalayan climbing at its most horrible.

It was brave and audacious of the four from Spokane to choose the 1971 French West Pillar for their attempt on the mountain. Roskelley, Chris Kopczynski, Kim Momb, and James

States might have opted to make their speedy attempt on the classic French first-ascent route of 1955, but instead ventured onto a much more worthy and terrifying objective, originally climbed by an 11-member team in nine weeks using bottled oxygen. Roskelley, in the blunt style that became his trademark, states in the *AAJ* that "we had chosen to raise ourselves up to the standard of the mountain, not to pull the mountain down to our level with large teams of climbers and Sherpas." The climb was highly significant for its time because of the small size of the party and the "self-sufficiency" of their style. This four-person team employed no Sherpas above the base camp, nor did they use supplemental oxygen.

In order to ascend and descend the route several times for acclimatization, as well as to stock higher camps, Roskelley's team fixed 1,200 feet of rope to Camp 4 at 25,000 feet. This rope was used in climbing the 1,000-foot crux, and to protect a traverse out onto the south face, aptly named by the first ascensionists the "Terrible Traverse." In describing the crux, Roskelley paints an eerie picture of tracing tattered nine-year-old fixed lines, clinging precariously to frayed aluminum caving ladders, and climbing past spent gear in his team's negotiation of this section of exposed thin face climbing.

On summit day, States tired and Kopczynski accompanied him down, while Roskelley continued on solo through difficult rock, mantling his way toward the summit. Momb was in base camp because his knees had already blown thanks to his converted ski boots. After capturing a few Kodak moments on top at 3:45 p.m., Roskelley began a grueling descent back down the ridge. Fighting off waves of sleep that threatened to smother him every 10 or 15 minutes, he finally staggered into Camp 4 at 10:30 p.m, after 21 hours on the go. Another 8,000-meter summit had been climbed by Americans, and this one in a lightweight style at the forefront of its era.

Makalu's West Rib was a jewel in John Roskelley's nearly unmatched crown of achievements (all without bottled oxygen) that included Dhaulagiri, Nanda Devi, Trango Tower, Gaurishankar, K2, Uli Biaho, Cholatse, and Tawache (despite several attempts at Everest without oxygen, that summit eluded him). A cutting-edge Himalayan mountaineer of rare qualities and exceptional power, Roskelley helped to pioneer the modern Himalayan ethos.

1994. EL CAPITAN NOSE ROUTE
FREE IN A DAY

STEVE SCHNEIDER

In 1958, when Warren Harding, Wayne Merry, and George Whitmore completed the first ascent of El Cap's Nose after 45 days of climbing spread over 18 months, they unknowingly created what would become possibly the most sought-after rock climb on the planet. Seventeen years

later, Jim Bridwell, Billy Westbay, and John Long used the Nose to set a landmark for big-wall speed by climbing the Nose not just in a day, but in a mere 10 hours. (The Nose remains a benchmark for speed climbing, with Tim O'Neill and Dean Potter's 2001 time of 3:24 hours.)

But the coveted first free ascent of the Nose eluded all the big boys of free climbing. Two distinct pitches repeatedly bouted all comers: the Great Roof (pitch 23) and the Changing Corners (pitch 30). When Lynn Hill pulled through these pitches and continued to the top in 1993, all heads turned to mark the event. The crux of the Great Roof was underclinging a crack so thin that it would accept only the tips of a climber's pinkies. Here, Hill's diminutive size came to her advantage. Her fingers fit the crack, and although there were long reaches between locks for a 5-foot climber, nothing could stop this force of nature. She had originally freed the Great Roof the year before in her first bid to free climb the Nose, only to fail on the Changing Corners pitch. Undaunted, she partnered with Brooke Sandahl in 1993 for another try. On the Changing Corners pitch, Hill found her petite frame suited to the terrain as she squeezed herself into the tiny, smooth corner that marks the crux. Inventing a bewildering "Houdini move" that enabled her to do a 180 in the corner, her battle was as much mental as it was physical. After three days of practicing the moves, Hill felt ready for a full redpoint of the route. On their subsequent ascent, Hill fired off the Great Roof first try. Hill methodically climbed the Changing Corners pitch (which some claim is as hard as 5.14b) and the remaining five pitches to lay claim to what is undoubtedly the hardest free climb of its length on Earth.

The next year, in 1994, Hill began training for what would be her toughest test ever. Her vision was to climb the Nose free in a single day. She soon realized that she had underestimated what it would take to free climb the Nose in 24 hours. When she arrived at the Great Roof in midday, it was hideously hot, and she repeatedly fell near the end of the traverse. Partnered with Valley veteran Steve Sutton, it was all they could do just to aid up the rest of the route that day.

September 19 found Hill back on the Nose, again with Sutton. She realized she needed to hit the Great Roof in the early morning hours, before the sun turned it into a sweatbath. Extrapolating downward, she started her ascent at 10 p.m., climbing through the night by headlamp. The initial pitches involve difficult slab climbing up to 5.12, followed by the pumpy hand and fist crack climbing of the Stovelegs. When she reached the Great Roof around 9 a.m., she made it on her first try. Moving steadily along, Hill and Sutton rested for several hours waiting for the Changing Corners to go into the shade. When Hill finally attempted the pitch it was still warm and she took three falls, wasting precious mental and physical energy. Even though she'd been climbing all the last night, she still managed to pull together a redpoint of the pitch. The final crux was the last pitch where a 5.12c section leads over a bulge with a minimum of small edges. Donning her headlamp for one last battle, she fought off her exhaustion from 3,000 feet of hard free climbing and just pulled through the final moves, arriving on top about 23 hours after starting her pilgrimage.

How astounding was her ascent? The German Huber brothers' day climb of Freerider is pretty notable; Tommy Caldwell's Salathé (5.13b) free in a day this year is inspiring; and Yuji Huriyama's recent day and a half near-onsight of the Salathé is completely outstanding. But until somebody else, male or female, repeats the Nose free in a day, Hill stands apart on a pinnacle of her own. Her effort on this one magnificent day marks the crowning achievement of her astounding career.

HIGH PRAISE

Celebrating 52 magnificent books from the Club's first century.

DAVID STEVENSON

"To this day mountain climbing remains the most literary of all sports. No other activity so compels its participants, from the international star to the weekend scrambler, to turn each personal conquest into public tale."

BRUCE BARCOTT, *"Cliffhangers," Harpers, August 1996*

As I considered the books of the American Alpine Club's first century, Barcott's observation rang increasingly true. What other outdoor literature could be this rich, diverse, and copious? His use of the word "compel" seemed equally appropriate. Very few authors have made their livelihood or fame in writing about climbing, nor have they sought it. Climbers write for personal reasons, just as they—we—climb for personal reasons.

The thing is, publishers don't print books for writers. Their business is in satisfying readers. That's where we come in, and in recent decades our ranks have grown faster than bolted routes on a limestone crag. Many of us were first lured into climbing by epic tales from faraway ranges; others of us first clipped a sport route then wondered how it was done before power drills were invented. Whatever sequence led you to the mountains, chances are good that eventually you cared almost as much for the diversity and history of our sport as you did for pulling the hard moves. And as the tendons age, the balance often shifts, and soon our library shelves grow heavier than our rucksacks.

In the great spirit of mountaineering itself, we bring you a celebration of influential works from our literary history. These books are guiding stars, some to my generation, some to yours, some to those that came before, and some to those that have yet to take reading seriously. Such was my goal in building this list of 50, er, classics. Even if you can't read all these books, at least have a look at what our comrades have been writing over the first 100 years of the AAC's history.

How does one arrive at a list to represent a whole century? My methods here have hardly been scientific or quantifiable, as literary judgments seldom are. Fortunately, I've been lucky enough to edit the *AAJ*'s book review section since 1996, so I began with a short list comprised from memory. I then consulted Neate's *Mountaineering Literature: A Bibliography of Material Published in English* (1986), scoured decades of *AAJ* book reviews, and began talking to people, from young climbers I met on a glacier in Alaska's Ruth Gorge to the venerable Nick Clinch, former AAC president and owner of a private collection of mountaineering titles ("some are pamphlets, you know") nearing 30,000 in number.

I called Nick, for example, when I became concerned that the developing list had too few entries prior to the halfway mark—1952. He assured me that such a disproportion was natural: there simply weren't that many books with mountaineering themes in print, nor were many people climbing back then. Furthermore, he suggested adding James Ramsey Ullman's *High Conquest: The Story of Mountaineering* (see 1941, below), a history that has all but disappeared today but was highly influential for two decades. A generation or two younger, I could not have known its influence without the benefit of Nick's experience.

Numerous e-mail messages were exchanged with Steve Hutchins, a reader of mountaineering literature. Steve's knowledge is not only wide ranging, but esoteric: "Look," he wrote, "at the binding of Beckey's first volume of the *Cascade Alpine Guide*. It's stitched and glued at the spine, not just glued. The story was that Fred insisted on the more durable and costly method, convinced that the books would be used in the field." Steve's suggestions were thoughtful and invaluable throughout the process and are woven into the list.

The purpose here is celebratory and emphatically nonhierarchical. The list is structured chronologically, meaning there are implied judgments about historical importance. While I showed favor toward titles by AAC members, it also happens that our membership penned the most interesting books about mountains and climbing—in short, we've been there, done that, and told the world what we've seen. In the event that a title has undergone various editions and revisions, I noted the first edition.

In Neate's preface to *Mountaineering Literature*, she writes: "A practicable definition of 'mountaineering book' continues to elude me." I now see why. These books are as wide ranging as are the reasons we climb. While I have tried to imagine what a consensus list might look like, the end result is personal. Your own favorites will inevitably be different. What I'm sure we have in common is our love for the hills and for climbing's rich literary history. We read to learn of our past, to understand the present, to inspire our future—and just for the sheer fun of it. So tie in; let the celebration begin.

1908. Ice-Bound Heights of the Mustagh: An Account of Two Seasons of Pioneer Exploration and High Climbing in the Baltistan Himalaya, FANNY BULLOCK WORKMAN AND WILLIAM HUNTER WORKMAN.

Four years before the founding of the American Alpine Club, a middle-aged American couple arrived on bicycles in Kashmir. Leaving their bikes behind, Fanny and William Workman proceeded to Ladakh and the Karakoram Pass. Thus began a fascination with the Himalaya that was to result in an attempt on Kangchenjunga (their first-ever climb!); a claimed, though later disproved, world altitude record by 56-year-old William of 23,394 feet on Pyramid Peak in 1903; and the true altitude record for women (22,810 feet) in Fanny's 1906 ascent of Pinnacle Peak. These and other heavily-supported adventures the Workmans shared in five handsome books, illustrated with Fanny's superb photographs and issued between 1900 and 1917. The one I've chosen to lead our list is the first of the five to be published within the Club's century. At 444 pages it is the largest of them all, and will take today's reader unfailingly to two remote worlds— to turn-of-the-century Mustagh, and to the mental and cultural landscape of these most unusual adventurers. The Workmans were original AAC members.

1911. My First Summer in the Sierra, JOHN MUIR.

    A founder and president of the Sierra Club until his death; Muir's early environmental activism led to the establishment of Yosemite as a National Park. Much less known is that Muir was a founding member of the AAC and Club president from 1908-1910. This book, published in 1911, was put together from notes and illustrations Muir made 41 years earlier. Muir was an excellent climber of his generation, and made numerous first ascents throughout the Sierra. His literary reputation, however, is based not so much on his descriptions of mountaineering feats but on his glorious evocations of the mountain world. For example, his meditation on what it would be like to gaze forever at Cathedral Peak: "bathed in such beauty, watching the expressions ever varying on the faces of the mountains, watching the stars, which here have a glory that the lowlander never dreams of, watching the circling seasons, listening to the sounds of the waters and winds and birds, would be endless pleasure."

1911. A Search for the Apex of America: High Mountain Climbing in Peru and Bolivia, ANNIE SMITH PECK.

    Here Peck describes numerous early climbs in the Andes, including the first ascent of Peru's highest peak, Huascaran, then thought to be the highest summit in the Western Hemisphere. Peck wanted to establish a new altitude record for climbers in the Western Hemisphere and a world altitude record for women. But Aconcagua turned out to be higher and Fanny Bullock Workman's ascent of Pinnacle Peak in 1906 would prevail. Peck was a fascinating figure, not only because she was a pioneering climber and a woman, but also because of her competition with Workman and the controversies that arose from her role as an expedition leader. Peck, like Muir, was a founding member of the AAC.

1913. The Conquest of Mt. McKinley: The Story of Three Expeditions through the Alaskan Wilderness to Mt. McKinley, BELMORE BROWNE.

    In 1912 Browne was turned back a hundred yards below the summit, an occasion Bradford Washburn has described as "the greatest heartbreak in mountaineering history." This book describes their epic attempt, which ended when a sudden storm snatched victory at the last moment. Browne wrote: "The last period of our climb on Mount McKinley is like a memory of an evil dream." Keep in mind that after a safe descent, the three-man team still faced a 250-mile wilderness trek back to Cook Inlet! Browne's book was instrumental in casting doubt on Dr. Frederick Cook's spurious claim of the first ascent. In addition, Browne was a strong advocate for the establishment of Mt. McKinley National Park, participating in Senate hearings in 1916.

1914. *The Ascent of Denali: A Narrative of the First Complete Ascent of the Highest Peak in North America,* HUDSON STUCK.

The subtitle says it all: This book is of great historical importance. Stuck was an Episcopal missionary—the Archdeacon of the Yukon—and had lived in Alaska for nine years at the time of the climb. On the first page he announces, "I would rather climb that mountain than discover the richest gold-mine in Alaska." His team was well prepared and blessed with excellent weather. Stuck describes the first view from the summit: "Never was a nobler sight displayed to man…. What infinite tangle of mountain ranges filled the whole scene until gray sky, gray mountain, and gray sea merged in the ultimate distance!"

1914. *Mountaineering and exploration in the Selkirks: A Record of Pioneer Work Among the Canadian Alps, 1908-1912,* HOWARD PALMER.

Besides Archdeacon Stuck's account of his McKinley ascent, another notable American mountaineering book appeared in 1914, this one reflecting the surge of activity taking place in Canada. Though Howard Palmer notched roughly 25 firsts in the Canadian Rockies, it was the Selkirks that captivated him. "The peaks within the loop of the Columbia rise from unfriendly terrain," wrote Club great J. Monroe Thorington, "but they were Howard Palmer's first and last love." He was, says Thorington, "one of that hard-bitten group ... whose amazing back-packing journeys through the passes of the Selkirks made mountaineering history just prior to World War I. They would leave Glacier House heavily laden, returning weeks later, their provisions exhausted but with victory on distant peaks." Palmer made more than 20 first ascents in the Selkirks, among them Mt. Sir Sandford, highest in the range. This attractive book, called "classic" by Thorington and "a model of its kind" by Henry Hall, is the definitive story of early Selkirk climbing. Palmer was President of the Club from 1926-1928, editor of the *AAJ* from 1930-1933, and served continuously on the AAC Council for 33 years.

1924. *Tales of a Western Mountaineer,* C. E. RUSK.

Rusk was one of the founding members of the AAC, associated with I.C. Russell and also with members C.H. Sholes and W.G. Steel, who had earlier established The Mazamas (Oregon). This delightful book is a landmark because it's the only book that tells the story of climbing in the Cascades—for its own sake, as sport—during the early part of the 20th century. Though Rusk led an expedition to Mt. McKinley in 1910 and played a role in disproving Dr. Cook's fraudulent claim (see 1913, above), his heart was always with the snowy peaks that range from the Canadian border south to Mt. Shasta. Fittingly, the ashes of Claude Ewing Rusk were carried to the top of The Castle, a rugged promontory near the summit of his favorite mountain of all, Mt. Adams.

1925. The Glittering Mountains of Canada, J. MONROE THORINGTON.

Thorington was one of the most important AAC members of all time, Club president from 1941 to 1943, and later editor of the *American Alpine Journal.* The Canadian Rockies were the favored playground of Club members in the early years, and this is the story of climbs in "The Canadian Alps" during the Club's second decade. In 1921 Thorington had co-authored with future Club president Howard Palmer *The Climber's Guide to the Rocky Mountains of Canada,* the first title in the AAC Climber's Guide series and a book instrumental in spurring the growth of activity in the Canadian Rockies. (A second *AAC Climber's Guide* by Thorington was issued in 1937, this one to the interior ranges of British Columbia; later editions of the Rocky Mountain guides were co-authored by future AAC president Bill Putnam.) *Where The Clouds Can Go,* the beloved autobiography of Conrad Kain, edited by Thorington and published by the Club in 1935, stands as another of his lasting literary gifts to the North American climbing community.

1932. The Teton Peaks and Their Ascents, FRITIOF FRYXELL.

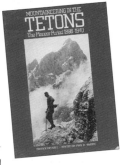

This history records the ascents from 1898 in a short, simple writing style later adopted by many guidebook writers. Fryxell notes in his introduction that during the year 1921 "not a single ascent" was recorded in the entire range. On the Grand Teton in 1931, first ascents of what became known as the Exum and Underhill ridges were made on the same day in July. In the closing sentence of his introduction, Fryxell presciently observes "...it is perhaps profitable to review the past, placing on record such facts concerning the Teton peaks and their ascents as may prove of assistance to the even larger groups of mountaineers who will surely come."

1935. Men Against the Clouds: The Conquest of Minya Konka, RICHARD BURDSALL AND ARTHUR EMMONS.

When Burdsall, Emmons, and company climbed this remote Chinese peak in 1932 it was the second highest mountain climbed to date, 24,892 feet. This was the highest Americans would reach until Nick Clinch's team succeeded on Hidden Peak in 1958. It was also an outstanding example of a small tightly-knit team doing it all—reconnaissance, Alaska-style load hauling, ascent of an unknown and challenging mountain—in a single self-reliant excursion. And it affected those who followed such things. Clinch wrote in *Classics in the Literature of Mountaineering,* "The ascent and the book served to spark the interest of American climbers in the great Asian peaks." While this may have been true for the cognoscente, most of the world let the Minya Konka climb come and go without recognizing it for the milestone it truly was.

1938. Sierra Nevada: The John Muir Trail, ANSEL ADAMS.

Adams' influence—on climbers, artists, environmentalists, and the American public—is so great as to be inestimable. Of all Club members his work is undoubtedly the most widely recognized and beloved. This enormous folio was beautifully produced with 50 huge black and white plates of the peaks along the crest of the Sierra. It is, according to Adams, "my best work with the camera in the Sierra." By coincidence, 2002 happens to be the centennial of Adams's birth year as well as the AAC's. Adams's is the more widely celebrated, with a variety of exhibitions and observances occurring nationwide, including the publication of Ansel Adams at 100, said to be his definitive volume (114 images), cataloguing the exhibition of the San Francisco Museum of Modern Art.

1939. *Five Miles High: The Story of an Attack on the Second Highest Mountain in the World by Members of the First American Karakoram Expedition,* ROBERT H. BATES AND CHARLES S. HOUSTON (AND RICHARD BURDSALL AND WILLIAM HOUSE).

It would be difficult to overestimate the influence of this climb and this book on the imaginations of American climbers. A relatively small party of Americans in excellent style make it to 26,000 feet on the Abruzzi Ridge, and a more illustrious group of climbers has never graced our membership (Robert Bates became an AAC president). This climb initiated an American fascination with K2 that would extend for 40 more years until Lou Reichardt (future AAC president), Jim Wickwire, John Roskelley, and Rick Ridgeway reached its summit on the sixth American attempt. The book was published by the AAC.

1941. *High Conquest: The Story of Mountaineering,* JAMES RAMSEY ULLMAN.

There have been more sophisticated histories written since, but when considered in the context of its historical moment this book stands out because it was the only game in town. American climbers coming of age in the 1940s and 50s were highly influenced, even inspired, by this book. Ullman was a writer who climbed, as opposed to the more typical climber who writes. His mountain-related titles include the best-selling novel, *The White Tower* (which the *New York Times* described as "…one of the best examples of sustained suspense I have ever encountered in fiction…"); a young-adults' best-seller, *Banner in the Sky* (made into the Disney movie, *The Third Man on the Mountain*); the biography of John Harlin (see 1968, below); and the official account of the 1963 American Everest Expedition.

1942. *The Manual of Ski-Mountaineering,* DAVID BROWER, EDITOR.

This pioneering instruction manual, which went through several editions, was the first of its kind in America. Though it didn't trigger the recent popularity of backcountry skiing, it shows an outlook toward winter possibilities that today seems quite modern. Besides Brower, contributors included AAC members Bestor Robinson, Richard Leonard, Ed LaChappelle, and Allen Steck, among others. Brower, like John Muir before him, was both an AAC member and leader of the Sierra Club. Steve Roper noted in these pages last year that Brower was "…the world's pre-eminent conservationist of the last half of the twentieth century." This book reminds us that first he was a mountaineer.

1949. *A Climber's Guide to the Cascade and Olympic Mountains of Washington,* FRED BECKEY.

This guidebook, third in the AAC *Climber's Guide* series (see 1925, above), is the original edition of what would burgeon into Beckey's three-volume, thousand-page opus, the Cascade Alpine Guide. It's these latter volumes that we commonly think of when we hear the term "Beckey's Bible." However, in his foreword to Beckey's *Challenge of the North Cascades* (see 1968, below) Harvey Manning called the 1949 edition "one of the most influential events in the annals of North Cascades travel. 'Beckey's Bible' as we called it, shaped the alpine lives of all of us"—and of thousands of climbers since.

1954. *K2: The Savage Mountain,* ROBERT BATES AND CHARLES HOUSTON.

The 1953 expedition was composed of many of the members of the 1938 group. This book tells their story and that of one of the most dramatic episodes—and certainly the most dramatic belay—in all of mountaineering history. Most readers of the *AAJ* will be familiar with the outline of events, and those who aren't should read about it for themselves rather than hear me summarize. I suspect most students of climbing history will agree with Nick Clinch when he says, "...in my opinion, the high point of American mountaineering remains the 1953 American expedition to K2." Like its 1939 predecessor, this book was published by the AAC.

1956. A *Climber's Guide to the Teton Range,* LEIGH ORTENBURGER.

This book, a work in progress for most of Ortenburger's adult life, was a labor of love. Ortenburger based his work on Henry Coulter and Merrill Maclane's 1947 guide, 67 pages published by the Dartmouth Mountaineering Club. By 1956 Ortenburger had climbed most of the routes in the book. Although there was a second edition of Ortenburger's *Guide* in 1965, there were also two "condensed" versions in 1974 and 1979, as well as what Jack Durrance and Hank Coulter refer to in the foreword to the third edition as the "Pink Monster Edition." It was difficult to keep the written record apace with the climbing activity. The third edition was finished in 1996 by Rennie Jackson five years after Ortenburger died, and weighs in at over 400 large-format pages. In the acknowledgments Jackson thanks the many rangers and guides and others who were helpful, a list which numbers well over 100 and includes dozens of well-known AAC members.

1956. *Give Me the Hills,* MIRIAM UNDERHILL.

This is the climbing memoir of Miriam O'Brien, gifted American climber and AAC member who was active in the Alps in the 1920s and 1930s. She was a fine writer, and this is a fascinating story. The stories of her "manless" climbs, including the first on the Grepon, and also those with guides—the great Armand Charlet among them—and future husband Robert Underhill, are fascinatingly rendered. Their climb of the Aiguilles du Diable traverse in 1928 is noted as one of the all-time 100 great climbs in the Alps by Silvain Jouty in his revised edition of Roger Frison-Roche's *History of Mountain Climbing,* as well as in Stefano Ardito's year-by-year chronology of great climbs in *Mt. Blanc: Discovery and Conquest of the Giant of the Alps.* Another lasting tribute to her climbing prowess is the route Via Miriam on the Torre Grande in the Dolomites.

1960. *Mountaineering: Freedom of the Hills,* HARVEY MANNING, ET AL.

Manning served as "chairman of the editors" for this collaborative effort by the Climbing Committee of the Mountaineers. Now in its sixth edition, with over half a million copies in print, it would be hard to overestimate its influence. The first sentence sets the tone: "The quest of the mountaineer, in simplest terms, is for the freedom of the hills, to be fully at home in the high wilderness with no barriers he cannot pass, no dangers he cannot avoid." In fact, many books on this list are indebted to this one, the first book published by The Mountaineers, whose subsequent book division has brought out more than 600 titles.

1965. *History of the Sierra Nevada,* FRANCIS P. FARQUHAR.

Though not a climbing history per se, there is much climbing recorded here, including chapters on the Whitney survey, Clarence King, and John Muir. Farquhar, who edited the *AAJ* from 1956 to 1959, covers the "human experiences in the Sierra Nevada from the time the Spaniards first saw it in the latter part of the eighteenth century to the present." As he notes, the characters who appear in this story are "strong, vigorous, and eager. They faced the unknown barrier of the Sierra and overcame it." In this description we recognize our predecessors and our direct connection to the age of exploration. Francis Farquhar wrote Sierra Nevada history in another way when he invited Robert Underhill to come to California and give a clinic on modern roped climbing. Held in the summer of 1931 and dubbed the "Palisade Climbing School," it concluded with the first ascents of Thunderbolt Peak and Mt. Whitney's east face, led to the first ascent of Yosemite's Higher Cathedral Spire in 1934, and planted the seeds that would ultimately bear fruit in the Golden Age of Yosemite rock climbing.

1965. *Everest: The West Ridge,* THOMAS HORNBEIN.

Hornbein's tale of his and Willi Unsoeld's first ascent of the west ridge and their harrowing bivouac while descending the south ridge is part of a larger story, that of the national expedition led by Norman Dhyhrenfurth that placed Jim Whittaker, the first American, on the summit in 1963. (The expedition's official account is *Americans on Everest,* by James Ramsey Ullman.) Hornbein's book is a thing of beauty, particularly in its first edition, 12th in the Sierra Club's Exhibit-Format Series, a lavish, massive book with production values rarely matched today. The obituary for Jake Breitenbach, killed in the Khumbu Icefall on the approach, never fails to move me deeply. This book spoke to a whole generation of climbers to be.

1967. *Ascent,* STEVE ROPER AND ALLEN STECK.

This marked the first of 14 volumes and has showcased the writing and photography of countless AAC members (without being a Club publication until the last edition, in 1999). Though Steck and Roper have been in charge from the beginning, other early editors included Edgar Boyles, Glen Denny, Dave Dornan, Joe Fitschen, Chuck Pratt, David Roberts, Jim Stuart, and Lito Tejada-Flores. I selected the first *Ascent* for this list not because it is necessarily the best, but because at that historical moment the editors had such an uncannily accurate sense of the climbing Zeitgeist. As David Roberts said in his foreword to *The Best of Ascent* (1993), "before *Ascent* we had no medium…in which to declare our passion." That first volume contains at least two lasting pieces for our history: Steck's own "Ascent of Hummingbird Ridge," and Tejada-Flores' "Games Climbers Play."

1968. *Challenge of the North Cascades,* Fred Beckey.

Beckey started contributing stories and photos of his climbs to the *AAJ* back in the 1940s when he was still a teenager. "My impression looking at these old *AAJs*," says Steve Hutchins, "is that this kid's ongoing articles must have electrified members and actually changed their consciousness about climbing's possibilities." This classic (Neate's label) autobiography spans only 30 years of Beckey's remarkable record—he's climbed steadily for 34 more years and, at age 79 shows no signs of stopping.

1968. *Straight Up: The Life and Death of John Harlin,* James Ramsey Ullman.

"There may never be another American climber who gets a carefully researched, full-on biography by a skilled and mature professional author." When Steve Hutchins wrote this it took me aback: climbers write about themselves, they write about other climbers. But how often does a climber attract a writer's interest; in other words, how often does a climber step outside our rather insulated world and into the public eye? "The result," Hutchins continues, "was not just a fascinating look at one of the most interesting personalities of an era, but a close-up of the phenomenon of California climbers/AAC members bringing their Yosemite technique to the Alps."

1968. *The Mountain of My Fear,* David Roberts.

This is the first book by one of our most lucid and distinguished writers. It describes the ascent of the west ridge of Mt. Huntington in the Alaska Range by four young men. The climb in and of itself is a remarkable achievement, but the writing sets a standard for clarity and beauty that has rarely been matched before or since. Not only was the climb accomplished in excellent style, but I remember thinking that it showed me what was possible for mere mortals such as myself. Bates and Houston, Hornbein and Unsoeld were gods to me at that time, but Roberts' story thrilled and frightened me because I could identify with it.

1969. *Minus 148: The Winter Ascent of Mt McKinley,* Art Davidson.

In 1967 Denali didn't see anywhere near the traffic it does today; even a summer ascent was newsworthy in the climbing world. This book describes the first winter ascent—nearly unthinkable at the time—its harrowing conditions, its tragic costs. This ascent marks a milestone in the history of our continent's grandest peak. Read it on a winter night in front of the fireplace.

1970. *Deborah: A Wilderness Narrative,* David Roberts.

Roberts' account of his attempt on Mt. Deborah with Don Jensen is filled with bickering between the two, horrifying crevasse danger, and very little actual progress on the climb. I remember finding this book unpleasant upon my first reading. Later, before my first Alaska trip, Willi Unsoeld, whom I regarded as the Oracle at Delphi, advised me to read *Deborah* before I left. In the light of Unsoeld's recommendation, I still found Roberts' tale unpleasant, but now it rang with truth. This is a cautionary tale.

1971. *Norman Clyde of the Sierra Nevada: Rambles through the Range of Light,* NORMAN CLYDE.

This is a collection of 29 Clyde articles and essays brought together in book form by Dave Bohn, with a prologue by Jules Eichorn and a long letter from Smoke Blanchard. Clyde died the following year, his ashes scattered by friends on the summit of Clyde Peak. Clyde accomplished some 96 first ascents in the Sierra Nevada between 1914 and 1939, mostly solo, and was a fine writer. This is something of an underground classic—only 3,000 copies were printed. As this one is hard to find, another selection of Clyde's writing is *Close-ups of the High Sierra* (1998).

1971. *The Challenge of Rainier,* DEE MOLENAAR.

Mt. Rainier has more glaciers than any peak in the contiguous United States: 35 square miles of ice, including 26 officially named glaciers. These facts, combined with its altitude and notorious weather, make it all the more surprising that Rainier receives as much human traffic as any other snowy mountain in America. A large number of American Himalayan climbers have worked and trained on Rainier, and the number of prominent AAC members who have a history with the peak is amazing, from John Muir to Ed Viesturs. Molenaar, a member of the 1953 K2 expedition and contributing artist to countless climbing books, did a thorough job of compiling the human history of exploration and tragedy on this great mountain.

1971. *Basic Rockcraft and Advanced Rockcraft (1973),* ROYAL ROBBINS.

These two slim volumes (167 pages between them) are as cleanly written as the style they set forth. As a climber starting out in the early 1970s I doubt I knew anyone then who didn't read these and attempt to commit them to memory. Sure, now we have sticky rubber and camming devices, but the foundations are all here, set down by Robbins 30 years ago. I read somewhere just last year of a novice climber in the Valley rapping off a route to consult *Advanced Rockcraft* on the shelves of the store, then jumaring back up to his high point with the beta. Robbins is better known for his climbing achievements and ethical stances, but his writing is a model of clarity.

1972. *Chouinard Equipment Catalog,* YVON CHOUINARD, TOM FROST, AND DOUG ROBINSON.

"What is a commercial catalog doing in the book review section?" Galen Rowell asked in his 1973 *AAJ* review—answering his own rhetorical question with, "It contains more information on the ethics and style of modern climbing than any other publication in our language." History has proven Rowell's observation to be right on. Usually when people refer to this catalog, it's in reference to Doug Robinson's essay, "The Whole Art of Natural Protection." (While I admire that article greatly, my personal favorite of Robinson's is "The Climber As

Visionary," first published in Ascent and later included in Robinson's collected essays, *A Night on the Ground, A Day in the Open* [1996]). Furthermore, the catalog had a higher consciousness that's hard to define; with its cover (a sixteenth century Chinese painting) and its pages filled with quotes from the Rolling Stones, Einstein, and Chouinard himself, this little catalog was way cool in the days before *way* ever modified *cool.*

1974. *The Vertical World of Yosemite,* GALEN ROWELL.

Readers of the AAJ are undoubtedly familiar with the work of Galen Rowell. As stunning (and relentless!) as his photographs may be, it would be a grave injustice to think of him simply as a photographer. This book, Rowell's first, has him wearing the hats of historian and editor, collecting in one volume many of the most important accounts of climbing in the Valley. Like many others, I'm partial to Chuck Pratt's "The South Face of Mt. Watkins" (which first appeared in these pages in 1965). I don't know many climbers of my generation—that is, the one starting to climb as this book appeared—who were not influenced by *The Vertical World.*

1975. *Downward Bound: A Mad! Guide to Rock Climbing,* WARREN HARDING.

Before Harding's death in February of this year I might not have included this one. But like the man, the book is a one-of-a-kind creation. It's funny, it has an edge, and it sometimes goes too far. But as Harding liked to remind us, we take ourselves far too seriously. In the void left by his passing, we have, at least, this book to remind us of that.

1976. *Climbing in North America,* CHRIS JONES.

Perhaps the most remarkable fact about this book is simply that there really has been nothing quite like it, before or since. Sure, people complained that it left them wanting more, but that seems appropriate given the nature of the undertaking. The breadth of Jones' research strikes me as staggering, and the dozens of references which follow each of its 22 chapters are indispensable and represent an enormous amount of research. But this isn't merely a dry list of historic routes; Jones' achievement here is his human history, his rounding out of our sense of these historic figures as people. Until compiling this list, I hadn't returned to this book in many years; now I can't pull myself away from it.

1977. *Climb! Rock Climbing in Colorado,* DUDLEY CHELTON AND BOB GODFREY.

Like Chris Jones' history, this book tells the human stories behind the climbs of its day. However, its photography had an even greater impact. Today we take for granted stunning photos of climbers leading that can only be taken by professional photographers on rappel. This book helped to launch the new era of climbing photography, displaying just how stunning the images can be when the photographer is focused on his art, not on participating in the climb. This year a 25th anniversary edition, edited by Chelton and Jeff Achey, follows up on the follows up on the evolution of climbing in Colorado so beautifully showcased in the first edition.

1977. In the Throne Room of the Mountain Gods, GALEN ROWELL.

In his review in these pages, William House, a member of the 1938 K2 team, expressed his boredom with the discussions of "serious internal dissensions." But Rowell's story of the failed 1975 American attempt on K2, rife with problems with porters and rifts within the team, is, I think, the first example of the new American expedition book: an attempt to tell the truth about a complicated and messy human scenario. House closed his review with the seeming grudging admission that it "may some day become a collector's item." There he was right. Rowell's attempt to tell it all, his great attention to history, and the larger format that nicely displays the photography for which Rowell would later become famous, all combine to make a great book out of a story filed with much unpleasantness. The photograph of Leif Patterson celebrating "the sight of green grass at Urdukas" just months before he would die captures a beautiful and redemptive moment.

1978. Mountain Passages, JEREMY BERNSTEIN.

Bernstein is a true Renaissance man: physicist, climber, and staff writer for *The New Yorker.* For the latter, he wrote about both physics and climbing. This volume, which was published by a university press, collects his mountaineering essays, many of which first appeared in *The New Yorker.* For that reason alone—as conveyor of our world to the larger reading public—this is an important book. Bernstein's portrait of Chouinard is probably his most widely known piece, but I'm particularly fond of his evocations of climbing in the Alps, which he accomplishes in a self-effacing style. When I climbed the Arête des Cosmiques on the Aiguilles du Midi just a few years ago, I remembered Bernstein's version of it and was grateful for the seed he had planted many years before.

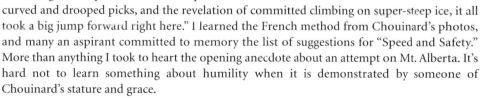

1978. Climbing Ice, YVON CHOUINARD.

Steve Hutchins notes: "This book had a tremendous influence on attitudes toward technique and equipment. (Take for example the amusing scramble by The Mountaineers to revise the snow and ice chapters in *Freedom* to incorporate the new knowledge—right down to the sudden appearance of French words and the undisguised copies of Chouinard's photos in line art!) Short axes, curved and drooped picks, and the revelation of committed climbing on super-steep ice, it all took a big jump forward right here." I learned the French method from Chouinard's photos, and many an aspirant committed to memory the list of suggestions for "Speed and Safety." More than anything I took to heart the opening anecdote about an attempt on Mt. Alberta. It's hard not to learn something about humility when it is demonstrated by someone of Chouinard's stature and grace.

1979. *Fifty Classic Climbs of North America,* STEVE ROPER AND ALLEN STECK.

This book, which begins by expertly considering just what might give a climb classic status, very quickly became a classic itself. Part history, part guidebook, this volume excels at both. Its influence was undoubtedly greater than Steck and Roper imagined. Critics called it "Fifty Crowded Climbs," but that hardly seems fair; we share the mountains with increasing numbers of people. There's only one route in here I've done twice—once five years before the appearance of this book, and once 10 years after; it wasn't crowded either time. "Our routes," the editors said, "are not the fifty classic climbs of the continent, but rather our personal choice...." This book invites us to try these, but the greater invitation is to make our own choices, our own lists.

1980. *Annapurna: A Woman's Place,* ARLENE BLUM.

In 1978 this all-woman group succeeded on Annapurna—the first time the peak had been climbed by Americans or by women. This is an important story not only because it broke down long-held assumptions about the ability of women to climb the highest peaks, but because holds up well as a traditional expedition tale of hard climbing, triumph, and heartbreak. The bibliography provides a thorough accounting of mountaineering and exploration books by women. Before this book fewer people believed that a woman's place could be on the summit.

1980. *The Last Step: The American Ascent of K2,* RICK RIDGEWAY.

The final chapter in four decades of American efforts on K2 ends in success. Just as members of the 1938 expedition returned in 1953 (see 1954, *K2,* above), a core from the 1975 team (see 1977, *Throne Room,* above) returned in 1978, led by Jim Whittaker. The expedition culminated in successful summit bids by Jim Wickwire, Lou Reichardt, Rick Ridgeway, and John Roskelley. The climb has undeniable historical importance, but as Whittaker says in his introduction: "The American ascent of K2 is a story about people." If this seems like a cliché, in Ridgeway's capable hands the human drama of this tremendous effort shines through.

1982. *A Walk in the Sky,* NICK CLINCH.

This is the story of the only American first ascent of an 8,000-meter mountain. Hidden Peak (Gasherbrum I) was first climbed in 1958 by Pete Schoening and Andy Kauffman in an expedition led by Nick Clinch, who later became president of the Club. In addition to its obvious historical importance, it should be noted that this was a small party of friends—"informally organized, almost entirely self-supported"—at a time when Himalayan expeditions typically were large national productions, heavily subsidized and publicized. Even though Clinch wrote the book in 1959, it wasn't published until 1982. He added both the preface and epilogue decades after the climb, words that strike the reader as modest and wise.

By the way, Hidden Peak wouldn't see a second ascent until Messner and Habeler would do a new route on the northwest face in 1975, alpine style and without oxygen, a pivotal event in Himalayan climbing.

1990. Eiger Dreams: Ventures Among Men and Mountains, JON KRAKAUER.

In this collection of 12 essays one should not expect the rough early scrawlings of a young apprentice. These are highly polished pieces, keenly observed and expertly described. One advantage this book has over the author's later works is the inclusion of a few lighter subjects. His portraits of the Burgess brothers and of the current climbing scene in Chamonix (circa 1989) are laugh-out-loud funny. Pieces in which Krakauer becomes the subject of his own work, such as on the Eiger in the title piece and on The Devil's Thumb, are drawn with the same dead-on, unflinching eye. As a prose stylist Krakauer is unmatched on this list.

1991. Mount McKinley: The Conquest of Denali, BRADFORD WASHBURN AND DAVID ROBERTS.

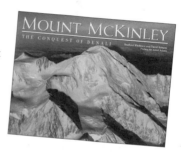

This book combines the work of one of our finest photographers with an equally talented writer. The effect is stunning: beautiful as an art object, immensely readable as a history. This is one of the finest coffee-table books ever published.

1992. The Ascent, JEFF LONG.

This fictional Everest expedition, set against the cultural background of Chinese-occupied Tibet, won the prestigious Boardman/Tasker Award for Mountaineering Literature, making Long the only American to receive this prize. Long's earlier novel, *Angels of Light* (1987), is also noteworthy. It presents a fictionalized version of Yosemite climbers and the famous airplane that crashed in the High Sierra loaded with drugs. In both books Long manages what all fiction writers attempt: to get at larger truths not so easily garnered from personal or historical experiences.

1992. K2: The 1939 Tragedy, ANDREW J. KAUFFMAN AND WILLIAM L. PUTNAM.

Written more than 50 years after the expedition, Kauffman and Putnam set the record straight. Before this book the general impressions of this climb were that Fritz Weissner made it to within 800 feet of the summit, that four climbers died, and that the reputations of two climbers, Weissner and Jack Durrance, suffered greatly in the aftermath. As the authors ask in their introduction: "But why bother to rehash a story whose broad outlines are known? Why set out to correct the innumerable factual errors found in virtually every available account? For two important reasons: truth and justice." This book brings closure to events that began to be resolved during Kauffman and Putnam's successful lobbying to bestow honorary AAC membership on Weissner. Between them Kauffmann and Putnam have 117 years of membership in the AAC.

1994. Camp 4: Recollections of a Yosemite Rockclimber, STEVE ROPER.

This is at once a history and a personal memoir of climbing in the Valley, particularly the years 1957 to 1971 when American climbers and their routes were setting the standard worldwide for big wall climbing. In his preface Roper wrote: "To put into print the recollections of a bygone era is like traversing along a frightfully exposed ridge.... No writer can deal with personal events without treading this...." One of the great achievements of this book (there are many) is just how successfully Roper walks that ridge: the personal is here, the history is here, and Roper is meticulous in keeping them clearly separated, even when they would appear inextricable, such as on his first ascent with Kamps and Pratt of the Direct North Buttress on Middle Cathedral in 1959. Robbins has called this the "best piece of extended writing about the early Yosemite climbing scene yet published," and Chouinard adds that Roper "has captured the real spirit of the Golden Age of American rockclimbing." They ought to know, they were there. Most of us weren't there, but when we read this book we wish, more than ever, that we had been. The book was awarded first place for non-fiction at the premiere Banff Mountain Book Festival.

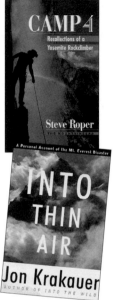

1994. *In the Shadow of Denali: Life and Death on Alaska's Mt. McKinley,* JONATHAN WATERMAN.

In Waterman's first two Denali books, *Surviving Denali* and *High Alaska*, he compiled statistics, provided climbing histories, and offered route information. *In the Shadow of Denali* complements these earlier two with its acutely observed rendering of personal experience on the mountain. At least two of the essays, "Lone Wolf (the Other John Waterman)" and "Winter of Our Discontent," about the first winter ascent of the Cassin, are highly memorable, even haunting.

1997. *Into Thin Air,* JON KRAKAUER.

This is an ongoing publishing phenomenon that's difficult to summarize succinctly. In a 1999 article in these pages, bookseller Michael Chessler wrote that at that time the book had sold close to 3 million copies and had grossed perhaps 50 million dollars. Chessler wrote "Some climbers will always admire [Krakauer] for his writing and his good works [donating a percentage of profits to the American Himalayan Foundation], while others will always feel that Boukreev's version [*The Climb*, with G. Weston DeWalt, 1997] was right." Whichever your view, *Into Thin Air*'s influence is undeniable. Krakauer asks the hard questions about the ethics of guiding on 8,000-meter peaks, and some will always hold that against him. But these are questions that deserve—demand, really—our consideration. This one is a benchmark, if for no other reason than the sheer numbers of people, mostly nonclimbers, who have read it and shaped their view of mountaineering by it.

1999. *Bradford Washburn: Mountain Photography,* ANTHONY DECANEAS, EDITOR.

I've been hesitant to include books from the past few years on this list, for who can say what their influence might be? But not much guesswork is required here: this book's place in history is guaranteed. Washburn's photographs have been a staple of the American climbing world (and these pages) for decades. Many a first ascent has been inspired by imagining a line over a brilliantly detailed Washburn black and white. This book is the most elegant showcase of his life's work.

1999. *Ghosts of Everest: The Search for Mallory and Irvine,* JOCHEN HEMMLEB, LARRY A. JOHNSON, AND ERIC R. SIMONSON, AS TOLD TO WILLIAM E. NOTHDURFT.

The most enduring mystery of 20th century mountaineering is whether Mallory and Irvine completed their ascent of Everest on June 8, 1924. As the whole world knows, an American expedition led by Simonson found Mallory's remains in 1999. This book reconstructs the 1924 expedition in light of the new evidence and tells its own story as well: the discovery of that evidence. Four or five books describe aspects of the Mallory discovery, but this one by the expedition's originators is the most thorough in its combination of historical perspective, first-hand experience, and insight. It's also beautifully presented.

1999. *Extreme Alpinism: Climbing Light, High and Fast,* MARK TWIGHT.

Twight articulates here what great climbers have understood intuitively. The book appears to be of the "how-to" genre but it's hardly for the novice, and though all climbers could learn something from these pages, it has a more important purpose. This book describes, clearly and with refreshing maturity and balance, the state to which our art has evolved.

⚹⚹⚹⚹

It's been a magnificent century. From the porter caravans of the Bullock-Workmans to the fast and light world of today's extreme alpine climbers, we've glimpsed the many faces of our alpine ambitions, and seen how right Bruce Barcott was in calling ours such a literary sport. And what about the future? Chessler pointed out in his "After Thin Air" essay that the market is there for our genre. Still, I believe what a literary agent once told me, that no art would be produced because someone had their fingertip on the pulse of the market. Good writing comes from the same place as good climbing, and one's heart should not be market-driven. When I look over the 2002 *AAJ* book reviews and wonder about the future, I see much for which to be hopeful: Sherpa people telling their own stories, Rick Ridgeway's poignant search for "the lost father" of his title, and Jon Waterman's grueling solo Arctic odyssey that turns into a thoughtful exploration of Inuit culture. Our tradition is rich and healthy. As climbers have stood on the shoulders of giants, so have our writers.

If I asked 50 climbers to name a book I left off the list, I would have 50 different answers and twice as long a list. Last May I was on the Ruth Glacier and made the acquaintance of a pair of young climbers who were doing the Cobra Pillar on Mt. Barrille. We were sitting around base camp eating no-bake cheesecake when I put the question of climbing books to them. "*On Edge: The Life and Climbs of Henry Barber* [Chip Lee, 1982]," responded Justin Talbot unhesitatingly, "that's a good one." It's a book I happen to know; I admired Barber tremendously, yet hadn't considered the book for the list. But now the book leapt up in my estimation. I liked the idea of this youth, a Connecticut kid, reading about Barber, another New England "kid" (the book ends when Barber is 28 years old!), and finding his inspiration there. And the proof was, here was Justin today on one of the great routes in the Alaska range. Literature and inspiration, influence and mountains: it's personal .

THE DEBT WE OWE
THE AMERICANS

The Alpine Club of Canada reflects on its mentor's centennial.

R.W. SANDFORD
Vice President, Publications — The Alpine Club of Canada

An early Alpine Club of Canada trip to Mt. Aberdeen, circa 1924. Photo: Brian Wyvill, Whyte Museum of the Canadian Rockies. Courtesy of *Canadian Summits: The Canadian Alpine Journal 1907-1994*

Without the influence of Americans, it may have taken a long time for Canadians to develop their own alpine culture. By accident and by design, Americans helped Canada become a world center for mountaineering. The first technical ascents of high mountains in Canada did not occur until the Canadian Pacific Railway granted easier access to Canada's western mountains in 1885. Though the earliest climbers were from Europe and Britain, it took only a couple of years for the Rockies and the Selkirks to be discovered by American tourists and adventurers. Many of these were mountaineers with experience in the Alps and in the Rocky Mountains further south.

A golden age of Canadian mountaineering followed the tracks west. American tourists would simply get off the train, walk or scramble to the tops of nearby mountains, and name them for their friends. Canadians, in the beginning, were not interested in mountaineering for its own sake. Most Canadian climbers were "inadvertent summiteers," climbing mountains mostly for such practical purposes as prospecting and surveying. They did not climb for sport. It took the death of an American climber, Philip Stanley Abbot near Lake Louise in 1896, to make Canadians aware of the stupendous mountaineering potential that existed in the West. Three years later, the Canadian Pacific Railway hired professional Swiss mountain guides and posted them at resort properties at Rogers Pass, Lake Louise, and Banff. Over the next 25 years, these guides and their descendents led more than 250 first ascents in the "Canadian Alps," often with American clients.

Decades of close association with European guides and American climbers helped make Canada the alpine nation that it is today. Through example and direct support, Americans encouraged a uniquely Canadian appreciation of mountain places and experiences. Watching Americans make history in their own land inspired Canadians to become upwardly mobile. Sometimes, as with the creation of the Alpine Club of Canada, Americans simply shamed Canadians into developing our own alpine culture.

A founder of the American Alpine Club, Charles Fay, climbed extensively in Canada in the years following the completion of the CPR through the Rockies. He was the leader of the expedition to Mt. Lefroy on which Philip Stanley Abbot became the first mountaineering fatality in Canada. Fortunately, Fay was not the kind to walk away from disaster or adversity. He made an impassioned defense of mountaineering at the inquiry into Abbot's death that put an end to the grumbling in political circles that mountaineering ought to be banned in Canada. Fay was also a member of the Anglo-American expedition that made the first ascent of Mt. Lefroy on the anniversary of Abbot's death, an expedition that opened the door to mountaineering adventure and exploration in the vast alpine regions north and west of Lake Louise.

When Charles Fay helped to bring the American Alpine Club into existence in 1902, he inspired Arthur Oliver Wheeler to try to create a sister organization in Canada. Wheeler tried for years to generate interest in a national mountaineering organization in Canada, but in the end was unsuccessful. It was only after Fay offered that a Canadian chapter of the AAC could be created to suit the needs of America's northern neighbors that Elizabeth Parker was able to wake Canadians from their apathy so they could realize the importance of mountains to their

Albert MacCarthy and Basil Darling on Extinguisher Tower, Mt. Robson ACC Camp, 1913. *Byron Harmon, Whyte Museum*

own identity. This, however, did not mean the end of the American influence on Canadian mountaineering.

When the Alpine Club of Canada was created in March of 1906, it had 117 members, 15 of whom were Americans. At the club's first General Mountaineering Camp held in the Yoho Valley in the summer of 1906, some 133 climbers graduated into membership of the club. Eight were Americans. Today, the ACC boasts some 6,000 members. Of these some 400 have American addresses. Though he is Canadian, the current president of the ACC presently lives in the U.S.

American influence on the ACC has been profound. The positive nature of this influence can be measured, to a real extent, by the number of honorary memberships that have been bestowed upon Americans. The AAC's founding president, Charles Fay, was elected an Honorary Member at the ACC's founding meeting in 1906. Early climber and photographer Walter Wilcox was made an honorary member of the ACC in 1909. Though she was not a noted mountaineer, alpine artist and naturalist Mary Vaux Walcott was made an honorary member in 1914. Albert MacCarthy was a member of a party that made the first ascent of Mt. Robson in 1913. He was made an honorary member of the ACC after making the first ascent of Mt. Logan in 1925. Climbers James Monroe Thorington and Kate Gardiner were made honorary members in 1945. Brad Washburn was similarly honored in 1967, followed by Henry Hall Jr. in 1975. In the long history of the ACC, there are few of any nationality who have done more for climbing or who are more respected in Canada than American William L. Putnam, who was presented honorary membership in 1985.

Perhaps as important as American ACC membership has been the American literary influence on Canadian climbing. Early books by Walter Wilcox drew the attention of the entire world to the alpine glories of Lake Louise. Climbers and adventurers of the caliber of Howard

Palmer and Lewis Freeman not only made important ascents in the Rockies and Selkirks, but also published enduring accounts of their adventures that helped establish a mountain literature genre in Canada. James Monroe Thorington became one of Canada's earliest and most highly regarded alpine scholars.

Nowhere has American involvement in Canadian climbing been more influential than in the writing of mountaineering guidebooks, a tradition that goes back to the first trail guide ever written for the Rockies, in 1897. This tradition comes full circle with popular contemporary guidebooks authored or co-authored by Americans on mountain ranges as accessible as the Alberta Rockies and as remote as the big walls of Baffin Island.

As a centennial gift to the American Alpine Club, the Alpine Club of Canada will be producing a beautifully bound edition of Alfred Ostheimer III's hitherto unpublished account of an extraordinary expedition he made to Jasper National Park in the summer of 1927. Fittingly, the publication of this joyful account of a summer of summits in the Canadian Rockies was funded jointly—by Cana-dians and our American friends. On this most important anniversary of the AAC, we hope our gift will become a lasting memento of a century of association and shared appreciation of the glories of Canadian peaks.

Top: Hans Fuhrer, left, and A.J. Ostheimer from *Every Other Day: The Journals of the Remarkable Rocky Mountain Climbs and Explorations of A.J. Ostheimer*. Edited by R.W. Sandford and Jon Whelan, with an introduction by David Dornian. Published by the Alpine Club of Canada in celebration of the Centennial of the American Alpine Club.

CHARLES F. FAY

JOHN MUIR

HENRY G. BRYANT

THE AMERICAN ALPINE CLUB

100 YEARS OF ALPINE LEADERSHIP

From social club to alpine warrior, the American Alpine Club's
presidents look back on a century of defining who we are.

There have been 32 presidents of the AAC, including me. Like me, many (perhaps too many) were trained in the law. A fair number were educators and medical doctors, and even one was a man of the cloth who gave sermons upon his descent from climbs in the Canadian Rockies. Some were highly accomplished climbers, while others were more hikers or men of science. And even though the Club at its outset admitted women into its ranks of members, only one president has been a woman.

The presidents have generally been a hearty and long-lived lot, with many accomplishing significant climbs while in office and after. Nearly all have served the club in a myriad of other capacities and responsibilities, both before and after their presidencies. If there can be one uniting thread that binds us all, it is our devotion to and love of the Club and of mountains.

The issues we have faced are often the same, seemingly unchanging: East versus West, age versus youth, and where and how to spend our money. Another preoccupying matter for many has been the Clubhouse, its existence, location, and operation. A persistent issue has been the establishment and securing of the endowment, which has probably been resolved through the creation of an Investment Committee mandated by the Bylaws. Another relatively recently "resolved" issue is that of the qualification for membership, as the Club has gone from a social organization with a membership in the hundreds to a social and service organization with a membership in the thousands.

Let us now hear from those who have led the Club over its first century. I'll quickly summarize the terms of office of the presidents who have passed away, and let all the currently living presidents speak for themselves.

JAMES FRUSH

CHARLES ERNEST FAY (1902-1907, 1917-1919)

Presidents have traditionally served for three years, but Professor Fay, our first president, not only served a six-year term but was redrafted for an additional three-year term. He had served as President of the Appalachian Mountain Club of which he was also a founder. He climbed primarily in the Canadian Rockies and had served as the American agent for the Duke of Abruzzi's Mt. St. Elias expedition.

JOHN MUIR (1908-1910).

Muir is perhaps our best known president outside the Club. While Fay was from and of the East, Muir was from and of the West. There would often be this alternating, from the West to East, of the geographical source of our leaders. Muir also complemented Fay's literary and social standing in climbing with his fervent conservation of the climbing environment.

JUDGE HARRINGTON PUTNAM (1911-1913)

Putnam oversaw the first major controversy handled by the Club: expelling Dr. Frederick Cook from AAC membership. Now, nearly 100 years after the founding of the Club, this controversy still rages in the minds of not just a few, and the board of director has dealt with the issue as recently as last year. Under Putnam's leadership the issues of a Clubhouse and library arose for the first time.

HENRY GRIER BRYANT (1914-1916)

Bryant oversaw the formal incorporation of the Club under the laws of the Commonwealth of Pennsylvania. The Montagnier Collection of alpine literature was accepted by the Club to form the base of its library.

LEWIS LIVINGSTON DELAFIELD (1920-1922)

Delafield's presidency found the Club for the first time formally sponsoring expeditions. The Club's first sponsored expedition was to Canada's Mt. Logan for which a clubwide, and worldwide, fundraising effort was undertaken. And our annual meeting under Delafield had the now-typical visit from our British climbing friends. Movies of the British Mt. Everest North Ridge expeditions of the early 1920s were shown.

REVEREND HARRY PIERCE NICHOLS (1923-1925)

Honorary Membership became an issue under the Reverend's presidency as it often has since. His urging of the election of Pope Pius XI as an Honorary Member came to naught as the Pope declined the honor. In his stead, the Board elected George Mallory. There was also significant growth under the Reverend's leadership as the Club membership rose from 126 to 144 despite the deaths of some eight regular and Honorary Members.

HOWARD PALMER (1926-1928)

Palmer was another lawyer, although one who didn't practice law. He was typical of many of the Club's presidents in that he wrote extensively on the alpine environment. His *Mountaineering and Exploration in the Selkirks* formed the basis for his compilation of the Alpine Club's first guidebook, that to the Rocky Mountains of Canada.

DR. WILLIAM SARGENT LADD (1929-1931)

Ladd oversaw the participation and the founding of the Union International des Associations d'Alpinism (UIAA) and the gift of our first clubhouse, an old fire station located on the upper East side of Manhattan. The gift generated the first major fundraising effort for the Club and the establishment of an endowment to help fund the upkeep of the gift. It was during his term that the first *American Alpine* Journal was published (1929).

HENRY BALDWIN deVILLIERS-SCHWAB (1932-1934)

Under deVilliers-Schwab's presidency the Club's membership increased past the magic number of 200. He was one of our most widely climbing presidents of this era with climbs throughout the world, including notable ascents in the Alps, New Zealand, Chile, Peru, South Africa, and Australia.

All photos from the AAJ article "Early History of the American Alpine Club," by Howard Palmer, which describes the "colourful background of the club, the commanding personalities of the founders, and the vicissitudes of earlier years..."

JOEL ELLIS FISHER (1935-1937)

Fisher oversaw the first and only proxy fight, or contested vote by the membership, in the Club's history. The goal of the dissidents was to require a bylaw amendment which would require that the annual meetings be held throughout the entire country and not merely among the major cities of the East. The proxy fight failed to obtain the amendment, but ever since the practice of the Club has been to attempt to rotate the location of the annual meeting.

JAMES GRAFTON ROGERS (1938-1940)

Rogers was our first Colorado president and was also the president of the Colorado Mountain Club. Under Rogers, the Club, and many of its members, were instrumental in bringing into existence the 10th Mountain Division of the U.S. Army.

JAMES MONROE THORINGTON (1941-1943)

One of the mission statements for our Club has always been the dissemination of information on the alpine regions, and yet the progress and financial success of our publications program has always been fraught with difficulties. Under Thorington, the Club became "the publisher of last resort" for mountaineers, ensuring that information was published which would otherwise not see the light of day. Thorington was perhaps the ultimate scholar of alpinism for the Club and involved in producing a long series of guide books for the Club. He also served as editor of the *Journal.*

JOHN CROWTHER CASE (1944-1946)

Case focused, as might be expected from the time of his presidency, on the furtherance of the 10th Mountain Division. At the end of his presidency, the Club membership had passed the milestone of 300 members.

WALTER ABBOT WOOD, JR. (1947-1949)

Wood focused greatly on the process of testing and certifying mountain guides. He himself was also a certified guide, having qualified in Switzerland. He also helped found the Arctic Institute of North America.

HENRY SNOW HALL, JR. (1950-1952)

Hall had previously served the Club for 15 years as its secretary and later became the Club's first Honorary President in 1974. His significant financial support helped not only the Club but many expeditions maintain solvency. Interestingly, he had been elected to Honorary Membership, a special category bestowed only by the board of directors, prior to his serving as president.

BRADLEY BALDWIN GILMAN (1953-1955)

Gilman was the only officer who sat in all four of the primary officer's chairs. He was intimately involved in uncovering and stopping, at the last minute, the plot by some members to attempt to obtain membership for a dog, a great difficulty in those days in that the application needed to go through the Board of Directors or, as it was known in those days, the Club's Councilors.

JOHN CAMERON OBERLIN (1956-1958)

When I was elected president of the American Alpine Club I was a resident of Cleveland, Ohio, and in those days I traveled to meetings by train.

Club affairs were then in disarray, lacking an editor of the *American Alpine Journal*, an administrative secretary, and a librarian. Leaders of the Sierra Club were pressuring the AAC to become a similar conservation oriented organization in a manner that unnecessarily cost the Sierra Club its tax-exempt status. Many western members were highly critical of the Club's operations but unresponsive when asked to make any helpful contribution.

The biggest accomplishment of my tenure in office was the appointment of H. Adams Carter, a close friend of Bob Bates, as editor of the *American Alpine Journal*. (Bob had himself been co-editor with David Robertson during an earlier difficult period.) The legacy of Ad Carter is so extraordinary as to place a heavy burden on subsequent editors to emulate him. The *Journal* is his monument and the most important continuing product of the Club.

An Expeditions Committee was inaugurated and I appointed George Bell its first Chairman. A Conservation Committee was also established, with Bill Child at its head. At the urging of Dave Brower, Corinne Albinson was made administrative secretary and took over the day-to-day operations at the Clubhouse. The Club's charter was dug out of the safe deposit box and examined by our former president Brad Gilman, a lawyer and a trust officer, who steered us in our conservation supporting activities without endangering our invaluable tax-exempt status. I myself went on a personal tour of our Western states and Sections (at my own expense) where such members as Pete Schoening, Raffi Bedayn, and Bob Craig made real efforts to be helpful.

With the Club's charter in mind, Ad Carter organized a small expedition to Chile (again, at our own expense with some contributions by other individual members) including Bob Bates and me to conduct a survey of Ojos del Salvado. There was a good chance it might turn out to be the highest peak in the hemisphere as Aconcagua had just been re-surveyed and drastically downgraded. Aconcagua retained its crown by a rather slim margin, but our survey was officially recognized by the Chilean government and the American Geographical Society.

The Club has come a tremendous distance since my day and it is to be congratulated on its successes. Old age does not bring any increase in wisdom but it does afford a certain perspective denied those who cannot look back down so many years.

There is simply no end to worthy causes the Club can be pressured to pursue, but it is always a mistake to "jump on one's horse and ride rapidly off in all directions." To stay focused on the objectives of the Club's charter will serve the great purpose of enhancing enjoyment of the high mountains for all of our members. To load us down with too much ironware and too much bureaucracy will cost us the freedom of the hills.

ROBERT HICKS BATES (1959-1961)

During my term of office the main issues concerned the New York Clubhouse and the cost to individuals to become members of the AAC. Increasing the membership was important too, and effort was made to get more young climbers as members. The Expeditions Committee was very active, and I tried to help with letters to the authorities in Pakistan, Nepal and elsewhere. The Club also worked with Mt. McKinley National Park people about establishing sound climbing regulations there. The *AAJ* and the *AAC News* were then the Club's major connections with its sections. Big issues, such as whether the Clubhouse should be moved, developed in the future.

My greatest challenge in AAC leadership was helping to solve a problem that threatened to split the club between East and West. Groups of fine climbers from both areas had been raising money to become the AAC expedition to climb the highest peak in Antarctica. Back then all flights to there were made by the U.S. Navy, and those with international implications were controlled by our state department. Here we had an advantage, for James Grafton Rogers, who had been president of the club from 1938 to 1940, was now an Undersecretary of the State Department. With his help we put together a meeting in Washington with representatives from the Navy and the State Department, and also from the two groups of AAC climbers. Rumors existed that Japanese climbers were already planning a similar expedition, but no official request had been made. At our meeting the state department and navy representatives strongly agreed that action had to be taken fast, for one expedition only, and that it must be an American expedition. It was left to me to decide who the leader of that expedition should be.

Obviously, the climbers from the East and from the West would need to be fused into a single party—if that could be done. Fortunately, I knew the man who could do it. He was an experienced climbing leader whose parties had included climbers from across the country. He was well liked by all for his judgment and sense of humor. The man was Nick Clinch, who was born in Texas, lived in California, and had good climbing friends everywhere. I called Nick, filled him in on the need to fuse the two groups into one, and assured him of the full support of all parties concerned.

The climbers of the two groups accepted Nick with acclaim, even as he accepted the position of leader. The result was a great success. The climbers became a fine team, making ascents of the highest peaks, with no accidents. Their success was extolled by climbers around the world. Not everyone was pleased, as I learned a couple of years later in Kathmandu, when a Japanese climber confided to me that the one great climb he had expected to make was the first ascent of Antarctica's highest mountain. But somehow the Americans had gotten there first!

CARLTON PERRY FULLER (1962-1964)

Fuller helped move the Club from an organization that focused primarily on the East Coast into a more national organization. He encouraged the 1963 American Mt. Everest Expedition that made the first American ascent and the first traverse of the mountain. At the end of Fuller's presidency, Club membership was over 600 in number and disbursed widely throughout the country.

LAWRENCE GEORGE COVENEY (1965-1967)

Coveney accomplished what was near impossible for many of his predecessors. He succeeded in having the Club hold its annual meeting in Seattle, which turned out to be the first of many to be held in the Seattle area. He was considered as a bridge between a number of young "troublemakers" and the Club's financial "establishment," and eventually helped bring the "troublemakers" into the positions of leadership in the Club, arguably co-opting them forever.

NICHOLAS BAYARD CLINCH (1968-1970)

My presidency was a study in transition. For many years a small group of Easterners had run the Club, rotating the various offices among themselves. They had met the challenges of the Club and American mountaineering, but suddenly everyone had done everything, except for two new younger Councilors, John Humphreys and me. Then John was killed in a plane crash. That left me. Carl Fuller called and said "they" wanted me to be president. I was dubious but he insisted and promised me "full support."

There have always been two basic conflicts in the American Alpine Club. West versus East and Young versus Old. With the recent broad growth in climbing and the moving of the Clubhouse to Colorado, conflict between West and East has been reduced, but Young versus Old continues. It always will.

The Young are active and have the problems and the Old have the experience and ability to deal with them. Unfortunately, the Old are not familiar with the current problems and the Young are ignorant of what the Old are doing to promote mountaineering. The most effective efforts are not always the most visible ones.

The most important asset the Club has is its name: The American Alpine Club. This, together with its history, makes it a formidable instrument for those willing to put forth the effort to use it. But it does not do things on its own. Someone—officers, staff, members—has to do the work.

In the late sixties the challenges were made more difficult by an increase in mountaineering and by the cultural changes in society. I was young and from the West and I personally knew mountaineers everywhere. I visited all the sections and, as I was "one of them," they listened to me regarding what the Club was trying to accomplish.

My objective was to bridge the gap between Young and Old, West and East, and use that instrument. With all of us working together we achieved such things as the Grand Teton Climber's Ranch. When there was a problem we would try to help, but frequently I would ask the person who brought it to our attention if they would be willing to tackle it in the name of the American Alpine Club and promised "full support." This used the two most important advantages of the Club, its name and the energy of its members.

Today the challenges are greater but so are the resources of Club. We have a vastly bigger membership base and a larger, more efficient staff. Even so, President Kennedy had it right. The Club is a wonderful instrument, but the members have to use it. You cannot leave things to others.

John Lathrop Jerome Hart (1971-1973)

The first major revision of the Club's bylaws occurred under Hart's presidency. He was also instrumental in arranging climbing exchanges with alpinists from the Soviet Union.

William Lowell Putnam (1974-1976)

Three main issues concerned me: the quality of mountain guiding, relationships with the U.S. Forest Service, and developing clearly written policy statements on issues affecting alpinists.

The late and much beloved Raffi Bedayn headed up the mountain guiding effort, and we failed to make much progress. Since the National Park Service managed most of the more popular climbing areas in the United States, and since they have a long-standing practice of dealing only with a single concessionaire for each park, we found two discouraging conditions. There was an established vested interest in maintaining the status quo, and it seemed to make little difference to the bureaucrats that we were offering a quality-assurance concept that had great potential benefits to the public. In later years, the American Mountain Guides Association started up completely independently from the Club. It seems to me that outsiders from the concessionaire guides founded the AMGA, and they have strived mightily to build a thoroughly trained roster of really good guides.

To establish relations with the U.S. Forest Service, volunteers from the Club's membership presented themselves to the supervisors in many of the national forests where climbing is a significant recreational activity. The objective was to have someone in regular contact with those supervisors who might insert a word of advice, the supervisor thus profiting from the experience of a knowledgeable mountaineer. These persons would be readily accessible to each supervisor to advise in resolving problems of access, camping, trail-making, etc.

To draft a series of statements that embodied the Club's well-considered attitudes toward ethics, access, environment, forest management, mining, registration, huts, and roads, I used some of the Club's most erudite members, led mostly by future president Price Zimmerman. In subsequent years my successors have encouraged further policy statements on other mountaineer-related issues as the need for a defined policy has become evident.

As we have found from our more recent and more intense involvement with issues affecting climbers, these long-standing, well-reasoned, and reasonable statements have been of great value in establishing our bona fides when dealing with land managers.

JAMES FRANCIS HENRIOT (1977-1979)

Many exciting and significant events occurred during my tenure, events that I look back to with sincere appreciation for the cooperation and support of our members. But what I particularly like to recall here are four issues that contributed to the sustainability of the Club, since they are very important as we move into our second century.

First, our outreach broadened to include a wider geographic spread. The strong formative influence of our East Coast location and membership shaped the Club into the powerful force that it became in the earlier years. But as the first president from the Northwest, I was pleased to set annual meetings and board of directors meetings at key places in the western part on the country, including Salt Lake City, the AAC's Climbers Ranch in Grand Teton National Park, Rocky Mountain National Park, and Mt. Hood. Similarly our membership continued to extend westward. Our membership peaked at 1,360 at the end of my tenure.

Second, younger members joined the Club, increasing their percentage in a significant fashion. This meant fresh blood with a younger generation bringing new ideas, lively commitment, and an orientation toward the future.

Third, the endowment fund was strengthened through a low-key campaign with the generous contributions primarily from board members and others. Over $100,000 was added to the fund when the campaign came to an end in 1979.

Fourth, the Club's participation in international mountaineering was expanded through participation in the International Union of Alpine Associations (UIAA) and mountaineering exchanges. In 1977 the Club hosted the UIAA General Assembly meeting at Pinkham Notch, New Hampshire, its first meeting in North America.

Amateur expeditions to Himalayan countries grew significantly during my term. The Club screened and approved qualified expeditions, facilitating their efforts to obtain permission to climb. The Club had participated in the first large international climbing meet hosted by the Soviet Union in the Pamirs in 1973. Thereafter the Club began formal climbing exchanges annually with primarily the Eastern European Socialist countries. I was very interested in exchanges, and at the conclusion of my term as president I became chairman of the Climbing Exchanges Committee for 14 years.

Let me conclude by saying that I was fortunate during my term as president to have the assistance and guidance of the immediate past president Bill Putnam, an Easterner, and an earlier past president, Nick Clinch, a Westerner.

The future is built upon the past. I am very happy in this retrospective to be confident of the American Alpine Club's solid future.

THOMAS CALLENDER PRICE ZIMMERMAN (1980-1982)

Having previously been chair of the Conservation and Access Committee, I was troubled by the Club's inability to lend significant material support to the activities it fostered, especially publishing, maintaining access, and granting climbing and research fellowships. To assure a reliable source of funds it was necessary to increase the Club's endowment, but to do this we had to win back the confidence of our principal donors, which had been forfeited by the raids on the endowment that had taken place in the past. A revolving fund was set up with the idea of putting publications on an independent footing, and a drive was launched to make good past losses to the endowment. With a giving record of 65 percent, equal to that of the best liberal arts colleges, the drive demonstrated the commitment of our members, but the confidence of major donors came slowly.

ROBERT WALLACE CRAIG (1983-1985)

Looking back, which is somehow getting easier than looking forward, I'm impressed that for the past 50 years the AAC has been in an accelerating state of transition, with the past 20 years being a time of such change as to make the earlier Club almost unrecognizable. Nevertheless, in spite of growth, of outreach, of unbelievable advances in climbing skills and expeditions to every-where, the original spirit of friendship, camaraderie, humor, and curiosity that animated the early American climbers still prevails and makes the Club a very good place to be. When I was asked to serve as president in 1983, I accepted with a sense of indebtedness for all the expeditionary opportunities, the friendships, the inspirations that the Club had offered.

My term was one in which we continued to encourage younger, very active (in several instances world class) climbers to serve on the board of directors and committees of the Club. I urged the election of more young women to take part in the work of the Board (and for this some Victorian types accused me of ulterior motives). Following on the shoulders of Miriam Underhill, Ruth Mendenhall, Joan Firey, and Dana Isherwood, more and more young women climbers have served to the present.

If I made one fundamental mistake during my term (and I'm sure I made several) it was to accept leadership of an innovative Everest West Ridge expedition (oxygenless, porterless—and, I later concluded, a bit mindless). On that occasion the past friendships of 35 years in the AAC came to the fore and provided me with the support and insights needed to try to do a reasonable job: curmudgeonly and kind Bill Putnam, the wise and Pickwickian Nick Clinch, the gentleman scholar Price Zimmerman, the street smarts aristocrat Jim McCarthy, and the tirelessly supportive Jim Henriott were helpful in so many ways that express the best in the AAC tradition. And then there was Bob Bates, who was always available for counsel and moderate restraint.

We began to explore the possibility of an American mountaineering consortium to increase the impact of the AAC's Committee on Access, to encourage broader use of the Club's growing and outstanding library resource, and to possibly open new membership pipelines. The idea was that regional clubs might be helped on their access issues and in turn contribute in the policy arena to goals of the AAC. This did not quite happen, but it sharpened thinking within the Club on how we might be more effective in pursuing policy goals within the U.S. Forest Service, the National Park Service, and in dealing with local governmental entities.

We initiated an effort to increase membership numbers in 1984, but found the qualifications required discouraged any significant gains. Notwithstanding, we did increase from 1,760 to 2,100.

JAMES PETER MCCARTHY (1986-1988)

One of the hottest and most contentious issues during my term was qualification for membership. As almost no one today will remember, the AAC was originally modeled on the Alpine Club (the world's original mountaineering association, founded in London in 1857). Membership was by invitation and two members had to propose a new member and the prospective member had to submit a résumé. In the very early days the council, and later the board, spent a good deal of time in reviewing such résumés. Later it became the job of the secretary and the membership committee to do so. It was my intention to do away with all that and accept anyone who had climbed for two seasons. This concept did not initially receive universally enthusiastic support from the board. Nonetheless, after several lively board meetings over a couple of years, the present structure of qualifications was finally agreed to.

Another agenda that was pursued at this time was an attempt to reach out to what we would call today the sport-climbing community. This started out as an attempt to protect the interests of our great women competitors, Lynn Hill and Robyn Erbesfield, who were active in European comps and who were subject to a good deal of rule manipulation. Despite several trips to Europe by me, the issue of fairness was not completely achieved during my term. Along these lines, a very expensive, and in the end fruitless, attempt was made to organize and fund a national team. Fundraising efforts came to naught and the effort had to be abandoned.

Armando Menocal, one of the founders of the Access Fund, is fond of twitting me these days. He claims that I was the grandfather of the Access Fund. There may be a tiny kernel of truth in his jibe. It is true that I let the members of the Access Committee of the AAC, the forefathers of the Access Fund, have considerable leeway during my term. It pleases me these days to see our club and the Access Fund acting in concert on important issues such as the bolting controversy.

GLENN EDWARD PORZAK (1989-1991)

At the start of my tenure as AAC president, the Club was faced with a six figure annual deficit, a dwindling endowment, and a static and aging membership of approximately 1,500 climbers. The Club was also embroiled in the numerous controversies surrounding the organization of the emerging sport of competitive climbing—an activity that was not understood (or particularly embraced) by the Club's membership base and was overwhelming the Club's limited financial resources. It was clear that if the Club was going to survive, it needed to get its financial house in order and make some dramatic changes. To do this, however, some difficult and unpopular choices had to be made.

First, we proposed and the board passed a balanced budget amendment. We then organized the initial American sport climbing team and helped set up the World Cup competitive sport climbing circuit. Once organized, however, the Club removed itself from any future financial and leadership roles in this sport. The Club then spun off its Access Committee into a new organization, the Access Fund. This latter move allowed the important work of climbers' access to continue with a new financial base, while at the same time enabling the Club to balance its budget.

The heart of the effort to change the direction of the Club, however, was centered on the need to relocate its Clubhouse. The time was long overdue to sell the New York headquarters and move west to the mountains, the geographic center of our membership base, and the greatest area of potential membership growth. At the same time, a move west would also enable the Club to reinvigorate itself with a new administrative staff. Perhaps most importantly, it would send a signal of a change in direction and that the Club would no longer be dominated by its "Eastern establishment." Rather, the Club's new direction would focus on membership benefits and service related issues to the climbing community at large. Highlights of that change in direction were our success in securing climbers rescue insurance for all Club members and upgrading the Teton Climbers' Ranch.

It took virtually my entire three-year term as president to build the consensus for such a move. Finally, the last actions I took at the final board meeting over which I presided were the introduction of the resolutions to sell the New York Clubhouse and move the new Club headquarters to Colorado. Both resolutions were approved unanimously. Little did I know then that those resolutions would embark me on a 10-year campaign to find the old junior high school in Golden; develop partnerships with the Colorado Mountain Club and the Colorado Outward Bound School in our new headquarters building; and finally raise and spend 8 million dollars to create a 40,000-square-foot complex now known as the American Center for Mountaineering.

The high point of my term as president, both literally and figuratively, was reaching the summit of Mt. Everest in May of 1990. As the first sitting president of an alpine organization to climb the world's highest peak, the ascent hopefully sent a message that the Club was composed of members who were active climbers.

John Edward (Jed) Williamson (1992-1994)

At the fall 1991 board meeting of the AAC, graciously held at Ad and Ann Carter's mountain retreat in Jefferson, New Hampshire, item eight of the agenda was clubhouse relocation. The minutes reflect "a straw vote clearly indicating that the board was in favor of such a move." At the December 1991 meeting, Honorary President Bob Bates moved "That the Board of Directors of the American Alpine Club sell the New York Clubhouse and relocate, the sale to be accomplished at a net gain to the club even after the cost of relocation." Unanimously carried. Then Jim McCarthy moved "That the next president should appoint a chairman and constitute a committee to oversee the sale and relocation of the American Alpine Club property." Also unanimously carried.

I was elected president at this annual meeting. My interest in taking this office was to help expedite such a move. I was among the few who had visited the New York office in recent years, and it had not escaped me, in looking at the guest book, that only six visitors (and not many members) had been to the headquarters in the previous few years.

Things moved quickly over the next year. Jim McCarthy and I were in charge of the "sell" end, while Glenn Porzak and Mark Udall would look for appropriate properties in the Denver area. The very short story is that the net result was a sale at a good price, with most of the proceeds going back into the endowment, and a good buy in Golden. This was followed by a successful Capital Campaign—and thanks to many, many good people. We bid farewell to Franc de la Vega, who had served 20 years as executive secretary, and Pat Fletcher, who had served nearly as long as librarian. I appointed Ralph Erenzo to become the managing director until, with Mark Udall and Bob Craig, I hired Charley Shimanski as the executive director to oversee the move west and set up temporary offices there until the completion of the American Mountaineering Center in Golden.

This was a large and rewarding task, but there were other matters as well. First, there was the ongoing struggle with our publications program—an issue that persists. Next, there were the feisty young sport climbers. As the AAC was the governing body for this budding enterprise, Jim McCarthy, Ralph Erenzo, and I headed up efforts to try to manage it. Will we ever forget that first American-sponsored competition on the outside of Snowbird Lodge? I also journeyed to Washington a few times to represent the club in discussions and committee meetings on Capitol Hill about the emerging topics of fixed anchors in the wilderness and paying for rescues. During this time I also helped form the Wilderness Risk Managers Committee, whose mission is to sponsor an annual educational conference for adventure-program administrators. I am still a presenter and the AAC representative for this issue-based gathering. Involvement in the AAC is like the Hotel California: you can check out—but you can never leave.

LOUIS FRENCH REICHARDT (1995-1997)

I joined the American Alpine Club in 1969 proud of climbs that would not even merit a footnote in the AAJ today, but happily did then. Shortly afterward, I joined Boyd Everett and his comrades for the first American attempt on Dhaulagiri, which was made possible by AAC sponsorship, as were all my subsequent expeditions to Asia. The AAC really captured my loyalty during this expedition by the extraordinary moral support that we received from Nick Clinch, Henry Hall, and others in the club after the avalanche that claimed so many of our lives. At a time when I could well imagine being subjected to an inquisition, the club was completely supportive. I realized then that a single life would not provide time enough to repay adequately this generosity.

For this reason above all others, it was a special pleasure to be asked to serve as vice president in 1991 under Jed Williamson. It was an exciting time to be involved with the AAC. Every board meeting was in Colorado, with half of the time spent inspecting empty warehouses or office buildings as potential future AAC headquarters. Every day of these three years was full of anticipation and excitement. The move to Colorado promised both opportunity and risk. Jed's superb judgment of people resulted in recruitment of two ideal people—Ralph Erenzo, who managed the move from New York as managing director, and Charley Shimanski, who took charge in Colorado as executive director. Glenn Porzak's judgment, patience, and persistence resulted in identification of a future headquarters with opportunities beyond our imaginations. Together these decisions went far toward ensuring the success of this exceedingly risky move.

With events so favoring success it was an easy decision when the nominating committee unexpectedly asked me to follow Jed as president. What possibly could go astray after so much positive momentum? How wrong I was! The first unimaginable challenge was the loss of Ad

Carter, who had contributed more than anyone else to the AAC through his editorship for more than 20 years of the *American Alpine Journal*. Ad's loss was not to the AAC alone, since he was the center of a network of informants on mountaineering throughout the world that was in danger of collapse. After serious arm-twisting, I persuaded Jed Williamson to step into the breach as managing editor. With advice from Yvon Chouinard, Christian Beckwith was identified as a worthy replacement for Ad as editor. As our recent *AAJ's* demonstrate, Christian was an inspired choice, rising to the challenge of reestablishing a network of informants as well as ably editing the *Journal*. Also critical for the success of this transition was the generosity of Yvon and many other members who provided a financial cushion for the *Journal* during these challenging years.

There were also many anticipated challenges associated with our move and commitment to our new headquarters. First, of course, was financial. In collaboration with our partners in the Colorado Mountain Club, the AAC embarked on an unprecedented fundraising campaign to raise the several million dollars needed to realize our vision for the new American Mountaineering Center. During my three-year presidency, this was a constant challenge that absorbed almost the entire effort of our executive director and required dedicated leadership from Mike Browning, Glenn Porzak, Jed Williamson, Nick Clinch, and many others. This campaign was only completed on my final day in office.

The promise of our new headquarters and the exigencies of fundraising forced us to consider seriously how we could remain relevant in the climbing and mountaineering communities when such a small proportion of active climbers were AAC members. As a first response, we discarded in 1995 our arcane membership requirements and committed ourselves to discounts and other policies to encourage membership by young climbers. Supported by local volunteers, the Club established new sections in the Southeast, Midwest, Southwest, South Central, Northern Rockies, and North Central regions of our country, so that sections finally covered almost the entire span of the United States. The demands of granting agencies also forced us to make a serious commitment to increasing the diversity of AAC membership. Among other actions, we established a new award in the name of our Honorary President Robert Hicks Bates to recognize exceptional skill and climbing achievement by a young climber. Through outreach, sections, staff performance, and effective advertising, our membership expanded by more than 2,000 from approximately 2,300 in December, 1994, to more than 4,300 in December, 1997. In addition, the average age of our membership declined by several years, suggesting that our outreach to younger, more active climbers had some success. Nonetheless, this average remained in the low 40s, a decade or more above the average age of the American climber.

Certainly the most persistently annoying challenge during my presidency was that posed by our publications program. While we felt committed to the *American Alpine Journal*, despite its cost, and to *Accidents In North American Mountaineering*, a dependable revenue source, increasingly painful financial realities led to the realization that neither of two able publications directors could turn red ink into black ink at such a small press. We only associated with The Mountaineers Books reluctantly, but this immediately benefited the Club, both financially and by reducing a major diversion of staff effort from our core missions. Despite this, our publications program has continued to challenge each of my successors.

Challenges to access were given momentum by responses of the National Park Service to the publicity and political pressures generated by a series of accidents and costly rescues on Mt. McKinley. Efforts to prevent implementation of discriminatory fees and access policies challenged the connections and diplomatic skill of our Board during my presidency. Our success in challenging access fees and unreasonable pre-registration requirements was real, but only partial. The December 1996 flood of Yosemite Valley provided the second major challenge of access and environmental policy. Despite openness and sympathy from Park Service personnel for our positions, it gradually became clear that other pressures had persuaded them to propose unacceptable plans for redevelopment that would compromise Yosemite Valley's environment and accessibility to climbers. Whether we would be more effective inside or outside of the National Park Service tent was discussed repeatedly at our board meetings during 1997. In the end, John Middendorf, Tom Frost, and others persuaded our board to challenge the National Park Service to be true to its own mandate—"to protect and preserve natural resources"— through support of a lawsuit, an unprecedented act for our small organization. The future would clearly show how right were Frost and Middendorf to insist on such a dramatic shift from our policy of exclusive reliance on dialogue and persuasion. At the time, though, I was relieved to pass the challenge of getting the most possible from a mixed policy of simultaneous cooperation in some areas and confrontation in others to my extraordinarily able successor.

In summary, the three years of my presidency were ones of transition dedicated to realizing my predecessors' vision for a new mountaineering center, to acquiring new members, and to ensuring that the AAC regain its position of leadership as an advocate for climbers throughout this country. While there were challenges and disagreements, it was a wonderful experience because I always received unstinting support from my predecessors and from the board. It seems to me very unlikely that there is another organization as united and supportive of its core missions as is ours.

ALISON KEITH OSIUS (1998-1999)

No question, the defining issues of my term were the Yosemite and the fixed-anchor crises.

Yet at the same time, gifts rained from the heavens. Another major event was a great act of generosity, when Lyman Spitzer— climber, professor, and leading astronomer—left the AAC a bequest. We put the funding into perpetuity and designated the income for climbing grants, policy work, and worthy projects.

Yosemite was a hot potato early on, two months after my installment, when we were petitioned to join a lawsuit set up by Tom Frost and others to protect Camp 4, the historic climbers' campground in Yosemite. The Park Service, reconfiguring the floor plan in the Valley in the wake of massive flooding, planned to abut Camp 4 with new concession-employee dormitories. In 100 years the AAC had never sued anyone, but it was with full support of the board and past presidents that we joined this lawsuit, the first climbing organization to do so.

At Tom Frost's behest, Dick Duane applied in the name of the AAC to have Camp 4 placed on the National Register of Historic Places in Washington, D.C. It was declared eligible for nomination, a major (and rather stunning) boost to our team. Its listing now is virtually complete.

The AAC also strove to protect the pine-filled, rocky Swan Slab meadow from being filled with buildings from the Yosemite Lodge complex. We joined in this effort with the Sierra Club, which achieved a preliminary injunction against construction from a District Court judge in San Francisco.

In the end, our cause prevailed without a courtroom battle. More important, Camp 4 was not only preserved, but newly valued: the Park Service—to its credit—accepted our views, and ultimately expanded it. Moreover, Frost, Duane, and Linda McMillan created cordial, collaborative relationships within Park Service ranks that still serve us well. Among their gains was strong support for a proposed climbers' ranch/campground near Yosemite Valley. In the tradition of Raffi Bedayn and Nick Clinch, they serve as problem solvers and liaisons with the climbing community.

I did not think anything could top the Yosemite problems, until four months later the U.S. Forest Service suddenly dictated that no fixed anchors were allowed on Forest Service wilderness land. No pitons, no bolts, no slings around trees for rap anchors; no placement and no replacement of existing anchors on these lands. The justification cited was the Wilderness Act of 1964 prohibited installations. That prohibition, however, we felt certain was intended to mean buildings and airstrips.

We mobilized, and published op-ed pieces in: *The Wall Street Journal, New York Times, Los Angeles Times, San Francisco Chronicle, Rocky Mountain News, Oregonian, Salt Lake Tribune, Idaho Wood River Journal,* and *Denver Post.* Two supportive editorials came out in the *Denver Post,* written by a staff writer who is also an AAC member. Many other AACers were active and energetic in using their excellent connections to friends in high places.

Lloyd Athearn, AAC deputy director, read through guidebooks and journals, and documented extensive fixed-anchor use prior to the Wilderness Act. Jeanne Klobnak, our legislative liaison, went to Washington, D.C., and researched the legislative and philosophical history of the Wilderness Act. We joined forces with the Access Fund, ORCA, AMGA, and NOLs in many sessions of information sharing and strategizing. Lloyd was our representative in a negotiated-rulemaking process between interested groups and the USFS. He worked closely with Sam Davidson, policy director for the Access Fund. (Creating a bridge with the Access Fund was probably the only goal in my term that I came up with—as opposed to it coming at me!)

And we also celebrated: co-hosting a party with Tom Frost to honor the nomination of Camp 4 to the National Historic Register. All the generations of climbers gathered in Yosemite, with a sense that everyone should speak and be heard. All knew that everyone here would never be together again. And since then we have lost Chuck Pratt, Warren Harding, and, most recently, R.D. Caughron. They were greats.

Last, we allowed Greg Mortenson of the Central Asia Institute, as a winner of the AAC Conservation Award, to seek funding from AAC members for his causes of education and health care for the people of the Himalaya. Members came through beyond anything we could have dreamed (I can only call it gangbusters), allowing him to open a whole new school for girls, which he named for the AAC.

I am often asked what it was like to be the first woman president. Far from resisting that, the Club sought it; I was asked to take that office. No one ever had a more sterling bank of advisors, or better backup.

C. JAMES FRUSH (2000-PRESENT).

I suspect I will be best remembered for being the President of the Club during its Centennial. Still, a number of important things happened during my term and, I must say, the same old issues continued to dominate.

After years of listening to widely varying opinions on "what the membership wanted" at Board meetings, we finally took some concrete steps to determine what it is the membership actually wanted. For the first time, the Club conducted a professional survey of its membership to learn about both its demographics and its members' needs and desires. The results indicated we are largely a group of middle-aged, well-to-do, white men who have climbed broadly around the world (no surprise). We most value the fellowship our club provides, and primarily support political and con-servation efforts. And the annual meetings are important: over half of our membership have attended one.

As usual, the publications program of the Club was in financial disarray, despite significant efforts by my pred-ecessors. In addition, the library was in need of some long-overdue improvements. The board agreed to take unre-stricted funds from the Club's investments accounts, including some of the "Clubhouse" funds, to correct the cash flow shortage the publications program had created and to bring our library into the 20th century as we entered the 21st century.

Also at the Clubhouse, Colorado Outward Bound was brought in as a partner, which resulted in the comple-tion of the American Mountaineering Center and the establishment of a conference center. Diligent efforts are being made to attempt to complete construction at the Golden Clubhouse by arranging and funding our museum.

Responding to our membership survey, the Club continued to increase its involvement in public interest activity, continuing our participation in the fixed anchor rule making process. We also became one of the leaders in interfacing and interacting with numerous land man-agers. We hired our first full-time professional lobbyist, located in Washington, D.C.

The Club's annual budget passed $1 million per year with a staff of more than 10.

Numerous other initiatives have been undertaken, including digitalization of the American Alpine Journal, the establishment of the Spitzer Climbing Grants, the establishment of the Piolet Society (a planned giving society), the creation of the American Alpine Club E-News, the initiation of the Club's Hut System, and the adoption of a Code of Conduct for Club members and staff.

Lastly, a new editor for our beloved *Journal,* John Harlin III, was recruited and appointed during my term. A president can perhaps have no greater legacy.

Such is the past, but what of the future? Seemingly ageless, some of the old tensions arise now and again to trouble us, such as East versus West and age versus youth. Also, the tension between our existence as a social club and a service organization occasionally causes conflict. We must strive to be both in this our second century. We cannot ignore our necessity to be active in the areas of public policy and land management. We must work with like-minded col-leagues in similarly oriented clubs to protect both the environment itself and our access to it.

We must grapple with the fact that we are both a fundraiser in need of contributions and a fund-giver helping climbers, researchers, and others active with alpine issues.

We must also struggle to remain relevant, particularly to young climbers, especially because of our demographic. To help, I've established our first Outreach Committee, with its focus on disadvantaged and minority youth.

We cannot and should not lose our roots. Tradition is a function of style. And as every climber knows, style is of utmost importance. Let us build upon our traditions, and with particular attention to style. With a comradeship which binds us all to the Club and to each other, as does the rope that joins us when we climb, we will move forward into our second century.

(I wish to give particular credit to Bill Putnam's Centennial History of the American Alpine Club *for providing the factual background on the presidents who have not presented their own thoughts.)*

DEGREES OF FREEDOM

*From dry tooling to figure fours, M-climbing in the mountains is
redefining the vision of what's a climbable line.*

RAPHAEL SLAWINSKI

Is it mixed? Rock? Ice? Neither? Routes like Mixed Monster on Mt. Wilson push the boundaries of how much (or how little) ice it takes to make a mixed route. Raphael Slawinski drytooling toward the dagger. *Eamonn Walsh*

"We cannot solve problems by using the same kind of thinking we used when we created them."—Albert Einstein

Mixed climbing has come a long way from its beginnings in mountaineering. The early mountaineer with his nailed boots "providing an equally good grip on rock and ice" (Heinrich Harrer, *The White Spider*, 1959) seems barely recognizable in the modern alpinist making rapid ascents of huge mixed walls from Alaska to the Himalaya. Certainly the pioneer seems to have little resemblance to the "M-climber" figure-fouring their way across an icy roof. In fact, aside from the fact that they both use some form of ice axes and crampons—and even this basic equipment is becoming increasingly specialized—do the alpine and M-climbers have anything in common? By recalling some milestone climbs, I will trace the evolution of mixed climbing into the multifaceted activity it has become.

THE BEGINNINGS: SCOTS AND NORTH WALLS

"It was half superb rock-technique, half a toe-dance on the ice—a toe-dance above a perpendicular drop. [Heckmair] got a hold on the rock, a hold on the ice, bent himself double, uncoiled himself, the front points of his crampons moving ever upwards, boring into the ice."—Heinrich Harrer referring to the first ascent of the north face of the Eiger, in 1938, The White Spider.

Mixed climbing as an activity practiced for its own sake originated in the early 1900s in Scotland. Seeking added challenge, Scottish mountaineers attempted summer rock routes in winter, a startlingly modern concept. Around the same time, the development of crampons (initially not adopted by the nailed-boot-shod

Eamonn Walsh approaching Mixed Monster, which requires two pitches of bare rock to reach the ice. *Raphael Slawinski*

Scots), helped inaugurate the golden north wall era in the Alps. On large alpine routes, mixed climbing was—and often still is—a means to an end, rather than an end in itself. Nonetheless alpine climbs of the 1930s, such as the north faces of the Eiger and of the Matterhorn, defined the state of the art in mixed climbing for decades to come due to their unprecedented length, sustained difficulty, and fearsome commitment. Not until the 1960s were mixed climbing standards raised again, on routes such as the Orion Direct on Ben Nevis and the Bonatti-Zappelli on the Grand Pilier d'Angle of Mont Blanc. By the end of that decade existing equipment and technique had likely been pushed as far as was possible. For an advance to occur, both would have to be reinvented.

THE INTERLUDE: WATERFALL ICE

> *"Apart from the loomingly obvious Cascade Icefall [...], nothing was done until the full potential of modern ice climbing equipment was realized..." –Bugs McKeith,* Canadian Alpine Journal, *1975.*

The breakthrough came in the late 1960s with the introduction of the curved pick by Yvon Chouinard and the Terrordactyl's radically drooped pick, by Hamish MacInnes. The new technology revolutionized ice climbing and paved the way for free-climbing on vertical ice. The revolution in ice climbing eventually would also alter mixed climbing beyond recognition. But ironically, the explosion of interest in waterfall ice initially distracted climbers from mixed climbing. By the early 1980s ice climbing, from being merely one of the techniques in the alpinist's arsenal, had evolved into a full-blown technical art. The skills gained on waterfalls also gave rise to a whole new generation of alpine climbs. Slipstream in the Canadian Rockies blurred the distinction between waterfall ice and alpine climbing; the Moonflower Buttress in the Alaska Range applied the highest levels of ice climbing skill to a major alpine first ascent; and the list goes on. Waterfall ice climbing, though initially pursued for its own sake, ended up revolutionizing alpine climbing.

AHEAD OF THEIR TIME: MIXED CLIMBING IN THE 1970S

> *"Without the Terrordactyl, we'd still all be swinging."–Duncan Ferguson*

For most winter climbers of the 1970s and 80s, vertical ice was the end of the rainbow. The one place where mixed climbing continued to advance was Scotland. Duncan Ferguson recently commented to me that, "even though credit for much of the impetus for modern ice climbing has gone to Chouinard and his curved tools, I strongly feel that it is the Scots and MacInnes in particular and [his Terrordactyls] that ushered in the birth of modern mixed climbing." Indeed modern mixed climbing in the Alps was not a native development, but arrived only when Rab Carrington and Al Rouse exported Scottish attitudes to establish their now classic route on the north face of the Aiguille des Pelerins in the winter of 1975. In North America Ferguson, who was years ahead of his time in his pursuit of mixed climbing, was likewise influenced by Scottish climbing: "I started ice climbing in about 1971.... After [a] short-lived fascination with steep and thick ice, I got frustrated with the clumsy and brutal nature of ice climbing...." But it was only after reading about Scottish climbing, "that I sorted out what I wanted to do with my ice

Suffer Machine, on the Stanley Headwall. The 1991 first ascent of this "unformed" ice route, which involved aid climbing to gain the hanging ice, represented a breakthrough in a climbable line. *Dave Campbell*

climbing—forget the 'thick ice' part of it and see how far I could go with a pair of Terrors and a new attitude and vision. A redefinition of what 'ice climbing' was.... Spent the entire rest of the season wandering around by myself and bouldering and traversing and soloing short mixed climbs. Rock climbs really, with a set of Terrors and crampons. Thin ice, snowed up rock, rock moves between patches of ice and pure rock...." It would be over a decade before Ferguson's redefinition of ice climbing would gain widespread acceptance.

Hard and fast: Alpine mixed climbing into the 1980s

> "*The wall was the ambition. The style became the obsession.*"–*Alex MacIntyre,* Shisha Pangma: The alpine-style first ascent of the South-West Face, *1984.*

> "*Winter alpinism is hard enough without the added dilemma of free-climbing ethics.*"–*Barry Blanchard,* Climbing #117, *1989.*

Perhaps because most alpine routes require some mixed climbing, the development of waterfall ice climbing had a more immediate impact on the sort of mixed ground being climbed in the mountains. It was only later that climbers began to seek out hard mixed ground at the crags. Thus in 1974 in the Canadian Rockies Jeff Lowe and Mike Weis applied the lessons learned on waterfall ice climbs such as the first ascent of Colorado's Bridalveil Falls to set a new standard

Raphael Slawinski attempting the second ascent of the direct start to Suffer Machine (M8) in 1997. This bolted variant was symptomatic of the next step in the evolution of mixed climbing: sport climbing with tools. *Dave Campbell*

of mixed climbing difficulty on the Grand Central Couloir of Mt. Kitchener. On the crux pitch, "with only knifeblades between frozen blocks for protection, the climbing was extremely nerve-wracking. Seldom would the tools penetrate more than half an inch before meeting rock" (Jeff Lowe, *Ice World*, 1996). The bar was raised again in 1978, when Jim Logan and Mugs Stump made the first ascent of the Emperor Face of Mt. Robson. Typical of alpine climbing with its overriding emphasis on getting up, they had no qualms about resorting to aid, yet the runout nature of the climbing also required free-climbing at a high standard. For three days they surmounted pitch after pitch of difficult, poorly protected mixed climbing, with considerable exposure to objective hazards and scant possibility for retreat. On the final day Logan took eight hours to lead the crux pitch, "at first around a roof with all tied-off pins, then onto a tied-off screw, then a bit of ice climbing…. At the top of the pitch I ran out of piton placements and ice, and set off for 30 feet of rock climbing on overhanging loose snow-covered rock with no protection" (Jim Logan, *Climbing* #52, 1979). The Logan-Stump remains unrepeated to this day, a testament to its difficulty and seriousness.

In the Alps the north face of the Grandes Jorasses was a forcing point for advances in alpine mixed climbing. In 1975 Nick Colton and Alex MacIntyre climbed a line of icy runnels and chimneys on the right flank of the Walker Spur. While the Colton/MacIntyre also comprises difficult ice and rock climbing, the main difficulties are mixed. When it was first climbed, the route was undoubtedly one of the hardest of its kind in the world. The Grandes Jorasses remained at the forefront of alpine mixed climbing into the 1980s with a number of difficult new routes: the famous No Siesta in particular was likely ahead of its time. Established in 1986 by the Slovak climbers Stanislav Glejdura and Jan Porvaznik, it featured much thin vertical ice, and difficult free and aid climbing on often poor rock.

One of the first routes to bring a higher standard of mixed climbing difficulty to the greater ranges was the Infinite Spur of Mt. Foraker (5304m) in the Alaska Range, established in 1977 by George Lowe and Michael Kennedy. In describing how they were motivated to attempt the route in pure alpine style in keeping with the new Alaskan idiom of "speed, commitment and technical competence," Kennedy could have been writing today. They encountered much 60-degree ice and rock up to 5.9. The crux was three pitches of mixed climbing high on the route: "My mind was clear and surprisingly calm as I visualized the way ahead, keenly aware of the chalkboard-screech of crampons on rock, the rattling thud of an axe in too-thin ice, a sling on a frozen-in spike, the dull ring of a bad piton behind a loose block, calf muscles screaming for relief, choking spindrift in eyes, throat, down the neck" (Michael Kennedy, *American Alpine Journal*, 1978).

In the Himalaya, large and technical mixed faces were also beginning to be climbed in alpine style. To name but a few: the Hungo Face of Kwangde (6100m) in 1982 by David Breashears and Jeff Lowe; the south face of Annapurna (8091m) in 1984 by Nil Bohigas and Enric Lucas; the Golden Pillar of Spantik (7027m) in 1987 by Mick Fowler and Victor Saunders; and the list goes on. The ultimate achievement in completely committed alpine mixed climbing was Voytek Kurtyka and Robert Schauer's 1985 first ascent of the west face of Gasherbrum IV (7925m). As described by Kurtyka, "the conditions on the face proved very difficult and dangerous.... Altogether, we climbed four pitches of [5.6]–two of them at 7100 and 7300 meters [...] without a single belay point. The real nuisance was the very deep snow on the mixed ground through which we tunneled vertically..." (Voytek Kurtyka, *American Alpine Journal*, 1986). The compact rock and light rack meant that retreat was not an option. Finding the difficulties of the lower face greater than anticipated, and trapped by a multi-day storm on the upper face, they ran out of food and fuel. Reaching the summit ridge on the seventh day, they spent another three descending an unclimbed ridge.

BOLTS AND FIGURE-FOURS: THE M-REVOLUTION

"It appeared to us that ice climbers had reached the limit of technical difficulty. After all, water can only drop so vertically, and ice can only be so rotten before it can no longer support the weight of the climber. So what was to be next?"
– *Jeff Marshall*, The Polar Circus No. 2, 1987.

"There are very, very few ice climbs in the world that are actually hard, but these mixed climbs, on the other hand, they were hard. You could pitch on them...."– *Will Gadd*, Rock and Ice #89, 1998.

Though mixed climbing had been going on in the mountains for decades, M-climbing, the new wave of technically extreme mixed climbing, grew chiefly out of waterfall ice climbing. Bored with the predictability of thick ice, climbers turned their attention to lines previously considered to be unformed. In 1991 in the Canadian Rockies Jeff Everett and Glenn Reisenhofer aided up a ropelength of rock to reach the hanging ice of Suffer Machine (200 m, WI5 A2); the following year in the Alps Jeff Lowe and Thierry Renault also used aid to connect the ice features on Blind Faith (400 m, WI6+ A2). Though initially such discontinuous ice smears were linked up with little regard for the style in which the rock was ascended, it nevertheless took a visionary attitude to even conceive of these mixed lines as potential routes. Lowe in particular was inspired by the possibilities and, with his 1994 ascent of Octopussy (20 m, M8) in Colorado's infamous Vail amphitheatre, the style in which a mixed climb was accomplished returned to the fore with a vengeance.

> *"Let's get real here. No one does a figure-four ice climbing." –Karl Nagy,* Canadian Alpine Journal, *1997.*

> *"The third time, however, was magic. This time I did a second figure 4 immediately following the first one, which allowed me to get a good stick higher up with my right tool." –Jeff Lowe,* Ice World, *1996.*

With its pre-placed protection, redpointing tactics, and exotic moves, Octopussy signaled a radical departure in mixed climbing. Technically, it was by far the hardest mixed climb yet made. The easy access, reliable protection, and lack of objective hazards freed climbers to pursue pure technical difficulty. This was of course similar to what happened in rock climbing some 10 years earlier, when the acceptance of bolt protection paved the way for sport climbing and, ultimately, higher technical standards. Vail continued to be a crucible for M-climbing with Will Gadd's 1997 first ascent of Amphibian (40 m, M9). Stevie Haston was at the cutting edge of M-climbing in the Alps, with routes like 009 (M8+) in 1997 and X-Files (M9+) in 1998. As the dry tooling craze took hold, mixed climbing began to look increasingly like rock climbing with axes and crampons. The athleticism of the new wave of M-climbing also attracted a new breed of participants, often superb rock climbers. With routes like Tomahawk (M11-) and Mission Impossible (M11) in the Alps, and Musashi (M12) in the Canadian Rockies, Robert Jasper, Mauro "Bubu" Bole, Ben Firth, and others are pushing dry tooling into a realm of previously unimagined technical difficulty. With the added catalyst of competition in the three-year-old Ice World Cup, the movement skills required for hard M-climbing have evolved far beyond the static positions of traditional mixed climbing: dynos, figure fours, heel hooks…. The equipment is evolving just as quickly: leashless tools, lightweight boots with integrated minimal crampons….

So what?

> *"The hype pretended that M7 or 8, or 12 for that matter, had never before been climbed until the current practitioners rap-bolted some overhanging choss heap, rehearsed it, climbed it, did photo shoots on it, and treated it as commerce." –Mark Twight,* Climbing #178, *1998.*

> *"009 had a crux dyno on it that […] will, by its very nature, eliminate 98% of the old ice climbers." –Stevie Haston,* High Mountain Sports #184, *1998.*

Hard mixed climbing at the crags is nothing new. Scott Backes recently commented to me, "the routes at the crags [are] why I am able to go into the mountains and do what it is I do. I've been climbing at two 27-meter quarries since the 80s. The quest for pure difficulty mostly on top-rope has led me to know as well as can be known the limits of adhesion and made the routes done high over gear thinkable...." What is new is the attention devoted to what before was considered mere practice. While some have deplored turning "ice climbing into sport climbing," it is worth recalling that the 5.12, 5.13, and 5.14 barriers were not broken by mountaineers rock climbing on rainy days for something to do. They were broken by climbers single-mindedly pursuing pure technical difficulty for its own sake. Similarly, M8, M9, M10, and beyond were climbed only when climbers divorced mixed climbing from alpinism and started mixed climbing for mixed climbing's sake. M-climbing has yet to approach the physical demands of the hardest rock climbs. But it has made a good start by jettisoning the traditionalist baggage of its mountaineering roots.

Nonetheless, one might question whether the pursuit of technical difficulty for its own sake is not missing the point. As Duncan Ferguson recently commented to me, "I strongly feel that the heart and soul of climbing, rock or ice or mixed, have to do with intimate adventure and challenges to the vision and spirit and are not necessarily fed by pure technical difficulty." More pragmatically, one might question whether extreme M-antics at the crag have any relevance for what goes on in the alpine realm. Certainly, after spending time at an M-crag witnessing the dynos,

The nine-pitch drips of Rocketman, 1999, an early application of new-wave mixed to a long route in an alpine setting. *Raphael Slawinski*

The seven-pitch The Day After Les Vacances de Mr. Hulot, on the Stanley Headwall, was the hardest traditional mixed route in the Rockies for years after its first ascent in 1994. It begins left of the lower dagger, traverses snow ledges, then finishes up the curtains. *Raphael Slawinski*

the figure fours, the leashless tricks, it is hard to believe that any of it will ever be used in the mountains. But even if not all of these techniques find their way onto alpine routes (some of them already have), the main import of M-climbing might be in breaking down psychological barriers regarding what is and what is not climbable. To quote Ferguson again: "I see the move onto modern mixed climbs (bolt protected or not) as being a healthy part of the process of raising standards— of forcing new lines of *vision*. The M12 [at the crag] directly translates into an 'impossible' M10 pitch way off the deck...." Or, as Mark Twight recently commented to me, "those mixed climbers participating at the highest levels of the discipline are too consumed by its demands to apply their skills in different arenas.... That said, 'new wave' mixed climbing must influence alpinism. Just as high levels of rock climbing ability obtained by sport climbing 'stars' raised overall standards for everyone, high levels of mixed climbing ability will raise the general level of every climber simply by existing."

This brings us to the thorny issue of bolts. Much of the recent push into extreme technical difficulty in mixed climbing seems inconceivable without them. Yet they remain controversial, particularly in the mountains. In the words of a staunch traditionalist, "[bolts] do not require any weakness in the rock or any skill to place, and they destroy the traditional challenge of mountaineering" (Mick Fowler, *American Alpine Journal*, 2000). Whether one considers bolts to be justifiable, particularly in the mountains, hinges on what one believes constitutes a route. Mark Twight recently summarized the dilemma to me thus: "The person who chooses to bolt insists that because he can climb a particular passage, a route exists, regardless of the natural opportunities for protection.... The person who chooses not to bolt insists that a route does not exist simply because he can physically climb there, natural opportunities for protection must exist also if the climber has need of same." Part of the reason why bolts have become an issue in mixed climbing is that rising standards have expanded our notion of what is climbable. Where it used to be that climbable and protectable lines more or less coincided, the new dry tooling skills have expanded our notion of climbable terrain far beyond what may be naturally protected. Conversely, it is absurd to pretend that mixed climbing standards would have risen as high and as quickly as they have without wholesale acceptance of protection bolts. Having said that, it would seem a pity if the challenge of mixed climbing were reduced to merely executing a sequence of difficult moves. As demonstrated by routes such as Robert Jasper's 1998 Flying Circus (145 m, M10), which only used bolts at belays, truly hard mixed climbing and bolts are not always inseparable.

Another criticism often leveled at M-climbing is that, as Topher Donahue recently commented to me, "most modern 'mixed' climbs have maybe one true mixed move on them, the rest [...] being dry tooling or ice climbing." While this characterization of M-climbing is certainly accurate, I would argue that M-climbing has given us a new perspective from which to look at the mountains in winter. It is also a perspective that is more relevant for alpine climbing. Rock that because of adverse conditions cannot be "rock climbed" often presents the greatest difficulties on alpine routes. Dry tooling skill acquired on M-climbing testpieces adds an awesome weapon to the alpinist's arsenal. From the new perspective, ice climbing, "true" mixed climbing, and dry tooling are all just different aspects of winter free-climbing.

Of course, unlike in rock climbing, the notion of "free" in mixed climbing is controversial. Mixed climbing involves the use of tools: whether or not leashes are used, one still brandishes a skyhook in each hand. To turn our backs on dry tooling and use our hands no matter what the conditions in the name of free-climbing seems a backward step, as dry tooling is an extremely effective winter climbing technique. But the use of tools does make it difficult to be dogmatic about free-climbing. (On the other hand, hazy though the free versus aid distinction might be in theory, attempting a sustained overhanging mixed route quickly makes clear the difference between relying on one's axes, crampons, and skill alone, and making progress by resorting to aid climbing tactics where one can rest on the gear.) Ultimately, the stand one takes on such issues hinges on what is thought to be "good" style. In alpinism, a climb was traditionally considered to be in good style if it was executed with limited means and, generally, "... with little of the frigging around normally associated with a major [...] ascent." (Dave Cheesmond, The Polar Circus No. 1, 1986). However, remarkably little attention has been paid to free-climbing ethics: on large alpine routes such considerations have usually taken a back seat to simply getting up. But alpinists have traditionally placed limitations on themselves to prevent "the murder of the impossible." If by placing a bolt one does not face up to the full "challenge of mountaineering," so also by pulling on gear one evades that challenge. (Seen from this perspective bolts are not an absolute anathema but just one more crutch, such as aid climbing, that we occasionally lean on.) By borrowing from the strict free-climbing ethos of rock climbing, the new generation of M-climbers has the ability to redefine what constitutes good style in alpinism. And finally, whatever one's stance on the importance of free-climbing ethics in mixed climbing, free climbing is almost always faster. And speed in alpine climbing is both good style and good sense.

INTO THE FUTURE

"I wanted one-arm pull-ups, big swings, speed, and see-through frozen lingerie." –Stevie Haston, High Mountain Sports #184, 1998.

"… I found myself back on the south face dry tooling some M5/6 pitches in the death zone at about 7600 meters." –Tomaz Humar, American Alpine Journal, 2000

Andy Parkin and Mark Twight's 1992 first ascent of Beyond Good and Evil on the north face of the Aiguille des Pelerins was an important milestone in alpine mixed climbing. They took 26 hours to climb 14 pitches of thin vertical ice and rock up to French 5+ and A3. As Twight recently commented to me, "when we started working on it […] there had not been many, if any, routes of that level of sustained difficulty combined with inobvious protection done in the Alps." The route's reputation kept it from being repeated until 1995, when taking advantage of good conditions Francois Damilano and Francois Marsigny made the second ascent. However, within the span of the few years since the route was first done, standards have risen to the point that the second ascent was quickly followed by further repeats, all parties completing the route in a day and dispensing with most of the aid. Even accounting for the fact that the original finish to the route is still rarely done, the quick transformation from feared testpiece to modern classic is remarkable nonetheless. Stevie Haston has also done much to bring hard mixed climbing to the mountains, with a strong emphasis on free climbing. His routes on the east face of Mont Blanc du Tacul, the 1994 Pinocchio (M6+) and the 1995 Scotch on the Rocks (M7), were both groundbreaking achievements. While they are not routes of the stature of No Siesta or even Beyond Good and Evil, they are nevertheless sustained multipitch offerings (around 350 meters in length) in an alpine setting, and they were established without bolts (in the case of Scotch, without pitons). In 1997, Robert Jasper added Vol de Nuit (M7+) to the right of Scotch, again climbing the route all free and without bolts. Each of these routes, when it was first done, represented a significant step forward in traditional (if not exactly alpine) mixed climbing. Yet within the span of a few seasons they had become trade routes, sometimes seeing multiple ascents within a single day—yet another stark proof of the rapidly rising skill levels. It is then perhaps surprising that a route like Vol de Nuit remains one of the hardest (quasi-)alpine mixed routes in the Alps. This is but one example of the striking disparity between technical standards at the crags and in the mountains.

In the Canadian Rockies, rising standards fostered on M-climbing testpieces are also having an impact on alpine mixed climbing. For instance when in 1996 Alex Lowe freed Troubled Dreams (150 m, M7) on the Terminator Wall, it was hailed as a major accomplishment. Lowe admitted to being "really pushed" on the crux, and the route went unrepeated. In 2000 Rob Owens, employing many of the new M-climbing techniques including figure fouring on lead above natural gear, added a direct start to Troubled Dreams called Stuck in the Middle. This more sustained variation quickly received several repeats but, tellingly, went nearly unreported. For the new wave of M-climbers, skilled in dry tooling, it was just another day out climbing. Dry tooling where a few years earlier climbers would have tried rock climbing and, failing that, resorted to aid, has also helped turn some alpine testpieces, like the Andromeda Strain, into trade routes. To some extent, a new generation of mixed climbs in the Canadian

Rockies is blurring the distinction between M- and alpine climbing. In the past few years a number of long, quasi-alpine mixed routes have gone up, many of them the work of Dave Thomson. The combination of technical skill and bolt protection has redefined the vision of what constitutes a climbable line. One of the best of the new routes, Rocketman (350 m, M7+), situated in a high glacial cirque, has bolts protecting the technical cruxes yet the easier climbing is quite engaging. When I free-climbed the route in a long day, the effort and focus required were no less than on many alpine routes, and the technical difficulty significantly greater. In a more traditional vein Steve House, with his new routes like the 1999 M-16 (VI, WI7+ A2) on the east face of Howse Peak, and the 2001 Sans Blitz (V, WI7 5.5) on the east face of Mount Fay, has done much to bring higher standards to truly alpine routes.

Climbers are also taking the technical skills acquired at the crags to the greater ranges. In 1996 Jack Roberts and Jack Tackle established Pair of Jacks (M6 WI5) on the north face of Mt. Kennedy (4238 m) in the St. Elias Range with the explicit goal "… of establishing a difficult new standard of [mixed] climbing via a new route on a beautiful mountain" (Jack Roberts, *Canadian Alpine Journal*, 1997). Climbing in a hybrid of alpine and capsule styles they covered 36 pitches of hard mixed ground. Yet Roberts admits to misgivings about their tactics. He recently commented to me, "hauling of packs in a major way, and bivouacking in portaledges, this does not constitute alpine climbing." Although an ascent dispensing with these would certainly have been in better style, the tactics used on Pair of Jacks probably represent a necessary step in the evolution of alpine mixed climbing. At some point, perhaps soon, climbers will be strong and fast enough to climb such routes in lightweight style. But when Pair of Jacks was

Raphael Slawinski on the first ascent of Mt. Rundle's Animal Farm (M10+), in 2000. At the time it was the hardest mixed pitch in North America, fully embracing sport climbing means to mixed climbing ends. *Darcy Chilton*

first done, a heavier approach was likely instrumental in Roberts and Tackle getting up the route, and doing it almost entirely free. Significantly, a very strong team later attempted to repeat their route in a single push and failed.

Single push style was successfully applied by Scott Backes, Steve House, and Mark Twight on their 2000 ascent of the huge and technical Slovak Direct route (5.9 M6 WI6+) on the south face of Denali (6194 m). Inspired by Voytek Kurtyka's concept of "night naked" climbing, they carried no bivi gear and blitzed the route in 60 hours of virtually non-stop climbing; the previous alpine-style ascent took a week. The following year Stephen Koch and Marko Prezelj upped the ante by climbing a new route on the southwest face of Denali in this style. They warmed up with the first free ascent of the Moonflower Buttress (M7?), accomplished in a 36-hour round trip from base camp. Moving on to Denali, they established Light Traveler (M8?) in 51 hours round trip from a high base camp, with Prezelj free-climbing the crux pitch on sight.

Modern mixed climbing standards are also making their way into the Himalaya. Many noteworthy climbs have been made; the few selected below merely illustrate the state of the art. In 1996 a strong French team, climbing in alpine style, climbed Extra Blue Sky on the north face of Kwangde beside the then unrepeated 1982 Breashears-Lowe route. The new route was described as steeper and harder than the north face of Les Droites. In 1997 Andrew Lindblade and Athol Whimp completed the much-attempted direct line on the north face of Thalay Sagar (6905m). Their route, which involved thin ice up to WI5 and cold rock climbing up to 5.9, was also climbed in alpine style. The big news in 1999 was Tomaz Humar's bold solo of a new route on south face of Dhaulagiri (8167m) with mixed difficulties up to M7+.

A direct comparison of the difficulties of crag and Himalayan mixed routes is of course highly problematical. A more meaningful assessment of the evolution of standards in Himalayan mixed climbing is provided by the recent repeats of some of the testpieces of the 1980s, and it would appear that even the repeat ascents have done little to lessen their reputations. Thus in 2000 a strong international foursome made the second ascent of the 1987 Fowler-Saunders route on Spantik. Describing the difficult and poorly protected mixed climbing they encountered, one of the members of the team wrote: "The moves, which years ago I would have dared to execute only if protected at least at waist level, were dainty in spite of the rare air and protection" (Marko Prezelj, *American Alpine Journal*, 2001). In 2001 the 1982 Breashears-Lowe route on Kwangde finally received a second ascent. The second ascent party took six days for the round trip, the same as the first, and avoided the thin ice crux of the original route. While today there is undoubtedly a broader base of alpinists climbing at a high standard, the Himalayan testpieces of the 1980s were so far ahead of their time that arguably they have yet to be surpassed.

In spite of the great advances in mixed climbing made over the last quarter of a century, one is struck by how slowly the technical standards in the mountains advance relative to standards at the crags. Whereas in the 1970s mixed-climbing standards did not appreciably differ between crag and mountain routes, today the gap between them has grown to such an extent that they almost appear to be different disciplines. While on the one hand this points to the immense possibilities for applying M-climbing techniques to the mountains, it also underscores the degree to which the high standards of M-climbing rely on a controlled crag environment. While the gap between the two is likely to grow, perhaps the rising standards at the crags will contribute to a corresponding rise in the alpine realm.

Ultimately, the ideal in alpine climbing has always been one of doing more with less. Aiding, bolting, fixing, jumaring, and hauling are often necessary taints, but taints nonetheless. Just as the development of ice climbing gave climbers the skills to create new alpine testpieces and turn old ones into trade routes, so the greatest contribution of M-climbing may be to give climbers the physical and technical means to reduce a major ascent to simply climbing. In fact, I believe that this process is already well under way.

While I have tried to plug the many gaps in my knowledge of mixed climbing throughout the world by extensive reading, in the end there is no substitute for first-hand experience. Thus I want to thank Scott Backes, Topher Donahue, Ben Firth, Will Gadd, and Jared Ogden for sharing their insights into mixed climbing. I particularly want to thank Aljaz Anderle, Duncan Ferguson, Jack Roberts, and Mark Twight for taking the time to answer my questions; Tom McMillan for suggesting the title; and Scott Semple for many thought-provoking exchanges and for suggesting the opening quote.

Mt. Rundle's Terminator Wall, home of (left to right), The Terminator, The Replicant, and Sea of Vapours. *Pat Morrow*

LIGHT TRAVELER

On a long Alaskan single-push ascent, it can feel like forever has come and gone already. Fighting off sleep and dehydration on new and newly freed routes up Denali, the Mini-Moonflower, and Mt. Hunter.

STEPHEN KOCH

Stephen Koch on the Mini Moonflower's Luna route, Mt. Hunter. Mt. Foraker is in the background. *Marko Prezelj*

Five. That is the number of times I have stopped. Stopped during the coldest, darkest, and most painful time on this journey. Stopped to kick the life back into my dying toes. It feels like I am lifetimes away from safety or flat ground. Here is the upper part of the Cassin Ridge on Denali's southwest face. Here is merely the aftermath of climbing this new route, Light Traveler, with Marko Prezelj.

Marko and I met in February 2001 at the British Mountaineering Council's International Winter Climbers' Meet in Scotland, a convergence of people from many countries to climb and discuss topics of concern. I was there representing the United States and the American Alpine Club after better-known and stronger climbers had been unable to attend. Though Marko and I didn't have the opportunity to climb together in Scotland, we shared a number of fine moments over libations at the local watering hole.

Marko Prezelj on the middle section of Luna. *Stephen Koch*

Once back in the States, I e-mailed Marko and so it was revealed that we both wanted to climb in Alaska, and that our approach to climbing was similar. We both liked to climb alpine style and with minimal gear. We both understood that the lighter you go, the faster you go, and the faster you go, the further you go. Language was not a problem: Marko's English is excellent. There was, however, a major difference between us: Marko's greater alpine experience. He has been on the cutting edge of alpine climbing for over a decade. Among many other climbs, he had climbed a new route to the south summit of Kangchenjunga with Andrej Stremfelj in 1991, an ascent that won the inaugural Piolet d'Or award.

I am better known as a snowboard mountaineer, and if something is possible to descend on skis or a snowboard, it isn't highly technical. Climbing with Marko, I would be able to see what I was capable of as an alpinist, on truly technical terrain, without the added weight of a snowboard.

Jack Tackle had given me the idea and encouragement for a new route on Denali. Jack is not only a huge inspiration but also a legend for his new and difficult routes in the Alaska Range. We work together for Exum Mountain Guides in the Tetons, and I trusted his eye for

Stephen Koch descending the Moonflower Buttress. *Marko Prezelj*

new routes. As we pored over photographs of Denali's many faces, we saw that the most logical unclimbed feature was to the left of the Cassin Ridge and to the right of the Denali Diamond. No one had been on the southwest face for 18 years—and there had been no new routes done in single-push style. This was my chance to complete a great climb, in the best style, with a stellar partner. I was ready.

Marko and I flew into base camp on May 26. After finding a deserted campsite we went to work setting up our tents and soon learned that Ian Parnell and Kenton Cool, our neighbors, were approaching their climbs in a fashion similar to ours.

Marko and I wanted to start by attempting a new route on the Mini Moonflower Buttress, a formation that had first been climbed by Parnell and Cool the week before. So we skied across the glacier, where fist-sized chunks of ice covered an area as big as a football field. I kept a wary eye on the hanging glaciers above as I pushed my anaerobic threshold to get through this area.

I gladly offered the first series of leads to Marko. Saying that Marko looks comfortable in the mountain environment is an understatement. He eats up vertical terrain like it is candy. After catching my breath at the top of the first pitch, I told Marko I would feel more comfortable if he put in a bit more gear (another piece!). "I will," he responded. "But more gear takes more time." I knew that might mean the difference between success and failure, but not having climbed with Marko until now, I didn't have the complete trust needed to accept his decisions without question. This would soon change.

Following the rope that snaked around the ice as fast as I could left me breathless at the belay. Yet we were finding our rhythm without even knowing it. The change-overs went smoothly and speaking was hardly necessary. We would comment on the high quality of the climbing or the view, but that was about it. Eating and drinking was done while belaying—we both had Petzl Reverso belaying devices, which allow the lead climber to belay the second with less attention to the rope, since the device locks up when the rope is weighted from below.

The climbing was mostly mixed with good protection in both rock and ice. As the angle kicked back past vertical, I encountered rotten ice. There were no good feet. Every time I kicked, my cramponed boot would slide through an airy mess, leaving all my weight on my frighteningly pumped arms. I was scared I could fall. Fifteen feet below I had equalized a Screamer shock absorbing sling on two pins, but I was above lower-angled rock. If I fell, I would bounce off, and though I would probably only break a leg, that could just as easily mean death up here. I was able to get a decent stick in better ice high above my head, but by now I was too pumped to use it, so I clipped into my teetering tool. As quickly as possible, I punched my fist through

the airy mess and slung all of the icicles I could, then added another Screamer to this, clipped it, and gently weighted the contraption with my cramponed foot. This allowed me to reach up high with my left tool for a solid stick.

Now on better ice, I was able to stem out onto the rock with one foot. Pulling the bulge felt great, and relief and gratitude washed over me. The anchor that I set up was good. Marko pulled up beside me. We were on our own and loving it.

It was still my lead. I sorted the gear and unclipped. Just as I started climbing I heard something from above. A huge mushroom the size of a small car was smashing the cliff above us, breaking into smaller pieces as it fell. It hit us just as I dove on Marko and the belay. After it had passed, we decided to continue. I flitted from one protected spot to another. We tried simul-climbing, but it didn't work well because the necessary gear was difficult to get.

Several more pitches of fun, difficult, mixed climbing and deep snow (including a tunneling section that Marko burrowed

Marko Prezelj getting close to the ridge on Luna. *Stephen Koch*

The route of Light Traveler, Denali. *Stephen Koch*

through) brought us to the summit ridge. It was double-corniced and nasty. Happy with our achievement, we rappelled directly down the face, reaching camp after twenty-three hours on the go.

This climb, which we named Luna after the moon and inspired by Lemon Luna bars, gave us the bond of trust needed to do further hard routes. Our confidence grew. A few days of rest while watching Ian and Kenton attempt the Moonflower Buttress of Mt. Hunter got us psyched for a go. The Moonflower entails difficult ice climbing along with a couple of A3 rock pitches on a huge granite- and ice-covered wall. Sharpening crampons and axes and adjusting the rack had us anxiously ready in the evening.

The Alaskan summer light is a key factor to climbing technical terrain without stopping. One can climb continuously through the night without the need for headlamps. On the Moonflower we would take bivouac sacks and a stove to melt snow for water.

We started climbing at seven p.m. After several great ice pitches, a mixed pitch brought us to the base of the Prow, one of the two pitches of aid climbing on the route. It was Marko's lead and he quickly climbed up using his picks in the thin crack. When he arrived at the belay, where it is normal to lower off and pendulum, he clipped in one rope for protection, down-climbed and delicately traversed from one ice patch to another without falling. This was the only pitch on which we hauled a pack; on all the others, the lead climber carried his pack. We did not bring jumars or aiders. We were climbing without any extra gear.

With one of the main technical pitches done, it was time to continue as fast as possible. The second would virtually run up the ice, doing anything to move fast and save time. The beauty of leading in blocks is that the leader is rested and ready to lead again after the second gets up and the gear is sorted. Our rhythm was "on" and we kept moving up the massive wall with, to apply a Twightism, a surgeon's brutal efficiency.

Mascioli's Mushroom, as it has been called since the death of Steve Mascioli in 1999, was a danger that we were wary of, but we were able to avoid it by climbing mixed terrain to the left of the normal line. This brought us to the Shaft, two pitches of vertical and overhanging ice that is the ice crux of the route. It was my lead and I was psyched. A rope frozen into the ice offered nice (albeit questionable) protection as I clipped sections of it with a quickdraw.

A few more pitches brought us to the next crux: the Vision, an aid pitch originally climbed with a pendulum. I got a small cam and piton in to safeguard my passage and then went for it. My feet were skating off tiny granite nubbins, but I hung on despite the weight of my pack and managed to reach the ice with a great yell of joy. We had done it! We had freed the aid sections of the Moonflower, the route that Mugs Stump pioneered and that had been called "The Nose Route of the Alpine World." Now all we had to do was get to the top of the buttress, but first we needed to get to the third icefield to melt snow for water.

We had been on the go for 16 hours with only five liters of water between us. We knew there was a good-sized ledge that Doug Chabot and Bruce Miller had chopped into the third icefield. Marko and I decided to push on rather than stopping at a less comfortable spot on the second icefield.

Arriving at the third icefield, we started chopping out a hollow spot to set the stove. It took quite a lot of time and work; the wind was howling and spindrift crept into every nook and cranny. I tried to light the stove. Nothing. Here we were, 20-odd pitches up the Moonflower Buttress with no sleeping bags and a stove that was spitting gas out the pump. My mental energy drained with the blood in my fingers as I tried to fix the stove. No luck.

We discussed our options: go up or go down. We would be descending the route anyway, so it made sense to continue as high as possible without water. We ate everything we could stomach and as much snow as our mouths could melt. I noticed a metallic taste in my frozen mouth and spit blood: I had been chewing my cheeks and tongue.

After paring our gear down to the absolute minimum, we took off, climbing with a sense of urgency we hadn't had before. A traversing pitch brought us to the exit pitches. From there we slogged up the upper snowfield, arriving at the Cornice Bivy, tired but happy, after 25 hours of climbing.

After a pow-wow, we decided that going to the summit would be too great of a risk; we were already pushing it by going without water for so long. Time to get off the mountain.

Eleven hours of rappelling brought us to bottom of the face. Though we had not made it to the summit, we were elated at our achievement and skied into camp just as everyone was getting up. Ian and Kenton prepared pancakes, an exchange that would become a regularity between us.

⚜

We were really tired and needed several days of rest. Had our expedition ended there, we would have been thrilled. Two good routes in the Alaska Range is a good season, but a new route and freeing the Moonflower felt superb. Our confidence soared.

Ian and Kenton set off up Denali to try a new route on the Father and Son's Wall. Steve House and Rolando Garibotti were waiting for good weather to try a single-push repeat of Foraker's Infinite Spur. Having people around climbing in a similar style was really inspiring. It felt like family. We were taking greater risks because climbing in the best style mattered. We were climbing on the shoulders of the great pioneers of the range: Stump, Tackle, Cassin, Haston, Scott.

In order to acclimatize better we planned to climb to the top of Denali. Slogging up to the 14,000-foot camp was the most unpleasant part of the journey so far. I don't like carrying or dragging much weight, but it was necessary if we wanted to spend much time up high on the

Marko Prezelj negotiating the Shower Pitch on Denali's Light Traveler. *Marko Prezelj*

mountain. Marko was ahead of me as we headed up to the 17 Camp. He reached it and passed me on his descent while I was still going up. At 17 I met my friend Forrest McCarthy, who invited me in for dinner with his clients. After dinner he offered me a place to sleep, which I gladly accepted. The following day I hiked to Denali Pass and climbed the ridge up to the plateau, and on the following evening from 14, Marko left at 3 a.m., reached the summit, and got back at 10 a.m. He was not going for a speed record—but might have beaten it anyway. He climbed the entire way in his down pants. "I was farting the whole way," he said later, "and was happy to have the company." When he took off his pants the "company" was still around.

The weather was continuing to hold. A four-day storm was forecasted but nothing happened. Every day was sunny. We rested, ate well, and caught up with friends over many chess matches and big meals.

Finally it was time to go. Our plan was simple. We wanted to leave 14 Camp, climb the rib to 15,500 feet, descend the Wickwire Route to the base of the southwest face, and climb a new route up the face to the top of the wall where it meets the upper Cassin Ridge. From there, we would continue to the summit. We left at 7 a.m., taking basically the same rack we had on the Moonflower Buttress but with a second pump and a bit more fuel. We had one 60-meter 9.6-mm rope with a 50-meter 5.5-mm haul line that could be used to rappel if necessary.

Getting through the lower Wickwire was both tricky and dangerous. Two scary crevasse crossings, some downclimbing below seracs, a rappel over a bergschrund, and a sprint under the big southwest face seracs brought us to the base of the wall five hours after leaving 14. We simul-climbed for about 600 feet to the bottom of our chosen line. The granite was of the highest quality I had seen anywhere.

As we got ready to start, my stomach was acting up, so I relieved myself, but the cramps wouldn't go away. This is what happens when someone is really scared, I thought, but I didn't feel scared; I felt excited. I would not have wanted to be anywhere else on this planet at that moment. That would soon change.

With my stomach feeling like it did and the route looking as steep as it did, I kindly offered the sharp end to Marko, who readily accepted. The route went straight up into a chimney that stopped and then to a left-facing corner with a huge roof. The wall looked smooth for the feet, and there wasn't much ice, either.

Watching Marko on this first pitch didn't help my stomach any. He skillfully worked his way up to and around the big corner. Once around, he let out a joyous and relief-filled scream. Marko later said this was the "hardest free pitch I have led in the mountains." He hauled his pack and I followed. I wished he had hauled my pack, too, for that pitch took more out of me than the diarrhea had. Can you say "flash pump"?

Marko led another two difficult pitches. There was a drip of water at one of these belays with which I wanted to fill our bottles, but the need to dodge careening ice chunks from high above made it difficult. The drip was good enough to drink from if I pressed my lips to the wall, but every time I tried I got a mouthful of silt and pebbles. I filled a couple of bottles so things could settle out before it was time for me to climb.

Marko handed me the rack and off I went. After about 30 seconds it was time to drop my pants again. My stomach was still not right. I hadn't shat myself in the mountains, and now was no time for that with well over 7,000 feet of climbing and a descent to go before any real cleansing would be possible. Fear was not part of my makeup at this point, but I was frustrated with my bad stomach and loose bowels. The only thing to do was to climb.

Marko Prezelj on the upper "snowfields" of Light Traveler. *Stephen Koch*

Light was still shining as I led. My second pitch was the "Shower" pitch. It started out innocently enough, a fine-looking vertical column with a blob of ice and snow at the top and roofs. Soon, however, I was forced to move left into vertical terrain with thin cracks. My pack was weighing me down. I hung it on a piece of gear and continued into the wetness. What started out as a drip that I thought could be avoided turned into a constant unwanted and potentially dangerous companion. My shell was in the pack, along with my belay jacket and balaclava. I was climbing in a Schoeller top that was getting soaked. By the time I made the belay my jacket was icy armor, not good with the sun setting and the pack not hauling well. The pack kept getting stuck during hauling, which meant that Marko had to manually help it. Marko was furious when he arrived, yelling, "Stephen, this was stupid." I was taken aback and hurt because it had been a difficult and serious lead. I was wet and cold and yelled back, "Stephen not stupid" and "Good job Stephen!" with, according to Marko, a cynical smile that made him realize he would have said the same thing if he were in my position. He immediately got where I was coming from and all was good again. I told him I hadn't hauled many packs and apologized. The temperature dropped in the Alaskan twilight but we were able to ward off the cold with movement.

We were moving so well on these pitches that neither of us put on our belay jacket. We ate and drank while belaying so as to not slow our progress. Climbing in blocks of three pitches each was working well and we were both getting good, difficult leads.

After the first several pitches the angle eased, but still there was not an easy pitch. Pitch after pitch, the climbing continued. Working our way up this endless wall into the unknown was thrilling.

We had been climbing through the night and now looked for a place to brew up. Our water was gone and we needed to hydrate. But we weren't finding any places to brew. It was cold now and stopping would mean no movement. No movement means getting cold to the core. The belay jackets wouldn't be enough, so we just didn't stop. It wasn't really discussed. Thirsty? Check. Tired? Check. Hallucinating? Not yet. Still enjoying the climbing? Check.

Marko was leading again. I really wanted to stop and brew. I was so thirsty and didn't want a repeat of the Moonflower dehydration session. Still, there was no good place to brew. We were looking for any flat rock or place to hold the stove. We didn't want to stand and watch the water boil. If we were going to brew, we wanted to at least be sitting.

The stone wasn't lacking much, even in the darkest twilight of the Alaskan night. The rock was made for drytooling. My warm feet were making me happy. Cold toes had always been a problem for me. Before this trip I put thermo-flex liners in my plastic shells. This combination, along with overboots, had me smiling with joy, the joy of knowing that on many other occasions I would be swinging my feet to force warm blood into drained toes. Not now. Everything on this expedition was going perfectly, from the landing on the airstrip to our freeclimbing the Moonflower, to now warm feet. The energy needed to swing a big leg like mine would be needed for breaking trail up higher.

I put my shell on and followed Marko up the first of two triangular icefields. After traversing leftward, we climbed together on easy terrain until Marko could find a belay. The rock quality deteriorated for several hundred feet, and I knocked off several rocks that narrowly missed Marko.

The pitches seemed endless and all we wanted to do was to find a place to brew up. We were going on 27 hours of straight climbing with our original five liters plus a couple of addi-

Marko Prezelj climbing the snowfields above the lower wall. *Stephen Koch*

tional bottles from the drip. This was not enough to keep properly hydrated, but even double that wouldn't be enough to keep hydrated with the energy we were expending at this altitude.

I led up snow-covered rock for 200 feet, where the angle eased. I wasn't going to stop until I found a place to rest and brew. Big boulders were sticking out of the snow, but they were all downsloping. Finally I decided to head for the biggest one I could see with the hope that it would meet our needs. It did. I climbed around to the top and sat down, bringing up the rope for Marko hand over hand (there was no place to anchor).

We each kicked out a place to sit, Marko below and me above with the stove. The first thing we made with our precious water was tea, black tea that neither of us wanted. We des-

Marko Prezelj on the crux first pitch of Light Traveler. *Stephen Koch*

perately needed to drink, but we had brought black tea instead of herbal tea. It was triple strong and we dumped it out. Hydrating is the number one thing we needed to do, and we had just dumped out drinkable liquids. Sometimes you just don't argue with yourself.

Sitting on our packs in the sun with zero wind, we enjoyed our spectacular position on this magnificent mountain. I thought about the other climbs done on this massive wall. The Denali Diamond, the Roberts-McCartney, the Cassin Ridge, and Mugs' solo of that route. These climbs and climbers set the path for us to follow. We were taking things a step further with the first new route done in single-push style. Below us we viewed the Valley of Death, waiting to see the inevitable serac avalanches sweep across. I kept melting snow, filling bottles. We drank. Finally, we ate: potatoes, garlic, sharp cheddar and tuna; two Ramen, six soups, many GUs and candy bars, two hot chocolates, two coffees for Marko, GU-2-0 drink supplement with electrolytes, bagels and cream cheese. Yummy in the tummy!

I would nod off for moments here and there, but neither of us were in a comfortable or safe enough position to sleep. I wasn't thinking about much more than trying to keep the pot from spilling over in the soft snow. Our fuel was down to about a third of a bottle. We would get one more brew stop. The warm sun filled us with energy and warmth, but now it was time to go.

On our way again at about 4 p.m., we realized the sun had softened the snow. Our crampons were balling up terribly. Every step required a blow to the crampons with the axe. We were roped together and swapping leads. After a few hours we got back into technical climbing. Marko led off on another beautiful mixed pitch. The Cassin Ridge was over to our right and the upper southwest face was to our left. Fatigue was setting into my head rather than my body; I was tired of belaying, tired of climbing, and ready to be done.

I pulled out the stove, only to discover that all the fuel had leaked out of the bottle due to the increased pressure from our rapid ascent. I hadn't let the pressure out after our earlier cooking session. Again we were nearly out of water and getting dehydrated.

The Alaskan night was upon us and we had to climb to the Upper Cassin on our own, as we had done on the entire route. We were not climbing on the backs of others who climbed days, weeks, or years before. We had no ledges chopped, steps kicked in the deep snow, or topo in hand. It was Marko and me, alone. There wasn't a third person to help break trail, talk with on belay, split the load with, or to snatch a nap while belaying. There was no napping while belaying. We had dived into the exciting unknown of a new route. Commitment was complete. If something went wrong, we had only ourselves to save us. Our margin of safety was small, but we would have had it no other way. We did not use any of our eight pitons. We had no jumars. We were going to climb the route, not jug. We hauled the pack on only three pitches.

Several more moderate mixed pitches and we were at the top of our route, where it meets with the upper Cassin. We left our 10-pound rope right at the top of the last pitch. Didn't even coil it; I just belayed Marko up and untied. I didn't have enough emotional energy to feel bad about it.

We had to keep it together. No water again. Low light, now breaking trail. We were on our own and feeling like the mountain was ours. We only had to get off it to feel good about it.

Marko got ahead while I stopped to swing my feet. My toes were cold. It would have been easy just to climb, not heeding the cold toes. But I knew better. That would have been lazy and we had done too much great climbing to get sloppy or lazy. It would have tainted the ascent to get frostbite.

Stephen Koch and Marko Prezelj after 50 hours on Light Traveler, Denali.

We were climbing with our belay jackets and balaclavas now. There were no places to stop and rest, and, even if there had been, we wouldn't have been able to use them. It was too cold to stop for more than a few minutes.

The light got low and all turned into a blue-gray haze, both inside my head and out. My peripheral vision was going, as was my ability to judge near distance. A couple of times I had to catch myself with my spike as I fell forward. If we had listened to our bodies, we would have fallen asleep every time we stopped, and then died from the fall.

After swinging my feet warm, I would begin hiking again, only to slowly have my toes get cold after an hour or so. The swinging was taking valuable energy away from me, but I would have to have enough. I have kept my feet warm in many cold situations; this would be no different. It seemed like forever had come and gone.

Marko waited and again we were together. He would lead, breaking trail for a while, then it would be my turn. No words needed to be spoken; we were saving our energy for upward movement. The thought of not being able to finish didn't creep into my head. I was suffering like never before, mentally and physically shattered, just wanting to get off this mountain. It was relentless and never-ending; the snow would go from névé for a few moments to breakable knee-deep the next. We didn't want to have to think any longer. Just get us off this face!

Finally, slowly, we worked our way up the Cassin to the summit ridge. Sunshine! Flat ground! Marko was sitting on his pack. I dropped my pack, sat down with a sigh of relief, and was startled as Marko knocked me over with a huge bearhug. We had done it. Our new route was nearly complete. All that remained was a fifteen-minute walk to the summit.

We were wobbly on the flat ground for the first few steps. On top we snapped a few quick photos and then were off. Forty-three hours of climbing, 48 including the "approach." It took us three hours to get back to 14, where we were treated to egg burritos and liquids from friends.

We were back. From where? A new route? Or an experience that Marko and I alone hold inside us? I have tried to explain certain aspects of the climb to people, but to go deep, I am not yet ready or able. Marko and I know what went on, and that is good enough for me. Now you know a bit about our adventure.

SUMMARY OF STATISTICS:

AREA: Mt. McKinley, Alaska Range

ASCENTS: Mini-Moonflower: first ascent of Luna (2,200 feet, V M7 WI6+ A0).

Mt. Hunter: free ascent of the Moonflower Buttress (4,500 feet to cornice bivy, M7 WI6).

Mt. McKinley: first ascent of Light Traveler (8,500 feet, M7+ WI6).

All ascents by Stephen Koch and Marko Prezelj.

EXTRATERRESTRIAL BROTHER

*Forty-six hours of magical mystery touring
on McKinley's Father and Son Wall.*

KENTON COOL

Kenton Cool kitting up and thinking about what's to come on the Father and Son Wall as it emerges from clouds just before their big push. *Ian Parnell*

"So there's no moraine at all?"

"Not a single stone," replied Ian. "You just fly straight to base camp, no porters, cooks, or even L.O.s. Basically no hassle. You just rock up, fly in, and then you have it in large style."

My eyes glazed over. We were sitting next to the world's biggest haulbags on what seemed to be the worst moraine in the Himalaya. Admittedly, India's Arwa Tower was impressive, but the amount of hassle and effort was telling. Physically fighting with agents--plus a nine-day approach from base camp--was not ideal.

A week later, still in India, Ian and I were sitting in a very similar spot in a very similar state. "So, when are we going?"

"Going where?"

"Alaska, you fool; this sucks!"

Seven months later Ian (a.k.a. Buba Smith) and I are sitting next to one another again. This time it's outside the Fairview Inn in Talkeetna, drinking beer and awaiting our burgers. "Beats Delhi, huh, Kenton?"

I couldn't really disagree. We had arrived only 24 hours previously and would be at base camp in less than 24 more. It was looking like a designer trip. I have a reputation for being excitable, and right now, with a few beers inside me, I was fully excited.

The following evening saw us step out of our plane and onto the soft snow. A gaggle of people with skis and gear were shouting and screaming. "Okay, New York Bushwhackers Expedition" boomed a rather short, attractive lady wearing what looked like carpet slippers. Four climbers almost jumped to attention before throwing their gear into the plane. "Hi, Ian," the woman said quickly before jumping into another chaotic scene of bodies and gear.

"That's Lisa, the base camp manager," explained Ian as we pulled our gear up to two empty campsites. After almost ten years of Himalayan climbing I had never seen a base camp such as this.

The next few days saw us sorting gear and eating (apparently we set a record for the amount of food brought in by a two-person team). Ian seemed to know most of the people at base camp and spent much time yarning. The big news was that one team was currently on the Stumps Route on the Moonflower and another was on the Wall of Shadows. Now, neither Ian nor I are superstars; we're not like the late Alex Lowe or the current Steve House. We're normal human beings, and all this talk of overhanging ice, killer mushrooms, five-day storms, and lightning-quick ascents was beginning to psych me out. It was time to go climbing.

The Mini Moonflower, as it became known during this trip, is a triangular buttress about a quarter of a mile past the Moonflower on Mt. Hunter. Ian had spotted it the year before and neither of us could believe that it hadn't been climbed. Such a buttress in the Alps would have six routes on it.

After sorting a standard rack and two 7.5mm ropes, we turned to our supplies: 30 GU energy gel packets and seven liters of water. We looked at each GU suspiciously. "You sure about these, Bubs? Doesn't look like very much to me!" Ian simply eyed them in silence.

Ian kicked up the initial slopes, went over the bergschrund, and put in a belay below a steep groove. Reaching the stance, I leaned over and muttered, "Here we go, Bubs, let's have at it!"

Ian led off over some interesting mixed ground, and the pitches quickly merged into one. The climbing was hard enough to be interesting but never desperate; it was very similar to French goulottes in Chamonix: squeaky ice, good rock, great climbing.

Kenton Cool enjoying pitch 8 of Kiss Me Where the Sun Don't Shine on the Mini Moonflower, Mt. Hunter. *Ian Parnell*

The plan was to climb during the night (remembering that it doesn't really get dark at this latitude) and rest in the daytime, using the sun to fight the cold. However, as night became day, the clouds rolled in and wet snow began to fall. The leads (we were climbing in blocks of three pitches) switched again, and Ian started up what was to be the crux—a steep ice runnel with a tricky mixed step at the top. I pulled up to Ian at the belay with a roar of delight: "Fantastic, man, fantastic."

But concern began to creep in as we got higher. Despite his list of outrageous ascents, Ian is relatively new to mountaineering. "What do ya reckon about the snow, Kenton?" We were worried about the upper slopes shedding on us. I'd heard nasty things about the Moonflower doing the same thing.

"Don't know, Bubs. Tell you what. We'll continue up and if it gets any heavier we'll reconsider."

Although we had scoped the route from below, a combination of the clouds and actually being on the route meant that routefinding was tricky. We were using a large roof as a reference point, but as the clouds were coming in and out, a rather ominous sight came into view. A huge ice mushroom could be seen to one side of the roof. I caught Ian's eyes and they said it all. The whole upper half of the route was threatened.

We said nothing as I racked up and continued, trying to move out of the fall line, which seemed impossible. Tiredness was setting in; it was 29-plus hours since we'd left base camp. Watching the rope inch out the belay plate was depressing, and all I could think of was my sleeping bag and killer mushrooms. (Ian had suffered broken ribs at the hands of a collapsing mushroom the year before.)

"Below!" screamed Ian. I looked up expecting to see crashing mushrooms but instead got a chestful of ice. "Arrgghh!" My hand felt like it had been squeezed in a vice. "Bastard, Ian, you bastard!"

"You okay?"

"Yeah, yeah, man." My hand was on fire and I couldn't move it. Shit, I thought, it's broken. My immediate thought was for the rest of the trip and all the money we had spent getting here. "Safe" finally filtered down. I gingerly dismantled the belay and began to climb.

Ian was concerned about my hand since it was rapidly swelling. Light was fading and it was snowing again—and it was my lead. "Any chance of you continuing, Bubs?"

"No sweat, man." He led another pitch toward the ridge, and we now seemed to be directly under the mushroom. The pitch finished on easy ground, and the ridge seemed to be only about 200 feet away. The condition of the snow prompted another discussion, and the ice prodder came out of my pocket. We forced a couple of mocha GU's down us, flushing them with the last water and started to descend. Fifteen rapid abs saw us back to the bergschrund and one last, long rappel to the skis.

Brits are famous for not being able to ski, and Ian and I are no exception. This, combined with Ian's low-quality bindings, meant that skiing with rucksacks was at best interesting. I'd turn around to see Ian sitting on his sack smashing his skis with his pole while screaming obscenities. We finally reached base camp in the early hours. A wave of utter exhaustion enveloped us both, but the ascent was in the bag and it was time for tea and medals.

After a few days rest we decided to go up the west buttress to look at a new route on Denali's Washburn Wall. Unfortunately, a three-day storm rolled in and we got no further than the 11,000-foot camp. On our return to base camp Ian bumped into "BenAndKevin" from New Hampshire along with Bruce Miller. "Don't worry, Kenton, I told them not to do the route on the Washburn Wall." Well, they did and called it Common Knowledge. Yanks for you!

The next week was spent sunbathing and eating at base camp, with a brief spell on the Moonflower, which we climbed with three points of aid. After this we geared up to go to the 14,000-foot camp on Denali.

Ian was quite right about no moraine, but he didn't mention anything about sledge pulling. Anyone on Heartbreak Hill when the Brits were around were in for a laugh. Ian seemed to take it quite personally in the way his sledge would overtake him and pull him off his skis. He lay there in a crumpled heap, close to tears through frustration. It was hard to imagine him cranking it out on steep ice, and I could only laugh. Three days later, after many such falls and even more four-letter expletives, we reached the 14,000-foot camp.

This high camp on the west buttress is beautifully located and overlooks Mt. Foraker and the very top of Hunter. We were positioned here to make an attempt

Ian Parnell on pitch 19 of "The Shaft" during an ascent of the Moonflower, Mt. Hunter. *Kenton Cool*

on the Father and Sons Wall, a wall which to date had only one route on it. The plan was to climb a line to the left of First Born (Steve House's line), join up with the north buttress route, and then traverse both the north and south summits. All this in a single push with no tent, no sleeping bag, no idea.

Leaving camp at 10 p.m., we descended to the top of Motorcycle Hill, and it was here that we got our first look at the wall (it had been cloudy on the way up). "It's a bit big, Ian!"

"Na, it just looks big; no bigger than Stanage" came the reply. We had stashed a bag with ropes and hardware at the top of the descent, but unfortunately a freeze-thaw cycle had occurred. Ian pulled a cam out of the bag and attached to it was most of the rack and a huge lump of ice. Meanwhile I was struggling with a rope that thought it could do the Indian rope trick. "Bollocks" was slightly understating it, I thought as Ian started chipping ice away. Not the ideal start.

Things went from bad to worse, and the descent rapidly became one of the most mind-numbingly frightening things I've ever done. The slope felt good to start with but quickly deteriorated to what felt like imminent death, all above a line of gnarly seracs. Finally I broke the tension. "Ian, I'm scared, I'm scared stupid; I don't like this at all."

"No, it's shit," he agreed. We decided to go to a slight depression and make yet another ab; this would be our third one, each one leaving us more and more committed. Finally, after using all but three feet of our ab tat, we reached the glacier. "Better not retreat off the route," Ian pointed out, looking forlornly at the tat.

As we moved quickly over the glacier, the wall loomed above us and a sudden realization of how remote this route really was sunk in. Although perhaps less than a mile from the west buttress, we could have been on the moon. The only feasible escape would be to exit via the Peter's Glacier. With no bivy gear, minimal food and fuel, it wasn't really an option. Cramming GU's and water down, I geared up.

The first 600 feet disappeared quickly as we moved together. The plan was to gain the center of the face via a series of icy runnels. I found myself eyeing a rather scary-looking icefall, the key to the line. "It's shit, utterly shit" Ian shouted down as he watched his tools track down in the mush. The ice had been fried by the sun, leaving a soggy excuse for falling blocks. "Don't fancy it, do ya, Kenny?" I didn't and I told him so. Back at the belay we had a

Kenton Cool belayed in deteriorating weather beneath pitch 13 of Kiss Me Where the Sun Don't Shine, Mini Moonflower. *Ian Parnell*

Kenton Cool looking for a way out 28 hours into Extra Terrestrial Brothers, Denali. Ian Parnell

The Mini Moonflower (left) and the real thing, the Moonflower Buttress, on Mt. Hunter. *Ian Parnell*

discussion on what to do, and out came topos and descriptions. Arms were waving here and there, and necks were craning. In retrospect 600 feet up a 6,500-foot wall and being lost already wasn't very good. Try left was the final decision, and thus began the magical mystery tour.

We moved quickly over moderate but interesting ground and soon gained a mixed spur that seemed to kick back into the middle of the face. The climbing was a mixture of icy runnels and easy mixed ground interspersed with gnarly steep snow. After a number of hours I ended up belaying underneath a short, steep corner, with the yellow plate of Ian's crampons inches above my head. "Watch me, Kenny!" His feet skated and so I placed his front points onto a micro edge for him. "There's nothing for my tools" he spurted as his left foot shot off the edge again. "I'm off, na I'm on, no I'm off." He wasn't; he was in fact grinning nervously at me. Sweat glistened on his face. It turned out that Ian had just sent the crux.

Thirty hours into our little jaunt we stopped for mashed potatoes and soup. It's surprising how comfortable it is sitting on two ropes halfway up a mountain. Sleep quickly overcame me. The only shelter we had was a bothy bag, and it was this, flapping in the wind, that woke me almost four hours later. "Four hours, you sure? It felt like ten minutes to me," Ian moaned. My mind was groggy from not enough rest. My senses slowly returned with depressing clarity, as my hostile surroundings closed in once again. Moving away from our little lunch spot was the psychological crux, but once moving again we passed the hours with little recognition.

The final hard climbing found us moving together over tricky ground. This was more out of laziness than forethought. Looking back on it, we were stupid, but normal reasoning had long since left us. It was turning to an ordeal, no longer fun. The final slopes up to the north ridge were never-ending and the thigh-deep powder was soul destroying. "Go, Ian, you're the man. Yeah, have at it, show it who's boss!" Upon hearing this, Ian would pull himself back to his feet and break trail for another eternity before collapsing again. It was only afterward that I confessed I was encouraging him only because I didn't want to break trail myself. It truly was an impressive sight. The final 300-foot slope up to the north ridge was horrendously loaded, and the wind was blowing spindrift over the top. The last 60 feet I had to climb totally blind. Pulling onto the ridge was like stepping into the heart of Hades. The wind was screaming all around us. We had intended to sleep in the sun on the ridge and then traverse the north and south summits, but the wind meant that stopping was impossible and sleeping would result in black digits or worse.

The ground was easy but I was unable to move across it; my body was hurting and my mind had gone numb. Figures kept dancing in my peripheral vision and I kept looking every which way. I knew there was nothing else up there, but I kept staring and saw nothing. "Ian...Ian" I found myself muttering. "This is fucking stupid," I screamed. I slumped down utterly spent, feeling frustrated and angry that Ian had brought me here. This was quickly superseded by a feeling of guilt; it was Ian's dream and I was in the process of shattering it. For me, continuing up was not an issue; it was time to drop onto the upper Peter's Glacier. I think with this realization my self-conscious gave up and my body stuck its finger up at me.

As we moved off the ridge and down onto the glacier, the situation seemed to improve. Out of the wind and with food in me, I started to recover. Ian had for the last hour or so been operating for the both of us. We plowed straight across the glacier, under a snub of rock above an icefall. The final push to the 16,000-foot camp on the west buttress was fine, previous stories of waist-deep powder proving unfounded. Reaching the ridge, we quickly located the fixed ropes on the headwall. I turned to Ian, who was grinning. We embraced and shouted into the wind, congratulating each other. Cramming the rope and gear into the sack, we clipped onto the fixed ropes and started to bum-slide almost down to the tent. We staggered into camp approximately 46 hours after leaving it. We got a number of strange looks from people looking as spent and as disheveled as we were. They had no idea, no idea at all.

SUMMARY OF STATISTICS

AREA: Alaska Range

ASCENTS: Extraterrestrial Brothers (VI, Alaska Grade 5/6, Scottish VII) on Mt. McKinley's Father and Sons Wall, in 46 hours round-trip from the 14,200-foot camp on the West Buttress, early June. Kenton Cool and Ian Parnell.

Kiss Me Where the Sun Don't Shine (Scottish VII) on Mt. Hunter's Mini-Moonflower in May. Also a repeat of Mt. Hunter's Moonflower Buttress. Kenton Cool and Ian Parnell.

WALLS IN SHADOW

Single-push climbing is out there, all right, but not beyond judgment.
Speedy climbing on the second ascent of Mt. Hunter's Wall of Shadows
and a new route, Common Knowledge, on Denali's Washburn Face.

KEVIN MAHONEY

The north buttress of Mt. Hunter. Wall of Shadows begins in the couloir on the left then takes to the face. *Kevin Mahoney*

Spindrift avalanches pass the door of our snow cave. A grin grows wide on Ben Gilmore's face as he raises his fist triumphantly. Two thousand feet up the Wall of Shadows we discovered this crystal cavern to enjoy shelter from the storm. We stumbled upon the cavern by the Force, that undeniable draw that leads one off route with blind faith that something will come together (a.k.a. fool's luck when you are desperate). It is 10 hours into our second day of climbing; during the last three hours snow has been falling, creating spindrift avalanches at regular intervals. BTUs, sweat, Gore-Tex, and spindrift have joined forces to soak through all my layers. We are at the top of the Crystal Highway and another open bivy, with spindrift filling my bivy sack, seems less appealing than it did while leaving our tent behind on the glacier. Light may be right, but spindrift sucks.

✻✺✺◈✺✻

This is our third trip to Alaska, which lately seems to be the only time we get to climb together. So it was easy for us to believe that we could pull off the second ascent of the Wall of Shadows with a scant alpine rack, two 7.6-mm 60-m ropes, four days of food and fuel, our sleeping bags, and bivy sacks. The A4 sections that Michael Kennedy and Greg Child experienced seemed to have ice on them, so we hoped it would go free or with very little aid since we were not prepared for anything more.

As Ben led up through the bergschrund, I recalled what Kennedy said about the first ascent: "It was the most difficult route in our combined 50 years of climbing." As the rope went tight and I started to climb, I wondered what we were smoking back on the glacier for us to

Ben Gilmore leaving the shrund on the Wall of Shadows. *Kevin Mahoney*

believe we could pull this off. A thousand feet higher we must have been smoking again, because after the first day we felt confident we would succeed. So far we had been able to avoid the first aid section, dubbed Coming into the Country, by climbing ice to its left. Then, half a dozen pitches of fun ice led us to Thug Alley, 200 feet of thin, plastic ice less than a yard wide. At the base of the Enigma, we chopped a bunk-bed bivy out of the ice.

Brew, dinner, brew, sleep, spindrift, sleep, spindrift, sleep. Finally we woke to a beautiful, cold morning. After drinking our instant oatmeal (the fastest way to get it down), we were ready to tackle the first real unknown, the Enigma (A4). Fortunately, it was Ben's block so I got to cheer him on, hoping he could find a way through the mystery that was just out of sight. A thin ice

Ben Gilmore on the Dry Heaves pitch (pitch 10) of the Wall of Shadows. *Kevin Mahoney*

runnel to a small roof ended with
a choice: left or right? After some
tenuous exploration, he settled on
a thin ice smear to the right.
Clearing off a dusting of snow,
Ben discovered an old rivet from
the first ascent. With a junk #1
TCU in, Ben stretched to hook a
front point in the old, sun-faded
tat, which got him high enough to
gain egg-shell ice that had separated from the rock. The angle was
only 85 degrees, so Ben figured it
was no harder then WI 5. He con-

Ben Gilmore (left) and Bruce Miller 14 hours into Common Knowledge
on the Father and Sons Wall. *Kevin Mahoney*

tinued with no gear for 30 feet on ice that was so thin that it required him to spread his body
weight over three points, since no single point would hold. Most people would call it WI 6X, but
Ben still thinks it was only NEI 5-. Finally, the Enigma was behind us and the rest of his block
went smoothly and ended at the Crystal Highway.

At first I was psyched to have this block, but as the snowfall increased and the spindrift
filled my jacket with regularity, I realized that justice had been served. Ben had had the crux pitch
so I deserved the crux weather while leading 80- to 95-degree plastic ice. Fatigue, chills, common
sense, and insecurities begged us to retreat; the thought of another spindrift-filled night loomed
over our heads. At one spot we went off route to explore the top of a diamond-shaped blob
frozen to the wall. The top had no potential, so I put in a rock anchor and started down the other
side; halfway down my boot broke through the ice to my knee: paydirt. Forty-five minutes later,
as we watched the spindrift avalanches pass the door of our snow cave, we were again optimistic
about our future. Tomorrow, the Somewhere Else Wall (A4).

❧❦❀❦❧

We wake to blue skies, just when we need it. Now it's my turn to sort out the other A4 section
of the route. I climb an ice runnel to a hanging snow-mushroom traverse, then pull on some
gear to get through the exit roof and gain ice for a belay. As Ben follows, his feet drop out from
under him. The huge mushroom drops away and he is left hanging from one tool slotted in a
crack. The next piece of protection is five horizontal feet away with blank rock separating him
from it. With no other options, Ben cuts loose for the heinous pendulum into the right-facing
corner. After pulling through the roof and settling into the belay, he finally starts to breathe
again. After some more mixed terrain that required pulling on gear to ease my nerves, we are
done with the Somewhere Else Wall. Ben leads us through the "dry heaves" and onto the third
ice band, where we join the Moonflower Buttress.

As we search out the best place to spend our third night, we hear voices. Doug Chabot
and Bruce Miller are finishing their second day cruising the Moonflower Buttress. I knew Doug
from Exum Mountain Guides, and we had met Bruce the previous year. We decide that we will
go to the summit together the next day.

The next day is clear and cold, and Bruce and Doug head out first for the Bibler Come

Kevin Mahoney on the crux Candelabra pitch of Common Knowledge. *Bruce Miller*

Again Exit. While we wait our turn for the first real pitch, Ben discovers his water bladder has leaked two quarts of water all over his down parka—a great way to start our summit push. We climb through three fun pitches to gain the upper slopes to the northeast ridge and join forces with Bruce and Doug to break trail to the summit on a beautifully calm evening with light clouds dancing in the setting sun to keep us in awe during the tedious post-holing. A quick celebration, one last photo, then back down the northeast ridge.

Nine rappels, courtesy of Bruce Miller V-thread Express, bring us back to our bivy on the third ice band and finally sleep. The next day, nineteen more rappels and we are back at our skis on the glacier, marveling in the glow of an anxiety-free night of sleep.

I wince at the dull thud of plastic hitting ice. My body and mind were just starting to unwind after leading the crux of Common Knowledge, a full 200-foot pitch of vertical to overhanging, sun-rotten, sublimated ice that Ben dubbed the Candelabra because of its resemblance to a huge candle dripping with melted wax. Bruce had already followed the pitch and is perched next to me for the bird's-eye view of Ben's stoic performance. Ben's crampon spring bails have compressed to the point of obscurity; tiny front points poke out beyond his plastic boots. With every kick of his boot the plastic sounds a dull thud that reminds Bruce and me that Ben is essentially campusing WI 6 at altitude with a pack on. Now, that is just the challenge; the truth is we are 2,000 feet up a 7,000-foot route, and every thud of plastic against ice means toe against plastic. Not one to complain, Ben admits that it is a little pumpy.

Backup plans are essential in the mountains. Weather, conditions, health, and psyche all factor into which route is appropriate. Our intent was to attempt a new line on the southwest face of Denali. We joined forces with Bruce Miller, who was in search of a partner. After a period of unstable weather and a reconnaissance, we chose a less committing route: an obvious ice line on the northwest side of the west buttress. Ben and I had thought of attempting the line the previous year but had turned around while on the descent to the base of the route. The ice had been so hard that our brand new Express screws had to be torqued into the ice with our ice tools. This year it is later in the season and the temperatures are much warmer. We hesitated, knowing that other very competent parties were eyeing the same route and each was likely to succeed. After giving it due respect, we racked up. With 9.4-mm and 8.8-mm 60-m ropes, a light alpine rack, and a stove with 22 ounces of fuel, oatmeal, and ramen we were off.

Ben Gilmore following the Somewhere Else Wall pitch after the Mushroom Collapse on Mt. Hunter's Moonflower Buttress. *Kevin Mahoney*

Bruce Miller leading the Waterfall Pitch on Common Knowledge. *Kevin Mahoney*

From 14,000 feet on the west buttress we descended 5,000 feet, around Windy Corner and down from Motorcycle Hill. Seven rappels brought us to the Peters Glacier, and we were now completely alone, staring up at our proposed route, hoping the needle of ice in the middle of the route was better than it looked.

Bruce led us up through the bergschrund, then we soloed the next 700 feet to the base of the first steep pitch. Ben led the first block of cruiser ice with steep steps to spice it up. At the base of the Candelabra, I took the lead. After leading up through the 200 feet of fun, tenuous climbing, I gave the rack to Bruce to share the wealth that continued for one more pitch. But first we have to suffer through the sound of Ben's boots thudding into the ice as he muscles his way up the Candelabra.

Bruce takes his block through cruiser ice and a few steep steps. Then my block starts with the Waterfall Pitch, a pitch of WI 4 that would be more at home in Crawford Notch, NH, than at 14,000 feet on Denali. By now the clouds that had blanketed the valley floor have crept up to us and are dropping snow on our parade, but we have become adept at climbing in spindrift. After a few more pitches of mellow ice, we are on the upper shoulder and into simul-climbing terrain. We debate brewing up since we have been on the move for 14 hours and are low on water, but we decide we can wait for a more protected spot. We must be fatigued and dehydrated to believe we can find a more protected spot on the broad, sweeping slopes of the upper north side of the west buttress. The next 3,500 vertical feet take much longer than it should, up through slopes of 55-degree blue ice and snow with a few belayed steep pitches up through a rock buttress with ice runnels guiding us. We finally reach the top of the buttress after 20 hours; here we spend the next two hours resting and brewing, trying to rejuvenate for the traverse back to the fixed lines.

The Washburn Face on Denali: (1) Common Knowledge and (2) Beauty is a Rare Thing, 1995. Kevin Mahoney

The technical climbing is behind us, but after 22 sleepless hours even horizontal ice with 2,000 feet of exposure gets your attention. Bruce and Ben go ahead while I lag behind, realizing with every step that, despite my exhaustion and desire to drink a gallon of Cytomax, I am turned on to a new style of climbing: single push, with the same gear that you might go out for a day of cragging with, plus a stove for a brew session. Many strategies are used to get up peaks or just to do cool routes like Common Knowledge, with no summit at the end. Yet to cover 7,000 feet of terrain and feel confident to handle whatever you may encounter is liberating and fun. Prior to attempting to climb a big route in this style, I was tempted to think that such tactics are outside the envelope of safety. Now I feel that it is out there all right, but judgment can keep it within the envelope. This self-awareness and decision making is one of the greatest attributes of alpine climbing.

SUMMARY OF STATISTICS:

AREA: Alaska Range

ASCENTS: Second ascent of Wall of Shadows (VI, WI6 mixed 5.9 A2) on Mt. Hunter's north buttress. May 15-18 up; May 19 down the Moonflower rappels. Ben Gilmore and Kevin Mahoney.

First ascent of Common Knowledge (V, WI 6R) on Mt. McKinley's Washburn Face (the northwest face of the west buttress). June 2; 26 hours round trip from 14,000-foot camp. Ben Gilmore, Kevin Mahoney, and Bruce Miller.

CIRQUETRY

Trundles from God and other tales of Speed and Freedom in the Cirque of the Unclimbables, Yukon Territory.

JONATHAN COPP

Tim O'Neill celebrating the first free ascent of Club International on Bustle Tower. *Jonathan Copp*

The Beaver roared, its circa 1957 pistons pounding as we looped skyward within a mountain cirque, trying to gain enough altitude to slide through a notch. Warren was on the headset barking to his co-pilot, "Whataya think? Got enough height? That glacial air is going to suck us right down once we pass the keyhole." One problem: I was the co-pilot. Staring out at the notch, I could scarcely see space enough between the menacing cloud mass and the serrated ridge for our burly little craft to fly. "Crap, I don't know!" Warren took us for a few more doughnuts around the cirque and then lined up to thread the needle. We were just skimming the bottom of the threatening cloud as ice and rain began to pelt us. "Ehhhaa, it's been a shit June, really a shit June. Feckin' rain every day."

I turned to look at Timmy O'Neill, Brooke Andrews, and John Abel, all of whom were piqued by the aerobatics and concerned with the weather report. Fact is, we hadn't expected anything less. It was the Cirque of the Unclimbables after all, darn close to the Arctic Circle, and wetter than many a rainforest. We had come to explore the cirque's legendary walls and

Josh Wharton on the first free ascent of the Original Route on Mt. Proboscis, which was also the first one-day ascent of the face. *J. Copp*

spires. As the float plane finally carved into Glacier Lake Basin, the Nahani River meandering into the distance like loose mercury, the high alpine Cirque of the Unclimbables winked at us through its bellowing cloak of cloud. We were psyched.

Fairy Meadows is the perfect name for the base camp where we finally dropped our gear and supplies. Marmots whistled their cheer. Gigantic, streaked boulders played architecture, while phantasmagoric cloud bundles wafted up valley to engulf our group and the wildflowers in sparkling dew and rain. But as the first weeks passed, our psyche began to turn inward with the acknowledgment of the hideous weather. Our first few attempts at the Lotus Flower Tower were wet, bracing jaunts onto one of the world's most sublime alpine spires. One day Brooke, Timmy, John, and I, fueled by a sucker hole of blue sky, went for the Lotus. I led the first few

Josh Wharton cleaning pitch 10 of Pecking Order on Parrot Beak Peak. *Jonathan Copp*

pitches in full raingear, snowmelt running down my sleeves and soaking me through. That day, by the time we were 400 feet up, snow had begun to fall. Brooke and John decided to rap. Timmy and I, because we figured it would be more fun to climb into the storm than to descend and go back to our nylon cells, kept going. But after several hundred feet, numb hands and slick rock drove us off. A few others had joined us in Fairy Meadows by then. Playing hackysac in the mud with the Welsh folk and drinking some corn with James and Francesca Garret, we were passing the days well.

As happens in life, when things get good, time flies (and so do the mosquitoes). When the sky finally cleared on July 18, we were running. Timmy and John, along with a handful of other teams, were gunning for the Lotus. Brooke and I, having made a few stunted goes at the classic tower already and not wanting to get in queue, headed for Bustle Tower, a chiseled 2,000-foot spire in the heart of the Cirque. Our goal: climb it and have fun. I usually

Josh Wharton midway up the first ascent of Pecking Order on Parrot Beak Peak. *Jonathan Copp*

climb with a sort of triage mentality. Free climbing is the ideal, speed the necessity, and survival mandatory. From this I find free climbing faster than aid climbing, thus enabling speed, which in turn puts us in less danger from a hungry storm, hanging serac, or falling rock. Brooke and I were well on our way up a route called Club International (V or VI 5.10 A2). To me it looked like the best possibility for the first free route on the tower. But as we buckled into the belay atop pitch four, a line of left-trending splitter cracks drew us out of the route's corner system and onto the headwall's face. The next four or five pitches held an amazing array of features, from perfect hands to a crux finger crack, into a wet groove, and through a wild off-width ear that culminated in an overhanging juggy roof. A few hundred feet above the roof we converged with Club International. From here moderate climbing led to the ridge and on to the summit. By now it was one in the morning yet still light enough to climb. Our goal—to climb it and to have fun—was, at least to Brooke, beginning to mutate, especially with the increasingly cold belays and approaching darkness.

Within a day and a half, the weather still holding, Timmy O'Neill and I were at this exact same belay. Having free climbed all of the aid on Club International to arrive in the upper dihedrals by the afternoon, Timmy and I were jazzed and movin'. We were doing handstands on the summit by 5 p.m. Club International went amazingly smoothly, the crux being a delicate 5.11b face traverse out of the main corner system and into a splitter finger crack. Brooke and my "major variation" that bends out on the left side of the wall is called Don't Get Piggy, 5.12a.

As Timmy and I ambled into Fairy Meadows, I spotted that look in Brooke's eyes. She was ready for another one. The question was, "was I?" The weather was still holding, and a lotus petal was perched on her lips. By 8 p.m. the following day we stood at the base of the Lotus Flower Tower. It was dry from bottom to top, and nobody's eyes but ours were on it. We made the bivy ledge by midnight and slept for the few hours of darkness that had finally found these northern territories. We woke to a pink flamingo band of clouds marching our way. "Damn, is the weather window closing? Let's go." Lotus's famous headwall is as lovely and as stately as can be imagined. Sections of delicate face climbing connect splitter crack systems. By 2 p.m. we were on the summit eating snow until our mouths went numb and realizing we were just in time.

Josh Wharton stopping the clock atop the first free ascent of the Original Route on Mt. Proboscis (shown on the right), which was also the first one-day ascent of the face. *Jonathan Copp (2)*

Chris Hampston on a pillar in Fairy Meadows, heart of the Cirque of the Climbables. *Jonathan Copp*

Top: The Lotus Flower Tower is on the left; Parrot Beak Peak is on the right, with Pecking Order shown.
Below: Josh Wharton sitting on Pins and Needles in base camp, Fairy Meadows. *Jonathan Copp*

After three weeks in the Cirque, it was finally time to wish farewell to Timmy, Brooke, and John. We had all summited the Lotus and a few other dreamy peaks and, well, I wanted to stay for more. Ha! No, I had really planned to stay a bit longer and climb with my friend Josh Wharton. But saying goodbye is always difficult—especially because I was left completely alone (but only for a day) within this majestic cirque, sharing the place only with those ancient goateed beasts chipping their hoof-marked trails into the snow and ice and earth.

I had another two weeks though—to sit in the tent and fester, I thought. But when the new recruits arrived, Chris Hampston, Kevin Cochrin, and Josh Wharton, they brought with them renewed energy and optimism. After humping beastly loads up into Fairy Meadows, Josh and I set our sights on Parrot Beak Peak, one of the largest and least explored walls within the cirque. I believe there was only one aid route on it, and that had been climbed just once! The line we were scoping took a meandering course up the center of the wall—delicate features, but all there.

One day, after one too many Scrabble tournaments, one less cloud floated in the boiling skies, so Josh and I made for Parrot. Our plan was to work out the first few pitches of the route, because they looked thin and might require a bolt or two, or some spice work. Once we were actually on the wall, though, perfect edges and thin features appeared in the bullet granite. Within a few hours we were 600 feet up the wall without having placed a single pin or bolt. We hadn't planned on continuing, but it wasn't raining or snowing yet, so in a handful of hours more we were 2,000 feet up, and I was drilling the first bolt, for a belay. Josh was down below shivering and I had a T-shirt on my head for a beanie: unprepared is an understatement. The next gust of wind held a few raindrops and, without any shell layers, we were outta there, but enthralled with how the route was going and looking forward to our next attempt.

Another morning of mediocre weather, after many days of bad weather, left Josh and me wondering if we shouldn't climb the Lotus. We figured we wouldn't need much if we climbed it fast enough, and maybe we could beat the looming afternoon showers. Four and a half hours after beginning, we were standing on top of the Lotus Flower Tower, grins as big as the mountains. We simul-climbed most of the route, hootin' and hollering to each other along the way. "Josh, don't miss the splitter hand crack through the roof!" "Jonny, these knobs are insane!" It was great making it back to camp for lunch and the drumming of rain on the taut nylon.

From the very first day Josh arrived, a main goal in the back of our minds was to free climb the original route on Mt. Proboscis in a day. The route had never been completely freed (although almost by Feagin and Blanchard), and the wall had never been climbed in a day, as far as we knew. The challenge was enticing, especially after kicking steps up What Notch and gazing out at the golden face. We made a few attempts at it, getting as far as the top of the icy notch before the next storm cycle rolled in.

When the second true weather window of my trip opened, Josh and I were in position for Parrot Beak Peak. Back up on that wild face with two ropes and no jumars, our progress was smooth, and we knew where to go, until we didn't. A few run-out face sections connected cracks and corners, and the final headwall plastered us into a left-facing corner running with snowmelt. Having freed everything up to there, we grappled with numb hands up the final four hundred feet of wet rock, trying to hang on for an all-free route. And we did, barely. By late afternoon we had made the top, navigating the bulbous snow features to find the true summit. We named the route "Pecking Order," 2,800 feet, V+ 5.11R. Two ropes, two bolts, two friends, one day. The highlight of the route came unexpectedly as I rapped off the summit headwall.

Sore fingertips and clear heads in the Cirque of the Unclimbables. Top: Josh Wharton after freeing the Original Route on Proboscis. Below: Josh and Jonathan in Fairy Meadows. Proboscis on the left. Lotus and Bustle on the right, *J. Copp*

Touching down on a nice ledge 180 feet off the anchor, I felt a queer vibration. Lifting my feet to peer down the wall, I noticed the ledge was actually a forty-foot-tall pillar, barely seated on this overhanging face. A rush of excitement and terror ran through me as I began work on this trundle from God. The towering flake would have been a nightmare to rappel past, so I had to, really! The monolith creaked as I wedged my knee behind it, and human-sized shards dropped from behind its middle. I glanced up at Josh, who was staring down wide-eyed from the summit, and felt a hesitation—almost a feeling that gravity could implode or seismic chaos could result from such a feature falling through space. But I couldn't stop now. When it finally gave, it fell like a man shot, headfirst until it was parallel with earth below. Then it released to drop into a deafening silence. It's that silence that I remember most, before the cacophonous explosion. People at base camp thought it was thunder, though the skies were clear.

We were giggling, but that goal in the back of our minds (Proboscis) was still there, buzzing away like a pesky mosquito. As the weather window was holding, we would give it a go. After one day of rest, we woke early and climbed from Fairy Meadows up and over What Notch and into the Proboscis cirque. By nine a.m. we were starting the first pitch of the legendary 1963 route, first climbed by the all-star team of Layton Kor, Jim McCarthy, and Royal Robbins. After only a few wet sections, we were into the meat of the climbing (two ropes, one liter of water, and no jumars). A splitter finger and hand crack soared for pitches up a streaked face. We grabbed knobs and edges when the crack pinched down. The crux fell into Josh's lead, and we both hung on for the onsight. Hats off to Josh, because it was spicy. After simul-climbing a long section and piecing together the final pitches, we stood on the catwalk summit at 5:30 in the afternoon. The Original Route—VI 5.12R. With sore fingertips and clear heads, we savored the silence of the place and the silencing of that buzz in our minds. The Snickers weren't bad either.

SUMMARY OF STATISTICS:

AREA: Cirque of the Unclimbables, Logan Mountains, Northwest Territory, Canada

NEW ROUTES: Parrot Beak Peak: Pecking Order (2,800 feet, V+ 5.11), Jonathan Copp and Josh Wharton. First free route on the wall. One day. Bustle Tower: Don't Get Piggy variation to Club International (2,000 feet, V+ 5.12a), Brooke Andrews and Jonathan Copp.

FIRST FREE ASCENTS: Proboscis: Original Route (VI 5.12R, 8.5 hours), Jonathan Copp and Josh Wharton. Bustle Tower: Club International (2,000 feet, V+ 5.11, approx. 10 hours), Jonathan Copp and Tim O'Neill.

SPEED ASCENT: Lotus Flower Tower (2000+ feet, V 5.10), 4.5 hours. Jonathan Copp and Josh Wharton.

All routes climbed in late July and early August, 2001.

HOLY BAFFMAN!

Speed climbing Mt. Asgard's Scott and Porter routes, Baffin Island.

CEDAR WRIGHT

Jason Singer Smith speeding up the 40-pitch Porter Route on the north face of Mt. Asgard. *Cedar Wright*

Three thousand feet and over 24 hours up the north face of Mt. Asgard on the second ascent of Charlie Porter's visionary wall route, tears were streaming from Singer Smith's eyes.

"Do you believe in fate?" I asked him.

"Believe in it? My whole life operates on it," he said between sobs. It had been one year to the day since Singer had been kidnapped by terrorists in Kyrgyzstan, and now here we were, committed to the point of no return, without a bolt kit, on the first-ever single-push of a Grade VII, and Singer had just been hit by a falling rock.

"This is what it's all about, Singer; we paid good money for this," I joked, staring up at the 14 pitches of wall climbing between us and the summit, then down the 30 pitches to the glacier below.

Our dreams had brought us here, but now our shared dream seemed more like a nightmare. Blame it on Peter Croft, who Singer and I idolized in our climbing adolescence.

He was the one who ingrained in us the importance of style. He was the one who sparked our dreams of becoming world-class speed climbers. Blame it on Robbins, Fitschen, Frost, and Pratt: they set the standard years ago, bringing the Nose down from 47 days to seven and a half. We wanted to take speed climbing to Baffin Island the way Robbins took wall climbing to Proboscis, in the Northwest Territories. We wanted to stake our claim in the history of style. Now all we wanted to do was live.

⁂

Four years on Yosemite Search and Rescue had given me plenty of time to hone my skills, and I had learned from the best, clocking speed records with the likes of Dean Potter, Timmy O'Neill, Ammon McNeely, and Singer. While I did get a buzz from rocketing up Grade VIs, I felt that even with one rope and no headlamp, the level of commitment was never that extreme, and I always considered the climbs training for something larger and more committing. Baffin Island hovered in the back of my mind somewhere between myth and legend, promising me the epic challenge I longed for.

Now, my dreams were becoming reality. Singer and I were going to Baffin Island, "the land that never melts," realm of Yosemite-sized big walls and no night. Actually, it was a dream, but the kind that you live while you are awake. Bouncing along on the air currents, I stared with anticipation out the window of the plane down onto the fifth-largest island in the world, a big-wall climber's paradise, with a thousand lifetimes' worth of rock. Had I known what the Arctic held in store for us, however, I might have asked the pilot to turn the plane around in mid-flight.

Our plan to go to Baffin was completely spontaneous. The late spring had proved fruitful for Singer and me, and we shattered several speed records: Southern Man and The Prow on the Washington Column, and Lurking Fear on El Cap, which we completed in 4:27, the second-fastest El Cap had ever been climbed. In the same day we linked up the South Face Route on Mt. Watkins with Lurking Fear for the first-ever link of those two walls. We topped out completely worked and yet hungry for something more. We wanted to suffer even harder.

While walking up to a roof crack, Singer said, "You know, we really should go to Baffin this summer."

I replied with an unequivocal "Let's go!"

Two weeks later, with some invaluable help from our friends and The North Face, Singer and I were on the plane.

Singer had already survived Baffin once, during his epic solo second ascent of Midgard Serpent on Mt. Thor ("Alone on Mt. Thor," *AAJ* 1999). I met Singer right after he returned from this legendary trip and was awed by his tales of walls even bigger than El Cap. I remember being impressed not just by his commitment to climbing Thor, but to going about it in good style. He humped all the loads the 15-plus miles to Thor, completely unassisted, and clocked the fastest ascent (12 days) of one of the most famous and formidable big walls in the world.

Now it was time for us to up the ante and leave the creature comforts of portaledges and haulbags behind. We made jokes about how it was going to be "Summit or plummet, do or die." They wouldn't have seemed so funny had we known what was in store for us.

⁂

We touched down in the isolated town of Pangnirtung. Like all of Baffin Island's outposts, there are no roads out of "Pang" and the only way in or out is by plane or boat—or, for the adventurous, by skidoo during the winter when the sea ice is frozen. The locals are Inuits, which translates as "the people," and they still hunt caribou, polar bear, whale, seal, and walrus as part of their daily diet. This is a people only decades removed from a nomadic hunting life. We paid our park fee, chartered a boat to take us and our 600 pounds of gear the 30 miles across the fjord to Auyuittuq National Park, and were soon waving goodbye to our boatman.

We packed up our first loads and began the three-day hike to Mt. Asgard, a trip that would become painfully familiar. Along the way we were forced to wade through countless streams fed by the hanging glaciers that surround the valley. We moaned and wailed our way through the ice-cold crossings and cried quietly under the burdensome packs. We passed the occasional trekker, but mostly we went at it alone, seeking comfort in a good book during the resting hours.

As fate would have it, I sprained my ankle at one of the stream crossings. I rested impatiently while Singer humped the climbing rack the last leg up the glacier to the base camp below Asgard. Luckily, a four-day storm ensued and not much climbing time was lost.

After two and a half weeks of carrying way more weight than I ever thought myself capable of, we were finally at base camp with all our gear. I had come this far and I had to try my best, but my ankle felt weak, and I wavered somewhere between nervousness and terror.

Our first goal was the Scott Route on Asgard. We awoke to clear but frigid weather and saddled up for our first climb. The 3,500-foot route was put up in 1972 in an epic 30 hours by Doug Scott, Dennis Hennek, Paul Nunn, and Paul Braithwaite. No bolts were placed. I had the pleasure of leading every pitch with Singer climbing simultaneously behind me. The first 3,000 feet go at 5.10 or easier, and we free-soloed most of this with the rope tied between us. I called for a belay on a couple of the upper pitches, including the classic and crux overhanging chimney (5.11), and Singer followed on jumars.

Three hours and 56 minutes after starting, we topped out on the north tower of Asgard, psyched to have finally climbed something, and in record-breaking time. We rapped contentedly back to base camp, for a tent-to-tent time that was half the previous fastest time on the route.

The next day we hiked three hours to the base of the north face of the north tower of Asgard, site of Charlie Porter's ground-breaking big-wall route of 1975. Doug Scott described the route in the book *World Mountaineering* (1998) as follows: "Using just one bolt and his ice axe, Porter gained the prominent dihedral to make a direct route to the summit. He made 40 pitches—the most remarkable achievement on Asgard, Baffin Island, and probably anywhere!" We took one look at the perfect overhanging dihedral that he had climbed, wiped the drool from our chins, and started making plans to climb it.

After motoring the Scott Route, we were perhaps overly confident. We mistakenly assumed that Charlie hadn't had any copperheads, so all we would need was a few pins. After all, Charlie had not had cams, so how bad could it be, with all of our modern tools? I remember saying that this was going to be like the Nose Route of Baffin, and we genuinely thought that we would climb it in about 12 hours.

A few days later we were standing at the base of the 2,000-foot "approach" to the 3,000-foot wall. On the approach, which most would consider part of the climb, we encountered quite possibly the worst climbing known to man, consisting of fresh rock fall/talus scrambling, and wandering, sand-covered 5.8. We free soloed all of this in our hiking boots, loaded

The approximate line of the Porter Route on the north face of Mt. Asgard. *Cedar Wright*

Cedar Wright stepping out of the chimney on the crux pitch (5.10) of the 3,500-foot Scott Route, put up in 1972 on the south face of Mt. Asgard. *Jason Smith*

down with 50-pound-plus packs, grimacing and moaning all the way. By the time we reached the base of the wall, we both agreed that we'd rather totally epic and spend 60 hours on the climb than bail. We hucked our Gore-Tex, boots, and other unnecessary gear off the approach, and watched in glee as it fell free for 1,000 feet, smashed into a 50-degree ice slope and then rocketed to the base.

Four pitches along, looking up at 60 feet of copperheading, we realized that, as we lacked enough copperheads, beaks, and pitons, we were completely underprepared. The diagnosis: Charlie Porter was bad ass. This became our mantra of suffering as we rapped the four pitches down the wall and 15 pitches down the approach. Along the way, we found Charlie's ice axe, film, and bolt kit. We were psyched to have found this little piece of big-wall history, but we both agreed that nothing was worth doing the approach again.

Twenty-four hours after leaving the tent, we returned, tired and dejected. The bad memories were already beginning to fade, however, and Singer and I formulated a plan to walk out the 30 miles to the park entrance, where we had more copperheads and pitons stashed.

We couldn't go home without giving it our best. The next day we began the hike out. The fun had ended long ago. We were now men possessed.

On the way out we ran into park wardens Daniel and Tommy, with whom we had become acquainted while ferrying loads. They had already impressed us with their generosity and impeccable knowledge of the park, and we were happy to have some contact with the outside world. Daniel entertained us with stories about clubbing seals and fending off polar bears, and Tommy made fun of our desperate appearance. They gave us rejuvenated motivation and things almost seemed fun again.

Five days and 60 miles later, we were back at base camp, just in time for a six-day storm. We were already on our last reserves of sanity, and our tent-bound antics would have made great blackmail footage had anyone been filming. I tried not to stress too much, but my nights were mostly sleepless, and my dreams anxiety ridden. We both knew that this would be the hardest, most committing climb of our lives.

On day seven we awoke to cloudless skies and began suiting up for battle. On the initial rappel down the bergschrund that brings you to the Parade Glacier, a van-sized boulder rolled across our rope, but, miraculously, it wasn't cut. A few hours later, as we neared the 2,000-foot "approach," Singer nearly plummeted unroped into a bottomless crevasse. Ravens circled above, ready to pick at our bones should things go wrong.

We looked up at the initial approach and realized that Charlie's fixed lines, which we had hand-over handed in a couple spots on the previous attempt, had been completely chopped by a catastrophic rockfall in the last few days. For 26 years the ropes had remained unscathed. We leave for a week, and come back to chopped ropes! Had we brought more copperheads on the initial attempt, we might very well have been wiped off the face. But, right or wrong, we had too much time and energy invested to turn back now.

With the increased burden of extra pitons, food, and water, our packs were even heavier, and now the approach was covered in a gritty layer of rock dust. Things were very grim, and we exchanged more than a few desperate looks. When we finally arrived at the base of the wall, we realized that the pillar we had lunch on during our previous attempt had been ripped off the face by the rockfall. The seriousness of our situation was highlighted by the occasional rock bullet whistling past our heads.

Singer chopped steps up the final ice cone to the base of the route proper. I followed it free and took a fall. Singer caught me on a hip belay without an anchor. We hadn't even started the wall climbing, and I was shaking visibly.

With rocks and ice rocketing down all around us, we cut our rest short, and Singer started up the first block of the climb, styling it in about four hours. I followed, removing the beaks and tied-off blades, and lamented the fact that my block was next, and that it started with the crux A4 pitch. Night fell as I got onto a fixed head placed the year I was born, and then placed one of my own. It was probably good that the darkness hid the string of junk gear below me. I placed two tipped-out beaks and 11 copperheads and clipped two fixed heads that Charlie left behind before I finally reached the A1 crack that marked the end of the A4 section. The sun rose on the glacier landscape below as I climbed another five hours, linking the strenuous and continuous nailing of pitches six and seven.

After nine and a half hours of leading, I was more than happy to pass the lead off to Singer. He toiled for another nine or so hours, taking us to the start of pitch 11 in a mix of dicey nailing and free-climbing.

"Can I send you up any gear?" I asked.

"Yeah, send me up the .38 Special!" he joked.

"Who needs a gun when you've got rock fall?" I replied.

With almost 24 hours behind us, I took over again and drunkenly started up pitch 11—only to find out exactly where the rockfall had come from. The next three pitches were completely buried in rock dust and littered with precarious, car-sized loose blocks. Rocks were whizzing past my head regularly now, and my slow and steady pace became frantic and furious. As I swam in vertical 5.10 sand with no pro, Singer let out a scream of pain. Hit in the knee by a softball-sized rock. Singer was understandably shaken, though conscious that the injury could have been much worse. Our lives flashed before our eyes more than once in those three pitches of rockfall climbing. We were like scared children.

We had been hauling up to this point, but now, with Singer injured and the loose rock everywhere, hauling was no longer an option. We gathered everything that we absolutely didn't need, including the trail line, the extra pitons, the Gore-Tex, and the extra hammer, and threw it into the abyss. Singer was incapacitated for leading, so now the burden lay upon me.

The next pitches were a blur of suffering and endurance. The routefinding was difficult and I bailed from several different cracks, logging almost 1,000 feet of off-route climbing. The constant movement kept me relatively warm, but Singer spent most of his time sitting at the belay shivering uncontrollably.

We began to wonder if hucking all our gear might have been a bit hasty. I looked down at the glacier 4,000 feet below and wished that I'd never come to Baffin at all. I just wanted off. I might have screamed for help if anyone could have heard us. We both knew that if I didn't find the route soon we were going to become permanent fixtures on the north face of Asgard.

Thirty-eight hours and 4,500 feet after beginning the route, I finally mantled onto the summit and into the sun. Singer asked me if, knowing what I knew now, I still would have climbed the route.

"No," I said. "But ask me in a couple of months and I'll probably say yes."

After a couple of hours of basking in the sun, we began the 20 rappels that led to base camp. The descent was sketchy, but compared to the climbing we had survived, it seemed like a walk in the park. Following the rappels was a mile of talus and two miles of glacier walking. After 38 hours in tight climbing shoes, we could barely walk. We cut the toes out our Five Tens, relieving the excruciating pain, then slipped and slid down the glacier, toes poking through our shoes. Fifty-four hours after departing, we stumbled joyously into base camp.

The next day we awoke to the worst storm we had seen in our month and half on Baffin. It was snowing sideways outside. If we had been another day on the climb, we would have been dead for certain. We both knew that we had expended every ounce, not only of skill, but of luck, in achieving this climb. We dreamed of sandy beaches and tropical sunsets.

We were down from the climb, but we had thrown off our boots, Gore-Tex, and backpacks, and with the storm raging we had no way to retrieve them, even if they were in a retrievable location. After two days of sitting out the storm, we began packing up. I clipped the entire rack to my harness, then packed all of our gear into stuff sacks and looped them over my shoulders with slings. With my painful makeshift backpack, I skated down the glacier in my running shoes and a fleece jacket. When I began to slide out of control toward one of the numerous crevasses, I would just lie down and dig the climbing gear into the ice.

On the three-day hike out, I was loaded down with most of the gear, and Singer limped out behind me. One night I awoke to Singer screaming frantically, "Where am I?" In his dream the storm had moved in while we were on the climb, encasing us in ice. He awoke, clawing furiously at his imaginary icy tomb.

Three days and 35 miles later, we were on the boat, motoring back to Pangnirtung and civilization. The sense of closure on the climb was beginning to sink in. Now I just had to survive the plane, then the car ride back to Yosemite, and I would feel like the expedition was a success. We were happy to be alive and eager to get back to the friends and family that we loved so much. It had been the climb of a lifetime.

⚛

Back in Yosemite I reveled in the simple pleasures of good food and a loving girlfriend. One day in the cafeteria I relayed my story to Tom Frost and TM Herbert. They both listened with wide-open eyes to my epic tale of speed climbing in Baffin.

"Good God, son" TM said when I had finished. "I'm going to have nightmares. You obviously need to be institutionalized."

A few weeks later, I ran into Peter Croft in Camp 4. "Nice work up in Baffin," he said. "I think it's really proud that you guys went for it in a push without a bolt kit." Here was my biggest hero, complimenting me on my climbing style. I couldn't help but beam with pride.

Now it all seems like a surreal dream, and I can almost reason that it wasn't actually all that bad, but I know that realistically, if it had been any worse, I wouldn't be telling this story. In the days that followed our return, the World Trade Center collapsed and America turned frantic and paranoid. In spite of this horrible tragedy, with my personal near-death experience behind me, I felt more at peace than ever before. Singer reacted differently, jumping on a plane to Thailand only weeks later in an effort to escape all the personal and national chaos that ensued.

As weeks turn to months and the details fade with each day, I long for the next fix, but I know that nothing will likely ever compare to Asgard. In the meantime I enjoy the sunny exposure and perfect cracks of Yosemite with a rejuvenated, child-like wonder, knowing that in the big picture all this nonsense about style and climbing is completely meaningless.

SUMMARY OF STATISTICS

AREA: Auyuittuq National Park, Baffin Island, Nunavut Territory, Canada

ASCENTS: Mt. Asgard: The Scott Route (3,500 feet, VI 5.10), Jason "Singer" Smith and Cedar Wright. The Charlie Porter Route (40 pitches, VII 5.10 A4).

PROJECT MAYHEM

Mastering the chaos during solo battles on
"the hardest big-wall route on the planet," Mt. Thor, Baffin Island.

JIM BEYER

Jim Beyer ferrying loads to the 3,700-foot west face of Mt. Thor, Auyuittuq National Park, Baffin Island, in the Nunavut Territory. Project Mayhem provided 4,300 feet of sustained solo climbing. *Jim Beyer*

All my carefully laid plans are unraveling into chaos. It's deep into my third night alone on Mt. Thor. Sitting on my camo bullet bag in my portaledge tent, I ponder the rivulets of water draining into the puddles on the floor. How am I to bivy in this mess? Should I sit up all night, or lie down in the water?

This won't do. Despite my cold and fatigue, I go out into the storm and lower my tent 30 feet, out of the cascade. This freight-lowering maneuver becomes an epic as my arms grow weak and wooden with hypothermia.

An hour later I'm shivering in my sodden pit, hips and shoulders in puddles of cold water. And for two nights and one day I lie in those puddles of despair, wondering what happened to my Baffin luck.

Things got off to a rough start in Montreal in July of 2000, when my car got tossed and most of my gear was stolen. I dropped $5,000 the next day replacing some of it, but many of the hooks, hammers, and "special effects" were homemade and not replaceable. I spent many evenings filing hooks, making gear, and worrying about what was missing.

The rock low down on Thor is problematic. It is gneiss packed with gray quartz that is both harder and weaker than Yosemite granite. Extremely expanding and loose, this rock has a big weakness: its brittleness. Thin expanding flakes break easily. Fat natural hook moves atop weathered "crumble cookies" explode when weighted, leaving blank rock or slopers that must be "enhanced" with a chisel. This route I'm on looks so big and continuously hard that El Cap's Reticent Wall—a hard, proud route—looks like baby food in comparison.

The wall above was terrifying and, filing new hooks at the base of the wall, I discovered my mind control was already wavering. The "pivotal moment" last year had occurred while I was drilling the belay bolt on pitch two.

The pitch had started with tenuous aid above two ledges and only got worse. After nine hours and a 50-foot runout on A5 (and a possible double-ledge fall), I finally found a decent knifeblade placement. Four hours later I was drilling that belay bolt. When I got there, I was so weak (with five bolts) that my normal A5 high was replaced with despair. I had overdrilled a second potential A5 crux down to A4 because of my faltering mind control. Furthermore, I was just starting up a huge route and was already worried that at my current rate I would use all my bolts before I got halfway. It was a huge mental battle. I needed to regain complete mind control (and stop drilling) or untie and "walk the wind" right now, before exhibiting further snail-eye. ("Snail-eye": Ever poke the eye of a snail and see it retract into its body? That's what your manhood does, figuratively speaking, when....)

Several pitches higher I led a fat pitch that took two days. The bottom half is quality A4+ techno aid with tiny heads, expando beaks, and hooks up to an expanding flake that was just good enough to call the runout over. A blank section succumbed to hooks, a few bathooks, and two quarter-inch bolts. Above this was a long, two-inch-thick expanding flake

Hauling the portaledge high on Project Mayhem. *Jim Beyer*

that disappeared, followed by a long hook traverse (A5) into a good corner.

Pitch followed pitch, day after day, week after week. High up the wall I realized that I had mastered the chaos. I realized that I was more comfortable on Thor climbing expando and dodging rockfalls than I was in America. I felt a strange detachment from reality. With each misadventure I stood back and said, "What an adventure," as if I was commenting on someone else's misfortune.

For me, climbing big walls is not a speed event. It is a way of life. While others play trendy speed-climbing or "free"-climbing games on easy big walls, I play a different game of big-wall ascent, with rules of my own choosing. Climbing is anarchy. End of lecture. I daydream of going to a different planet that has mega big walls and spending a year on the face—just climbing, hauling, and taking rest days as needed.

While free climbing (5.9R) up to Hrungnir "Ledge," I realized it was not a place I could afford to fall, as my protection was sketchy. A huge double roof below with multiple sharp edges would not be kind to my 9-mm lead line if I hucked. (I had extended my 11-mm lead line with

Looking up pitch 22 from the belay. *Jim Beyer*

my 9-mm tag line to finish a 250-foot pitch.) I was standing on dirty slopers with my left hand pimping an arête when my right hand pulled off a flake. The flake knocked my hand off the arête. I felt myself going off backward and time stood still as I slapped my left hand back onto the arête as my right caught a small crimper. I pulled back in and the "shake" didn't skate my feet off. A six-inch jet of blood spurted out of my hand with every heartbeat, and the arête was immediately covered with red. Blood poured off my elbow and sprayed into the air. The animal within took over and free-climbed like a man possessed for about 20 feet until a solo backup knot on the harness stopped him. At this point my mind was able to regain control. I've had my share of injuries, but never did blood spray out of my body. I pressed my hand against my mouth and immediately got a mouthful of rich blood. I swallowed. It tasted really good.

This shocked me. I swallowed another mouthful before reaching for the tape clipped on my harness. I surveyed the trail of blood to the stained arête while licking my arm and beard clean.

An hour later I was hauling the pitch in a daze when my bags stuck. I jacked the haul system from 3:1 to 5:1 and it seemed to work for a while, but after 40 feet of increasing difficulty, I broke out of my daze. I realized that my 25-foot-long chain of six haulbags was not jammed against the double roofs below. Perhaps my old lead line (chopped by a loose flake on pitch 6) was stuck instead. This rope was dangling from the top haulbag in the chain. I set a rappel to check it out and brought two rope bags to pad the sharp edges below. Once on rap, I dropped in at speed without padding any edges. I quickly confirmed that, indeed, the dangling rope was stuck some 400 feet below. All my other long ropes were in play and to organize a 400-foot rap would be too slow. I tied my 50-foot ninja cord to the 230-foot mystery rope I was on and salvaged what I could. The stuck rope was incredibly taut, for I had hauled 40 feet of stretch out of it. I looked up my rappel line to the roofs and saw a big white puffy wad on the edge of the lower roof. This puff was my rappel rope sawing on a sharp edge. If my rappel rope separated, I'd get a quick tour of the lower face and make it to Valhalla before dinnertime.

I froze and tried to estimate my danger. The damaged section of rope was far above me, but even from here it looked bad. I clipped an ascender into each rope and reviewed my options. It appeared that staying clipped into both ropes would be safest, so, with some trepidation and a lot of innocence, I cut the taut rope and was catapulted upward. It was like falling up. There was a second of float, then a short fall downward.

And so I hung for a while as I'm wont to do and just laughed as I waited for my little dose to cut in. There is so little sweetness in this life, so when my adrenaline rush cut in I just enjoyed the moment. Looking down at my hand, I realized that I had not dropped my knife or cut anything important (like my rope) during that out-of-control maneuver. And then I started laughing like a psycho.

Go Abe was a Japanese solo climber who attempted, over the summers of 1996 and 1997, to climb a new route on Thor just to the left of my route. When just 45 feet or so feet above Hrungnir Ledge while leading an easy corner, he pulled off a dangling flake that chopped his 10-mm lead line. He did not survive his 40-foot ledge fall, and he died alone. I'm sure the Valkyries came and carried him off to Valhalla, for solo on Thor is certainly battle. Only those who perish on the field of battle go to Valhalla. I honor this warrior and admire his complete commitment to his chosen solo mission.

I was just 250 feet right of Go Abe's gear stash and death bivouac chaos. My food and water were mostly gone, and I hoped he had enough to fuel my solo mission. I led a 250-foot traverse (off route) to get to his gear but was dismayed to find no food or water. Parks Canada did the body recovery but left most of his gear—the stuff I rooted and looted through. His portaledge camp had been destroyed by rockfall and he had worked the upper headwall from a boulder cave. How he planned to climb the virtually ledgeless overhanging headwall (1,800 feet) without a portaledge has troubled me since first I saw this epic possibility.

I had been looking up at the overhanging headwall for over a month now. It was the perfect venue for me: extremely overhung and very blank with only enough features to suggest a possible line. It looks like terrain on Reticent Wall or the Black Canyon's Happy Trails, except far steeper and longer.

I decided to drill a bolt on the first headwall pitch. This was decided before I even started up the route. The reason is silly, but internally accepted. While Go Abe perished on an easy

The west face of Mt. Thor, showing the line of Project Mayhem, climbed solo during 2000 and 2001. *Jim Beyer*

pitch, just 250 feet left of me, my pitch will prove to be more extreme. I refused to be killed in a situation similar to Go, because stupid people would lump us together. For a person outside the tribe, this might seem strange, but pride sometimes requires a man to die, and sometimes it requires him to live.

And so I started up the pitch (A4+) by climbing loose blocks (A3+ with a possible ledgefall) to a corner and finally a blank arch. A trenched circle-head blew in the arch but I didn't huck, as my adjustable daisy shock loaded on a nearby funky knifeblade that held. After the bolt, marginal knifeblades driven straight up under thin expanding flakes led to a double-bolt belay—a rare treat to ease my troubled mind.

A blank corner above led to expanding roofs and blocks. Four placements into the crux (A4+) the wire tore out of my trenched (chiseled), small aluminum head and I dropped into space. I wasn't scared. My mind instantly focused on my good belay anchor, and I just kicked back and enjoyed the 25-foot ride. Back in the old days, I seldom fell while big-wall climbing. Young and cocksure, I thought it was because I was good. Now I fall on every wall and know it is because the difficulty has increased to the point where cutting-edge gear and skill is not enough. Luck is also required—and required on a regular basis.

With two pitches fixed on the headwall, I looked forward to getting another load of ice chunks in the morning, then committing to the headwall and moving up to my high point. A big storm moved in overnight, however, and dawn broke bitterly cold and snowing. This didn't deter me from the day's agenda, and mid-day found me unroped, crossing exposed, snow-covered scree and rock with a huge load of ice chips in a blizzard. One slip and I'd be over the edge. It was surreal in the half-light and blowing snow. It was so real yet I felt totally disconnected from reality. But I heard a voice on the wind and I listened. It was my three-year-old daughter. "Don't fall, Papa," she pleaded.

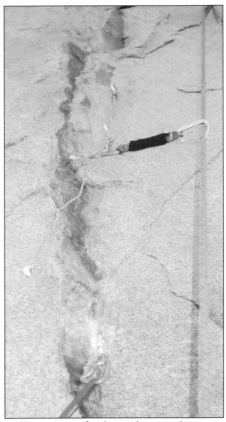

Back at the ledge/tent I piled in and resolved not to commit to the headwall until the weather broke. Five days later the snow tapered off but the weather was not much improved. Daytime highs of 50° Fahrenheit in August had become highs of ten degrees in early September. All my water was frozen. I had plenty of gas and ice, but only seven days' food. Still, I was eager to finish my route, even though I knew it would take a couple of weeks.

On the morning of the sixth day of the storm I decided that if I were to have any chance of summiting this year I must climb today and the storm must clear today. I knew that once I committed to the headwall there would be no

A close-up view of techno aid on Mt. Thor's west face. *Jim Beyer* chance of retreat, as each pitch on the headwall (except the last) overhangs 25 feet. I jugged the two pitches, cleaned one, and racked up. It had taken five hours. Every rope was sheathed in one-and-a-half inches of rime. Every knot was frozen hard. Everything was coated in rime, and still it stormed. I was shivering uncontrollably in the bitter wind. The pitch above looked A5. Would I be able to stand on dicey hooks while shivering this badly? Would my rope, frozen stiff as a wire cable, even hold a factor-two fall? A rip to the belay was definitely possible. I realized my best chance on the headwall would be to abandon my circuitous techno aid and drill the direct linkages with bat-hooks. This would get me on top, but it would also degenerate my proud route.

This was the hardest decision of my life, as I wanted to complete this route in the best style I could and in a single push. Yet I realized it was September above the Arctic Circle and it was not going to warm up. It was all too much. When my analytical side did the math, it didn't add up. Then my aggressive side cut in with: "This is what we want. How far have you come because of me? I will bring us through this, as always. I will carry you and in the end you will thank me." Then I did the math again.

It was desperately cold. I couldn't just hang around. It was either up or down. I felt sick to my stomach. I decided not to "think this through" but to "go with my instinct." My instinct felt I would not survive the headwall in these conditions with the food I had unless I abandoned style and drilled it up.

An overhanging web, high on Project Mayhem. *Jim Beyer*

I rappelled into the vapors. Eventually I felt a strange enchantment as I realized that I would live to see my children. I was supremely happy, as I had almost just given up that hope. But as I struggled out of my frozen outerwear I knew that I would have an opposite and equal reaction the following day: depression.

Two days later an eight-day storm broke, but the temperature never did rise in the following two weeks. I was bummed that my route would require two summers instead of one. This taint will bend climbers against my proud route and me. But I accepted my destiny.

The following day I traversed to Go Abe's stash and grabbed an ice hammer and ice screw. His crampons would not clip to my boots. I soloed unroped with a small pack, for I had left everything behind except a micro rack, rope, lunch, and one liter of water. I expected to make my riverside campsite that day as I had previously read in an old magazine that two members of the 1985 American Direct team had traversed off and returned via this "ledge."

I made fast progress until Hrungnir Ledge became an overhanging wall. A forlorn 9-mm rope with multiple deep core shots was fixed between widely spaced quarter-inch bolts. I slid across this marginal rope. The next pitch wasn't any easier as I traversed snow-covered slabs 10 feet above a sharp edge, looking at the death fall. I reached easy ground as night fell, so I crawled into a crack and shivered all night without bivy gear.

At first light I downclimbed 1,000 feet on Hrungnir Ledge, but it ended abruptly on a blank 2,000-foot wall. I re-ascended 500 feet to a mixed gully and climbed without crampons and with but one primitive tool four pitches of 5.10 M6 to the shoulder. I took one fall on an ice screw while crossing an easy ice gully, but that was trivial compared with the shakefests I endured on the unprotected slabs and bulges above.

One snow-covered slab was particularly memorable. Small stones were frozen onto the slab, and these I cleared of snow, mantled, and stood on. While on a 50-foot runout I encountered an "impossible move." No holds and no possible friction on the wet slab. I couldn't down climb, and a big fall in this situation would be fatal. I packed snow onto the slab as a hold and—supergripped—mantled onto it.

After two of my coldest nights in the mountains and two-and-a-quarter days of alpine terror, I reached the base.

For this year's attempt I prepared in a manner similar to the year before by soloing a hard El Cap route in the spring—this time a new A5 variation to Surgeon General. I also soloed an A6a test piece—Canyonland's Outlaw Spire—that required not only extreme aid expertise, but an ambivalence toward life that is refreshing. Pitch two (A6a) on Cult of Suicidal was a full 90-foot runout with ground-fall potential. It was at least one full grade harder and more dangerous than anything on Reticent.

In mid-July, two weeks after leaving Montreal and after many days of load-carrying, I set out for Hrungnir Ledge. I drop in with six raps and do eight roped traverse pitches to my route. I rope up on the traverse as the conditions are sketchy with three inches of snow on three inches of ice on loose scree, which all lay upon wet, dirty slabs. I adopt a climbing mode of fixing my lead line to an alpine belay anchor, then returning for my 65-pound load of food. This works for me because I get to kick steps with only 20 pounds, then follow the pitch with the big load in a set of steps along a horizontal rope fixed at one end. I slide an ascender for a belay.

While traversing an icefield just five feet above its bottom edge, I suddenly find myself falling down a gully atop a thin slide of snow, ice, and scree. I flash upon my anchor-protection-system and come up with "probable death fall." My anchor is a one-by-one-by-three-foot boulder lying on loose, 35-degree scree. My fixed line stretches 150 feet horizontally across easy snow/ice without intermediate protection. I am clipped into this rope via a single ascender, and the edge of Hrungnir Ledge is but 40 feet below me. Instantly I rock my long axe from swagger stick to self-arrest position. Just before insertion I flash on angle of insertion, depth of insertion, and body position. It is at this moment that I realize I am falling down a rock gully. I don't think an ice axe self-arrest will work. While face down in self-arrest position—riding this rapidly accelerating debris—I look down over my left shoulder and spot a boulder, three feet above the gully, three feet left of the gully, embedded in gravel and coming up fast! Instantly I drop my axe and throw a four-point dyno for this boulder. My hands land on either side of the boulder and I am in a point of balance when my 65-pound load drives me hard into the boulder. I am fully amped and hold on.

"I stuck it with both hands," I say slowly as I look below. There is not another sizeable boulder above the edge of the 2,000-foot wall. I survived this fall in the no-fall zone only because I reacted instantly, figured out a new plan of action, threw a big old busta move, and stuck it—all in a couple of seconds. If one hand had missed I would not have had the strength to hold the impact of my falling pack and me.

A strange moment of sweetness follows as I realize I'm in the zone, climbing well, and will live to climb those A5 pitches on the headwall.

After ascending to my high point of the previous year and fixing an A5 pitch, I set out on what turns out to be the crux pitch. Two beak-and head-seams lead to a small roof that provides only a circle-head and bad blade stack. Further heads lead to delicate hooking on loose flakes. Thin natural hooking up to the natural belay is the technical crux (A5c). It is an 85-foot runout airfall. I've put in shorter runouts elsewhere that were rated higher (A5+) but they were ground-fall routes.

The weather breaks the next day, and for a week it's stormy and cool. Although I am on an overhanging wall, I am constantly damp from condensation—I'm climbing in a cloud. I take one day off but climb all other days. One day is particularly miserable, so I quit after five hours.

During this period I am distressed to note that what appeared to be a knifeblade crack from the ground is in reality a thin dike of black crystal. I do more drilling than expected here, but still end up with long Reticent-style A3+/A4a pitches.

After 18 days on the wall, I reach the summit. I believe my route, Project Mayhem VII, 5.10c A5c, is the hardest big-wall route on the planet. Sixty-six bolts and about 35 bat-hooks were drilled. It has five pitches of modern A5, three pitches of A4+, nine pitches of A4, and one-and-a-half pitches of 5.10c face climbing. I hiked 175 miles and spent 57 days on the face and three months alone over the summers of 2000 and 2001.

After cleaning up the base of Thor, I raft out with most of my gear in a tiny Kamikaze raft I had carried in. While rafting below the last major portage, I miss an eddy and am swept into a rapid I had not planned on running. I jump out into the shallows, but while I struggle with my raft in waist-deep whitewater a wave breaks over my raft and carries away my only paddle. I jump on my raft, and, lying face down on top of my packs, insert my index fingers into the half-inch holes provided for the optional oarlocks. I then balance my overloaded raft through the rapid and four-foot standing waves chasing my lost paddle. The river separated into multiple braided channels, and I never saw that paddle again. I floated the remaining eight miles to Overlord out of control.

SUMMARY OF STATISTICS

AREA: Auyuittuq National Park, Baffin Island, Nunavut, Canada

NEW ROUTE: Mt. Thor: Project Mayhem (VII 5.10c A5c), Jim Beyer solo, three months total during the summers of 2000 and 2001.

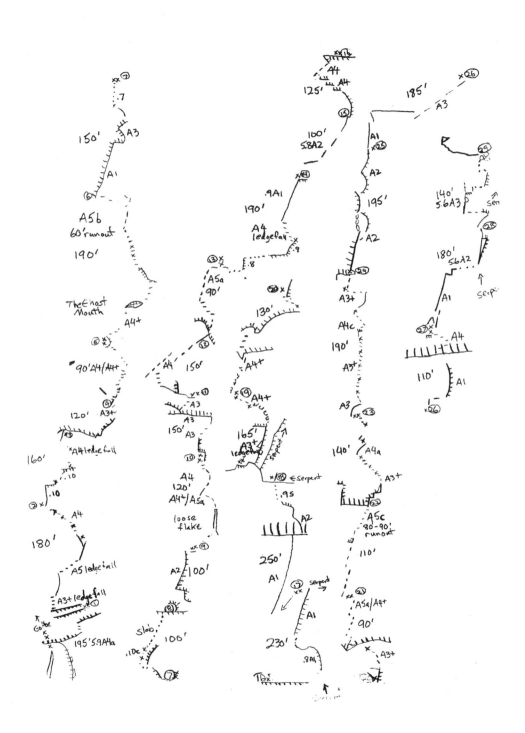

TRUE VALUE

*Finding beauty and danger on the first alpine-style ascent of Torre Egger
and a new route on Cerro Fitz Roy, Patagonia.*

TIM O'NEILL

Tim O'Neill flashing the V-for-victory on the Tonta Suerte route, Cerro Fitz Roy. *Nathan Martin*

I blindly struggle to find a small foothold on life. Exposure looms like a vulture circling fresh road kill. My heavy pack plus a pair of clunky boots multiplied by total exhaustion equals "freaking desperate." The rain that scared us away from our second attempt on Fitz Roy's massive west face is still fresh on the granite. Things are slick, serious; we are unroped. "Nathan where's that edge you used?" "Put my boot on it—now!" "Hold on dude," he answers distracted, his words directed somewhere else. I figure he's getting his footing, preparing to spot me if I pitch; perhaps he's wiping off the grit from the hold. I'm getting pumped. "NATHAN," I shout. He pushes my foot into place, holds it and then sheepishly offers, "Sorry dude, I was busy digging out a sweet one." He holds up a striking black, quartz crystal. At once I forgive him. Beauty and danger are synonymous in Patagonia. Isn't that why we came?

Nathan Martin and I met up in Puerto Natales, on January 11, 2002, amidst the cigarette smoke and garbled Chilean Spanish of Ruperto's Bar. Nathan had been hard at work in Moab, Utah paying for his trip ahead of time, a fascinating concept. I spent December kayaking on Chile's pristine, rain forest-edged rivers that run below snow capped Andean giants. A dream to paddle internationally became realized. Now it's time to dream again. With our Patagonian dreams encompassing towering spires, impossible scale, and certain anguish, they often border on nightmares. We arrive in Argentine Patagonia, and particularly Chalten, the town several miles downhill from the climbing, to vomiting, laughter, and friends. We will depart two months later in the same fashion. We've been hearing mixed reports about the weather. "Nope nothing, no summits for anyone," said a pair of disheartened South African climbers. "Dude, I heard Jarred and Tofu scored a half dozen summits," Nathan piped in. Either way, it's not cool to miss the often - solitary windows of opportunity in Patagonia. If you do miss one, you feel like a schmuck, silently chastising yourself for blowing it; wishing you were there instead of elsewhere

Tim O'Neill on the final mixed pitches before the summit mushroom on their alpine-style ascent of Torre Egger. *Nathan Martin*

Nathan Martin in the 5.10 handcracks on the 15th pitch of Tonta Suerte, Cerro Fitz Roy. *Tim O'Neill*

missing out.

Five days later we are missing out, big time. We humped killer loads from Campamento Bridwell seven hours up the Torre Valley's dry glacier to our favorite ABC, Noruegos. Being builders by trade we've a penchant for constructing bivys. Immediately we break ground on our third spec home, having built two here during the 2000 season. Excavating, laying stones, and eventually collapsing inside. In the morning the sky is weird, wind and drizzle spook us. We descend to Bridwell. In the morning sun an empty camp causes us to scream in unison, "Shit, we're blowing it." We re-ascend hurriedly from Bridwell to Noruegos for a spot of lunch. This time we continue walking over to the west face of Bifida, at 4:30 p.m., in a white-hot, ozone hole induced furnace. The idea to climb the peak was spontaneous and we carried virtually no information regarding our proposed first ascent. This would set the tone for our entire trip. At midnight, exhausted, we dig in the snow with a pilfered shovel, make a bivy platform, brew hot tasteless crap, and get pelted by falling ice all night. We wake to splitters-ville, magnificent

blue skies. At 8:15 a.m. in a methamphetamine-like daze, we speed climb half a pitch on Bifida's striking west flank before the weather window slams shut on our little fingies. Ouch, what a bitch, it's a bail festival. We retreat from the face, and hike up and over to our stone condo at Noruegos in a blistering gale. Below Standhardt's east face we ponder the fate of a Spaniard who perished in a crevasse in this identical spot last month. We stop to gape at Torre Egger's ferocious east aspect, crane our necks to listen to Pete and "Moch" suffer. They are descending from over a thousand feet up with their haul bags and ropes from a free attempt that only failed because Mother Nature didn't want them to play any longer. I console us with a weak spirited, "At least we aren't up there hating it like those guys." Not yet.

On the veranda at Noruegos the following day, over tea and Austrian-style hot cakes, Pete and Moch give us

Tim O'Neill exploring mixed ground on Torre Egger. *Nathan Martin*

the green light, their topo, and well wishes for our proposed first alpine style ascent of the Torre Egger. They are over it, beaten down by the unpredictable weather, and descend to Bridwell Euro style, wearing only tightie-whities below the belt. Sitting in the proud Cerro Torre throne and gazing at nothing in particular, I am stuck by the immensity of this place. It seems endless in every regard, no limit to any alpine inclination—I feel like a kid in a candy store, only a kid with wooden teeth and a bovine network of stomachs. "It's time for this baby to have its umbilical cord severed," Nathan declares, startling my attention back to Noruegos. He's referring to the Egger's previous eight ascents all employing fixed ropes and siege tactics. "Sure Dude, sounds feasible," I chime in, although I nervously recall not signing on for an ascent of Torre Egger during this tour of duty. We dry our clothing and equipment in the sun and prepare to enter Patagonia's no mans land in the early morning. It has been almost nine years since someone has stood atop the Torre Egger's phantasmal ice mushroom, or for that matter even made

Tim O'Neill jugging with the Beast on pitch 18 of Tonta Suerte, Cerro Fitz Roy. *Nathan Martin*

it halfway up the formation. Sleep comes slowly; I roll another smoke.

Our first attempt ends at the beginning of the 2002 Austrian variation, 800 feet above the glacier, just to the left of a hanging serac so massive it seems continental. The badly drawn topo leads us astray; or are we just dense? We spend hours reconnoitering a massive section of black and orange rock. The sky darkens, the clouds loom, I preach doom, and we rap at 5 p.m., disgruntled and tired. The walk across the glacier to our "casa de piedra" in blustering rain is numbing. Already our second failure and we've only been here one week. We hardly speak except to ask rhetorically, "Why are we here?" The answer of course does not exist. Living the question will have to suffice. Tomokadzu Nagaoka, who epitomizes the Zen alpinist, awaits us at ABC. We find him lying on the ground ensconced in a pitifully tattered bivy sack, sand blasting his exposed face. He and his partner have also failed. They were attempting an alpine style ascent of Exocet on Standhardt's east face; falling ice and severely deteriorating conditions forced them down. "Tomo" is smiling in fact he always smiles—and from it radiates his absolute strength of character. His eyes alone speak volumes on patience, passion, and persistence; his English doesn't allow much more. Though he has no Patagonia summits that I am aware of, Tomo, with his incessant drive, becomes my focus for inspiration.

Again we rest in sun having climbed the previous day in shit. We're busy blowing it once again. You feel impotent when given the opportunity to score, only to limp back to camp unadorned, no summit hash mark etched on your sword. Timing is everything here; it's a mix-

The Torre group, standing proud. *Nathan Martin*

ture of 75 percent luck and 25 percent wisdom. If you're off it can shatter your confidence and whittle away your strength until you simply vanish in a cloud of remorse. "What would Tomo do?" becomes my mantra. On January 22nd at 5:30 a.m. we begin climbing on Torre Egger for our second attempt and do not stop moving for the next 60-plus hours. I experience transformation on so many levels I feel like a stranger; surely *I* wouldn't have chosen such insanity.

We enjoyed our few moments on top of the Egger's towering, ephemeral ice mushroom peering into a whiteout. A storm had been increasing for several hours and our 1 a.m. breach onto the summit coincided with its apex. Nathan had just spent the last two-plus hours leading up the mushroom, climbing the most difficult alpine pitches of his life. All of his accumulated skill and strength were required to keep him alive. Torre Egger's top marked the passing of the final boundary, as we became the sixth and seventh persons to have climbed all three of the Torre Group. "How do we get down?" I yelled to Nathan as much as to myself. He tersely answered, "I don't know, I haven't had the chance to think about it." We decided to chop a bollard, our first ever. We simply stamped down the unconsolidated rime ice and freshly fallen snow to form a 10-foot semicircle about a foot deep. As Nathan dropped over the edge into darkness I belayed him from the other side of the shroom with our 60-meter static rope, and waited for the snow to slice through.

"The snow's beginning to stick to everything Tim; careful climbing in those boots," Nathan warns from his single-cam anchor situated thousands of feet above the barren glacier. It's 4:30 a.m. and the wind desperately wants to scour us off the face. I think of sleep, a warm bed with my woman; hell I'd settle for a gravel bed in a rock-hewn cave with Nathan, but that is momentary folly. I am abruptly brought back to our ludicrous position on Torre Egger's east face as a gust whips a frozen aider, stings my face. We began descending over three hours ago and still have a mountain of rappels left before we reach the relative safety of the glacier. We want nothing more than to continue down, but a granite flake 50 feet away has different plans; perhaps it needs companionship, or a trophy. I navigate across broken, slick terrain, to free the snagged cord. Foolishly I drop the end below me instead of carrying it back. As Nathan tells me that the cord is trapped again I realize how truly alone we are in this horridly inhospitable place. I am an alien. I traverse through tombstone-sized teetering blocks another time and pull with all my spite as Nathan yells for me to use my knife. It pops free before I can finish the math on how many raps we'd have with a single rope. When I down climb to the belay I ease onto it in relief.

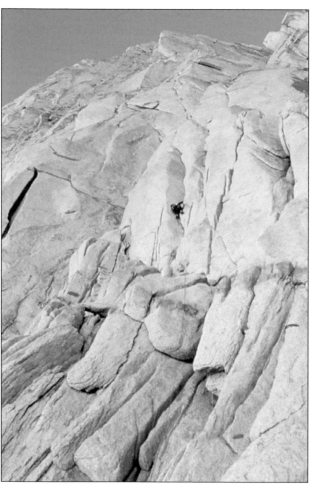

Tim O'Neill getting into Tonta Suerte's off width on the west face of Fitz Roy. *Nathan Martin*

Tim O'Neill approaching Cerro Fitz Roy via the Sitting Man Ridge on their second attempt. *Nathan Martin*

"The sky is starting to lighten in the east." I look out to the horizon to verify Nathan's report and we're reassured by the promise of a new day. It's amazing what confidence the light brings—it scares away the bogeymen, the monsters of the night. For hours we've been rappelling past the previous day's labors. I blankly recall the chimney that I ascended using an ice axe in one hand and chalk on the other, the hook move that broke apart as I grabbed onto the holds above. Oh yeah, there's where Nathan chopped the ice ledge we stopped on last night, no, that was two nights ago. As Nathan toils below me smacking pitons and stoppers into icy cracks I sway back and forth poised on a ledge. Fatigued beyond belief I clip myself into the belay; moments later I feel my legs buckle as I instantaneously fall asleep. How sweet is luck and for whom does the bell toll? Music from a phantom DJ plays in my head. I can swear that I hear the Beatles, I even ask Nathan, who's a rope length away if he hears the eerie melodies. He doesn't even hear my question; perhaps he hears Led Zeppelin. Spindrift avalanches roll down upon us incessantly and fill our hoods, sometimes even our mouths. I watch as the wind plays with them. The snow cascading off the enormous hanging serac mesmerizes me as it is blown back up and redeposited above in a perpetual, transitory dance. It is the frozen smoke rising from an eternal ice furnace. If there is a god this is it.

Back at Bridwell the celebration is unanimous. Almost everyone has summited, the Brazilians, Chileans, Brits, and a slew of Americans. Success also relates to a safe return to base camp; to see your friends' faces is victory. Nathan, spurned on by the absence of tobacco, arrived in camp several hours before me. He's already buzzing hard on a liter of "Gato Negro," but with-

The Torre Group from the Bridwell Base Camp. *Nathan Martin*

in minutes I am on his heels, due to an ultra susceptibility caused by super fatigue. Soon I am "stick in the eye" drunk. The happiness of being surrounded by close friends, sharing drink and food overwhelms me. I lie down on the ground and pass out.

⁂

The following day, descending to Chalten to rest and to escape from the proximity of the peaks, we run into Isaac who is gathering climbers to search for his overdue friend. The news that Frank Van Herreweghe is missing sobers us, makes us fearful. We stand in the pouring rain speechless and exhausted. I stare into blank tired faces then at the running muddy water at my feet. Two days ago Lorne Glick and Mark Davis last heard Frank while they were climbing the Super Couloir around 5:30 p.m. Frank was rope-soloing the California Route, which joins into the top of the Super Couloir at the Three Towers section, and asked them about their nearness to the summit. They never saw him. A severe storm, the same one we encountered while descending the Egger, enshrouded Fitz Roy the night Frank would have been descending, and the storm remained for two full days. Because it is impossible to scale the peak to search for him, many of us do what we can and circumnavigate it looking at the advanced base camps and scanning the approaches. The mood in Chalten is somber. The weather is indifferent; it continues its cycle of randomness.

⁂

After several days recuperating below at Camp Madsen we cannot ignore the continued opportunities of stable weather. It's time to attempt our next objective, a new route on the monstrous west face of Cerro Fitz Roy. Two years ago we watched from Noruegos as Kevin Thaw and Alan Mullin climbed the Czech Route on Fitz Roy's west face. I was intrigued then by a prominent series of dihedrals that shot straight up from the crest of a striking shield of gray from the Czech Route's sixth pitch. Kevin peered up into this system and provided us with key information regarding the improbable gaping off-widths that loomed above. His foray unlocked the secret to opening up this alpine passage: bring multiple pieces of wide gear—really wide gear.

Our first attempt, on January 31, ends atop Sitting Man Ridge, our ABC for the route, which lies 1,000 vertical feet above the Torre Glacier. After spending 17 hours trapped in the confines of our bivy sacks we ascend a few hundred feet up a severely broken rib on Fitz Roy's northwest flank before clouds, rain, and wind force us down. Back in Bridwell I feel lethargic, my mind and body crying out for rest. The good weather does not capitulate to my demands and forces us back up valley. The most direct line, our chosen approach, teems with an abundance of objective dangers. What is normally steep snow interspersed with shattered rock outcroppings has deteriorated under persistent sun into giant expanses of mixed terrain and falling rock. I grow to despise this section of the earth, likening it to an unrelenting root canal without anesthetic.

On our second attempt, on February 5, under building pressure and bluebird skies, we roll the dice at the base of Sitting Man Ridge. It's noon and what's left of the snow sticks to my dull crampons as we start up. An enormous rock scar in the middle of the approach intermittently releases worrisome slides of exfoliating debris. I hear the nauseating whirl of a dentist's

The west face of Fitz Roy, showing Tonta Suerte.
Nathan Martin

drill. Sculpted boulders surround our ABC and from the hollows that pit their tops we collect rainwater and brew Nescafe mochas. At 9 a.m. the next morning we depart from ABC equipped with bivy gear and a change in plans. We opt for a stay on Déjà Vu ledge at the base of the gray shield. After navigating hours of vertical talus and connecting sketchy unroped bouldery moves we arrive at the proper base of the wall. Two pitches later we reach the ledge and settle down for the night. In the morning we climb to the top of the gray shield and are afforded a quick preview of what lies ahead before rain soaks our hopes and us. Exasperated and feeling beaten down, we drop to Bridwell in a storm that saturates us to our cores. In Chalten we play soccer, eat meat, talk on the phone to our families, and try to act like normal people. It doesn't work. Unbelievably when the sky opens we once again race up to our gear stash on Sitting Man Ridge.

"I will never ascend to this ridge again," I silently vow. It is February 15 and as we deftly retrace familiar hazards a fundamental part of me is bewildered by our third attempt. An inner force drives me so strongly that I disregard an intensifying disgust of this warfare with the mountain. My front points slip off an edge. Regaining my focus, I leave fear and doubt below. At 1:30 a.m., after a one-hour respite, we shoulder our packs and silently stride off toward infinity. In total darkness we ascend to the wall. I hear my breathing, hear loose stones turning under Nathan's boots. As night becomes day we approach our high point, then stop on a rounded ledge to brew up and smoke. I take us up the first series of new pitches, thanking the fact that I ran back to Bridwell two days earlier to retrieve our forgotten three pieces of wide gear. We are going speed style, in blocks with the second jummaring with an unwieldy pack. I run it out, in love with the sunshine, feeling connected to the stone. Nathan takes over his second block of leads and I begin to pencil a topo. "There's three to choose from," Nathan cries out, describing the cracks that await him in the section we thought may be welded shut, not a weakness to prey on. With dusk descending we pull over the west face ridge onto a 60-meter long rolling ledge. We fix a rope length above and decide to wait for light. By 3 a.m. I swallow a gulp of water melted from dirty ice then pass out and wake up, pass out and wake up. In the morning we stir out of the cold night, swollen and sore. By the time we reach the summit at 5:30 p.m. we are incredulous that our luck has held out. A storm's been threatening all day in the west, hovering above the icecap, and doesn't spoil our summit dream.

The legendary Torre Group: Cerro Torre, 3127m; Torre Egger, 2899m, showing the Martin-O'Neill ascent route; and Cerro Stanhardt, 2799m. *Nathan Martin*

The time we spend on top is filled with gratitude, awe, and Tomo-sized smiles. The unity of these experiences transcends friendship, goes beyond the tangible, the known. Through them we view the alternatives to the status quo, perhaps even perceive true value and vitality. Our descent of the Super Couloir from Fitz Roy's summit will be the most horrific experience either of us has ever had to endure. Encountering Frank's body 15 rappels below in the dead of night, grinding through carabiners and belay plates with grit embedded, sodden ropes while praying that the falling rock isn't stamped with our number. We then mistakenly walk out for 12 hours down the Polone Valley, having missed Paso Cuadrado, over unstable, treacherous glacier and talus. Eventually night descends and we collapse into it far away from our ethereal summit, far away from even ourselves.

There is a duality that exists in all forms of life, an unlikely synthesis of opposites. In mine it has never been more distinct than when I am climbing in places such as Patagonia, where beauty and danger combine.

SUMMARY OF STATISTICS:

AREA: Argentine Patagonia

ASCENTS: Titanic variation (1200m, VI 5.10 A2 WI6) on Torre Egger's Italian-Austrian route. Nathan Martin and Tim O'Neill.

Tonta Suerte (1800m, VI 5.10 A1 WI3) new route on Cerro Fitz Roy, February 17. Nathan Martin and Tim O'Neill.

BARBAROSSA

When getting up is not nearly enough:
the first ascent of Yamandaka, in the Indian Karakoram.

MARK RICHEY

The north face of Yamandaka, Peak 6218m. Barbarossa ascends the prominent central buttress. *Mark Richey*

Braced precariously at the edge of the waterfall, Mark Wilford hesitated for a terrifying moment to assess the situation. He fought to maintain his footing on the slick, algae-coated rock, while glacial-fed water blasted over him, stretching his rappel line bowstring tight. His next actions would be critical. Fifty feet below, the waterfall plunged into a deep, ominous pool, how deep he didn't know. "I'm cutting my pack loose," he yelled up in a desperate voice. Fearing he might drown in the churning Maytag below, he wanted every opportunity of escape. Then he unlocked the screw on his rappel device and disappeared over the edge. A day before we had been the first to stand atop a magnificent mountain in the Indian Karakoram—and now we were caught in a nightmarish descent of a water-filled canyon. How the hell have we ended up here, I thought. With more than 50 years combined experience in the mountains, we surely could have avoided such a predicament.

Our international expedition of eight had arrived at base camp some three weeks prior at the head of the Phunangma Glacier, a remote and unexplored region of northern Ladakh, in India. Our leaders were the legendary climber-explorer Sir Christian Bonington and his good friend and companion of several Himalayan adventures, Harish Kapadia of India. It was Harish's connections and intimate knowledge of the big Indian ranges that opened the doors for our unique opportunity. Other than the highest peak in the valley, which we named Argan Kangri (6789m), the plan was simply to climb whatever looked best.

Having no photographs of the region, our expedition was truly exploratory, which meant we could easily have found ourselves surrounded by unappealing mountains of crumbling rock or impossible icefalls. Fortunately that was not the case, and we were delighted to find dramatic-looking peaks with knife-edge ridgelines and steep granite walls. It was like being in the Alps for the first time—only all the routes were unclimbed and none of the mountains had names.

Our group included Jim Lowther, also from the U.K.; Divyesh Muni, Cyrus Shroff, and Satyabrata Dam from India; and my partner Mark Wilford and myself from the U.S. Captain Vrijendra Lingwal of the Ladakh Scouts would serve as expedition Liaison Officer. Two friends of Harish's, Dr. Burjor Banaji and Suman Dubey, would accompany us as far as base camp. The expedition was organized to allow maximum flexibility of the various teams to explore and climb as much as possible. Wilford and I were immediately drawn to the north face of Peak 6,281 and its striking central pillar, and we at once made it our primary objective. Although the weather was warm and stable when we arrived, it soon began to show signs of deterioration and colder temperatures. A race was on between our time to acclimatize and the encroaching winter conditions.

On September 8, after a few days acclimatization at 17,000 feet at our communal advanced base camp, Mark and I traversed to the base of Peak 6281 with heavy packs. We carried five days of food, fuel to melt water for seven, two ropes, and a light technical rack, including ten pitons, three ice screws, and some wired nuts and cams. We carried no étriers or hauling devices. We also took a tiny tent in hopes of finding ledges large enough to erect it. As we reached the base of the face it began to snow, so we made camp beneath a huge boulder.

The morning of the 9th dawned partially clear; yet despite a fresh plastering of snow we started up the initial ice slopes leading to the prominent central rock buttress. After six long pitches of low-angle ice, with some easy rock, we reached a large notch in the ridge that we called First Tower. Unable to find an adequate bivy, we rappelled one ropelength to a small rock ledge. Inside our tiny tent with the stove brewing, we felt almost removed from the towering ridge above us. Fickle weather kept us in the tent till noon the next day, but at the first

Glacier Camp on the Phunangama Glacier. *Mark Richey*

signs of clearing we hurriedly packed our gear and started up. No sooner had I begun the first pitch than full blizzard conditions ensued.

Moderate mixed climbing, interspersed with sections of scary, loose blocks, typified the initial terrain. We managed just three pitches in full winter conditions before an unlikely bivy spot atop a precarious ice mushroom appeared beneath an overhanging wall. We hacked and flattened the mushroom until it was large enough for our perch. With part of the tent hanging over the void, it was not hard to imagine the horrifying scenario should the ice mushroom collapse during the night, sending us instantly to the end of our tethers, trapped in our sleeping bags in a tent filled with all manner of paraphernalia. We tied our boots securely to the belay and fortunately the night passed uneventfully.

We awoke early to cloudless blue skies, and with great optimism I set off on the lead. Two technical rock pitches followed, involving tension traverses and a short section of aid. A third, easy pitch led to the prominent snow ridge marking the top of the second tower and the beginning of the final pillar, the obvious crux of the climb. It was about 1 p.m. and the afternoon sun was just upon us. The pillar was compact granite without a clean crack system. I started up a thin seam that led up the left side of the pillar, first free climbing, then aiding, digging ice from cracks to find placements for knifeblades and small wired nuts. Suddenly, a television-sized block dislodged from my hand pressure, sending Mark scurrying to the far side of the belay ledge as we both watched the spectacular missile explode 3,000 feet down the face. To my horror, I saw that the block had nearly severed the rope, just ten feet from my end. After re-tying and chopping off the end of the rope, I continued up the seam to where a shallow ramp broke across a blank wall. A pendulum off a knifeblade led to a small stance, then a delicate traverse, with my crampons scraping on small edges, took me to a final overhang and a hanging stance. I had one remaining carabiner!

Mark lowered out the haulsack with what little rope remained, and we watched it swing into space, arcing across the smooth wall. Following the traversing pitch on jumars with a heavy sack was awkward, hard work and meant leaving several of our precious pitons. Another pitch of similar climbing followed and it seemed to deliver us through the steepest part of the pillar. Mark took over the lead, working his way up mixed ground to a steep slab and a bit more aid. As the sun dipped behind neighboring peaks and the cold began to creep through my clothing, I prayed for a good bivy ledge. Arriving by headlamp, I found Mark busily chopping away at a 50-degree ice slope. After two hours we produced a pair of narrow ledges, two feet wide, that we could barely lie down on. Too tired to cook or eat, we melted a liter of water and settled into our sleeping bags on the tiny perches. During the night, wind-blown spindrift avalanches began to pour down the face with regularity, building up and forcing us off the slippery ledges. To make matters worse, I began to have severe coughing fits. I assured Mark it was not altitude related, just a cough aggravated by the dry, cold air and my heavy breathing. Secretly I worried that it might be the onset of pulmonary edema.

We had both managed a bit of sleep when morning dawned gray with menacing black clouds on the horizon and a stiff cold wind out of the west. My coughing seemed to have subsided for the moment but I was tired from the hacking. We could retreat and it would likely take all day—or we could go for the top. It appeared we might summit that day, hopefully before the storm hit. It seemed a pity to retreat, being so close, and, with the season well advanced, we both knew we would not be back. The decision to continue seemed easy, but it was imperative we make the summit that day as we couldn't bear the thought of another open bivouac. Wilford, in the lead now, started off on a scary, tenuous pitch, hooking axes on a film of ice and deftly mantling onto a snow-covered slab.

Above, a long series of snow-covered ramps led left to a steep corner and finally the summit icefields. I

Mark Wilford follows on the third day of the ascent. *Mark Richey* jumared up to Mark as he announced excitedly that the summit was in sight. And then he was off in full ice-climbing mode, armed with two axes and three screws for a 200-foot pitch of bullet-hard water ice. We had been certain in base camp that it would be névé. Mark climbed smoothly, and at the top of the pitch he belayed at a small rock outcropping. On the next pitch he had to run out several hundred feet of sixty-degree ice, placing just one screw, saving the other two for the belay. By now the cold, lack of rest, and altitude were starting to take their toll as swirling clouds and blowing snow enveloped us. The storm had arrived.

As we sorted the mess of frozen ropes and gear at the belay, we wondered if our companions far below could see us nearing the summit. A final hundred feet of ice led to the summit cornice, where Mark traversed left and glimpsed our anticipated descent down the northeast face. He hollered down a frightening description of unstable cornices above death-trap gullies. After traversing back right under the cornice to its narrowest point, he managed to

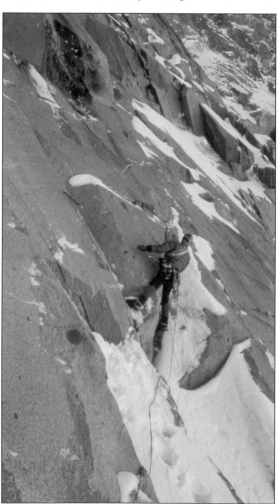

Mark Richey leading across compact granite on day three.
Mark Wilford

chop a body-size notch, plant his axes in the soft snow, and bellyflop onto the summit snowslope, just 40 feet below the true summit. By the time I reached Mark the storm had achieved blizzard status, and after scraping out a tent site we collapsed inside, exhausted. It snowed all night and into the morning, dumping over a foot of snow as my coughing fits intensified, keeping me and Mark from any sleep.

By noon the next day the skies showed signs of clearing, so rope-less we climbed to the true summit, shook hands, snapped some pictures, and marveled at the awesome view. All around were range upon range of unclimbed mountains and unexplored valleys. And far below were our companions, waiting, wondering what we were up to.

After a lengthy discussion we decided our original plan of descent down the northeast ridge to the Phunangma Glacier was too risky given the amount of fresh snow and avalanche danger. We opted instead to go down the gentler south face to a smooth, disarming glacier we could see below, hoping that the glacier descended into a valley that eventually would lead us back to Arganglas and our base camp. We lacked a map, however, so in reality we could only guess how the glaciers and valleys connected.

Three rappels got us to easy down-climbing and the long glacier. By mid-afternoon we reached the snout, and our valley appeared to curve toward Arganglas, just as we had hoped. With a little luck, a leisurely walk would see us back in base camp by the next afternoon in time for beer and celebrations.

We couldn't have been more wrong. Snow-covered talus and towering boulderfields blocked our way and slowed progress to a crawl. By nightfall we found ourselves only a few miles below the glacier, exhausted but at least safely camped in a serene meadow. We ate our last bits of food and in the morning were awakened by a curious, marten-like creature that seemed fascinated with his strange visitors. In the cool dawn, tired but happy and completely unaware of what lay in store for us, we headed down the picturesque valley. Although seemingly out of danger, we both suffered from that uneasy feeling one gets when you sus-

The second bivouac. *Mark Richey*

pect something very wrong is in the making. We both questioned why such alpine meadows were completely devoid of livestock or herders.

By mid-morning we had our answer. Our gentle valley funneled into a deep, narrow gorge, plunging down and out of sight. "We're fucked with a capital F," Mark declared. There was no way we were going back up and over, and it was now day seven on five days of food. We had to commit to the canyon and hope it would lead us down.

At first the descent went well, as we hopped from one side of the glacial stream to the other and scrambled down short cliffs. It was really quite beautiful, with the sheer, red-colored canyon walls above us covered with magnificent rhododendrons. Brightly colored birds darted about.

But soon the canyon walls began to close in and the stream rushed stronger. "Ever done any canyoneering?" I asked.

"Not till now," Mark said as we rigged a rappel down the first of many waterfalls. The anchors were the tricky part, as we had to search, sometimes in vain, for cracks in the compact, polished rock. Once, at the lip of a 70-foot fall, we piled the largest boulders we could move,

Mark Wilford descending into the unknown. *Mark Richey*

slinging the base of the stack, and lowered over the edge. Then things got worse. The canyon became a water-filled channel with no place to stand. We were forced to our knees to prevent flipping over on the greasy surface, as we lowered down in the turbulent water, hoping we'd find a stance for the next rappel. It was like being flushed down a giant toilet. That's when we came to the waterfall with the deep pool.

It seemed an eternity as I waited for Mark to appear on the other side of the canyon, and I recall thinking to myself: What if he doesn't make it? Do I try the same thing? Then I saw him on the other side of the pool, giving me the big thumbs up. Moments later I found myself in the cascade, repeating the same crazy antics. After I joined Mark, we spread our gear out on the rocks to dry—and rest and assess the damages. Mark's camera was destroyed but fortunately all our film was dry. We continued, making more rappels, with more wading through deep pools and channels. Exhausted, we began falling ass over teakettle on the greasy rocks.

About then we came to the end of the line. We stood together on a boulder at the lip of a huge waterfall as mist from the crashing water filled the air. Beyond, the sheer canyon walls twisted steeply down and out of sight. We gauged the falls to be about 200 feet high, the length of our remaining rope. Peering over the edge, Mark said slowly, "We could be trapped down there and no one would ever find us; we'd just slowly starve to death if we couldn't get out."

There was no way to break the overhanging waterfall into two rappels—and coming back up the rope was out of the question should the canyon below prove impassable. It seemed we were trapped. It was now late in the day and getting cold, and it looked as if it might rain. Anxiously, we searched the canyon walls for a weakness. One side of the canyon overhung radically and was smooth, with few cracks. On the opposite side a steep slab led up to a vertical wall where a series of giant blocks, precariously cemented in place with mud, formed a slight weakness. We had five carabiners, half a dozen nuts and pitons, and no slings. We stripped the leashes and straps from our crampons and ice axes to make crude runners, ditched unnecessary gear, and prepared for the final roll of the dice. In mountain boots and soaking wet underwear, Wilford started up the first terrifying-looking pitch. A hundred feet up he squeezed into a chimney, placed some marginal gear, hung his pack, and started up over the blocks. The first one was about the size of a grand piano, and the only way up was right over it. I held my breath; it held. Next was a short roof followed by 15 feet of dead-vertical climbing on loose, sandy flakes. After a brief pause the familiar "I'm goin' for it" floated down, so I moved as far left as possible and braced myself. With the gun to the head, there are few climbers smoother than Wilford, and he pulled through the steep wall flawlessly. Shortly, I joined him at the belay; amazingly all the blocks had held. "That was the scariest pitch I've ever led," he said. And this coming from a climber who had made a career of bold solos and first ascents.

Two more steep pitches led to third-class terrain just as it got dark. Following faint ibex trails, we skirted the shoulder of the canyon rim until finally emerging on the mountain slope. Beneath us were cliffbands and stacks of house-sized boulders. We didn't dare risk negotiating the loose terrain at night and so settled into another bivy on the hill with just a liter of water and no food. Our concern now turned to our comrades on the other side of the range. Surely they must be worried, and we feared they would soon alert the military base to dispatch a helicopter—and that was the last thing we wanted. At least we knew that Chris was not one to panic, having been in similar situations many times before.

At first light we descended the final slopes with care and at last arrived in the Nubra Valley. Several times we heard the chop-chop of helicopters and feared they were searching for us. From

The scene of the epic during Richey and Wilford's descent. *Mark Richey*

the valley floor we got a good look at our descent canyon; we had been within 600 feet of easy ground but had made the right decision: the final section was a continuous waterfall.

A few hours walk saw us to the first bridge over the Nubra River, where a military sentry was posted. We were met with warm smiles, congratulatory handshakes, and a welcome platter of fried bread and hot tea. We inquired if anyone spoke English. "Yes, English, yes," responded the senior-looking soldier, and we launched into our story in an effort to impress upon our host the importance of contacting the army base in Diskit. We had met with the friendly and accommodating General Ashok Dugal at the beginning of the expedition and were anxious not to inconvenience him or his men in any way. After about five minutes of one-way conversation it became apparent that our host didn't understand a word of what we were saying, and so we gave up and enjoyed the bread and tea. Soon a porter we recognized from base camp showed up; he didn't speak English either but was obviously relieved and happy to see us. Finally, after flagging down a Jeep with an interpreter, we learned that Harish and Chris had sent him down from base camp to look for us. If there was no sign they were to launch a search on the next day! Relieved, we sent the porter back to base with a note that we were safe and would take a few days rest in the Yarab Tso Inn.

Hitching a ride up the valley, we were picked up by an American tourist en route to Srinagar. She was quite excited to hear of our adventure until all of a sudden her face dropped and she said, "You have no idea of what's happened, do you?" The date was September 15. To our disbelief she vaguely described the shocking terrorist attacks of September 11. Without phone, TV, or newspaper, it took several days, listening to crackly broadcasts of Voice of America, before we could piece together the horrific details.

Back in base camp we found Chris, Jim, and the rest of the team fighting deep snow and

Ladakh monastery. *Mark Richey*

avalanche conditions on Argan Kangri. At last altogether in base camp, we enjoyed a hearty reunion. Mark and I were quite moved to learn that on the seventh day of our ordeal they had built a stone altar and prayed for our safety; I suspect those prayers helped see us through. Our Indian friends had made first ascents of two other lovely mountains, Abale Peak (6360m) and Amale Peak (6312m) while Harish was busy exploring some high passes and valleys to the west. There were still plenty of interesting, objectives, but in light of the volatile international situation we decided to cut the expedition short. Besides, winter seemed to be coming early to the Karakoram—and we'd had enough.

In keeping with local tradition, and with Harish's help, we named the mountain Yamandaka after a fierce yet benevolent Buddhist deity. Our route was named Barbarossa after the book we'd been reading. Barbarossa was the German code name for the invasion of Russia during World War II, undoubtedly one of the most brutal campaigns in the history of warfare.

SUMMARY OF STATISTICS:

AREA: Arganglas Group, East Karakoram, India

FIRST ASCENT: Barbarossa (1200 meters, VI 5.9 A2) on the north face of Yamandaka, Peak 6218m, near the Phunangama Glacier, from September 9-13. Descent of the south face to the Shingskam Topko Valley, September 13-15. Mark Richey and Mark Wilford.

Unraveling the Mystery of Lhotse Middle

Think all the 8000-meter summits have been climbed?
Then you need the vision to see a peak like Lhotse's middle summit, Nepal.

Yuri Koshelenko

The previously unclimbed 8414m summit of Lhotse Middle from the point of reaching the ridge. *Yuri Koshelenko*

The history of the Himalaya and Karakoram says that there are only 14 summits with altitudes higher than 8000 meters. But massifs are not Egyptian pyramids, and a mountain is often crowned by several summits. Kangchenjunga has the most of all: five peaks. Each of its summits was climbed separately. According to a list compiled by Reinhold Messner, the Lhotse massif has three obvious summits: Main (8501m), East (8414m), and Lhotse Shar (8386m). Lhotse East has another name: Lhotse Middle, the 26th summit on the Messner list.

My impressions of Lhotse were shaped mainly by my friend and coach Alexander Pogorelov. He took part in the first south wall direttissima on Lhotse, in 1990. Alexander didn't reach the summit as did Karataev and Bershov, but his group came very close to success. Pogorelov, Turkevich, Kopeyko, and Hitrikov were the first to reach the 8350m point. They fixed ropes on the most difficult part of the route, from 7600m to 8100m during four days, and then moved in alpine style, practically without food and bivouac gear, having only two ropes and a short ice-axe. Pogorelov and his friends spent three nights at an altitude higher than 8000 meters. Carving their way up the snow ridge, they rushed to the summit with all their strength. Lhotse's knife-sharp ridges above 8000 meters were dangerous and exhausting work in a snow trench. The climbers performed huge efforts that were technically difficult, then they descended by a miracle after 10 days on the wall.

As always, there are inspiring people in climbing, mountaineers who generate ideas and are able to light others by their fire. People gather in their magnetic field to accomplish the hard work. The idea of climbing Lhotse Middle belonged to Vladimir Bashkirov. The way to Lhotse Middle was not easy, although Bashkirov's first suggestion about the route contained inside itself today's success. Nevertheless it took several expeditions for climbers to understand the beauty and clarity of the new line. This was not a standard solution of the Lhotse Middle problem, but on closer examination it turned out that it was the only answer.

First to make the attempt was the 1997 Russian Lhotse Middle Expedition. Unfortunately, it finished tragically for Bashkirov. Shortly before the Lhotse expedition Vladimir Bashkirov had been working as a guide on an Indonesian expedition. Vladimir died, probably due to coronary deficiency, during the descent from the Main Lhotse summit. That year climbers only glanced at the ridge that leads to the east, to the uncertainty.

In 1998 Bashkirov's friends organized an expedition to reach Lhotse Middle via Lhotse Shar. The expedition partially succeeded: Sokolov, Timofeev, Foigt, and Vinogradski only reached Lhotse Shar's summit, but it was a success in itself.

In 2000 two expeditions intended to ascend Lhotse Middle. In the spring it was the Georgian-Russian attempt, again via the Main summit. Then, in the autumn, the expedition of Russian Ministry of Emergencies planned a dizzying route on the south wall of the Lhotse massif. This expedition ended tragically, too: Vladimir Bondarev died in an avalanche.

These attempts caused some resonance around the world, and in 2001 three expeditions intended to reach Lhotse Middle. Korean and Spanish teams planned the traditional traverse. The Korean climbers set their base camp under Lhotse Shar, but after they had examined the situation, they moved their BC to the Khumbu Glacier. A Spanish pair of climbers planned to set their Camp 5 behind the Lhotse Main summit and conquer Lhotse Middle from there. It's not a secret that climbing the ridge full of roofs and cols at an altitude of 8400-8500 meters is very difficult technically and, above all, is a psychological problem.

The Russian team had experience from the previous year and perspective on the route to the Middle summit via the Kanchung (northeast) wall. This was the route originally proposed

Traversing the Kanshung slopes of the Lhotse massif on May 24, 2001. *Gleb Sokolov*

by Vladimir Bashkirov, but many climbers thought it was too ambitious because of the high risk of avalanches on the northeast and north slopes of Lhotse massif. Nobody knew where the gate was to the Kanchung wall: via the South Col or via the north ridge of Lhotse Main. The important traits of the northeast wall route are its logical line that leads directly to the Middle summit without any intermediate points, and its protection from the Nepal-side winds that are prevalent here. During a traverse, it's psychologically easy to turn back after an intermediate summit is reached, such as Lhotse Main or Shar. But on the northeast wall there is only one target—if we turn back, then we lose the summit. It is useful sometimes to drive oneself into a corner where the only exit is to climb.

⁂

When planning a great achievement we have to understand what is the main objective. Any additional goals always decrease the probability of victory. One characteristic of our expedition was that we refused any extra objectives. There would be no traversing or climbing of vertical walls. We used extra oxygen, and Himalayan, not Alpine, tactics. The previous expeditions' experience persuaded us on this strategy. Looking at our photos, we understood that reaching Lhotse Middle is a very difficult problem. The Kanchung wall looks harsh, and the most difficult climbing waited for us near the summit. Later, when we looked at the summit from the east side of the South Col, our impression about the difficulty of the route became even stronger.

Our expedition reached a base camp on the Khumbu Glacier on April 1 before ropes had been fixed. Other expeditions didn't hurry to start their ascents. Our group together with Simone Moro and Denis Urubko fixed ropes to Camp 3. The west slopes of Lhotse shined in a black reflection without snow. By the end of April the route to the South Col was done and our group (Gilin, Ermachek, Sokolov, myself) had ascended to set up Camp 4. Meanwhile two other groups (Timofeev-Vinogradsky-Bolotov-Kuznetsov and Cherny-Elagin-Yanochkin-Volodin) descended to Deboche for a rest. (Editor's note: the team members are briefly profiled at the end of this article.) In spite of Sherpa help we had to carry loads of up to 17 kg. It felt heavy for a first ascent above 8000 meters. When I'd reached the South Col, our tent was already installed; Gleb Sokolov and Denis with Simone had set up the camp. There was not much snow; it seemed like we were on the debris of a shipwreck due to previous years' accumulation of expedition garbage.

The main task of the advance group was to find a gate to the Kanchung wall of the Lhotse massif. We did this task not so well, partially due to the bad weather, partially due to insufficient acclimatization (we hadn't used extra oxygen yet). On May 1 Sokolov, Gilin, and Ermachek carried some loads to the east side of the South Col and descended. I waited for Timofeev's group to help them. Next day we five together had reached our loads and atmospheric conditions allowed us to have a good look at the rock walls of the Middle summit. This view didn't give us any optimism. There was no way that was pleasing to us because the slopes were too steep and they were dangerous due to avalanches. Sergey Timofeev decided to seek a way via the north ridge of Lhotse Main. I was advised to descend, and my friends put on oxygen masks and went up along the Geneva Ridge. May 2 and 3 they carried gear and ropes to about 8100m.

In the next days the weather grew worse and Cherny's group couldn't ascend above 7300m (Camp 3). The three of this group descended to the BC while Vladimir Yanochkin remained in the Camp 3 intending to move at his own risk. He didn't have a radio and we could only get information about him from other expeditions. Yanochkin only reached our ropes at 8100m and his words about the closeness of the Middle summit were taken by a majority of our climbers with some amount of distrust.

On May 10, after a rest in Deboche, our group began ascending again. We had to find a way from the north ridge to the inside corner that lead to a drop in the ridge between the Main and Middle summits. After the bad weather all the upper camps were covered deeply with snow, and we as the leaders had to work with a spade. The biggest surprise waited for us at the South Col. Yanochkin didn't tie the door to our tent as required (he said he wanted to help us get in the tent) and wind and snow had made use of it before us. When I looked inside, I saw some emotions on Gleb Sokolov's face as he tore ice from our sleeping bags. This was a depressing picture: a snowdrift inside the tent had melted a little and our warm clothes and sleeping bags had permafrost and a moist freshness.

Nikolay Gilin (left) and Yuri Koshelenko on the highest point of Lhotse Middle–the big firn roof, on May 24. The ridge leads to Lhotse Shar. *Gleb Sokolov*

We spent a night and in the morning reached 8100m. The weather was not so bad; the wall of Middle summit was sometimes visible. East and northeast slopes were overlain with fresh, free-flowing snow. Moving toward the Kanchung wall was like suicide. Gleb Sokolov ascended along the ridge for reconnaissance; Gilin and I took photos and movies; Ermachek was next to us. Then Gleb called down. There was a gendarme in the ridge like a column. I attached myself to the rope and ascended into the cloud. To the right overhung a huge ice serac, downward a steep ice slope. It was impossible to know distances inside the strong fog that blends with the white slopes. We talked with Gleb and decided to go farther. But above the gendarme the slope became steeper and more difficult. I returned into the cloud. It was an incredible feeling: the crisp slope, a serac whose wall led into infinity, and us—two living points on the huge unconscious area of this mountain.

Moving by touch under the overhangs of fragile blue ice along the narrow strip of loose snow, I compared my steps with the inside voice of my heart. The oxygen mask disturbed me and made technical actions difficult; I removed it often. Snow was sometimes so loose that together we began to slip to the edge of the ice slope. I touched the snow with my hands and asked it not to fall into an avalanche. The most dangerous place was where the ice serac ended. The ice wall lost its steepness there, turning into the slope. At some moments I felt I would lose my balance, but it ended well. Our rope stopped five meters from the firn. Gleb fixed the rope using a pair of firn anchors and we had a chance to catch our breath. Thirty to 40 meters above us hard firn turned to a downy snow slope. We stayed. This seemed like the natural break line of possible avalanches. We looked to the east and saw between clouds our future route and Lhotse Middle's summit. We realized clearly that the route was real and the summit could be reached. We returned to the South Col. During the night the weather turned into a storm; it seemed like the Earth began to rotate faster. But yesterday we had met the summit face to face and it did not seem so bad. We needed two to three days of good weather above 8000 meters and we'd reach it.

In the camp at 6400m we met Timofeev's group. Our words about the situation had a double effect. I can't say that their reaction was joyful—we didn't reach the inside corner, didn't perform our task. But we had found new facts about the route, and they gave us hope for reaching the summit.

Victor Kozlov told us by radio that the weather over the next few days would be bad and Timofeev and his group should descend to BC with us. But other news was good, because on May 16 we got the permit for Lhotse Middle in a ceremonial atmosphere. Victor Kozlov's joy was the greatest. He had been pressing for this permit for several years.

Our schedule was corrected due to new circumstances. Though our tactics were slightly changed, our strategy remained invariable. On May 17 Yanochkin and Volodin carried loads to the beginning of the ropes we had fixed; on the18th Bolotov and Kuznetsov ascended further, as did Timofeev and Vinogradsky on the 19th; Sokolov and Koshelenko had to start their ascent on the 20th, but at the insistance of Nikolay Gilin we started a day later. Ermachek descended to receive medical treatment. Vasily Elagin was now in our group, but ascended only to 7000m; he refused his attempt because he had caught a chill and didn't want to slow anyone on their way to the summit.

In the meantime our success was increasing. Yanochkin and Volodin had made two cargo ascents to the gendarme and descended. Bolotov and Kuznetsov passed 300 meters of the slope; next day Timofeev and Vinogradsky helped them. Their group had reached the inside corner and set Camp 5 at the beginning of the traverse of the Kanchung wall (8120m).

The leading group now had a chance to reach the summit, but the most difficult part of the route was still ahead of them. On May 23 our three reached the South Col. There it was slightly windy, but not bad weather for 8000 meters of altitude. We hadn't any radio contact with Timofeev's group. The base camp couldn't contact them, either, but we explained this by an influence of the north ridge between us. The common excitement grew. This feeling was like a rush to be in that day with our friends, our hopes of their success, our concerns about their fortune, and our sense of nearing the final outcome. Clouds covered the valley below 6000 meters, and Gleb started another discussion about the character of the monsoon.

At 17:00 we heard at last from our leading group. Audibility was very bad, but we made out an occasional word. We in our tent and the people in the base camp wondered out loud what they could be saying. At 18:00 Timofeev confirmed than a group was descending from Lhotse Middle's summit. After accepting our congratulations, he answered our questions about the route condition and fixed ropes; he also told us to bring two more ropes.

At 5 a.m. our three left Camp 4 on the South Col and ascended the Geneva Ridge to the north ridge, reaching Camp 5 at 7 a.m. The sun was already high, but clouds covered the valleys. Our way shone in the sunrays. It was warm and calm. We congratulated our friends again on their ascent, and learned that they hadn't climbed the big firn roof on the summit, being afraid of it falling. They advised us to avoid it as well. Evgeny Vinogradsky and Peter Kuznetsov told us that two ropes would be enough and we could pick up the ones they had dropped by the wayside.

We descended along a serac. The snow conditions were excellent in comparison with my previous experience. During a week of a good weather the snow had consolidated. Avalanche danger remained, but didn't appear as fatal. We passed the snow slope quickly and started ascending along rock ledges covered with snow to the center of the inside corner. Our leading group gave us good tracks, but we still needed to move carefully. There was very difficult climbing, especially in the beginning of the inside corner. I found the rope that was promised and cut about 70 meters off of it. Gleb carried the next rope. Nikolay Gilin shot video. We had passed by the snowed rocks and reached the ridge. The beautiful tower of Lhotse Middle was now in front of us. Its shape was like tongues of flame with the scroll of the summit roof. To the right and below, touching slightly the line of clouds, was the pyramid of Lhotse Shar. The rope led us to the base of the tower. Our friends' tracks meandered fluently on the snow ridges, disappearing on the rocks and showing up again. This pointed spire was definitely the key to the route. Later we were told that Alexey Bolotov, who lead the difficult sections, climbed 12 to 15 meters of vertical rock wall after two unsuccessful attempts. This was the most serious obstacle on the way to the summit. Alexey did it by free climbing without any protection. He had lead out all the rope and then fixed it by a firn anchor in the horizontal firn that turned to the scroll of the summit roof. This was the point where the fixed ropes ended.

Our group decided to improve the result and to risk reaching the summit roof. I dropped my oxygen cylinder, took Gleb's ice axe as a second and five firn anchors, and started to traverse the snow ridge's wall. All the time I expected to find loose snow but found strong firn instead. I lead the rope to its end, and Nikolay Gilin brought me the next rope. The roof's 80-degree wall was seven body lengths high. The roof looked like half of a funnel. Thin fragile edges curved to the north. Some deep breaths for sure, then some light steps to the center of the roof. I fixed the rope by a firn anchor, but there was no assurance that this snow cap wouldn't fall down with a hiss. Some moments later I found that the world didn't turn over. Gilin and Sokolow were near me. Gleb was sitting like a cowboy on the ridge when snow begun sliding down from under his boots, but he caught his balance. We had been taking photos but every moment felt like we were on a sinking ship.

We returned from the Lhotse Middle summit, and I enjoyed the beautiful moments of having reached my destination. We took pictures of the summit with our tracks leading to it, and felt the magical clarity, the sunlight, and the intense feeling of gratitude to Him, the Creator of all that is good. It was absolutely clear from here that the world is round.

Returning from the summit, with the big firn roof marking the summit visible in the background. *Gleb Sokolov*

A telephoto view of Lhotse Middle from the north ridge of Lhotse Main. *Yuri Koshelenko*

On May 27 at 11:00 Yanochkin and Volodin, moving along fixed ropes, reached the summit. The weather was already unstable and they had to carve their way anew in many places. The five-year history of attempts on Lhotse Middle had ended. A number of favorable conditions had come together to help us: the right choice of route, a good team from many Russian regions, good financing by Russian businessman Pavel Kadushin, and good circumstances.

Our manager Victor Kozlov headed our expedition and film crew. Due to his efforts we got the permit for Lhotse Middle from the Nepal Ministry of Tourism.

Nikolay Cherny was the most experienced climber among us. He had taken part in the first Soviet Everest expedition, in 1983. He was our sport leader and permit leader on Lhotse Main (the Nepal Ministry of Tourism didn't give at first the permit for the Middle summit, so we had to buy a permit for the Main Lhotse to get a chance to start climbing). Nikolay endured all the difficult, barely noticeable job of ruling the porters, Sherpas, kitchen workers, and other problems with base camp and expedition loads. A very wise man.

Sergey Timofeev combined the jobs of leader of his group and captain of our team. On May 16 he became the leader of the route on Lhotse Middle. We got the permit directly in our base camp on Khumbu glacier from the deputy Minister of Tourism.

Evgeny Vinogradsky, Alexey Bolotov, Nikolay Gilin, Jury Yermachek, and Sergey Timofeev are climbers from Ekaterinburg. They are skilled high-altitude climbers and have a rich Himalayan history. Their most significant climb was the first ascent of the west wall of Makalu. Vinogradsky has climbed Everest four times.

Vasily Elagin, Vladimir Yanochkin, Victor Volodin, and Nikolay Cherny are from Moscow. Their high-altitude experience commands respect, especially Cherny's and Elagin's ascents.

Gleb Sokolov on the summit in an uncomfortable position on the edge of the big firn roof.   *Yuri Koshelenko*

Peter Kuznetsov from Krasnoyarsk had a first ascent on north wall of Everest.

Gleb Sokolov first started high-altitude trophies on Khan-Tengry and Pobeda peaks on Tian-Shan. From 1996 he took part permanently in Himalayan expeditions.

Many of these climbers had taken part in attempts on Lhotse Middle. Sergey Timofeev together with Bogomolov and Babanov lowered down from Lhotse Main the dying Bashkirov.

Igor Borisenko from Moscow and Sergey Shakuro from Novokuznetsk together with producer and author Victor Kozlov made a film.

I didn't have any previous ascents above 8000 meters and was considered by the experienced high-altitude climbers as a debutante dark horse, whose incompetence could be dangerous.

SUMMARY OF STATISTICS:

AREA: Nepal Himalaya

FIRST ASCENT: Lhotse Middle, 8414m. The route is about 3,000 meters. Everyone used extra oxygen above 8000 meters. Nine climbers reached the summit between May 23 and May 27: Alexey Bolotov, Petr Kuznetsov, Evgeny Vinogradsky, Sergei Timofeev, Yuri Koshelenko, Nikolay Gilin, Gleb Sokolov, Vladimir Yanochkin, and Victor Volodin.

THE SHARK'S FIN

After beating back dozens of the world's best climbers, Meru's central peak finally succumbed to an unrelenting soloist. Indian Garhwal.

VALERI BABANOV

As far as I knew there had been about 15 attempts on India's Meru Central, otherwise known as the Shark's Fin. This was my second. The first had been in the spring, when there was much snow on the wall. Now, at the end of August, it was greatly changed. The snow on the glacier had thawed and the lower part of the wall was nothing but black rocks. It was obvious that the first 300 to 400 meters would be especially dangerous. Stones fell constantly from the wall.

In contrast to the spring attempt, I would be following the right buttress. I thought the new route would be a little easier than the spring one, and it was also a logical line that was perfect for a solo ascent. The overall height from the glacier to the summit was a little more than 1,500 meters. The total length of the route would be closer to 2,000 meters. Taking into account all the mistakes of the spring expedition, I had brought about 500 meters of 5 mm Kevlar static and 8 mm dynamic rope. I would fix them on the lower part of the wall.

On September 1, my old friend Igor Zdhanovich and I moved onto the glacier under the wall. Igor helped me drag part of the equipment up there, but then I began to work alone. The route went up steep and shattered rock slabs covered in loose stones. The climbing was delicate. The weather was unstable, and as a rule it snowed in the afternoons. In two days, September 2 and 3, I reached a height of 5500 meters and fixed some ropes. On September 4, I came down to base camp at Tapovan to have a rest in rain and snow.

Over the next week, I went up the wall again, but unstable weather kept me from making much progress. At the end of September 9, I reached a rock shoulder at 5600m and decided to organize a high camp there in preparation for a spurt toward the summit. A rock wall more

Hauling gear at circa 5800m on Meru's Shark's Fin during the spring attempt. *Valeri Babanov*

At 5500m on the way up the Shark's Fin, Meru Central. *Valeri Babanov*

than 100 meters high barred the way to the ice. But I would decide later how to overcome the wall. Now I had to go down to ABC for the portaledge and for extra food. I decided it would take two or three days to pass the rock band and reach the ice wall, which led in about 700 meters to the crest that joined the central and north summits.

Early on September 14, I began to climb the fixed ropes. But soon heavy clouds came crawling in and it began snowing heavily. The next day, back in ABC, it snowed from noon on. I sat and thought only about the ascent. I could not think about anything else.

It was getting colder every day.

On the night of September 15, hurricane winds shook the tent. It seemed the weather was getting worse. What would it be tomorrow?

On the morning of September 16, the sun shone. But high winds blew huge snow "flags" away from the crest and the wall, and I needed to wait. My instinct whispered that a radical change would come over the weather.

The next morning, September 17, held no clouds in the sky, while only a weak wind blew. That day I headed up toward 5600m, where my high-altitude camp would be.

⚜

September 21. I have had a day of rest at 5600m, as I needed to gather strength after three days of solo work fixing 250 meters of rope on the wall above.

It was 9 p.m. local time and 10:30 p.m. back in Omsk. Everybody was going to bed, but I would have to spend a long and dangerous night on the north face of Meru Peak. I couldn't fall asleep. I was getting more excited with the approach of midnight, when I would start up toward the summit.

I cooked soup and sweet tea. I analyzed my actions so far—waiting at basecamp for better weather, finding a good high camp, fixing ropes on the rock wall—and came to the conclusion that they were correct, based upon my knowledge, skills, and instinct. The day of rest had come to an end, and the time of consideration was over.

It was absolutely dark, with a weak wind blowing, as I crawled out of my sleeping bag. I breathed the cold air and began to put on all the necessary things: warm fleece jacket, windproof suit, and light down coat. My motions were quick and confident, the result of many years of climbing. I left my crampons off because the first 150 meters of the ascent would be through rocks.

It took me a little time to pack up my rucksack. My equipment consisted of two 60-meter ropes, a Gore-Tex bivouac sack, two pairs of Polartec gloves, some rock pitons, 10 ice screws, Friends, half a liter of hot tea, and little loaves of chocolate. The rucksack weighed a little more than 10 kg. I tried to imagine the ascent above 5800m step by step in order to make sure that I had everything I needed.

At midnight I radioed Igor at ABC telling him I was ready to go up in two minutes. We had agreed that he would be on the radio all the time so I could get in touch with him in case of need. Then I snapped jumars on the rope, which led from the tent straight into the darkness, and began the ascent. My light jumped all over the rocks. The night world surrounded me. Everything outside this spot of light seemed to me a different world. I tried not to be afraid. I did my work and went slowly up, stopping often to keep my strength for the coming day.

Soon I put on my crampons because the next part of the way would be covered with ice. It took me much time and physical effort to pass this part.

At about 2 a.m. I reached the end of the fixed ropes. It was getting colder. I had to keep my toes moving to keep them from freezing. I went on with the ascent with the help of ice axes and without rope for the first 100 meters. As it got steeper, I wanted to use the rope because it was getting too dangerous. The darkness and soundlessness of night increased my fear. The black sky looked like a dense material decorated with silver stars. It seemed that I was in the middle of an alien world, and I felt my loneliness and isolation so heavily that I had to ask Igor to hold up a light for me to see. Soon a little luminous spot appeared far below. Oh, my God! How far from me it was! Like the light of a distant planet!

I continued up and up. Why was I on this huge ice-covered wall? Was it an aspiration to prove something, or some kind of obsession? I couldn't find an answer.

My axes broke through a thin crust of ice and I tried to hook the safe ice under it. I moved mechanically, losing track of time. Driving ice axes and crampons became my existence. Strong blows, short stops, and breathing were the means of survival. Little by little, the ice grew steeper. At one point, I climbed a short vertical "neck." To the left and right, the ice ran up even steeper. I felt as if I was in a subway tunnel made of ice, while 1,000 meters of air strained at my feet. The only safety among this danger and tiredness was the knowledge of relief ahead.

Only the rustle of snow flowing away from the wall broke the silence. All other sounds seemed to be frozen. From time to time I switched my headlamp to a longer beam, but it didn't reveal any more of the chaos of the ice couloir. It was very difficult to guess the distance to the summit or to orient myself among the huge ice fences that crossed the wall many times. During daylight they had seemed lower. The night changed everything.

Dawn drew near. I had worked almost eight hours, and the altimeter showed a height of more than 6000m. Behind me the two-headed massif of Shivling was visible in weak morning

The climbing between 5600m and 5800m, with the Shark's Fin keeping company above. *Valeri Babanov*

light. It seemed I could touch it. Here, in the Himalaya, it felt like I did not belong to myself. There were other laws that I could explain only with the help of intuition or instinct. These laws of the mountains ruled me and I had no opportunity to change them.

In another second, light enveloped the very top of Meru Peak. I could distinctly see every rock on the sharp crest leading to the summit. The dark blue sky contrasted with blinding white summits under the morning sun. The great snow cornices were scarlet, the ice slope was gold and crimson. Huge mountain chains melted away in the distance. I stood on steep ice and couldn't tear myself away from the magnificent view and magical colors.

The air warmed quickly. It didn't seem so terrible as at night. My eyes began to close as I climbed again, and the tiredness rolled like an ocean's wave. Almost in despair I realized that I could do nothing about it. It was so far to the summit. I had to gather all my strength to go on. As I climbed my organism mobilized. I wondered where the energy and self-control came from.

Finally I grew excited. My summit was not far off. The slope going to the right was not steep, but it met a seemingly impassable obstacle: the crest that joined the central and the north summits of Meru Peak. Around me was the first world—the real world. Then there was the second world over the crest—the invisible world, the world that had existed only in my imagination for many months. The world I was aiming for.

I climbed under the crest as high as possible. There were only two meters of overhanging snow above my head separating me from the exit on the crest. The last ice screw was about four meters down. If I fell I would fly down for eight or nine meters. So I tried to consolidate my position with the ice axes: I dug at the ice about my head and caught on some at waist level. Suddenly the snow gave way, and I barely had time to catch onto something with the ice axe–the

The yellow portaledge high camp at 5600m. *Valeri Babanov*

sensation was very unpleasant.

It became clear that I would not get through this cornice directly, so I began gingerly traversing to the right. I did not know what my feet stood on, and my ice axes held onto emptiness.

I felt like a tightrope walker struggling to keep in balance. As I twisted an ice screw into the hard snow with my left hand at waist level, I realized that it would not bear even my own weight, but at least I could hold onto it. My stretching right hand managed to turn in a second ice screw. I changed hands. The rope was not clipped into the ice screws because they were of no use. Now I struggled to make a breach in the snow cornice with the ice axe in my right hand. The bright sunlight dazzled me. Then I swung my axe on the other side of the cornice and pulled very carefully. I felt that the ice axe would hold me. I tucked my legs under and drew myself up. The entire load was on my right hand. I drew the left hand up so I could lean on both hands, then pulled up and crossed onto the other side.

In this extreme telephoto, Valeri Babanov is visible in the shadowed snowfields in the upper right. *Igor Zhdanovich*

Freedom! I couldn't believe it. Overcoming the crest had taken greater mental and physical effort than had climbing half the wall. I lifted my head. The north summit of Meru was guarded by almost 100 meters of rocky wall, but a crest led toward Meru Central's nearby summit, just 100 or 200 meters away. I called Igor on the radio. He told me that he had seen everything with the help of high-powered binoculars.

I tried to find safe ice in the crest with my ice axe and eventually found something like ice, so I placed an ice screw there and fixed the rope for my descent. I would go up without luggage. I had left my rucksack about 10 to 15 meters below and had no wish to go down to get it.

Slowly I began moving toward Meru Central. There were huge snow cornices to the left,

The cornices under the summit ridge, at 6225m. *Valeri Babanov*

The ridge between Central and North Meru. *Valeri Babanov*

and the average angle was about 45 degrees. The crampons held splendidly in the hard snow, leaving hardly a track. All my attention was concentrated on my feet. The snow slope below impressed me greatly. I saw how smoothly it fell away, then it dropped steeply to the right toward the Kirti Bamak Glacier. The glacier, rounding the Meru Massif from the south, seemed less big because of its remoteness.

My lungs heaved from lack of oxygen. Besides the view, I couldn't think about anything except breathing, my sore throat, and the fact that every swallow hurt terribly. I was very tired and had to stop every 30 or 40 steps. So that I wouldn't fall while resting, I drove the ice axes as deeply as possible, then sat on my knees and took a firm stance with my front points in the hard, steep névé. Each time, I didn't want to move again. Only occasionally did I glance toward the summit.

What would I find up there? A mysterious entrance to another world?

There was one more stop on my knees, and at last I got up. But there was nothing above my head. I realized that I was standing on the central summit of Meru, at the top of the Shark's Fin. The altimeter showed 6310m. It was 1:40 p.m. My strength felt restored because the work had been done and it would not be necessary to go up any more.

I turned and looked about. There were mountains and only mountains across the horizon. I wished I could stamp this magic world in my memory forever. But the window of favorable weather would close very soon. Clouds already were running toward the summit of Meru from the south, and from time to time the summit was covered with gray, impenetrable mist.

It was time to go down. I began the descent toward the rope I had fixed. The opposite end of the rope disappeared into the deep, dark face. It would be a long and dangerous descent.

For the last time, I feasted my eyes on the country that spread out below. There was something unreal in the colors. I tried to take a detached view of myself from the height of this world, but it was in vain–something prevented from it. Maybe I was not yet ready to fully feel the mountain world. Maybe I needed to return.

I reached the 5600m bivouac at about 7 p.m., worn out to my limit. I wished only to drink, lie down, and not move. Because I had

Valeri Babanov in Kathmandu. *Babanov collection*

had no time to stop, I had eaten only one chocolate loaf and taken only a few sips of water during the whole day.

Now I needed to cook and drink, but I got into the portaledge and fell asleep. I napped about 20 minutes, enough to restore a little of my strength. I got up, gathered some snow, and began to cook. At last I had enough to drink and subsided into sleep. My sleep was the sleep of the man whose dream has come true.

SUMMARY OF STATISTICS

AREA: Garhwal, Indian Himalaya

FIRST ASCENT: Shangri La (2,000 meters, ED—5C/6A A1/A2 M5 75 degrees), Central Meru Peak, Shark's Fin, 6310m. September 17-22, 2001. Valeri Babanov, solo.

Special thanks to Igor Zhdanovich for his help during the time of the expedition.

Thanks to Lidia Fedorova for translating from the Russian.

AND THE BLIND SHALL SEE

Thanks to new techniques and dedicated doctors, the end is in sight for the epidemic of needless blindness in the Himalaya.

GEOFFREY TABIN

Dr. Sanduk Ruit restoring vision in Tibet. Dr. Ruit was the first Nepali doctor to perform modern cataract surgery with a sight restoring lens implant. In 1995 he co-founded the Himalayan Cataract Project with Geoff Tabin, dedicated to eradicating needless blindness in mountainous Asia. *Michael Amendolia/Network Photographers*

The expedition begins with the usual frenzied packing in Kathmandu. Each box is carefully labeled. We double-check all the necessary equipment, as there will be no chance of getting supplies along the way. We fly first to Lhasa and then over spectacular unexplored mountains to land in Xining, in the Tibetan populated Quinghai Province of China. We proceed in old Chinese jeeps across the rugged landscape of the Amdo region, one of the poorest places in one of the poorest countries in the world. This is the area where the current Dalai Lama was born.

Our jeep bounces along a heavily rutted road winding along a high plateau. On both sides unexplored 6000-meter peaks rise steeply. A few scattered settlements of bare wood and mud hovels cling to the steep hillsides adjacent to the road. White Buddhist prayer flags flap in the wind on top of each box-like dwelling. Yaks and goats graze on the sparse grass in the brown remnants of barley fields. At nearly 15,000 feet the temperature dips below freezing every night. There is no electricity or even firewood to be found in this region. Cooking is done over open fires of dried yak dung.

Life is harsh here, particularly if you are blind. And the high Tibetan plateau has one of the highest rates of cataract blindness in the world. The two local doctors whom we brought to Nepal for basic training in cataract surgery have pre-screened patients and tell us that there are more than 300 people in the county of about 800 households who are totally blind from cataracts in both eyes.

Our bus moves off the rutted dirt track and on to the pavement of Golog, the only large settlement for several hundred miles. Many of the buildings are Chinese prefab concrete blocks and most of the officials are Chinese, but the population is overwhelmingly Tibetan nomad. We pull up in front of the county hospital. Our team includes my partner, Dr. Sanduk Ruit, a Nepalese ophthalmologist, two nurses and two technicians from our eye hospital in Kathmandu, plus the two Tibetan doctors, Dr. Wong and Dr. Sangye whom we have been training. Here we will also work with and teach two local nurses and two assistants.

My interest in international medicine grew out of my climbing trips in Nepal and Tibet during the 1980s. In 1981 I left medical school to join an American climbing team attempting to make the first ascent of the east face of Mt. Everest. I vividly remember seeing a blind mid dle-aged man being led with a stick by a small child. When I looked at his eyes I saw that his pupils glowed an eerie white, rather than the normal black color. I soon learned that this was the appearance of an absolute cataract. After completing medical school I worked as a general doctor in Nepal. I was frustrated that most of the medical problems I faced were the result of public health issues and could not be "cured" by a doctor. Then I watched a Dutch team

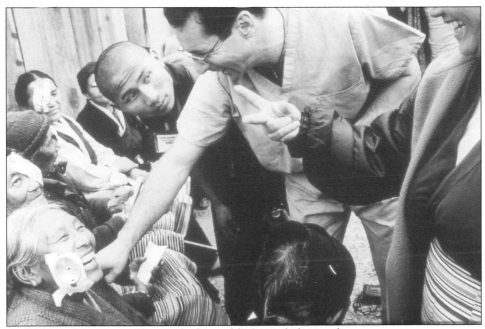

Geoff Tabin in Golog County, Tibet. *Michael Amendolia/Network Photographers*

Dancing the joy-step upon seeing the world anew. *Geoffrey Tabin*

perform cataract surgery. I witnessed a miracle. A woman from my village, who had been totally blind, had her sight restored. She went from living the life of a neglected house-plant, kept in a dark corner of the house and occasionally carried out to spend a few hours in the sun or go to the bathroom, to having her life returned. She was no longer a burden and could return to being an active member of the family, cooking and caring for her grandchildren. I returned to complete an ophthalmology residency in America and a fellowship in corneal surgery under Professor Hugh Taylor in Melbourne, Australia, one of the leaders in the worldwide fight against needless blindness. More than 90 percent of the blindness in the world is preventable or treatable. In mountainous Asia over 70 percent of the blind people can have their vision completely restored with cataract surgery.

During my fellowship year I was sent to Nepal to work with Dr. Sanduk Ruit. I was amazed by his skill: He is a master surgeon. Ruit trained at the best hospitals in India and then spent two years studying microsurgery in the Netherlands and Australia. He became the first Nepali doctor to perform modern cataract surgery with a sight restoring lens implant. Previously all doctors in the region sliced the eyeball in half, pulled out the entire lens, sewed the eye shut with crude sutures and gave the patients thick, coke bottle, glasses that provided some focus but also a lot of distortion. It is not surprising that the second leading cause of blindness in Nepal (after cataract) is bad cataract surgery. Dr. Ruit adapted modern techniques to his environment and perfected high volume delivery of high quality cataract surgery in remote regions at a cost of less than 20 dollars per surgery. I stayed in Nepal after my fellow-ship working at the eye hospital in Biratnagar and teaching Dr. Ruit's technique. When I returned to America in 1995 we formed the Himalayan Cataract Project, dedicated to eradi-cating needless blindness in mountainous Asia.

Rumors of this camp began circulating in the Golog County several months ago. Hundreds of elderly Tibetans and their families have gathered around the hospital. Their gazes combine a mixture of hope and doubt. No one has ever been cured of blindness here before.

The hospital has the sickly smell of many such Third World facilities, a mixture of the acrid odor of stale urine with the rich scents of excrement and antiseptic. The halls and tables are dusty. Filthy IV tubing and dirty needles litter the hallways. A welcoming committee of flies buzzes in every room. There is no heat. The power is out.

As the portable microscopes, generator, and other supplies are unloaded, Dr. Ruit looks across the barren dirt courtyard of the hospital and gives me a broad smile. Pointing at the blind crowd, he excitedly exclaims that everything is perfect. "This is where the people need us."

Twelve hours per day for the next three days Dr. Ruit and I operate side by side without any high tech equipment beyond a microscope. When the generator fails we keep working on eyes illuminated by assistants holding flashlights.

Technicians inject local anesthetic and prepare the patients for surgery. When a case is finished the patient is rolled off one side of the table as the next patient is rolled on. The face is painted with antiseptic and the surgery continues. The turnover time between patients is less than a minute. Dr. Ruit sustains a pace of seven perfect surgeries per hour for the 12-hour operating day.

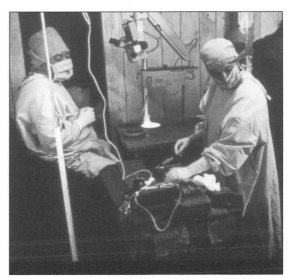

"There is a new sky for my eye! I am free from the hell of darkness!" exclaims Sonam Dechen, moments after the white gauze patch has been removed from her left eye. Tears of joy stream down her bronzed cheeks. Yesterday the 63-year-old widow was unable to see the shadow of a hand moving in front of her face. Today she can see well. With no living sons she had no one to take care of her, often going days without eating and falling in ditches. "Now," she proudly states, "I will be able to take care of myself."

In three days Dr. Ruit and I perform over 200 "miracles" in Golog. On the fourth day the local doctors begin operating on the second eyes of patients who have had sight restored to one eye. I assist at one microscope. Dr. Ruit continues restoring sight to the blind at his table. Dr. Sangye sits in the surgeon's chair and stares intently through the microscope. His eyes are focussed. An enormous turquoise charm box filled with Buddhist prayers bulges at the chest of his surgical gown. He tentatively scratches at the surface of the patient's eye with a blade. I encourage him to use a little more force. The initial incision is eventually made, but he has difficulty removing the cataract. We switch seats and I complete the case. After a few tries he is able to perform each step of the procedure. Ten eyes later he completes an entire surgery without my help.

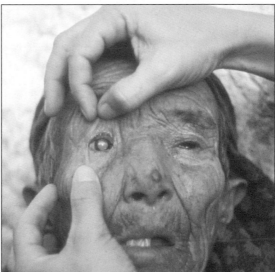

On a visit to Tibet's Golong County, Dr. Ruit and Dr. Tabin, along with their two surgeons-in-training, performed 506 cataract surgeries in nine days, with no infections or serious complications. *Michael Amendolia/Network Photographers*

In nine days a total of 506 cataract surgeries have been performed. There are no infections and no blinding complications. More importantly, Dr. Wong and Dr. Sangye have each completed more than 75 successful cataract surgeries. We donate the microscopes, surgical instruments, and enough lenses for each doctor to restore sight to another 500 people.

The total cost of the skills transfer including bringing the local doctors to Nepal for training, transporting our team to Golog, buying all the microscopes and surgical instruments to donate, and restoring sight to over 500 eyes is less than $25,000. In Tibet there are no services for the blind. Sightless people require family members to care for them, an enormous economic burden. The life expectancy of the blind in this part of the world is less than half that of sighted people the same age. After surgery most patients can return to work or traditional roles within their family.

Over the past seven years we have trained 16 doctors to perform modern cataract surgery from Tibet, two from Sikkim, three from Bhutan, and one from Northern Pakistan. In Nepal, where we have worked with dozens of ophthalmologists to improve their cataract surgery skills, the number of cataract surgeries performed has increased from 15,000 in 1993 to more than 97,000 in 2001. Although other people and organizations have been working in the area, it is Dr. Ruit who is most responsible for the increase in quality, which has led to the increased volume of patients who come seeking surgery.

We work closely with several other non-government organizations, including The Central Asia Institute which helped us begin our work in northern Pakistan, SEVA, The Fred Hollows Foundation, The Christofel Blinden Mission, The Tibet Fund, Tibet Development Fund, and The Tibet Vision Project. Finally, we have had great support from other American and Australian ophthalmologists and several of the large ophthalmic pharmaceutical companies.

One-day's supply of post-operation happiness among Golog County's Tibetan nomads.
Michael Amendolia/Network Photographers

We are now branching out beyond simply teaching cataract surgery. In Nepal we are training ophthalmic assistants as primary care health workers and setting up primary eye-care health clinics. We run a two-year course in conjunction with Kathmandu University that trains eye-care workers to refract and give glasses, screen patients, and treat common diseases and infections. The ophthalmic assistants refer serious and surgical problems to doctors. This will have an impact on preventable etiologies of vision loss. For instance, the leading cause of blindness in children is Vitamin A deficiency. More then half a million children go blind worldwide from lack of Vitamin A each year. Once blinded, the child's sight is lost forever. Prevention only requires a 75-cent pill to be given by the local health care worker once per year. The ophthalmic assistants are also playing a major role in preventing vision loss from Trachoma, the world's second leading cause of blindness, and from blinding corneal infections.

On the other end of the spectrum we are sending some of the best young ophthalmologists in Nepal for fellowships in America or Australia where they learn state of the art subspecialty care. We have trained doctors in corneal transplant surgery, retinal surgery, glaucoma management, and pediatric ophthalmology in the past three years. These doctors are returning to become the teachers of the next generation of ophthalmologists in the region. In the next few years we are planning on starting a full three-year ophthalmology residency program at the Tilganga Eye Centre in Kathmandu.

We are also mentoring several poor hospitals, working with them to help them become financially self-sufficient. At our base hospital, the Tilganga Eye Centre in Kathmandu, our surgical programs function without outside support through a cost recovery model where the wealthier patients help defray the costs for the destitute. Our full charge for cataract surgery is around $120 (U.S.). Nearly half of the patients in Kathmandu pay this fee. One quarter pay a lesser amount and one quarter receive totally free care. With high volume surgery and a material cost for each cataract surgery of less than 20 dollars this cost recovery system works in even the most impoverished regions of Nepal.

Seven years ago our task of overcoming preventable and treatable blindness in mountainous Asia appeared more daunting than any overhanging rock-and-ice wall I have seen. However, like a big climb that is slowly surmounted one step at a time, we are progressing one doctor and one eye at a time. We are far ahead of my most optimistic expectations from when we started our work. At our present rate of progress, mountainous Asia should be self-sufficient in cataract surgery within the next five years and able to eliminate the backlog of cataract blind within 10 years.

For more information please visit our website: www.cureblindness.org

Any contributions are most appreciated. Tax deductable contributions to:
The Himalayan Cataract Project
c/o Geoffrey Tabin, M.D.
Dept of Ophthalmology—University of Vermont College of Medicine
1 South Prospect Street
Burlington, Vermont 05401
Tel. (802) 847 3843

RELEASING BELLAVISTA

Seventy years ago the Tre Cime Group in the Dolomites was home to the world's boldest and most overhanging aid climbs. The overhangs are still there—and so is the boldness—only now they're beginning to go free.

ALEXANDER HUBER

The Tre Cime di Lavaredo, in the Parko delle Dolomiti di Sesto of the Provincia di Bolzano. The 500-meter Bellavista route is shown on the north face of the Cima Ouest. *Konrad Kirch*

Most of us like to be cozy and warm, and prefer the weather fair and dry. I said most of us, because there is a small group of human beings who—at least at times—like it different. The members of this obscure sub-species revel in the cold and rave about steep, loose, difficult rock. After weeks in centrally heated and fully insured civilization they get fed up and start dreaming of freezing, shattered dolomite and dubious pieces of protection. They are looking for the enchantment of an adventure strong enough to withstand the drudge of everyday life.

By now you understand that I am talking about alpine climbers, those people who have a hard time understanding why some folks call rock "bad" when they actually mean "loose."

Those people who feel marvelous when perched among the tottering phone booths of the Tre Cime, and who find exactly what they are looking for in the preposterously dynamic north face of the Matterhorn.

However, when I set out in February 2000 to scare myself on the north face of the Cima Ouest, in the Dolomites, the quest for adventure was not the only reason. Six years earlier, with the Spanish climber Lisi Roig Alegre, I had done the Swiss-Italian Route, a classic that goes free at 5.12. A real gift. It also gave me the opportunity to spend hours looking at the huge roof to the right of the Swiss-Italian Route, an upside-down world that cast its spell and refused to release me. I had an inkling that the great roof of Cima Ouest might be the home to one of the world's craziest freeclimbing lines. But it took a few years for me to return to the Tre Cime. Too many dreams, goals, and plans were buzzing around my head, crying for realization, and elbowing out the idea of the great roof each time it rose to the level of consciousness.

Its turn came during a long stretch of cold turkey after an injury in the fall of 1999. I had squashed my right index finger and was afraid to lose an important part of my life—climbing! Although Doc Hochholzer, the famous Teutonic finger guru, assured me that my days on the rocks were not yet numbered, gnawing doubts persisted. For five months I was completely out of commission, reduced to immobility. After this I couldn't think of a better jump-start for my life than a real adventure.

It turned out to be pure fun. Instead of putting up another direttissima, I wanted to do a winter solo following a natural line with only nuts and pitons. Bolts would be allowed only at the belays. I was very scared and had to mobilize all my skills not to make unhealthy contact with the snow-covered talus under the wall.

The route was loose to my heart's content, challenging, and wild. After the five days on what I named Bellavista, my thirst for adventure had been quenched—and I also knew that every meter of the route could be climbed free. Maybe hard—very hard!—but possible. A free ascent of this huge roof became my obsession: a 5.14 route up the loose dolomite of Cima Ouest's gloomy north face!

I was not ready yet. After the long break enforced by injury, my arms were in such a sorry state that three months of training would in no way build the strength I needed for this roof. I had to postpone the project. The summer of 2000 at least made it clear that climbing wasn't a thing of the past; a visit to Yosemite gave me the confidence that really hard climbing would soon be possible again. I had a goal and knew what to do. So, back home again, without hesitating, I entered the circuit of torture chambers, training rooms, and plastic walls. If you want to climb really hard—in the mountains, too—you have to build a solid sport-climbing basis. In spring I started to slowly but steadily increase my performance level on the crags. I began to re-enter the realm of 5.14, where the holds get really small, the overhangs truly steep, and the moves extremely athletic.

⁂

At the beginning of June I feel ready. It is a cold day when Matthias Leitner, from Graz, and I cross the frozen snowfield under the wall to place the necessary protection for a free attempt. The feeling of fear is much more intense than during my solo, and I seem to have picked a very bad day. Then comes the first pitch I did on aid in winter. I am drained from the free climbing below, but Matthias' enthusiasm is unperturbed. Totally cool, he drapes himself with the necessary paraphernalia—hammer, knifeblades, Lost Arrows, angles, nuts, skyhooks, étriers—and takes off into an upside-down world. Aiding has almost nothing in common with "proper" climbing—you move like a caterpillar at the pace of a snail—but it is in no way boring, even if it lasts for a long time. After two days Matthias and I manage to struggle out of horizontal purgatory. We have climbed Bellavista, leaving all protection and the ropes on the route. From the tiny lake under the face we stare up spellbound to the overhanging amphitheater glowing in the sunset. The stage is set for the rehearsal.

Two big questions are waiting for an answer. Am I physically capable of pulling it off? And how do I protect the 55 meters of roof? To preserve the original state of Bellavista and the challenge of the route, I have decided that placing bolts is not an option. In an era governed by numbers, I have to make a statement—to prove that there is a way out of the blind alley climbing is stuck in today. Borderline moves: okay! Fun in our sport: okay! Still, for many of us climbing is more than a sport. Why not consciously renounce the safety of bolts and instead rely on our mental strength, our skills, and our willingness to take risks? These are qualities that every climber needs on the big alpine routes.

A week later I am back on the face. Goal number one is to improve the protection by placing reasonably good pitons, especially in the difficult pitches of the giant roof. But even systematic scanning of the compact yellowish-gray rock proves fruitless: long stretches of the most difficult ground yield only to stoic hooking, stretches that will have to be free-climbed without protection. On the thin line between sticking to the rock and yielding to gravity, the fear of impressive falls is ever-present. Some of them are really long—to the displeasure of the knifeblades ripped from their shallow cracks, sending the unhappy climber on another long, plummeting trip into space. The dreaded zippers rob me of more and more points of protection.

Three weeks later, Guido Unterwurzacher is nice enough to suffer through my first attempts to free the roof. For 10 meters, pitch number six follows a break under a six-meter ceiling, from where the line of least resistance leads through the roofs. At first sight it is hard to believe it could go free. But again and again, the fingertips slip into the junctures between the huge blocks forming this inverted world. At the end of the traverse there is even a resting spot, just enough to shake out the burning forearms, to clip the rurp for some imaginary protection, and to sort myself into the microledge before cranking through to a two-finger pocket, just making it to the second one—and catching sight of the large holds at the belay. But the forearms are running hot again, incapable of letting go and reaching out. I cling to the pockets for a few more seconds. "Aaahhh," I scream as my body sails through the air, tearing the rurp and two knifeblades from their precarious placements and catapulting them against my forehead despite the helmet. Another jerk, then I find myself swinging in space. My eyebrows are drenched with blood, but Guido answers my worried look with a casual, "Just a small cut. You still look good enough."

I jumar back to the belay. Twenty minutes of relaxing, then the next attempt. Having skillfully done away with the need to clip the last three pegs, I can spare my strength this time. Just cool it! Right hand on microledge, pocket with the left. Don't think, just do it. I feel the big holds at the belay in my hands: the first pitch of the roof is cracked. Guido follows on jumars, experiencing the joys of abruptly increased exposure. Now every action is doubly planned and triple-checked. I, too, am feeling the stomach butterflies, for on the second roof pitch the protection is significantly thinner. When the first attempt ends abruptly six meters out from the belay, the only knifeblade between me and Guido also loses contact with the rock. After this scary screamer, my muscles seem to have entered the same state of disruption as my shattered nerves. No wonder the left foot slips from a hold just four meters from the belay on the last half-hearted attempt of the day. "Aaahhh," etc. etc. Amen.

A week later. More and more pegs have resigned their service as pieces of protection, but the second pitch has also succumbed. The next item on the agenda is the redpoint ascent of all the pitches in a day, starting from terra firma. So as not to make things too easy, I've decided to get rid of the hanging belay between the first and the second roof pitch. To call it a proper free ascent, we would have to climb all of the 55 overhanging meters in a single uninterrupted push—quite a challenge for my poor forearms.

Attempt number one. Matthias has volunteered to come along. This is good, because he knows the route and is aware of the fine points of belaying it. The initial pitches yield without draining us physically and mentally. I feel strong and the conditions are just right—dry and relatively warm. I start up the roof. Although there is nothing to lose, my body is vibrating like an electric eel. Just short of the old belay, the mental maelstrom starts churning: "You'll never make it today!" Another one of those screams discharges my anger while I swing 200 meters above the talus.

We still have a chance. As so often, the nervousness has vanished after the first fall and the arms seem strong enough for a second try. Half an hour. After the traverse to the left I calmly manage to pull over the roof and reach the resting spot with the large holds at the belay. One-third of the stretch is covered. I manage to shake out the forearms, to steady my breath, and to reduce the heart rate. I set out, following the path of my thoughts. Above and below

Alexander Huber on the sixth pitch (5.14b) of Bellavista. *Heinz Zak*

Alexander Huber on the eighth pitch (5.11c) of Bellavista, on Cime Ouest. *Heinz Zak*

have ceased to exist, the exposure has vanished, the quality of protection has become irrelevant. Everything is under control. One hard sequence after another gives in to my unwavering determination. I reach the pin eight meters out from the belay, clip it, and immediately climb to the resting spot a meter to the left. Again I take my time to lower the heart rate and loosen the arms. The crux. A traverse to the left, eight meters long with no pro to go for. You must pull it off in an athletic, dynamic fashion, not giving gravity a chance, spooling off the sequences like a gymnast doing his well-rehearsed Olympic program. "The foothold doesn't work!" Thoughts reappear. There is a mistake in the sequence. I must try to correct it! But how? At least do something!

"Aaahhh!" The colossal arena amplifies my scream. Strain and fear burst from my body while it plummets toward the ground. The rope goes taut, transforming my fall into a huge pendulum. Matthias, too, has taken a beating. He was hanging three meters below the roof when the force of the fall hit and catapulted him against the horizontal ceiling. We're through for the day. Let's get out of here as fast as possible!

Back in the valley I decide to prepare the next attempt more thoroughly. Every mistake could mean the loss of more points of protection. Two more days of training in the route, bouldering out the moves, and internalizing the program. Then back to serious business, this time with Gernot Flemisch.

The cold turns out to be an advantage. The body doesn't overheat even when working hard, and the fingertips stay dry. Again the crux. The hands are shaking and, despite the low temperatures, sweat beads my brow and the tongue sticks to the palate. Sport climbing at 5.14, with gadgets from the bag of aid-climbing tricks as protection. Reaching far to the left, I touch the first good hold, go into an undercling, and manage to sink my hand into a big hole—the resting spot. Stomach cramps, burning forearms, my spirit on the verge of surrender—and still 10 meters to the belay, 10 long meters that won't forgive any mistake. Inch by inch I force myself upward—from resting point to resting point, filled with fear of failing so close to the goal. Then the last move. The left foothold is dubious, but I can't afford to hesitate, as the arms are approaching the final stage of exhaustion. Staking everything on this last chance, I make myself go on. At last, the handhold! My horizon and release.

The way to the top is open, today, on July 18, 2001. My adventure has reached its conclusion. At last the giant roof of Bellavista has been climbed free.

SUMMARY OF STATISTICS:

AREA: Tre Cime di Lavaredo, Dolomites, Italy

ASCENT: Cima Ouest, north face, Bellavista (500 meters, VI 5.12a/A4 or 5.14b). First ascent March 15-20, 2000, Alexander Huber (solo). First redpoint ascent July, 18, 2001, Alexander Huber. The pitch list: 5.12a, 5.11a, 5.10a, 5.11c, 5.11d, 5.14b, 5.13b, 5.11c, 5.11a, 5.10c.

Translated by Nicholas Mailänder

CLIMBS AND EXPEDITIONS

2002

Accounts from the various climbs and expeditions of the world are listed geographically from north to south and from west to east within the noted countries. We begin our coverage with the Contiguous United States and move to Alaska in order for the climbs in the Alaska's Wrangell Mountains to segue into the St. Elias climbs in Canada.

Unless noted otherwise, accounts cover activity in the 2001 calendar year (January 1-December 31). First-person accounts from winter 2001-2002 activity and shoulder-season areas (e.g., Patagonia) are included when possible. Winter climbers and those returning from the southern hemisphere can help us in future volumes by submitting accounts as soon as possible. We encourage climbers to submit accounts of other notable activity from the various Greater Ranges to help us maintain complete records.

For conversions of meters to feet, multiply by 3.28; for feet to meters, multiply by 0.30.

NORTH AMERICA
CONTIGUOUS UNITED STATES

Washington

Nooksack Tower, south face. In July Ben Manfredi and I teamed up to try a beautiful new face in the Mt. Shuksan region. The face is the seldom-seen steep "back side"—the south face of Nooksack Tower. The route is directly above the East Nooksack Glacier. The face presents as much vertical relief as the north aspect of the Tower but is steeper.

We made camp on the shoulder that divides the Price Glacier from the Nooksack Cirque area. Downclimbing and one rappel took us to a small pocket glacier. A short couloir led down onto the edge of the East Nooksack Glacier. We ascended the glacier, climbing through icefalls of varying complexity. We started the climb on the right side of the south face. We front-pointed for a short distance up a couloir and then exited left onto a sloping belay ledge, where ice tools and crampons were exchanged for chalk bags and rock slippers. The first several pitches angled slightly left and up, passing a short overhanging bulge and eventually leading into a depression. Simulclimbing led up and left out of the large depression to the left-center portion of the south face. The rock we encountered was extremely poor and afforded limited protection opportunities. From the left half of the face we pushed directly up, eventually reaching a small tower. After a rappel, an easy section of fourth-class rock led to the summit. The route (V 5.10- snow/ice to 55 degrees) was done in 12 pitches with a 200-foot rope and some simulclimbing. We quickly descended the standard north face route on the "front side" of the Tower and pulled into camp, drained after a 17-hour push, and enjoyed caramel candies from the local supermarket.

JENS KLUBBERUD

Mt. Hardy, The Disappearing Staircase. It was amazing that a feature as compelling as the northeast buttress of Mt. Hardy could have not been climbed by 2001. Perhaps it was its perceived isolation, since it is almost 10 miles from the road to its base via the Pacific Crest Trail. However, the summit is less than a mile from the North Cascades Highway, and a direct cross-country approach is mild by Cascades standards, due to its position east of the crest.

On August 19 Dan Aylward and I climbed the northeast buttress in a 21-hour round trip from the car, which we left at the Easy Pass trailhead. A thousand feet of moderate climbing along the edge of the prominent gully splitting the lower apron led to the steep upper headwall. The six upper pitches were, for the most part, directly up the buttress crest. The final two involved a traverse 40 feet to the right after a blank face forced us off the direct line. An additional 800 feet of moderate climbing on an elegant knife-edge ridge led directly to Mt. Hardy's 8,080-foot summit. The route was climbed hammerless. Aid was necessary for cleaning, but the second was able to follow the aid section free (IV 5.10c A1). Photographs and a topo are available at the website http://www.saarch.com/forrest/hardyfull.htm

FORREST MURPHY

The Kloochman, Traverse; Goose Egg Mountain; The Talon. The Kloochman is an enigmatic massif in the southern Washington Cascades. An old volcanic intrusion, the mile-long north-south-trending wedge has a main south summit, a prominent north summit, and three lower towers to the north. On May 9 Stoney Richards and I completed a traverse of the formation from the north (IV 5.9R/X, 26 pitches), climbing up and rappelling or downclimbing each tower, then descending from the south summit by the south ridge. While linking several old routes on the towers, we climbed 16 new pitches on Tower 1, Tower 3, and the north summit. Although the Kloochman is known for its extremely poor rock, many of the pitches had fair-to-good rock, although long runouts were the norm. The north summit provided the most enjoyable climbing and led to a spectacular knife-edge ridge, which took us to just below the main summit. One can un-rope and walk for over a quarter of a mile across the main summit area.

Also of note in the area is a new seven-pitch sport-and-trad odyssey, called Ride the Lightning, on the 800-foot south wall of Goose Egg Mountain. The small rock sliver named the Talon also has two new routes, the Direct South Face and the North Face, making four routes now to the summit of this elusive spire.

JOSEPH PURYEAR, *AAC*

California

YOSEMITE VALLEY

Yosemite Valley, various activity. (Editor's note: Several of the ascents mentioned in this summary, particularly new routes, appear in greater detail as individual reports below.) In 2001, Yosemite continued to be an arena of significant free-climbing and blazing speed ascents. On the free climbing front, two new ascents were made on El Capitan. In the Spring, Tommy Caldwell and Nick Sagar became the first to free the Muir Wall—their free variation goes at 5.13+ and is reportedly the most sustained free line on El Cap. In September, Germans Alex Huber and Max Reichel established El Corazon (5.13b R) on the southwest face.

Although specifics are lacking, on the far right side of El Cap, Jim Bridwell established Welcome to Afghanistan, a relatively short (about 10 pitches) route with climbing to A4/5. Over 13 days in May, Jim Beyer soloed Slacker's Toil (VI 5.9 A5B), a four and one-fourth pitch variation to Surgeon General/Lunar Eclipse. Ammon McNeely continued his string of impressive ascents, establishing Known Offender (V 5.11b A3+), on the Super Nova Wall, with Jennifer Kelly in November. Unreported from April 2000, McNeely and Cedar Wright put up High Line (VI 5.10R A4). The route is between Crack the Whip and Dime Bag, in the Super Nova area.

In June, Germans Gabor Berecz and Thomas Tivadar made what is probably the second ascent of Genesis (VI 5.11 A4) on El Cap over six days. They report: "We found the free parts not so hard. The harder aiding is often on very tiny features, which maybe won't hold more ascents in the future."

Leo Houlding and various partners, including Jason Pickles, Kevin Thaw, and Cedar Wright, worked a desperate free project called The Prophet. The route is based on Bad to the Bone except for the first pitch (Eagle's Way). Five pitches, up to Bad to the Bone's sixth belay (guidebook topo), have been freed. Thus far, pitch five is the crux at E8 6c (5.13b). Pitches have been re-led on each attempt, no fixing, and have good belays but some dangerous runouts. On some of the old "protection" bolts, Thaw says, "Hard to say how good they are, a fall would certainly test them...."

On May 16, Brits Houlding and Pickles climbed the incredible, sustained West Face of Leaning Tower, freeing all but the initial bolt ladder at 5.13b (or E7 6c). Houlding writes, "The initial insanely steep bolt ladder remains an aid pitch and will never go free (so prove me wrong)." A few days later they climbed the route in 1 hour and 59 minutes, a new speed record.

Many protagonists of modern speed-climbing in Yosemite, like Timmy O'Neill, Dean Potter, Steve Schneider, Jason "Singer" Smith, and Cedar Wright successfully exported their skills to the world's great alpine areas. Reports on their incredible ascents are found elsewhere in this journal.

O'Neill and Potter made an incredible enchainment of the Northwest Face on Half Dome, the South Face on Mt. Watkins and the Nose on El Capitan, becoming the first to make a one-day (23:45) ascent of three Yosemite grade VI walls on different cliffs.

The long-standing speed record on the Nose finally fell—three times. First, O'Neill and Potter climbed it in 3:59:35. Two weeks later, Hans Florine and Jim Herson upped the ante, going at 3:57:27. O'Neill and Potter answered a few days after, further raising the bar in establishing the current record of 3:24:04.

In an impressive link-up, Jim Herson and Peter Coward climbed the Salathé on El Cap and the Regular Route on Half Dome in 23 hours. They didn't jumar any pitches, because, writes Herson, "Pete hates to jug and I don't know how to jug." Herson tried, "much to Peter's dismay" (because of the time factor), to free the Salathé in the process. He didn't quite pull it off.

On El Cap, several routes saw their first one-day ascents. Two were by Brian McCray and Ammon McNeely: Get Whacked (VI 5.10R A5, in 12:47) and Plastic Surgery Disaster (VI 5.8 A5, in 21:37). McNeely also climbed, with Jose Pereyra and Chongo Chuck, Lunar Eclipse (VI 5.10 A4) in 19:47.

Other speed records made on El Cap in 2001 include: Flight of the Albatross (14:50; variation for first 6 pitches; Florine, McCray, Kelly Simard), Muir (19:56; Nils Davis, McCray), New Jersey Turn Pike (16:09; Heather Baer, Florine, Schneider), Zenyatta Mondatta (26:25; McCray, Pereyra), Mr. Midwest (7:40; Hans & Jacqueline Florine, Schneider), East Buttress (2:05 CTC; Smith), and Lurking Fear (4:27; Smith, Wright).

Notable records on other Valley formations include Southern Man on Washington's Column (2:38; Smith, Wright) and the East Buttress of Middle Cathedral (34 minutes—1:15 car-to-car; Smith). Also, on Higher Cathedral Spire, Andrew and Matt Wilder set records on the Regular Route (37 minutes) and the East Corner (1:15).

The best documentation of Yosemite speed climbing action, including these ascents, is found on Hans Florine's site, www.speedclimb.com.

KELLY CORDES, *AAC*

Leaning Tower, West Face. On May 16 Jason Pickles and I climbed the West Face of the Leaning Tower free except for the initial insanely steep bolt ladder. Royal Robbins called the Tower, first climbed by Warren Harding in 1961 with heavy use of bolts, "the steepest wall in North America." The Tower's west face is comparable in angle to Kilnsey North Buttress but a thousand feet high. Harding's rusty bolts were replaced by the American Safe Climbing Association in 1997, a commendable effort.

We began free climbing where the bolt ladder ends at a small ledge in a shallow, steep groove. The 160-foot crux pitch (5.13b or E7 6c) leads one to Ahwahnee Ledge, a five-star perch named after the exclusive hotel in the Valley. The pitch can be broken in two, utilizing the "gay belay," at 5.13a (E6 6c). A unique and enjoyable hanging ramp pitch, then a full 60-meter stamina fest, both around 5.12c (E5 6b) bring you to the big roof. Its size is deceptive, but when you pull into its depths, all becomes clear: about 20 feet of horizontal laybacking, then another 20 feet of bridging up a 45-degree overhanging groove. Every hold is a jug, and it's a wild pitch, extremely exposed (5.13a or E6 6c). A final typically steep corner completes the outstanding, sustained route. The incredible view of El Cap obtained from the summit makes the final mantle perhaps the most spectacular topout in the world. Achievable in a day and of a semisport nature, this route is set to become a classic of its grade.

Several days later we made the fastest aid ascent of the same route while retrieving a jammed rope. Our time of one hour and 59 minutes sheds an hour and 20 minutes off the previous speed record. The same afternoon Jason caught his bus out of the Valley.

LEO HOULDING, *United Kingdom*

El Capitan, Muir Wall. "Oh my God, he's actually going to step off this ledge!" This was my thought as I watched my partner, Tommy Caldwell, step off a ledge and free-climb at the top of El Capitan. We had been on El Cap a year earlier, doing the Nose in a day, but free-climbing, rather then pulling on the gear at this height, was a new experience.

After Tommy introduced me to free climbing at the top of El Capitan, it occurred to me that I could be a good partner to free the Muir Wall with him. Tommy's two previous attempts were ended by bad weather and a partner bailing. For me this could be the opportunity of a lifetime.

The real crux would be convincing my expecting wife Heather to let me cross the continent for the attempt. No problem. So it was that during the last week of April we started working on the upper pitches. We made sure the crux pitch, two from the top, would go. It did, at 5.13+. We would each free climb the entire route. If one of us fell, whether on lead or second, he would lower to the bottom of the pitch and reclimb it.

The first pitches, including a 5.9 chimney and two wet, sloppy 5.12 pitches, had us off to an exciting start. Having only four trad routes under my belt, and knowing that the first 5.13 pitch was next, I was beginning to think I was up there to belay Tommy on his free ascent. When I made this suggestion, Tommy calmly replied, "We could go down if you don't think you can climb it." The gauntlet was thrown.

After trying the 5.13 pitch, going down, and resting, I managed to get through it. We were ready to blast through the next five pitches, getting us to Mammoth Terraces. Prepped for the next 5.12 pitches, I had gotten into the swing of things, Tommy was gaining confidence in my chances, and we were moving faster. Just in time, too, as we were approaching the 5.13 pitches leading out of the corners and onto the steep face of El Capitan. The sweep of The Nose jutted out below us, as we traversed through the final handholdless moves.

After rapping down in the twilight, we knew the time had arrived to commit to the route. After a day of hauling five days of supplies and resting, we started early, jumarring to our high point. The next few pitches were fun, warming us up for the 5.12 pitches necessary to complete the free variation.

It being a busy Saturday in Yosemite, the death-block pitch was especially nerve-wracking. Tommy or I (probably I) dislodging this car-sized block down the face would not have made for a successful adventure. Relieved to complete this pitch, we set up our first bivy. But not wanting to face a 5.12d dihedral, which loomed above us, first thing in the morning, Tommy climbed it before settling into his sleeping bag for the night.

Despite Tommy's coaching, I had to start the day figuring out how to move up the dihedral, and it took a few attempts before it finally went. I arrived at the ledge, and once again my partner amazed me by stepping off the ledge and free climbing 2,400 feet above the ground. It was my turn, and I gingerly moved onto the overhanging 5.12a, feeling like I was leaping out of an airplane. This, followed by a runout 5.11, left me ready to call it a day. Not Tommy, though. He climbed to the final crux pitch and sent it before nightfall. I had another stimulating morning start to look forward to.

Knowing that the hard climbing was behind him, Tommy broke out the cell phone and called home to say he had almost sent the route—just one 5.10 pitch to go, and he had done it!

Laying on the ledge listening to Tommy's excitement, I tried to find reasons why I could fire the 5.13c crux, despite having never climbed a crack that difficult, despite having spent two days on the wall, despite being so far up.

After I made three tries Tommy told me to come down and rest. I know that he was ready to stay there for me until I could do it. But how long would that be? He stood on the small ledge and said nothing. I thought of the liebacking of small pin scars and long lock-offs, while Tommy sent positive, relaxing energy by being content to wait. A few minutes later, after I'd done the lock-offs, I heard Tommy yelling; knowing that we now had it! The most continuously difficult free line up El Cap, The Muir.

NICK SAGAR, *Nova Scotia*

Half Dome-Mt. Watkins-El Capitan Blitz. In October Dean Potter and I became the first to climb three Grade VI Yosemite walls within 24 hours. We started on Half Dome's 2,000-foot Northwest Face. Approaching via the Death Slabs we arrived at the base at 7:00 a.m., rested, ate, and hydrated. We decided on a midmorning start in order to have daylight on The Nose, at the end of their marathon 24 hours. Blasting at 10:15 a.m. with a handful of cams and stoppers, I led the first of two blocks. Clipping only fixed anchors and other fixed gear, we simulclimbed to the Robbins Traverse. Potter swung into the lead as I prepared to jumar a fixed line. As I readied the jumars I hastily slapped the jug on the rope but neglected to engage the trigger. I watched it cascade 1,000 feet down the face. Undeterred, we barreled up the Zigzags, passing a party of Japanese, and topped the route in 2 hours and 12 minutes. We coiled the cord, shoed our feet, and sprinted down the cables and back to the base.

After recovering the dropped jumar from a bush and deeming it okay, we hastily descended the Death Slabs and jogged four miles up Tenaya Canyon to our next Grade VI, the South Face of Mt. Watkins. This would be our second time on the South Face, and again we planned on only two blocks to cover the 2,000+-foot wall. As the wall became shady I took the first lead, as it favored my free/aid style. We switched leads at the base of the crux aid pitch, as Potter grabbed the rack and launched into the remaining predominantly free pitches. We donned our headlamps on the last pitch, topping out in 5:15, creating a record in the process. Even though we had walked to the top of the formation the previous night to stash water and shoes, we became disoriented as we ran out to Highway 120, where Potter's rig was waiting. We burned a half-hour of precious time locating the faint trail. Upon reaching the van I reracked, Potter drove, and both of us devoured as many calories as possible in the 45-minute respite. Parking in El Cap Meadow under a star-filled sky, we had less than 10 hours remaining to ascend the longest of the walls. We chose The Nose as the finishing leg because of our familiarity with the route, this being our third time on it, and for its proximity to the road.

A team of Koreans was at the start of the first pitch just after midnight but kindly yielded the right-of-way. The Nose required four blocks, with me leading the first, to the pendulum at the top of Sickle Ledge. Due to extreme exhaustion, simulclimbing was kept to a minimum, and the majority of the route was short-fixed. With a #1 Camalot as the biggest piece Potter led the Stove Leg cracks, finishing his block on top of The Boot. In the middle of the Great Roof pitch the sky began to lighten as I closed in on Camp V. We passed a party of three at the Glowering Spot, and with Potter in the lead we simulaided out the summit headwall bolt ladder and collapsed on top. In 23 hours and 45 minutes we had climbed more than 80 pitches and 7,000 vertical feet.

TIM O'NEILL

El Capitan, Nose, speed record. On October 15 Dean Potter and I went sub-four hours on El Cap's 3,000-foot Nose, cleaving 23 minutes off the record of 4:22, set nearly a decade ago by Peter Croft and Hans Florine. This was our fourth ascent of the route together but our first time climbing it in daylight. We alternately led, in four leader blocks. With me taking the first block and Potter simulclimbing behind, we reached Sickle Ledge in less than 20 minutes. We switched leads for pitch six, above Sickle Ledge, and Potter swung into the Stoveleg Cracks. I lowered out with a 5-millimeter cord, and we simulclimbed through the Stovelegs. We had cut a 140-foot 10-mm rope specifically for the ascent. Potter rope-soloed the Boot, pitch 17, which marked the end of his block, as I simul climbed up the bolts below and waited until he pendulumed across the King Swing, snagging it first try. I then blasted toward Camp IV, short-fixing the rope at the end of the Lynn Hill traverse. Potter lowered out with the 5-mil, jumared the fixed line, popped the knots at the belay, and joined me as I wove my way through Camp IV to the Great Roof. As I jumped onto my trusty cam hooks at the apex of the arching roof, Potter slammed in a nest of camming units and hung tight till the rope was fixed and he could lower out. We simul-climbed through Camp V, using direct aid when necessary, and switched leads at the top of the Glowering Spot, pitch 26. Potter took us to the summit, short-fixing the majority of the upper pitches, with me jumaring maniacally behind. We simulaided out the headwall bolt ladder and tagged the top-out pine tree in 3:59:35. Haggard but grinning we had broken the greatest of the rad-dad, old-school speed records on El Capitan.

Two weeks later, on October 28, Hans Florine teamed with Jim Herson and took an additional two minutes off the record, coming in at 3:57:27. Potter and I answered back on November 2 by slashing off another 33 minutes, for the current record of 3:24:04.

TIM O'NEILL

El Capitan, Tempest. June 9, 1999: I am in a doubly overhanging dihedral, approaching The Eyrie. Lulled by the morning sun, I contemplate the sand running over my knee. Suddenly, the body-sized arrowhead flake I am hooking explodes out of the corner. The sharp edge of the block rolls over my stomach and in a haze of motion sails past Valerio Folco (CAI), who is oblivious, writing in his diary on the portaledge. I jumar past the tear in my lead line and tie in farther from the end. We camp at the Eyrie. To the east is a subtle buttress that is the most consistently steep feature we can see. We say nothing, the language barrier keeping talk to a minimum, but we each silently conclude that it will be our next adventure: a third ascent of Tempest. Information about Tempest was sketchy and hard to come-by. One person dismissed the route as a bolt ladder. Others claimed the route was one of great difficulty, having stymied many attempts, "the most sought-after route on the Captain." It turns out that the Tempest's first-ascent team (Jarrett, Hornibrook, and Lloyd, 1993) had previously done many big-wall FAs together. What impresses me about Tempest, in addition to the superb, audacious line, is the quality of the FA. The positioning of fixed belay anchors shows great skill and care. Where rivets exist, they are spaced at impressive distances, similar to Reticent Wall.

Val gave me the jobs of recruiting a third climber and finding a photographer. In October, as Bruce Bindner led the second pitch, Val remarked, "Bruce is the perfect wall climber." The three of us alternated leads. I wanted to lead the pitch called Tom, and Val wanted to lead Killer Whale. That made it easy to decide which pitches we would each lead. Jerry Dodrill and Marco Spataro filmed us on the initial pitches, and again at the top.

The route retains much of the character of a first ascent, with grassy cracks being commonplace. There is a lot of climbing up small (and very large!) detached features. Since there is as yet no published topo, I shouldn't say too much more. I think that Sea of Dreams will never be equaled when it comes to beauty of line and fun climbing, but Tempest stands out in that, along with Reticent, it will probably be one of the last independent lines created on El Capitan.

THOMAS I. MCMILLAN, *AAC*

El Capitan, Slacker's Toil. Slacker's Toil (VI 5.9 A5b) is a four-and-a-fourth-pitch variant to Surgeon General/Lunar Eclipse. My variation climbs an A5 pitch and an A4+ pitch on a super-loose feature, The Great Sword. I basically soloed the lower half of Surgeon General, including Eric Kohl's A5 crux pitch, then headed out right, then up into the Great Circle. After climbing Lunar Eclipse's Milky Way pitch, I climbed straight up to the Devil's Brow and off via Lunar Eclipse. My new A5 pitch and Kohl's old A5 pitch are both technically harder than the Reticent crux, but Reticent is longer and therefore harder.

JIM BEYER, *AAC*

El Capitan, El Corazon. On September 7 Max Reichel and I looked for a new free-climbable line on the southwest face of El Capitan. We found it and reached the top on September 14. We used aid on some sections during the first ascent but returned for a completely free ascent. We placed new bolts on belay stations but did no other bolting. Pitons and birdbeaks placed during the first ascent were left as protection for the free climb. I returned to the route three more times (six days, total) to work on free climbing certain pitches. On October 3 at 10 a.m. Max and I started, at the base of the Salathé, to redpoint the route in a single push. On the first day I climbed 17 pitches and bivied on the Gray Ledges. On the second day I climbed up to the Tower to the People. Then after an early start I reached the top on the third day at 9:45 a.m., having redpointed all 35 pitches in less than 48 hours.

The new line El Corazon combines the Salathé, Albatross, Son of Heart, and Heart routes, plus some established variations that link the freeable sections of the existing routes. The Heart is the most obvious feature on El Capitan, marking the center of the southwest face. Through the middle of the Heart goes the classic aid route Son of Heart, known for its frightening, claustrophobic chimneys. For 300 meters this corner-and-chimney system rips through the overhanging wall above the Heart, making it a natural line for free climbing. But the giant roof of the Heart itself seemed to be an insurmountable obstacle. The solution is Albatross, which passes the very right edge of the Heart to a traverse up and left leading back to Son of Heart, which you join 100 meters above the overhangs of the Heart.

ALEXANDER HUBER, *Germany*

Super Nova Area, High Line. On March 20, 2000, in the Super Nova Area near the Rostrum, Ammon McNeely, and Cedar Wright established High Line (VI 5.10R A4). The route is located between Crack the Whip and Dime Bag. The climbers report "This route has a little of everything. Do not attempt it unless you are a very experienced wall climber. The crux is on almost every pitch. Tons of beaking, including the Squeakin' by Beakin' pitch, which starts with a 20-foot roof in which it takes hours to get peckers tied off at the eye hole to stick, and if they don't, you get slammed into the wall. Don't forget to mention the death blocks that are lurking on the last three pitches. Overall, it's a classic."

AMMON MCNEELY AND WWW.ROCKANDICE.COM (NEW ROUTES PAGE)

SIERRA NEVADA

Incredible Hulk, Doodad, Mt. Bandaloo (Pt 10,002'). Between August 2 and August 22 I traversed the Sierra Nevada from Twin Meadows to Hetch Hetchy, via Matterhorn Canyon and the Grand Canyon of the Tuolumne River, with members of the dance troupe Project Bandaloop, at times numbering as many as 12. On August 3 Heather Baer, Greg Bernstein, and I climbed the red dihedral on the Incredible Hulk, a great route with an amazing crux pitch up a vertical corner. On August 9 six of us climbed the normal route on the Doodad, then four members danced a quartet on the south face of this outstanding Sierra pinnacle. Next, we found an overhanging crack on the spire's north face, which I led and named Fractal Wind Currents (5.11a). Over the next two days all members of our troupe climbed Matterhorn Peak by the normal route. In lower Matterhorn Canyon, during a recon, I had spied a beautiful dome that we christened Mt. Bandaloop. This appears on maps as Point 10,002, one-half mile southwest of Miller Lake. It is almost 10,002 feet high and mostly vertical, but I could find no trace of recorded climbing activity. During August 12 and 13 Jeff Schoen, Deb Wolfe, Heather Baer, and I made the first ascent of the west face (5.10, A1). The crux was a 150-foot vertical crack splitting a wave of glacial polish. Because of vegetation we were unable to free this one section. We called the route Who's Your Doodaddy? In the third week of September, I made the 20-mile approach with Greg Sonagere and Heather Baer, and, after some scrubbing, freed this stellar crack at 5.12a. It is the most stunning splitter I have seen in the Sierra backcountry. Our Bandaloop group continued our journey, which included a wild eight-person vertical dance performance off the summit of Wildcat Point and a wonderful wet journey down the Muir Gorge of the Tuolumne River.

STEVE SCHNEIDER, *AAC*

Conness, Plan B. In June Paul Teare and I went in to Conness with a plan to climb the Harding Route, while keeping a keen eye on the possibility of something new. We realized our fate when we saw two climbers above us heading toward the Harding Route. Something new it would be. We were drawn to two prominent orange corners at about midheight on the right side of the southwest face. A short first pitch up a right-facing corner puts you at the base of a beautiful dogleg finger crack. Another easy pitch up and left aligns you with the leftmost of the two prominent right-facing corners. A short undercling and funky lieback on featured, clean rock takes you to the corner. From the top of the corner, an undercling left puts you on a nice ledge. Follow the ledge right for about 60 feet until you reach a thin crack leading to a small, steep left-facing corner. This steep corner ends for 10 feet and begins again higher. Linking this gap with very interesting face climbing is the crux of the route. This route is very clean and well worth repeating. After returning home and researching Conness, we found that the prominent corner to the right, which shares the same dogleg crack, is the Rosy Crown Route, which also looks great. Our route, Plan B (V 5.11-), is seven mostly 60-meter pitches.

JIMMY HADEN

Tehipite Dome, Wall of Ages. Last summer John Fehrman, Bryan Sweeney, and I completed a route (Wall of Ages V-VI 5.11+ A0) up the main south face of this magnificent dome in Kings Canyon

National Park. This three-year project had involved Richard Leversee, Mike Davis, Scott Thelen, and Brandon Thau on two previous forays. While the route can be approached from the valley floor, it is in the best interests of future parties to rap the route and climb out. The climb is 23 pitches long, free at mostly 5.10-5.11, except for one short tension traverse and one short bolt ladder that spans a blank bulge. A spacious wooded ledge, Sherwood Forest, offers bivy options at the midpoint, though the final complete ascent was done in a long day. There are now several independent finishes on the upper section of the formation that alone are worth the hike in.

DAVE NETTLE

Citadel, Nothing But Time. On September 2 Jimmy Haden and Michael Pennings climbed a new route on the north face of the Citadel. Their route, Nothing But Time (IV 5.10+) starts just right of the low point of the face and climbs the leftmost of three parallel cracks through an obvious, large roof.

MICHAEL PENNINGS

Angel Wings, South Arête, Original Route. In February 2002 Jason Magness and I made what we believe was the first winter ascent of the South Arête of Angel Wings, in Sequoia National Park. After an 18-mile snowshoe approach, we pulled off our plastic boots, put on the rock shoes, and started climbing 5.10 off the snow. The route is on clean, golden Yosemite-like granite and follows a nearly continuous crack system, all the way up to the 5.11+ Black Roof.

We led in blocks, French freeing when necessary for speed, and my leads got us to the Black Roof. Jason Magness then took over and with a few pulls got through the roof and traversed straight right to a chimney. The chimney, presumably dry in summer, was a raging creek. On sparse and marginal pro, Jason ascended the chimney with his back pressed against the wall, water cascading over his back. When I reached his belay, Jason poured so much water from our only chalk bag I expected to see fish.

A wet sitting bivy ensued, and by the next morning we were eager to reach dry ground. We decided the Rowell-Jones 1971 line (V 5.11+) would offer the quickest way to the summit plateau. Full of ice, flowing water, and squeeze chimneys, it was the wrong choice. Without an axe or crampons I tried to chimney above the ice in plastic boots, eventually wriggling out of the chimneys, after two pitches, into a lower-angle gully filled with snow. The ice I knocked down shredded the ropes and nearly took out Jason. Finally we emerged from the gully and after a rappel and another gully attained the summit plateau.

CRAIG CLARENCE, *AAC*

Mt. Stewart, Patterson Bluff, Amphitheater Wall, Arctic Lake Wall, Mt. Newcomb. Mike Pennings and I established a direct line (Fallen Angels, IV 5.10+) to the west summit on the north face of Mt. Stewart, following a prominent crack system that widens enough at one point to inspire the pitch name The Sleeping Bag Simulator. The climbing is on clean, solid rock, and most of the ten pitches are consistent 5.10.

Brandon Thau, Joe Reichert, and I linked up ten long pitches of steep, sustained free climbing with a short bolt ladder (perhaps freeable face climbing) on Patterson Bluff. Our

on a small buttress, between The Crystal Line and Times Lost. A bolt 15 feet off the ground marks the start. Pitch 1: Climb the buttress (5.6) to a tree-covered ledge. Pitch 2: From the left end of the ledge climb up and left past two bolts to a clean right-facing dihedral. At the top of the dihedral move right through overlaps past three bolts (5.10) to a leaning, left-facing dihedral. Belay at its top. Pitch 3: A short 5.7 crack leads to a large left-leaning ramp. Climb above the ramp, trending up and right to a circular break in the horizontal roof that forms the bottom of the large headwall in the middle of the face. Pitch 4: Move over the bolt-protected roof (5.10a), then connect cracks and seams to a ledge with a pine tree in the middle of the headwall. Pitch 5: Climb straight up to a mantle, then left on a dike, and surmount a bulge, passing two bolts. A right-facing dihedral takes gear well but closes down for the final 5.10 move off the headwall. This brings you to a large sloping ledge, I'itoi's Patio. Pitch 6: Scramble up easy ground for a full pitch, trending left towards an obvious water stain. Pitch 7: Climb a crack and pass four bolts on an arête left of the stain to a ledge with large oaks. (Note: You may be able to scramble to the summit by climbing the tree filled gully left of this pitch.) Pitch 8: Move right out onto the face, passing some flakes (5.6), to a large ramp and cross the route Born of Water. Pitch 9: Instead of climbing the ramp head straight up to an undercling/overhang (5.6). Up and right leads to the summit plateau. Bring a full rack of cams, nuts, and slings. Tri-cams may be helpful.

MIKE STRASSMAN

Baboquivari Peak, Cloud Man Got Angry. In March Jackie Carroll and I added a four-pitch variation, Cloud Man Got Angry, to Born of Water. The variation is definitely a better alternative. Start 30 feet right of Born of Water and slightly downhill, in a vertical open book. Pitch 1: Climb the book and, passing cactus, head to another dihedral, which has grass in it. Passing a few bolts (5.9) gets you to an excellent finger crack in the dihedral. Belay on a ledge at the top. Pitch 2: Climb straight up and pass a roof on its right (5.9). Weave up ledges past a bolt to a belay stance. Pitch 3: Climb past nine bolts to a water groove. Belay at its top. Pitch 4: Follow 10 bolts out and left on steep rock with great holds. A 5.10a friction move ends the difficulties at a ledge called I'itoi's Balcony. The fourth pitch can be climbed without trad gear if you are comfortable on easy runouts. From the left end of the Balcony, join the 5.7 dike pitch (pitch five) of Born of Water.

MIKE STRASSMAN

Utah

WASATCH MOUNTAINS

Devil's Castle, Evil Eye In September Glen Henshaw, Jonathan Smoot, and I climbed a new route on the 800-foot north face of Devil's Castle in the Wasatch Mountains. Beginning at the lowest point of the face we ascended indistinct cracks 120 feet right of the Black Streak. The climb, Evil Eye, is seven pitches long (up to 5.9R), involving sections of good and bad rock.

BRIAN SMOOT

DESERT

The Desert, Various Activity. In Canyonlands National Park two new routes were established in the remote Dabneyland. Says Steve "Crusher" Bartlett, "These towers are named after Walt Dabney, the park superintendent who instigated the strict climbing regulations in Canyonlands in 1995." One of the new routes, Chocolate Starfish, was aided solo by Bartlett in the spring. The route traverses a 120-foot, A1+ horizontal roof crack—perhaps the longest roof crack in the U.S., surpassing the popular 80-foot Crackhouse in the Gemini Bridges area near Moab. The other route, Northern Frights (5.11), was climbed by Bartlett, Ralph Ferrara, and Eve Tallman in March. The tower is located south of the various captain formations, about halfway between Monument Basin and White Crack Campground.

On the north face of Zeus in Taylor Canyon, Jason Jones and Nick Branscomb established a four-pitch new route, Seraphim (5.9 C2), which was mostly aid, probably during the year 2000. In April 2001 Jim Beyer soloed Cult of Suicidal (VI A6a 5.9) on the west face of Outlaw Spire. Three bolts were placed on the four-pitch route, which sports a 90-foot runout with ground-fall danger on the crux second pitch.

In remote Crips Hole west of the Gemini Bridges on the Island-in-the-Sky, Andrey's Tower was climbed in July by Jimmy Dunn, Hellen Heaven, Billy Rothstein, and Danny McCann. The 250-foot spire was named in honor of Andrey Barbashinov, a mountain guide from Kazakhstan, who was visiting the U.S. on the Anatoli Boukreev exchange program. Andrey, the first person to summit Denali in 2001, was so excited about climbing in Canyonlands that he rescheduled his flight home in order to meet Jimmy Dunn in Moab. While driving south from Wyoming on a motorcycle, he was killed when a truck hit him. The Russians Are Coming was climbed free at 5.10+.

A dramatic tyrollean traverse was made on Frog on a Lily Pad—from the frog to the lily pad. The frog and the lily pad are landforms that tower over the west edge of Moab Valley just above where the Colorado River leaves the Moab Valley and enters the canyons. The first ascent was made by Chris Kelly and Lee Kelly in March.

On the Island in the Sky Paul Ross and Colin Downer established Keswick Lads' Day Out on the 280-foot Tombstone. The 5.10, C3 route ascends the tower's east face, one crack system left of Family Plot. Both climbers come from the town of Keswick in the English Lake District. In June, in the same area, Ross and Jeff Pheasant put up Pearly Gates (250' 5.5 C1) on Lost World Butte. The route faces south and is located right of Gateway to the Lost World. Ross says, "One of the easiest climbs in the desert, and it takes one to the top of a beautiful butte with excellent views." Lost World Butte is just over one mile north of the Tombstone. Also on the butte, in November, Ross and Layne Potter established If (named for a Rudyard Kipling poem). The route ascends an east-facing crack system at the west end of the butte (260' 5.9 C3). Paradise Lost (a.k.a. Kipling Groove) was established on the butte between Mirage Crack and Gateway to the Lost World (320' 5.7 C2), by Ross and Layne Potter in October. A final route, Road Not Taken, was established on the butte in November and ascends cracks right of If. The route, named for a Robert Frost poem, is a 300-foot climb rated 5.10.

On Castleton Tower Paul Ross and Jeff Pheasant introduced girdle traversing to the Colorado Plateau when they established the Bjørnstad Traverse (a.k.a. Girdle Traverse of Castleton Tower) April 13-14. The route is 900 feet long (9 pitches, IV 5.10 C2). The climb begins and ends at the

Kor-Ingalls south face route and uses four pitches from established routes and five new pitches.

On the Ruminator Tower in the Lake Powell area, Eve Tallman and Ralph Ferrara established Captain Piggly Wiggly (5.10+R) in September. The tower is 200 feet high and is climbed from the north side. Its location is approximately three-fourths of a mile east of the Hite Marina turnoff from Utah 95.

In the North San Rafael Swell, Mallory's Mountain Marmalade (a.k.a. 3M) was established on Outhouse Tower in April 2001 by James Garrett and Sheridan Potter. The route ascends the 200-foot spire left of Chopped Sand, climbing the middle of the south face at 5.9 A1+. On James' Tower (a.k.a. The Light Bulb) Chris Andrews and Mark Rosbrook established Sheepish Stair (310', 4 pitches, 5.10 A2+). The route begins opposite the original ascent line. The team also climbed a 5.9 one-pitch variation they dubbed No Name Woman, which begins one crack system left of Sheepish Stair. The spire is obvious high on the west Wingate buttress 0.8 mile up Buckhorn Wash from the San Rafael River BLM campground.

On Towers of the Virgin in Zion National Park in April, Craig Luebben and Mark Beardsley established a major new line up the Towers of the Virgin: Chainsaw (1600', 11 pitches, V 5.11R). Attempts had been made on the route by Luebben with Paul Midkiff in 1985, with Beardsley in 1992, and with Silvia Luebben in 1997. To reach it, park near the maintenance facility behind the old visitors' center and walk to the end of the road. Follow Oak Creek upstream, taking the right fork. Pass waterfalls on the right and continue up a sandy, brushy hill to the right for about 500 feet to the start of the climb. This is an area left of Nu Gah's Wall. In May Ammon McNeely soloed Space Shot (V 5.10 C2) in 3 hours and 57 minutes, likely the fastest solo.

COMPILED PRIMARILY BY ERIC BJØRNSTAD, *AAC*

Canyonlands, San Rafael Slabs. Located 15 miles west of Green River, Utah, just south of I-70, a new climbing area has been opened on the Eastern Reef of the San Rafael Swell. Paul Ross and Layne Potter have made four new routes, ranging from 1,200 to 1,800 feet in length, up to 5.9 in difficulty. For those who need a change from strenuous vertical cracks, these open slabs provide fine situations, a feel of mountaineering, and great views toward the La Sal Mountains and Canyonlands. The rock is sandstone and surprisingly sound. The quality of these slab routes, in particular Surfing the Swell (1400' 5.9R) and Reefer Madness (1800' 5.9R), is comparable to the best granite slab routes of Whitehorse Ledge in New Hampshire. Protection, however, is sparse and confidence on slabs is a benefit. The descents from the routes climbed so far have been back down the ascent route, as the summits of these slabs overhang the canyons behind by about 400 feet.

PAUL ROSS

San Rafael Swell, Cinquenta Tower. On November 3, the day after my 50th birthday, Tim Toula and I made the first ascent of this tower. Paul Ross and I had climbed the first two pitches the day before. The flat-topped tower is located on the north side of the San Rafael River, across from Mexican Mountain and El Sombrero, and can be reached by hiking the closed, unimproved road for about two miles from the gate (before the abandoned airstrip). The four-pitch route (III /IV 5.10 A1) ascends the left side of the south face to bolted belay ledges. The final pitch is an overhanging hand crack that spit out Texas Tower Tim Toula, giving it the A1 rating. A great tower summit with views in all directions!

JAMES GARRETT, *AAC*

ZION NATIONAL PARK

West Temple, Full Steam Ahead. Between Gettin' More Western and Back Where It All Begins, this route climbs 13 new 60-meter pitches to join Back Where It All Begins for a final three pitches to the summit. It was soloed on January 10, 1999, by Ammon McNeely and graded VI 5.10 A4. The first and fifth pitches are the cruxes, with ledge- and ground-fall potential. McNeely writes, "Placements are fragile and the route should only be attempted by an experienced sandstone wall climber." A topo was left at the visitors' center.

FROM WWW.ROCKANDICE.COM (NEW ROUTES PAGE)

Colorado

Seven Castles Area, Under A Winter Sky. On January 5 I soloed a four-pitch route in the Seven Castles area north of Basalt. Under A Winter Sky (III 5.9X) climbs the main chimney system on the left side of the wall. It then breaks left to gain the prominent stepped corner system. It continues up the corner system for two more interesting pitches. I descended by rappelling the route. The Seven Castles area consists of many 180-meter walls beckoning to be climbed.

JOSH GROSS, *AAC*

ROCKY MOUNTAIN NATIONAL PARK

Otis Peak, various new routes. On the south face of Otis Peak, just west of the Otis Flower Tower, we climbed what we think are a number of new routes. If you see the area, you will understand why it is hard to identify specific formations—there are so many! With Joe Vallone, Bill McKnight, Vladimir Broz, and Mark Hammond, I put up five routes of grades II and III ranging from 5.8 to 5.11R.

KEITH GARVEY

Long's Peak, The Diamond, Bright Star. Bright Star was first climbed by Ed Webster and named in honor of Lauren Husted. A variation was free climbed by Charlie Fowler and Scott Cosgrove, but they avoided the meat of the route. Cameron Tague and I followed the original Bright Star a pitch farther in 2000, eventually joining The Yellow Wall. Last August I recruited Roger Briggs, the Diamond master who was celebrating his 50th birthday and 89th ascent of the wall that summer. All nine pitches of Bright Star are sustained and somewhat runout 5.11+. Cameron had fallen to his death crossing Broadway, below the wall, a few weeks after our climb in 2000, but his confident image was with me every move of what even Roger feels is one of the finest climbs on the wall. We left the Bright Star name, but added Cameron's name to the list of Bright Stars.

TOPHER DONAHUE

Long's Peak, The Diamond, The Honeymoon is Over. For the past two years fellow Diamond lover Eric Doub had been calling and sending topos of a possible 5.13 on the Diamond of Long's Peak. He'd put considerable work into the project, which he'd named The Honeymoon is Over. He told me of clean, steep rock, devious cracks, thin faces, and just about everything else that a climber dreams about. It sounded like this route had it all. Since my first experience on the Diamond at the age of 12, I had gained great respect for this wall. Sudden thunderstorms and high altitude make any route an adventure. With these elements added in, a route such as Eric's seemed quite intimidating. But with the Diamond staring at me through my back door, I had to give it a try. In early June my dad and I hiked up to the route. Being a former guide on the Diamond and a long-time climbing partner, my dad had as much enthusiasm for the route as I did. Starting at 2 a.m. we got to the base just before first light. After climbing the fourth-class North Chimney, we arrived on Broadway with plenty of daylight ahead of us. However, early season conditions turned the route into a waterfall. After five pitches we headed back to the comfort of home.

For a month and a half I thought about the climb. I had not seen the entire route, but what I had climbed was everything Eric had said it would be. In late July I headed up again. After wearing my dad out the first time, I chose as my partner the next obvious choice, my girl-friend Beth Rodden. Although never having been at 14,000 feet or climbing in an alpine environment, she was excited about going up there. Getting on Broadway at first light again, we had a full day ahead of us. The wall was much drier than before, and it looked like a great day for free climbing. The plan was for me to lead each pitch and for Beth to jumar with the pack. The first four pitches (shared with Eroica, followed by five independent pitches) were straightforward and went quickly. The next two pitches were the crux and took everything I had. Little did I know that climbing 5.13 near 14,000 feet would be so taxing. Luckily, it was a weekend, and we were not alone. Shouts from nearby climbers, hikers, and especially Beth gave me the motivation to send. The next two pitches took the rest of my energy. I nearly fell countless times, and the only thing holding me to the rock were shouts of encouragement from below. With only a 5.12 pitch left I was completely exhausted.

After a rest and more encouragement from Beth, I couldn't turn back. As I started climbing, my arm cramped every time I bent it. Each crack looked like a dead end, and I could not find a line that seemed to make sense. I wandered over the face for a long time until I spied a camouflaged bolt and a fixed nut, both from Eric's attempts. They tipped me off as to where I should go. I hit the highest point of the Diamond just as my gas tank hit empty. My screams of success were carried off by the wind.

TOMMY CALDWELL, *AAC*

BLACK CANYON OF THE GUNNISON

North Chasm View Wall, Roasted Pork. In September Nick Meyer and I made the first ascent of Roasted Pork (IV 5.11 A1) on the far left side of the North Chasm View Wall. We approached the climb by descending the Cruise Gully. We then skirted the entire North Chasm View Wall and climbed the gully used to approach A Moveable Feast. A detailed description of this approach can be found in Black Canyon Rock Climbs. We climbed the gully for 100 feet on fourth-class rock. On the left is a large slab, which we continued up with some 5.9 climbing. At the top of this slab we noted a stuck rope and several cams that had apparently been left as rappel anchors. It appears that the party before us retreated below a pegmatite band on the second pitch. We climbed through the horrendously rotten peg band via unprotected free climbing and aid. From the top of the pegmatite the route continues into a steep 5.11 corner and then into another difficult thin crack. We resorted to several moves of aid on this pitch. Once easier ground was gained, we traversed to the right on pegmatite to access a prominent corner system. We followed this corner for several pitches to an overhanging finger crack. We chose not to climb this crack, as it was full of hundreds of wasps. Instead we down climbed and tensioned to the right to gain a right-facing corner system. We followed the corner for several hundred feet to a large undercling flake and followed it to the top. We thought we had joined No Pig Deal for its final pitch, but after speaking with Jonnathan Copp, we think that the routes are independent lines.

ROBBIE WILLIAMS

North Chasm View Wall, Rotten Piggy. In September Chris Kruthaupt and I climbed the new route Rotten Piggy between No Pig Left and No Pig Deal. It begins in a large gully/chimney system 100 feet to the right of the Comic Relief buttress. Ascend the vegetated gully via third-class climbing for 500 feet to gain a large ledge. From this stance climb up and right in a hand crack with big loose blocks to a spacious ledge. Traverse directly to the left and up to another ledge. Move right, traversing and down climbing, to gain a deep chimney. Climb this evil-looking chimney with poor protection and loose rock for two pitches. Near its top exit right to gain better rock and more enjoyable climbing. From the top of this chimney the climb wanders from system to system, generally trending right. I believe the route crosses No Pig Left and then continues up between No Pig Left and No Pig Deal.

ROBBIE WILLIAMS

Painted Wall, Journey Through Mirkwood. In August Jonathan Copp and I descended the S.O.B. Gully at 3:00 a.m. hoping to make the first free ascent of Journey Through Mirkwood on the Painted Wall. This 2,000-foot route was one of the few older routes on the Painted Wall that had not been free climbed. Tom Pulaski, Jimmy Newberry, John Pearson, and John Rosholt made the first ascent over three days in 1977. For many years it saw few ascents. As we descended the S.O.B Gully first light awakened the canyon, and dawn illuminated the aptly named Painted Wall looming above us, dubbed for the many rotten pegmatite bands scarring its face. The pegmatite may compromise the rock's structural integrity, but it gives it the flavor and excitement of no other rock wall. Jonathan and I began our climb at first light, simulclimbing the first three pitches. We carried only a rope and a small rack. Several more long, moderate pitches took us to just below the crux of the route, the Roofs of Mordor. This was the only section of the route that we were unsure about climbing without aid. I stared up at the roofs, a bit intimidated, but as Jonathan climbed to the belay he had the look in his eye! I knew we would not only finish the climb in a day, but it would go free. Jonathan took the sharp end, making short work of the crux pitch. The climbing through the roofs was gymnastic and powerful. Climbing through the final moves near the top of the overhang, Jonathan's feet cut loose, forcing him to climb on small holds hanging from his hands. Somehow he held on, and as I yelled up encouragement, I wondered if I would be able to get up this pitch. When I arrived at the belay, I applauded his

Andy Donson in the Black Hole, South Chasm View Wall, Black Canyon of the Gunnison. *Jonathan Copp*

impressive lead, and we both screamed with excitement. Regardless of our sense of accomplishment, we still had over 1,200 feet to go and not a lot of daylight. Luckily, the climbing above was relatively moderate, and we were able to finish in four long pitches. We were happy to have completed the first free ascent of a climb on the Painted Wall, without fixing ropes, working pitches, or adding bolts.

ROBBIE WILLIAMS

South Chasm View Wall, The Black Hole. After years of longing gazes and idle dreaming, Jonathan Copp and I found ourselves looking up with apprehension at the vast leaning dihedral of The Black Hole (ca 2,000' V+ 5.12b). A wide crack, at first green with slime, continued up to a large roof about 400 feet up. This feature, which looms over the lush meadow at the base of the South Chasm View Wall, had repelled attempts by a number of suitors, earning the title The Janitor's Victim's Corner. We had obtained this worrying information, along with a crucial Big Bro, from Jeff Achey over breakfast an hour earlier.

Things started badly. Fifteen feet off the deck I was pumped silly and about to call it a day. However, a more direct approach—taking the slime head on—paid off, and I soon found myself, coated in green paste, belaying off the fixed hex that marked the high point of earlier attempts. The next two pitches of offwidth were dirty but dry. This short day climaxed in a roof crack demanding wide hands, wide stems, and our remaining drive. We fixed our 60-meter lines end-to-end from a small ledge above the roof and just made it down to the slabs above the meadow. We recrossed the river and hiked back up to the north rim for a brew and some sleep.

On the following morning, May 27, we were back at our high point. The pitches from here to the rim were a huge contrast to the horrors below. No wideness, just perfect clean rock, allowed us to run out rope-stretching pitches. One notable pitch had us contemplating retreat, but we got lucky. An overhanging flared seam, more akin to a pitch on the Squamish Chief than in the Black, succumbed to an improbable lieback sequence and became the second crux of the route. The hard climbing ended at the upper meadow, where we traversed left to join the last pitches of Astrodog. Thanks to Ralph Burns for saving our arses and driving us back to the North Rim.

We abandoned the bolt kit with our packs at the bottom of the route, through laziness rather than ethics, and got lucky. However, if you're planning on trying one of the other unclimbed lines in the vicinity, you'll probably be psyched to bring the kit along.

ANDY DONSON, *ex-pat United Kingdom*

South Chasm View Wall, Goldberg Special, Shadowboxing. During two days in October Heidi Wirtz and I free climbed the lower part of the Goldberg Special on South Chasm View Wall, joining Astrodog for the upper pitches. The crux A3 aid pitch went free at around 5.13- and required triples of the .00 TCU. It's likely the first 5.13 in this adventurous canyon. A few weeks later I returned with Jared Ogden and added a direct finish to the upper pitches of a mysterious aid route. After replacing a couple of 1/4-inch bolts, we climbed the 12-pitch line we call Shadowboxing, starting with the Goldberg Special crux and ending with a 5.12 direct finish that entails huge fall potential in 5.10 and 5.11 terrain.

TOPHER DONAHUE

Stay Puft Buttress. The Stay Puft Buttress (1,700' V 5.10 A1) was established by Josh Borof and Paul Emrick on June 19, in scorching hot weather. The route starts on top of the huge boulder about 400 feet from the river in the S.F.O.B. Gully and ascends the first buttress downstream of the South Chasm View Wall. The lower portion features shade, nice cracks, and a 50-foot runout 5.7 slab off the belay. Higher, the route swings onto the sunny west face and involves a 15-foot section of dirty A1. Cleaned it should go at mid-5.12. The main theme of the route is mossy 5.10 offwidths, so stay puft.

JOSH BOROF

Wyoming

GRAND TETON NATIONAL PARK

Mount Owen, North Face. On August 15 Tobey Carmen, Eric Draper, and I climbed a probable new route (IV/V 5.9) on the north face of Mt. Owen. We began climbing a hundred feet or so to the west of the lowest point of rock on the north face. We belayed about ten pitches of 5.9 and easier climbing, through mostly clean and enjoyable rock, from the ground to the point where we joined the established North Ridge Route and continued to the summit. It took us roughly 20 hours to complete the ascent and descent, car to car.

NATHAN BROWN

SOUTH FORK OF SHOSHONE RIVER

South Fork Ice Routes. In April 1999, while flying over the South Fork near Cody, I discovered a new arena of ice. A day later we began the epic approach, six miles into the Shoshone Wilderness. We named the first and largest amphitheater Garden of the Gods; it hosts one of the largest concentration of icefalls on the South Fork. Andy Cowan and I spent two days climbing in the area, establishing new routes in the Garden of the Gods and Garden of Eden amphitheaters. All routes were between WI3 and WI5+. The remoteness and commitment level kept me out of the area for another year. I returned in January 2001 with Solon Linton, Kristine and Cole of Missoula, and Mike Snyder from Cody and established more great, pure lines. The climbing is some of the best I have ever done, and the ice is just plain big! During the past two trips the following routes have been established: Sucker Love (WI5), Forbidden Fruit (WI4), Redemption (WI5), Revelations (WI5), Wet Dreams (WI5), and Tales from the Crypt (WI3). The climbs range from one to four pitches. With so much ice still to be pursued, there's no doubt that new routes will continue to go up for many years, along with a few great mixed climbs.

With the last few years being very dry, Cody locals have ventured farther into the South Fork's depths. First ascents are limitless for those who want to get in there and get after 'em. New routes are going up all the time, such as Spying and Flying (7 pitches, WI5), Wyoming Rodeo (WI5 M5), Top Hooker (3 pitches, WI5), Roeshamboe (WI5), and Dragon's Tail (WI5+). These are just a few routes established by Mark Devries and me. Photos and route descriptions can be found at www.coldfear.com.

AARON MULKEY

WIND RIVER MOUNTAINS

Squaretop, East Face, The Miscreant Line and The Conveyor Belt. Two routes were established in August 2000 by Tod Anderson, Skyler Crane, James Donnell, and Ernest Moskovics on the left side of the east face of Squaretop. The lines, climbed by different pairs, are predominantly independent and about V 5.10d. Both routes follow right-leaning cracks and dihedrals for 18 pitches (2,200'). At the end of the tenth pitches, the climbers bivouacked. The climbing is reportedly excellent, on solid rock with generally good pro.

WWW.ROCKANDICE.COM (NEW ROUTES PAGE)

Mt. Hooker, Loaded for Bear. I wasn't sure if I'd get my Czech friend Jakub Gajda to accompany me on another climbing trip, and I wasn't sure that I was ready for another adventure. But by June I was excited for another trip. It had to be short and cheap, since I only had ten days off work and very little dinero. I turned my attention toward an unclimbed feature I had seen in the Wind River Range—Mt. Hooker's east face. The east face is separated from Hooker's better-known northeast face by a broad couloir. The face comes to a point with diving-board overhangs. Its shallow grooves would be ideal for Jakub to practice his newly acquired skill of placing heads.

We rented a horse for the gear and hiked 18 miles to a lake, just off the Bear's Ears Trail, at the base of the awesome feature. From our camp on top of a big flat rock, we scoped a great line that split the wall. The highlight was what looked to be a succulent hand-crack that ran for two full pitches just below the blocky tip. We fixed two lines over the bottom slab pitches, which Jakub described as some of the most fun friction he had ever done. The next morning we packed the haulbag and headed up. Jakub's memory must have been giving him hunger flashbacks, for although the wall was only 1,200 feet high, he wouldn't stop packing until the huge bag was bursting.

The alpine granite was spectacular. The third and fourth pitches were beautiful shallow grooves that required several 'biners worth of heads. Lugging our massive bag-o-rations we moved steadily. A small traverse at the top of pitch four brought us to the bottom of what we'd thought was the great hand crack. "Oh sheet," said Jakub. "Hand crack, my azz." The crack turned out to be a nasty little offwidth. We suffered through that evening and into the morning before we perched below the summit overhangs. I led the last pitch over the upside down stairs, and finally a heart-stopping mantle put us on the summit.

We unpacked the haulbag and noticed that we still had five beers, three-quarters of a pack of Oreos, a tin of sardines, cheese, and ten liters of water. We had gone heavy; we had gone Loaded for Bear (V 5.9 A3).

BRENT EDELEN, *AAC*

Mt. Hooker, Pay to Play. On their first trip to the Wind River Range in late August, Chattanooga climbers Jim Hewett and Neeld "Off the Couch" Messler established a new route on the Northeast Face of Mount Hooker. In nine free pitches and four of aid, Pay to Play (VI 5.11 A3) ascends the face between Brain Larceny and Red Light District, continuing straight up from Der Main Ledge to the top. It was completed over five days of climbing in good weather, with the team enjoying about four hours of sunlight each day.

A day of scoping revealed many potential lines. A distinct roof crack attracted the team's attention, along with a line of corners and cracks with just one blank section. Pitches one through three climb moderate cracks topped by an awkward 5.9 squeeze/offwidth. Pitch four, the free-climbing crux of the route, blasts through the offwidth roof crack and up a lower-angle squeeze to the bottom of the blank section. The next pitch involves slabby face climbing, protected by two 5/16-inch buttonheads. The sixth pitch and aid crux comes next, a seam with thin nailing to a string of bat-hook holes, protected by one rivet, that leads up and right to the next feature.

The left-facing dihedral of the seventh pitch continues to arch left until it becomes the traversing roof beneath the eighth pitch. Two crack pitches then gain Der Main Ledge. The eleventh pitch traverses up and left to gain the left-facing corner that leads to the top in two final pitches.

The climbing is, for the most part, straightforward and enjoyable, though there are some loose sections. More good routes await climbers willing to brave the inconvenient approach and possible bad weather.

JIM HEWETT

Cathedral Buttress, Northeast Face, The Flight of the Golden Camalot. Around to the right from the Orion's Reflection wall is more good rock, though the wall is not as high. There Jason Keith and Alan Hunt established The Flight of the Golden Camalot (IV 5.11). The route begins with a ramp, followed by a step left. Pitch two ascends steep cracks. A hand traverse left (5.10+)

avoids an offwidth. The route's crux is a 5.11 finger crack in a corner. Above are occasional 5.10 and much high-quality 5.8.

JOE KELSEY

Cirque of the Towers, Warrior I, Northwest Face. In late August Brian Edmiston and I, both from Carbondale, Colorado, freed the 60-foot A3 hook traverse on the stunning 1,000-foot Northwest Face route on Warrior I at IV 5.11R. No bolts or pins were placed. First climbed in 1970 by George Lowe and Jeff Lowe at IV 5.9 A3, the Northwest Face involves mostly straight-forward jamming on stellar battleship-gray granite. I took one 25-foot penduluming leader fall on the crux second-pitch (the site of the hook traverse) and returned to the belay before heading back up to link the delicate edge sequence together. Although the climbing is otherwise not difficult (5.9 with two small sections of 5.10), and the upper dihedral is one of the most commanding features in the Cirque, neither of us could find any information about previous free ascents of this outstanding route.

JONATHAN THESENGA

Cirque of the Towers, solo traverse. Squinting into the sun, I stood on the top of War Bonnet gazing across at what I had just traversed, the Cirque of the Towers in the Wind River Mountains. Above me cumulus clouds benignly drifted by, resisting the afternoon weather pattern that usually transforms them into angry thunderheads. Two weeks before, after climbing the classic War Bonnet route Black Elk, I was zapped by lightning. Today I was suffering from another environmental hazard, severe dehydration.

From a climber's perspective the Cirque of the Towers is the most impressive feature in the Winds. In a three-mile semicircle that rises above picturesque Lonesome Lake to elevations as high as 12,406 feet, the 11 granite spires contain a perfect blend of cracks, edges, and friction.

Much of what has been climbed in the Winds has been loosely recorded and often under-rated. For all I knew Fritz Wiessner had done the Traverse in the 1930s wearing hob-nailed boots. I decided to add the modern car-to-car element, which added 16 miles to the adventure.

On August 14 I left the Big Sandy trailhead at 2:00 a.m. I arrived at the base of Pingora as it was getting light and followed the South Buttress to the summit. I rappelled to the notch to the west of Pingora and climbed the classic East Ridge of Wolf's Head. I continued to Overhanging Tower, Shark's Nose, Block Tower, and WatchTower. I chose the path of least resistance, soloing some established routes and improvising other routes. I descended by both down climbing and rappelling. The rest of the traverse is a scramble over the summits of South Watch Tower, Pylon Peak, Warrior II, Warrior I, and War Bonnet.

I remember downclimbing from War Bonnet's summit by liebacking a minivan-size boulder. I remember it suddenly starting to roll. The next thing I remember is coming-to 30 feet lower and scrambling down the ridge. Regaining control over my runaway body I realized I must have blacked out due to my severely dehydrated state. Having watched too many Hollywood movies, I thought, "Am I alive or did that boulder roll over me, and now I am just an invisible spirit like Bruce Willis in 'The Sixth Sense'?"

Finally, I got down to the trail and a stream. With a belly full of power gel and water I started jogging back to my car. Coming out of my stupor I laughed at myself for thinking I was dead. As

I turned a corner I saw a hiker walking towards me. Anxious to prove my connection with the living, I stared at the man, waiting for him to notice me. But within 20 feet he still had not looked in my direction. I felt a twinge of panic as he drew within a few feet of me; still giving no indication of my presence. Suddenly, he glanced up. "Hey, how's it going?" he questioned.

"Great, just great," I yelled, not thinking about the Traverse, but ecstatic to be on this dusty trail in the middle of Wyoming.

Statistics: 19 miles, 11 peaks, 7,500 feet of elevation gain, 5.8 difficulty, 12 rappels, 16.5 hours.

DAVE ANDERSON, *AAC*

Lost Temple Spire, north face, Separation Anxiety. For years climbers have admired a 220-foot crack that splits the face to the left of the Lost Temple Spire's north prow. On August 2 Jason Keith and Dave Shewell reached this crack by first climbing two pitches of the North Prow route and traversing left on a big ledge. They traversed another 25-30 feet, then passed a 5.10a roof and climbed a 5.9 fist crack. This brought them to what they named The Pitch of a Hundred Hand Jams—only a few face holds and finger jams in the 220 feet. A 5.9 pitch brought them back to the North Prow. They named the route Separation Anxiety, (IV 5.10).

JOE KELSEY

North Continental Tower, Little Sandy Buttresses. Near the head of the Little Sandy Valley is what appears to be a trio of impressive towers on the Divide to the east. Fred Beckey and Bob Stevenson named the central, highest one Continental Tower when they climbed it in 1967. Its southern neighbor has been climbed and called South Continental Tower. Given the view from the valley, it is natural that the northern formation (12,080+') would be called North Continental Tower, though it is really not a tower but a protruding fin. Tower or fin it appeared to be the most difficult of the three and as of last summer remained unclimbed.

On August 27 two Jackson Hole 16-year-olds, Trevor Bowman and Nick Stayner, climbed the North "Tower" by its southwest buttress and north ridge. They began by climbing a flake that led to a short 5.8 dihedral and a sloping ledge. They worked left to a larger ledge and followed it past a discontinuity to a prominent right-facing dihedral. This dihedral led to the fin's spectacular knife-edge crest. The first of three pitches on the crest involved a 5.9 move onto an 18-inch ledge and a crawl. The final pitch (5.7) regained the crest from an exposed ledge on the crest's east side via the right of two dihedrals. Bowman and Stayner named their route Aristeia (III 5.9), which in The Iliad means "One's greatest moment in battle."

On the Little Sandy Valley's west side are formations that have collectively been called the Little Sandy Buttresses. Between the two main buttresses is a cluster of three pinnacles. Before their Continental Tower climb Bowman and Stayner climbed these pinnacles. They climbed Tower 11,440+', the highest and northwesternmost of the cluster, by a contrived but pleasant route on the west face—a pitch on an arête, a descent from the arête, and a pitch on the main summit's west face (5.6). They then climbed the most conspicuous tower, the eastern of two 11,320+-foot towers—named King Cone by an earlier team who climbed a different route—also by two pitches on its west face (5.7). Finally, Bowman and Stayner climbed the western Tower 11,320+', the central tower as seen from the valley below, by one easy pitch on its west ridge (5.3).

JOE KELSEY

Alaska

BROOKS RANGE

Brooks Range, first complete traverse. In September of 2001 I completed the first crossing of the North American Brooks Range, from Point Hope to the Mackenzie River. This crossing required many expeditions over a number of years. Viewed from Point Hope in the west, the route proceeds to the source of the Ipswik, across the Wulik Peaks and the Delong Mountains to the source of the Kugururok. It continues along the Kugururok to the Noatak and than through the Noatak basin to Portage Pass and the upper Alatna. It then reaches across the Killik Basin to the Okomilaga, Chandler Lake, and Anuktuvuk Pass (by way of Kollutuk). I had lived in Anaktuvuk Pass in my teens and it was here that I first conceived of the project to comprehensively explore the entire range. In those days, hunting caribou and traveling by dog sled, I traveled as far as the Killik in the west and the Itkillik in the east. I made the first historical winter ascents in February of 1966, and two years later began a series of summer mountaineering expeditions that spread eventually throughout the entire range and into Canada. Countless peaks were climbed, passes crossed, and icefields explored. It was an orgy of mountain exploration that I thought was perhaps historically obtrusive. Like many mountaineers of that time I was desperately trying to touch something that no other human being had touched. And whereever I went there was always someone not far behind me.

In the 1980s and 1990s a good deal of time was spent in the Franklin and Romanzof icefields, climbing the most appealing of the ice peaks. Much of the eastern half of the route across the entire range was accomplished in this period. Looking east from Anaktuvuk Pass the route continues into the Anaktiktok Basin and through the Nanushuk, Itkillik, and Atigun Basins. It then proceeds up Accomplishment Creek over the summit lake, down the Ribdon headwaters to the upper Wind River and down the Ivishak. From here a pioneering descent of the Echooka was made with Deirdre Hammond. But the main route east follows the upper Canning and crosses the icefields of the upper Jago to find the most northerly point on the American Continental Divide (1991). The route goes south of the Continental Divide here into the upper Sheenjek at the fork of the great arch. A pass into the upper Kongakut leads to a region of limestone river tunnels. The lower Kongakut turns to Pagilak Creek and the Yukon border. The softer contours of the British Mountains then loom along the Malcolm River to Sheep Creek and the Firth River. We crossed from the Firth to the Babbage in 2000.

In September of 2001 the final expedition crossed the Barn Range through the canyons of Fish Hole Creek and a succession of passes to the Blow River at the very end of the mountains. Geologically, this point is the eastern edge of the Brooks Range. We ended at Bonnet Lake. The Richardson Mountains beyond had been crossed from the Mackenzie in 1999. A great deal of knowledge was acquired in the course of these expeditions in fields ranging from linguistics to natural history and geography. Many persons contributed to our success. I feel compelled to mention most especially Rebecca LeCheminant, Ruthmary Deuel, Craig Deutche, Patrick

Colgan, Walter Rogers, Paul Lencioni, Peter Balwin, Ed Hartley, Deirdre Hammond, John Morry, Olive Morry, John Hugo, and Pat and Clem Rawert.

DENNIS SCHMITT

HAYES RANGE

Peak 12,360' South Ridge. In mid-April Jon Miller and I left Fairbanks for a climb of the obvious line on the south face of Peak 12,360'. Situated between Mt. Hayes and Mt. Shand, this unnamed peak is the third highest peak in the Hayes Range. We flew into a small tributary glacier that feeds into the Black Rapids-Susitna Glacier pass, landing at about 5,500 feet. After bundling the plane up for a few nights, we skied up to the base of a prominent couloir that intersects the south ridge at about 9,000 feet. We climbed unroped up the snowy couloir to the ridge, then continued on ice and snow to the south basin at about 10,000 feet. The next morning we climbed hard snow and rime ice up the southwest ridge from the basin. At one point unstable rime mushrooms required a rappel from the ridge onto the west face. From there we followed hard water ice and more rime to the summit, feeling the altitude in our low-life Fairbanks lungs. We made the mistake of descending directly along the east ridge to the col between Peak 12,360' and Whale's Tail, the next small peak toward Aurora Peak. This required steep downclimbing on icy slopes and several rappels. (It would have been better to walk down the northwestern slopes and traverse easy ground to the col.) From this col we downclimbed to the basin, returning to our tent just at dark. The next day we descended to the plane, warmed it up, and flew back to Fairbanks. We believe that this enjoyable line had not been climbed before.

KEITH ECHELMEYER, *Alaskan Alpine Club*

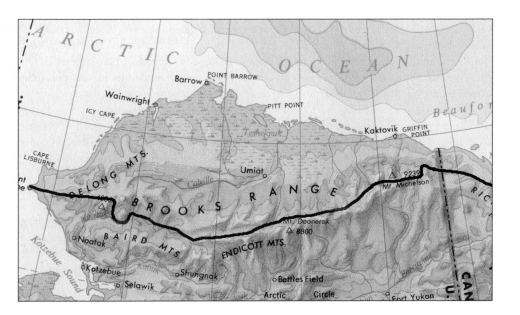

ALASKA RANGE

Denali National Park and Preserve, summary. The 2001 climbing season finished on a great note this year, with safe and successful experiences enjoyed by climbers, guides, and pilots, as well as the National Park Service. In fact long-time park employees indicate that the 2001 season was one of the most enjoyable seasons to date. The weather in June was "clear" throughout the month, with climbers summiting the mountain on all but three days. Air taxis were able to fly in and out of the Kahiltna base camp with very few delays. There were new routes and numerous repeat ascents of hard climbs made by experienced teams blessed with stable weather.

It was also a great year for the wilderness, thanks to the labors of park staff, as they led a passionate environmental-awareness campaign. These determined efforts by rangers and volunteers in weighing trash, numbering fuel cans, and educating the public on human waste disposal made a huge difference in returning Denali to its pristine state. Despite a record number of climbers, many seasoned veterans agreed that the mountain was the cleanest it has been in modern history.

A partnership with the American Alpine Club in the development and use of the Clean Mountain Can, and in the purchase of biodegradable waste bags, helped in the effort to explore new methods of human-waste disposal. The AAC grant provided financial support for a pilot study involving rangers and volunteers, as well as guided and non-guided expeditions. Nevertheless, with the growing number of climbers, we are still seeing occasional abandonment of caches and improper disposal of human waste. The mountaineering staff issued nine citations for waste-related violations.

It was a relatively quiet rescue season. Not only were there no fatalities in the park; no climbers or backcountry users suffered critical injuries. On the topic of search and rescue, the South District was given the task by Congress of completing a cost-recovery study that looked at a variety of rescue-related financial issues.

Rangers carried out 11 mountaineering patrols on Denali, and also patrols into the Ruth Glacier and Little Switzerland. Mountaineering volunteers again provided invaluable support to rangers on Denali. Their experience and expertise enabled mountaineering patrols to professionally carry out rescue and environmental-education efforts.

A record 1,305 climbers attempted Mt. McKinley, with a record 772 reaching the summit. Four expeditions attempted climbs during winter months, though only Masatoshi Kuriaki reached a summit, climbing Mt. Foraker on March 31, 2001, via the Southeast Ridge. The average trip length for an expedition on Mt. McKinley was 17.1 days. The average age of a Denali climber was 36 years. The oldest climber was 70, the youngest 11, both record-breakers. Women comprised 10 percent of the climbers on Mt. McKinley, and 45 percent were successful. Guided clients accounted for 18 percent of climbers on Mt. McKinley; clients and guides together accounted for 25 percent of the climbers on the mountain.

A total of 189 summit ascents were made during May, 549 in June, and 34 in July. The busiest days on the summit of Denali were June 4 (69 climbers) and June 8 (68 climbers). There were only three days in June when climbers did not reach the top.

Climbers came from 39 nations. After the United States (with 765 climbers), the other nations most represented were United Kingdom (65), Japan (48), Switzerland (45), Canada (44), Korea (40), France (37), Finland (34), and Germany (31).

On Mt. Foraker 11 climbers summited out of 40 attempting the peak.

The view of Mt. Foraker from Light Traveler on Mt. McKinley. *Stephen Koch*

DENALI NATIONAL PARK

Mt. McKinley, Zanto's Riches. Torrey Riches and I summited the North Peak of Denali on May 15, via the Northwest Buttress. We spent 11 days acclimatizing on the West Buttress and three days climbing the Northwest Buttress. Our original plan was to make the first alpine ascent of the 1982 Bocarde Variation. However, when we arrived on the lower Peters Glacier the 1982 variation was out of shape. We spotted a new line approximately one-half mile up the glacier. The new variation, Zanto's Riches (Alaskan Grade 4) climbed 5,000 feet of new terrain through a glaciated plateau, a steep headwall, and an icefall. It connects with the original Northwest Buttress route at the top of the first rock pyramid. The crux of the variation is a 55-degree ice headwall, which we named Toydoy's Headwall. We slept at 12,000 feet and 16,500 feet. After summiting the North Summit on a low-visibility day, we returned to our high camp and the next day continued to the 14,000-foot camp on the West Buttress. During the climb we subsisted mainly on GU. By the time we reached the safety of the West Buttress, we had exhausted our three-day supply of food and fuel.

The North Summit of Denali has no crowds and has stunning views. The most inspirational part of the climb was proving to ourselves that out there on huge and popular peaks there are still unclimbed lines that moderate climbers can do in style.

AARON ZANTO, *AAC*

Mt. McKinley, Father and Sons Wall, Extraterrestrial Brothers; Mt. Hunter, Moonflower Buttress; Mini-Moonflower, Kiss Me Where the Sun Don't Shine. British climbers Kenton Cool and Ian Parnell established Extraterrestrial Brothers (Alaskan Grade 5/6, Scottish VII) in early June on Mt. McKinley's Father and Sons Wall, in a 46-hour round trip from the 14,200-foot camp on the West Buttress. In May they also established Kiss Me Where the Sun Don't Shine (Scottish VII) on the Mini-Moonflower, and repeated Mt. Hunter's Moonflower Buttress. A full account appears earlier in this journal.

Mt. Hunter, Wall of Shadows Variation; Mt. McKinley, Common Knowledge. British climbers Ben Gilmore and Kevin Mahoney made the second ascent, with a variant start, of Wall of Shadows (VI, WI6 mixed, 5.9 A2), the Child-Kennedy 1994 route on the north buttress of Mt. Hunter, from May 15-18 (descent May 19). The pair then joined with Bruce Miller to climb a new route (Common Knowledge, V WI6R) on Mt. McKinley's northwest face of the west buttress (a.k.a. Washburn Face) in a 26-hour round-trip push on June 2. A full account appears earlier in this journal.

Mt. McKinley, Light Traveler; Mt. Hunter, Moonflower Buttress; Mini-Moonflower, Luna. In mid-June American Stephen Koch and Slovenian Marko Prezelj established Light Traveler on Mt. McKinley's southwest face in a 51-hour round-trip from the 14,200-foot camp on the West Buttress. In May the pair established Luna on Mt. Hunter's Mini-Moonflower and in early June made an all-free ascent of Mt. Hunter's Moonflower Buttress. A full account appears earlier in this Journal.

Mt. Foraker, Infinite Spur, fast ascent. Steve House and I climbed the Infinite Spur on June 9 and 10. We carried little in the way of gear, because we are lazy and could not be bothered carrying tents and sleeping bags. This allowed and forced us to move at a steady pace. Our speed was the result of such a lightweight approach but not the goal. We carried an MSR XGK stove, 33 ounces of fuel (used half), 40 GUs each, eight packages of soup, some Halvah (sesame seed paste), map, compass, altimeter, GPS, radio, an 8.8-mm rope, six screws, five cams, stoppers, slings, biners, a tarp for emergency and wind shelter, and Polarguard parkas. We each carried a small daypack.

I led the first block, which was 10 pitches of rock to 5.6/5.7 and easy mixed climbing. Steve led the second block, mostly steep snow and moderate ice, with one short WI5 pitch. By simul-climbing we climbed the spur in six "pitches," though one "pitch" gained 900 vertical feet. We reached the end of the spur (at ca 15,000') after 13 hours of climbing. We spent 3 hours and 45 minutes at a flat spot drinking and eating. Then I led three more pitches on moderate ice. We continued roped for a while, then unroped below the east summit and climbed on to the top, stopping just before the summit for a hot drink. We summited at 8:15 a.m., 25 hours after starting.

We descended the Sultana Ridge, which took an additional 20 hours, including one more brew/hydration break, to return to Kahiltna base camp.

The route proved to be easier than we expected and involved much snow climbing, something I get bad allergies from. Nevertheless, we enjoyed the climb, mostly because of scenery beyond belief. The descent of the Sultana provided some of the prettiest views. Another pair started on the Spur the same day we did, but there were no other parties on the mountain, which made the experience richer and more special (even more so when compared to the

Denali cattle drives). However, our approach was rather unromantic, in that with our lack of equipment we could not spare the time to contemplate our surroundings. Our experience was thus not as textured or rich as it might have been. This was the price we paid for the ease with which we managed to climb.

ROLANDO GARIBOTTI, *AAC, Club Andino Bariloche*

Mt. Foraker, southeast ridge, winter ascent. On the morning of February 8 I departed base camp (6,550') on the southwest fork of the Kahiltna Glacier. I made Camp I at 6,400 feet below the base of the southeast ridge in the evening. My route began at the middle of the base of the southeast toe. I carried loads from 6,400 feet up the toe to 8,100 feet and made my first snow cave (Camp II) on February 18. I knew that even a few inches of new snow on the avalanche slopes ahead would prevent me from making the climb. I traversed quickly through this area between 8,800 feet and 9,250 feet, which is safe, with stable snow conditions. On February 23 I moved camp up to a snow cave at 9,780 feet (Camp III) on the southwest side of the ridge. The snow cave took four and a half hours to construct. Eleven days of continual storm kept me in the cave. I made Camp IV at 11,300 feet, between blue ice and cornices, on March 17. On March 21 I moved camp up to 13,200 feet (Camp V, snow cave). This highest camp was one hour from the base of the ridge, so on March 23 I broke trail to the base of the ridge to facilitate my summit attempt. On day 46, March 24, I attempted to reach the summit but stopped at 13,900 feet because of high wind. Four days of storm kept me in the snow shelter. On day 53, March 31, I departed high camp at 7:35 a.m., arrived on the summit at 2:34 p.m., and was back in high camp at 7:10 p.m. I stayed on the very peak for only seven minutes. The conditions were blizzard, strong northwest wind, and a temperature of -20°. On the summit day I covered approximately 4,200 feet, with knife edges, cornices, and a 30- to 40-degree slope on the final 3,000-foot climb. Crevasses were obvious, so I traveled without poles. On April 5 I departed high camp in the morning, after three days of storm. On day 66, April 13, I arrived in base camp in the afternoon.

MASATOSHI KURIAKI, *Japan*

Mt. Foraker, Infinite Spur variation. The sun is setting, and the cold is creeping down the Kahiltna. It is May 16, and Eamonn Walsh and I have just been spit out of the last plane of the day at Kahiltna base camp. We stare up at the Moonflower Buttress of Mt. Hunter, which stands front-row center in this arena. The Moonflower will be first, then the Infinite Spur on Foraker. But failure on the Moonflower quickly teaches us about moving efficiently in Alaska, so we take a day of rest, then begin our long journey up the Infinite Spur. We have planned for a 10-day round trip. We climb the Spur despite nasty storms, deep snow, being caught in avalanches, heavy packs, and cold. We free the route without hauling our 55-pound packs. We suffer like we never imagined possible. We fly out spending less then three days in base camp.

We did a new variation on the Infinite Spur by staying on the rib proper. It may have been a bit slower but proved to be the best climbing on the route. Above the icy rib the route is blocked by a rock buttress. On the first and second ascents the teams skirted the buttress to the right on snow slopes but then encountered loose 5.9 rock. Last year's third- and fourth-ascent teams avoided the bad rock by going left around the buttress but found snow and ice climbing that was unaesthetic and slow. We went up a gully that splits the buttress and offers three really good pitches up to AI4. Subsequent ascents this year went our way as well.

Above the buttress previous and subsequent parties have gone left on snow slopes to reach the base of the dreaded Horizontal Ridge. We went straight up the rib and had four more pitches of primo mixed climbing up to M5. Recommended.

ROB OWENS, *Canada*

Mt. Hunter, Moonflower Buttress, fast ascent. From May 16 to 19 Doug Chabot and I climbed The Moonflower Buttress, to the summit, in a record "fast and heavy" 83-hour round trip. Our strategy included jugging difficult pitches and hauling, among other things, our garage-sale tent, which we couldn't set up on two of the three nights. We both agreed the route lived up to its reputation as The Nose of ice climbing.

BRUCE MILLER

Mt. Hunter, Mini-Moonflower. In May two new routes were established on Mt. Hunter's north buttress, which has become known as the Mini-Moonflower. This spur peak is actually a facet of the northeast ridge, and previous ascensionists (1999 *AAJ*, p. 252) have also called it the northeast buttress of Mt. Hunter. The pyramid-shaped subpeak is northeast of Hunter's north buttress, just past the large, obvious icefall. New routes were established in 2001 by Kenton Cool and Ian Parnell, and by Stephen Koch and Marko Prezlj. Accounts from each party appear earlier in this journal.

Paul Figg in a snowstorm during day 2 of The Prey, on the east face of Mt. Hunter. *Malcolm Bass*

Mt. Hunter, east face, The Prey. It all happened rather fast. Paul Figg and I arrived in Alaska on May 13, and two days later we were on the West Fork of the Tokositna, watching Paul Roderick's plane disappearing down-glacier. We were the second climbing party ever to land in the cirque under Mt. Hunter's east face, the first being Tackle and Donini en route to Diamond Arête. The cirque is a serious place, swept by avalanches and tight for landing. We did as Tackle advised, and, dispensing with any sort of base camp, landed, packed, and racked, intent on going

The Prey on Mt. Hunter's east face follows the center buttress, with the Diamond Arête to the left. Most of The Prey stays on the left (back) side of the buttress. *Paul Figg*

over the top to the Kahiltna. We had seven days' scant rations, nine days' gas, and a bivy tent. Thirty minutes after landing we crossed the bergschrund.

Our aim was to climb one of the two prominent buttresses to the right of Diamond Arête to the east ridge. We chose the rightmost of the two, as the left buttress, although its lower third was split by a compelling icy couloir, had a long section of corniced ridge at midheight.

The first day gave moderate snow climbing, interspersed with short, steep, rocky steps, initially up the right side of the buttress, then across the crest into a shallow couloir on the left flank. We found a good tent site under a serac just below the crest. The next day began with a late start and a deviation onto the crest and the world of frozen froth. We hastily returned to the shallow couloir, vowing to keep off the mushrooms. Back in the couloir we moved together, placing intermediate gear against the threat of being knocked off our feet by the hissing spindrift avalanches. The climb's crux began, just before midnight, where the couloir petered out in a basin of steep, insecure snow beneath a steep headwall. A worrying struggle got us to a belay beneath a promising chimney/groove system. Three superb pitches of snowed-up rock, thinly iced mixed ground, and excellent steep blue ice, overall about Scottish V, took us onto the horribly mushroomed crest and into the sunlight of our third day. Tired and dehydrated we stopped to brew, but grew paranoid about what the sun would do to our flimsy perch and moved on. The climbing on the crest was grim. Belays were nonexistent, and the ice had far too much air in the mix. We were now level with the east ridge, which was far away to our right. At three that afternoon, 24 hours after leaving our last bivy, we reached a rocky outcrop below the crest, chopped a totally inadequate tent ledge, and got into the tent. Two minutes later we got out and chopped some more.

The fourth day started with the most photogenic pitch I've ever seen. On a sunny morning, high on a new route in the fabled Alaska Range, a cascade of blue ice flows between glistening walls of white granite. A pity that we packed the camera up on day two. This cover-pitch led us through the outcrop to more insecure snow. Four pitches later we joined the east ridge as it swept up from our right, and were rewarded by massive views of Denali's south face.

The climb up the east ridge to the summit was straightforward. We bivouacked once and reached the summit at 8:15 p.m. on day five. We stopped on top just long enough to let our photographs of the west ridge blow away, and then descended to the plateau.

Our descent of the West Ridge route took place nearly entirely in thick cloud and light snowfall. Route finding in these conditions was hard; we often had to sit for hours waiting for a brief clearing in order to set our course. The compass proved essential. On some days we were able to move for only an hour or so. However, our limited food supply encouraged us to keep inching down rather than sitting it out. We eventually reached the Kahiltna Glacier in the afternoon of day 10 and trudged round to base camp and the gluttonous joys of a cache bag full of bagels, eggs, and smoked salmon.

We called the route The Prey (Alaskan 5, Scottish V, 900m to East Ridge).

MALCOLM BASS, *Alpine Club*

Rick Taylor high on the south ridge of Mt. Hunter during the first ascent of the Corliss-Taylor Route, with the Happy Cowboy Pinnacle/Traverse in the background. *Greg Corliss*

Mt. Hunter, Corliss-Taylor Buttress. From May 13-21 Greg Corliss and I climbed a new route on Mt. Hunter that is essentially a variation of the existing South Ridge route. The climb rises in the middle of the south face, between the southeast spur and the south ridge. The route starts at

8,300 feet, in the gully below the hanging glacier to the left of the southeast spur. After crossing the bergschrund, the route immediately takes a snow ramp up and left for 1,000 feet and then traverses pretty much up and right through rock bands, snowfields, and mixed ice to join the original South Ridge route at 11,500 feet. The difficulty to this point is 5.8 WI3. Most of this climbing was straightforward in fun alpine terrain. Where our route joins the South Ridge route, we found a bent ring angle piton, looking very old, and a Lost Arrow, looking newer but still dated. We wonder if the pins were from the original Waterman ascent.

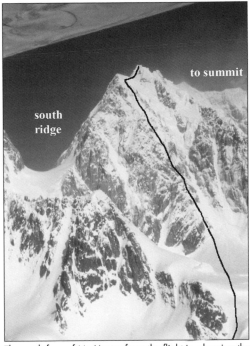

The south face of Mt. Hunter from the flight in, showing the Corliss-Taylor Route between the south ridge proper and the southeast spur on the south face. *Rick Taylor*

The true character of the route becomes clear in the snow climbing along the upper south ridge. The difficulty and associated pucker factor are almost entirely dependent on snow conditions. Surreal is the best way to describe the pinnacles and cornices that we found. We experienced mainly deep sugar snow and bottomless conditions, similar to temperature-gradient crystals. At times these conditions pervaded through the entire snowpack, while at other times we were able to dig deep and reach stable and firm snow. Progress was generally slow and required laborious trenching and swimming, while attempting to evenly distribute body weight over a snowpack that was extremely weak in compressive strength. The snowpack was most challenging at the steepest part of the arête, where in places it was armpit deep. These conditions resulted in much suffering and much trenching, especially past the Happy Cowboy Pinnacle (have spurs on for this pony) and the Changabang Arête. The climbing was exposed, marginally protected, and "heady." These sections did, however, provide one heck of a view down plunging couloirs to the glacier 5,000 feet below. Cornices were unstable, and we each experienced a cornice fall (ride 'em cowboy) on this part of the ridge. Conditions were consistent on the South Ridge from 11,500 feet to the summit plateau. We reached the summit after six days and descended the Southwest Ridge in three and a half days. On the descent poor visibility made navigation and route finding challenging. We found the descent to be involved and continuous from top to bottom, with a great deal of downclimbing and six to 10 rappels.

RICK TAYLOR, *AAC*

Thunder Mountain, Deadbeat and Ring of Fire; Mt. Huntington, West Face Couloir. "Sweet Jesus, man, this blows. I hate alpine climbing." It had become our trip's mantra. But short memory resulted in Scott DeCapio and I climbing three routes from the Tokositna Glacier, all in pure alpine style, of course. We climbed light, leader and follower both with packs, and all free.

On the night of May 27 we headed for the obvious couloir right (east) of the central-spur rock buttress on Thunder Mountain's 3,500-foot south face. (The bottom of the couloir is labeled "3" in the photo on p. 205 of the 2001 *AAJ*.) After soloing 1,000 feet to the first ice step of the couloir's left fork, we roped up. The next 1,500 feet rose at 50 to 70 degrees, with vertical steps. It was followed by a broad basin leading left, toward the summit, that was unseen from the glacier but offered 700 feet of phenomenal mixed climbing. Even the steep exit bulges had bomber névé. We finished with obligatory scary snow groveling and a short, scrappy Grade 6 mixed crux. A final 200 feet of nasty snow swimming brought us to the summit, eight hours and five roped pitches after starting. Thunder had reportedly been summited only once before, and the topo map didn't indicate easy ground up top, yet we had convinced ourselves we could simply walk off. Feeling idiotic we rappelled the route as the sun gained the couloir, thus descending in terror, along with chunks of snow, ice, and rock. Relieved, we reached our skis 14 hours after leaving and named the route Deadbeat, after our hero and role model in "The Big Lebowski." And perhaps after ourselves.

After a meager, failed attempt on the narrow cleft in the rock buttress immediately left (west) of the British couloir route Dream Sacrifice, site of Malcolm Daly's epic fall and rescue

Look out below! Scott DeCapio entering the crux roof section of Ring of Fire on Thunder Mountain. *Kelly Cordes*

in May 1999 (2000 *AAJ*, pg. 206), we returned on the night of June 1 to try again. Scoping the route from below, we assumed the climbing leading to the obvious crux rock band would be easy. Time for new binoculars. Between moderate sections we found considerable Grade 6 terrain. At least it was mostly quality climbing… mostly. The crux was a desperate pitch of overhanging roofs and flakes, a full grade harder than anything until then, though with good pro. My joy at having a top rope for Scott's brilliant lead soon ended. The next pitch, though at least a half grade easier, was gripping—steep and stacked with death blocks. Scott belayed in a narrow funnel below me, the only available spot, hiding behind his 15-pound pack. A worthless, overhanging, shite snow-ice-mushroom offwidth against smooth rock finished the pitch. Moderate ground led to a full-on battle through steep, unprotectable hell-snow and the summit. We were worked, and after 17 hours and nine pitches of character-building effort we relaxed and brewed for two hours on top.

We rappelled and down-climbed Deadbeat in the shade, hitting the skis 24 hours after leaving. I'd been saving a route name from one of my favorite Johnny Cash songs. The name seemed fitting: Ring of Fire.

Paul Roderick then flew us to Mt. Huntington, which supposedly hadn't been climbed in under a day. It was an obvious candidate for a lightweight sprint. But we did know that its summit is notoriously hard to reach. We left our 8,200-foot camp at 10:30 p.m. on June 8, crossed the 'schrund an hour later, and roped-up at the prominent ice ramp/couloir splitting the west face. Motivated by pizza and beer, we figured if we pulled this off, we could feel good about flying out. The couloir, with fixed pro and bomber moderate ice (a couple of steps of WI4, then easier), was a blast. Five hours from camp, we were starting up the broad summit slopes. These final 1,000 vertical feet proved terrifying, unquestionably the most challenging climbing of the route, with steep, unconsolidated mank snow, worthless ice, cornices, and, of course, no protection. Vertical trenching through collapsing sugar. At least we were tied together for the potential 4,000-footer. Now I understand why folks sometimes stop at, ahem, "the end of the difficulties" on Huntington. We summited at 7:30 a.m. but, not psyched about any descent route, we were unable to enjoy the spectacular view. The sun would hit the face in a few hours, and at this point in the trip we felt worked. Scott's deadpan statement said it all, "I want my mom so bad right now. I hate alpine climbing." The downclimbing part of reversing our path was a bit unnerving, but 16 hours after leaving camp we were back, enjoying whiskey and a fresh bag of Twizzlers. In an unprecedented display of will power, I had kept them unopened for a final celebration. "Yeah, ya know, alpine climbing ain't so bad."

KELLY CORDES, *AAC*

Thunder Mountain, Walk of the Schnitzelkings. On April 6, 1999, German climbers Christoph Duepper and Thomas Traxler climbed the right-hand fork of the split couloir to the right (east) of the central spur—the Lightning Spur—on Thunder Mountain's south face. This is the couloir starting at the "3" on p. 205 of the 2001 *AAJ*. After 1,000 feet the couloir forks. The route Deadbeat ascends the left fork, while the German route goes right. Duepper and Traxler climbed much of their 3,000-foot route unroped, encountering mostly 50-degree snow except for four short pitches of 80- to 90-degree ice. After about six hours of climbing, they reached the narrow col atop the couloir and rappelled.

TALKEETNA RANGER STATION FILES AND *High Mountain Sports 232*

Ruth Glacier, Peak 10,370'; Peak 11,300' attempt; Moose's Tooth, Shaken Not Stirred. On May 15 Jared Ogden and I were dropped by Talkeetna Air Taxi on the West Fork of the Ruth Glacier. Our plan was to try the east face of Mt. Huntington, but the weather was not cooperating. On our second day in camp we climbed a couloir in the middle of the east face of a 10,370-foot peak just north of our camp. The knife edge ridge at the top involved a mandatory rappel, and since there was no anchor, we think we may have done a new route. We turned back in a whiteout about 200 feet below the top and had an exciting descent down a different route from what we climbed. After an aborted attempt on the Southwest Ridge of Peak 11,300', during which a snow cave collapsed on us, we packed up our sleds and headed down to the Ruth Amphitheater, where the weather was clearly better.

Peak 10,370', a bump along Mt. McKinley's Reality Ridge, directly north from the standard base camp on the west fork of the Ruth Glacier. *Mark Synnott*

We bivied below Mt. Barille and the next day made the long climb up to the hanging glacier below the south face of the Moose's Tooth. We lay around in our bags for a few hours, then at 3 a.m. began climbing a gully called Shaken Not Stirred. Conditions were excellent. Most of the climbing was straightforward, with the exception of one difficult chockstone capped with an overhang of unconsolidated sugar snow. We arrived at the Englishman's Col at about 9 a.m., having simul-climbed most of the route. From there, rather than heading left to the west summit and a descent of the west ridge, we headed right, toward the middle summit. The first pitch from the col onto the ridge was very difficult, involving vertical climbing on unconsolidated snow and ice, but it deposited us onto a wild Peruvian-style ridge. After more simul-climbing we reached the middle summit about noon. We paused briefly, then continued along the ridge. Our plan was to continue traversing until we found Ham and Eggs, a popular route that has fixed rappel anchors. Unfortunately, we had only brought one 8-mm rope and a small rack. There is a lot more ridge up there than we thought, and a lot of gullies that all look the same, so when we arrived at one with a rappel sling around a horn at the top, we dropped in. One thousand feet down, we got cliffed out by a 1,500-foot wall and realized we'd have to climb back up. Then a storm blew in. We had to climb some hard mixed pitches to get back to the ridge, all done in a whiteout with spindrift pouring on our heads. We eventually found the salvation of Ham and Eggs, but with only one rope we had to do a lot of downclimbing and install many V-threads to get down.

Mark Synnott, *AAC*

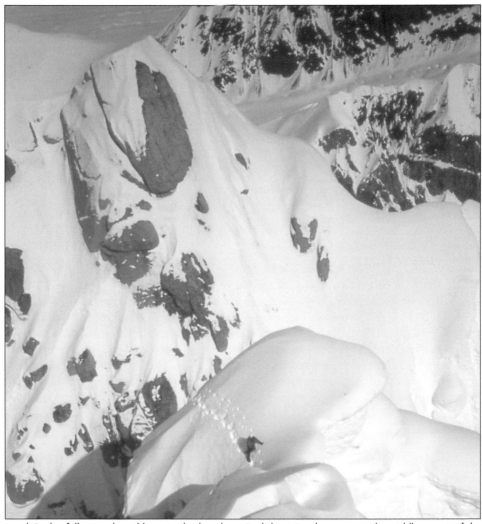

Jared Ogden following the wild corniced ridge above Englishman's col en route to the middle summit of the Moose's Tooth during the first ascent of Shaken Not Stirred. *Mark Synnott*

Peak 11,300', Baja Lime. Dakota Soifer and I, both of Boulder, Colorado, decided to vacation on the West Fork of the Ruth Glacier in May 2001. We finished finals, packed our gear, and flew to the Last Frontier.

On our second day on the glacier we "warmed up" on the Southwest Ridge of Peak 11,300'. Though the summit was capped by wind slab that deterred us from the true summit, we both had fun in incredible weather. The next day was spent eating egg sandwiches with never-ending Baja lime sauce, sunbathing, playing rummy, and eyeing our new obsession. We had stopped in the National Park Service library before leaving Talkeetna to get route information. We weren't sure what to do in the West Fork and wanted to know what was available. Seeing no routes drawn on the south face of Peak 11,300' on the library map and seeing a nice line, we decided to give it a whirl. The line is just to the right of the obvious pillar in the middle of the south face. It follows mixed ground interspersed with steep snow, traversing slightly eastward to meet the southeast ridge at about three-fourths of the height of the face.

We weren't off to the best start. On May 15 Dakota caught me on a hip belay at 4 a.m. as I tried to tiptoe across the bergschrund. Skirting the bergschrund to the left using a finger crack brought us to the base of steep snow/névé. At the top of the wide couloir we moved right through four pitches of 70-degree mixed climbing to the crux pitch, a loose 5.9 corner with bad gear placements. This was followed by easier ground, with just a few hard sections and a few pitches traversing on thin, slushy-snow-covered slabs. After about 20 pitches we hit the ridge. To our dismay we found that this side of the summit cone also had windslab protecting it. We decided to let it bar our way and started down the face. Many rappels, a few stuck, and some downclimbing deposited us back on the West Fork of the Ruth Glacier. Our roundtrip time was 19 hours. Pictures we have since seen suggest that the face usually has much more snow.

BEN HOYT

Moose's Tooth, Direct East Pillar (a.k.a. The Beast). On the 5,000-foot east face of the Moose's Tooth, site of the historic The Dance of the Woo Li Masters (Jim Bridwell and Mugs Stump, 1981), Bridwell and Spencer Pfingsten established the Direct East Pillar, a.k.a. The Beast (VII A5 5.10b WI4+ M6). The route, which took 29 days of effort in 2000 and 30 in 2001, is essentially a direct start to the 1981 route, joining it halfway, via the rock pillar to its left. Rotten rock was common. The key pitch, the 18th or 19th of the 44, involved 70-degree rock covered with unconsolidated snow, with no protection for 200 feet. This pitch, which forced the team to retreat in 2000, linked the new line to the 1981 route. Bridwell says it is the most difficult route he's ever climbed.

PERSONAL COMMUNICATION WITH BRIDWELL, AND *CLIMBING*, AND *ROCK AND ICE*

Cathedral Mountains, various first ascents. From June 28 to July 18 British climbers Lindsay Griffin, Geoff Hornby, Dave Wallis, and I visited the Cathedral Mountains, a small offshoot of peaks to the west of Mt. Russell. Heart Mountain is the main peak named on maps. The peaks are bordered by Cathedral Creek to the west, and it must be wondered if these were the original Cathedral Spires (the name now given to the Kichatna Spires). From a gravel airstrip and hunting lodge established by Clark Engle in the 1960s, a track led approximately five miles to an old trespass mine by the edge of Boulder Creek, about two miles north of the snout of the range's main glacier. The mine site was used as a base by our team.

We made 18 probable new routes, including 15 probable first ascents of peaks. However, hunters and prospectors have been active in the area, and Heart Mountain has been named, so it is possible some of the peaks had seen unrecorded ascents. Names are provisional and altitudes very approximate. From the trespass mine (ca 3,300 feet), Heart Mountain and Point 6,765', farther along the ridge to the southeast, were climbed via the col between them. We climbed Point 6,765' twice. The second time we continued south on the ridge, over three crumbling rocky summits, Points 6,700', another 6,700', and 7,000', to reach Point 7,236'. We traversed Point 7,236' by ascending the north ridge and descending the south ridge to a col. From this col we traversed Point 7,400' from north to south. In a 14-hour push we climbed the northwest gully of Heart Mountain and traversed the ridge, first southeast, then south, for approximately three miles to Point 7,880', taking in eight summits. We climbed Point 6,805', which overlooks the Purkypile Mine to the north, from a snow basin to the east. From a glacier camp at 6,200 feet, about two miles up the main Boulder Glacier, we climbed Points 7,900' and 7,600' on the south bank of the glacier. We named Point 7,600' Mount Alyssa. The highest mountain of the region and the only one known to have had an ascent, Point 8,500', was climbed via a southeast-facing gully. We descended the line of the original ascent, the northwest ridge, to a col connecting the head of Cathedral Glacier with a high glacier basin on the north side of the mountain. From here Point 7,825' and two other peaks, 7,800' and 7,700', were gained by traversing a snow-and-rock ridge west. Despite a height of 7,825 feet assigned to the most northerly of these three peaks, the middle one appeared to be the highest. We reversed the ridge and followed it to its eastern end and the summit of Point 7,900'. A snow gully allowed a descent to the high glacier basin, which was crossed and the camp on Boulder Glacier gained. These peaks were climbed in an eight-hour push. The 1,000-foot south-facing rock pillar below the summit of Point 8,500' was climbed and the snow-and-rock ridge above followed to the summit for the third ascent of the peak. During much of the trip clouds developed in the afternoon and led to light rain or snow, which sometimes became heavy. Temperatures were far from extreme, usually hovering close to freezing. This meant good snow conditions never really occurred.

BRIAN DAVISON, *United Kingdom*

Mt. Red Beard, West Ridge. In early May Jamal Lee-Elkin and I, unable to fly into the Hayes Range because of uncooperative weather, flew into the Yentna Glacier south of Mt. Foraker. The Yentna is a relatively unvisited area, probably because the peaks, ranging from 8,000 feet to 13,000 feet, are much smaller than their neighbors around the Kahiltna. We opted for the Yentna on the advice of Paul Roderick, the owner of Talkeetna Air Taxi, who has occasionally flown parties into the glacier.

After an attempt on a nice peak directly above our base camp at about 4,000 feet (aborted due to foul weather), we packed light and headed out for another attractive peak just south of base camp. The route followed a long west ridge, with a subsidiary summit at about 6,000 feet, a rock ridge with several large gendarmes, and final shoulder and summit ridge above the gendarmes—the entire ridge was about 4,000 feet long. Conditions were difficult, with deep snow and much post-holing before we reached the rock ridge. We bivied just below the ridge in a snow cave, believing further bivy sites would be few and far between, as turned out to be the case. The next morning we followed the ridge, with one 5.8 move and a spectacular, airy traverse around the largest gendarme, protection on the snow traverse being afforded by perfect granite flakes. Communication, on the other hand, was less than perfect, Jamal being on one side of the gendarme and I on the other. Above the gendarme the climbing was straightforward, though the weather was hot. The rarely-had views of Foraker and the Revelations from the summit were impressive.

Jamal named the peak Mt. Red Beard, in honor of his friend and climbing partner Ned Greene, who had a large red beard. Ned was the caretaker of the Harvard Cabin on Mt. Washington; he died last winter when an ice dam exploded and swept him 800 feet down Damnation Gully. Mt. Red Beard is nine miles east (91 degrees, to be precise) of Mt. Russell, the most frequent Yentna climbing destination. Its elevation is approximately 8,600 feet, and it is located in square seven of the Talkeetna D-4 map.

JIM LARUE, *AAC*

Glacier 1 (Fake Peak Glacier) Peaks. From June 1-22 British climbers Mike Fletcher, Richard Leech, Oliver Shergold , and I visited the unfrequented Glacier 1 (a.k.a. Fake Peak Glacier). In the prevailing fine weather we made seven ascents, five of which we believe to be of new routes. Glacier 1 rises gently east from Glacier Point at the southern end of the Ruth Gorge and is famous for a diminutive rock spike on its southern rim known as Fake Peak. This 1,675-meter point's fame derives from its identification as the site of Dr. Frederick Cook's photo of him posed triumphantly on what he declared to be Mt. McKinley.

After Dr. Cook, the next recorded visit to Glacier 1 took place in 1977. Local climber Brian Okenek, approaching from the Ruth, made the first crossing of the col at its head and descended the Coffee Glacier on the far side. In recent years, though, several parties have been diverted to the glacier to make ascents of Fake Peak for its history, and one or two ski descents of an easy glaciated peak, Sholes (1,890m), were made by parties organized by Paul Roderick. The first technical climb from the glacier basin was made in 2000, when Geoff Hornby (U.K.) and Mike Smith (U.S.) made the first ascent of Tassles (2,090m) via the aesthetic west couloir. In March 2001 a guided party from the Alaska Mountaineering School climbed Fake Peak by its northeast ridge.

Flown in by Talkeetna Air Taxi director Paul Roderick, the 2001 British party established base camp just below Cook's Col and the site of his "upper world" panorama. The two most attractive peaks on the eastern rim of the glacier, Glisen and Lee (both ca 1,920m), were our main objectives. After a repeat of the easy southeast face of Sholes and a reconnaissance to the col south of Lee, we made the first ascent of Lee on June 5. Fletcher and I climbed the straight-forward 45-degree, 550-meter west-northwest couloir, which led directly to the summit, while Leech and Shergold opted for the steeper north face via the northwest couloir. All arrived on the summit within minutes of each other and descended the west-northwest couloir.

On June 9-10, while Fletcher and Leech made a ski trip to the Ruth Amphitheater, Shergold and I climbed Glisen in a 28-hour round trip from base camp. Leaving camp at 4:00 a.m. we first followed a deep avalanche runnel in a 50-55-degree subsidiary couloir on the west face, with a loose mixed exit onto the south ridge. After a couple of wet granite pitches we gained access to a traverse line onto the middle of the west face. There a succession of interest-ing mixed pitches, interrupted by the usual almost-bottomless Alaskan snow, led over a rock tower to the summit crest. This proved broad and relatively cornice-free, and we reached the summit at about 5:00 p.m., after 13 roped pitches above the head of the initial couloir. On the descent (downclimbing and rapping) we discovered a ledge system, hidden from below, by which we could have avoided the crux section. We regained the top of the couloir at 11:00 p.m. The walls of the couloir were plastered with potentially dangerous snow formations, one of which collapsed and swept the lower gully shortly before we arrived. We waited for colder con-ditions, but a thin cloud cover hindered a freeze, and our packet of biscuits and liter of water each were running thin (we had anticipated being out for six to eight hours). Shergold and I therefore rappelled the steep mixed pitch into the upper couloir at 2 a.m. and started a roped descent. We were back at camp by 8:00 a.m. on the 10th. Glisen is a fine summit, and we feel that a competent party could climb it much faster. We graded the 650-meter West Face Indirect Alpine TD (Scottish V mixed).

On June 13 all four of us climbed Fake Peak by its south ridge, and the following day Leech and I climbed the northeast ridge of Sholes over various small northeast shoulders to join the normal route (at which point we descended).

Attention now turned to peaks at the back of the Balrog Glacier (the west arm of Glacier 1). Early on the 15th Leech and Shergold began up the southeast couloir on Point 7,470', which stands on the watershed between the Balrog Glacier and the upper Coffee Glacier. They reached a point approximately one-third of the way up when the side wall avalanched below them, sweeping their tracks. To continue would have meant reversing the route later in the day, and with temperatures barely dipping below freezing they descended. The following morning Fletcher and I visited the same area and ascended a side glacier northwest of Sholes. Finding good conditions we made the first ascent of Point 5,800'+ via the southwest face to the southeast ridge. After descending to the side glacier we continued south toward the steep upper section of the northwest face of Sholes, but the expected consequences of imminent sunshine prompted a retreat. On the 20th, with Leech and Shergold in the lead, all four of us made the first ascent of the northwest face of Sholes (AD)—a nice line, though then in poor condition. In the upper section five long pitches of 70-degree and steeper snow, with two delicate cornices, led to the summit slopes.

With much snow having disappeared from rocks at lower altitude, a trip to a now-denuded Cook's Col led to the discovery of sections of Cook's old box and one or two other artifacts. However, the highlight of the trip was the first plastic sledge descent from the summit of Sholes, by Leech and Shergold on June 17. New Wave plastic sledging in the Alaska Range could come of age during the next few years—the Sultana Ridge on Foraker, for example, being an eminently suitable target.

LINDSAY GRIFFIN, *United Kingdom*

RUTH GORGE

Mt. Barille, Northeast Pillar, Baked Alaskan. Eighteen-year-old Scotty Thelen and I left Valdez at noon on June 29 and raced to Talkeetna to catch Talkeetna Air Taxi into the Ruth Mountain House. The whole state had had a month of predominately clear weather, and with any luck I could squeeze another trip in. An earlier trip into Little Switzerland left me wanting more. After landing we packed the sleds and headed around the corner to the base of the Cobra Pillar, only to find fixed ropes on the Austrian route. The Cobra scared us off, so we skied back around past the Russian route, Forever More. Just past a steep drainage is a smaller face on the shoulder of Barille, the northeast pillar. We quickly agreed on a route up the corner on the edge of the face. We fixed the scary bergschrund crossing and, after 40 hours of funky weather, headed up with a large rack. The Ruth had taught me the value of large pieces, and the rack included gear up to a #5 Camalot and a #7 Big Bro. Steep, shallow hand cracks led to easier climbing and great ledges. Five pitches led to a perfect bivy ledge, where we strung the fly and waited out weather until morning. Further moderate climbing took us up a large chimney and up the face proper to steep double cracks, where we were glad to have the large pieces. We topped out on the pillar's large table-like top, 1,500 feet from the summit of Barille but an obvious ending point. We enjoyed the view and waited for evening cooling, since our descent route was exposed to snow and rock fall. Seven 60-meter rappels dropped us right back to our start, with no rock fall. The cloud ceiling descended with us, and that was it for our Alaskan summer. Our route, Baked Alaskan (IV+ 5.10 A2) had superb crack climbing of every size and great ledges. After a number of trips I'm finally feeling somewhat comfortable in the Land of the Giants.

BRIAN TEALE

Mt. Barille, East Face, Orgler-Bonapace, probable third ascent. On June 21 Ken Sauls and I flew into the Ruth, where we made a second ascent of the 1988 Orgler-Bonapace East Face route on Mt. Barille. Just gaining the rock was tricky, involving a complicated icefall at the base of the mountain. About 280 feet up the rock, at the start of huge dihedrals, weather moved in quickly, so we fixed our ropes and left a small amount of gear at this high-point.

A few days later, on about July 1, we returned to good cracks and a mixture of free and aid climbing. Ken led the first block of about 10 pitches in eight hours. By 11:15 p.m. we were on a reasonable ledge, when small clouds dropped a little precipitation. Snail eye clouded my vision. "Ken, I don't know about this," I said. Ken replied, "If we're gonna climb this peak, we're gonna have to deal with some weather." I imagined a soaking-wet rappel epic down the grainy granite we had just climbed. When we opened our pack, we found that one of our water sacks had leaked its entire contents onto Ken's fleece jacket. "Jingis," Ken stated. Now we had only four liters of water, instead of six. Then it was my turn to lead. It was good free climbing up cracks and chimneys, pitch after pitch, fixing short where possible and aid soloing. With dawn approaching we reached the first pendulum point. I tensioned off 70 feet before gaining a series of small ramps and ledges that led toward the target crack system. Within 10 feet of the crack was a chimney, and I crawled in. Yahoo! After several more fine pitches and another series of tension traverses, at about 1 p.m., about 24 hours after starting up, we were seated on top of the first-ascent team's first bivy ledge. We lazed in the sun and drank nearly all of our water. By 3 p.m. we switched leads, and Ken set out onto the upper half of the wall. We were so thirsty we drank water trickling down the rock. Ken, like a bulldozer, kept the upward progress happening. His shout of "Line fixed!" broke my delirium, as I fought and struggled with the back-breaking pack. Instead of hauling, we had the second jumar with the pack. By 4 a.m. we reached the first-ascent's second bivy ledge, at the top of the face proper. We ate our last few energy bars. Belaying Ken became torture, as I could hardly stay awake. Every 10 minutes or so I would feel dizziness. Many outstanding 5.9 and 5.10 rock pitches zigzagged us to the top of the east face of Mt. Barille. By 10:30 a.m. we were on top of the formidable rock wall.

Up the steep snow face Ken went, into the mist, until I could hardly make him out. We stood on the flat snow summit with no view except thick Alaskan fog. What now? We were in a frightful position; no food, no bivy gear, and fog preventing us from going farther. Feelings of impending doom: Are we gonna perish here? We lay down and rested. My weariness prevented clear thought. Small things seemed impossible. Then false starts in the fog and snow, huddling from the wind and rain in an alcove, trying to nap, until the mist settled a little around midnight. Suddenly we could see Mt. Dickey. Realizing we could leave this cold place and make it to base camp got us going. We managed to figure out the descent—down the southwest ridge, through the Sheldon Amphitheater, and around into the Gorge and our camp by Dickey.

Variable stone quality, a couple of whippers, and some heart-pounding rock fall kept the descent interesting. We returned to camp 64 hours after leaving.

JON ALLEN

Mt. Barille, Feeling Randy. On April 22 Sean Easton, Dave Marra, and I flew into the Ruth Gorge with aspirations to climb new routes. We decided to "warm up" on the southeast buttress of Mt. Barille. Two days after landing I started up the first pitch, quickly discovering that we were on our way up an enormous pile of gravel. Sean climbed the second pitch to confirm it, and Dave the third. Had it not been for the arrival of our first storm we would have surely abandoned the route. We pushed on in foul weather, because we were on the only safe line in the Gorge.

We spent 11 nights on the wall, but for 4 days we were stormbound in the portaledge. The route was climbed in 15 pitches, primarily aid climbing. Most of the rock was horrible; in places we aided off pitons placed, snow-picket fashion, at the back of a hole dug with hammers. At one point we removed a 3/8-inch bolt by hand, after hauling on it. At other times we couldn't even get bolts in, as the rock disintegrated as we pounded them.

We started the route at an obvious notch 200 feet above the 'schrund, then climbed a short offwidth to face climbing that led to the left side of a large roof. Traversing under the roof we passed it at its apex, then entered a left-facing corner. The corner led to a snow patch 1,000 feet up. We then worked left to another chimney/groove system for 300 feet. Then back right onto the headwall and a straight-in crack for 300 feet. Straight up till we reached a small ridge that took us to the summit.

We named the 850-meter new route Feeling Randy, in honor of our pilot from K2 Aviation. Randy saw us returning from the climb and tipped his wings. An hour later he landed in front of our tent and handed us a pizza. We rated the route Rockies 5.9 A2 [*a Canadian sandbag rating for hard routes with loose rock—editor*]. However, the rating will probably change as our bolts erode out over the next few months.

We attempted a couple of other routes but found similar or worse rock and poor snow and ice conditions. We flew out on May 17.

CONNY AMELUNXEN, *Canada*

LITTLE SWITZERLAND

Dragon's Spine, Apocryphal Arête. I went to Little Switzerland for the first two weeks of June. There Adam George, Ben Lamm, and I climbed the Dragon's Spine. We climbed the south-facing slab to the left of the major dihedral that splits the wall. We named the route the Apocryphal Arête and rated it 5.10cR WI0-. Our route, unfortunately, didn't top out. We got to a small platform 30 feet below the actual top of the formation, but were stopped by snow, lack of balls, and fatigue. I say lack of balls because we could have gone up a steep slab that was clear of snow but opted not to chance a big fall. "I know I've done boulder problems that high and harder than that," I told Ben and Adam, "but there's no way I'd go up that here." Ben tried to traverse around to the north side, but that's where he encountered the snow. Oh, well. Then began our hellish descent. "I love alpine climbing, except for the going-down part," Ben kept saying. He was getting dehydrated, and kept repeating himself, and eventually started mumbling incoherently to himself. The next two tent-bound days did nothing to improve his sanity. He patrolled our campsite, on the hour, looking for yetis. "They'll get us if we're not careful!" he said. "If I hadn't killed that one that stole my harness, we'd be fine. But they're a revenge-minded lot!" After a few weeks back in civilization Ben got a bit saner, but then he bought a motorcycle, and it's been downhill since.

Route description: Begin by hiking up a steep grassy gully for 200 feet to a chimney with old pitons. Rope up. Climb the chimney to a small roof. Traverse right (5.10). Rope drag gets bad, so belay at a bad stance (125 feet). Climb up and then out left onto shitty rock, continuing up until you find a good stance. There aren't any, really. This is the only bad-quality pitch (175-200 feet). The next pitch begins on the same bad stuff but ends on a nice ledge (200 feet). Climb a wide chimney (175 feet). Climb up and left into an offwidth (100-125 feet, 5.9+). Belay where the crack splits. Climb up and right in the narrowing, increasingly flared crack (5.10R); finish on a ledge (190 feet). Climb up and right in a right-facing dihedral (200 feet). Climb to a large ledge and begin up a right-facing dihedral. Belay on a pillar below a left-facing, overhanging dihedral (200 feet). Climb up and left in the dihedral to a small roof. Pull the roof (5.10), then scramble up and belay (100 feet). Climb mostly fourth class towards what looks like the top. Eventually you get to a right-facing dihedral. Climb it to a ledge, keep going up, and pull over left to the top of the pillar where we stopped. It's only 20 or 30 more feet, but without a bolt it would be a V2 highball friction-slab problem. Rappel to the left.

BRIAN SOHN

Middle Troll, south face; The Throne, Smaug's Hoard. Eric Sullivan and I flew to Pika Glacier on August 9 and glassed The Throne's south face. We skied to the base and found a start for our line: a left-facing, right-leaning dihedral system toward the west side of the face. The snow apex at the left edge of the face is the base of the first pitch.

Our second day was a whiteout until late afternoon, when we climbed the first pitch on aid, past hanging moss gardens, and fixed a rope. The 11th dawned clear, and we climbed the south face of Middle Troll (IV/V 5.8). Immaculate dark granite for 1,200 feet led to the summit—a spectacular diving board jutting from the apex of the west face.

On the next day, after we jumared The Throne's first pitch, Eric attempted a hook traverse on aid but took a short fall and skinned his knuckles. I took the lead and pendulumed to a crack to the left. I climbed a slab to an overhang and pulled over (5.10). Above was 30 feet of thin face climbing on flakes, with no protection. Forty feet above my last piece and looking down at a huge ramp, I traversed right to a ledge and pounded in pins. Eric put a nasty core shot in the rope jumaring the pitch, so we called it a day.

The 13th dawned clear, so we hustled to The Throne. I led the third pitch free (5.9+), over a thin slab to a huge, bomb-bay chimney. The fourth pitch entered an overhanging dihedral system that continued for two pitches, through three large roofs. Eric led next, freeing a rotten offwidth, then aiding through a mess of loose blocks on leapfrogged cams and grinding nut placements (A3) to relative security, traversing a 20-foot horizontal roof to a spectacular hanging belay on the rightmost corner of the roof. We fixed a rope and headed home.

It then stormed incessantly for days—rain, snow, and tent-rocking wind. The only respite was downing Southern Comfort in a cold horizontal rain while taking sled runs.

On the afternoon of the 18th it suddenly cleared. We had to get our gear regardless, so we rushed to the wall and jugged our four pitches, pulling the ropes up after us. Eric took the fifth pitch, using aid to pass a double-roof system. There is a wonderful flake just to the right that in dry conditions would probably go at 5.9. Eric finished the pitch (A2) with free moves onto a small sloping ledge. I led the last pitch, an awkward little chimney to a sloper traverse (5.6). We rejoiced at our new route, Smaug's Hoard (V 5.10R/X A3), then made several involved rappels and hopped enormous 'schrunds in a waterfall-filled drainage on The Throne's west face. It had cleared for less than four hours but was storming again by the time we reached camp.

We celebrated with moldy bread, burritos, and the last of the Southern Comfort. Another 40-hour storm dropped almost a foot of snow. Our DGA plane showed up eight hours late on the 20th, and we enjoyed spectacular views of Denali and The Ruth on the flight out.

This report is dedicated to the memory of Matt Porter (24) of Trapper Creek, who died September 13 in a single-car accident near Whitehorse, Yukon. He was a fun, buoyant Alaskan spirit we met on The Pika during our stay, and he will be missed by the Alaskan climbing and skiing communities, as well as by all who knew him.

SAMUEL JOHNSON

Royal Tower, Spam and Legs. Memories of fear and exhilaration lingered as I waited out the storm. What a climb our new route was! For 26 hours of continuous climbing, the ice, rock, and snow of the Royal Tower demanded our concentrated energy. My partner Eric Seifer and I got a full-value climb; a 2,500-foot Grade V that went at M5 WI4 5.8 A2.

Spam and Legs ascends the left Royal Tower, as seen from Pika Glacier, by the right hand of two parallel couloir systems—the couloir immediately right of Boomerang Buttress (photo p.207, 2001 *AAJ*). About three-quarters of the way up the couloir, after it widens from a ribbon, the route exits right across rock to reach the upper snowfields. Kicking steps up the slope, we used sparse rock protection for a running belay.

We began at 8 p.m. on May 21. Our first difficulty was crossing the bergschrund of rotten snow. Eric swam and slithered tenuously between rock and delicate vertical snow mushrooms on the left side of the 'schrund. Once we were across, the race began as we fed our calves 800 feet of moderate mixed terrain with marginal alpine belays.

In the thinnest section of the couloir and the darkest hour of the northern night, Eric scrapped his way up the crux pitch. Barely attached to the wall he pounded pitons in a shallow groove smeared with sublimated ice. Frazzled from the M5 section, he handed me the rack and looked at an upcoming blank section. "Do you think it'll go?"

"No problem," I responded, though I didn't have a clue, really. I had him lower me and used big-wall tricks to pendulum across the face. Finally, at the height of my arc and with my body fully extended, I stuck my tools into ice and heaved us back into the game.

In the gully above we climbed two beautiful sections of WI4, in each a lack of anchors necessitating some simul-climbing. Finally the couloir widened, and we traversed right for two pitches across loose 5.8 rock, until we reached snowfields. It was cake to the top, until I almost fell in the summit cornice crevasse.

We were so far up and so vulnerable. The view was powerful, as seen through the lens of the journey. Down and down now, descending through the steep fear. We stuck our ropes on the first rappel, forcing me to ascend them and move the anchor. We fixed gear for 15 rappels and each of us fell asleep while waiting for the other.

Down safely and out of the way of the storm and accumulating spindrift, I could let go and feel the weight of our adventure sink in.

RIVER (JAMAL) LEE-ELKIN

Middle Troll, Chaos. On June 9 we climbed what we hoped was a new route on the west side of the Middle Troll in Little Switzerland. The route follows the normal route, via a hidden couloir, to the ridge crest, just below the main rock buttress on the west face. From here, instead of continuing up the rock, we traversed along a terrace to the south and climbed directly up the secondary snowfield, stopping 20 feet short of the small col between the Middle Troll and a smaller peak to the south.

From here a chimney gave good climbing and access to the summit ridge. Unfortunately, due to double-sided cornices on the ridge we had to climb below the crest on mixed ground. With some interesting climbing, and tunneling through one section, we reached the final summit block. Because of deteriorating snow conditions and a small slide on the summit slope, we decided not to continue up the final 30 feet to the summit proper.

Descent was down the western buttress. Our ropes became irretrievably jammed, and we had to chop them. Not only were they brand new; it meant the end of our trip.

Since we experienced poor snow conditions and loose rock on much of the climb, we did not grade the route, as difficulty would vary greatly with conditions.

MARK CLIFFORD AND WILL STANTON, *United Kingdom*

South Troll, Pure Retro. In June Brian Teale, Kirsten Kremer, and I completed a new route (Pure Retro, V 5.10+) on the obvious west pillar of the South Troll. It is immediately right of a twin crack I soloed in 1988. The approach is easy and obvious, with steep snow climbing beginning at the bergschrund. The route follows a high-quality crack system and is possibly the best rock climb in the area. Steep snow and ice lead to classic flakes, which lead to splitter cracks on the pillar. The route is safe from falling objects, although the summit snowfield, which sits on a granite slab, is somewhat tenuous. Descent was via rappels on my old route, which we beefed up, providing an excellent way off the spire. Avalanche exposure in the lower gully is high late in the day, and descending the couloir in the early evening was dodgy. Both the 1988 route and the 2001 route should become classics. We spent 14 hours on the ascent and descent. We left a topo in the Talkeetna Ranger Station binder, which also includes the previous routes I've done on the formation.

PAUL TURECKI

KICHATNA SPIRES

Kichatna Spire, As Good as It Gets. In July Nathan Martin and I completed a new route up the center of the central buttress on Kichatna Spire's east face. This was the sixth ascent of the peak, with each ascent creating a new route. The east face is the mountain's most continuously steep and largest face, rising 3,000 feet above the Shadows Glacier. Ours, the fourth route to ascend this face, rises directly to the summit. It is more than half free climbing and is composed of generally very good rock, though it becomes a bit flaky on pitches 12 and 13. From there to the

Kichatna Spire, showing, (1) East Face Pillar, 1982; (2) East Face, 1982; (3) As Good As It Gets, 2001; (4) East Buttress, 1992; (5) Northeast Couloir to North Ridge, 1966. *Jay Smith*

summit the climbing is mixed, involving rock, snow, and easy ice.

We first attempted this route in July 2000, in capsule-style with a portaledge and haulbags. This attempt failed after we spent 11 days on the face and completed nine 60-meter pitches. From our high point we had hoped to complete the route in a single push, leaving the ledge and haulbags to be picked up during the descent. We climbed only two and a half of the days, the remaining days being spent cooped up in the ledge trying to stay dry in torrential rains. Water poured in through the fly's clip-in loop, ran down the straps, and flooded our 3-by 6-foot home. This occurred after meticulous preparation to safeguard against this exact scenario, which I had experienced before on Middle Triple Peak. The best laid plans…. Stubborn and determined though we were, retreat became a dash to safety after five days of continuous downpour turned to snow. As water froze and turned to massive, life-threatening sheets of ice, we rapped. We descended in crampons down overhanging rock walls covered in verglas and flowing with icy waterfalls. Full survival mode.

Two weeks later the snow level dropped to 3,500 feet. Jay Hudson came to our rescue two days past our intended pick-up, after four attempts to fly in. We were the last climbers in the Alaska Range, and he wanted to quit worrying about us. This was nearly his demise. Upon landing, his plane sunk in the mushy snow, its wings iced up, and visibility diminished as darkness closed in and snowfall increased. On our fourth attempt to take off we became airborne but could not gain altitude. The iced wings, tail wind, and payload kept us mere feet above the crevasse-and-rock-strewn glacier at over sixty m.p.h. Jay turned to me and said, "We're not out of this yet!" But there's a good reason why we fly with Hudson, and before long we were talking about beer and showers.

Though I had just experienced one of the worst expeditions of my 20 and we had spent weeks on our backs, after two beers we were making plans for the next year. Hudson wasn't sure

As Good As It Gets: Nathan getting ready to bail (above) after five days of torrential rain at the highpoint of the 2000 attempt. Now it's snowing and everything is turning to ice. *Jay Smith.* Jay Smith on pitch 6 (5.10) leading to the blade cracks up and right. The headwall looms above. Taken during the unsuccessful attempt during July, 2000. *Nathan Martin*

that he wanted to be included and walked out of the Fairview shaking his head and mumbling about selling his planes and taking up fishing.

In 2001 we were back but had just missed one of the finest spells of weather in recent history. People had been summiting left and right in Alaska, while I'd been working the Eco-Challenge in Fairbanks. A month of fantastic weather was coming to an end. Though it had rained for the past two days, Hudson flew us in through improving skies. Within 24 hours we had BC established and four pitches fixed. Then it rained for eight days. On day 10 we started our alpine style attempt and 52 hours later were back on the ground. Our ascent had been completed in rain, snow, and swirling clouds, the summit reached in a total whiteout, and the descent made in a raging storm. The wind had howled, and our ropes hung up. We had given it our all, and we were successful. Thank God it was over. Yippee!

As Good as It Gets (VI 5.11c A3+), completed on July 10, is named for the quality of the climbing—also for the atrocious weather the route was climbed in.

JAY SMITH, *AAC*

Bastion Spire, Slovenian-Alaskan Route; Garvey Spire. Tim Ciosek (U.S.) and I spent 25 days on the Cul de Sac Glacier (a.k.a. Cool Sac) in the Kichatna Spires. We came to the glacier on June 6 and had amazingly good weather and conditions. On June 9 we climbed a new route on the west face of Bastion Spire–the Slovenian-Alaskan Route, IV 5.9 easy mixed, 750 meters. We spent 12 hours on the face, climbing and descending. We found easy mixed climbing in soft snow, with a lot of bad rock sections (5.9) on the lower part of the wall. On the upper part we had solid rock. On June 20 I soloed the southeast couloir (II, 600m) on Sunrise Spire. I started in the middle of the day, so I had soft snow in the couloir. After 40 minutes I reached the ridge but didn't go on to the true summit. We also climbed the spire between Bastion and Skuzerian Peak. We had no information about anyone climbing that spire before. We found an easy couloir up to the ridge and grade IV and V on the ridge to the summit. We named the spire Garvey Spire, after the late Steve Garvey, a well-known Alaskan climber. We left the glacier on July 1. It's an amazing area with tons of possibilities for new routes.

KLEMEN MALI, *Alpine Club of Slovenia*

WRANGELL MOUNTAINS

Peaks 9,035', 9,400'+, and 9,436', first ascents. Peak 11,000', attempt. On June 2 Kelly Bay of Wrangell Mountain Air flew me into the upper Nikonda Glacier at 7,200 feet for reconnaissance. I soloed the east face of Peak 9,035'. The climb started with easy snow, to around 8,000 feet. From here the slopes continually steepened, and I climbed a couple of mixed pitches to reach the summit ridge at 8,700 feet or so. I followed the broken rock ridge with some fifth-class moves for a couple of pitches, before it became easy snow again to the high point. I tried to stay in safe terrain, because of extreme avalanche conditions. On the summit ridge the slopes settled with me, and when I returned to camp I noticed that the whole northeast face of the peak had slid. That was my other choice of a route!

In late August I returned with Kevin Smith to attempt the peak I had been scouting in June. This time we had to hike in to reach my previous camp at 7,200 feet. It took two and a half torturous days to walk in from the Nabesna River landing site at 2,800 feet. We spent most of our time in the creek and climbing the canyon walls with heavy packs. The weather

Peak 11,000'+ in the Wrangell Mountains, taken from the lower glacier on the north and west side of the peak. The attempted route follows the west ridge running from right to left. The still-virgin summit is hidden behind the leftmost high point of the ridge. *Danny Kost*

Pure as the driven snow: Just another 11,000-foot virgin summit in the Wrangell Mountains. Photo taken from the north showing the north face and east ridge on the left. *Danny Kost*

for the rest of the trip was unsettled. It started out clear and extremely windy. On August 28 Kevin soloed Peak 9,436' northeast of camp while we waited for the winds to subside. On August 29 the two of us climbed Peak 9,400'+, which is exactly two miles east of the terminus of the Nikonda Glacier. On August 30 we tried for an early start on our main objective, Peak 11,000+, but again the winds and weather were unsettled. We waited a few hours, and the weather looked better, so we gave it a try. We ascended from camp on a long snow ridge. At around 8,700 feet, we were forced to do a few pitches of fifth-class rock before getting back on snow. At 9,000 feet we began a long traverse across moderate slopes, past Peak 9,903'. We then ascended a short slope to re-access the ridge proper and followed the ridge to around 10,500 feet, where the ridge narrowed to paper thin. It was extremely corniced, and the right side of the ridge was maybe 60 degrees, with the left side approaching vertical. We traversed the ridge on the right side for a few pitches before I decided to turn around. There was nothing but clouds in every direction, and we heard thunder in the valley to the east. It was a tough decision to turn around within an hour or so of the summit. As we were getting off technical ground onto the easier ridge, the summit disappeared in the clouds. After descending for a few pitches we were caught in a total whiteout, with high winds and blowing snow. This continued until we reached base camp. After an hour or so in camp, the clouds lifted again. We'll have to return to finish the last 400 feet to the summit. I believe the ascents we did make were all firsts.

DANNY KOST, *AAC*

Peak 9,200'+. In mid-June Paul Claus landed Bill Chapman and me on the western end of the Nabesna Glacier at around 7,400 feet. We came to climb the peaks on the ridgeline between the Kluvesna and Nabesna glaciers. We climbed at night due to snow conditions. On the first night, June 17, we attempted the east face of a 10,000+-foot peak above camp. We climbed steepening snow and ice to around 10,000 feet, where we set up a belay beneath an overhanging serac. This serac was constantly spitting out spindrift. We started up steep ground around the serac, but it was apparent that we were moving too slowly. We needed to be off the face before the sun hit it at 7 a.m. The face was sliding frequently during the day, so we turned around. Little did I know that, because of weather, this was to be our best night of climbing. On the night of June 18 we ascended Peak 9,200'+ about a mile south of camp. We skied up to around 9,000 feet southeast of the summit. From here we went over Peak 9,155' and followed the ridge to the summit of Peak 9,200'. A steep traversing pitch brought us under the summit block, and a short, steep snow pitch to the summit's narrow ridge. We alternated standing on the summit. The climbing was marginal, due to warm temperatures and rain.

On the night of the 19th we attempted another 10,000+-foot peak about four miles northwest of camp. We skied to a saddle at 8,400 feet, about a mile from the peak. Here we sat waiting for the weather to break, but it only got worse. The weather was again bad on the 20th. On the 21st we skied around to attempt the peak again. We reached a saddle on the north ridge at 9,040 feet. Here the wind and snow pinned us down for a couple of hours. As it subsided we decided to attempt the ridge. However, the loss of time, as well as deep snow on the ridge, forced a retreat from around 10,000 feet. Our pickup was scheduled for the following day, but the wind shifted to the north. Fires were burning in the interior, the glacier had smoke down to the ground, and we were only able to talk with our pilot by radio as he flew over. Luckily, the winds shifted, and we were picked up late in the evening. I believe the ascent we made was a first.

DANNY KOST, *AAC*

Peak 9,072' and Peak 8,778', corrections. On page 218 of the 2001 AAJ first ascents of Peaks 9,072', 8,625', and 8,778' were reported. In 1995 Alaskans Danny Kost and Harry Hunt reached about 10,000 feet in an unreported attempt on the then-unclimbed northeast ridge of Mt. Natazhat. In the process they climbed Peaks 9,072' and 8,778', which lie on this ridge and must be summited to continue to Natazhat. The 1997 AAJ (p. 189) reported a successful ascent of Natazhat's northeast ridge, in April 1996, by Hunt and fellow Alaskans Paul Barry, David Hart, and Dave Lucey. They also climbed Peaks 9,072' and 8,778'. Burch and Taylor's routes (2001 AAJ) on these peaks were probably new but not first ascents of the peaks, and thus their naming of Peak 9,072' may be inappropriate. Their climb of Peak 8,625', however, was likely a first ascent.

CHUGACH MOUNTAINS

Mt. Sergeant Robinson, north face. Cash Joyce and Carl Oswald, who has been extremely active in putting up routes in the western and northwestern Chugach over the last few years, did a 12-hour blitz of the previously unclimbed north face of Mt. Sergeant Robinson (10,450'). The route was about 4,500 feet long, mostly a straightforward snow-and-ice face with alpine ice as steep as 80 degrees. It is probably the fastest way up the mountain from the highway and a good alternative to the knify, long, and loose north ridge. While the hangers in the area might seem frightening from a distance, the route is mostly free of objective hazard. The 13-miles up Glacier Creek is far easier by snow machine or skis in winter than as a summertime trudge. The climb also typifies the potential of these mountains—big ice faces, terrifying rock quality, and relief on the scale of famous big routes in the Canadian Rockies.

EVAN PHILLIPS

Cantata Peak, North Ridge. On August 5 Ryan Campbell and I headed to the south fork of Eagle River, intent on checking out the unclimbed 4,000-foot north ridge of Cantata Peak (6,450'). After hiking six miles we gained a hanging valley above Eagle Lake and gained the ridge through swirling fog. The first half of the ridge was mostly tenuous fourth-class scrambling with one roped pitch (5.4). At 5,000 feet we donned rock shoes to climb a short 5.7 chimney/offwidth. We continued, simul-climbing, until the ridge became a terribly exposed knife-edge. A rappel off a gendarme and a beautiful 5.5 traverse on the crest of the ridge brought us to the chossy upper ridge. Five hundred feet of easy but exposed scrambling took us to the summit. We descended the popular west ridge and cruised back to the trailhead, arriving after 14 hours on the go. The climb was similar to the East Ridge of Edith Cavell, but with crappier rock and a shorter crux. We rate the route III/IV 5.7.

EVAN PHILLIPS

ST. ELIAS MOUNTAINS

Mt. Hobbs; Middle Peak. In early April Ruedi Homberger, Reto Reusch, and a friend they call Gonzo made the first ascent of a 10,500-foot peak between Celeno Peak and Ultima Thule Peak. They accessed the peak from Canyon Creek Glacier and named it Mt. Hobbs, for an Ultima Thule Outfitters cat who has more than nine lives. They then attempted a peak they were calling Middle Peak, but were forced to retreat by avalanches. Charley Sassara and Carlos Buhler also attempted this peak but encountered similar hazards.

BASED ON INFORMATION FROM PAUL CLAUS AND RUEDI HOMBERGER, *Switzerland*

University Peak, South Face; Barnard Glacier, ascents and ski descents. On April 1 Paul Claus dropped Bob Kingsley, Lance McDonald, John Whedon, and me at 7,000 feet, below the south face of University Peak. We had come to the St. Elias Range to attempt the first ascent of this 7,200-foot face. As skiers we were also drawn to the fall line, unbroken from top to bottom. God's own ski shot! Paul had attempted the face several times and generously passed one of his dreams on to us. It felt great having the Claus clan behind us. For the next four days we watched the face, skiing some sweet powder to gain different perspectives on our route. We climbed the bottom quarter one afternoon to an overhanging outcrop that offered the only semblance of protection for a tent on the entire face. A forecast from Paul was for the weather to "fall apart in the next day or two." We decided to go for it in one push.

April 6 was spent maximizing caloric intake. At 10:30 p.m. we left camp in a light snow. The full moon had risen over Mt. Donna, surrounded by a huge halo. All of us expected this to be just a little full moon ski tour. We reached the outcrop in three hours. As we brewed, stars appeared overhead. Continue we must. Dawn found us covered in frost and level with the seracs that hang from the south ridge. Snow conditions were optimal: six to eight inches of sloughed powder over ice. At around 8 a.m. we traversed left, hoping to find a place to chill on the ridge. Exposure there was even greater: huge granite cliffs dropped to the Hawkins Glacier. At 10:30 a.m. we finally reached a level spot at the very top of the south face. We were still roughly 300 vertical feet below the summit but decided to save our energy for the descent. We climbed down into a tight tube, where we found good ice for a V-thread. A 200-foot rap brought us to skiable snow. The first few thousand feet were 50 degrees or more, tapering to 45 degrees below. As we relaxed on the final 40-degree powder, Paul's Beaver rounded the corner, carrying the next of several University Peak ski-descent teams.

Just before dark a knock on the Megamid had us revelers tipping over assorted kettles and bottles. Paul, after swapping planes, had cut his engine near the summit and coasted into the

Left: Base camp beneath the 7,200-foot south face of University Peak. The highpoint of the various ski descents was the final rock outcrop 300 feet beneath the summit. All skiers followed the main snowy face, some on the left, some on the right. *Dave Hanning* Right: John Whedon during the first ski descent of the south face of University Peak (from 300 feet beneath the summit, with some rappelling). *Lorne Glick*

alpenglow to bring us congratulatory beers. On the 10th, with six days left, three of us (Lance had frostbite) made a plan with Paul for a pickup to the east. We crossed an easy pass east of University via a straight and narrow glacier. After setting up camp at 7,000 feet on the main Barnard, we skied several 10,000-foot peaks. Incidentally, Paul, having flown very near the summits of the peaks in this area with an accurate altimeter, thinks that actual elevations are higher than those listed on maps. He believes that University Peak is almost 15,000 feet high, rather than the accepted 14,470 feet.

LORNE GLICK

University Peak, south face skiing. Shortly after the above ascent and ski descent, on April 18, Brad Barlage and Dave Hanning climbed high on the south face and descended on skis. Barlage turned around about 1,000 feet from the summit and skied the face from 13,780 feet. Hanning reached about 14,300 feet. After nearly disastrous attempts to ski from higher, he down- climbed to the ledge from which Barlage started and skied from there. Hanning writes, "However, the face itself still has not seen a summit. This jewel will shine brightly among the many in the University Range of the Wrangell-St. Elias Mountains until someone comes to claim her." The team skied many chutes in the area as well, and ski-toured in the western Wrangells.

On May 13 the husband-and-wife team of John Chilton and Lisa Korthals also climbed high on this face and skied down. Photographer Blake Jorgensen and Chris Korthals, Lisa's brother, who served as a safety guide for Blake, were also on the trip but did not ski the face. Chilton and Lisa Korthals reached a high point of about 13,500 feet. Writes Chilton, "It seems both the previous descent parties climbed and skied the climber's left side of the face. Being two weeks later in the year, with the sun packing more punch everyday, we felt there were more threatening objective hazards on the left side and elected to tackle the face from the climber's right side. During our descent slides scoured the left side three times. I read my inclinometer eight times that day, and every time it was between 48 and 52 degrees, for over 7,000 vertical feet." Both parties experienced frigid nighttime temperatures but observed considerable solar warming of the snow during the day.

BASED ON REPORTS FROM JOHN CHILTON, BRAD BARLAGE*, AAC, AND DAVE HANNING*, AAC
*RECIPIENTS OF AN AAC/HELLY HANSEN ADVENTURE GRANT

Baldwin Glacier: Peaks 10,460', 9,450', 10,142', 9,100'. On June 14 Marcus Collins, Phil Fortier, Greg Mueller, and I flew in to the upper Baldwin Glacier with Ultima Thule Outfitters pilot Paul Claus. With our base camp located at 8,000 feet, we climbed several nearby peaks. We made the first ascent of Peak 10,460' by its glaciated west face. The route consisted mostly of 40- to 45-degree snow and bare ice, with a short and notably steeper section of ice around mid-face. After this ascent, we skied across the glacial valley to the west and climbed Peak 9,450' by its south ridge. The most aesthetic mountain of the area is Peak 10,142', of which we made the second ascent by the unclimbed west face. The west face contains a glacial tongue that flows steeply down the edge of a cirque from the summit. The route began with several pitches of moderate ice, followed by long slopes of frozen snow (40- to 50-degrees) interspersed with short bare sections. After summiting we began an unknown descent down the south ridge, where we linked steep snowfields between the cliffs along the ridge. We also skied up Peak 9,100' via its west side. The final summit ridge consisted of traversing a cornice and scrambling on a loose rock spire. In addition we climbed an unnumbered peak immediately south of Peak 10,460' via a seven-pitch ice climb on its north face. The route, on almost entirely bare 50- to 60-degree ice, led from mid-face to a breech in the cornices about 300 feet below the summit. A short section of 40- to 60-degree snow led to the double corniced top of the peak. We had very good weather for most of the trip, but this created soft snow and some faces never froze. Our team flew out to the Chitina airstrip on July 3.

DAVID BURDICK, *AAC*

ALASKA COAST MOUNTAINS

Mendenhall Towers, Rain, Heavy at Times; Rabbit Ears, Who Needs Cable? Over a 10-day period from June 18 to 27 Ryszard Pawlowski (Poland), Dave Sorric, and I put up a new route on the north face of the Mendenhall Towers (6,980') in the Juneau Icefield. The route follows the prominent arête on the north side of the highest tower for 2,500 vertical feet. This was the third attempt in as many years by Sorric and myself, the previous two having been stifled by bad weather, the usual crux of climbs in southeast Alaska. As in the previous years, once the awaited weather window arrived, Northstar Trekking helicopters flew us from Juneau to the north side of Mendenhall Towers.

After fixing four pitches we spent three days waiting out the weather. We then climbed

another two pitches and secured the haulbag at our fourth pitch, as it started to rain again. We retreated to the ground. After we spent two more days in the tent, the weather improved, and we made our way to a prominent saddle about one-third of the way up the arête, where we bivied. After a 6 a.m. start we reached the summit around 9:30 p.m. and finally returned to the bivy site at 6 a.m., 24 hours after leaving. After a short rest we descended to the glacier.

We named the route Rain, Heavy at Times in memory of the dismal forecast we constantly heard on our previous two attempts. We rated it V 5.10d, with snow and ice to 60 degrees. The route involved 24 pitches and 14 rappels. We used a 70-meter rope, which future teams should take into consideration, especially when following our rappel anchors.

The rare good weather also allowed Dave Sorric and I to put up a new line on the north face of Rabbit Ears, west of Mendenhall Towers. The route ascends the north face to the left of the prominent dihedral that was first climbed by John Svenson and others. In keeping with the Rabbit Ears theme, we called the route Who Needs Cable? It involved eight pitches up to 5.10b.

Mendenhall Towers, Rain, Heavy At Times shown. *Jacek Maselko*

JACEK MASELKO, *Poland*

Canada

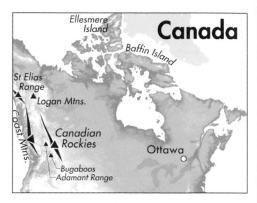

ST. ELIAS RANGE

KLUANE NATIONAL PARK RESERVE

Mountaineering summary and statistics.
During the 2001 climbing season 42
mountaineering expeditions registered in
Kluane National Park Reserve. A total of 163
persons spent 2,872 person-days in the
Icefields. The weather was again typical of the St. Elias Range, "unpredictable." Some expeditions
hit it lucky and had few weather days, while others waited out long periods of poor weather.
Avalanche conditions seemed to be greater than normal, with many teams reporting a very
weak layer in the snowpack throughout the Icefields all season long. Some teams wisely decided
to abort or change their planned routes because of this phenomenon.

As is the norm, most expeditions focused on Mt. Logan, though only the King Trench
and East Ridge routes were attempted. Of the 23 expeditions on Mt. Logan, 11 reached one of
the main summits (Main Peak, East Peak, or West Peak). Successful expeditions took from 13
to 24 days to reach a summit, depending on weather and the team's abilities. Other mountains
that had climbing activity included Queen Mary (six expeditions), Mt. Lucania-Steele (four),
King Peak (two), Kennedy (one), Walsh (one), Vancouver (one), and Pinnacle (one). The
Icefield Discovery Camp was in operation again; its location may be the reason that Mt. Queen
Mary was a popular destination. Only four guided expeditions were in the Icefields. There were
also three ski-tour expeditions into the St. Elias Range. Of note was a traverse of Mt. Logan—
up the East Ridge and down the King Trench—by a keen crew from British Columbia. Another
B.C. crew ski toured the St. Elias Range from Kluane Lake to Dry Bay, Alaska. And a B.C. couple was successful on both Mt. Logan and Denali this season.

Only one major search-and-rescue operation occurred. The incident involved the loss of
Kurt Gloyer, one of the premier mountain pilots in the area, when his aircraft crashed upon
take-off after picking up two climbers near Mt. Kennedy. The climbers survived the crash, in
which the aircraft ended up 30 meters down a large crevasse, and were rescued the next day.
Other incidents were of a lesser nature, such as frostbite and altitude sickness. In each case the
climbing party was able to get itself to its base camp.

Scientists were also at work on the slopes of Mt. Logan. Because of the altitude and cold,
Logan's ice and snow have never melted. Glaciologists took ice cores from the Logan plateau
and from these cores can obtain a history of the earth's climate. The team established two
camps, one on the Quintina Sella Glacier and the other near 5330m on the upper plateau.

Anyone interested in mountaineering in Kluane National Park Reserve should contact
the Mountaineering Warden and ask for a mountaineering package. The Warden can be
reached by mail (Kluane National Park, Box 5495, Haines Junction, Yukon, Canada, Y0B 1LO),
by phone (867-634-7279), or by fax (867-634-7277.) Information can also be obtained from
the Kluane National Park website at http://www.parkscanada.pch.gc.ca/kluane.

RICK STALEY, *Mountaineering Warden, Kluane National Park Reserve*

Mt. Kennedy, north buttress, ascent and pilot's death. On July 10 Bill Pilling and I flew with Kurt Gloyer to climb the north buttress of Mt. Kennedy. We decided to carry over the top and return via a scenic and easy route over nearby Mt. Alverstone. Bill had descended the north side of Alverstone in 1995. We started up on July 15 with six days of supplies and climbed through most of the sustained 50- to 65-degree ice that makes up most of the first half of the route. Our expectations that July would be the best time for this route were fulfilled, as we found more ice and little of the deep snow that has plagued April to June attempts. No bivouac sites appeared until we made it to a tiny ice spur to the right of the main prow. After we chopped a site and re-hydrated, it was early morning, and we took a rest day. On the 17th we continued up more sustained ice and snow to the upper rock band, the crux section of the route. There we worked ice runnels and ramps across smooth granite. As midnight approached we bivouacked under an overhang. After a short sleep I led the crux rock section, somehow pinching a nerve that weakened my right foot. Bill led one more mixed pitch and reached snow slopes. After a few more pitches we stopped early to give me a chance to rest and stretch my back. In the morning I felt better, but Bill volunteered to keep leading. He balanced this nobility with a few route-finding mistakes. We got back on track and climbed snow slopes, digging in near the summit. Unfortunately, a wind came up, and we experienced the same problem that Tackle and Roberts had there in 1996, as spindrift poured down and pushed in our tent. We escaped to the summit and an extensive view.

We descended to camp on the Cathedral Glacier at about 11,800 feet. Storm and whiteout then kept us there, as our supplies dwindled. As our pickup date approached we stomped a note in the snow asking for food and gas. The skies cleared during the day on the 26th, our pickup date. At about 6 p.m. Kurt Gloyer flew in and found us. He circled twice to scout our situation and landed near us. He had noted crevasses below, but felt there was enough take-off room to clear them. I don't know why, but we didn't get in the air before those crevasses. The FAA later said that the skis and prop broke off on a slight rise of snow. We plummeted into the last crevasse, stopping about 80 feet down. Kurt died shortly after the crash. Bill and I huddled, injured, in the plane. The next day a combination of U.S. military, Coast Guard, Kluane Park rangers, and Gulf Air personnel collaborated on a safe and efficient rescue. We are forever grateful for their efforts, and we mourn the loss of Kurt, a great pilot and exemplary individual.

ANDY SELTERS, *AAC*

ELLESMERE ISLAND

Manson Icefield, ascents and exploration. From the village of Grise Fjord we made a month-long unsupported ski tour and exploratory mountaineering trip from April 28 to May 24. Our group consisted of Marek Vokac and Lars Tore Ludvigsen from Norway, and Marshall Netherwood and myself from Canada. Each person skied with a pulk containing all supplies for our 300 km tour. The pulks weighed between 60 and 70 kg apiece.

We walked and skied frozen Jones Sound for 55 km to the Jakeman Glacier, one of the few named glaciers flowing from the Manson Icefield. The Manson Icefield extends over approximately 6,000 square kilometers, with over 50 glaciers reaching the ocean. The widest glacial snout reaching the sea is nearly 15 km wide. We skied up the Jakeman, taking the left fork, and after four days were situated well into the icefield. From two camps seven summits were ascended with skis and crampons.

Everyone made numerous penetrations into crevasses, usually when not wearing skis and typically while on summits or ridges. The visits were only up to the armpits, but the crevasses were certainly deep and wide enough to kill. Polar bear protection included two shotguns, noisemaker pistols, bear spray, and a camp perimeter trip-wire alarm system. No bears and no tracks old or new were seen.

The weather was mixed. It began with −30ºC night temperatures and ended just above freezing a month later. About 30 percent of the time the icefield was covered in clouds thick enough to be considered whiteout conditions. Moderately strong winds were common from all directions. On the last night, near Grise Fjord, a tent pole was bent by the wind.

On the return route we descended a different glacier to a brackish lake dammed by the Jakeman Glacier. A side trip into Fram Fjord included scrambling up two minor peaks. Our last ascent, starting from three kilometers west of Anstead Point, was up an unnamed 1111m peak at the southern edge of a small unnamed icefield.

Table of peaks climbed and their locations:

DATE	MOUNTAIN	ELEVATION	UTM EAST	UTM NORTH	ROUTE
May 6	Peak 1 (glacial dome)	1368m	518035	8511790	Traverse of western slopes
May 7	Peak 2 (Hyperbolic Ridge)	960m	517897	8521634	Up SW ridge, down NNE ridge
May 10	Peak 4	1347m	513575	8525398	SW slope
May 12	Peak 5	1334m	511962	8528548	SSW ridge
May 12	Peak 6	1340m	513904	8530484	West ridge
May 19	Peak 8 (boundary pt. of land claim GF-23/49A)	741m	496300	8496500	SSW ridge
May 19	Peak 9	457m	490500	8491500	NE slopes
May 21	Peak 10 (Fielder Icecap)	1111m	480430	8493145	SSE slopes

All UTMs are NAD 27 in zone 17X
Altitudes from GPS and corrected to measured sea level difference

GREG HORNE, *Alpine Club of Canada*

BAFFIN ISLAND

Cambridge Fjord, Alain Estève Peak, Sous l'œil de Nanouk. Combining their experience of polar deserts and of mountains all over the world, climbers of the French High Mountain Military Group (GMHM) went to the Canadian north and climbed a virgin peak during their three-weeks spring trip. The route is more than 1,000 meters high and is situated on the unexplored Cambridge Fjord, on the northeast side of the island. The peak was found during an aerial reconnaissance in April. We called it Alain Estève Peak in the memory of a friend who died on a Norwegian icefall four years ago.

The expedition began on May 19 at the small village of Clyde River. Inuit hunters drove us with snowmobiles for two days on the ice cap to the fjord. We were lucky to observe a seal hunting and to see (far from us!) two polar bears. We arrived at the base camp in a storm. A few minutes later we were alone, 300 km from the nearest established settlement.

During the first week the weather was awful. Nevertheless, during the few moments of blue sky we managed to fix 400 meters of rope on the wall. During the second week the sun came back. The entire team climbed to the top of the ropes, leaving only belay anchors behind. The first bivouac was on the first shoulder. On the second day we reached the second shoulder, facing the overhanging part of the upper mountain. We fixed two pitches before sleeping. On the day after, despite snowfall in the morning, we fixed seven pitches.

The next day was the hardest. The moves were intricate, but we succeeded in freeing them. On the last day, June 1, the bags were hauled and the last 50 meters easily climbed. Because of bear tracks around base camp, we called the route Sous l'œil de Nanouk (Under the Eye of the Bear).

ANTOINE DE CHOUDENS, *French High Mountain Military Group (GMHM)*

Turnweather Glacier, Sangtraït. When Frank Van Herreweghe (Belgian, but Catalonian citizen) and I arrived at Auyuittuq National Park, we felt really happy. After months waiting for this moment, finally we were in Baffin, ready to enjoy this unknown land. We arrived in the beginning of July at Pangnirtung. We spent 10 days carrying our stuff from Overlord to the Turnweather Glacier. It's a hard trek with weight—not too long compared with the approach to Asgard or Thor, but steeper and long enough.

Turnweather's 1,155-meter Sangtraït route. *Silvia Vidal*

Silvia Vidal on Sangtraït, belay 10. *Frank Van Herreweghe*

We knew about the first route on the wall, Insumisioa, climbed in 1995 by a Basque-Catalonian team. We also consulted the rangers' office, where climbers register ascents. There we learned of two attempts—a Canadian attempt in 1999 and an earlier Japanese attempt.

We put our base camp at the Turnweather moraine and started to fix the first 250 meters of the wall. It was difficult to choose a line because we didn't have much information about the previous attempts. Finally we decided to start on the east buttress on the north face. We climbed 19 pitches, two having been climbed by the Canadians and having bolted belays and one having been climbed by the Japanese. The other 16 pitches were ours. We spent 15 days living on the wall capsule style (three camps), climbing and suffering from rain and fog. The result is a new route called Sangtraït (blood blister). The blood blister appeared after I smashed a finger with the hammer. I also broke my finger.

Sangtraït has 1,155 meters of aid and free climbing (A4 5.11a 60-degree snow). The first 150 meters are on a 40-degree snow ramp. Then the rock begins, being a bit loose for the next four pitches. After this we had to cross a 60-degree snow ramp, after which the rock becomes better and better until the top. We rapped down the wall, taking 24 hours. It was hard to cross the ramps, lowering our haulbags, because after 15 days there was no more snow, just loose rocks. Chaotic!

After opening this new line we had time left, so we hiked through the main valley to visit mounts Asgard and Thor and see how beautiful they are. We spent two months on Baffin Island, enjoying the landscape, the people, and the climbing. But most important was to enjoy all this with Frank. Always happy, always there.

SÍLVIA VIDAL, *Spain*

Mt. Thor, Project Mayhem. On July 28 Jim Beyer soloed to the summit of Mt. Thor after completing what he calls "the hardest big wall route on the planet." The route has five pitches of modern A5 and three pitches of A4+. By comparison, he says the hardest El Cap routes have two to four pitches of A4+ to A5. He reports: "Although I have climbed at least three routes (solo first ascents, unrepeated) with harder pitches (Cult of Suicidal, A6a, on Outlaw Spire in Canyonlands; and On a Tear and Parallel Reality, both A5+, on Sextant Spire near Shiprock), I believe Project Mayhem (A5c) is harder because it is long and continuously difficult." Project Mayhem, he feels, "is truly a route worth dying for." His story appears earlier in this Journal.

Mt. Asgard, Charlie Porter Route and Scott Route, fast ascents. Taking Yosemite speed-climbing tactics to Baffin Island, Jason "Singer" Smith and Cedar Wright made the second ascent of the revered Charlie Porter Route (VII 5.10+ A4) on Mt. Asgard in an incredible 38-hour push (54 hours round trip from base camp). They also repeated the Scott Route (3,500', 5.11) on Asgard in 3 hours and 56 minutes. A full story on their remarkable trip appears earlier in this journal.

LOGAN MOUNTAINS

Bustle Tower, Lotus Flower Tower, Parrot Beak Peak, Proboscis. In the Cirque of the Unclimbables Jonathan Copp made a series of impressive ascents with various partners. With Brooke Andrews he established the Don't Get Piggy (V 5.12a) variation to Club International, and with Tim O'Neill made the first free ascent of Club International (V 5.11b). The routes are also the first free ascents of 2,000-foot Bustle Tower. He and Josh Wharton then climbed the famous Lotus Flower Tower in 4 hours and 26 minutes. Copp and Wharton also established Pecking Order

(2,800', V+ 5.11R) on Parrot Beak Peak, also in a day. After a rest day, the pair made the first all-free ascent of the Original Route (2,000', V 5.12R) on Proboscis, onsight, in a day. A full account of this trip appears earlier in this journal.

Terrace Tower, The White Tower first free ascent, and Light in August. Yan Mongrain and I arrived in the Cirque of the Unclimbables on July 28. On August 10 we brought our gear to Terrace Tower, a squat, flat-topped spire near Bustle Tower, to just "have a look." We were attracted to The White Tower on Terrace Tower, first climbed by Paul Friberg and Kurt Blair in 1997 and rated III 5.11 A1. The route ascends the left side of a prominent white pillar, with the steepness of the wall giving it a Rostrum-like feel. After our mandatory groveling through two loose, grassy pitches, Yan led the first of the steep, enjoyable pitches, a perfect crack in a left-facing corner. I then set off on what we thought was the A1 section, an imposing dark, wet-looking overhang. It was dry enough to free, although we

Terrace Tower's southeast face, showing (1) The White Tower, (2) Light in August. *Jay Knower*

could easily picture the roof being very wet and therefore unfreeable. Sustained, slightly loose 5.9 climbing brought us to the summit. We rated the route III 5.11, and thought that the A1 roof was not much harder than the rest of the route. After asking around camp and reading route information, we determined that the route had not been freed prior to our ascent.

While on The White Tower we spied a possible line to the right of the prominent pillar. We fixed ropes on the first two pitches, pitches shared with The White Tower. The third pitch proved to be the crux, and on our first attempt I fell onto a poorly placed .75 Camalot. I then aided to a good anchor, and we cleaned and worked the section on toprope. Dirt in the cracks and the subtlety of the moves required us to resort to this maneuver. An onsight ascent would certainly be a feather in one's cap! After pulling the rope, Yan led the pitch. Above this pitch the crack widened to an awkward, overhanging chimney, which finally led to a belay on a huge wedged block.

We had been climbing on the right side of the prominent white pillar. Above the block we could stay on the right side of the pillar and surely top out without much additional difficulty (the right side showed evidence of a previous, probably aid, ascent), or we could veer left up a steeper crack system splitting the pillar itself. We headed left, up very steep hand and finger cracks, passing three roofs along the way, giving ourselves three added pitches of sustained 5.11. The last pitch looked relatively easy, and we wearily congratulated each other on our new route, thinking the ascent was in the bag. The last move before the summit, however, presented a serious problem: a sloping, slightly overhanging mantle onto a grassy ledge. After much difficulty and many expletives, the move was accomplished by a dynamic lunge into a moss-filled crack, fingers buried in mud and moss, and the adept use of a knee. Yan and I named our route Light in August (8 pitches, IV 5.12-).

JAY KNOWER

Mt. Proboscis, Piton Karmik and various repeats. The story starts from a discussion we had with Paul Piana and Todd Skinner in Greenland, in the Tasermiut Fjord, in 1998. They told us about Proboscis and their route Great Canadian Knife, and we learned of possibilities for new routes. So last year on July 10 Thierry Bionda, Antonin Guenat, and I were at the Geneva airport, ready to visit the land of gold for a six-week trip. The trip was organized from Switzerland with Warren LaFave of Inconnu Lodge.

Four days later the magic of a helicopter brings us to the base of the southeast face of Proboscis, with our gear and food. We contemplated some lines, but when we looked closely, there were bolts or belay anchors. Finally, we chose the left pillar. There is no route on this side of the wall, it dries quickly, and the rock seems solid. There is no risk of rockfall, as in the central part. After two days of continuous rain the sun came out, and six days of perfect weather awaited us. Six days later our route, Piton Karmik (550 meters, VI 5.10b A3), is finished. The rock was as good as we expected, and the crack systems were clean and nice to climb. The route was mostly aid climbing, with some free pitches.

Three days later, after a friendly visit from a grizzly bear that we witnessed from the top of our route, we started the Great Canadian Knife (VI 5.13b). On the 26th we fixed 200 meters and came back the day after to finish the route. We stopped one and a half easy pitches before the end of the route because of a heavy hailstorm. Now we decided to come back to civilization. By the 29th all our gear was on What Notch pass, and we took it to base camp in Fairy Meadow. On August 2 we climbed the Lotus Flower Tower's Southeast Face route (V 5.10) on a rainless day. The climb is very amazing and dry except the first two pitches. After some days of boul-dering with locals we climbed the route Jonny Copp and Tim O'Neill freed one week before, Club International (V 5.11b) on Bustle Tower's south face.

We took the next helicopter out and went fishing and climbing near Whitehorse until our return to Switzerland.

DENIS BURDET, *Switzerland*

Phenocryst Spire, The Hustler. Mark Reeves and Steve Sinfield, supported by the Welsh Sports Council, arrived at Glacier Lake on July 30. They slogged to Fairy Meadows, set up camp, and waited most of a week for better weather before climbing the classic Lotus Flower Tower in about 12 hours.

After a couple of rest days under blue skies, the Welsh team went to what they think is Phenocryst Spire. They fixed three pitches up a clean white rock pillar. The next night they slept at the base and woke to rain at 3:00 a.m. One and a half hours later the rain ceased. They climbed nine pitches above the fixed three, gaining a 16-foot square subsummit at the top of the white pillar. They had freed all pitches onsight. The sky grew dark, rain fell, and they began descending the route. They placed three bolts for rappelling (one of which can be clipped for pro on pitch 7). The Hustler (1,500', V 5.10-R) involves clean granite slabs and corners, some avoidable loose rock, and runouts on the harder sections.

BASED ON REPORTING BY MARK REEVES AND MOUNTAIN INFO, *High Mountain Sports*

COAST MOUNTAINS

SQUAMISH CHIEF

Warriors of the Wasteland, Second Ascent. Warriors was a communal effort that spanned over 20 years, with over 10 people involved in the ascent. At IV 5.12c it was first completed and free climbed continuously by Matt Maddaloni and Ben DeMenech in September 2000. Colin Moorhead and I did the second ascent in July 2001. Warriors starts by coinciding with Western Dihedrals for two pitches of steep 5.10+/5.11- slab and face climbing. Then more 5.11- face and crack. Pitch four gets real, with a sustained 5.12 ultrathin crack. The fifth pitch, the crux, is a steep, difficult face. (The rock to the right looks easier.) Pitch six is an incredibly burly, over-hanging corner (50 meters, solid 5.11). This is followed by a rather unpleasant traverse right along a dike into a corner. The finish is on Colin's awesome 5.10+ Cloudburst. Colin and I climbed Cloudburst, mostly in the rain, freeing most of it. With the exception of Scott Cosgrove's free version of the Grand Wall, we deem it the most difficult free climb on the Chief.

STEVE SEATS

Alaska Highway, free solo. In July I was walking up the North Walls trail with my shoes, chalk bag, and the ashes of my friend Ben DeMenic. The plan was to climb Angel's Crest, a 15-pitch 5.10, and scatter his ashes along the way. I'm not sure what I was thinking, but I found myself at the base of Alaska Highway, a 5-pitch 5.11+ I'd climbed with Ben a few years before and had done a few times that summer. I had been toying with the idea of soloing the route for some time. I knew it was dry, I knew the weather was only going to last another day or two, I knew I'd already cheated the first crux (it would be an awfully stiff march up that trail all alone and empty handed). One question remained: Can I get to the top without falling off? I ran over the route in my mind: I'd felt supersolid on the last few goes. I took the bag of ashes out of my pocket and put a large pinch in my chalk bag. "Bet you never thought you'd do this one," I said. The first pitch is always a struggle, it involves weird (classic Squamish) tree-humping through a roof. It went smooth. The second is the crux for most people. It's way steep, way awkward, and way physical. It's also the type of climbing I find I'm best at. It went too quickly. The only part that was at all scary was the last 30 feet of 5.8 face climbing. I'm an awful face climber. I dug a little hole at the top to put Ben's ashes in. Then I said goodbye. The walk down was weird, dreamlike but hyperfocused. Kind of sad and lonesome, too. The locals seemed to think it was the first free solo of the route, when word got out. This surprised me; I figured Croft had most likely done it and maybe somebody else as well. All in all, I don't care. It was a fun solo and it's a great route. It was also the last time I climbed with Ben.

STEVE SEATS

Monarch Mountain, central Coast Range, March. There is only one route on the south face, shown. *Guy Edwards*

Coast Range B.C./AK, first complete ski traverse. From Feb. 2 to July 17, 2001, we traversed the spine of the Coast Range Mountains from Vancouver, B.C., to Skagway, Alaska. The trip was 2,015 km. in length, and was done primarily on skis.

The Coast Range is a very rugged range that receives a lot of precipitation, and thus is very heavily glaciated. Many of the sections of our route had been traveled before by such explorers as Dave Williams, Markus Kellerhas, John Baldwin, John Clark, and others. However, the 400 km section from Bella Coola to Terrace, as well as sections near the Iskut River, Stikine River, and Whiting River had not previously been traversed.

Guy Edwards, Lillouet Icefield, Feb. 20. *Dan Clark*

The route, following the major icefields, peaks, landforms, or towns, was: Mistys, Garibaldi Divide, Pemberton, Lillooet, Homathko, Klinaklini, Monarch, Bella Coola, Tweedsmuir Divide, Mt. Atna, Terrace, Shames Mountain, Kinskuch, Cambria, Salmon Glacier, Eskay, Hoodoo Mountain, Choquette Glacier, Great Glacier, Devil's Thumb, Sheppard Peak, Wright Glacier, Taku Glacier, and Juneau Icefield. We finished the route by hiking the Chilkoot Trail to the headwaters of the Yukon River.

The whole route was traveled in a self-propelled manner except for the crossings of the Iskut River, Stikine River, and the Whiting River. Twenty four food caches were prepared, nine of which were placed by helicopter or ski plane.

We climbed 14 peaks en route, including first ascents of Stadium Peak and Peak "Such A Long Journey." As well, we made four attempts on the Devil's Thumb, but were not successful—blaming it on the limitations of our lightweight ski gear. Numerous steep slopes, icefalls, glaciers, and other obstacles were encountered and negotiated—the trip was a mountain traverse.

Initially four people started: Dan Clark, Vance Culbert, John Millar, and myself. After one month, while skiing down to the Homathko River, Dan Clark was badly injured in a fall and could not continue on the trip. Kari Medig continued with the group as a new fourth member from the Klinaklini Glacier to Terrace. In Terrace, Kari departed, and Lena Rowat joined as the new fourth. On the Stikine River, Cecelia Mortensen joined as a fifth, traveling all the way to Skagway. From the Taku River to Skagway, Heather Culbert also joined us.

Highlights included repeated bathing in icy rivers and glacial ponds, being tent-bound and food deprived for four days on the Klinaklini Icefield, cracker crumb wars, seeing the south face of Monarch Mountain, traveling the Cambria and Juneau Icefields in whiteout conditions unable to see anything, negotiating the avalanches through the "Wicked Valleys," skiing bare glacial ice, shoulder stands, and enjoying the wilderness of southeast Alaska and northwest B.C. Living as a small contained group with little outside

Coast Range Traverse, Vancouver to Skagway.

The southeast face of Devil's Thumb, Alaska, in early June, during the complete Coast Range Traverse. *Guy Edwards*

contact for five months was a challenge in itself.

Thanks to the Shipton-Tilman Award (W.L. Gore), the Canadian Himalayan Foundation, and other private companies for assistance.

Guy Edwards, *Canada*

Mt. Tiedemann, South Buttress Integrale, correction. On page 110 of the 2001 *AAJ*, Simon Richardson writes that the South Buttress Integrale of Mt. Tiedemann had not been repeated. In fact, Bruno Boll, Daniel Hamman, and I climbed the route in July, 1998 (see 1999 AAJ, page 272). We were inspired to do the route by Jim Nelson (member of the first ascent party), who provided us with photos and route information.

Forrest Murphy, *AAC*

Adamant Range

Gothic Peak, south face; The Stickle, south face. Fred Beckey recruited and led our party from Squamish and Pemberton, B.C. into the Adamant Range this summer. The trip produced two new high-quality free climbs on good granite. Our first and main objective was Gothic Peak. Fred's photo of its aesthetic virgin south face helped inspire us to board the chopper and do our duty by exploring the vertical world. Andre Ike and I found a continuous dihedral system that went for six pitches up the southeast corner, before hitting the fat white feldspar band that wraps the entire summit. An upward and leftward traverse through this band led to an exit corner and the summit, eight pitches later. The climbing went free at 5.11a, with the crux on the first pitch, although a 5.10+ offwidth on the third pitch provided the most entertainment.

A good variety of corner cracks and face climbing made up the rest of the route.

Later that week John Chilton and Lisa Korthals climbed four new pitches up the south face of The Stickle. Their attention then turned elsewhere (base camp in Thor Meadows is a distracting place), and they offered the unfinished Stickle line to Andre and me. We obliged, and by late afternoon the next day we were on its summit, with Lisa and Johnny yodeling at us from the summit of neighboring Mt. Adamant. The route followed a steep, crescent-shaped corner for three pitches of 5.10 to a ridge, for two pitches of mid-fifth, and finally a beautifully exposed headwall for two more ropelengths with moves up to 5.11-. This put us in a little notch on the summit ridge where we discovered a perfect 5.9 handrail that led directly to the summit. We each led and down-led this pitch, as there was little available for an anchor on the summit, and the notch was the ideal spot to rappel from. That night, and for the second time that week, we had the pleasure of experiencing darkness through the sketchy

Andre Ike, last pitch of the Stickle. *Jon Walsh*

maze of crevasses on the Adamant Glacier. It's amazing how fast snow bridges and footprints melt at 30 degrees in the middle of August. For topos and more info on these routes, check out Dave Jones' new guidebook, *Selkirks North*, due out in spring 2002.

JON WALSH

PURCELL MOUNTAINS

THE BUGABOOS

Bugaboo Provincial Park Mountaineering summary and statistics. The 2001 Bugaboo season was blessed with good weather but not many new routes. Rather, a number of older classics were dusted off. Early July saw an attempt at the completion of an aid project on the Pigeon Feathers by a team of locals that ended in a med-evac when one member of the party broke an ankle as the result of a ledge fall. Members of the same team nearly completed a new line on the Minaret of South Howser Tower. The ice route Ice Hose on South Howser was in shape most of the summer, allowing several ascents by alpine ice aficionados from around the world and even from Canmore, Alberta. All Along The Watchtower on North Howser saw an ascent by a Kiwi/Canadian team. Among the most in-vogue classic routes were the Southwest Corner of Snowpatch Spire and the Beckey-Chouinard on South Howser, which never seems to lose appeal. In addition the Northeast Ridge of Bugaboo saw at least three to four ascents a week in late July and all of August. Several parties were benighted on the Northeast Ridge due to under-estimating the commitment this classic route demands. The only other med-evac of the summer was the result of rockfall in the Bugaboo/Snowpatch col. The victim escaped with only minor injuries. The oldest climber was 76 and was not Fred Beckey. During mid-August a team of 17 women known as Girls-Rock ruled the Applebee campground and completed everything from Wildflowers on Snowpatch to the Beckey-Chouinard on South Howser. Some men were afraid, while others were delighted. A lone Minnesota climber attempted a burly aid line on the east face of Bugaboo Spire, only to be defeated by a week of poor weather at the end of July. Hence he called his effort Unfinished Symphony. Rumors of a new and improved rappel route on Snowpatch Spire proved to be true. The creator is unknown, but suspected to be Joe Benson. Several speed ascensionists found that running shoes are not appropriate for approaches in the Bugaboos, resulting in many a hairy descent from the Bugaboo/Snowpatch col. Overall, a good season was had in the Bugaboos, with many good stretches of weather and a busy campground and Kain Hut throughout July and August. No incredible epic Krakauer-type stuff to report— just, lots of good alpine granite climbing that is truly world-class.

WAYNE J. SOBOOL, *Bugaboo Ranger and ACMG Member*

Bugaboo-Pigeon-South Howser-Snowpatch enchainment. I realized I was super-anxious to climb in the Bugaboos when I arrived at the Applebee Campground five days before my partner was scheduled to arrive. I figured I would keep myself busy hiking around and scoping out routes, but soon discovered solo potential. A lot of the classics were within my comfort level, from 5.4

Aaron Martin on Retinal Circus, The Minaret. *Zack Smith*

to 5.9. After climbing the northeast ridge of Bugaboo Spire and the west ridge of Pigeon Spire, I saw potential for an amazing day involving numerous classic alpine granite pitches and four of the best summits in the Bugs. On August 8 I awoke at 5:30 a.m. and was out of camp by 6:00. After repeating the northeast ridge of Bugaboo and west ridge of Pigeon, I journeyed to the South Howser. Soon I found myself on the ultraclassic Beckey-Chouinard, doing hand jam after hand jam. A few hours later I was sitting on an amazing summit in a spectacular granite arena. The next goal, Snowpatch Spire, was staring at me from across the glacier, but I had to get off the Howser Tower first. I had brought one 60m, 7.5-mm line for rappelling, but after asking around camp, I wasn't sure one 60-meter rope would cut it. Turns out one rope worked until the last rap. My rope went from the last rock anchor to the top of the 40-foot bergschrund. Luckily, I had collected enough bail slings and 'biners that when all were tied together they extended the last anchor enough to put me into the 'schrund. I showed up at the base of the Kraus-McCarthy on Snowpatch, gulped the last of my water, and began climbing again. At around 6:00 p.m., 12 hours after I had set out, I stumbled back into camp and slept like a baby.

AARON MARTIN

South Howser Tower, The Minaret, Retinal Circus. In early August Aaron Martin from Mammoth Lakes, California, and I, from Moab, Utah, visited the Howser Spires in the Bugaboos. Before I arrived, Aaron had a huge solo day linking four major formations (see above). Two days after hiking in we started up a striking line on a feature called The Minaret, which is a turret of steep, clean granite attached to the South Howser Tower. We decided to attempt this route with a minimum of equipment: a double set of cams up to three and a half inches, eight pins, one hammer, a 9mm lead line, a 7mm tag line, and food and water for one day.

Zack Smith on Retinal Circus. *Aaron Martin*

This style looks good on paper, but you usually get skunked trying it. This time we scored, though. Someone else had attempted the line before but had bailed about eight pitches up, placing bolts and leaving pins and stoppers. This helped us tremendously, because we would often short-fix off their anchors and lead in blocks. The climbing here was sustained and mostly high-quality free and aid. The crux free climbing went to Aaron—flared runout liebacking above an uninspiring TCU belay. We topped out on the Minaret at dusk, all smiles but ready for it to be over. However, with our rack we felt it unwise to try to rap our route, and other routes that end here are about 20 pitches long, leaving us little choice but to continue to the summit of the South Howser Tower. The guidebook said something about a few low-fifth-class pitches leading to the summit, so we figured we would be fine. Several hours and a thousand feet later, in the dark, we would joke about this. We discovered solid 5.10 climbing and circuitous route finding.

The sky, however, felt it was showtime. Simulclimbing and short-fixing along the exposed ridge, I would sometimes stop moving and stare at our first sight of the northern lights. A half-moon of Halloween orange highlighted the distant peaks and valleys. In another direction a meteor shower was exploding with streaks of light lasting several seconds. We motored along and after dozens of false summits we found the real one, 15 hours after we started.

Early the next morning the perfect weather broke into a violent lightning storm just hours after we touched down. We fled our exposed bivy and began a heady descent to Applebee Campground, stumbling and laughing at each other. We decided to name the entire experience Retinal Circus.

ZACK SMITH, *Uninhabited*

CANADIAN ROCKIES

Canadian Rockies, various activities. In the front ranges a dry winter, followed by a dry spring, made for great rock climbing in the summer of 2001. Taking advantage of the good conditions, visiting New Zealand climbers Mike Brown and Steve Eastwood established The Corrupters (500 meters, 5.10 A2) on the northwest face of the Ship's Prow above Canmore, in an impressive one-day effort. Further details are lacking, but it is likely that their route follows the obvious wet corner on the right side of the face. The corner, which had previously been attempted, is dry only in the driest of summers.

In the main ranges, in contrast, early summer was snowy and wet, and even by late July many of the big peaks had not yet come into condition. Finally, in early August an extended high-pressure system settled over the range and shifted the summer alpine season into high gear. Unlike many of the Rockies' major north faces, the mile-high north face of Mt. Temple is easily visible from a highway and accessible by a two-hour walk. As a result it has some ten routes and variations on it and might have been considered climbed out. But last August Josh Briggs and Rob Owens found a major new route near the left end of the face. The East-Northeast Buttress (IV 5.8) climbs the prominent prow between the Aemmer Couloir and the Sphinx Face. The crux is six pitches of 5.6-5.8 on good quartzite. The route joins the classic East Ridge route near the top of the Aemmer Couloir. Offering good climbing with few objective hazards, the ENE Buttress should become a popular objective.

In his Selected Alpine Climbs Sean Dougherty describes the east face of Mt. Woolley as "an obvious target for a route" that had been overlooked, as "most people are more interested in the big routes over the other side of Woolley Shoulder" (meaning Mt. Alberta and North Twin). In late August Ben Firth and I took the hint and bivied below the face. We had hoped to follow the aesthetic central rib, but the limestone on the rib, although of good quality, turned out to be blank and very steep. As a consolation prize, we climbed the snow-and-mixed couloir immediately left of the rib to the south ridge, which we followed to the summit (III 5.10).

On the repeat front Eric Dumerac, Jeff Nazarchuk, and I made the third ascent of the Lowe-Hannibal route (VI 5.10+ A0) on the remote north face of Mt. Geikie. The mountain has aptly been called the dark horse of the Canadian Rockies. It offers challenging climbing on excellent quartzite on a grand scale, yet many climbers remain unaware of it. The three of us climbed the route over two days in early August, freeing all but two points of A0. We were not the first to call it the best alpine route they had done in the Rockies. Several of the Rockies' other classic big routes also received ascents, including the North Face of Mt. Bryce and the Supercouloir of Mt. Deltaform. A strong twosome from south of the border made the long approach to the still unrepeated North Face of North Twin but did not set foot on the face, owing to rockfall and wet rock.

The ice season was a strange one. Many areas like Kananaskis Country and the Ghost Valley in the front ranges, as well as Field and Mt. Wilson in the main ranges, were unusually lean. Old faithfuls, like Professor Falls and Oh Le Tabernac, did not form for the first time in years. Yet areas like the Terminator and Stanley headwalls enjoyed above-average ice conditions. Go figure.

The season got off to an early start, with The Replicant (145 meters, WI5+) on the Terminator headwall and Nemesis (140 meters, WI5+) on the Stanley headwall receiving multiple ascents in October. The first major new route of the season came at the end of month, when Briggs, Virginia Buckley, and Eamonn Walsh climbed Virgin No More (130 meters, WI6R). This Curtain Call-like route is located high in the bowl between Mt. Epaulette and the Kauffman Peaks and is obvious from the Icefields Parkway. It had been looked at for years, but the four-hour approach had repulsed previous attempts. The first crux pitch consisted of "mushroomed, chandeliered, hollow, and thin [ice], very technical and hard to protect." This section was followed by a strenuous free-standing pillar. A few weeks later Rene Cote, Doug Sproul, and Jon Walsh put up another major route across the bowl from Virgin No More. Named Choksondik (225 meters, WI5) in keeping with the theme of the area, it was climbed from a bivy at the base and was described as "a very engaging climb on very thin, rotten, and air-filled ice."

Further north Peter Kottegen and Dana Ruddy climbed Power of the Gospel (140 meters, WI5) to the left of Echo Madness in the Stutfield Glacier cirque. This beautiful valley is surrounded on three sides by hanging glaciers, which feed a multitude of impressive waterfalls. Unfortunately, though, most lines are threatened by serac fall. While the glacier-topping Power of the Gospel appeared to be relatively benign, the first ascensionists cautioned, "this…is something individuals will have to judge for themselves."

In the Bow Valley the bowl between Castle and Protection mountains has long been known to contain quality ice, but the four-hour approach has kept climbing activity to a minimum. In November Grant Meekins and I bivied in the hanging valley, intent on the second ascent of the impressive Superlight. Instead, we found two good new routes. Smothered Hope (120 meters, WI5) climbed steep ice in a deep gash, passing under a couple of chockstones for ambience. The real gem, however, was Guinevere (160 meters, WI5R M4+), a "cool line with lots of varied climbing."

On the solo front Mike Verwey made the first solo of the remote Gimme Shelter (300 meters, WI5+) on his third attempt. He had attempted to solo the route last year and the year before but both times retreated after only a couple of pitches. Adding to its seriousness, the route is threatened by a band of seracs. A few years ago Guy Lacelle was retreating from a solo attempt on the neighboring Arctic Dream when he barely missed being killed by serac fall down Gimme Shelter.

Impressive though all these firsts were, the ice season was marked more by a change in attitudes, which combined with a relentless rise in standards, often reduced what had previously been major endeavors to half-day outings. The once-feared Stanley Headwall, home to such classics as French Reality (145 meters, M5 WI5+), Nightmare on Wolf Street (180 meters, M7+ WI6), and Suffer Machine (200 meters, M7 WI4+), served as the stage for much of this dramatic advance. Due partly to the paucity of ice in other areas, local climbers converged on the headwall through November and early December. At times there would be nearly 10 cars parked at the trailhead in the predawn darkness. The early starts were required to avoid being scooped on the route of choice, not in order to finish before dark. On the contrary, long ropes, rising abilities, and a certain irreverence for earlier standards made for some very fast ascents. For several weeks French Reality was climbed almost daily, with some ascents taking less than six hours car-to-car. Nightmare on Wolf Street also received numerous ascents. Jason Billings and Owens cleaned up on Suffer Machine, freeing the bolt ladder on the original start at M7. The free version of the route immediately received further ascents.

From fast ascents of individual routes, one obvious progression was to link-ups of several routes. Kim Csizmazia and Will Gadd combined the classic Sorcerer (185 meters, WI5) and Hydrophobia (125 meters, WI5+) in the Ghost Valley during the short days of late November. The two routes had first been linked solo by Joe Josephson. Using a 70-meter rope and leading in blocks, Csizmazia and Gadd completed their link-up in less than 11 hours car-to-car, with no soloing. In late March, after Gadd returned from the Ice World Cup, he and Scott Semple made the first link-up of Polar Circus (700 meters, WI5), the Lower and Upper Weeping Wall (via the Weeping Pillar, 350 meters, WI6), and Curtain Call (125 meters, WI6). Once again using a 70-meter rope and block leading to good advantage, they completed the link-up in 13:16. In early April visiting climbers Rolando Garibotti and Bruno Sourzac upped the ante by making the first linkup of Polar Circus, the Lower and Upper Weeping Wall (via the Left-Hand Side {180 meters, WI4} and Teardrop {170 meters, WI6}, respectively), and Slipstream (925 meters, WI4+) in 15:15 car-to-car. They soloed all of Polar Circus and all but the last pitch of the Weeping Wall, and roped for only a few pitches of Slipstream. This link-up of three ultra-classic routes had been the subject of talk for years and had previously been unsuccessfully attempted by several strong teams.

RAPHAEL SLAWINSKI, *Canada*

Mt. Geikie, Lowe-Hannibal Route. Most Canadian Rockies peaks consist of limestone, some solid, most crumbling. But hidden in the backcountry of the Tonquin Valley near Jasper rises a subrange of quartzite peaks. The gem of the area is the massive north face of Mt. Geikie. Not surprisingly it was George Lowe who, with Dean Hannibal, pioneered the classic route on the face in 1979—750 meters of rock leading to 750 meters of mixed ground. The guidebook calls the mountain the "dark horse of the Canadian Rockies." While its north face is not as well known as those of Alberta or North Twin, it is definitely one of the grande course routes of the Rockies. The list of unsuccessful aspirants reads like a Who's Who of North American alpinism: Dave Cheesmond, Barry Blanchard, Scott Backes…. Between the route's sustained technical difficulties and the Tonquin's notoriously poor weather, it took three determined attempts before Sean Dougherty and James Sevigny succeeded in making the second ascent of the Lowe-Hannibal in 1989.

Eric Dumerac, Jeff Nazarchuk, and I made the route our objective last summer. We eased the pain of the 30-kilometer approach by having gear ferried on horseback to a fishing camp on the Amethyst Lakes. With light packs and in perfect weather we hiked over Maccarib Pass and got our first view of the face. By early evening we were pitching camp at the edge of the moraine. The solitude was intense.

It was still dark the next morning when we made our way across the glacier to the base of the face. The moat below the described start had opened up, so we made for a dihedral farther left. Jeff volunteered for the first lead block. Changing into rock shoes he stepped over the moat and onto perfect quartzite. Another 1,500 meters of it soared above into a cloudless sky.

Jeff disposed of pitch after pitch, while Eric and I wheezed our way up the lines. (For the sake of speed we compromised on style, and the seconds jumared with the packs.) By early afternoon we reached large ledges and the last water for a while. After re-hydrating, Eric took off on his lead block. As evening shadows fell across the valley, we made our way onto the steep headwall, the crux of the route.

We spent the night on separate ledges and awoke to another cloudless dawn. It was my turn up front, and I eagerly led off. Pitch followed pitch, and by midafternoon we stood at the base of upper face. We unroped and scrambled upward. We had hoped to run up the mixed ground, but the snowfields and ice strips were mush. As we traversed back and forth looking for a break, a wet slide engulfed Eric. It seemed wiser to rope up again. Eric took over the lead, and as another evening fell we continued simulclimbing over rock, snow, and ice. We were hoping that our gully would go, as by now we were wet and did not relish the prospect of spending the night standing on steep ground. But a hidden traverse delivered us onto the summit snowfield, and some time after midnight we finally stood on top. We were too keyed-up to sleep, so we dug a trench into the very summit and waited for dawn.

The descent of the west ridge was long but uneventful, and by early evening we were back at our tent. The following day we staggered under heavy loads back to the road. By the time we reached Jeff's minivan our feet were so sore we could barely walk. But the high lasted at least as long as the blisters.

RAPHAEL SLAWINSKI, *Canada*

Mt. Temple, east-northeast buttress; Squashed Bones. This beautiful line ascends the buttress between the Aemmer Couloir and the Sphinx Face on the north side of Mt. Temple. It compares in quality with, and is only slightly more technical than, the classic East Ridge. Most of the technical pitches have amazing rock quality and are well protected. The route hits the upper East Ridge route below the Black Towers. The objective hazard is low and crampons and ice axe are not needed until the East Ridge is intersected. It is probably the first route on Temple's north side to dry up in summer.

Traverse east from Lake Annette, staying low, moving past the start of the Greenwood-Jones and the Sphinx Face. Ascend to the col that marks the crest of the buttress between the Aemmer and the Sphinx. Start climbing (low fifth class) on the left side of the buttress, aiming for the right-leaning gully that situates you behind a prominent pinnacle. Eventually you reach a large ledge just to the right of the crest and below the start of the steeper climbing. Climb a 20-meter steep section to another large ledge. Move left on the ledge until a weakness in the headwall is found immediately right of the crest. (The overhanging face left of the crest is an obvious barrier.) Climb three and a half pitches, mostly 5.7 or 5.8, following obvious weaknesses on the right side of the crest. A fifth pitch (5.8), climbed on the crest proper, provides amazing exposure down the steep face on the left. A short sixth pitch on loose black rock gains fourth-class terrain that is best negotiated on the right side. Several short, steep sections lead to a final steep wall of horrendous rock. Climb easily left of the steep wall and gain the upper east ridge below the start of the Black Towers. Either follow the ridge to the summit or bypass the Black Towers by traversing the east face and gaining the popular East Ridge route. Take a set of nuts and cams up to three inches. No pitons were used, but a few may be useful for the Black Towers. We climbed the route on August 5 and rated the difficulty IV 5.8.

ROB OWENS, *Canada*

Mt. Babel, east face; Mt. Louis, east face. Kevin Thaw and I arrived in the Canadian Rockies on August 1 with two weeks set aside for an alpine climbing holiday. It seemed that the weather was less unsettled on the more southerly peaks in the foothills, so we drove up to Moraine Lake to have a look at the east face of Mt. Babel. The weather was good, so we bivied and left Moraine Lake around 7 a.m. It took about three hours to get to the first pitch of the climb, partly because we headed up the wrong gully toward the base. The face was dry but covered with an immense amount of loose rock. I was twice hit by rocks, one of which broke my baby toe. We simulclimbed the first half of the route and pitched out the second half. We reached the top in about eight and a half hours, having made an all-free ascent. The descent is long and complicated and was further slowed by my toe. Also, the guide-book almost led us astray by warning, "Don't be tempted to peel off to the east too soon–you'll end up climbing back up to the ridge line." In fact, the descent never drops off to the east but remains on the spine of the north ridge until you reach a huge gully right before the Tower of Babel. We made it back to the car just as it became pitch black at around 10 p.m.

Next we headed to the east face of Mt. Louis, a 2,000-foot face that, as far as we could find, did not have any routes. We had hoped to tackle the clean headwall in the middle of the east face, but when we got there we found it to be much steeper and blanker than anticipated. Instead we chose a line running directly up its right edge. We soloed the first half of the climb, at up to 5.7, and simulclimbed the upper section, at about 5.9, with most of the 5.9 being found in the last 700 feet. The quality of the route is high, with many moderate pitches of clean face climbing and little loose rock. Total climbing time was about three and a half hours. We did find one piton halfway up and a few old pieces of tat low down, so are not certain we climbed a new route.

MARK SYNNOTT, *AAC*

Cryophobia, showing the belays. Hydrophobia is left. *Sean Isaac*

Waiparous River Valley, Cryophobia. In February 2001 Shawn Huisman and I completed the first ascent of Cryophobia (V M8+ WI5+), the name meaning "fear of ice," located in the remote Waiparous River Valley near the Ghost. We began working on this project the season before, but the route melted out by late December from warm Chinooks, so we returned the following year to finish it. It required over 10 days of work to aid, equip, and redpoint this futuristic line. It links thin ice smears with long stretches of overhanging rock on the 240-meter ice-streaked wall immediately right of the classic hard ice route, Hydrophobia (V WI5+). The approach itself is an epic ordeal involving a one and a half hour drive from Canmore on rough dirt roads, an hour on an ATV Quad Runner, and an hour bush-whack. This may well be the most sustained multipitch sport mixed route around, with its seven pitches going at M4, M7+, M8+, M7, M7+,

M6, and WI5+. Every pitch is truly mixed, whether it is hooking an ice seam in a crack, stemming to basketball-sized ice blobs splattered onto the wall, or swinging onto free-hanging daggers. Due to the compact nature of the limestone, protection consists primarily of bolts that were placed on lead, aid-point style. Repeat ascents need only quick draws, a few midsize Camalots, and ice screws, including stubbies.

Sean Isaac, *Canada*

Sean Isaac on Cryophobia, Ghost River. Hydrophobia is the thick ice to the left. *Brad Wrobleski*

Greenland

WEST GREENLAND

Akuliarusinguaq Peninsula, first ascents and Bylot Island (Baffin), traverses and first ascents. After our successful first ascent of the North Wall of Sanderson's Hope in 2000, we wintered the boat in Aasiaat, West Greenland, and the crew for 2001 assembled there in early July for another Tilman-type expedition. We sailed (or rather motored as there was no wind) to the Akuliarusinguaq Peninsula (72° N) for our first objectives: some remote unclimbed 2000m summits near the ice cap. These were located further inland from the region we explored during 1998.

After an exacting walk-in carrying skis, climbing, and camping gear, we reached the main approach glacier on the third day. We skinned up this on our skis to establish a high camp. This was now new territory and I cannot begin to describe the feeling of knowing you are somewhere nobody has ever been before in the whole history of God's good earth. Over the next two days we made the first ascents on ski of six 2000+m summits and one at 1885m. The descent down the glacier and back to the boat only took two days as this time we found a better way round the snout of the glacier.

Next, it was round to the Upernavik area (73° 45′N) where Mat Goodyear and Andy Prosser put up two new rock climbs in this area of huge potential. Both were climbed from the boat. Warm Up (300 meters, British HVS 5a) lay on Kingigtoq Cliff and Out of Retirement (400 meters, VS 4c) was at Sarqarssuaq. The Old Man had joined them and was stretched on one pitch of 4b/c after all these years of retirement from serious climbing. At Upernavik Mat and Andy flew home and Polly Murray, the first Scotswoman to climb Everest, and Tash Wright flew out.

We made our way toward Bylot Island (north of Baffin) sailing and motoring well north to get over the top of the Middle Pack, a field of pack ice that stays stubbornly in the middle of Baffin Bay for most of the summer. We were eventually stopped by pack ice ca 50 km short of Bylot Island. After two days drifting and waiting we finally managed to get round this by going first southeast, then west. We anchored off Bylot Island before being beset in the bay by pack ice next morning. We finally made our way northward to the Cape Liverpool area where Tilman had started his traverse in 1963.

From here Peter Maxwell and I repeated H.W. Tilman and Bruce Reid's north-south traverse on skis. It still took us 10 days, as the bigger glacial streams were difficult to cross especially with our "sleds" (really glorified toboggans). In the process we made the first ascent of eight unclimbed peaks, some on skis, some climbing. These were not technically difficult ascents, but the continual crevasse systems in this glacial land were a menace. The women had started off earlier and made an alternative north-south traverse—the Murray-Wright traverse—touching Tilman's route at one point for a few kilometers when reaching their intended initial glacier proved impossible. They made a longer and faster traverse, mainly skating on their telemark skis. Unfortunately, having taken too little food with them, they were not able to climb any peaks and nearly starved waiting two days on the beach at the end. We were all collected by boat, the remaining crew having brought it round to Pond Inlet for us.

We then sailed back to Upernavik for some more crew changes, made our way down the west coast of Greenland to Paamiut, and then back to Scotland across a stormy Atlantic.

BOB SHEPTON, *United Kingdom*

Sanderson's Hope, northwest face, new route. On July 2 the yacht *Northanger* set sail for Greenland from Port Kirwan, Newfoundland. On board were the captains/owners Keri Pashuk and Greg Landreth, climbers Chris "Beeker" Romeskie and I, and crew Angela Rivers and Duncan Kemp. The crossing to Faeringehavn took place during eight days of calm, with beautiful sailing among the sea birds, whales, and Newfoundland fishermen, who were shocked to see a sailboat so far off shore. A day later we were in Nuuk, the capital city, where final preparations were made for the long trip ahead.

Duncan completed his part of the journey, returning to Victoria. Northanger and crew continued for 18 days up the west coast, stopping occasionally to stretch our sea legs and do some exploring along the way. We sailed as far as 800 miles north of the Arctic Circle to the land of the midnight sun, our "planned" climbing area. Unfortunately, while there were many cliffs, the rock had the consistency of porridge. The sea was dangerously thick with both ice and massive icebergs, making for an easy decision to head back to Sanderson's Hope, the most impressive objective we had seen on the way "down north" (Newfoundlanders call north down and south up).

Sanderson's Hope has an amazing northwest facing sea cliff, which received its first ascent in the summer of 2000 by the Reverend Bob Shepton's "crew" (I say crew reluctantly because his crew flew to Greenland, bypassing the sailing experience.) A stunning prow remained unclimbed and became our objective.

We obtained a secure anchorage in view of Sanderson's Hope and sailed to the wall for a dramatic step off the bow onto rock. Greg, Beeker, and I spent a few days sorting and preparing gear, then fixing ropes before committing to the wall. The climbing was free but for 15 points of aid. The rock was generally solid with many cracks, but there were also features on sections of blank face. However, the initial cracks entailed some digging with a nut tool to obtain good protection and/or finger locks. In total, the ca 800-meter face took 10 days of effort with five nights on the wall (six days climbing, three days hauling, and one day off due to rain). Four 3/8-inch bolts were placed for our two camps and four 1/4-inch bolts were placed on lead for protection. Everything was hauled to the top and we walked off the back, greeted by Keri and Angela with champagne and cake. We christened our route Down North (V 5.10+ A1).

With the darkness descending and the chill of a coming winter in the air, we headed back down (or was that up?) the coast. From a small village called Attu, we crossed the North Atlantic again, making a more direct passage to the East Coast of Labrador. The crossing took six days and this time included stormy weather and intense sailing, with more than a few crew members seasick.

Overall, an amazing and challenging adventure with some great friends, lasting three-and-a-half months…and did I mention the romantic nature of a sea-faring life? Angela and I are now planning a life together.

JIA CONDON, *Canada*

SOUTH GREENLAND

Igdlorssitt Havn, Cape Farewell, new routes. At the western end of Prins Christian Sund is an anchorage at the entrance to a valley. Marked on the map as Igdlorssitt Havn, it is unclear whether this local name refers to the anchorage or the valley. Arriving from the village of Aappilattoq, an hour-and-a-half away by fishing boat, it becomes obvious that Igdlorssitt Havn is the name of the magnificent 800-meter tower just one-and-a-half kilometers inland on the eastern side of the valley. Its granite headwall, bathed in evening sunlight, is akin to the world famous monoliths of Yosemite, Baffin, and Patagonia. The primary objective of our expedition, however, was to climb previously virgin granite faces and peaks at the valley head, a four-hour walk up the glacier. Photographs taken on a previous expedition to the valley in 1992 promised plenty of potential.

Unfortunately, the initial section of the glacier that had been frequently traveled during the 1992 expedition was dangerously crevassed, and on closer inspection the rock quality of the peaks and faces in question was poor in comparison to the main face above base camp. Instead, attention was focused on the main face of Igdlorssitt Havn, and on the extensive sea cliffs and walls immediately east of base camp. The only known rock route in the valley was established on the main face of Igdlorssitt Havn in 1996 by a team of Croatians. The route, called Ujarak after a boat that picked them up at the end of a long 12-day wait when their lift failed to materialize, weighed in at VI+/A3. It was 24 pitches in length and took them six days to climb as a team of four. Keen to explore new ground and avoid pitches of A3, our team blitzed the area climbing 16 new routes, one on the main face, others on the flanks and the rest on some impressive local sea cliffs.

After a number of attempts, the new route on the main face was finally completed in one push from August 12-14 by Max Dutson and Dave Lucas. Wonderful World was 800 meters, 23 pitches, and British E4 6a C1. On July 29-30 Richard Garnett and Mark Harris climbed the long ridge that lies behind the main face of Igdorrssitt Havn. It gave much easy and loose climbing with numerous gendarmes. A little right of Wonderful World but slanting up right in the upper section is Action Man's Purple Head, a 1000-meter-long 23-pitch route at E2 5b put up over August 1-2 by Garnett and Harris. Later, Harris with Dean Grindell linked the start of Wonderful World with Action Man's to give Wonderful Purple Head (25 pitches, E2 5c). The easy-angled, right hand flank of the main face gave A Long Walk to Freedom, an excellent route with superb situations at HVS climbed on August 2 by Grindell and Mark Shea (1000 meters, 25 pitches). On the right side of the left wing of the main face, Matt Heason and Adam Jackson put up the 11-pitch Cryptic Crossword (500 meters, 11pitches) at E3 5c, a route that was repeated on a number of occasions during the trip. The route was first completed in 12 hours on July 29. Other routes were climbed on the sea cliffs and walls above, which lay to the east of base camp. These were two to five pitches in length. Some were on wonderful golden granite with difficulties up to E5 6a. We enjoyed mostly fine sunny weather during our stay at base camp from July 27 to August 18, apart from the period August 3-9. Full copies of our expedition report can be emailed to anyone interested in organizing a trip to Greenland. Contact: mathew.heason@cgey.com.

MATT HEASON, *United Kingdom*

The southeast face of Los Capitanos on south Greenland's Pamiagdluk Island, showing (1) Easy or Squeezy and (2) Aquasky. Right: Gabor Berecz leading, Toni Lamprecht belaying pitch 18 on Easy or Squeezy. *Thomas Tivadar*

Pamiagdluk Island, South Greenland, first ascents. The Greenland Bigwall Expedition spent six weeks between the end of July and September in South Greenland. Our aim was to push the complex limits in one bigwall route without bolts. Accordingly we had a team of four strong climbers with different specialties, from 5.14 sportclimbers to multiweek A4-A5 Himalayan big wall climbers, and everything between. The four Munich-based members were: Gabor Berecz (45), Günter Dengler (32), Toni Lamprecht (30), and myself (41).

After a complicated journey—without helicopter!—to the islands of South Greenland, we made a three-day tour in our small raftboat from Aaplagtoq to find good, high, untouched walls. We found the best choice with bad Greenland weather to be the 1,100-meter southeast face of a 1190m "new" mountain we named Los Capitanos, on the island Pamiagdluk. After transporting our equipment to the island we built our base camp in the "Antonio Valley" approximately an hour walk to the face. Nice and very stormy weather alternated every two to three days. We did everything by ourselves, without any help of tour agencies, ships, helicopter, and satellite-telephones. We told nobody where we were.

For the first route we climbed a free line at the highest part of the over two-kilometer-wide face. We worked with fixed ropes because of the stormy weather; all together we spent seven days on the route. We made the top by a polar storm and rappelled down in heavy waterfalls by night. The 28-pitch climb has excellent granite and we called it Aquasky (VI 5.11).

In the following six days we climbed in extraordinarily good weather a 25-pitch route we called Easy or Squeezy, by some hard "limit pushing" parts without drilling (VI 5.12b A4c). At the end we climbed the trio Berecz-Lamprecht-Tivadar, a shorter alpine route on the north-west-shoulder of the peak Frenchbird (Kaempleplade 8pt. III 5.10b).

The goal of our expedition was to not use bolts in our climbs. The protection was always traditional. We just left on our rappel line between the two climbs a single 8mm bolt each 60 to 100 meters. Our climb was supported by the DAV and the Sektion Bayerland.

THOMAS TIVADAR, DAV *Sektion Bayerland*

EAST GREENLAND

Trillergerne Mountains, Fox Jaw Cirque, Tasiilaq Fjord. The Fox Jaw Cirque lies seven kilometers beyond the head of the Tasiilaq (a.k.a. Ammassalik) Fjord, ca 80 km from the settlement of Tasiilaq. Leaving Reykjavik in Iceland on June 23, Katy Holm, Andrea Kortello, Dave Thomson, and I arrived in Tasiilaq four days later after sailing with the French-owned yacht, *Vagabond*. After some final shopping, *Vagabond* took us to the head of the Fjord and we spent the next week reconnoitering the area. We decided to make the East Trillergerne Peak, which lies north of the Fox Jaw Cirque, our first climbing objective.

From our valley base camp we accessed the Trillergerne peaks by ascending a terminal moraine for ca 300 meters, then continuing up the ridge until we were below the north side of the Fox Jaw Cirque. Here, we crossed a glacier to the peaks. We climbed the western peak to the first ledge system, then traversed across this to reach our peak. At this point we rapped straight down, fixing lines as we went. Next day we re-ascended to our high point and continued scrambling for ca 100 meters, after which the climbing became moderate. With eternal Arctic daylight we continued through the "night" and reached the summit at 3:00 p.m. on July 16. We feasted on breathtaking views of glacier-fed fjords and numerous virgin summits. The route was rappelled and the glacier reached after 44 hours of non-stop climbing. We christened it Lithographic (16 pitches, 5.10 A0).

Katy, Andrea, and Dave next went into the Fox Jaw Cirque. Their chosen objective was not to be taken lightly. After five days working the route they had still not been able to free the first pitch. A shower of rain brought them back to camp. Two days later we all returned to the cirque. On our second day back Katy freed the pitch. At this point Dave left for Canada. On August 2 we decided to "go for the top." By midnight, after consistently demanding climbing, we reached an impassable roof. This, and the return in August of some night-time darkness forced a decision to descend. This partially completed route has nine pitches up to 5.11c and A0.

We returned to the Trillergerne peaks for our final climb. Starting our ascent as before, we continued up on the western peak. Carrying a tarp and a stove we aimed for a patch of snow about halfway to the summit. Initially we hoped to climb all the way to the top but by the second day realized it would take several days due to the complexity of route finding. As we hadn't budgeted for this, we focussed on a nearer goal. We reached the top by 3:30 p.m. on August 9, then rapped the route, spending one more night on the mountain. Calleditas has 13 pitches up to 5.9.

Back in camp our bodies were exhausted and although we still had time for another climb, we headed out to the village of Kuummiut with some local fishermen. Here we spent five glorious days with locals, who invited us into their homes. We ate whale steaks and fresh fish and were allowed a small insight into Inuit life. During the five weeks we spent in the area, we had only three days of rain. This is really unusual for the region.

KAREN MCNEILL

Trillergerne Peaks (high on left) in the Fox Jaw Cirque, from the valley floor. *Karen McNeill*

Fox Jaw Cirque, Tasiilaq Fjord, first ascent of The Incisor. As part two of the Year of the Snake Expeditions 2001, I arrived at Kulusuk in July. I then took a boat through a maze of icebergs to the small village of Tasiilaq, also known as Ammassalik, home to about 2,500 Inuit people and a few Danes. Greenland is owned and governed by Denmark and my Danish contact, Hans Christian Florian, one of the top doctors in Greenland, wasted no time accentuating my jet lag even further with strong Danish pilsners. My plans to get to the fjord were quickly set after a couple of phone calls. For a small fee I hitched a ride in a helicopter on its way out to the area, arranging for a boat to pick me up on the coast several weeks later.

We flew over endless mountain ranges surrounded by dark ocean fjords dotted with huge tooth-like icebergs. As soon as I stepped out of the helicopter, it raced away. I stood alone, some distance from the base of a tower that resembled a gigantic fang from a fox's jaw. Shuttling loads, I soon had all of my gear at its base. The reason I had chosen this tower was not only that it was the most prominent and beautiful in the area but also because I thought I might be able to climb it without standing in aiders. My goal was to free climb the entire route on sight without any aid, solo.

The first half of the tower looked like wonderful free climbing. It also looked like I would have to shuttle loads up fixed lines; relentless and painstaking work. Starting at the very base of the tower, the first ca 300 meters of climbing ranged from 5.6 to 5.10 and was mostly high-quality cracks mixed with some desperate face moves here and there. It took me two days to climb, fix ropes, shuttle loads, set up a portaledge camp, and pull up all my ropes.

From there, the wall got much steeper. It looked like there was at least another 300 meters of climbing to the summit. The weather stayed sunny and breezy, like early spring in Yosemite. It was the middle of Arctic summer and I had 24-hour daylight with sun hitting me about eight hours a day while up on the wall. From my portaledge camp, I climbed four more pitches in the next two days (nine pitches total so far). All the pitches were climbed free with no falls. There were a couple sections of 5.11 and lots of spicy 5.9 and 5.10. Teetering blocks, expanding flakes, and pieces of creaking, balanced rock required meticulous climbing.

On my fifth day on the tower, and my eighth day in the fjord, I ascended the four fixed ropes to my high point, pulled the last two up with me and set up my solo belay system. It took only two more pitches to reach the summit. Unfortunately, on these last two pitches, my goal for the style that I wanted was interrupted. On the second-to-last pitch the crack narrowed to a hairline seam. Difficult nailing for at least 10 meters would be necessary, whereas free climbing this section would involve spicy stemming and face climbing. It seemed my safest choice would be to aid this section first.

After nailing a bunch of blades, I then down aided, leaving in the pins. I then free climbed the pitch. I used the same tactic on the last pitch. I summited on the morning of my ninth day in the fjord just minutes after midnight, then took a rest day to hydrate before leaving my portaledge camp and rappelling with all my gear. I named the ca 550-meter route Tears in Paradise (11 very long pitches, VI 5.11 A1) and the tower The Incisor. There was no evidence that it had been climbed before.

The scariest part of the whole trip happened later, while ferrying heavy loads back across one of the glaciers. The glaciers were quite dry, with only small sections of thick, frozen snow remaining in places. Crossing at night when they were most firm, I unfortunately fell in a crevasse about half a meter wide and seven meters deep. The huge haul bag on my back stopped me. My feet dangled below. I felt helpless at first but was able to roll out using my ice axe and pole. It was one the scariest moments of my life. Finally I was able to hitch a ride from a fishing boat two weeks before my scheduled pick up. Of course, Hans Christian had more Danish pilsners waiting.

Tears in Paradise, The Incisor, Fox Jaw Cirque. *Mike Libecki*

MIKE LIBECKI, *AAC*

Staunings Alps, Great Cumbrae Glacier, first ascents. Following previous Scottish Mountaineering Club expeditions to the Staunings Alps of Northeast Greenland in 1996 and 1998, our party of six (J. Fairey, C. Jones, C. Ravey, B. Shackleton, N. Walmsley, and me) was lifted by helicopter from the coastal airstrip at Mesters Vig to the Great Cumbrae Glacier. Base camp was established on July 23.

Over the next 25 days the weather remained mainly fine and stable with only two days of bad weather. In the warmer hours snow conditions would deteriorate and slopes and couloirs become dangerous, but 24 hours of daylight allowed us to move around in the colder periods (night time temperatures were around -5°C), when the snow was stable. However, there were several nights when it was even too warm to do this.

The surrounding glaciers were explored on skis and a number of unclimbed peaks noted, some of which were not shown on the maps in our possession. On July 26, climbing as pairs, the whole party made what we believe to be the first ascent of Keswicktinde (2380m) on the ridge between Tupilaq and Sefstromsgipfel. An easy couloir followed by two steeper pitches of ice led to a col, from where the northwest ridge, heavily corniced and steep in places, was followed for 10 pitches to the summit snow cone (650 meters, Grade AD).

On July 28 a new route was established on Sussex (2330m) from the Great Cumbrae Glacier by Shackleton and me. The line followed the far left-hand branch of the couloir between Sussex and Sydney. This was easy at first, after which there were several pitches of steeper ice to a col. Two pitches up a steep ice slope, followed by five pitches of rock on the southeast face led to the final ridge section above the south face. One rock pitch put us on top (650 meters, D). Sussex had only received one previous ascent, in 1963 from the northeast (AD).

The first ascent of a fine rock spur (the Jones/Fairey Spur) above Great Cumbrae Glacier leading to unclimbed summit (2570m) just north of Sefstromsgipfel was completed by Fairey and Jones on July 28-29. The 550-meter route had 27 pitches and was graded ED. The pair descended by rappelling into a couloir to the south, after which one climber was avalanched 300 meters and finished up unharmed in the rimaye. He was rescued from this point by the other five members.

On August 10 Fairey and Jones made the first ascent of a small peak at the junction of Little Cumbrae and Cantabrae glaciers. Pap of Cumbrae (1695m) was climbed via its southeast ridge, giving four pitches on rock (200 meters, AD). On the same day Ravey, Shackleton, Walmsley, and I made the first ascent of Mearsfjeld (2100m), a peak on the ridge between Little Cumbrae and Cantabrae. From Little Cumbrae Glacier we climbed a couloir, which steepened at the top to exit on to a col beside a square rock peak. From here the easy southwest ridge was followed to the top (400 meters, PD). On August 13-14 Fairey and Jones made the first ascent of Tandlaegetinde (2350m) via the south face. This is a peak on the ridge between Tupilaq and Sefstromsgipfel, and the 400-meter route gave 15 pitches of rock at an overall grade of TD.

Attempts were made on the south face of Sussex, a 700- to 800-meter difficult rock wall; a new route on Sydney, which was terminated only 60 meters from the summit due to unstable snow; the unnamed square rock peak, where we got to within a couple of pitches from the summit before loose rock barred the way; and the west ridge of Emmanuel, where 12 pitches were completed at an overall TD before an impasse was reached one-third of the way up the ridge. There is still much potential for new rock climbing in this area.

COLIN READ, *Scottish Mountaineering Club*

Top: Peak 2680m, the highest summit in the Rignys-Bjerg area of northeast Greenland, still unclimbed. Bottom: Approaching Narwhal Tooth Peak from the northeast on the Broadway Glacier. *Jim Gregson*

Rignys Bjerg area, various first ascents. A group consisting of Norman Vernon (co-leader), Robert MacCallum, Dave Rothery, Graham Poole, Sandy Gregson, and myself (co-leader) flew on 30 June from Isafjördur, Iceland to Constable Pynt, Northeast Greenland in a Twin Otter before flying on to Broadway Glacier at a rendezvous fixed with a Royal Navy group at N69°12' W26°45'. Over the next 16 days (nights in practice!) the Tangent Rignys Bjerg Area Expedition 2001 explored, skied, and climbed peaks bordering Broadway Glacier and two of its side branches, the West Side Glacier and Hole in the Wall Glacier. Other ski tours revealed many unclimbed peaks still available in the Rignys Bjerg area. The group made first ascents on the South Side Traverse—Whiteliner Peak, 2000m, Centrepoint 2025m, and Dumperfjeld, 2030m—a fine outing. From Hole in the Wall Glacier, the excellent northeast face and ridge of Majordomo Peak 2310m was done, with a complicated descent of the north face through seracs and crevasses. Starboard Ridge, the north arête of Anchorman Peak, 2340m, gave a very

The first ascent of Harpoon Ridge, Narwhal Tooth Peak, 2360m, in the Rignys Bjerg area. *Sandy Gregson*

good climb, mostly on snow/ice with a short rock band high up. The most impressive climb completed was the Harpoon Ridge (north arête) of Narwhal Tooth, 2360m, a beautiful peak. This gem—a Biancograt of the Arctic—had an approach complicated by weakly bridged crevasses leading to a lower section studded with pinnacles, turned on the west side, then a switchback ice arête in a very exposed position to a final "calotte" of hard ice protected with ice screws to gain a fine summit. Descent was made by the interesting west ridge (this mountain also has a very impressive and unclimbed north face). Other peaks climbed were Jack Tar Peak, 2045m, by the south face and ridge; Farawa' Peak, 1910m, by the Zorro Route (east face); and attempts on another two abandoned due to unfavorable conditions. A long ski tour to Col Beyond, 2385m, at the head of West Side Glacier, running up to the Inland Ice revealed the huge Sorte Brae Glacier system with hundreds of difficult looking virgin peaks lying west of the Rignys Bjerg ranges. Note to would-be visitors: the rock in these areas is of a very suspect nature—giraffe-like tendency definitely needed! The Tangent group had only two short periods of poor weather with snowfall during their trip before Twin Otter pickup late on the evening of 15 July for direct flight back to Akureyri in Iceland.

JIM GREGSON, *Great Britain*

In the northern Lindbergh Mountains. Top: Qaqaq Walker, the right-hand peak, was climbed by the right-hand ridge. Qaqaq Endean is left, climbed via left ridge. Middle: Qaqaq Cater on left was climbed by central snow arête. The right-hand peak is unclimbed. Bottom: Confluence of Lanchester and Hurst glaciers. *Jonathan White (3)*

Northern Lindbergh Mountains, first ascents. On June 22 British climbers, John Booth, Brian Combs, Richard Denison, Ian Jones, Dominic Matters, and I departed Akureyri airport, Iceland, in a reserve Twin Otter, the normal plane at that time being "stuck in Greenland." We refuelled at Isafjordur, then flew directly to Greenland, reaching the limit of the pack ice in approximately one hour and landing after a further 20 minutes. On reaching the Kronborg Glacier, we had turned inland and flew approximately northwest over Gunnbjorns Fjeld and the Kong Christian IV glacier to land at 69° 07'N, 31°02'W on the previously un-named Lanchester Glacier. Weather conditions were perfect and our equipment dump had been located by the pilots prior to land-ing. About 20-30 cm of snow (now consolidated) had fallen in the three weeks since its deposit.

We spent the first one-and-a-half days establishing base camp, then embarked on our first ascent. This first peak was climbed by all six members (on two ropes) as a day ascent from base. In the following three days, we first split into threes, then pairs, to make five further ascents, missing one day due to bad weather. On the fifth day after our arrival we split into two groups of three and went exploratory ski-touring on adjoining glaciers. The group making the northern tour explored two glaciers and made one ascent, whilst those on the southwestern tour visited the western rim of the Southern Lindbergh Plateau and made four ascents (including a second ascent). On returning to base, a group of three made a further day ascent.

After another rest day due to poor weather we set off in two groups (four and two) on four-day exploratory ski-tours to the west. During this period we made a total of 12 ascents, mainly in pairs. These included a number of nunataks on the edge of the icecap. On one summit we found a survey pin drilled into loose rock. This is believed to have been placed in 1934 by Martin Lindsay's team during the leveling of "The Monarch" (a.k.a. Gunnbjorns Fjeld). After two further rest days due to poor weather we set off on the last of our four-day ski-tours in two groups of three. These took us to the east and southeast, where we made three further ascents. The final attempt at a day ascent from base camp was aborted due to poor weather, and the team was collected by Twin Otter after 23 days on the glacier.

Although most peaks involved some ski-mountaineering, all climbing was done on foot, using crampons as appropriate. Plans to utilize traction-kites for glacier travel were hampered initially by lack of wind, and subsequently by our abilities at kite flying and skiing in lace-up boots. Both improved toward the end of the trip.

Weather conditions were typically excellent with only four days of bad weather out of 23. Recorded temperatures ranged from +10°C to −16°C, though wind-chill could bring this down to −30°C. There was very little wind during the first half of the trip, but it became much stronger during the second half.

The team also had a well-defined environmental strategy. Snow was melted using solar ovens wherever possible, reducing the fuel usage to less than 20 liters of SBP/Coleman fuel. All solid waste was contained and removed from Greenland. Food and packaging waste was taken to Isafjordur for domestic disposal, with all solid human waste repatriated to the U.K. We believe we were the first expedition to repatriate all its human waste.

In summary, this was a highly successful expedition, during which extensive exploration was made of an area ca 1300 square kilometers. A total of 28 peaks were climbed, including 25 first ascents and subsidiary summits. The terrain was largely on snow and ice, with the poor quality rock avoided wherever possible. Route grades ranged between Alpine F and AD. Snow conditions varied considerably in the region, though generally improved closer to the icecap (hard ice in places). Around base camp most snow slopes consisted of a three-centimeter crust overlying 20-30 cm of powder, which in turn lay on a firm base. When moving in boots or crampons, the top crust broke about 75 percent of the time, so glacier travel was made entirely on ski, using pulks to transport food, fuel, and equipment. Significant first ascent and new route potential remains in the Northern Lindberghs, particularly at the unexplored northern end of the nunataks.

JONATHAN WHITE, *United Kingdom*

NORTH PEARY LAND

North Peary Land, first ascents, a traverse of the peninsula, and confirmation of the world's most northerly peak. Our nine-person Return To The Top Of The World Expedition landed at Frigg's Fjord, then traversed the peninsula to the north, going up the Syd Glacier, across the Polkorridoren, and down the Nord Glacier. Along the way five climbers (John Jancik, Joe Sears, Vernon Tejas, Ken Zerbst, and I) made the second ascent of Helvetia Tinde on July 17 via a new route up the east ridge. The ca 1920m summit of Helvetia Tinde was first climbed in 1969 by the British Joint Services Expedition and is the highest peak in the most northerly mountain range on earth, only ca 750 km from the geographic North Pole. We carried the Joint Services British flag to the summit of the highest peak in the Roosevelt Range 32 years after they carried it there. The next day all nine team members (David Baker, Terri Baker, Jancik, Jim McCrain, Jim Schaefer, Sears, Tejas, Zerbst, and myself) made the first ascent of the highest unclimbed peak in the most northerly mountain range on earth.

Our aim, on reaching the north coast, had been to locate and climb the northernmost mountain on earth. During the next five days we recorded altitudes of summits, altitudes of saddles, and GPS readings for 14 peaks. On July 23 four team members (Sears, Tejas, Zerbst, and myself) crossed the sea ice at Sands Fjord to make first ascents of four peaks (Peaks 1, 2, 3, 4) on Cape Christian IV. The following day David Baker, Jancik, McCrain, and Schaefer made the second ascents of two peaks (Peaks 5 and 6) previously climbed by the 1997 Euro-American Expedition and claimed by them as the most northerly mountains on earth.

On July 25, Sears, Tejas, Zerbst, and I climbed Peak 5 with all but Zerbst continuing across Peak 6 and a small point called Peak 7 to make the first ascents of Peaks 8 and 9. The final peak of that day (Peak 9) was farther north than any other known summit. We continued east along the coast to Cape Morris Jesup, where we were to meet our airplane. There McCrain climbed a small hill and Tejas climbed four other summits to collect measurements. Upon our return to the United States, we submitted our data to several authorities and agencies in Denmark and the United States, asking help to determine what is a peak and what is a sub-peak. With all the peaks on both sides of Sands Fjord lying within the same minute of latitude, this decision led to much debate. The consensus was that Peak 6, at 83°, 36.427' north, is the actual summit of the most northerly mountain.

Six members of this expedition had been together in North Peary Land in 1996 as part of the American Top Of The World Expedition. During that expedition, we had walked across the sea ice to Kaffeklubben Island and then on to Oodaaq Island, considered the northernmost land on earth. In the spring of 2001 we compared readings with staff members at both GEUS and the Danish Polar Centre, and found discrepancies. On the flight to North Peary Land in 2001 we were able to fly over these islands and determine that our 1996 island is a new island. It has been confirmed by the Danish Polar Centre as the new most northerly land on earth. More information at www.2001topoftheworld.com.

Steve Gardiner

North Greenland

Warming Land exploration and first ascent. There is a picturesque valley in the extreme north of Greenland that is reminiscent of the Yosemite in California, with vertical walls topped by ice capped domes and mesas. It is intermittently intruded by glacial arms and is punctuated by a sublime chain of lakes. A 3,000-foot castle peak stands monolithically at its head. The triangular peninsula in which this valley resides is called Warming Land. Our *National Geographic* sponsored expedition in July made the first crossing of this peninsula from Saint Georges Fjord to Hartz Sund and back again. A subtle divide in the central valley sheds to an eastern and a western river. A second western river feeds from a second picturesque mountain valley adjacent to Saint Georges Fjord. We began at the mouth of this second western river. It appeared uncrossable but for the natural bridges cut into the limestone bedrock. The expedition proceeded across a natural bridge and was on its way. The favor of fortune at that river was to repeat itself throughout.

The weather was fair and an easy route was found through a ridge of pyramids to the central western river. This river led us into the central valley. An advance base camp was established in three days at the eastern lake at the heart of the central valley. From here we set out down the canyons of the eastern river to Hartz Sund. A solo climber made the ascent of the monolith from the west side through a succession of walls, chimneys and shelves. He reached the summit as the first snow storm of the day began to clear. After two more snow storms and 22 hours of exploring all members were back at advance base camp. In good weather we returned to Saint Georges Fjord across the grain of the ridge country and over a fine, high pass at the margin of the western icefields. A maze of corridors through the miniature ice caps led to an ice-dammed lake and the headwaters of the second western river. We discovered another sequence of limestone tunnels in the upper regions of this river. One day down the river took the expedition back to the west coast. We departed from the same alluvial shelf along Saint Georges Fjord where we had arrived two weeks earlier. Personnel included National Geographic writer Gretel Ehrlich, National Geographic photographer David MacLean, CBS correspondent Bill Gasperini, ornithologist Betsy Fejkis, Dr. Miki Rifkin, Dr. Frank Landsberger, Patti Scott, Jeff Scott, Chuck Stielau, and myself as leader.

Dennis Schmitt

Mexico

CHIHUAHUA

BASASEACHIC WATERFALL
NATIONAL PARK

El Gigante, La Conjura de los Necios. As we boarded
the plane for Mexico at the beginning of November, we had one desire: that this trip would not
turn into another epic. The goal was El Gigante. It was late at night when our seven-man team
reached the village of Basaseachic, setting up base camp at the San Lorenzo Ranch, a few miles
from El Gigante—as the crow flies. The only thing missing was a sign saying "Welcome to
Climbers' Paradise."

The next morning Kurt Albert, Hans Martin, and Mariucz set off down the canyon to the
base of El Gigante, equipped with bivy gear and a video camera. By the next afternoon they
were back. Hans Martin put the camera on the table, and we peered at the monitor. We could
make out Kurt in front of a thicket of bushes. Slowly the camera swung upward, and the thicket
was replaced by a jungle. Bizarre cactuses and palm trees towered overhead. Lianas were draped
over them like snakes. "Terrific plants," commented Holger, "and where is El Gigante?" The
camera swung farther upward, and Kurt explained dryly, "That's El Gigante." A vertical jungle.
We thought of opting for an easy escape, maybe a cute little first ascent at the entrance of the
gorge. The discussion was ended by a secret poll the next morning. Kurt put his helmet on the
table. Everyone wrote "Yes" or "No" on a slip of paper. Not even Steven Spielberg could have
produced more suspense than our voting procedure. The first three slips said "No," the next
three, "Yes." The last slip would be the tiebreaker. And the winner was…El Gigante! This last
vote sealed our fate. No relaxed climbing, no floating up immaculate, sunny rock.

Everything then went downhill, literally. Kurt's suggestion had sounded exciting back at
the ranch—that we rappel to the base beside Piedra Volada, Mexico's highest waterfall, with a
1,600-foot drop. First we would tie together 500 meters of caving rope (also our rappel line)
and lower our 300 kg of haulbags in one big bunch. As I leaned cautiously over the edge, I realized
that this might be quite serious. Only a few feet below the face curved away in a huge overhang.
The canyon bottom was hidden in mist. Kurt was hanging at the belay by the drop-off, the wind
blowing his hair upward. He looked like the devil himself at the entrance to his preserve. It was
dark by the time the baggage, Mariusz, Holger, Klaus, and I reached the floor of the gorge. Hans
Martin wanted to toss the rope and come to our gorge base camp with Gunda via the more
conventional route the following morning. The next day before Kurt started rappelling he wrote
Hans Martin a note and left it at the belay: "Hans Martin, it is 7:00 a.m., and I'm starting down.
Please don't cut me off. Cheers, Kurt."

Wielding machetes Klaus and I cleared a way to the start of the climb. Instead of the
customary missiles, the leader sent down a bizarre selection of plants. But we couldn't leisurely
swing from branch to branch up the wall. On the contrary, the climbing was hard from the
start, with lots of sections of 5.11 and 5.12. Except that here the leader first had to unearth
holds, while dirt poured onto his face and into his clothes. He soon looked like a miner. I asked
myself which was worse, sailing through the stormy Drake Passage or climbing these hanging

gardens. After cleaning and protecting each pitch we climbed it free. Believe it or not, the hard pitches offered the best climbing. The days were short and it was dark by six o'clock. We never did more than three pitches a day. Until we were halfway up the wall, we rappelled back to base camp every evening, leaving fixed ropes. The next day another team jugged up and struggled a little farther. Only after a week of hard work was the haulbag up at half height.

It couldn't go on like this. One morning Holger, Kurt, Klaus, and I ascended the ropes with a minimum of gear, food, and water for three days, wanting to go for the top alpine style. While we tried to escape upward, Mariucz, Gunda, and Hans Martin took down the fixed ropes and packed gear out of the gorge. The climbing became worse the higher we got. The rock was dangerously loose. Kurt was leading a body crack when a pillar the size of a phone booth he was leaning against suddenly moved. Instinctively he swung to the other side, and only a pillow-sized block whizzed past Klaus, Holger, and me. If it had been the phone booth, we would have joined its downward trip. We were engaged in a war of nerves. Night was coming fast as we traversed around a leaning pillar the size of a church tower in a near-vertical hanging garden. Kurt crawled behind man-sized palm trees jutting from the face. Their leaves, sharp as knives, cut our hands and arms. We rigged a rope bridge from the tower to the garden and hauled our packs and haulbags across to a bivy spot. Holger wedged himself behind a palm bush, and Klaus huddled on a sloping grass shelf, while Kurt and I wedged ourselves between a tree and the rock. The situation might have fulfilled a botanist's dream, but for us it was a nightmare. Our only goal was to get off this face as fast as possible. Holger crawled up the next pitch, done in from the bivy. Loose rock crumbled under his feet. Five pitches below the summit we came upon Carlos Garcia's route and followed it up the only logical line through the headwall. When we topped out just before dark, after nine days on the wall, El Gigante had its first free climb and the madness a name: We called the route La Conjura de los Necios—The Conspiracy of Fools (880m, 23 pitches 5.13a).

STEFAN GLOWACZ, *Germany*

El Gigante, Blade, Scars, and Stars. In November 2000 I returned to Mexico with Jakub Gajda and Gareth Llewellin to attempt El Gigante. The month-long journey was wrought with near-death encounters and bucketsful of snakes. But we succeeded in establishing a new route on the monstrous monolith. The line ascends the 2,800-foot southwest face, ascending to a huge ledge and then following the left-most waterfall stain. The climbing was sustained hard aid. This previously unclimbed side was a little looser than expected. We climbed wall style, heavy and molasses-slow, averaging a pitch a day. After we spent 14 days on the wall, Blade, Scars, and Stars (VI 5.9 A3+) was finished. The route tops out at a place similar to Zodiac on El Cap, 1,000 feet shy of the summit proper. We were probably the first Australian, Czech, and American team to climb El Gigante.

BRENT EDELEN, *AAC*

Basaseachic Waterfall, Soy Caliente. Morgan Black, Aidan Oloman, and Sean Easton established Soy Caliente (5.11, A1, 9 pitches) ground-up over two weeks in November and December. Forty 3/8-inch bolts and 20 rivets were placed. Thirty meters were A1, the rest free. Rock quality was variable. We don't recommend a repeat of this route. The route goes up the wall 100 meters right of Basaseachic Waterfall. It is the fourth route on this formation, the other three being left of the waterfall. There are many large formations in Basaseachic Waterfall Park, but much of the volcanic rock is soft and loose. Topos, accommodations, information, and helpful assistance can be obtained from Don Fernando at Rancho San Lorenzo, located at the end of the road in the park. Thanks to the Canadian Himalayan Foundation for a grant.

SEAN EASTON, *Canada*

The Cascade Wall, Kola Loca. Zack Smith and I climbed a line, Kola Loca (V 5.10 A2+), on The Cascade Wall of Basaseachic. The route ascends the prominent dihedral system some distance left of the waterfall and the prominent black streak. Climbers since have called this a rappel route. We fixed the first three pitches, then spent two nights on the wall while climbing the last four pitches. The route was mostly aid, with a little dirty free climbing. Nel, the curator of the local curio shop, has the only detailed topo in existence.

BRENT EDELEN *AAC*

ELSEWHERE IN MEXICO

El Cerro Blanco, Irritilas (Nómadas) and Lluvia de Estrellas. This is a brief account about the lovely land and people of the states of Durango and Coahuila, México. Desert lands with multicolored sunrises and sunsets and incomparable beauty. The Peñón Blanco massif, better known as the Cerro Blanco, is one of the most accessible walls in México. It is a granite massif with 400 meters of vertical rise. Located in a desert zone where the temperatures in winter reach 28ºC (85ºF), it is best visited between the months of October and March. To reach Cerro Blanco you must take the national highway, Durango-Cuencame No. 40, to the town of Yerbanís where you turn toward Peñón Blanco until reaching Pueblo de Nuevo Covadonga and encounter the gap from the west of the rock massif. The Base Camp is two kilometers from the base of the wall. It is important to arrive with all of the food, fuel, and water you will need. This is a destination for adventure climbing. It is a one-hour approach to the base of the wall. All of the routes have been established and equipped in Yosemite style: Ground-up free climbing, placing bolts where there are no cracks for protection. There is trad, sport, and bouldering. There is vast potential here.

Cerro Blanco. *Luis Carlos Garcia Ayala*

In December 2000, Jorge Colín and I climbed a seven-pitch route that we called Irritilas (Nómadas) [Irritated (Nomads)] (350 meters, V A1 5.11). Spending three days on the wall, we climbed with clean protection and bolts. Those who conquer the desert can experience excellent granite and feel the climatic contrasts. You can also contemplate the beautiful sunsets and share with the people of the States of Durango and Torreón.

In November (2001) I was drawn back by a strong attraction to the desert and especially to a massif of granite rock that rises between hills, spiny bushes, orange colored blocks of granite, and a night sky teeming with thousands of stars. This is the place to live a good adventure. This time I was accompanied by James Scarse, an American climber interested in getting to know the area and opening a new free route. We spent two days on the wall climbing some exceptional pitches with a few bolts and fascinating rock features. We made the first ascent of Lluvia de Estrellas (Rain of Stars) (300 meters, V A1 5.12+). In the Piedra Partida campground, where there is an enormous boulder perfectly split in two, waited some friends from Torreón, Monterrey, México (City), South Africa, and Switzerland. It's a magical place.

LUIS CARLOS GARCÍA AYALA, *Mexico*

Tatewarí, Cola de Venado. The Cumbres de Monterrey "la Huasteca" National Park (la Huasteca refers to the region around the Gulf of México) is located in the metropolitan area of the city of Santa Catarina in the state of Nuevo León. Once in the park you have to follow the paved road (3 km) until it turns to gravel. Once on the gravel road follow a sign on the ground that says "Virikuta." This road enters another canyon that leads to the ranch of Don Simón Loera Correa. This Señor Simón is the rural Judge and it is important to let him know the length of your stay in the area.

The canyon is surrounded by a great massif of limestone rock that reaches over 500 meters in height. The area possesses vast potential for multi-pitch climbing and is only 20 minutes from the city of Santa Catarina. On the rock wall Tatewarí (Grandfather Fire), 550 meters tall, is the first route. Because it is a desert zone the best months to climb are October until April, the others being very hot. It is advisable to arrive with all of your food, water, and fuel when entering the park.

The Cola de Venado route on Tatewarí in La Huasteca National Park. *Luis Carlos Garcia Ayala*

On the first ascent of Cola de Venado, Tatwarí.   *Carlos Garcia*

Last October I was invited to get to know the canyon. I returned in December with Francisco Trad to equip and do the first ascent of Cola de Venado (Stag's Tail) (550 meters, V 5.12d). The ascent was done from the ground up, placing bolts from hooks. The work took us five days of climbing and staying on the wall. There are 10 pitches of 55 meters each and 115 bolts on excellent, featured limestone. Rap the route to descend.

After the first attempt we left the route equipped and returned to México City. Last March I returned to free the route and confirm its rating. This time Rodney Blackmore, from the U.S., and I simulclimbed the route without falls in a total of five hours, greatly enjoying the climbing. From the summit the landscape is spectacular and you can see three enormous virgin walls awaiting their first route. There are two other areas of the park for sport climbing in the zone of Guitarritas and various others around la Huasteca. There is enormous potential for further climbing in the area.

LUIS CARLOS GARCÍA AYALA, *Mexico*

Iztaccihuatl, El Orgasmo del Cerdo and Oz. El Orgasmo del Cerdo is more than 700 meters high, but only 300 meters are technical, with 200 meters of scrambling and occasional 20-meter fourth-class steps. It rises from the west glacier and was opened by Leonardo Torres, Gustavo Montalvo, and me in April. We climbed the route unroped, in less than five hours, because we found no way to safely use the rope we were carrying. You start at 4,500m on a 70-meter water-ice fall, with a 60-degree-ramp in the middle (WI3). You continue up a rocky ridge for another 300 meters, encountering fourth-class on two 20-meter steps. You then gain the base of a 40-meter icefall that is WI3. Once past the icefall, you ascend 80 meters of mixed terrain, which averages 50 degrees but is easy; pass more fourth-class terrain; and end on a 35-meter high serac, which may be AI3 or AI4, as it has 25 feet of vertical ice. From here to the summit is 120 meters of easy, though crevassed, terrain.

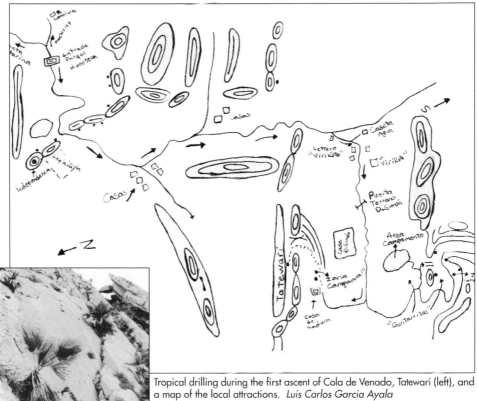

Tropical drilling during the first ascent of Cola de Venado, Tatewarí (left), and a map of the local attractions. *Luis Carlos Garcia Ayala*

The summit is at 5,260m. The descent involves a 45-degree ramp for 100 meters before you gain a tricky ridge of sand and rock.

In October, with Salvador Camacho, I opened the route Oz from the northwest glacier. The technical part of Oz is 330 meters long (WI-4 M3), but to get to it you have to make an ascending traverse from 4,600m to 4,800m on 40-degree ramps. Above the 330 technical meters you ascend 60-degree ramps for another 200 meters to the top. The total altitude gain for this route is thus 730 meters, not including the approach.

For both routes there is an approach, starting at 3,600m, that takes about four hours. They are among the hardest routes on our Mexican mountains. Our ice is tropical ice, and the rock is volcanic and tends to be unstable. The routes on the northeast side of Iztaccihuatl are committing, as they lack belay points for a secure retreat.

ALEJANDRO PEREZ RAYON, *Mexico*

Peru

CORDILLERA HUAROCHIRÍ

Nevado Sullcón, north face; Nevado Vicuñita Sur, southeast face, southwest face. Unusually bad weather and deep snow were a constant handicap during the 2001 climbing season in central Peru. In May J.P. Perret and I attempted Pariacacca Norte (5701m), but deep snow forced us to abandon our climb. In early June we explored for routes up Nevado Sullcón (5650m). I returned three weeks later and on June 26, with Damián A. Vargas, tackled the steep north face. We reached the summit, a first ascent, up steep ice and a narrow snow ridge. In mid-July Bruno Castro and I made an ascent of Nevado Vicuñita Sur (5500m). We gained the summit via the southeast face, but

had to make a hasty descent due to strong snow squalls. On August 28, Alejandro A. Vargas, his son Damián, and I revisited the mountain. We climbed its southwest face by way of a steep gully and the west ridge.

ALBERTO MURGUÍA, *Club de Montañeros Américo Tordoya, Lima*

Pyramide de Garcilaso attempt. *Jeremy Frimer*

CORDILLERA BLANCA

Santa Cruz Norte, west face attempt; Pyramide de Garcilaso, east face attempt. Jay Burbee (Canada), Michel van der Spek (Netherlands), and I (Canada) spent June in the Cordillera Blanca, where we began with an attempt on the unclimbed west face of Santa Cruz Norte (5829m). Uncharacteristic of the region, the weather was not good. In marginal weather we climbed a runnel on the right side of the face (the first one that completely avoids the prominent rock band at three-quarters height). Eight pitches were climbed, principally on ice and snow of varying quality and as steep as 60 degrees, as well as minor mixed sections. We topped out on the west ridge at 5700m late in the day and retreated to avoid an unplanned bivy. Our climb is not to be considered a new route, since it does not connect with an established route (the west ridge remains unclimbed) or reach the summit.

Next we unsuccessfully attempted a route on the unclimbed east face of Pyramide de Garcilaso in the Paria Gorge. The easiest approach to this face seems to be straight up the valley headwall, but is exposed to ice and stone fall. We took the quickest route, which climbed a glacier, formed entirely by icefall, traversed a bombarded scree ledge, and climbed one pitch of Grade 3 ice up the toe of the glacier. The east face of Pyramide de Garcilaso contains about a dozen steep ice streaks and runnels. We chose what looked to be one of the easier ones, a water-ice line descending from the col between the north and south summits. From a bivy cave at its base Jay led the first pitch in the dark of early morning, fighting with an eight-meter vertical pillar. Three more pitches up excellent 45- to 70-degree water ice and snow led to a 20-meter vertical ice curtain at 5500m. The lower part of the ice sheet was thick and of good quality, but higher the ice became thin, detached, and rotten. The underlying and surrounding rock was not of good quality, making the climbing somewhat unprotectable. An attempt to aid the curtain on ice tools was abandoned just below the point of no return. A safer but more complicated descent route below the east face of Paron, on rock slabs and steep grass, was used to regain the valley.

JEREMY FRIMER, *Varsity Outdoor Club (UBC)*

Nevado Quitaraju, south face. Brits Nick Bullock and Al Powell opened a new route on the great south wall of Nevado Quitaraju (6040m). This route is to the right of the Slovenian line (the only previous route on this wall). The first climbers explained that it took seven hours to cross the barrier of seracs

Top:Jay Burdee on the still-unclimbed west face of Santa Cruz Norte. Below: Southern Discomfort on the south face Siula Grande (see pg 304). Jeremy Frimer (2)

at the base of the wall. The new route is primarily glacial, with sections of 75 to 80 degrees and some of 90 degrees, as well as mixed climbing. Bullock and Powell reached the summit on July 23 after two days of climbing.

JUANJO TOME, *Peru*

Tuctubamba, Middle Earth. Clay Wadman and I tried the prominent couloir on the right, climbing ca 300 meters and reaching the rock band before rappelling the line of ascent. We found conditions that varied from one-inch ice over rock to perfect névé to bottomless snow. The crux involved thin, 75-degree ice protected by knifeblades. On our descent we used primarily knifeblades and small stoppers, but placements were difficult to find, as the rock is compact.

Topher and Patience Donahue did the probable first ascent of a line that is hidden to the left behind Tuctubamba, and Clay and I repeated it two days later. Middle Earth (IV 5.8 WI5, ca 400 meters) lies in a cleft and deposits the climber on the saddle between Tuctubamba and Taulliraju. Another 70 or 80 meters of moderate snow climbing takes one to the summit. Pitches two and four were the cruxes. The first crux involved rock climbing to access a tenuously adhered, five-meter vertical pillar, while the second involved vertical ice for 15 meters, protected at the steepest part by rock gear in the wall. Conditions were generally excellent, as was protection. Middle Earth is a recommended route to a great summit and lends itself to being climbed from Punta Union in a day.

CHRISTIAN BECKWITH, *AAC*

La Esfinge, Via Gringos. On June 17 Joe Vallone and I, both of Colorado, began to climb the south face of La Esfinge (The Sphinx). Funded by an American Alpine Club Youth Fellowship Award, our team of two set out to make the first all-American ascent of this Peruvian gem. The Sphinx is perched three hours north of Huaraz in the Cordillera Blanca, humbly located beneath the proud faces of the Huandoy group.

The route entailed 14 days of ferrying loads, fixing pitches, and varied climbing on immaculate golden granite in an unbelievable setting. Our route, Via Gringos, is to the right of a route put up by a Spanish soloist several years ago. It began with a technical face pitch, which punched through several roof systems on hidden crimpers and required delicate face climbing. We rated the pitch 5.12a; the difficulties are protected with bolts.

We pushed upward for seven more pitches, navigating a maze of thin seams and difficult corners. The major difficulties were not in the climbing of the natural lines, which were there, but rather in the relentless cleaning of malevolently vegetated cracks. Future teams will surely find the gear placement and climbing more entertaining without the bushwhacking through the high-altitude jungle we encountered.

As we continued we rested each night looking at the single, tattered photo of the face we carried. "Somewhere up there is a big ledge"—we reaffirmed this glimmer of hope daily, after dumping dirt from our trousers and before passing out wincing in pain. To reach the big ledge, we continued forging our way up several difficult pitches involving A3+ hooking and sizable fall potential. Along the way bat-hooks were used to link natural placements and bypass plants that were too dense to be removed and too prickly to touch.

On the sixth day Joe led across what we dubbed Jose's Roof Traverse. Mostly protected by large camming units, the roof required awkward moves, and much of the climbing was done while dangling from a crack. The pitch required a nearly horizontal traverse that finished under a small roof.

After an incredible hanging bivy several hundred feet from friends on a neighboring route, I led into the exit pitch of Jose's Roof Traverse. Varied climbing eventually brought me to an A2 knifeblade seam and an even more spectacular hanging bivy. Our pace of one grueling pitch per day began to wear our nerves thin, but after a long A3+ pitch the following day we finally rested in the comfort of the big ledge. However, the grim reality was that we were only halfway up.

On the ninth day I ventured into what we called the Railroad Cracks, a pair of parallel cracks. From the ground we had been sure that the cracks would be finger and hand sized perfect for free climbing. Despite our optimism, however, the cracks turned out to be closed seams that would hold no gear of any kind. Once again I was reduced to hooking far above the bolt I had placed. The slow pace, coupled with untimely losses of both drills, forced us to escape from our initial line and look for a quicker path to the summit. We joined a route (Todos Narcos, I think) a hundred yards or so to the right and quickly gained elevation the next day. Before retiring the next day we hauled to a high ledge, where the angle of the wall eases, and managed to climb two new pitches below the gleaming headwall at the top of the face.

The following day we finished the route and enjoyed a quiet, warm sunset over the Cordillera Negra. Over tuna fish and tomato sauce, we soaked in the soft rays of the sun as it drifted out of sight, all the while exchanging casual conversation about one of the toughest climbs we had done together. Via Gringos (The Way of the Gringos) is VI 5.12a A3+ route that was completed in 17 pitches, over two weeks, gaining the summit at around 18,000 feet.

ZACK MARTIN

La Esfinge, Mecho Taq Inti? Our team was two women, Tanja Rojs and Aleksandra Voglar, and I, Andrej Grmovsek, all from Slovenia. After acclimatization on Vallunaraju (5686m) we put up base camp under La Esfinge on July 11. Because of many articles in recent climbing magazines, we were expecting big crowds on and under the wall, but we were all alone. In the month of our stay under La Esfinge, only a few parties came and climbed the classic 1985 route.

Our plan was to put a new route on the wall, but the wall was almost full of routes. Nevertheless, we found a nice unclimbed line

La Esfinge, Mecho Taq Inti? *Andrej Grmovsek*

on a very steep buttress on the far left side of the east wall. The wall is highest there and faces south-east. We started 50 meters left of the route Cruz del Sur. We climbed mostly free but used aid while cleaning dirty cracks or placing hand-drilled bolts. We used mostly natural protection, which was hard to place. The cracks were dirty, filled with earth and plants, and also flared. That's why it was much easier to free climb, with runouts, than to use aid. The women found the climbing hard and climbed two pitches with aid, at 6b, A2+. We placed 13 bolts for belays on the lower part of the route and 9 on the pitches. On the lower part of the wall we fixed ropes and returned to the base every night. We had problems with weather, which is not typical for this mountain at this time of the year. During our 16 days under La Esfinge we had six days of snow, wind, and cold. In five climbing days we fixed six 60-meter ropes. Then in one day we climbed the upper wall to the summit. We named the route Mecho Taq Inti?, which in Quechua means "Where are you, sun?" It's 800 meters long, 15 piches, Grade VI.

After two weeks of resting and healing a heel injury, I returned to the wall with Tanja in August. Our plan was to free climb the harder, steeper first half of our route (we free climbed the upper part during the first ascent). I climbed it free, despite strong wind and cold. The difficulties were up to 7b (obligatoire 7a), with some long runouts. (1. 6c, 60m; 2. 7b, 60m; 3. 6c+, 60m; 4. 6c+, 60m; 5. III, 20m; 6. 6c, 60m; 7. 7a, 60m; 8. 6a+, 30m; 9. 6b+, 60m; 10. 6a, 60m; 11. 6b, 60m; 12. 6b, 60m; 13. 5c, 60m; 14. 6a+, 60m; 15. 6b+, 30m.) After a day of rest we also climbed the 1985 route (free onsight, at 7a). Of course it was snowing from the midpoint to the top. Then we took two days of rest and tried Cruz del Sur, a route that was climbed last year by a very strong party, Slovenian Silvo Karo and Italian Mauro "Bubu" Bole, and rated 7c+. We climbed it in three days. On the first two days we returned to the base by fixed ropes. We were really getting

Pitch 9 of La Esfinge's Mecho Taq Inti? (Where Are You Sun?). *Andrej Grmovsek*

tired, because we climbed so hard day after day. Except for the second pitch, which I needed to first nail (I climbed it on my second try), I climbed the route free onsight. I think the first-ascent climbers overgraded the route. It is only a little harder than Mecho Taq Inti? and not as serious.

ANDREJ GRMOVSEK, *Planinska zveza Slovenije*

Caraz II, south face variation. After we returned from the Huayhuash we climbed in the Blanca. Viktor Mlinar and I decided to climb the Fisher-Warfield-Sheldrake route on the south face of Caraz II (6020m), also called Caraz de Santa Cruz. The route was climbed in 1986, graded alpine TD+, and is 700 meters high. The first-ascent team ended the route at the east ridge, about 300 meters from the summit, and descended by rappelling the route. They spent three days round-trip. The wall faces more southeast than south, so it receives sun until noon.

On August 3 we started from our bivouac site at around 3 a.m. Luckily we passed the very broken glacier and climbed the lower, easier part of the route unroped, in ideal conditions. Halfway up the route we started to place protection. We climbed mixed pitches (Scottish V). Conditions on the upper part of the wall were bad. We needed four hours to climb the last three pitches on a snowy crest to reach the east ridge. We were happy, but realized that it was too soon to celebrate. The ridge is very corniced, and it took us another four hours to climb to the summit, which we reached at 2 p.m. The weather was still nice, just a bit windy. I don't know where exactly the Fisher-Warfield-Sheldrake goes in its upper part, but I think we climbed a different line.

The southeast face of Caraz II, showing (1) the approximate line of Superduper Couloir, 1998; (2) The Fisher-Warfield-Sheldrake route; (3) the Mlinar-Jost variation, 2001. Descent is behind left skyline. *Viktor Mlinar*

We started to climb down the original 1955 route (Huber-Koch, 800 meters) but had to make two short rappels—one in the upper part to overcome a 25-meter vertical step and the second to pass the 25-meter bergschrund. After 16 hours we reached our bivy site. The next day we descended to Laguna Paron and via Caraz returned to Huaraz. We took three days for the whole trip.

MATIC JOST, *Slovenia*

Artesonraju, northeast face. In June 2000 Spaniards Nemisio Matalobos and Angel Terrain established a ca 800-meter route rated alpine D (55 degrees) on the northeast face, which is accessed from the upper Santa Cruz Valley. The route lies between the 1965 Hartman-Reiss-Schatz-Steiger Route and the East Ridge (Janis-Lowe-Lowe-Ortenburger, 1971). It starts from the same snow slopes as the 1965 route, then crosses the rock rib on the couloir's left side to gain snow and ice that leads to the summit (6025m). It might be better thought of as a variation to the 1965 route.

MOUNTAIN INFO, *High Mountain Sports 227*

Chacraraju Oeste, south face. In the first week of August Steve Moffat (New Zealand) and I climbed what was most likely a new route (600m, WI5 5.9 mixed) just to the right of the 1982 Yugoslav route on the south face. This side of the mountain has over ten established routes. Our route choice was not determined by logic but rather by adventure. The thin ice-filled gully we chose was quite threatened by unconsolidated snow flutings on its sides and by a 30-foot corniced roof laced with large icicles. The climbing was enjoyable, for the most part made up of moderate, 50- to 70-degree, thinly iced granite slabs, with a few vertical sections of water ice and mixed climbing. The crux was a rotten 40-meter icicle at about 18,500 feet. Having underestimated the amount of rocky terrain on the route, we progressed slower than expected. We only had knotted slings for stoppers and a spare pick as a piton. We did not summit the peak, but reversed our route from a junction with the ridge near the low point between the two west summits. After 17 hours or so we safely made it back to our camp in the bergschrund, only to have our luck run out. Once we were in our tent the entire route ripped in a slide of ice, rock, and snow, most likely triggered by a falling cornice. Eventually the lip of the 'schrund broke, and we were buried, tent and all. We dug ourselves out and hightailed it back to the lake in an exciting snow storm. The south face in general seemed to be dry compared to conditions reported in most first-ascent accounts—further evidence that things are warming up in the Cordillera Blanca.

JOHN VARCO, *AAC*

Editor's note: This is likely a repeat of an existing route, There are already 10 "established" routes on this face, and their exact location is somewhat vague as conditions change from year to year.

Huandoy Sur, No Fiesta Hoy Dia. I noticed the northeast face of Huandoy Sur the first time I visited Peru, in 1990. It is clearly visible from the approach to Pisco, looking steep and difficult. Five years later I climbed a new route on it, Oro del Inca, which crosses the steep rock band and follows ice directly to the top. But the rock face to the right was untouched.

This year I had no intention of continuing my solo ascents in the Cordillera Blanca. I came with Urban Golob, also from Slovenia, but after acclimatising he had to give up due to health problems. So, solo again. The weather was not perfect, but good enough, and I started climbing early in the night on July 4. The approach had changed since 1995: the glacier was much easier now.

I started right of my 1995 route. After an easy icefield I found a good path to the rock and mixed ground of the route's central part. I used ice tools on rock (dry tooling). The rock was solid in difficult sections but worse on easier ground. Some short icefalls helped me avoid difficult rock. The upper icefield was relatively easy, although steeper than the lower one, but the 150 meters above were really difficult. I hoped to find a steep gully through the overhanging seracs above the icefield, and there were possibilities. But the quality of the black ice, combined with powder snow, was so bad that I had to descend more than 100 meters before finding a way through the seracs on the third attempt. It was still hard and risky, passing overhanging ice, but the top was too close for me to return without reaching it. I reached it in fog and snow at about 1 p.m., after seven hours of climbing, and immediately started to descend the French Route (Astier, 1979) on the same face. The descent took five hours.

I named the route No Fiesta Hoy Dia (ED sup, AI6+ M5/6 WI5). There was a relatively large amount of ice on the face this year, and it probably made the central rock easier. But the final seracs were probably harder than usual.

This is my fifth new route on big walls of the Cordillera Blanca (four solo): Huascaran, Chacraraju, Huandoy (two), and Chopicalqui. I consider NO Fiesta Hoy Dia my hardest solo in the Andes.

PAVLE KOZJEK, *Slovenia*

Palcaraju Oeste, Ratz Fatz. On the west face of the west summit (6110m) a new route, Ratz Fatz (500m, TD-), was established by Chileans Eduardo Mondragon, and Martin Waldhoer on July 25, 2000. The route begins just right of a prominent rock spur near the bottom of the face and takes a fairly direct path to the top. Most of the climbing was 45- to 60-degree snow, with some 65-degree mixed climbing midway and a 75-degree exit on flutings. Although they used the Ishinca Valley for their approach, they traversed the northwest ridge (towards Tocllaraju) from the summit, before descending a couloir between seracs. The couloir led to a glacier, which they crossed to the base camp used for Tocllaraju's normal route.

MOUNTAIN INFO, *High Mountain Sports 223*

Editor's note: this may have been climbed more than once before.

Huamashraju, west face. On August 4 Toma Erovnik (Slovenia) and our new Canadian friend Bruce Gordon climbed a new route on the west face of Huamashraju (5434m). They left Huaraz in the morning. After four hours of walking they reached the foot of the west wall. They climbed the central part of the wall, a five-pitch new route, about 200 meters high, that ends at the top of the rock wall. The difficulty is UIAA V to VI. They descended by rappelling the rock wall. In the evening they returned to Huaraz, where we met and celebrated.

MATIC JOST, *Slovenia*

Chinchey Group: Shahuanca, Cherup II, El Roca del Cuyé Loco. In the Chinchey Group, up behind Huaraz, the French alpinists Clément Guntz and Hugo Robin made what they think may be the first ascent of a peak they called Shahuanca on July 25, 2000. The peak, which is labeled 5,383m on the 1939 Deutschen Alpenverein map, lies east of Chopihirca (5057m) and Catac, in what appears to be the Shahuanca valley. The route ascends the west-southwest side of the peak, is 1,000 meters long and AD+ in difficulty. On August 2 Guntz soloed, a possible first ascent, the Northwest Arête of Churup II (5461m), from Q. Cohup at ca 4000m. He descended the face to the right. Guntz, Robin, and Joel Menard also established a new 500-meter rock route at El Roca del Cuyé Loco, near Churup, climbing a series of left-facing corners through a roof. The route appears to be called Le Pilier du Hamster Fou.

Based on correspondence with CLÉMENT GUNTZ, *FFME, France*

Churup, 496spa-smos. On October 2, I placed my tent at the upper Churup Lake and the next day broke trail to the base of the wall, where I left ropes, harness, and ice ax. On October 4 it took 1 hour and 30 minutes to return to the base, thanks to the trail I had opened. From the bottom of the face I climbed the obvious couloir to the right. This couloir comes to an obvious intersection. To the left, leading directly to the summit, is the Princesa Malinche route. To the right is Fear, a route up a mixed dihedral. I began by trending slightly to the right and then straightened my line and ended below a promontory to the right of the summit. From this point I took less than ten minutes to reach the summit. Descent was by the Fear route; the rappels are in place. (I used two 60-meter ropes.) I found good ice conditions, the average slope being 70 to 80 degrees, with two sections of 85 degrees. Equipment left: one ice screw, one pin, four slings. The route is named 496spa-smos (V AI4, 450m), on the southwest face of Churup (5493m).

RICHARD HIDALGO, *Peru*

Cashan Este, Mathi, Matias. In July 1998 I departed from Olleros and walked toward Rurec's Quebrada (creek), before arriving at Tararhua Lake (4400m), where I set up my tent. From there I went to the southeast face of Cashan (5723m). I climbed in a couloir, to the right of a buttress that passes through the center of the face. I surmounted a section of 75-80-degree verglassed rock below a serac barrier. After surmounting a bergschrund I traversed to the left across a snow slope that took me to the southeast ridge. I crossed the ridge and continued on the 70-degree southwest face to the summit. I called the route Mathi, Matias (500m, MD-, 70-80 degrees). Descent was via the northeast ridge and the crevassed southeast glacier. It took all night, and I came back to camp early the next morning.

RICHARD HIDALGO, *Peru*

Ocshapalca, Variante Peruana. Guillermo Mejia and I installed the tent at the moraine camp in September 1998. Our new route on the south face of Ocshapalca (Variante Peruana, 650m, ED-) begins to the right of the central buttress and the Alquimia Route. We climbed straight toward 5881m summit, joining the American Route for the top third. The descent to camp was by the Alquimia Route, after we made a bivouac in a cave 50 meters from the summit. *(Editor's note: is likely a repeat of an existing route.)*

RICHARD HIDALGO, *Peru*

Nevado Kayesh, Italian Route variation attempt. In June Guillermo Mejia and I set up a tent on the glacier, a half-hour from the bergschrund of Kayesh (5721m). We started up the German line, then followed the fixed Italian ropes (1973) until they ended. We continued for one more rope length up a couloir with hard ice until we reached a rock wall, at the bottom of which we bivouacked. All night it was snowing. The next day, leaving gear at the bivouac, we went as light as we could. We climbed the 40-meter wall, which was covered with snow and verglas, exposed and difficult to protect. We then traversed to the left over a hanging serac (soft snow, 60 degrees). We continued to the ridge, which we gained as high as we could, since it was double-corniced. We reached the ridge from the bivy site in three ropelengths, approximately 70 meters in a straight line. We descended the same line. It would be possible to climb the route in a day by going light. The route (400m, MD+) has eight pitches, of which we believe the last four are a variant of the Italian route.

RICHARD HIDALGO, *Peru*

Punta Numa, So Long Fox. An Italian pair opened an impressive route on the Punta Numa (baptized by Eloy Callado and Cesar Pedrochi after they made the first ascent on August 19, 1997). Roberto Iannilli and Luciano Mastracci climbed a line to the right of the Monttrek Route. They summited on August 2. They graded the route 7a, A3+ and called it So Long Fox. The first half of the route ascends compact plates; the finish is wild. The climb is complicated by the compactness of the rock. The rare cracks are too closed for nuts and are full of moss. The route was left partially equipped, and the belays are equipped with pitons or bolts. Fifteen bolts were used for protection and three for aid. To repeat the route carry nuts; cams, including the biggest; a variety of pitons; and small carabiners.

JUANJO TOME, *Peru*

CORDILLERA HUALLANCA

Nevado Huallanca, Koso. Between the cordilleras Blanca and Huayhuash is the small Cordillera Huallanca. Although it does not rise above 6000m, it offers beautiful mountains with glaciers and rocks. David Rodriguez Lopez climbed the mountain known as Cumbre de los Burros or Nevado Huallanca (5470m), the highest summit of the Cordillera Huallanca. The route, completely on glacier, starts near the west side of Collado de los Burros, next to a small lake. The route is approximately 500 meters long and is graded MD, with 70-85-degree snow and ice. The descent was by rappelling the route. The name of the route is Koso.

JUANJO TOME, *Peru*

CORDILLERA HUAYHUASH

Nevado Yerupaja Grande. Equadorian Santiago Quintero climbed the west face of NevadoYerupaja Grande (6634m). The main summit of Yerupaja had gone many years without an ascent until Santiago climbed it solo on July 4. The ascent and descent took him 17 hours. He followed the Northwest Ridge route, which was opened as far as Yerupaja Norte (6430m) by R. Bates and G. Dingle and completed to the main summit by D. Wilkinson and R. Renshaw. Because of the changing morphology of the wall, Quintero followed a route that is completely different from the original route. Although we cannot talk of a new route, we must mention that what Santiago climbed was for the most part unknown terrain, while being practically free of objective dangers. The difficulty is ED.

JUANJO TOME, *Peru*

Siula Grande, south face, Southern Discomfort; other peaks. In July Jay Burbee (Canada), Michel van der Spek (Netherlands), and I ventured to the eastern side of the Cordillera Huayhuash. Ten hours of dusty buses from Huaraz to Huallanca to La Union to Baños to Queropalca put us just 12 kilometers from the Cordillera. From a base camp at Laguna Siula (4300m) we climbed the left (south) side of the badly broken Sarapo Glacier in two days, making use of narrow passages between seracs and large crevasse fields. Most previous parties approached the right side of the glacier and reported mid-fifth class rock pitches below the glacier. Our route, however, was nontechnical, aside from one 50-meter, 55-degree, ice pitch at 5000m. We placed a high camp at 5500m in the isolated basin below the north face of Carnicero, the northeast face of Sarapo, and the south face of Siula Grande. On July 8 we climbed the northeast face of Sarapo by the Bachmann-Lugmayer line on the far left side of the face. The route involved eight rope lengths of 45- to 55-degree snow to gain the east ridge, which was narrow and corniced at first but became broader after 90 meters. In places, a long crack in the snow five meters below the cornice revealed either imminent cornice collapse or severe avalanche hazard. We decided to tread lightly on the cornice, and no incident occurred.

After rejuvenation at base camp, we returned to our high camp for our main objective, the south face of Siula Grande. Despite the notoriety of Siula, its south face remained

unclimbed. Our principal source of information was a mislabeled postcard. The south face is threatened by seracs largely on the right and is steep and rocky on the left, so we chose a route up the center. After four pitches of 55-degree quality blue ice, the angle steepened. Ice bulges and runnels as steep as 80 degrees led, in two more pitches, past the serac level and onto a snow slope at just over 6000m. As the sun was setting we happened upon an excellent bivy location, a steep crevasse eight meters wide. Its upper wall overhung and spilled large icicles onto the lower lip of the crevasse, effectively sealing it off. After a little shoveling we could safely unrope and stay dry without bivy bags. On the second day we crossed the bivy crevasse and attempted a direct finish but were thwarted by poor ice conditions (30 centimeters of rotten ice atop hard, brittle ice). We made a 150-meter traverse to an alternate finish, in hope of finding better conditions. Being in steep, south-facing

Siula Grande's south face, Southern Discomfort. *J. Frimer*

terrain we had been climbing in the shadow of Siula. To our short-lived delight, the sun now rose above the ridgeline at noon—only to set behind a cornice five minutes later. Several more ice pitches led to steepening mixed terrain above. We attempted to veer right but were met by the 60-degree sugar snow flutings for which the area is famous. I began a hair-raising tunneling traverse of the seven deep flutings separating us from a snowy shoulder of the east ridge. Fluting crests

Siula Grande's west face: (1) Simpson-Yates descent; (2) Noches de Juerga, 2001; Buhler-Price, 1999; (3) Simpson-Yates, 1985. The north (left) ridge was first climbed in 1936 by Awerzger-Scheider. *Jeremy Frimer*

were up to three meters deep and of particularly poor quality snow. In failing evening light on July 14 we reached the East Ridge route at 6250m. Having left our bivy equipment below, we were wary of a cold night and decided to retreat without summiting. Even so, I became hypothermic after making the final rappel to our traverse track. In my mentally weakened state I constructed perhaps the sorriest belay I've ever trusted. Ice screws were later removed by simply pulling straight out. The new route is named Southern Discomfort (ED-, 650 meters). We spent the next week thawing, while hiking the enjoyable Huayhuash circuit, where we met the Slovenian team that had just succeeded on a new route on the west face of Siula Grande. The team thanks Mountain Equipment Co-op and The Canadian Himalayan Foundation for generous support.

JEREMY FRIMER, *Canada*

Siula Grande, Noches de "Juerga." On July 3 Viktor Mlinar, Tomaz Zerovnik, Aritza Monasterio, and I left Huaraz and took a bus to Chiquian, where we hired donkeys to get to the Cordillera Huayhuash. From July 4-6 we marched to base camp, which we placed at 4,300m, half an hour from Lake Sharapococho. The weather was bad, with snowfall. From BC we saw only Yerupaja, Sharapo, and Trapezio. We used the bad-weather time for BC settlement, resting, and planning. We decided to put a tent with food and equipment under the wall. On the 10th, accompanied by our cook Marselindo, we carried heavy rucksacks to the base of the wall, at ca. 5,200 meters. Marselindo turned back, while we set up a tent and settled down for sleep. From BC to the tent was a six-hour walk. The next day we returned to BC to rest. The weather was odd.

On July 14 we left for the tent under the wall. Crevasses looked strange, so Viktor and Toma roped. After a hard beginning over the crevasse, with some dry tooling, Viktor traversed a snow mushroom to a steep icefield and beyond to the first rocks (Scottish VI). He placed a bolt, fixed a rope, and roped down. The first 55 meters of the huge wall was climbed. We slept in the tent under the wall. The weather was beautiful.

We started at night on the 15th; helped by the fixed rope. The slope beyond was a constant 65 degrees. The hardest pitches ascended a vertical icefall with very hard ice. We intended to bivi halfway up the wall, but when the sun got to the wall, ice and rocks started to fall. We were at ca 5800m and very exposed, so we quickly settled for a bivouac in a snow mushroom on our left. We took a little nap on a small shelf. It was very uncomfortable. The weather was beautiful. Next day in the morning we first descended 40 meters. The day's first pitch was led by Viki, the next by Aritza; then I took a pitch that involved a steep section with bad ice. The next pitch looked hard. I placed a bolt and roped down to a safe overhanging rock. We decided to bivi there and for four hours dug a shelf. With the sun, rocks and ice started to fall, but we were safe. The weather was good.

On July 17 we started at night. We left sleeping bags, bivi sacks, and food at the bivi site. We first ascended the fixed rope, then easily traversed left. The next two pitches combined bad vertical ice with rock. Aritza climbed more ice and a precarious mix with bad protection (Scottish VI). When I joined him a collapsing snow mushroom just missed us. We were surprised, as the wall was still in shade. There were only steep snow gullies and huge cornices left to overcome. Aritza took two more pitches, and finally Viktor masterfully traversed to the ridge. At 5:30 p.m. we stood at the top of the wall. We were 50 meters vertically and 200 meters horizontally from the summit of Siula Grande. We prepared for a bivouac in snow holes on top of the cornice. It was cold, the wind was blowing, and our sleeping bags were far away. We kept moving our fingers and tried not to sleep. At about 4 a.m. it started to snow. First we thought it was coming from the fog but soon found it getting serious.

We descended our line of ascent. We made 21 rappels: 13 from ice screws, 3 from bolts, 1 from a piton, and 4 from snow sabers. It was constantly snowing, and avalanches were

Before the traverse that leads out of the wall on west face of Siula Grande. *Victor Mlinar*

burying us. Fortunately, the wall is too steep for a big avalanche. At 2:30 p.m. we got to the tent under the wall, tired but happy and safe. In the morning we descended to BC, leaving wet ropes and the tent. New snow covered our tracks on the glacier, but we had no major problems. It snowed all day, and in BC it was raining. Finally, base camp, beer, Cuba libres. Then rest, rest, rest. The weather was beautiful. Marselindo retrieved our equipment from the base of the wall. He is 62 years young and walks so fast that we had problems catching him. He is quite a legend. We were waiting for donkeys on July 21, and the weather was sunny but windy. We returned by another path to Cajatambo, the nearest phone and road. On the 24th and 25th we rode back to Huaraz. And finally we chose the name of the route: Noches de "Juerga" (27 pitches, 1,000 meters, ED 65-90-degree ice; mixed Scottish VI).

MATIC JOST, *Slovenia*

On thin ice in the middle of the west face of Siula Grande. *Victor Mlinar*

Central Puscanturpa, Insumision. Spanish climber David Rodriquez Lopez opened a route, Insumision, on Central Puscanturpa (5442m), a beautiful mountain. The route ascends an oblique couloir that goes almost directly to the summit. The 450-meter route was ascended and descended in less than a day and is graded D, snow 65 degrees.

JUANJO TOME, *Per*

Brazil

Salinas, various routes. Salinas is known as the best place for long, adventurous routes in Brazil. It's only a three-hour drive from Rio, but the place is wild and peaceful. Just a small village with a café and a small grocery store. It's possible to ask for meals at the Refugio de Agua, a place like paradise an hour and a half from the wall. Salinas features steep granite domes from 400 to 700 meters high, with little equipment needed. There are a few bolts in the slabs. Almost half the routes have been opened by Sergio Tartari, the owner of the Refugio de Agua and the "seigneur"of Salinas. Sergio, who is one of the most "complete" climbers of Brazil, can be of great help with advice on equipment and approaches, which are not always obvious.

The 400-meter Capacete route at Cerj can be a good introduction to local rock and protection, as can the 700-meter historical Leste route at Pic Major. Otherwise the best routes, according to many Brazilian climbers, are Decadence Avec Elegance (17 pitches, all free up to French 7a+) and Paradoxo. Decadence Avec Elegance, which we opened in 1999, was so named because we came with a power drill, and Sergio was jealous. We gave it to him one day, and he quickly bolted some belays!

EMMANUEL RATOUIS, *France*

Bolivia

Northern Apolobamba. In July 2000 over four-weeks, Paul Bielen, Peter Boerstoel, Michael van Geemen, and Peter Valkenburg climbed 17 peaks above 5000m in the northern Apolobamba region, including one probable first ascent and six possible new routes. The Dutch team started from a 4880m camp on the shores southeast of Lago Chucuyo Grande. From there they ascended the short west ridge of Chucuyo Grande (5530m) and repeated the south ridge of Palomani Grande (5769m). They established the first route on the south face of Flor del Rocca Sud (300 meters, D 60 degrees), battling deep powder snow. On July 11 Boerstoel and Valkenburg opened a new route, the Central Pillar (300 meters, D+/TD-), on the east face of Nevado Saluyo Sud (5800m), finding mostly solid rock up to V+. At the same time Bielen and van Geeman established the Southeast Spur (300 meters, D) on the north peak (5770m) of Nevado Saluyo. They found mixed climbing up to IV- and 70 degrees, with awkward, deep powder snow. This pair then repeated the 1980 Italian West Ridge route on Chaupi Orco (6044m, the Apolobamba's highest summit) and opened a four-pitch route of very loose rock (IV/V) on the west face of Montserrat Norte (5650m). On July 15, on the southwest face of Sorel Este (5471m), a possible new route (300m, TD-) was made by Boerstoel and Valkenburg. They found good conditions, with a hard-ice 70-degree crux high on the face between two serac barriers. On the southwest face of Ascarani (5580m) the group repeated the 1996 Currie-Ryle route (300 meters, D 55 degrees).

They then moved camp to near the Paso de Pelechuco road crossing, a location allowing good access to the Katantica Group. On the west face of Katantica Oeste (5630m) they repeated the 1992 British route (350m, D-). Boerstoel and Valkenburg made the first ascent of 5610-meter Kantica Central's south face (200m, D+ 65 degrees) during a traverse from Katantica Oeste to El Presidente. The route on this peak's west ridge was repeated, along with those on the southwest ridge of Pelechuco Huaracha (5650m) and the west ridge of Katantica Estes (5590m). Boerstoel and Valkenburg made the possible first ascent of a 5470m, previously unnamed, summit on July 27. From the Pelechuco Road about one kilometer west of Agua Blanca, this summit is easily seen. They climbed solid, compact rock on the 550-meter north face, with a short crux of 6a (French). They called the peak Pico Pedros and descended the east flank.

MOUNTAIN INFO, *High Mountain Sports 223*

Chearoco Valley. During five weeks in the summer of 2001 a British female team comprising Adele Pennington, Catrin Thomas, Nancy Brooks, and I enjoyed a successful expedition to this remote and underdeveloped region. Although the trip was hampered by extremely bad weather, the team managed to establish one possible first ascent, make several new routes, and attempt others during only 13 days of good weather. The team established their base camp at the head of the Chearoco Valley, after a two-day approach walk from Lloco Lloconi. There is limited information on both Chearoco (6104m) and Chachacomani (5998m). Both apparently receive few ascents because of difficult access and lack of information. To the best of the team's knowledge the only previous expedition to this area had been by a Reading University team in 1962. During the team's stay they did witness a German commercial company trying both Chearoco and Chachacomani, and they learned that a German Youth Expedition had been there a few years earlier, but no further information was available.

After exploratory work Thomas and Gilbert made the first ascent of 5520m Dome 1, via its south ridge (PD). The pair detoured from the final summit ridge due to poor snow conditions. After descending through patches of wind slab, they continued into the main glacier bowl and picked a route through large crevasses to the summit. Pennington and Brooks carried out a reccon on the north ridge of Chearoco, reaching a high point of 5630m, and another reccon on Quellani, reaching a high point of ca 5315m.

Thomas and Gilbert had planned to attempt the south ridge of Rumca I (5240m). The pair made good progress onto the ridge via the western face, but was soon forced to abandon their attempt by poor rock. They retreated and traversed onto the south face. They made excellent progress up the face directly to a high point of 5040m, through mixed terrain and ice-smeared rock (Scottish IV/V), before being caught in collapsing debris, which caused a hasty retreat. Thomas, Gilbert, and Pennington made another attempt on Rumca I via the east ridge. Having crossed a complex glacier system to gain access to the ridge, the team made good progress but was forced to turn back at 5360m.

Two 50-meter rock routes were established on excellent granite low on Quellani, but further exploration for rock climbing proved futile. Thomas, Gilbert, and Pennington then made an ascent of Quellani (5912m) from the north. A short, steep 50-meter slope led to a scramble to the summit. Weather-worn slings on the summit indicated that this was not a first ascent.

However, an amazing route (PD). The weather broke, with nine consecutive days of snow. With time running out Thomas, Gilbert, and Pennington made a final attempt on Rumca III via the stunning south face arête but felt they would be taking an unnecessary risk to continue under such conditions.

DI GILBERT, *United Kingdom*

The south face of Illimani, near La Paz, showing Nada es Seguro, 2001. *Karen McNeill*

Illimani, Nada es Seguro. On April 25 Bruce and Sheila Hendricks and I took the 3 p.m. bus from La Paz to Cohoni. During the ride we chatted with locals and were able to hire an arriero (mule/horse driver), whose horses would carry our equipment into Illimani. Before we left Cohoni repeated emphatic instructions were given to our companions to ensure that they took us to the rarely visited south side of the mountain. Several hours later we realized that our instructions had been misunderstood, and we were heading to the base of the regular route. Bruce and Sheila took over navigating and led the way to the south side of Illimani. Minero Mesa Qala is a dilapidated mine at the base of the mountain. Arriving at dusk we set up camp among the ruins. Our arriero descended so that the horses could feed at a lower elevation. During our hike the mountain had tricked us with lines that appeared to be on the south face, but from the mine we had a better view of the south face and discovered that the features were part of the southwest face. We awoke the next morning to blue skies and feasted on the views. A good portion of the day was used to memorize details of our chosen route, which was the westernmost (leftmost) line on the south face proper.

By 3 p.m. our companions arrived to ferry remaining equipment around to Puente Roto. Our intentions were to meet them late the following day after descending the west ridge. After their departure we began the hike to the base of the route. It took three hours to traverse moraine, cross smooth slabs of granite, and ascend a glaciated snow cone. The top half of the route sported a large snowfield, so it was decided to climb during the cool of night. Using head-lamps to light our way, we began to climb pitches of ice, using rock anchors. Unfortunately, by dawn we were only ten pitches up and still had a lot of elevation to ascend. The technical crux of the route had been the first pitches of waterfall ice. We decided to continue up, knowing that it would be possible to move more quickly through the alpine bowl. The conditions varied from deep, unconsolidated snow to smatterings of shallow ice and several broken rock bands. As the afternoon wore on the blue skies departed, and clouds descended upon the mountain.

The summit ridge was reached by the evening of the 28th. As we arrived a storm began swirling spindrift in our faces and reduced visibility, so we dug a snow cave and spent the night crammed in our packs. By morning visibility had improved somewhat, and we were able to proceed along the ridge, being careful not to walk off into space. As the summit was gained, the weather deteriorated again, and hailstones violently stung exposed skin. We spotted footprints and began to follow them down. Luck was not on our side, though, as the prints vanished in the wind. For a second night we were forced to dig a snow cave. During the evening the clouds momentarily lifted, and we were given a clear view down the mountain. With no tent or sleeping bags to keep us warm at camp, we stayed put. By morning the clouds had descended once again, but we were able to find our way down. At Nido de Condores a local guide, who had awaited our arrival, fed us hunks of bread and cheese that we washed down with numerous cups of tea. Feeling refreshed the three of us hiked back to Cohoni and spent a final night there before catching an overloaded bus back to La Paz. The bus ride was the crux of our entire adventure. We called the route Nada es Seguro ("nothing is certain"), 1,450 meters, V WI3+.

KAREN MCNEILL, *Canada*

Condoriri Group, Huallomen, southwest face, Bon Anniversaire Annick. In 2001 I spent a few days climbing in the well-known Condoriri group near La Paz. The snow/ice conditions were very good considering we were there at the end of July. With a friend, Martin Imgrüth, I climbed a route on Huallomen's southwest face that would appear to be a first ascent. It is an obvious line cutting through the rock face. When I talked about it with the guides in La Paz no one could tell me if it had already been climbed. The best information I managed to get was from Jose Camarlinghi, of Andean Summits, who told me that it was previously a Bolivian guide's project that he didn't complete. Jose said he hadn't seen this line in such good condition for many years.

After walking 20 minutes up the Tajira glacier we turned left to reach the base of the triangular face. To get to the bottom of the line we climbed a snowy couloir for 200- to 250-meters. The first pitch followed a diagonal ramp, from left to right, leading to a chimney. We belayed with two pegs at the base of the chimney. We climbed the vertical chimney (UIAA IV+) on poor rock and then a thinly iced gully to belay on friends. Following up the gully it steepens to 75-80 degrees and then a snow wall of 85-90 degrees. Belay on ice screws. The gully continues with good ice then a very steep mixed section. Belay on cams. From there the ascent became easier up a gentle snow couloir leading to a section of poor rock. After this last rope length the couloir continued for 150-200 meters only interrupted by a little mixed section. The last difficulty is a poor rock chimney (UIAA IV) leading to a saddle. From there the view is very impressive. We then followed the

Low on Bon Anniversaire Annick. *Martin Imgrüth*

Huallomen: (1) Bon Anniversaire Annick; (2) unknown route; (3) British route. *Jacques Pahud*

saddle ridge to the base of a rock tower that we avoided to the right by an easy section that leads to the upper slopes of the normal route. We descended by the normal route after reaching the end of these slopes having decided not to follow the ridge to the true summit of Huallomen. This route is about nine rope lengths from the start of the diagonal traverse to the saddle. We found poor rock sections, poor and thin ice, steep snow sections, and very little in the way of good protection except at the belays. All this made the ascent a bit exposed, although the hardest sections are not very long. No material was left on the route. With more ice and less snow it could be easier to protect. We called this route Bon Anniversaire Annick.

To the left of the start of the route (traverse) there is an ice line going up to the left which seems to have been climbed. We found the hole left by a snow-stake at the top of the last chimney (saddle). That led me to think that those who climbed it carried on by the upper part of the line we climbed. From the base it seems the easier and more obvious way to finish this ascent.

JACQUES PAHUD, *Switzerland*

Cuernos del Diablo, north face; Gigante Grande, Via Loco. On May 26 Brent Loken, Bruce Hendricks, Brent's father, and I drove in Brent's jeep from La Paz to the Quimsa Cruz. We stopped for the night in the tawdry mining town of Viloco, where we were able to convince a few locals to put us up in the Evangelical Church and to porter to our base camp. Bruce and Brent had decided to put our base camp at Taruca Umana Pass. This site makes good granite accessible but is a half an hour from water. In the vicinity of the pass we climbed a number of one- to three-pitch routes. We found that it was comfortable to climb in the sun on north-facing rock, but that south-facing rock was darned cold. Many of the cracks were filled with dirt and moss, but the granite itself was perfect. The best-looking reasonably accessible peak for longer routes was Cuernos del Diablo, and twice we climbed there. Our first climb on Cuernos led on new ground for about five pitches on the left side of the north face, with climbing up to about 5.10a. The approach had proven to be more complicated than it appeared, though, and with daylight dwindling we retreated. Two days later we came back to Cuernos and started up a route to the right of our first attempt. After Bruce started with a Tuolumne-like left-facing corner, we veered left onto unclimbed ground, with face climbing and then cracks that were sometimes dirty and up to 5.10. Then we connected, we believe, with a 1987 German route known locally as La Clasica for the last couple of beautiful hand- and fist-crack pitches to the top (IV 5.10-). It seems that no one had climbed the highest of the 30-foot tall splinters that make up the horns of Cuernos.

Brent then drove out, while Bruce and I took the bus from Viloco south to Laguna Laram Khota, a lake with a roadside view of the southwest face of Gigante Grande (18,858'). Two obvious ice gullies split the lower cliffs of this 2,100-foot face. The right-hand one had been done in 1993, while the shorter but much steeper left-hand one was unclimbed. We hiked in with two porters, finding that Yossi Brain's guidebook is wrong in recommending that you hike around the east side of the lake. We camped on dirt below the glacier beneath the face. As we scouted the face the upper snow slopes avalanched down the route in the afternoon sun. We decided to spend the next day just watching the face to see if this was common, and scouting the descent. That day was colder and the face did not avalanche, but we agreed to either be out of the couloir by 3 p.m. or else hide to the side until after sunset.

   We started an hour after dawn on June 4. The first pitch was on thin, moderately steep ice with solid metamorphic rock but poor protection. As the chute twisted and steepened, better cracks appeared, but Bruce still had to work carefully on the crux fourth pitch. He started out on slightly overhanging rock that led immediately to a head-wall of vertical mixed ground. After another pitch or two it was near 3 p.m., and we hid off to the side under an overhang. Nothing came down, and at dusk Bruce headed off for what proved to be the last surprisingly difficult pitch, a tenuous one with near-vertical "snow-ice." From there we climbed and belayed into the night on moderately demanding ground by moonlight, encountering some of the worst rock anywhere and feeling the effects of dehydration from not bringing a stove. We reached the summit ridge around midnight. The continuation to the top would have been moderate, but over complex ground with loose rock, so we elected to descend. Contrary to Brain's guidebook, the "northwest ridge" we descended is a complicated face that requires weaving around cliffs and lots of loose rock. Our descent included about five rappels, and we made it back to our camp at dawn. We named the route Via Loco, and Bruce thought it might be the most technical alpine route in Bolivia.

ANDY SELTERS, *AAC*

Top: Cuernos del Diablo north face, two routes by Loken, Hendricks, Selters. Bottom: Gigante Grande's southwest face: left is Hendricks-Selters, 2001; right is 1993 route. *Andy Selters (2)*

Argentina

NORTHERN ARGENTINE ANDES

Cerro El Cóndor and Cerro Vallecitos, exploration and ascents. In January 1998 I directed an expedition to the high barren zone of the Catamarca province, in the northern Argentine Andes. We opened trail in virgin territory with a Ford XLT F-100. The route was difficult, but we managed to ascend to 5000m on the northern slopes of Cerro El Cóndor, an enormous volcano near the Argentine-Chilean border. This was the highest virgin peak outside Asia—or so we thought. Argentine maps mark its north peak as 6373m and its south peak as 6350+m. We erected a camp at 5400m. The next day I reached 5700m, and Ruth Reynoso managed to reach ca 6,000m on the crater's rim. We descended for a break before the second attempt. Unfortunately, we had to abandon our attempt because of problems with logistics and the support team. On the way down we found motorbike trails that made us wonder about a previous ascent or attempt. Some time ago later I received word from a French resident in Argentina, Henri Barret, who gave me important information, previously unreported, about El Cóndor. In April 1996 he made a reconnaissance using motorbikes and a pick-up with a man called Walter. In October 1996 he came back with Walter and his wife. He erected a camp at 4200m and from there made the second ascent of Cerro de la Laguna Amarga, 5007m (*AAJ* 1997, p. 242). He ascended to 5,000m on El Cóndor's northern slopes with a quadrocycle (four-wheel ATV). From there he departed early in the morning, ascended a steep slope, and reached the crater's rim at 6000m at 3 p.m. At 3:30 p.m. Barret and Walter reached the south summit, the highest they say, without finding traces of previous ascents. They stood 30 minutes at the summit looking at the enormous crater and the lunar landscape. The next day they had a difficult descent with the pickup. On October 1998 they attempted the north summit, reaching a glacier, but were stopped at 6000m by chaotic blocks and snow patches. So El Cóndor wasn't virgin, as we thought. In April 1997 Barret solo (Walter was sick) ascended Cerro Vallecitos (6168m, also a volcano), which lies entirely in Argentina, near the border with Chile, some kilometers North of El Cóndor. He found traces of a pre-Columbian ascent but not of modern ones.

MARCELO SCANU, *Argentina*

CENTRAL ARGENTINE ANDES

Aconcagua, overview. The official season for climbing Aconcagua is from November 15 to March 15. The Parque Provincial Aconcagua had had 4,434 visitors as of March 7, 2002. Nearly 88 percent of the climbers were non-Argentines, and 410 Argentines tried for the summit. Unfortunately, there were three casualties and 120 rescues and extractions. The first death was German Herbert Springer, who had a heart attack. The same problem struck Englishman Paul Whitehouse on February 15, 2002, when he attempted the Polish Glacier route. Argentine guide Gustavo Lo Ré was found dead on February 28. He was last seen on the 22nd when he tried to reach the Horcones zone by a nontraditional route, alone. He fell 200 meters. The mountain, by its normal route, isn't difficult, but the weather (this is an El Niño year) and high altitude make it dangerous. Next year should see an increase in outsiders because of the Argentine peso devaluation. The park will be open this winter (Southern Hemisphere), but no rangers or rescue services will be available, so anyone challenging the mountain in winter will be on his own. A strange "record" was achieved in the first week of February. A New Zealand party had supper on the summit! They were dressed for the occasion, and the record was accepted by the Guinness Book of Records as the "Highest Supper on Earth." It's a strange world.

MARCELO SCANU, *Argentina*

Cordillera de Olivares, Nevado de Bauchaceta. A group composed of Miguel Beorchia Nigris, Luis Pontoriero, and I arrived at the post of Tocota in the last days of January 2002, thanks to the help of Gendarmeria Nacional (Border Police). From there we had a bad mule ride to the Quebrada de Chita. After the awful ride, which resulted in scars in unpleasant places, we retreated because of doubtful weather and bad conditions. However, I found a beautiful paleolithic spear point.

From Chita we went to Las Flores, where a Gendarmeria unimog took the group to the Quebrada Pismanta and the post of the Muñoz family. On January 26 the group began the ascent to base camp. The next day Beorchia Nigris quit because of a stomach disease, but we others continued, reaching base camp at Dos Quebradas (3825m) on January 28. This creek is beautiful, with much animal life (we saw guanacos and seven condors at the same time) and petroglyphs. On January 30 we attempted Nevado de Bauchaceta. At 4400m my companion descended due to fatigue. I continued, ascending the great massif and reaching the minor northwest summit of Nevado de Bauchaceta (5,036m S30°28'16.7" W69°38'23.1") at 4:20 p.m. This was the second ascent, and I took a variant to the first ascent 13 years before. I continued to the highest (southeast) summit despite fierce winds. After descending to a col, I ascended a ridge that ended in the big broad summit (ca 5100m, 5158m by GPS, S30°28'55.8" W69°37'38.1"), reaching it at 6:20 p.m. This was a first ascent, correcting a misunderstanding in the 1990 *AAJ* (p. 202). I descended, reaching camp at 9:30 p.m.

Afterward we had bad weather, certainly because of the El Niño phenomenon. On February 3 my companion descended because of illness, and I attempted another mountain, but descended because of bad weather that continued for two days, with rain and snow. On the 6th Mr. Muñoz and his 10-year-old son rode by horse to their post, where I rejoined my teammate. We ate goat barbeque, drank wine, and smoked Havana cigars, raising our cholesterol, alcohol, and nicotine levels to Argentine standards.

MARCELO SCANU, *Argentina*

Cordillera de Colangüil, Cerro de la Quebrada Seca. A group from the nearby city of San Juan was active in this mighty and relatively untrodden zone in mid-January 2002, having as a goal the highest summit, Cerro del Lavadero (6122m). They took the Rio Lavadero route, but bad weather prevented them getting higher than 5,000 meters. They did ascend four virgin 4000m peaks, the highest of which was the Cerro de la Quebrada Seca (4735m).

MARCELO SCANU, *Argentina*

Argentine Patagonia

CHALTEN MASSIF

Torre Egger and Fitz Roy, Tonta Suerte. Tim O'Neill and Nathan Martin made an alpine-style ascent of the 3,300-foot Torre Egger via a combination of routes (VI 5.10 A2 WI6) in 59 hours from the glacier. They then established a new route on Fitz Roy's massive 5,500-foot west face, Tonta Suerte (Dumb Luck, VI 5.10 A1), in a 57.5-hour round-trip push. They are the only the sixth and seventh climbers to summit Cerro Torre, Torre Egger, and Cerro Standhardt. A full account of their Patagonia adventures appears earlier in this *Journal.*

Cerro FitzRoy's southwest face and Aguja Poincenot showing, (1) Tonta Suerte, 2002; (2) Slovak Route, 1983 (Orolin, Galfy, Petrik); (3) Southern Cross, 2002. *Rolando Garibotti*

Cerro Torre, east face. In late October and early November Italians Paolo Calza, Mauro Giovanazzi, Walter Gobbi, and Ermanno Salvaterra attempted a new route on the east face of this peak, via a completely independent line. After fixing the first 300 meters they got on the wall on October 27, establishing themselves at their first portaledge bivy, which they christened "Dalai Lama." Over the next week they managed to climb another 450 meters, reaching a point where the wall kicks back, not far from the base of a very large ice chimney on the upper third of the wall. At a small ledge they again set up their portaledge camp, where they were pinned down by a fierce storm for four days. Gobbi and Salvaterra became intoxicated with propane from their stove, so on November 3 they all decided to retreat.

ROLANDO GARIBOTTI, *AAC, Club Andino Bariloche*

Torre Egger, Italian Route/Titanic Variation. On December 31, Michael Mayr ("Much") and I made our first trip to Norwegian Camp. We originally intended to attempt an alpine-style ascent of Badlands, but after inspecting it decided to look at the nearby and Italian routes. Since the lower portion of was not formed, and the upper portion of the Italian route looked wet and dangerous, Much and I decided to try to combine the two. After 16 days of bad weather we finally began climbing. Although we had looked for the driest option on the face, we still got really wet. On this short attempt we climbed about 200 meters. On January 18 the weather was good again. Leaving bivi gear behind we continued for one more pitch up the Italian route. Much then led two new pitches to the top of the buttress. One more pitch, and we were 10 meters from Titanic. Titanic follows a right-facing dihedral that was streaming with water, so we climbed a considerably drier left-facing dihedral. We climbed this dihedral for three pitches, to where Titanic tends to the left. We continued up the dihedral for one more pitch. Here Much first tried climbing right but ended in a cul-de-sac, before finding a solution to the left. The next pitch followed a perfect open-book crack for about 25 meters and then exited around a sharp arête. From here it was short and easy to the snowfield. The weather looked nasty, and it was time to descend again, but we had completed a new variation and learned that climbing Torre Egger alpine style was possible. The rest of Titanic looked like it wouldn't present too much of a problem. Now we needed weather that would allow another attempt.

Back in Norwegian Camp we told Timmy O'Neill and Nathan Martin that they should have a go at our line. We gave them a topo of our variation.

I doubted that we would get another go at the mountain before the end of our trip, but two days later the clouds broke again. Much and I were still really tired, so we spent one more day resting, but then were at the base of Torre Egger again. In 12 hours we climbed to just above the snowfield and the Bivi del Canto.

And once again the clouds came rolling in. Earlier we had seen Timmy and Nathan just above us. They were trying a similar line to ours and started a day earlier. It looked pretty certain that they would make the summit. Much and I decided to bivy, although we had not intended to. It was a bitterly cold night without bivy-gear, and the next morning the weather became worse—snow, spindrift, and wind. We started to descend and at the snowfield saw Timmy and Nathan three pitches above us. Good to see that they were okay, because that night had been really tough. Timmy and Nathan had reached the summit. Much and I decided to return next year and try to reach the summit.

We free climbed every pitch, and we intend to climb the entire route free and alpine style. Much and I believe that the style in which a mountain is climbed is the most important thing. Torre Egger has had six ascents, and progress is only possible regarding style.

PETER JANSCHEK, *Austria*

Aguja CAT, Mate Humo. This obscure tower, located at the northern end of the Cerro Torre group between Aguja Cuatro Dedos and Cerro Domo Blanco, saw a new route by Austrians Tommy Bonapace and Christian Zenz. Their line, which they completed in late March, climbs the steep east face and involves 11 pitches with difficulties to 6/A1. Theirs might be the first ascent of this peak, as there is no clear historical record of any previous ascents. They named their route Mate Humo.

ROLANDO GARIBOTTI, *AAC, Club Andino Bariloche*

Cerro Pollone, lower south buttress of east summit; Beg, Borrow, or Steal. Blair Williams and I arrived in El Chalten on January 7. The next day we arranged for horses to carry our bags to Piedra del Fraile, our planned base camp and a pleasant place that is well worth the little money to stay there. The next few days were spent carrying loads to the end of Lago Electrico, our planned advanced camp for climbing on the Marconi Glacier. But after talking with German climbers, we thought we would have better success if we had an advanced camp by Paso de Cuadrado. They had already built a snow cave there and were kind enough to let us move in as they were moving out.

After an icy attempt on Guillaumet's Fonrouge route, we returned and completed the 13-pitch route. We were treated to amazing views of the surrounding mountains and the ice cap, then rappelled down the Amy Couloir. The next morning we awoke to clouds and wind, so we rolled over and stayed in bed. By 8:00 the clouds had cleared and the wind died, so we packed up, hiked to the snow cave, and picked up our stashed gear and continued to the base of the La Granja route on Aguja Pollone's east ridge. The route offered amazingly varied climbing. Everything from thin cracks to slabs to liebacking arêtes. We topped out around 6:00 p.m. and had an absolutely amazing view of big Fitz Roy. After too many summit photos we made five long rappels to the base.

After heading to town for beer and pizza, we were back in the spacious cave, waiting for the weather to clear and, sure enough, it cleared.

We had been eyeing the lower southeast buttress of Cerro Pollone's east summit and thought it was the perfect time to go for it. After a casual three-hour approach, we got a close look at the unclimbed face. We saw obvious cracks leading all the way to the top. Without even a photo we started up. One crack led to the next, with ledges almost every 200 feet. We came across signs of the only previous attempt at the face. An Italian team had tried the face earlier in the year but were stopped by ice in cracks. The last bolt they placed was at the base of a 60-foot offwidth that may have been another reason they retreated. I found the pitch to be quite enjoyable and reminiscent of a Yosemite 5.10a offwidth. We felt confident that we would make it to the top if the weather stayed good. One pitch after another led us to the top of the lower southeast buttress of Cerro Pollone's east summit. We chose to go no farther, as we felt we had reached the summit of the piece of rock we chose to climb. We made eight 60-meter rappels, using a few nuts but mostly threads and slings around blocks. We named the route Beg, Borrow, or Steal. We thought it was in the mid-5.10 range and around 1,500 feet long. We used no pitons or bolts (except the Italian bolts) and thought the route was a classic alpine rock climb.

The north face of Cerro Fitz Roy, Aguja Mermoz North, and Aguja Guillaumet, showing (from left to right), Slovene route on the west pillar of Mermoz, 2002; the French route, 2002 (Arpin et. al.); Tehuelche, 1986 (Italians Sterni, et. al.), the dotted line. *Rolando Garibotti*

Mermoz, showing, (1) Padre Viento, 2001, Donahue-Ogden; (2) Andy Parkins solo; (3) Tiempo Ensueños, 1983, Donahue-Harvey (no bolts); (4) Albert-Arnold 5.12; (5) The Gambler on Guillaumet, 2001, Donahue-Ogden. *Topher Donahue*

On February 4 we returned to snow and cold in Seattle. This seemed ironic after three weeks of perfect weather in Patagonia. I thank the American Alpine Club for awarding me a Mountaineering Fellowship Grant and their continued support of climbing youth.

MICHAEL SCHAEFER, *AAC, The Kascade Trad Klan*

Aguja Mermoz, northwest crest. On October 21 Vasja Kouta, David Pehnec, and I arrive at base camp, Piedra del Fraile. The weather is bad. First we attempt Supercanaleta on Fitz Roy but turn back a few pitches above the block. Later, conditions on that route are still not good, and we change the plan. The weather is Patagonian.

On November 9 the weather becomes good. We are a little late, but we leave Piedra del Fraile anyway. At midday we are at the base of the northwest crest of the Mermoz. The first few pitches are in a great crack. After that we arrive at a snow gully, which leads to the top of the first tower. In the evening the weather becomes worse, so we fix a rope on the left side of the slope and descend to base camp. For the next few days the weather is still bad.

We have had enough waiting, and early in the morning on November 13, despite strange weather, we leave base camp. It is quite cold with a little snow and the wind is getting stronger. After just a few pitches in icy cracks, ending at the top of the next tower, we descend to base camp again. In the next 10 days the weather is befitting to Patagonia, with a lot of precipitation. We even have snow in base camp. Our expedition is coming to an end, and we have just a few days.

We try again on November 23. Today we are only Vasja and me. David has leg problems.

Jared Ogden on the first ascent of The Gambler on Guillaumet. *Topher Donahue*

Because of the recent snow, cracks are snowy and icy, and we move slowly. In the afternoon it becomes colder. We reach the summit ridge by nightfall. The wind is getting stronger, so we retreat from that point. We rappel almost all night. Early in the morning we are in base camp. *(Editor's note: This summit ridge has several blank gendarmes and might not be climbable without heavy drilling.)* The Northwest Crest of Mermoz is over 1,000 meters high, and we graded it VI+ A0 V-IV 70-degree snow/ice.

ZLATKO KOREN, *Slovenia*

Mermoz, Padre Viento; Guillaumet, The Gambler; St. Exupery, east pillar variation. Jared Ogden and I arrived in the Fitz Roy region on December 1 and found several unclimbed ice lines in condition. On the east face of the Mermoz we did the first ascent of Padre Viento (1,800', M6 WI5+), to the left of the Red Pillar. On the left side of the east face of the Guillaumet, we found The Gambler (1,800', M7 WI6+). With overhanging ice and five pitches of M7 mixed climbing, it could be the hardest mixed climb in the area. Both routes end on heavily gendarmed ridges, and neither reaches a true summit, just the top of a wall. On St. Exupery's east pillar we climbed a new four-pitch M6 start to the 2,500-foot Regular Route and free climbed the rest of the 5.11 A1 route at very wet 5.11+.

Cerro Fitz Roy, north face. During January Frenchmen Jerome Arpin, Sylvain Empereur, Yannick Ponson, and Lionel Pouzadoux climbed a new route on the north face of Fitz Roy. They spent a total of six days working on the route and fixed ropes to pitch 20 (around 800 meters of rope). They summited late in the evening on January 22, 2002. Their line starts just right of the Polish route and reaches the Grand Hotel, a big ledge halfway up the face, in about 16 pitches. There it crosses Tehuelche and climbs a crack system just right of Tehuelche's most obvious feature, Marco's Dihedral. They climbed a total of 32 pitches (1,200 meters), with difficulties up to 6b+ and A2+. They descended the route. For a repeat they recommend taking three or four sets of cams, stoppers, some copperheads, many pins, and a few hooks. Belay anchors are in place.

ROLANDO GARIBOTTI, *AAC, Club Andino Bariloche*

Fitz Roy, Supercanaleta. Max Berger, Jérome Blanc-Gras, and I made a winter ascent of Supercanaleta on Fitz Roy on August 9. Ours was the third or fourth winter ascent, the first reported winter ascent having been made by Argentine climbers.

Conditions were okay. We climbed everything with ice axes and crampons, even pitches indicated on the topo as rock. Our dry-tooling experience allowed us to go faster. We climbed the route in just over 26 hours. We didn't sleep, taking only two hour-long breaks during the 46-hour round trip. Because it was too cold to sleep, we didn't have sleeping bags or a tent, just bivouac bags. We tried the route once before the successful ascent but were stopped by bad weather after a 1,000 meters. We reached the summit at 2:30 a.m., with a full moon and no wind, just very cold temperatures (about -30°C). It is a very beautiful route, varied and continuous, with hard parts all along the climb. To see photos of the Supercanaleta go to http://www.mountain-ski.com/photo/expedition/2001super-couloir/

ERWAN LE LANN, *France*

Fitz Roy, Supercanaleta and Californian Roulette; Cerro Torre, Compressor Route; free-solos and speed-solos. The pressure is rising. Clear skies move from the south, and brilliant stars appear overhead. In under three weeks in Patagonia, I have soloed Fitz Roy and Cerro Torre. Already I have far exceeded my expectations, yet I still search for something within these mountains.

My first and only objective was to solo Fitz Roy. I arrived at its base and waited for three days until conditions were perfect. I rested, gaining strength and confidence, and became obsessed with "light is right." Leaving most of my climbing gear and warm clothing, I carried only one quart of water and no bivouac gear. Two hours before dawn I stood before the Super-canaleta (VI 5.10 WI 4) and felt naked staring up at its 6,000-foot face. A wave of shivers rose up my body, and I subconsciously committed. Entranced by the fact that any mistake meant death, I sunk my ice tools so aggressively that I scarcely noticed blood soaking my mitts, leaving blotches on the ice. The sight drove me even deeper into a calm, decisive survival state, and I moved as if in a dream, free soloing through thinning ice and beautifully split alpine granite. Just under six and a half hours later, at 10:14 a.m., I awoke on the summit, crying and laughing, screaming "Fitz Roy" over and over.

Five days later I awoke again. Writhing in and out of the fetal position, exhausted and freezing, I lay cocooned in a tinfoil survival blanket at the Col of Patience, 1,000 feet up Patagonia's most formidable peak, Cerro Torre. I'd just speed-soloed the Compressor Route (VI 5.11a

A2 WI 4), capped by its mushroom tip, in eight and a half hours, and returned to the "Bus," a natural ice cave where I now waited. I sat up into a meditative pose and tried the yoga technique Heated Breath. I focused on breathing into my lower abdomen with resistance in the back of my throat, imagining my heart pumping strongly, forcing warm blood to the far reaches of my extremities. My body did heat up a little, and I maintained the pose for a few hours, but fatigue and the presence of four Russian climbers, properly equipped, huddled together snoring, threw off my concentration.

The Russians had planned to be halfway up the route, leaving me their bivy gear, so I could wait and descend the glacier with them safely. A sudden storm stopped them, and they wisely decided to wait, leaving me with the choice of an open bivouac or descending the glacier unroped. Panicked thoughts caused me to lose control of my meditation and talk to myself. "You don't want to lose your toes, Dean." "You can't cross the glacier alone, that's how soloists die." "The crevasses don't care how well you climb." "Food, warmth, sleep…I'm freezing." I laughed at the contrast of how warm I was, in the early morning sun, when I started rock climbing from here. Untethered for the entire climb except the final Bridwell pitch, I was only connected by a few millimeters of sticky rubber and half-finger holds as I went through the free cruxes. The haunting image of my single etrier sailing away in the wind of the brewing storm, before Maestri's endless bolts, recycled through my mind's eye. My legs were cramped from overkicking through the ice towers and high-stepping into single slings up hundreds of bolts. Hours later, with the storm undoubtedly upon us, I was way colder than before, and I cracked. Throwing the dice, I packed my frozen gear and left the Russians. I rappelled blindly into clouded darkness. At the bottom of the rappels I rationalized that it was the coldest part of the day, and the ice bridges were as frozen as they would be. I started walking, and within a few steps my right leg plunged into an airy hole, as I struggled not to go in. Totally tuned to all of my senses, I moved deliberately across the glacier. Pushed by the wind, I arrived at my stash under a boulder and passed out.

Ten days later I'm back at Fitz Roy, this time poised at Polackos base camp, directly below an obvious line on Fitz Roy's southwest side. This couloir was attempted in 1970 by Argentines, who joined the 1967 California route but did not reach the summit. It has been attempted many times and is named after one of the people who died on the route, Pippo Frasson Couloir. I feel strongly for all who have gone before me and give thanks, knowing I am standing on their shoulders. Staring up at its looming serac and 7,100 feet of elevation gain, it's easy to see why the route hasn't been completed. I clear my mind of every distraction and open my soul to the energies of the mountains. I need to be sure of what I'm seeking by entering the world of solo alpine climbing. Last night I asked myself why, and could not answer with words. This morning I sit totally alert at 1:30 a.m., buzzing with every emotion, tapped into my intuition and feeling every fiber of my body pulsing with strength I never felt possible. I realize that, so far, death consequence is the only thing that brings me close to my potential energy. I put it all toward moving up, and start. I open my mouth and screech a piercing cry, which focuses me on my outer breath, a technique used in martial arts, in lethal battle.

My mind becomes empty, and I move without a flaw up 4,000 feet of crack systems, ramps, and polished slabs on either side of the gully that marks my way. I am forced to smear through holdless sections up to 5.10+ in order to stay out of the fall line. I switch into leather boots and crampons, and my world turns vertical, as I delicately pick my way up a 100-foot, 90-degree, three-inch-thick ice smear. Melting water flows between the ice and rock, and every minute or two I am showered with blasts of graupel. I sink my tools and hang straight-armed until things stop falling and calmly tack my way up the impermanent flow. I mix-climb for another thousand feet, to the Italian Col. I traverse toward the start of the California Route and continue climbing, all free-solo, carrying only essential rappel gear (100 meters of 6 mm rope, stoppers, hexes, one ice screw, V-thread, three small Camalots, some sling, four locking 'biners, and eight Neutrinos). On the summit slope I lose control of my breath, my heart rate accelerates, and I feel dizzy and nauseous. My thoughts twist, and I wonder, "Is this the big one?" Unable to regain my composure, I stop, eat the rest of my food, drink some water, and pop three aspirin. "I pushed too hard," I think but still stumble toward the top. Almost crawling, I reach the summit, completing the first integral ascent of Californian Roulette (VI 5.10+ WI5).

After an hour basking on the top, I down climb to the edge of the summit ridge and start rapping. Two raps down, I pull my ropes and, blinded by the sun, only hear something falling. A toaster-sized block hits my leg, and my world goes black. I come to from the noise of my own screaming. My pants are ripped and bloody, and swelling stiffens my leg. In shock, I peg-leg for 30 more raps and hobble across the east-side glacier, passing several soft, melting ice bridges on my stomach because I can't jump.

I reach the snow caves at Paso Superior at dusk, hoping someone is there to help me, but everybody is gone. Captured by survival instinct, I move until I am warm, then lay down and sleep, continuing this cycle all night long, until I reach the camp at Rio Blanco at 4 a.m., 24 hours from when I started. I fall asleep in one of the log huts and am soon awakened by friends and taken care of. Though injured I enjoy a rare time of being content doing nothing, savoring each moment I'm alive.

DEAN POTTER

Cerro Domo Blanco, Son of Jurel; Aguja Poincenot, Southern Cross; Cerro Piergiorgio, attempt. In January 2002 Jonathan Copp and I arrived in Chalten intending to climb a new route on the west face of Cerro Piergiorgio. We never succeeded in this goal, but we completed two new routes on other formations.

During reconnaissance of the west face of Piergiorgio we decided that an alpine-style first ascent would be unlikely. Few crack systems extend from bottom to top. New routes would certainly be possible but for those with the patience, fortitude, and stubbornness to carry heavy nailing racks and fixed rope up to the base. We decided to attempt the original route, Greenpeace (M. Manica and R. Vettori,

Aguja Poincenot: Southern Cross, 2002, Copp-Taylor. Left: Cerro Fitz Roy: Tonta Suerte, 2002, Martin-O'Neill. *Jonathan Copp*

1985). It appealed to us because of its continuous crack systems and its position on a sweeping buttress not unlike El Cap's Nose. The route had been attempted several times since the first two ascents in 1985, but to our knowledge there had been no subsequent ascents. We attempted it three times. The weather was perfect during our final attempt, but about five pitches below the top I dropped my helmet after refastening the buckle improperly. We climbed two more pitches, and I belayed with my head in a hueco to avoid the detritus that Jonathan was sending down. The final pitches looked easy enough, but the chimney was choked with ice and other loose, blunt objects. We bailed.

During our attempts on Piergiorgio we often looked south at the northwest face of Cerro Domo Blanco, and drooled. Many vertical crack systems were spread across a broad, 600- to 650-meter face. We had not heard of any route on the wall. We wanted to climb a crack system up the center of the face but noticed that our snacky-cake supply

Above: Jonathan Copp working to get gear on Domo Blanco's Son of Jurel. Below: Copp jugging on an attempted new route on Cerro Piergiorgio. *Dylon Talor (2)*

Cerro Piergiorgio from the approach to an attempt on the right-hand side. *Jonathan Copp*

was severely diminished. We trekked to Chalten to resupply, and the weather became perfect. The following morning we hiked to our base camp, ate dinner, napped, and started hiking again at 3 a.m., January 30. We retrieved our gear from a cache along the Marconi Glacier and continued toward the wall through a section of tricky, involved glacier travel. The glacier was continuously about 45 degrees steep and crevassed all the way to the base of Cerro Domo Blanco.

We began climbing just after noon, with Jonathan taking the first block. His pitches were excellent, with many finger cracks in dihedrals, accompanied by easy aid and tricky climbing through a wet roof system. I began my block of leads around 7 p.m. A few loose, wet pitches led to more steep hand-size splitters as a storm blew in. I aided iced-up three-star cracks and, in the wee hours of the morning with freezing feet, turned the leading over to Jonathan. He led into the blowing wind and snow, while I whimpered at the belay. It turned out we were only two pitches from the top. Though bailing had crossed our minds, it was in fact easier to "retreat upward" to the top of the wall and search for an easier way down. When Jon finished the last pitch by using a #4 Camalot as an axe to chip holds up an ice runnel, he yelled "rope's fixed" though he had no anchor--just a stance made by a foot in a hueco and an elbow braced against the ice. I jugged up on his no-anchor anchor unaware of our predicament until yelling from above informed me of some startling specifics. Once at the top of the wall, we forwent the

Dillan Taylor approaching the about-to-be-realized Son of Jurel route on Domo Blanco. *Jonathan Copp*

stormy summit in classic modern alpine-climbing style. We rapped down the wall to the right of our route, Son of Jurel (V 5.11 A2ish), so named because we were nearly forced to "kneel before Zod," but we also ate our share of the canned, minced fish-product.

Returning to Chalten, we found ourselves in a multi-day international party binge. Nearly every bottle of Cerveza Quilmes in Chalten was consumed. Eventually, improving weather and guilt over our wretchedness forced us back into the mountains, this time to Camp Bridwell. After one night we moved to the Polacos camp directly beneath Aguja Poincenot. We spotted a splitter crack system on the southwest face, to the left of the Fonrouge-Rosasco route.

Early on February 17 we approached the north face of Poincenot via the couloir separating Poincenot and the Desmochada. We simulclimbed up a ramp system similar to the start of the Carrington-Rouse, but around 300 meters lower. The climbing was fairly easy for the most part, with occasional moves of 5.9-5.10. At the top of the ramp system, we traversed right onto the southwest face. My block ended and Jon's began near the base of the splitter crack system that we had seen earlier. We had joked that the cracks would be knifeblade seams, so we were surprised to find mainly hands and fists for nearly 300 meters, with a few tricky sections. I got to jug several three-star pitches. At sunset Jon completed his last headwall lead by penduluming left to a dihedral, which finishes at the top of the Carrington-Rouse ramp system. On a spacious ledge we brewed up, ate our BBQ chicken meal, and spooned, sans bivy gear, for a few hours. My snoring and shivering caused Jonny to initiate hot-drink preparations at 4:00 a.m. The wind had picked up considerably. After several hundred feet of simulclimbing we were lost somewhere left of the Fonrouge-Rosasco and Whillans routes. After a strange tunneling pitch and a

Dylan Taylor fully commited on the descent from Southern Cross, Aguja Poincenot. *Jonathan Copp*

rappel from a rope wrapped over a horn, we were beneath the summit. We ate a celebratory Snickers on top and rappelled the windy north face 100 meters left of Old Smugglers, destroying our third rope of the trip in the process. We called the route Southern Cross (3,700', VI 5.11 A1) because we began on the north side of Poincenot and crossed to the south side, and because we viewed the constellation during sleepless bivies. Furthermore, we had the CS&N song in our heads. Jonathan and I thank the American Alpine Club Mountaineering Fellow-ship Fund, as well as the Mugs Stump Award, for helping support this adventure.

DYLAN TAYLOR, *AAC*

Aguja Saint Exupery, north face and east face variation. On January 16, 2002, Americans Lorne Glick and Mark Davis climbed a new variation to the Kearney-Harrington route on the north face. They started on the Kearney line, then climbed a steep crack system left of Bienvenidos a Patagonia, joining the Italian east face route after climbing 120 meters of virgin terrain.

ROLANDO GARIBOTTI, *AAC, Club Andino Bariloch*

Chile

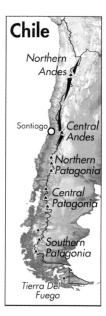

NORTHERN ANDES

Puna de Atacama, Peaks 5376m and 6070m, Veladero, Bonete, Reclus.
On the high-altitude plateau of the Puna de Atacama, in November 2000,
Britain John Biggar led a group (Brits G. Biggar, P. Clarke, P. Gilbert, and
B. Powling and Peruvian D. Aurelio) that made many ascents. They used
a 4WD vehicle to establish a base camp at 4700m southwest of Bonete
(6759m). In windy weather and with base-camp temperatures never
exceeding 0°c, they made five ascents of non-technical peaks, walking on
scree and occasionally snow. Peaks 5376m and 6070m (which could
logically be called Veladaro Northeast) were climbed, probable first
ascents. There were no signs of previous visits. The ascent of Peak 6070m
was by the southwest ridge. They also made ascents of Veladero (6436m)
and Bonete (6759m; FA 1913, Walther Penck, Germany). On Bonete
several members were blown off their feet on summit day. To the west of
Bonete, the group made a repeat ascent of Reclus (6335m).

MOUNTAIN INFO, *High Mountain Sports 230*

Sierra Nevada de Lagunas Bravas. Three years ago John Biggar's book High Andes came out, listing three 6000+-meter peaks in South America as having "no known ascent." "No known
ascent" is not the same as "no ascent," and I figured these peaks were probably already climbed.
They are technically easy—make that technically trivial: volcanic desert peaks formed of low-
angle rubble without snow. Two of the three are on the Chile-Argentina border, which was surveyed long ago. Incas visited summits all over the place. Still, it was a good excuse for a trip. I
hired a Chilean driver to check out the access and wrote Santiago for permission.

Paul Morgan, Paul Doherty, Tony Brake, and I spent five days climbing Sierra Nevada de
Lagunas Bravas (6155m), one of the last three South American 6000-meter peaks with
"no known ascent," per Biggar. We began from a base at about 4400m and put camps at 5100m
and 5550m. Sierra Nevada is a typical Atacama Desert volcanic peak, with very little snow and
ice. The footing was high-altitude dirt and scree from base camp to summit, though some
route-finding was involved. We summited on December 12, 2000 and found no sign of a
previous ascent on the rock-strewn summit. We checked both summit hillocks, which are on
the international border—the named summit and one of identical height a few meters to the
northwest. (Both hills are shown on the Chilean topo map, where the one is named.)
After checking with John Biggar and with locals in Copiapo and Caldera who would be likely
to supply transportation for modern climbers, we believe this to be a first ascent.

ROBERT AYERS

CENTRAL ANDES

Peaks in the Cepo and Quempo chains. I accompanied Fernando Montenegro (Santiago) in several forays into these two rocky chains located in the Santiago hinterland, east of the ski resort of Farellones. The peaks we chose were small by Chilean standards but were hitherto unclimbed. On January 24 we started from the Arenales valley and traversed Alto de la Jarilla (4050m) and Salazar (4020m). The latter peak demanded rope work under its summit. Both are in the Cepo chain. In December we went to the Quempo chain and climbed Sargento del Quempo (4156m). A week later we re-entered the Arenales valley and on December 28 traversed Lagruca (4109m) and La Laguna (4182m), five first ascents in all. In January 2002 I went, now alone, to the ski resort of Portillo and from the international border pass of Lomas Coloradas made the second ascent, and first by the unstable east flank, of Charqueado (4515m). An attempt on unclimbed, unnamed, and quite difficult Peak 4587m failed.

EVELIO ECHEVARRÍA

Northern Patagonia

LAKE DISTRICT

Cochamo, Cerro Trinidad. I climbed in Cochamo in 1999 and 2000, staying two months each time. The first year four Brazilians and I put up a new line on Cerro Trinidad (800m, 5.11 A4), calling it Mucho Granito Arriba. The follow year we visited the area again, but climbed in two teams. Two of the strongest climbers in Brazil, Sergio Tartari and José Luis Hartman, opened Tabanos na Cara (700m, 5.10c A3+) on the central pillar of Trinidad and Além da Laca (400m, 5.12c) on the lower Trinidad tower. They also opened another four routes: Mister M (500m, 5.10a), Velho Alerce (300m, 5.11, A3), and two two-pitch crag climbs. Stanley Costa and I opened Vozes da Grota (330m, 5.11c A2+) and made the first repeat of the just-opened Basque route Euskal Perestroica (900m, 5.10b A3) on Trinidad's main tower, freeing five of its eight aid pitches, upgrading it to 5.12 A2+. After that we did the first repeats of Além da Laca and Mister M and made an unsuccessful attempt on another tower.

MARIUS BAGNATI, *Brazil*

Cochamo, Cerro Trinidad and neighboring peaks. (Editor's note: In the 2001 AAJ, p. 300, Ian Parnell gives a summary of a traverse of many ridges in the Cochamo area by Lucy Regan, Brian Bigger, and James Marshall. More information on the traverse is presented here.) In January, after attempting to complete the right side of the central pillar of the north face of Trinidad (we tried in April 2000 but retreated from pitch 9), we decided to concentrate on an alpine traverse of the Trinidad horseshoe. Skirting the base of Cerro Trinidad, we scrambled up the loose descent gully on the mountain's north side. With much cursing James led the HVS pitch of Stirling Moss in very cold conditions to breach the difficulties on the east face of Trinidad. Meanwhile I climbed the northern subsidiary peak (unnamed, 1479m, almost certainly climbed) and returned to second Stirling Moss. With inquisitive attention from a condor, we scrambled to the summit of Cerro Trinidad (1720m). The summit domes of Trinidad and its neighboring peaks are relatively flat but are separated by deep gullies, requiring abseils onto knife-edge ridges, then easy but exposed climbing and scrambling up the other side. Heading south along the crest, we climbed two peaks (1703m and 1717m) in this manner. They had probably not been climbed, and we named them Cerro Concepcion Torre Norte and Cerro Concepcion Torre Sur. We then reached the unclimbed final southeastern peak of the horseshoe near the col at its center, and here we bivouacked.

In the morning we scrambled easily to the southeastern summit (1678m), which we named Cerro Romané, before descending its west ridge and reaching the southern col (1390m) by about midday. Views south revealed an apparently untouched and hidden valley with great potential for big wall and alpine routes. To the southwest an incredible curtainlike wall of rock links the southwesternmost peak of the Trinidad horseshoe to an unclimbed and snowbound peak (1897m) and eventually to Cerro Torrecillas (1809m) and Cerro Estraido (2098m), both unclimbed.

At about 2:00 p.m. the team crossed the col and started up the first mountain on the west side of the horseshoe. After crossing deep banks of snow, which contained fresh puma tracks, we encountered a 15-meter step. An excellent VS pitch up the rightmost arête of the buttress provided the solution, with great exposure from the deep gully below. Lucy returned to the col feeling ill, leaving James and me to continue the traverse. Easy scrambling led to a second step, giving a corner pitch of Severe, before we broke right up a lieback crack and through a short overhang at about HVS and HS. It was a short distance to the first summit (unclimbed, 1747m), which we named Cerro Alerce. We then traversed to the remaining subsidiary summit, Cerro Laguna (1708m). A cairn was discovered, which we later learned marked the first ascent of this peak, by its slabby northeast face. The final northern peak in the horseshoe, Pedro de Gorila (1761m, previously climbed by the northern wall) was protected by a south-facing wet, over-hanging 80-meter wall. Aid climbing was not feasible with our lightweight rack. We retraced our route, descended to the col by about 7:00 p.m., and slept there. In the morning the team descended north into the valley and followed the river, with some entertaining wading and jumping.

BRIAN BIGGER, *United Kingdom*

CENTRAL PATAGONIA

Bahia Murta Region. Between December 30, 2001, and January 12, 2002, David Wood and I climbed several unclimbed summits in the Tres Arroyos region near the small Chilean town of Bahia Murta. This area offers extensive climbing on heavily glaciated peaks, and to the best of our knowledge had not received previous climbing attention.

We established a base camp in Estero Sur at the lake (elevation 1100m) marked at the head of the drainage on Chilean IGM maps. During our two-week stay we climbed three summits from this base, despite generally poor weather. On January 2 we climbed the obvious high point of the ridge-like summit located southeast of the lake. We climbed this peak by following the northwest ridge through moderate terrain, which we later rappelled in a blizzard. We estimated the altitude of this unmapped peak as 2042m. High pressure moved in on January 4, allowing us to climb the beautiful triangular peak at the head of the drainage. Our route followed the north ridge, climbing through generally solid fourth- and mid-fifth-class granite. Both the route and the summit provided spectacular views of the northern ice cap and Monte San Valentine. We estimated the elevation of this unmapped peak at 1950m. Following five days of low pressure and poor weather, we climbed Peak 1942m directly southwest of the lake. We followed the northwest ridge, which offered enjoyable climbing over easy snow and rock.

SCOTT NUISMER, *AAC*

Southern Patagonia

TORRES DEL PAINE

South summit of North Tower of Paine, Maury the Jewish Tapeworm; Central Tower of Paine, Bonington-Whillans Route first free ascent; South Tower of Paine, Andrea Oglioni. This was a season of prolific activity in Patagonia, in both the Torres del Paine and Fitz Roy massifs. As Timmy O'Neill put it, it was Camp 4 South. Slack lines and alcoholism enhanced rest days, just as Yosemite-style techniques added bold, fast, and free alpine ascents to the history of these amazing mountains. This generation of climbers was inspired by accounts of early ascents in Patagonia. While these accounts have fueled a quest for enlightenment in the mountains, this generation has added their own elements of style: fast, clean, free, and most important, fun.

Shortly after returning from South America I was at Whitney Portal talking to fishermen who had ventured up to see the sights. My partner mentioned I had just come back from two months in Patagonia. "Oh, rich parents, huh?" was the response. I find it indescribably admirable and enlightening, not to mention admirably irresponsible, that people living on less in a year than some people's monthly car payments can scrape together the means to provide an experience that will last a lifetime. I guess you can explain it as willingness to sacrifice material need for spiritual necessity. Maybe that's part of the reason for the new style. Can't afford ropes? Bring just one. Can't buy pitons or bolts? Climb without them. Luckily, promotional credit card rates abound, and airfare is cheap.

This was the story for Zack Smith and I, who, lacking rich parents, were forced to explore the less-agreeable alternative of menial labor for pittance wages. Still, we rolled our dice and won—left LAX on January 10, 2002, and summited the North, Central, and South towers of the Torres del Paine by the 17th. Our first climb was a new route to the south summit of the North Tower. We took a line just to the left of Cornwall up a fantastic system reminiscent of the Enduro Corner on Astroman. Four pitches of offwidth, finger, and hand cracks deposited us on the South Ridge, which was about 1,000 feet of mostly easy climbing to the summit. We named the route Maury the Jewish Tapeworm (IV 5.11) in honor of Zack's ravenous parasite. Our second was the 2,500-foot Bonington-Whillans (V 5.11) on the Central Tower. This was the first route to the summit, full of history and wooden pitons. Thanks to warm, windless weather, a late start, and Drum cigarettes, we accomplished the first free ascent of the route and of the formation. Instead of a thin nailing roof midway, we took a 5.11 face variation to the left. Although definitely the trade route, the Bonington-Whillans features impeccable granite and an amazing locale. Two days later we climbed Andrea Oglioni (VI 5.11-), the ultra-classic 3,000-foot north ridge of the South Tower. All pitches were climbed onsight in blocks, with some short-fixing and lots of simulclimbing. The North Tower took three and a half hours, the Central four and a half, and the South six. A testimony to splitter weather: we were able to roll and smoke on every summit. You know you're trad when you smoke the topo.

After an interim including lots of chess, box wine, and a basecamp asado, Zack and I attempted a free variation to Adrenalina Vertical on the North Tower. Unfortunately, Zack violated the first rule of trundling (do not trundle on yourself) and injured his hand. Consequently we were forced to retreat to the comforts of base camp and the med kit. A few days later Brittany Griffith and Annie Overlin joined me in the French Valley, and we climbed the standard route up the Shark's Fin (V 5.9). It was their third day in Chile.

Lots of talented climbers made good use of this sunny season, and I'm sure our efforts will be lost among a multitude of ascents. However, there is one important issue I want to share. As climbers we gain an amazing reward in our pursuit of mountain adventure. Ideally, this is a pure nature experience in which we push our physical and emotional limits for a brief glimpse of our connection with the earth, while pacing our creativity to the rhythm of mountain processes. This requires a special interest in the natural world and a heightened awareness of its environs. What I'm trying to say is this: We get a lot out of being in the wilderness, and this, like everything else in nature, must result in an ebb and flow, a constant recycling of energies and balance. We are lucky to see nature unclothed but must also be aware of our role as its stewards. It is up to us to carry out our trash, remove fixed ropes and unnecessary gear. Become aware, and act appropriately. There are too many mounds of shit and wads of toilet paper adorning base camp forests. Take a small shovel, bury your waste, and burn your toilet paper. If you must fix ropes, remove them when you leave. This is an appeal that benefits us all. We must show respect if we are to be respected. Preserve the experience for others and help our world maintain its natural balance.

SEAN LEARY

North summit of North Tower of Paine, free ascent. On February 17, 2002, Allison Pennings and I climbed a new route on the west face of the north summit of the North Tower of Paine. Our route follows the route Adrenalina Vertical for two pitches before traversing left 40 feet into the obvious body slot. Above the body slot the route continues straight up. We both free climbed the entire route, which went at 5.11+, and was done in a day without bolts or pitons. On the previous day, February 16, we managed to free climb the Bonington-Whillans route on the Central Tower, with Michael leading all pitches. The crux pitch was a variation to the original route. Instead of climbing out the roof to access the Red Dihedral, we continued up to the left of the roof for about 35 feet before moving right into the dihedral. I believe this is different from the way Sean and Zack went on the first free ascent (it sounds like they traversed right 5 or 10 feet above the roof). Our variation was 5.11.

MIKE PENNINGS

(Editor's note: Allison Pennings was likely the second woman to summit the Central Paine Tower. Italian Ginella Pagani summited the tower in 1987, with Ermanno Salvaterra.)

North, Central, and South Towers of Paine, solo link-up. On February 16, 2002, I awoke in Campamento Japanese at 2:00 a.m., got caffeinated, and departed camp at 3:00 a.m. I intended to make a solo link-up of the Towers of Paine. With just over a week to go before my departure to home in California, I knew this would be my final try. I planned to climb all three towers by their normal routes in as continuous a push as possible. I started climbing up the North Tower via the Monzino route at 8:30 a.m. and summited at 9:11 a.m., for a time of 41 minutes. (Two weeks earlier I had made the climb in 35 minutes.) I roped up only for the initial 70 meters.

After descending the North Tower I began climbing the Central Tower via the Bonington-Whillans route at 9:55 a.m. and summited at 5:14 p.m., for a time of 7:19. On the summit ridge I encountered newlyweds Mike and Allison Pennings, who were on their way down after summiting a few minutes earlier.

A brief weather check on the summit revealed completely clear skies, with a view to the Pacific Ocean, so I began the committing rappels down the south face of the Central Tower. A 2,000-foot descent down the Grupo Ragni route, with 16 rappels and some scrambling, landed me on the big walkway that crosses the west face of the Central Tower at about 10:30 p.m. I hunkered down for the night in just my clothes. I do not think I slept, but I got some much-needed rest. At 7:00 a.m. on February 17 I got moving again under perfect skies. I continued my descent, pioneering a way down a 400-foot face that landed me in the large couloir between the Central and South towers.

At 10:25 a.m. I started up the Asti route and summited the South Tower at 7:50 p.m., for a climbing time of 9:25. After 15 minutes on top, with the weather still holding, I began my descent and arrived at the bottom six hours later at about 2:00 a.m. At 6:00 a.m I staggered back into Campamento Japanese, for a round-trip time of 51 hours from base camp to base camp.

This was my fifth attempt to make the Tower Traverse (or link-up). Along the way I climbed the North Tower four times, the Central Tower twice, and the South Tower once. I also endured three open bivouacs, two full-blown epic retreats from near the Central Tower's summit, one life-threatening rockfall, and an emotional rollercoaster. It is the first traverse/link-up of the Towers of Paine, solo or otherwise.

STEVE SCHNEIDER, *AAC*

PINGO VALLEY

La Mascara, Ilusiones and Duncan's Dihedral; Paine Chico, West Face; Cuernos. In early January 2002 Englishmen Andy Cave and Leo Houlding did the second ascent of and free climbed the route Ilusiones on the east face of La Mascara. Ilusiones was first climbed in January 2001 by Spaniards Alonso, Martos, and Pelaez. Cave and Houlding found it not to be extremely hard, managing to free it all at around 7a (5.12a), with some bad loose rock. They fixed 140 meters of rope on a rainy, windy day and came back down, then two days later climbed to the summit in nine and a half hours, descending in four hours.

Also in early January 2002 Dave Hesleden and Simon Nadin (U.K.) did the second ascent of Duncan's Dihedral (700m, 6b+ A1) on Mascara's south face. This route was first climbed by J. Copp and J. Merriam (U.S.) in 1998. Hesleden and Nadin found very cold conditions upon turning to the south-southwest side, as well as much loose rock.

Later in January Heslesden and Nadin climbed Paine Chico (also known as Almirante Nieto) via a couloir on the right side of the west face and then a snow ramp leading back to the left. They also did a five-pitch route immediately left of the prominent gap between the Cuernos. They found belays in place for the first three pitches but not beyond.

ROLANDO GARIBOTTI, *AAC, Club Andino Bariloche*

SOUTH OF PAINE

Cerro Panchote. The first winter ascent of Cerro Panchote, a triple-summited glaciated peak, occurred in September 2000, reports the Spanish magazine *Desnivel.* The peak was climbed in a three-day round-trip from the coast by Sergio Camacho and a partner. They used a fishing boat from Puerto Eden for the approach.

MOUNTAIN INFO, *High Mountain Sports 230*

TIERRA DEL FUEGO

Monte Ada. On Saturday, February 3, the rather grandly titled British Darwin Range Expedition 2001 arrived in the city of Ushuaia in Argentine Tierra del Fuego. For an expedition with such a large name we were rather short on members. In fact only Andy Parkin and I made up the climbing part of the team. Our objective was an unclimbed peak in the Cordillera Darwin in Chilean Tierra del Fuego. With the help of Celia Bull, her ocean-going yacht *Ada II*, Celia's sister Elaine, and my wife Jane, we were able to access this incredibly remote mountain range.

On the 13th we anchored the yacht at the head of a fjord next to the dramatically located Estancia Yendegaia, having battered our way west along the Beagle Channel. The Estancia's resident gaucho, Jose Alvarao, offered his services and horses to transport us inland to the mountains. By the 16th Andy and I had set up a base camp in dense southern beech forest on the Rio Neimeyer, about 10 miles north of the Estancia. A reconnaissance up the valley revealed the Bove Glacier with, at its head, Monte Bove (2400m) and the peak we had come to climb.

On February 18 it rained all morning, before clearing and allowing us to make a carry up onto the glacier. Once above the snout we moved easily up the gently angled ice, which was virtually free of crevasses and debris, to the head of the dry section of the glacier. We stashed our climbing kit, tent, stove, gas, etc. under a boulder and returned to base camp. Indifferent weather confined us to base camp for three days. Then we decided to go up regardless and get a feel for the mountains and our route.

On the 22nd the weather was showing no signs of improvement, but we left anyway, carrying personal gear and food for five days. When we reached our stash at the boulder, we loaded our rucksacks and headed for the upper part of the glacier. Soon it was necessary to rope up, and we went through a moderately crevassed section before the glacier leveled out. The weather had cleared, and we were treated to full views of our mountain and the route we wished to climb. The east side of the mountain sported a prominent buttress that dropped right to the glacier. The buttress was steep but offered many lines up systems of icy runnels, which led to a very steep rock headwall at the top, capped with rime. We spotted a couloir splitting the upper headwall; it looked like it would provide a climbable way to the summit. We set our alarms for 2 a.m. and went to sleep.

We were away at 4 a.m., leaving the tent, spare food, and gas on the glacier, intending to bivouac above. We crossed the bergschrund at the base of the buttress at first light and moved quickly up snow slopes to the right of a nose of rock. A little higher the ground steepened and we moved rightward, following the line of least resistance into a broad couloir. We roped up, and it began snowing. Spindrift avalanches started pouring down from above. I led a difficult pitch across to the right side of the couloir and up a steep corner. By now we were very cold and wet. Andy led a particularly difficult traverse back left to regain the center of the couloir above its steepest section. Above there were many pitches of steep, insecure snow and ice climbing between interconnecting runnels, as avalanches continued to pour down. As the light began to fade we were forced to dig a hole into a small cone of snow. We dug a small chamber, which we could sit inside and escape the worst of the weather. Our feet protruded outside and were continually swept by avalanches.

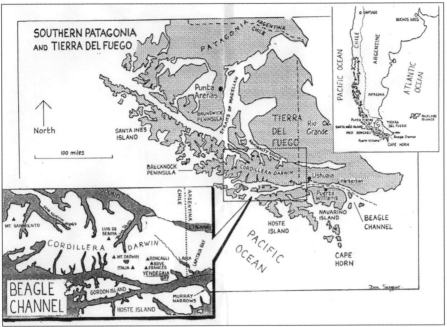

Tierra del Fuego and the Monte Ada region (Yendegaia Bay) visited by the British Darwin Range Expedition 2001. Monte Ada was climbed by Andy Parkin and Simon Yates. *Don Sargeant*

The night passed slowly, as somehow we slept. At first light the weather was no better, and we discovered a pool of water had formed under us. We were now both soaking but felt we should carry on. By the time we started climbing the morning had almost passed, but the weather had begun to improve. After two pitches the sun came out, and Andy suggested leaving the bivouac gear and going for the top. We debated for a while, as we would then have to abseil the face, and we had initially planned to descend another ridge. However, once we were free of the weight of bivouac gear we began to move much quicker, and the decision felt like the right one. Andy led two long pitches to the base of the headwall, which overhung as we had suspected. A steep gully, which gave a superb pitch of climbing, cut through the headwall. I had the pleasure of leading the gully, and then Andy continued to the top, which he reached at 6:30 p.m. on February 24.

The summit was windswept, covered in rime, and shrouded in mist. Slowly the mist began to lift, revealing the Cordillera Darwin in all its glory. We never had a complete panorama, but by waiting we eventually obtained views in all directions. To the north were the three summits of Roncagli, forming a definite chain. To the south was the squat mass of Monte Bove,

Andy Parkin climbing above the bivouac on the second day on Monte Ada. *Simon Yates*

to the southwest Monte Frances and Italia, and in the distance the northwest fork of the Beagle Channel, sparkling in the evening sunlight. The peak we climbed lay between Roncagli and Monte Bove and marked the watershed between the Bove and Dartmoor glaciers. It was on no map. The peak was somewhere between 2,000 and 2,300 meters high. It was previously unclimbed.

We soaked up the views for a full hour before turning our attention to getting down. We abseiled from the summit ridge, following the line we had climbed through the evening, continuing after it became dark. When we reached the steep section in the

Monte Ada: The Parkins-Yates route follows the rib dropping directly at the viewer in the center of the northeast face. *Simon Yates*

broad couloir that had given us problems on the way up, we abseiled straight down, hoping to gain the glacier quicker than by following the traversing line we had come up. We soon found ourselves on an open snow slope, which we down climbed until two abseils were needed to clear a band of seracs at the base of the face. Then we walked back across the glacier to our tent, arriving at 2:30 a.m. After a late start the next day, we slowly made our way down the Bove Glacier. The weather deteriorated once more, and we soon found ourselves walking in pouring rain, once again wetting all the kit that we had managed to dry during the previous day's sunshine. We finally reached base camp at 8 p.m.

For us the climbing was over, although we did spend two more weeks in the area, sailing farther west along Beagle Channel, exploring numerous fjords and the climbing possibilities they offered. The potential for ice and mixed climbs of up to 1,500 meters was almost limitless.

We were lucky in a number of respects. Only after we had made the decision to go did we find out that we would be able to use horses to get supplies to base camp. This saved us a lot of time shuttling loads. The site of base camp itself was determined by how far Jose could take the horses, not any decision on our part. In fact the camp and its relation to the Bove Glacier turned out to be perfect, as did the approach up the Bove Glacier. Finally, our decision to keep going through truly awful weather during the first day of the climb was crucial to our success. We could have waited a long time for a window of perfect weather!

We would like to name the peak Monte Ada, after Celia's yacht. The route is 900 meters, alpine ED, VI in grade. As such, it is the first technical route in this mountain range, where many peaks that offer walks to the summit wait to be climbed. The climbing itself felt very Scottish in terms of climate and conditions, but we have both spent time previously in the Paine and Fitz Roy areas of Patagonia and found the weather in this part of Tierra del Fuego to be much better than those regions.

SIMON YATES, *United Kingdom*

Antarctica

SOUTH GEORGIA

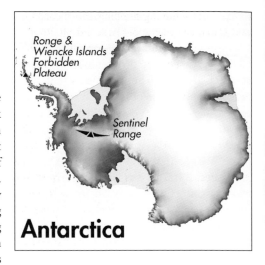

Ronge &
Wiencke Islands
Forbidden
Plateau

Sentinel
Range

Antarctica

Three Brothers, first ascent. Sailing aboard the yacht Pelagic, Alun Hughes, Skip Novak (captain of Pelagic), and I arrived at South Georgia with the aim of making a five-part series on sailing, climbing, and the history of wildlife on the island for Welsh television. The unclimbed Three Brothers were on my list since I first spotted them while working as harbor master on South Georgia during 1990-91. The 1991 South African Mountain Club Centenary Expedition led by John Moss had a go at the highest peak and got as far as the col. They reported straightforward skiing across the Neumayer Glacier. However, after a dry winter and a hot summer the glacier was now as dry as a bone and constant zig-zagging was required to make any progress. It took us a week to ferry everything in to the mountain, carrying roughly three loads each in order to establish a well-stocked camp below the headwall leading to the western col. The site was at an altitude of ca 450m and was occupied around January 18. The three of us were then stuck for a week of constant bad weather in a two-man tent.

We eventually received a forecast that a weak ridge of high pressure would arrive on what would effectively have to be our last day. We started at 4:15 a.m. but the weather was still bad with lots of spindrift avalanches being blown across the face in high winds. Al and Skip decided against it and turned back. I managed to work a way through the lower icefall and across the bergschrund via a hole to get onto the face. I climbed this in difficult conditions to the col. The weather then started to improve as forecasted, so I began to move eastward towards the summit tower. My planned approach via the southern ridge looked too steep to solo, so I traversed shale terraces and ramps to the crest of the north ridge. I then followed this on fairly steep glass-hard ice, past two false summits, to the main top at 2040m, arriving at around 12:15 p.m. on January 25. The summit has five high points, all about the same altitude within 70 meters. They were icy with a covering of hoar frost and dropped away spectacularly to the east. The western flanks were more slabby.

I traversed all five high points, crossing an à-cheval section and descending some precarious awkward steps, then began the descent. Instead of following my line of ascent I went directly down the icefields below the north ridge, then traversed around to the col at a lower level. I then reversed the face below the col, sticking to the rocks as much as possible to minimize any avalanche risk. I reached the others at 5:30 p.m.

CRAG JONES, *United Kingdom*

Nordenskjold attempt and Normann ascent. John Griber, Hilaree Nelson, and Rick Armstrong along with film crew Tom Day and John Teaford, made up a strong U.S. team, led by Doug Stoup that visited the island in October and November. They traveled aboard *Golden Fleece* and had ambitious plans for filming climbing, snowboarding, and skiing on the island's highest peak, Mt. Paget, as well as on Nordenskjold Peak and Mt. Roots. This group arrived to find the thinnest snow cover in the mountains for over 20 years and experienced atrocious weather for most of the trip.

On November 2 Stoup, Griber and Armstrong attempted Nordenskjold Peak. Climbing in very high winds Stoup and Armstrong turned back after frontpointing over 1000m of hard blue ice at around 55 degrees. Downclimbing from this point still took them around three hours. Griber continued on, reaching the summit ridge at around 2135m. Though only 200 meters below the top, changing conditions dictated descent, which amazingly Griber decided to do on his snowboard. Watched by the rest of the team, Griber descended the extremely icy face in around 15 minutes. Stoup, who has made a number of difficult snowboard descents in Antarctica, described it as, "One of the most amazing things I have ever seen." The next day their base camp tents were destroyed, hit by winds measured at over 70 knots. The team retreated to the boat. They then changed plans to make shorter ship-based forays.

One of these forays, on November 15, produced the second ascent of Mt. Normann (1265m), by a new route. Stoup, Armstrong, Nelson, and Griber climbed the 1200-meter east face of Normann to exit on to the narrow east ridge, which they followed to the summit. The climb gave over 1000 meters of 50-degree snow and ice, beginning at the water's edge, like all of their climbs. Most of the descent was done by ski or snowboard. Mt. Normann was first climbed in January 1991 by members of the South African Mountain Club Centenary Expedition aboard the yacht *Diel*. Stoup's team went on to do a number of other shorter climbs and ski descents on features close to the shore in Larsen Harbour, and spent time studying and filming the island's wildlife, before returning to Ushuaia.

DAMIEN GILDEA, *AAC, Australia*

THE MAINLAND

Sentinel Range, overview. In the 2001-02 season 67 climbers, including only four women, attempted Vinson by the normal route. Sixty reached the summit, producing a success rate of 90 percent, slightly lower than usual. No new routes were climbed in the range during the season, though the experienced Antarctic guide Dave Hahn, guiding a geological excursion, summited a number of minor points in the Marble Hills area.

There was only one expedition attempting anything other than an ascent of Vinson Massif by the standard route. The Omega Shinn GPS Expedition proposed to take an accurate GPS height reading of the summit of Mt. Shinn. In 1998, when I wrote *The Antarctic Mountaineering Chronology*, a reference book on ascents made in Antarctica, I realized there was no single, accurate, and accepted figure for the altitude of Mt. Shinn, supposedly the third highest peak in Antarctica. The figures given in various publications range from 4800m down to 4650m. The latter would make it the same height as Mt. Craddock, supposedly Antarctica's fourth highest peak.

The original surveys of the high Sentinel peaks in the early 1960s put *Vinson Massif* at 5140m, later changed to 4987m after a resurvey in 1979 and the republishing of the USGS topographical map to the area in 1988. The second highest peak, Mt. Tyree, was reduced to 4852m, but no new figure was given for Mt. Shinn.

The USGS publication *Geographic Names* of the Antarctic, by F.G Alberts (2nd ed. 1995) gives no numeric height for Shinn, but says, "A mountain over 4,800m…." The USGS

The west face of Vinson Massif (4897m) from the Branscombe Glacier, as seen from just below Camp 1 on the normal route. *Damien Gildea*

Geographic Names Information System website has no numeric figure for Mt. Shinn, similarly stating: "A mountain over 4800m...." The 1988 USGS topo of the area, *Vinson Massif*, has no numeric altitude figure on Mt. Shinn, as it does for most of the high peaks. The June 1967 issue of *National Geographic* features Nick Clinch's expedition that made the first ascents of Vinson, Tyree, Shinn, Gardner, and others. It puts Shinn at 15,750' (ca 4802m) but those figures were taken on the original 1960s surveys, since amended.

I felt that Shinn was probably lower than 4800m, though higher than 4600m. The Omega Foundation, an organization that supports science in the polar regions, agreed to an expedition that had as its primary aim a new, accurate GPS reading taken on the summit of Mt. Shinn. I was joined by Mike Roberts, a professional guide from New Zealand with 11 previous Antarctic expeditions to his credit.

We procured a Trimble 5700 Total Station GPS receiver, the successor to the 4800 model used by Washburn's team on Everest in 1998 and a NOVA crew the previous year on Vinson—who recorded Vinson at 4901m. The plan was to climb Shinn by the normal route, measure it, climb *Vinson Massif*, then sled 45 kilometers north to attempt the first ascent of Mt. Anderson (4157m), the highest unclimbed mountain in the Sentinel Range. To gather enough accurate data, a recording session of at least six hours on the summit of Shinn was deemed to be necessary. Data would be downloaded through the website of the Australian Land Information Group (AUSLIG) to give an Above-Geoid figure (GPS figure), and then post-processing by AUSLIG would produce a figure comparable to traditionally surveyed Above Sea Level figures.

The expedition's November 16 start was delayed by two weeks due to the failure of Adventure Network International to procure sufficient aircraft to begin operations for the season. The expedition landed on the ice at Patriot Hills on November 30 and reached Vinson Base Camp the next afternoon by a combination of DC3 and Cessna flights. We started up the lower Branscombe Glacier within hours of landing, stopping at the usual Camp 1 site that evening and proceeding to the usual Camp 2 the next day. After four days of storm we made

Above: Camp 1 on the way to Mt. Vinson and Mt. Shinn. Below: Mt. Shinn (ca 4800m), Antarctica's third highest mountain, from the west. The normal route roughly follows the right skyline, starting from the Vinson-Shinn Col, just visible at the far right edge of the picture. *Damien Gildea*

a route through the seracs at the top of the headwall beneath the Shinn-Vinson Col and established Camp 3 in the usual position. After deciding that more acclimatization was needed for our summit stay on Shinn, a partial ascent of Vinson's normal route was planned for the next day. In good weather, progress was slow, but we decided to continue to the summit and with two Norwegians made the first summit of the season. Upon return to Camp 3, other teams had arrived and planned to summit the next day. However two days of very bad weather with high winds, low visibility, and some snowfall followed, necessitating regular forays outside to dig tents out of severe drifts.

December 10, the 11th day on the mountain, dawned beautifully clear with only a light wind, so we set off in down suits for Shinn at 9:45 a.m. with the GPS unit and a small summit tent for the Shinn summit data session. At 2:30 p.m. we were around 100 meters below the summit on the southwest face when we encountered severe windslab avalanche conditions, a result of the previous two days' storm emanating from the northeast. Attempts at traversing around this area proved fruitless and we were forced to descend.

At Camp 3 Roberts learned of a medical emergency in his family that necessitated his return to the United States immediately, so we descended to Vinson Base Camp on December 11. Most parties were now ready to leave for home. I endeavored to find help to complete the Omega project on Shinn but though a guide was very willing to do so and Omega offered to fully cover his changeover and insurance costs, ANI would not allow him to stay.

The failure to accurately measure Shinn was particularly disappointing given the observations made with wrist altimeters on Vinson and Shinn. On Vinson (4897m or 4901m) our altimeters (mutually calibrated at previous known points) read 5130m—roughly 230 meters "high." At their high point on Shinn—estimated to be 100 meters below the summit—my altimeter read 4750m. If one subtracts the same discrepancy from this as found on Vinson—i.e. 230 meters—one could estimate our "real" high point as 4520m. If our estimate of distance below the summit is correct, then Mt. Shinn is only 4620m. Even if allowances are made with the altimeter readings and our judgement of distance to the summit, Shinn is still substantially lower than 4800m and possibly lower than 4700m. It is evident that significant work of this nature still needs to be done in this area.

DAMIEN GILDEA, *AAC, Australia*

THE PENINSULA

Wiencke and Ronge Islands, various ascents and scientific program. An international expedition comprising myself as leader and skipper, co-skipper Dave Hildes (Canada), Peter Taylor (US), Grant Redvers (NZ), Jon Millar (Canada), Elliot Robertson (UK), David Fasel (Switzerland), Fraser Bernie (Scotland), Andy Mitchell (UK), Lena Rowat (Canada), and Penny Goddard (NZ) spent 10 weeks sailing and exploring the Peninsula in the yacht *Gambo*. The weather and sea-ice conditions over the 2001-2002 summer were apparently exceptionally bad, giving record snowfalls, high winds and bad visibility. For these reasons we never ventured further south than the Lemaire Channel, but we had a fantastic time. We made three successful ascents on Wiencke Island, two of which are likely to be first ascents:

The yacht *Gambo* awaiting the return of intrepid explorers along the shores of the Antarctic Peninsula. *Alun Hubbard*

the first (or northernmost) of the seven sisters of the Fief Range (ca 1200m by its northwest ridge, a mixed route of between 30 and 60 degrees with a crux steep rock pitch on very chossy rock); the "shroom" (ca 900m) on the Wall Range, climbed via "Crag Jones" gully (opposite Noble Peak) to a nasty corniced ridge heading up left (north); Luigi (1400m) by its east ridge via an exceptionally good ski route (we may claim the first snowboard ascent and descent) with a 300-meter snow climb up to 50 degrees to the summit. Other projects on Wiencke Island failed due to exceptionally poor weather windows, but to keep sloth at bay we made almost daily ascents of the popular Jabet Peak (550m).

The team made a ski traverse onto the Peninsula Icecap Plateau via a route from the Orel Ice Fringe to the Downfall. Unfortunately, we were weathered off three-quarters of the way across the Downfall at the crux, before we could get fully established on the Peninsula and achieve an ascent of Mt. Walker. However, we made two possible first ascents: Stolze Peak (ca 1580m) on skis, and the westernmost peak of the Laussedat Heights. We also made the second ascent of Mt. Hoegh (890m) in conjunction with members from the British Army Antarctic Expedition (but led by the *Gambo* crew). The previously unclimbed Mt. Britannia (1600m) on Ronge Island was ascended via two routes. The first and more technical took place via the east ridge directly opposite Danco Island; and the second, via the southeast ridge, was achieved mostly on skis.

The majority of our scientific work was concentrated into two to three weeks at King George Island. Whilst *Gambo* was moored in Maxwell Bay, numerous field parties completed a surface and basal topographic survey of the Warzawa Icefield by Radio-Echo Sounding and GPS. We took GPS fixes at numerous rock outcrops in Admiralty Bay to ground truth and constrain 1950s aerial photography. We took a temporal and spatial suit of sub-glacial and supra-glacial water samples to assess for minor and trace metals, and other run-off nutrients. We also collected over 50 samples of glacogenic material for extremeophile microbe analysis.

ALUN HUBBARD, *Wales*

Antarctic Peninsula, various climbs. The British Army Antarctic Expedition aboard the John Laing made the second ascent of Mt. Johnston (2,304m) and conducted exploration of the high Peninsula areas, including the Forbidden Plateau. A climbing party of nine from this team reached the summit of Johnston on December 28, nearly 44 years after the first ascent in January, 1957. They later joined with members of the group on *Gambo* for a number of ascents (see above).

Elsewhere, the regular commercial climbing trip run by Australian company, Aurora Expeditions, operating aboard the ship *Polar Pioneer*, once again managed some interesting climbing, attempting the first ascent of the southernmost peak on Ronge Island, where they were turned back just below the summit due to windslab avalanche conditions.

DAMIEN GILDEA, *AAC, Australia*

Middle East

TURKEY

Mt. Ararat, northeast rib/face. On July 27, a group of climbers from five countries made an ascent of the northeast flank of Mt. Ararat (16,940') near the borders of Armenia and Iran in northeast Turkey. The team was comprised of Marcelo Buraglia (Columbia), Khoo Swee Chiou (Singapore), Tunc Findik (Turkey), David D. Keaton (US), Nasuh Maruhki (Turkey), Ricardo Torres Nava (Mexico), and Fernando Gonzales Rubio (Columbia). One of the expedition goals was to help raise awareness and support for several charities including the Babu Chiri School in Nepal and the Istanbul-based AKUT search and rescue team. The ascent alternated between a rib of funky rock and a series of snowfields. A short section of 50-degree ice led to the summit icecap and the east summit, which was traversed to reach the main top. The line, vexed by rockfall, may not have seen a previous ascent. Western climbers have typically been restricted to the mountain's southern route, but the lesser known northern approaches offer new route possibilities including the unclimbed and horrific looking Ahora Gorge. A more detailed report can be found at www.holy-landexpeditions.com.

DAVID D. KEATON

IRAN

Mt. Ararat from the northeast. The climbing route follows snowfields on the rib descending leftward from the summit. *David D. Keaton*

Alam Kuh, north wall, new route, second winter ascent of the face, and historical reporting. A joint team comprising members from two Iranian clubs (Arash Group and Damavand Club) led by Mohammad Mousavinejad, spent 16 days in February opening a new route. Anjoman, named after the newly (2000) formed Anjoman Kuhnavardi Iran (The Iranian Alpine Club), is the first new route to be climbed on the north face of Alam Kuh during the winter. Alam Kuh (4850m) is the

The summit of Mt. Ararat in eastern Turkey following a rare ascent from the northeast. *David D. Keaton*

third highest summit in Iran (after Damavand, 5671m, and Salavan, 4900m) but its 500- to 600-meter granite north face is undoubtedly the most prestigious in the country.

Alam Kuh was probably first climbed by the Bornmuller brothers (two German botanists) in 1902 via the easy south flank. The second ascent was made in 1933 by the British explorer and mountaineer, Sir Douglas Busk, via the east ridge (Siah Sang). The first ascent from the north came in 1936 when Gorter and Steinauer climbed the north ridge, separating the north and northwest faces. In 1951 Jalil Katibei and Mohammad Ali Tafreshi climbed the north wall of peak Shakhak. That was very astonishing in those days. This route has not been repeated yet, though some climbs of the easier ground to the right of the route have been done.

To the left of it (not seen in the photo) on the same day Naser Fallah, Ali Asghar Ordookhani, and Mehdi Sedghi Nejad climbed the steep snow slopes of the face between peak Shakhak and peak Siah Sang. This route probably has not been repeated. The first route on the true north face of Alam Kuh was first climbed in 1964 by German, Herman Rost and Iranian, Amir Alai. Two years later Blassier, Fresafond, Parat, and Valencot from a French expedition climbed a second route on the north face and in 1969 the Poles, Dobek, Wroz, and Waligora, added a third. The early 70s saw a spate of new routes on the previously unclimbed northwest face (Italians in 1970, Poles in 1971 and the first all-Iranian route in 1973). Poles returned to the north face in 1973, when Stama and others climbed the Great Roof. After the Islamic Revolution in 1978 the mountain was left for a while to Iranians. In 1983 a team led by the late A Azizi completed the first Iranian route on the north face, while over three years from 1982-84 Asgari, Babai, Mohammadi and others put up the Arash Route. From 1988 to 1991 several short routes and important variants were established by Iranian climbers. However, 1991 was notable for the first winter ascent of the north face.

Attempts at a winter ascent go back to 1974 (Poles). From 1980 to 1991 a handful of Iranian climbers tried the wall and all failed. One was killed and a number suffered frostbite. The main difficulty is the cold, with temperatures down to −40°C at night and −20°C during the day. Powder snow avalanches also provide regular problems. In winter of 1991 another large Iranian team tried the wall, only to complete three pitches of the Arash route in 20 days on the mountain. One member, Ishkhan Ebrahimi, suffered severe frostbite, which resulted in the amputation of all his toes and some of his fingers. However, in this large team there remained one determined climber. Mohammad Nouri wanted to climb the wall at any cost. He eventually

The north face of Alam Kuh in winter, Iran. Routes: (1) Katibei-Tafreshi, 1951, on Shakhak, was remarkable for its time; (2) Anjoman, 2001; (3) Rhost-Amiralai, 1964; (4) French, 1966; (5) Arash, 1982-1984; (6) Polish, 1973; (7) Polish, 1969; (8) German pillar, 1936. *Ramin Shojaei*

soloed the Arash route in four days. Since then several alpinists have attempted the face but failed...until the winter of 2001.

On February 6 the team (comprising Mohammad Moosavi Nejad—leader, Ramin Shojaei—technical leader, Ara Megerdichian, Esmail Motehayer Pasand, Kazem Faridian, Mohammad Nouri—cameraman, Ali Parsai, Abbas Aghasi, Abbas Mohammadi, Mahyar Pour Abdolah, Afshin Lahouri, Mehdi Broumand, Omid Amohammadi, and Ali Haji Saeed) reached Alamchal, the cwm below the face. While the others erected a hut below the face, Megerdichian and I started fixing the first pitch below the Golesang, the névé at the base of the wall. The following day I fixed another 200 meters of rope to the base of the wall.

The next day Faridian, belayed by Megerdichian, took the lead on the first pitch of the main wall. Near the start he fell on rock that was not so steep and injured his ankle. After carrying him down to Roodbarak in one and a half days, three team members, along with five new ones, came back. Meanwhile Megerdichian and I had stayed behind and led the first two pitches on the main wall.

A further pitch and a half were climbed over the 13th and 14th, after which it snowed for two days. Five members left. With Nouri filming, Megerdichian and I continued climbing over the next few days and on the 20th I completed the fifth pitch to reach the less steep, loose summit rock band. I placed the Iranian flag at the high point and then climbed down 10 meters to install a safe belay. That day we cleaned pitches four and five but due to snowfall left the remainder to be cleared on the following weekend. Our route Anjoman was graded VI A3 5.8.

While we were on the wall Mohammadi and Nouri took two days off to repeat their 1990 first winter ascents of the Haft Khanha peaks (ca 4700m). They were away from Alamchal camp for two days and climbed three peaks. At the same time Amohammadi and Saeed climbed the nearby Shaneh Kuh and Miansechal peaks (4300m).

RAMIN SHOJAEL, *Iran*

Africa

EGYPT

Red Sea Mountains, an historical overview and recent first ascents. Following the discovery of an old book by G.W. Murray entitled Dare Me To The Desert (1967), in which the author describes his explorations of Egypt's Red Sea Mountains in the 1920s and 30s, Di Taylor and I decided to follow in his footsteps. Delving into archives revealed that Murray was a Director of the Egyptian Desert Survey in the early decades of the last century. He was

also a respected member of the Alpine Club and the Royal Geographical Society, the latter awarding him their Founder's Medal. He served as an officer in the Northern Red Sea Patrol in the 1914-18 war and was awarded the Military Cross. Not only did he obviously know his subject well, scattering his pages liberally with unclimbed or otherwise attractive peaks, but very few climbers seemed to have been there and possibly none since the 1930s. We were hooked.

Our first attempt in 1988 was turned back by endless sandstorms and unexpected military checkpoints. Our second attempt in 1996 was an almost equal disaster. Despite sponsorship by Egypt's Tourism Authority and an Egyptian travel agent, the military refused to recognize our permits to what is a closed area of the Nubian Desert near the Sudan Border. Our planned exploration of the other parts of the Red Sea Massif was also inexplicably cut by the travel agent from five weeks to one—not much time for 600 miles of mountains.

Nevertheless, we located many of Murray's more northerly peaks in the Eastern Desert and managed to climb briefly on some. The granite was not perfect but definitely climbable and good in the water-worn gullies, where some Bedouin hunting routes exist. We also discovered that the renowned Italian climber, Emilio Comici, had been there in 1937, climbing several peaks the same year as Murray. The most interesting seems to be Gebel Shayib (2187m) the highest on the Egyptian mainland, climbed by Murray on April 26, 1922 and by Comici on April 29, 1937. The Austrian Alpine Club also climbed several peaks in this area during 1931. Adjacent to Shayib, Gebel Qattar (1963m) and other summits just to the north were climbed by Comici in 1937 (all these mountains in this area are accessible from the coastal resort of Hurghada). Gebel Gharib (1750m) is a couple of hours drive further north again. First climbed on the remarkably early date of April 29, 1823 by British explorer J. Burton, the peak was also climbed twice in 1937, first by Murray on February 22, then by Comici on April 3—a busy year for Egypt's mountains In addition to these existing routes, all this area offers interesting exploration potential with climbs up to 900 meters in length, some of which could be good quality. Intrigued by our discoveries, and in honor of Comici, some Italian climbers visited this area in autumn 2000, making some new ascents.

In spring 2001 we decided to try our luck a third time with the mysterious "forbidden" southern peaks. Here, not far from the disputed border with Sudan, lies Murray's "unclimbable glass dome" in a remote part of the desert. Nearby, just above the wild and empty coast, are the Farayid Mountains "the most aggressive in Egypt." This dramatic massif is also the location of Murray's rock bridge "which seemed to sway in the throb in the wind" and the Berenice Bodkin, "sharper and more vertical than the Aiguille du Géant, rising exactly on the Tropic of Cancer," which Murray "left alone in its austerity."

After considerable preparation with a new travel agent and some last minute fears that the trip was going to fail yet again due to continuing Egyptian military intransigence, we finally got our permits—all five of them. We were also given an escort in the form of a soldier "for our security," before finally making it into the desert together with climbing friends Mark Carr and Christine Evans. Driving the two vehicles, which were compulsory for a journey through this remote area, were Tamer El Sayed and Hany Amr, the directors of two Egyptian safari companies (Nomad Adventure Tours and Dune Desert Adventures), both keen to extend their desert knowledge.

Due to last-minute permit problems, our planned 17 days visit had shrunk to 10. This left us with about a week in the desert, 600 miles south of Cairo. It's a particularly wild and beautiful area nearly 500 meters above sea level, studded with large acacia trees, supporting herds of gazelle and, nearer the coast (four days' camel ride), scattered families of sword-carrying Ababda Bedouin, eking out a hard traditional life of camel breeding and charcoal making.

Our first objective, Gebel Sila'i (baldhead) "as sheer and smooth and unclimbable as The Hill of Glass" (756m) proved unexpectedly easy: Murray had failed to find the one reasonable route up this ca 300-meter-high, atrociously exfoliating, granite dome. It will be an excellent "trekking peak" if the area ever opens up, with magnificent panoramic views in all directions. A black basalt intrusion may offer a possible direct route but even it is obviously loose in places due to the extremes of temperature.

The Rock Bridge was truly spectacular; a ca 50-meter flying buttress of bizarre shape and proportions "like a tea cup handle" as Murray described it. We did a 250-meter route up the crag, climbing through the arch to the summit, extracting the maximum enjoyment from this most unusual rock architecture. The temperature on the top (in mid March) was 100°F. The climb was straightforward but as on Sila'i, the granite was disturbingly creaky.

Elsewhere in the massif of The Farayids (1366m), known as Mons Pentadactylus ("five finger mountain" to the Romans), there are numerous other impressive peaks with cliffs up to 300 meters high. Situated on the Tropic of Cancer, the Berenice Bodkin (1230m) is one of them but we only had time to find a way in to its base for future reference. It's definitely climbable from the northeast and the steep 150-meter upper cliff may be of better rock. On its north side slabs sweep up into a vertical, or possibly overhanging, headwall, in total 300 meters high. Just north of The Bodkin (also known as The Dagger of Berenice) the steep cliffs on the south face of Purdy's Peak (height unknown) looked equally, or even more, impressive. Whether or not any of these cliffs are climbable by a sane person is another matter. The only way to find out is to get on them.

Despite its brevity, it was a fascinating trip, allowing us not only to experience the joys of exploration and the ascent of new climbs, but also and equally importantly, to spend a little time with the Bedouin. Living four days' camel ride from the coast, they are still leading a traditional life. However, changes are inevitable—a new international airport is under construction 100 miles away on the coast, near Mersa Allam. New Red Sea coastal resorts for divers and sun-seekers are rapidly spreading south towards the area we visited. No doubt permits will be relaxed and the timeless solitude of the desert, its mountains, wildlife and people, will be faced with the arrival of mass-tourism as visitors escape the coast for desert safaris. It could spell the end for the people and wildlife, though if organized with forethought and consideration it could also be an opportunity for a new beginning. It will certainly allow the climbing and trekking community easier access. We are hopeful that our report to those concerned with Egypt's tourism and environment will contribute to protecting the future of this unique area and its indigenous people.

Useful contacts If you plan to go 'off road' you will almost certainly need permits, in which case you will need the assistance of an Egyptian tour agent. Permits, transport, and provisions for the above trip were arranged by Tamer el Sayed, Nomad Adventure Tours, 155 Al Sudan Street, Mohandessin, Cairo, Egypt, e-mail: nomad@sitravel.com.eg; in co-operation with Hany Amr, Egyptian Adventures, 58 Abdullah abu el-sude St, 1163 Heliopolis, Cairo, Egypt, e-mail: hanyamr@hotmail.com. Both these companies would be pleased to quote you for desert tours such as The Western Desert Oases, Gilf Kebir (SW Desert), Sinai, The Red Sea Mountains etc. Allow one month (maybe longer) to obtain Permits.

TONY HOWARD, *United Kingdom*

MALI

Hombori Mountains, new route. From November 20 to January 14 my brother Michael and I visited the Hand of Fatima in the Hombori Mountains. On Kaga Pamari we established a new route up the center of the southwest face, completing the line in the first week of December. The route is 400 meters in length and follows a crack system (finger to shoulder width). The maximum difficulties are French 7a. All belays were bolted, but nuts and cams are needed for protection. The route is situated just left of the 1993 Albert/Arnold line, Wanangaba Maby.

                                                              JENS RICHTER, *Germany*

MADAGASCAR

General information. For a selection of topo and photo diagrams, look at the two websites, www.madamax.com/camp-catta and www.campcatta.com. Local climbers and Camp Catta staff are encouraging exploration of the giant boulders around the forest, some 40 to 50 meters high. Last season there was a lot of bouldering carried out around Camp Catta and if development continues, the site could gain international recognition for its bouldering alone.

                                                            GILLES GAUTIER, *Madagascar*

Tsaranoro Be, new routes. The prominent series of corners that form the right side of the Yellow Pillar left of Gondwanaland was climbed in May by South Africans, Alard Hüfner, Mike Mason, and Matthew Munting. This "classic" line had been attempted on several occasions before by climbers of high caliber such as Arnaud Petit, but the highest point gained appears to have been approximately halfway up the route. Reports suggest that heavily vegetated cracks had put off a number of climbers. Christened Vazimba, the new 800-meter line was climbed in 18 pitches with difficulties up to 7a maximum. Camalots to size 5 are required.

A month later a Spanish-Swiss team comprising Toni Arbones, Benoît Dormaz, and Miriam Richard completed a sensational line up the front face of the Yellow Pillar left of Vazimba. Vazaha M'Tapitapy (Crazy White Men) is 650 meters in height and 16 pitches in length, entirely equipped with 160 stainless steel bolts. The team appears to have terminated their route at the top of the pillar, though it would be possible to continue up to the summit by following the last few pitches of Vazimba. The climbing is very sustained with 10 of the pitches 6c or above and the crux eighth pitch thought possibly to be as hard as 8a. Local activists report that this may be the best line to date in the country.

Right of Gondwanaland the 1999 Swiss Route, Norspace (Walter von Ballmoos/Stephan Salm: 16 pitches; 7a max) was re-equipped by von Ballmoos, with Jürg Bernhard, Andreas Bähler, Curdin Gliott, and Viktor Schwarz. Originally, the 73 protection bolts were placed with a hand drill making the Swiss party the only team since Albert and Arnold on their first visit in 1995 not to use a power drill to create a first ascent on the big walls of Tsaranoro. After consultation with Salm, von Ballmoos decided to re-equip the route, bolt for bolt, using a power drill and the best quality long-life bolts. It took five days with one rest day to complete the job, climbing twice up to pitch six, then finishing the rest from above. However, one bolt was added to pitch six. Then on a subsequent day von Ballmoos redpointed the route, except for a rest point on pitch 9 and pitches 14 to 16, where ropes had been left for the team to finish this section in the dark. The grade was confirmed as solid 7a (in August 1999 Misako Koyanagi, Jim Haden, and Mike Libecki climbed all the difficulties at 5.11c/d before rappelling from the top of the 14th pitch, while on the second complete ascent—in 2000—Alexander Buzinkay and Rado Staruch felt the protection to be very well spaced and rated the crux as 7a+).

Norspace was attempted in October by the British climbers mentioned below. Incidentally, the name comes from a young boy who was at Camp Catta at the time of the first ascent. At the same time as the Swiss were at work on their route, the all-female team sponsored by The North Face was creating Bravo les Filles. The young lad was always talking about "norspace" rather than "north face" and the name stuck.

GILLES GAUTIER, *Madagascar* AND GRZEGORZ GLAZEK, *Poland*

Lemur Wall, new route. To the right of Pectorine, in the vicinity of the huge broken flake, Swiss climbers, Jurg Bernhard and Andreas Bähler, created a new four-pitch route christened, La Voie Plaisir des Guides Suisses. The climb was put up on the 26th September and has difficulties of 6c, 6a obl. The pair set out to create a real 'plaisir' route and the result is a very well-equipped sport climb with 14 bolts on the crux pitch. However, the route was opened from the top.

Traditionally, routes in the area were opened from the ground up. The first to be equipped by rappel, Tsaky-Tasky on Lemur Wall (Duteurte/Tiberghien, 1998: 7a+), came in for some criticism. Local climbers comment that this criticism was well-founded as the route was disappointing and showed the first ascensionists' lack of experience. However, they feel the new Swiss route is different, as it is an excellent climb, strongly recommended, and has already seen around a dozen repeat ascents. They are quite happy for routes to be opened in this fashion, as long as the result is a very good climb that is accessible to many visiting parties.

MOUNTAIN INFO, *High Mountain Sports*

Tsaranoro, various climbs and new routes. Dave Kenyon and I arrived at Camp Catta on September 19. Our first three days were spent repeating the excellent existing routes, Alien II (350m 6b), Croix du Sud (300m 6b+), and Pectorine (250m 6b/A0) on a variety of crags to get a feel for the place, the coarse granite, the style of climbing, and the intense heat.

September 24-27 were spent on the water-streaked dome of Vato Varindry, a boulder by the standards of the area being a mere 320 meters high and 600 meters wide with only two existing climbs. During those days we opened a new route from the ground up, the local ethic. The result was a seven-pitch 6c (maximum and obligatory), which we called Malagasy Maroto (Madagascan Hammer) in memory of the happy hours Dave spent hand drilling on pitch two.

September 29 saw us going for the alpine start in order to repeat the superb Out of Africa (600m, 14 pitches) on Tsaranoro Kely. A fantastic route, that saves its 7a+ crux for the last pitch. The ascent took us eight hours and the abseil descent a further two hours. After a brief look at the new route potential on the right hand section of Lemur Wall and Mitsin Joarivo, we decided once more to focus our activity on Vato Varindry, where we spent five days opening an eight-pitch (325m) route, on which the first five bolts were placed from skyhooks. The result, Karma Chameleon (7a+max/6c obligatory) was finally completed on October 7.

October 8 started early in order to attempt the bold and impressive Norspace on Tsaranoro Be. We backed off after six pitches due to Dave's fingers and my head being in bits. The climbing up to that point was good but worrying due to the slightly friable nature of the rock and the scarcity of bolts. A bit of traffic should result in the route becoming a classic. We salvaged the day by repeating the highly enjoyable Le Cas Nullard (a classic 450m 6a) and traversing Karambony in order to look for the further new routing projects.

Oct. 9 and 10 saw Dave desperately trying to re-grow his finger tips, whilst I opened up the amenable Lemurs Ripped my Flesh (220m, 6b+ max or 5+ with two points of aid) on Karambony's lower slabs (Editors note: it appears that the first part of this route, as far as the half-way ledge, had previously been climbed four years ago by Gilles Gautier with his daughter and named Baba Kely, 5+).

October 11 and 12 saw the drilling continue as we ascended a groove line high up on Karambony to produce the jolly Le Mur Lemur (100m: 6b+ max and obligatory). Our final route before the tortuous journey home. In total we repeated five of the Massif's 28 routes and climbed four new lines (22 pitches, 1000m) on which we placed 120 protection bolts and 42 belay bolts over the course of 13 days new-routing in the baking sun. The members of the expedition would like to thank the Karabiner Mountaineering Club, Bendcrete Climbing Walls, Fuji, and Hilti for their generous support that helped to make this expedition a success.

DUNCAN LEE, *England*

The Sea Cliffs, new sport routes. Michel Piola and Benoit Robert returned to the North Coast for a couple of weeks during June and July to create 66 new pitches on Madagascar's northern limestone in the vicinity of Diego Suarez. These new sport climbs are at the two venues; Montagne des Francais and Nosy Hara. The popularity of this area is increasing fast and in addition to the new Piola routes, other climbers added a further 14 pitches.

However, environmental agencies such as World Wildlife Fund and Conservation International are trying to obtain a marine reserve status for the archipelago. Fortunately for climbers, the protests of local people have been heeded and it is thought that both Nosy Andantsara and Anjombavola should receive a special status that will allow tourist activities. Nosy Hara is still under discussion, as so far the proposed special status is likely to allow only access to the beaches and not the cliffs. Either way, it is possible that much of the interior of the island will remain totally preserved.

GILLES GAUTIER, *Madagascar*

MOZAMBIQUE

Sitting Chief. I was part of a joint Mountain Club of South Africa/British Mountaineering Council expedition to northern Mozambique and we were successful in climbing our objective, Sitting Chief (local name, Murupie). We had quite an adventure getting there with 10 of us in two cars. One car was a double cab Toyota Hilux and the other an old Land Rover Forward Control, which although big and slow, is strong and has loads of character.

Just before the Zimbabwe border, the head gasket of the Hilux blew, so nine of us and all our big wall gear and equipment squashed into the Landrover for a very slow drive through

Zimbabwe, Tete Corridor, Malawi, and finally Mozambique. After five days of travelling we eventually arrived at Lalaua, a village near Sitting Chief. About an hour later and to everyone's amazement, Pieter Martin arrived in the Hilux. He had stayed behind in Masina to get the head gasket fixed and then drove 2500 km on his own to catch up with us.

The Administrator in Lalaua would not give us permission to climb the dome, as according to a Dutch company, who had carried out a survey, the neighboring area contained valuable minerals and no one was now allowed to enter. We therefore drove three hours on bad roads to the capital city of the north, Nampula, where we spoke with the Governor. He gave us permission to climb.

The climbing on Sitting Chief looked as though it would be interesting from a distance, as the face contained huge huecos. We split up into four parties and attempted different lines. It turned out that after a couple of pitches the rock became covered in thick lichen, which made for unpleasant climbing. All attempts were aborted at various heights. Next, we focused our energies on reaching the summit via a huge corner system. This provided for some interesting climbing up corners and chimneys at about grade 23. Pieter Martin, Peter Robins, and Dave Turnbull were first on the summit, followed by Leo Houlding, myself and Mark Seuring. The day before Ben Bransby and Andrew Donson had reached a point one pitch from the summit before turning back as it was getting late. Matthew Munting and Izak Steyn retreated from their route.

We then headed off to Mlema 3 to do some real climbing on African Light, the route that Mark and I had opened in 2000. However, it rained (yes, rain in the middle of winter). Andy, Ben, and Dave spent a miserable night bivouacking in the rain at the base of the climb. They had planned to bivouac on Bundu ledge but the rain caught them three pitches up and as it was getting dark, they abseiled down and sat out the night in the rain. With spirits dampened and the weather looking grim, we headed off to lake Malawi. Here we relaxed in the sun and did some kayaking with Kayak Africa.

After another three days of traveling (by now we were well accustomed to this), we arrived at Blyde River Canyon. Here, we opened some amazing routes. This was definitely the climbing highlight of the trip. A couple of climbs at 26 were opened on sight. Then onto the Restaurant, where after two days of clipping bolts it was time for the British contingent to leave South Africa, everyone in agreement that we had enjoyed a great time together and got on very well.

ALARD HÜFNER, *Mountain Club of South Africa*

Commonwealth of Independent States

RUSSIA

CENTRAL CAUCASUS

Ushba Region, overview. The region of Ushba is the heart of the Caucasus. Baksanskoy ravine is rather wide, limited by Mt. Elbrus on the one hand and the peaks of the Main Caucasian mountain range on the other hand. There are more ravines downstream of the Baksan River; they also lead to the peaks of Main Caucasian range. They are Yusenghy, Adel-Su, Ader-su, Tutu-su.

Baksan is the most popular region of the Caucasus. There are lots of hotels and mountaineers' centers here. The most difficult and interesting peaks of the region have wall heights from 700 to 1700 meters. Mountaineers began developing this region at the end of the nineteenth century, but the main classical routes were formed in the 30-60 years of the last century. At present time there are not so many chances to open some new routes, but they still exist. The best known peaks of the region are: Elbrus (5642m-W, 5621m-E), Ushba (4710m), Shkhelda (4320m), Shurovsky (4259m), Ullukara (4302m), Free Spain (4200m), Coockoortlu (4639m), Juhntugan (3991m), Bashkara (4241m), Chaten (4368m), Nakra (4451m), Donguzarun (4468m), Ullutau (4207m), Jaileck (4533m), Tutu (4460m), and Cheghem (4461m).

A Prielbrusie panorama of the Ushba region. *Yuri Koshelenko*

All these mountains (with the exception of Elbrus and Juhntugan) have difficult mixed walls. There is only a little part of the region in the panorama below. The photo was taken from the mountain ridge that separates the Adel-Su and Ader-Su valleys.

YURI KOSHELENKO, *Russia*

WESTERN CAUCASUS

Fisht-Pshekhasu region, overview. This is a wild region with boundless forests, wild animals, and cave plateaus, just 50 km from the Black Sea. Fisht (2864m) is the first mountain in the Western Caucasus where there are glaciers. This region is interesting by its great opportunities for first ascents, and a lot of them are in free climbing style. The western walls of Fisht Mountain and the southwestern face Pshehasu are practically undeveloped by climbers. Elevation of the walls are unknown exactly, but I think they are from 200 to 800 meters. The walls were molded from the lime of the ancient ocean Tetis. Their latitudinal extension is about 15 km. Two of the strongly pronounced peaks are in this panoramic photograph. Pshehasu is at the left and the North Tower of Fisht Mountain is on the right. Meanwhile, the region of Fisht is well known among speleologists because the inside part of the massif is the prototype of Swiss cheese. There are only two tourist huts in the eastern and western sides of this mountain region. But climbers are not so often here.

YURI KOSHELENKO, *Russia*

In the Vodopadnvi region of the western Caucasus: the 700-meter-high Pshehasu Wall is on the left, and the 500-meter-high Fisht North Tower Wall is on the right. Both are unclimbed. *Yuri Koshelenko*

KYRGYZSTAN

WESTERN KOKSHAAL-TOO

West Komorova Glacier, new routes. During the month of July, Scott Decapio (USA) and I (Canada) traveled to Kyrgyzstan and climbed in the remote, military-restricted West Kokshaal-Too range in the Tien Shan Mountains on the border with China. I had visited this area in 1998 and had wanted to return to attempt the stunning unclimbed southeast face of Kizil Asker.

Constant storms kept us from even trying our main objective. However, the high precipitation created excellent summer ice conditions. We managed to climb three new alpine ice and mixed routes in three weeks. All three routes went completely free in day-trip-style without bolts. Our warm-up climb was the first ascent of the east face of Pik Gronky (second ascent of the mountain). Silent Bob (700m, IV WI4) began with a 250-meter strip of grade 4 ice then finished on a 50-degree ice face and elegant snow arête to the 4950m summit.

Next, we made the second ascent of the 600-meter Ochre Walls. A long couloir with 70-degree bulges split the lower section of this vast, orange-hued rampart. Where the couloir pinched off, we found three stellar mixed pitches consisting of narrow ribbons of thin ice lacing smooth granite slabs. South Park's chubby second-grader, Eric Cartman, provided the inspiration for the name; Beef Cake (600m, IV M5 WI4).

Our last climb was the type of line that I had always dreamed of finding: a 700-meter goulotte of ice slicing an unclimbed granite buttress. We cruised up into the gully on easy snow, moving together until the ice steepened. I took the first lead up grade 4 water ice. Scott followed through negotiating thin runnels pouring over short, steep steps. Above his belay, a meter-wide vein of gray foam was smeared in the back of a vertical corner. I stemmed up this strenuous pitch placing stubby ice screws in the frothy ice. More moderate terrain led to a body-width pillar tucked in the back of a chimney. Scott gently tapped up the loosely adhered column and pulled over a scrappy chokestone capping the slot. Above this last crux, we simulclimbed five pitches of 50- to 60-degree ice, punctuated by a few short-lived cruxes over rock steps plastered with sun-rotted snow-ice.

We tagged the top of a small, unclimbed peak on the jagged ridge of The Unmarked Soldier Group, then immediately began the descent. A long traverse put us above a broad couloir that looked like it would deliver us down to the glacier. Scott made the first of many V-threads just as the dark storm clouds began to boil overhead. Multiple rappels spat us out on the opposite side of the mountain from our highcamp. We slogged around to our tent arriving 17 hours after leaving. We named this last route Royale with Cheese (700m, V M6 WI5) and christened the minor summit Pik Mikhail (ca 5100m) in honor of our guide and base camp cook. The expedition was supported by the Polartec Challenge Award, Mugs Stump Award, AAC Lyman-Spitzer Grant, and the Canadian Himalayan Foundation.

SEAN ISAAC, *Canada*

Beefcake, above, and Scott DeCapio climbing it. *Sean Isaac*

Royale With Cheese is the obvious couloir, above, on Pik Mikhail, circa 5100m. Below: Approaching the Komorova Glacier and the West Kokshaal-Too range from base camp on the Kyrgyzstan side. *Sean Isaac (3)*

Chon-Turasu Valley, attempt on Koroleva and ascent of Molodezhnyi. In August I climbed with Graham Holden in the Chon-Turasu Valley of the Western Kokshaal-Too. We reached our 3300m base camp by Ural Truck in a problem-free three-day drive from Bishkek. We intended to climb new routes on Pik Dankova (5982m) or Pik Chon-Turasu (5728m), but a reconnaissance showed the lines on the east side to be rather serious, so we switched to the southeast ridge of Pik Koroleva (5816m) via Pik Tsandera (ca 5400m).

We acclimatized by attempting unclimbed Pik ca 5400m south of Pik Alpinist, turning back on the convoluted summit ridge in deteriorating weather. We were then confined to camp for several days as heavy snow fell in the mountains. As the weather cleared on August 17 we waded through the fresh snow to make a determined attempt on Pik Koroleva. We endured two stormy nights on the high col at the base of Pik Tsandera before continuing up enjoyable mixed climbing on the ridge. Despite the lowly 4A grade given to this ridge on its 1969 first ascent, we were brought to an abrupt halt by a loose rock tower at ca 5150m. As a consolation, on August 22 we made the first British ascent of Pik Molodezhnyi (5338m), via the northeast ridge.

During our stay we met two teams from the Moscow Railway Institute, one having trekked over passes and the other having unsuccessfully attempted piks Dankova and Chon-Turasu. Both teams planned to walk over the Borkoldoy Massif to Kara-Sai.

Potential new routes remain in the Chon-Turasu area, but many

Top: Trapez, Chon-Turasu Glacier, and Alpinist, from ca 5400m on the summit ridge. Middle: Molodezhniy and Alpinist from upper valley below Tsandera. Molodezhniy northeast ridge on the left, and circa 5400m in the center. *Paul Knott (3)*

(including the outstanding 2,000-meter-high east rib of Pik Koroleva) are more committing than existing lines.

PAUL KNOTT, *United Kingdom*

Kyokkiar and Sarybeles Mountains, first ascents. In August-September John Allen (UK), Peter Berggren (Sweden), Hilda Grooters (Holland), Tim Riley (UK) and I all climbed in the Gori Sarybeles and the Khrebet Kyokkiar of the far Western

Dankova from the northeast. *Paul Knott*

Kokshaal-Too. We were almost certainly the first mountaineers, either local, Soviet or Western, to visit these ranges of 4000m peaks on the Chinese border. We traveled by truck in one long day from Bishkek to Chatyrtash, an abandoned settlement in a border valley. Two local soldiers rode by to check us out and we discussed approaches to our range We had to cross the Ak-Sai river, then kilometers of foothills into the Kyokkiar. We decided to drive along an established road south of the range to get a different view. Three hours later the track petered out but there in front of us appeared another ridge of steep sided, snowcapped summits, rising straight out of a broad grassy valley.

We made camp and spent the next few days climbing four peaks in what was labeled on the map as the Gory Sarybeles. Three routes were straightforward and the easiest to their respective summits, while the other reached one of the two most strikingly sharp summits along the ridge. We never touched the numerous rock faces, which offer countless more routes.

We then decided to shift venue back to the Kyokkiar to give us enough time for xploration. Half a day after leaving the Sarybeles, we were guided to a yurt on the banks of the Ak-Sai, where there was a family with horses for hire. With a price agreed and a number of horses gathered, we were guided into the range along hunters' trails and left at a camp which clearly wasn't the one we'd intended.

The next two days were spent scouting a route to transfer our camp to the main valley, where we found a clear mountain stream. Our tents were surrounded by steep limestone walls hundreds of meters high. After a reconnaissance up the main valley toward the higher summits, Pete, Tim, and John moved camp to below a 1300-meter face, while Hilda and I climbed an easy summit up a side valley in a day trip from the main camp.

Tim, Pete, and I made an attempt on the high face, failing at 4600m due to lack of daylight. During our retreat we had to abseil 100 meters down glacier-smoothed slabs, which would block an ascent to the upper glacier.

With Tim and Pete keen to explore the valley that Hilda and I had previously visited, we transferred camp in poor weather, pitching our tents below one of the combes we had viewed while climbing the mountain in this valley. The next day a late start and higher than anticipated difficulties prevented a planned ascent of a couloir, which I had estimated at Scottish III/IV.

Instead we climbed an easy gully to the plateau, Hilda and I retreating just before we reached the top due to an electrical storm.

The following day Tim and Pete made an early start for the couloir while John, Hilda, and I descended. Tim and Pete reached us just before dark, big smiles on their faces after completing the best technical climbing of the trip.

The Kyokkiar does not compare in size or seriousness to the main area of the Western Kokshaal-Too. The peaks are on average 1000 meters lower, but the weather seems considerably better.

CLIMBING SUMMARY:

GORI SARYBELES:
Pt 4435m, northwest slopes, August 31, Gerrard and Grooters, Alpine F
Pt 4550m, northwest Face and north ridge, August 31, Berggren and Riley, AD+
Pt 4275m, northeast Ridge, September 3, Gerrard and Grooters, F
Pt 4375m, southwest Ridge, September 3, Gerrard and Grooters, F
On September 3 Berggren and Riley retreated in poor weather 200 meters up the obvious narrow couloir in the valley face of Pt 4275m (Scottish V)

KYOKKIAR:
Pt 4445m, Southwest Ridge, September 11, Gerrard and Grooters, F
Pt 4200m, Left-hand gully ascended to summit plateau, September 17, Berggren and Riley, 300m, Scottish 1
Pt 4200m, Couloir climbed to just below the summit plateau, September 18, Berggren and Riley, 500m, TD, Scottish 5
An attempt on the northwest face of Pt 4765m via the obvious ramp-line to a shoulder and then the upper snow slopes to the summit ridge was halted at 4600m.

DAVID GERRARD, *United Kingdom*

ALA ARCHA

Free Korea Peak, first ascents. On January 6-7 I climbed a new route, solo, up the center of the north face of 4750m Free Korea Peak. I spent one night on the face and another at the top. My route was a substantial variant to the 1975 Popenko Route. I was back on January 22 to climb another new route, solo, on the north face. It took me five and a half hours to climb this 900-meter ice route of 50 to 80 degrees. I named the route Barbera.

ALEXANDER RUCHKIN, *Russia*

Pakistan

HINDU RAJ

Kampur, attempt. In August and September Pete Linkroum, Jacob Moore, and I explored the Ishkoman region of the Hindu Raj. Our plan was to attempt Jutebar Peak (ca 5600m) near Darkot Pass, but due to poor conditions we turned our sights to a new line on Kampur (5499m), climbed in 2000 via the northwest face by Carlos Buhler and Ivan Dusharin (see 2001 *AAJ*). We started up the northwest face on September 10 but after six days tent-bound due to bad weather, bailed to base camp. There was no chance for a second attempt, as we were forced to leave because of the terrorist attacks on September 11. A tense exit ensued and we finally reached the U.S. on September 22.

CHAD MCFADDEN, *AAC (Recipient of an AAC Lyman Spitzer Climbing Grant)*

From Gashuchi, looking up to Chushubalstering, 6158, in the left background. Various routes ascend Areri, 5700m, left; Denis, 5800m, middle; Areri, 5700m, right. *Hervé Qualizza*

Kai Zom, Areri, Kamaro Zum, Ulumeshpati; new routes, first ascents, and various attempts. My first time in Hindu Raj was in 1999 with the "International French Expedition." We had the information from B. Domenech, who made some photos from the area one year before. Some of us were on the Makutchum base camp, and the others just onto the bottom of the incredible north face of Chushubalstering. Everyone tried to make the first ascent, but the mountain and the weather were stronger than us.

This year we decided to come back on the same BC. We planned to climb in two teams, Nicholas Fabbri, Clément Flouret, and Jéroma Huet as one team; Juliette Géhard and me as another. Hindu Raj is a perfect massif to climb: not very high (6800m maximum), "human faces" (except the Chushu, around 1500 meters), very easy approach (two or three days for BC, less for the mountains), and a lot of unclimbed summits or free faces. The massif looks like some place in the Alps, with wilder places of course, and the only difficult thing is to walk on unknown moraines without tracks or any trails. Do it yourself and enjoy!

So everything began by finding the summit we wanted to climb. The three guys started to go on Ulumespati, a 6175m with a 900-meter long snow slope. Two days walk is needed to cross the enormous glacier and the moraine. At the bottom, some big crevasses and quiet long snow bridges were "interesting." Early the morning, they climbed fast and joined the flat area just under the last wall. Unfortunately, the wind and maybe a too-fast acclimatization stopped them just at the end. It was the second climb from 1963.

During this time Juliette and I were opening two new routes on two 5000m summits. The first one was the Kai Zom, climbed the first time by Japanese expedition in the 1960s(?), and the other was an unclimbed summit by its north face. We called it "le Trident."

Top: the summit ridge of Kamaro, with Kamaro North in the foreground. Bottom: from the Grand Couloir Central on Kamaro, with Chushubalstering in the left background; Makutchum is the snowy background peak in the middle. *Hervé Qualizza*

After a big party on the BC, with sitar and drums, eating goat and French fries, we went to more serious things. The dream team climbed the Areri, a 5700m peak with 1700 meters of fantastic pillar, two-thirds of it increasingly difficult rock climbing, to finish with an easy snow ridge … and the rising sun. The descent took a long time, rappelling down with a shorter and shorter rope.

The two lovers decided to try an unknown 6000m, and missed—too dry, too steep, and too tired! Two days after, we were on the first meters of the Kamaro Zom. Maybe unclimbed by this face, we tried along a giant couloir. At the end, and after six pitches of quite mixed and steep climbing, we had the biggest surprise of the year: the end of the route was not a flat area like I had planned, but a snow ridge becoming warmer and warmer with the noon sun. After two hours more, we turned our back on the summit and missed it by a few meters. The sun finished his job by increasing rock falls and melting the snow so much that water was running on the couloir.

The day after, everybody was dancing again at the BC. Jay, Nico, and Clem opened a rock climbing route up by the BC, and I went with Juliette trying the Ulumeshpati. Like the others, we took two days to arrive on the bottom because of the snow. Bad weather was coming, and the conditions were different. The nice snow slope had become a horrible mirror of black ice. Early the morning, we waited for the stars but the snow was falling again. At 7 a.m. we decided to try something. We climbed slowly on the dark ice, and made many pitches.

Then we waited for the rain to stop. Eight days sleeping in the wet tents, eating peanut butter, playing cards, and listening to music. And like an incredible dream, the sun came back exactly the morning when the porters came back.

There are so many things to do in the Hindu Raj. Two valleys more to the east, 14 unclimbed summits; on the back side of Makutchum, Chikari, or maybe near the Koyo Zom…I will be back!

HERVÉ QUALIZZA, *France*

KARAKORAM

Passu Sar, attempt. Believing it to be still unclimbed and therefore one of the highest unclimbed summits in the Karakoram, a five-man Australian team led by myself booked Passu Sar (7478m). This peak is situated between Shispare and the Batura Group. However, shortly before leaving home, we learnt of a German expedition (reported in the 1995 *AAJ*), who appeared to have climbed Passu Sar in August 1994 and not the lower Passu Diar (a.k.a. Passu Peak, 7295m), which lies a little to the east. Checking with a local high altitude porter in Gulmit, we were able to confirm that Dirk Naumann, Ralf Lehmann, Volker Wurnig, and Max Wallner had indeed made the first ascent of the higher peak, using skis for much of the ascent and bypassing the lower peak by going through a high shallow saddle to one side.

We set up base camp in June close to the Passu Glacier but instead of finding the lower glacier just badly crevassed, as we had expected from information provided by the Alpine Club of Pakistan (which organized a successful expedition to Passu Diar in 1996), we discovered a giant icefall starting at around 4200m and having over 800 meters of vertical gain. On closer inspection we realised that the route was very complex, dangerous, and just not possible for a lightweight effort, so we abandoned any further attempt. The previous winter had been very dry and knowing this, we had arrived early to profit from whatever snow cover remained. However, it appears that a succession of dry years has taken a severe toll.

DAMIEN GILDEA, AAC, *Australia*

Sub-6000m peaks (Karakoram and Hindu Raj), attempts and ascents of new routes. On June 5 the Korean Five Peaks Expedition set off from Seoul for the Karakoram and Hindu Kush. The seven-man expedition, led by Gi-seok Seo, set out to make ascents of five peaks less than 6000m. These peaks were Khache Brangsa (5560m) and Ghonoboro (5500m) above the Arandu Valley, Mustum (5620m) and Shikari (5928m) in the Yasin Valley, and Bubulimotin (6000m) in the Hunza Valley.

First ascents were made on the North (5350m) and South (5560) peaks of Khache Brangsa in semi-alpine style. On June 15 base camp was established at 3800m and on the 18th ABC at 4300m. Chang-ho Kim, Seoung-mook Im, Gi-heon Jang, and Seong-moon Choi reached the summit of the North Peak on the 28th. The team bivouacked for the night at the 5240m col between the North and South Peaks, and the following day Chang-ho Kim and Seong-moon Choi reached the summit of the South or Main Peak. They spent three consecutive days climbing this new route, which was named Gosanja and rated 5.9 and WI5 M4.

From the Khache Brangse base camp, Gi-seok Seo, Chang-ho Kim, and Seong-mook Im climbed on the northwest face of Ghonboro in semi-alpine style. The climb took them three days. On the first night they bivouacked at 4900m and on the second at 5380m. The following morning the weather deteriorated into heavy snowfall and subsequently rock fall increased down their line. They were only able to reach 5380m, just 120 meters shy of the summit. The 1350-meter route was named Great Balor and rated WI4 M6.

A few weeks later team members, Gi-seok Seo, Seong-mook Im, and Myeong-hee Lee nearly climbed Mustum Peak in the Darkot region of the Hindu Raj. They climbed in alpine style. From an ABC they first bivouacked at 5100m, then climbed up into a couloir, where they bivouacked again at 5350m. They were finally stopped just 50 meters short of the summit on the evening of the third day, retreating due to an increasing night chill factor and lack of provisions and equipment. Once again, the team exercised care on the potentially dangerous descent. They rated the climb 5.9 M5 WI4.

On July 29, Chang-ho Kim and Seong-moon Choi climbed Shikari in alpine style via the northeast couloir. They spent three nights and four days completing the first ascent of the northwest route, Goxienzi, a 2000-meter wall rated M4 WI4. From ABC, the trio climbed 1,500 meters on their first day and on the second made the summit and retreated to a snow hole about two-thirds of the way down to their previous night's bivouac. On the third day they descended to their first bivouac site, where they rested. They then continued further west along the ridge and down a less steep slope to regain their base camp. Later, the Korean Five Peaks Expedition was forced to retreat from Bubulimotin due to unfavorable weather conditions, falling rocks and injuries to three of their climbers. The team returned to Seoul on August 28th.

PETER JENSEN-CHOI, *Korea*

Editor's note: Khache Brangsa was almost certainly a first ascent and it is most likely that the summits of Ghonoboro and Mustum have never been visited. 5928m Shikari or Chikari was first climbed in September 1999 by Slovenians, Jernej Bevjk, Jernej Brescak, and Matej Kovacic via the north ridge, finishing up the northwest face. However, prior to their ascent the three had climbed the 1,400-meter central couloir on the east face as far as the north ridge.

Ogre, second ascent and Ogre III, first ascent. On July 21 the team of Urs Stöcker, Iwan Wolf, and me stood on the summit of the Ogre (7285m). Having succeeded on the first ascent of the extremely difficult Ogre III (ca 6800m) on July 1, we concentrated on climbing the Ogre. Since the first ascent in 1977 by the two British climbers Chris Bonington and Doug Scott, all other attempts at climbing the mountain—more than 20 expeditions—had been unsuccessful.

On July 18, after two days' preparation, the team left base camp in uncertain weather for their summit attempt. On July 20 we reached the top of the south pillar at 6500m, after having climbed 28 pitches. The following morning at 2 a.m. they began the final, decisive stage. Climbing the steep (up to 55 degrees) icefield was very strenuous. It led to the start of extremely hard climbing up the final buttress to the summit. This proved to be UIAA VI and A2 at over 7000m. Strong wind and extreme cold made the last meters to the summit challenging. At 3:30 p.m. we were on top. After 24 years....

THOMAS HUBER, *Germany*

Baintha Brakk, attempts and second ascent. Four expeditions attempted 7285m Baintha Brakk (The Ogre) last summer and although talented groups from America, Austria, and Slovenia all failed, a three-man Swiss-German team achieved the highly coveted second ascent after an interval of 24 years. No new ground was climbed, but their success was arguably the most notable mountaineering achievement during the entire 2001 season.

Thomas Huber (Germany), Iwan Wolf, and Urs Stöcker (both from Swizterland) arrived at base camp (4500m) on June 7 to find three Americans, Hans Johnstone, photographer Ace Kvale, and Mark Newcomb, already at work on the South Pillar. Huber and friends therefore decided to concentrate on the unclimbed Ogre III, for which they also had permission. Their successful ascent, in itself a very major achievement, is reported below.

On June 30 Johnstone and Newcomb reached the top of the South Pillar (fifth ascent) and bivouacked. On the 1st July they headed up and across the large snow/ice field towards the summit tower but were caught in a snowstorm and retreated. They descended to base camp and then left for home. It was now the turn of the Swiss-German team. The three left their 5000m advanced base (Camp 1) on July 8, climbed the 300-meter couloir to the notch on the pillar crest and fixed 10 pitches. These included the crux, which Huber, now well-acclimatized, was able to redpoint at VIII+. Next day Stöcker and Wolf fixed rope to the proposed site of Camp 2 at 5900m, where they established a portaledge. A bad storm now moved in, the climbers retreated and subsequently were unable to regain the portaledge until the 18th.

On the 19th Huber, Stöcker, and Wolf climbed eight more pitches and established the portaledge (Camp 3) at 6200m. The following day they reached the top of the pillar in five more slabby pitches and then climbed the icy crest above to make Camp 4 (a bivouac under the portaledge fly) at ca 6500m. To the end of the rock section they had climbed 26 roped pitches. A 2:00 a.m. start on the 21st saw the three climbers ascending rightwards across the giant snow/ice field, reaching its apex at 8:30 a.m. In strengthening winds they tackled the summit buttress, following the line taken in 1977 by Bonington and Scott. Difficult mixed ground led to the three hard rock pitches, on which the alpinists discovered old pegs and confirmed the grade as VI and A2, with a long and tricky pendulum. The three reached the highest point at 3:30 a.m and on the following day rappeled 800 meters down the South Pillar to arrive safely back on the glacier by mid-afternoon.

Prior to this activity a two-man Italian team of Alois Brugger and Hans Kammerlander was at base camp, planning an alpine style ascent of the Original British route.The pair were on the mountain in early June, having established an advanced base below the face at 5000m. Their best shot took them to 6200m but the weather was unsettled and the route threatened by snow and serac avalanche. They retreated from their high point (below the plateau) on the 21st. A second foray up to advanced base on the 24th showed more than half-a-meter of fresh snow lying as low as 5000m and with time running out, the pair abandoned any further attempts.

Elsewhere on the mountain a very strong four-man Slovenian team, comprising Urban Azman, Tomaz Jakofcic, Silvo Karo and Peter Meznar, attempted the unclimbed south east pillar leading to the virgin East Summit (7150m). This is a route that has been attempted on numerous occassions from the Choktoi Glacier. The Slovenians arrived at their 4600m base camp in the middle of June and spent the next month attempting the pillar. They managed to climb the difficult 700m rock section above the col and reached a high point of ca 6350m at the base of the large snow field but very bad weather drove them down.

MOUNTAIN INFO, *High Mountain Sports 233*

Ogre III, first ascent. Thomas Huber, Urs Stöcker, and Iwan Wolf made the first ascent of Ogre III, the ca 6800m West Summit of Ogre II (6960m), now considered a distinct top. The Swiss-German team first inspected the approach on June 13, finding the glacier difficult (some short ice steps of 80 degrees) with dangerous seracs. Fresh snowfall kept them away for a few days but on the 20th they were ready for an all-out attempt. Carrying 28 kg sacs they reached the top of the 1000-meter-high snow/ice couloir (60 degrees maximum), which leads to the base of the very steep southeast pillar at ca 6000m. Unfortunately, they were more or less immediately forced to retreat in a storm. The next attempt saw five pitches fixed up the initial diedre in the steep rock pillar. The first three of these gave sustained climbing at VI and A2 with a section of A3, while the fourth, at V and AI, involved a pendulum. Not having enough food or gas for a summit attempt, the three descended to base camp.

Leaving at 2:00 a.m. on the 30th, the three reached the top of the couloir and their already established 6000m camp at 8:30 a.m., then jumared to their high point and fixed four more pitches (all free with difficulties up to VII). This put them at around 6400m and they returned to camp. The following morning, July 1, they had reached the top of their ropes by 5:00 a.m. The upper section of the pillar included an 80-meter chimney and some very difficult mixed climbing, which led to the final, small, snow-domed top of the West Summit or Ogre III. The climbers reached the highest point at 2 p.m. and spent a further five hours descending to their 6000m camp in a snowstorm.

MOUNTAININFO, *High Mountain Sports 233*

Ogre's Thumb, new route. Italians, Matteo Castelnuovo, Guiseppe Lafranconi, Alberto Marazzi, Simone Pedeferri, and Marco Vago, put up a new route on the South Face of the Ogre's Thumb (ca 5500m). Ragni sul Filo (700 meters) has 18 pitches with difficulties up to F7c and A2. The new line lies towards the left side of the face and joins the Original American Route at a terrace, some pitches below the top. The summit was not reached. Stances were bolted and a few protection bolts were placed but mostly the climb requires natural gear. It is reported to have one pitch of 7c, one of 7b, two of A2, a few pendulums and the rest 6b and above.

MOUNTAIN INFO, *High Mountain Sports 233*

Latok III, west face, attempt and tragedy. A strong Russian team met with tragedy during their attempt on the unclimbed 2,000-meter-high West Face of Latok III (6949m). Igor Barikhin, Mikhail Davy, Sergey Khadzhinov, Alexander Klenov, Alexander Ruchkin, and Alexander Odintsov established base camp on June 22. This was the same site used by Ruchkin and Odintsov for their 2000 attempt (see 2001 *AAJ*). Subsequently, while waiting for some delayed baggage, all climbers made an acclimatization ascent of a small subsidiary summit of the Latok group, which they refer to as Latok VI. The party slept the night on the top.

The capsule attempt on Latok III began on July 7, the team spending two days climbing and hauling equipment to the top of the ice slope below the start of the big corner system. Realising that stonefall in the corner was no less dangerous than the previous year, the team decided to pursue a more sheltered line up the flank of the pillar to the left. By the night of the 10th they had established a portaledge camp half-way up this wall. Unfortunately, the rock was far from good, making solid protection difficult to arrange, and there was still a problem from stonefall. On the 10th Odintsov was hit hard in the back by a rock and although there were no breaks, he was badly bruised, making further climbing difficult. On the 15th, now some distance above their 2000 high point, the weather deteriorated and it snowed for the next one-and-a-half days. However, by the evening of the 18th the Russians had reached a prominent elongated snow patch situated below the upper pillar and christened The Tomahawk. The climbing to this point had not been excessively difficult but almost constantly dangerous due to poor rock and stonefall.

The following day they moved up to ca 6200m, a point estimated to be two days' climbing from the summit. Barikhin was last man, jumaring the ropes and removing protection and belay anchors. As he ascended the last rope and the rest of the team were preparing a site for the night, a large rockfall suddenly cut loose from the summit ridge. Blocks flew past in all directions, but cowering close to the rock the five climbers at the proposed camp site avoided being hit. However, when calm returned, they realised the rope below had been cut and Barikhin had disappeared. The following morning the team abandoned the climb and descended, finding Barikhin's body just 20 meters above the rimaye at the bottom of the face.

MOUNTAIN INFO, *High Mountain Sports 234, and RISK*

Biacherahi Central Tower is in the middle of the photo. The Kurtyka-Yamanoi-Yamanoi route ascends the south face following the left skyline buttress from the snowy col. *Yasushi Yamanoi*

Biacherahi Central Tower, south face, first ascent. Voytek Kurtyka (Poland), Taeko Yamanoi, and I (Japan) visited the Choktoi Glacier. Voytek and I planned to try the north face of Latok I but the weather was so bad, we couldn't do it. Instead, the three of us climbed the South Face of Biacherahi Central Tower (ca 5700m). We completed the 450-meter route at 5.10 and A2 over six days in August. We spent four days fixing seven pitches above the col and on the fifth day jumared those pitches, then climbed the last four pitches to the summit. We spent no nights on the wall, only at the col, which was five hours above base camp. Half the route was loose, sometimes with large flakes of unstable rock.

YASUSHI YAMANOI, *Japan*

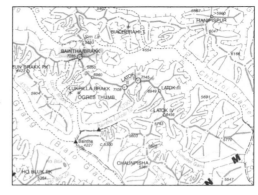

Shipton Spire, Inshallah, third ascent. Cecilia Buil, Nan Darkis, and I did the third ascent of Inshallah (1,350 meters: 5.12 and A2) on the south east face Shipton Spire. Darkis and I attempted to free climb most of the 30 pitches we led. Buil aided three pitches. We spent seven days fixing and hauling 300m+ before finishing the route in

a six-day push. We climbed through the last two days and two nights without sleep or much food, in order to finish the route. Unfortunately, we were unable to do the last two pitches because of an approaching storm and had to settle for a high point 50m below the summit. The route mostly consists of brilliant crack climbing, ranging from 5.8 to 5.11 hands to fists. There is minimal face climbing.

LIZZY SCULLY

Shipton Spire, Women and Chalk, first ascent. Italians Mauro "Bubu" Bole, Mario Cortese, and photographer, Fabio Dandri, put up the impressive all-free Women And Chalk on the South East Face roughly mid-way between Inshallah and the line of the 1992 American attempt. The team acclimatized around base camp in unsettled weather, before starting the first pitch on July 26. By August 10 they had completed the first 500 sustained meters and moved a portaledge camp on to the face in a little alcove at the top of pitch 14. Five days later they reached the summit ridge and junction with the 1997 Ogden/Synnott route, Ship of Fools. To that point the team had climbed on 13 days with Bole leading all 29 pitches on-sight, including

Mauro "Bubu" Bole, on Women and Chalk, Shipton Spire. See route line on next page. *Fabio Dandri*

Shipton Spire, showing the Women and Chalk route. *Fabio Dandri*

the crux 16th pitch, a 30-meter rounded jamming and layback crack dubbed the California Crack and rated F8a. At various stages during the ascent Bole then re-led a number of pitches for the camera. Twenty-three of the 29 pitches were 6c or above with 13 of these either 7b or harder. Some but not all of the belays were bolted (by hand) and two bolts plus a number of pegs used for protection (the protection bolts were used on pitches two and five, both 7b+, where there were very wide cracks). The climbing took place from approximately 4500m to 5700m with a total of 1100 meters of rope fixed, and the high point on the snowy summit ridge appears to be less than 150 vertical meters below the top of the Spire.

Bole averaged no more than 100 meters of climbing per day and on a number of days was only able to direct his energy to leading one hard pitch. He fell once, when a hold broke on one of the less demanding pitches around half-height. However, deciding that he had made a mistake with the line, he lowered to the belay and led an adjacent crack, thus upholding the on-sight ethic for each pitch of the final climb.

And the name of the new route? In Bubu's words, "Women and Chalk are the two essential elements in our life. There is always some chalk on our hands and a woman in our hearts, though to tell the truth, if it were the other way around life would be a lot easier."

MOUNTAIN INFO, *High Mountain Sports 234*

KARAKORAM-HUSHE REGION

Denbor Brakk, west face, Dancer in the Dark. In July Marcin Tomaszewski and I, both from Poland, arrived in the Nangma Valley. First we aimed for the west face of Amin Brakk. This wall harbours a couple of A5 routes and is said to be 1,600 meters high. No way! The wall is not much higher than El Cap, so the routes have to be much shorter than claimed. However, they all look hard. For our line we picked the prominent bulge (shown on the photo in *AAJ* 2000, p.119), followed by the immaculate nose of Amin lying to the left of all previous routes.

Marcin led two pitches of mixed and one of crumbling rock to the base of the huge bulge. There was no protection between belays. We hung a portaledge ready with food and water for something like three weeks of action. The wall above looked pretty blank, but we thought we might be able to link some small features with bat-hooks until we reached good prominent formations 250 meters higher. The features were there all right but they were all as loose as hell. Big blocks started cracking off the wall under the pressure of pitons. We started drilling, not only between features but also along them. We realised there was much more rock that would require drilling, so after breaking a couple of bits, we gave up. Seven days of work for nothing.

Of alternative venues Nawaz Brakk looked wet and loose, while Brakk Zang was already crowded with routes. However, across the river from camp was Denbor Brakk, a beauty with three steep distinctive west pillars more than 450m high. After studying the wall we opted for the central pillar. The first crack, which looked through binoculars like a perfect splitter, turned out to be flaring and slightly off-width with crumbling sides. It took some time to adjust to this type of formation. We followed cracks, mostly on aid due to their character. In order to try to stay on the prow of our pillar, we sometimes had to leave one crack system and pendulum to another.

We passed through the big A-shaped roof a little over halfway up and established our high camp just before the rain set in. Wearing rock boots, Marcin first tried to free the pitch above but fell due to poor rock. It was back to using aiders. Above, I began my lead with a simple 10-meter crack, followed by a very fragile traverse requiring the smallest Aliens and HB Offsets under thin expanding flakes. I needed to break off part of the flakes, because they were so thin at their ends they wouldn't hold half my weight. The traverse first curved slightly up, then down where it ended at a blank wall. After a pendulum I found a nice and easy off-width leading to the "hanging castle," a huge granite flake improbably sticking out of the wall. I went behind to find that the only attachment of the castle to the wall was at its base, where it sat on a 30-centimeter-wide and seven-meter-long sloping ledge. I moved up very carefully and after a tight chimney and beautiful hand traverse reached a belay. Marcin disappeared into the rain above my head and after his lead we fixed three ropes and descended to our high camp.

The next day was full of surprises. First we encountered a hard long pitch, where we thought we would find easy ground and then the top was inaccessible from our side. Fortunately, Marcin managed to find a small cave-like passage to the final summit block. According to the locals Denbor had never been climbed but on top we found battered slings and later learned that the peak had been climbed several years earlier from the southeast (the Gentian Traverse) by the British female climbers, Libby Peter and Louise Thomas. We took GPS measurements (a reading with five satellites indicated 4865m—i.e. more than 100 meters higher than Brakk Zang), summit photos, and happily began rappelling toward the foggy and rainy valley. Dancer in the Dark was rated VI A3+ 5.10d and was completed in eight days from July 18-25. There are 11 pitches.

KRZYSZTOF BELCZYNSKI, *Poland*

Denbor Brakk's west face, showing (1) Dancer in the Dark and (2) Against the Grain. Dancer in the Dark is described on the previous page. *Krzysztof Belczynski*

Denbor Brakk, west face, Against the Grain. During August I traveled to Pakistan with Damien and Elise Kelly, Jim Martinello, and Jason Sinnes, all from Whistler and Squamish, British Columbia. The party of four left me in the small Balti town of Kande and continued to the Charakusa Valley to climb new towers near K7. In one long day Alika, the Sadar of Kande and owner of the K6 hotel, and six other porters helped me get my four haulbags into the Nangma Valley and up to Amin Brakk's base camp. Here I discovered an unclimbed overhanging face more than 450 meters high on the central Denbor tower right opposite camp. A Polish team had attempted Amin Brakk's unclimbed nose but decided that drilling the blank overhanging prow for the first five pitches wasn't worth it. Instead, they completed a new line on the central Denbor tower, climbing to the left of the main overhanging face. They named their route, Dancer in the Dark, after a Bjork film (see previous page).

I first climbed one pitch on Nawaz Brakk next to Amin but was continually bombarded by rock fall, so I set my sights on Denbor's steep blank face. I soloed three pitches and spent one last dinner with the Polish climbers before they left for home. I would now ascend my lines and commit to the wall. The first three pitches involved hard overhanging seams with Birdbeaks and heads. After that, two pitches of hook traversing brought me to a major off-width that ran straight up the vertical prow for another four pitches. I had used one rope for a Tyrolean across the river and left it fixed. Another was fixed between two very steep pitches, so I could rappel the blank overhanging rock after summiting. One night a storm blew in, covering my portaledge with snow and blowing one of my two remaining ropes 30 meters to the left around a couple corner systems. I spent the entire next day bolting sideways to retrieve my ropes. At the top of pitch eight I pendulumed into the Polish line and climbed two variation pitches from here to the top. After being on the wall for eight days, I re-ascended two previously fixed pitches and led three new pitches to the top. Since there was no protection for the last seven meters I climbed unroped to the summit horn. I had given my Trango boots to a porter who had lost his shoes after falling into a river, so I therefore had to climb the whole route in plastic boots. I climbed the last seven meters barefooted. Sitting alone on top, gazing at Himalayan peaks, I felt very exposed. I rappeled the Polish route and traversed to my fixed line through the overhanging lower section. The 13-pitch route, which I named Against the Grain, has a grade of VI A4 V2.

Three days later I met up with my friends in the Charakusa valley and repeated Nazar Brakk (a.k.a. Luxor Pyramid) with Elise Kelly. This ominous peak towering above K7 base camp has some amazing 5.10 razor ridge climbing. The end of our trip involved some bouldering and new route scoping, then it was time to head to Thailand and enjoy some sunny sport climbing.

MATT MADDALONI, *Canada*

Drifika and Kapura, attempts. A six man Dutch team comprising Fedor Broekhoven, Coenradd Doeser, Wouter Dorigo, Bas Henzing, Martin Jongmans, and I were unsuccessful in our main objective, 6544m Kapura, south of the Charakusa Glacier. This beautiful unclimbed rock and ice pyramid lies immediately west of 7281m K6 and had received no previous official attempt. We tried the west flank and northwest ridge, finding the climbing overall to be approximately Alpine AD with ice up to 60 degrees and one rock passage of IV/V. We were stopped at ca 5800m by very deep and unstable snow. However, we did manage to attempt other peaks in the area, achieving moderate success.

We tried nearby Drifika (6446m) by several lines. Two attempts were made to climb the long southeast ridge in its entirety but this proved too time-consuming. There was a rock overhang of IV/V and ice up to 65 degrees. At the beginning of the ridge we climbed a small top, which we christened Pic Caro (ca 5800m). We then tried to bypass much of the lower ridge by climbing a 600-meter couloir up the left side of the east face (TD: ice to 80 degrees and mixed Scottish II) to gain the upper southeast ridge at 6100m. However, once on the crest desperate snow conditions halted any further progress above 6200m. The Original Route up the north ridge was also attempted but again dangerous snow conditions forced a retreat.

Prior to our attempt on Kapura we managed to climb an unnamed 5800m top that stands just south of Poro (6295m). The ascent was made via the south face and southwest ridge (D: ice to 55 degrees and rock to IV+) and the peak christened Minka. We also repeated the 1988 British Route (Bunnage/Hamilton) on the north ridge of Nazar Brakk (ca 5300m), climbing the original aid section free at F6a using only natural gear. This route has now become quite popular and something of a classic of the Charakusa. It was also climbed by Canadian (see above) and Italian parties while we were in the valley.

BART HERSMUS, *Holland*

Link Sar and smaller granite towers in the Kondus Valley, attempts. In May-June Steve Larson, George Lowe, Joe Terraveccia, Andy Tuthill, Eric Winkelman, and I explored several possible first ascent routes on Link Sar (7041m) in the Kondus Valley. This valley was only re-opened to climbers in 2000, when another group of Americans climbed the Tahir Tower (see 2001 *AAJ*). In

Link Sar, above, and the "Drus," below. *Steven Swenson*

1979 a Japanese expedition made the first and only attempt on Link Sar during the period between 1974, when the Karakoram re-opened, and the mid 1980s, when the valley was closed again because of the Siachen conflict. Subsequent to its closure the Pakistan military constructed a road alongside the Saltoro and Kondus rivers and then finally several kilometers along the east side of the Kondus Glacier.

The team, barring myself who was delayed leaving the U.S. due to work commitments, established base camp during the third week in May next to the road and directly opposite the glacier below Link Sar. Larson, Lowe, Terraveccia, Tuthill, and Winkelman then followed the 1975 Japanese route across the Link Sar Glacier and up a gully on the left side of the main glacier draining the east flank of Link Sar. They continued along the left side of this glacier to a small basin below the southeast face, then moved left from the Japanese Route, which is exposed to considerable serac danger from above, to the base of a couloir. Although photographs in our possession appeared to show this might be free from serac danger, once they were able to see clearly into it, they observed a serac wall partway up that threatened the entire route. They retreated to their camp in the basin and later that night a large avalanche came out of the couloir and blasted their tents. Deciding that the route was too dangerous, they descended to base camp.

I arrived at base camp late on June 10, two days after arriving in Islamabad, to find the rest of the team now attempting two rock towers further up the valley. These were ca 5200m and situated on the southeast side of the Kondus Glacier about 10 kilometers up valley from base camp. The higher tower to the left they called the Dru because of its close resemblance to the Chamonix peak, and the spire on the right they called the Candy Stripe, due to parallel snow-covered ramps near its summit.

From a camp at ca 4300 m George and Joe tackled the south ridge of the Dru while Steve, Eric and Andy attempted the south face of the Candy Stripe Spire. George and Joe began their route on the west side of the ridge but retreated after some very close calls with large falling rocks that chopped a rope. They made a second attempt that began earlier in the day to avoid rockfall. They climbed a total of eight or nine pitches (5.9 to 5.10+) before retreating due to very friable rock.

Steve, Eric , and Andy left early on June 10. After a brief ice bombardment in the gully to the left of the Candy Stripe, they escaped onto a terrace system and bivouacked at the base of the difficulties. They planned to follow cracks and weaknesses up the center of the face, leading to a prominent peapod-shaped corner at about half height. Because the route looked highly featured and continuous, they limited themselves to free climbing gear, hoping for a rapid ascent.

Next day Andy led the first block of five pitches, consisting of moderate cracks and ice encrusted chimneys (5.7-5.10). After a ca 12-meter leader fall he was able to move right to the base of the peapod corner. Here, Steve took over and due to the compact and seamless nature of the corner was forced to climb several difficult and run out pitches on the right hand wall (5.10-5.11). It became increasingly clear that they had underestimated the difficulties and the amount of gear required, so late in the afternoon they decided to rappel off, rather than spend the night in slings. Their high point was about two-thirds of the way up the wall from the start of the difficulties.

Candy Stripe, showing the high point of the attempt. *Steven Swenson*

The five climbers returned and George and Joe left for home. I set out to reconnoiter a new line on Link Sar that I thought may be a safer route for a second attempt. I crossed the Link Sar glacier and climbed up a gully on the right side of the main glacier that drains the east side of Link Sar. This gully led to a large, beautiful, heather bench full of wild flowers. I followed it up left then back right to a possible campsite directly below the east face of Link Sar.

Andy, Eric, Steve, and I headed back up on June 19 for another attempt. The proposed route followed a complex set of ridges, ramps, and gullies that we hoped would avoid the serac danger that seemed to ring the upper part of the mountain. After camping at my previous high point, we climbed up to a col and then along a crest to the top of a rock tower, from where we could get a good view of the route. Unfortunately, we could now see that it was also exposed to serac fall, so we retreated.

After several days of bad weather we left base camp on June 24 to reconnoiter the north side of Link Sar. We headed up the Kaberi Glacier toward Chogolisa and camped on a spur of rock, noting that so far all the potential routes we had seen on the north face had been exposed to dangerous serac fall. On June 25 we climbed up through an icefall toward the pass that drops into the Charakusa Valley. The weather was not clear and we could only get brief glimpses of the face but from what we could see the ground above contained several large active ice cliffs that were funneling debris into a narrow chute near the bottom, where we would be forced to climb. We returned to base camp on the 26th and left for Skardu on the 27th.

This area is very accessible, being a one-day jeep ride from Skardu. With a short approach, it offers considerable savings in both time and money, since hiring porters is not necessary. There may be safer routes on Link Sar than the ones we explored. Arial photos might prove of great assistance but could be difficult to obtain given the peak's close proximity to the line of control in Kashmir.

STEVEN J. SWENSON, *AAC*

India

Ladakh▲East Karakoram
▲Lahaul & Spiti
Pakistan ▲ Himachal Pradesh
▲Kumaun & Garwal
Delhi Nepal

India

General Overview. Out of approximately 140 expeditions visiting the Indian Himalaya (ca 105 of these coming from local mountaineers), around 60 (19 of which were foreign) were to routine peaks such as Kedar Dome, Jogin, and Stok Kangri, and are not covered in this report. There were no expeditions to Sikkim.

At least two expeditions to the newly formed Uttaranchal State, attempting peaks on the boundaries of the Nanda Devi Sanctuary, faced serious permit problems. Generally, approaching peaks on Sanctuary walls from the outside was permitted. Many expeditions have made ascents in the past, for example Changabang from the north and Nanda Devi East from the east. However, the new state authorities stopped a Korean and an American expedition, which were attempting Dunagiri and Kalanka respectively. The Americans reached their peak after long delays but the Korean team had to change plans and attempt Nilkanth instead. Future expeditions to the Uttaranchal States (consisting of Garhwal and Kumaun regions) and particularly to the peaks on the rim of the Nanda Devi Sanctuary should be careful in assessing the situation when they apply.

HARISH KAPADIA, *Honorary Editor, The Himalayan Journal*

The Indian Mountaineering Foundation, new appointments. During November elections for the President and the Governing Councils of the Indian Mountaineering Foundation were held in New Delhi. The current President, Shri N. N. Vohra, was elected unanimously for a two-year term. Twelve other members were elected and Shri H. C. S. Rawat and Ms. Rita Marwah were appointed Vice-Presidents. Shri N. N. Vohra is an experienced bureaucrat and a senior official who has served in various high capacities with the Government of India. With his knowledge of Government workings he has been instrumental in solving various matters and in helping to promote mountaineering in the country. With Mr. Vohra at the helm the IMF should be in safe hands.

HARISH KAPADIA, *Honorary Editor, The Himalayan Journal*

KASHMIR

Nun, Kun, and Kashmir peaks. Due to the troubles in the state of Kashmir no expeditions were permitted to the popular peaks of Nun and Kun. Similarly, no climbing has been allowed in the entire area of Kishtwar. Both southern Zanskar and Kishtwar have been affected by the terrorist activity in Kashmir.

HARISH KAPADIA, *Honorary Editor, The Himalayan Journal*

EAST KARAKORAM

Singhi Kangri second ascent, and other peaks on the Siachen Glacier. It is reported that an Indian Army expedition, organized by the Corps of Engineers and led by Col. Dinesh Kumar, made the second ascent of 7751m Singhi Kangri close to the head of the Siachen Glacier. In the process members of the team also made the first ascent of a subsidiary 7195m summit, which they refer to as Mercury. The report suggests these two summits were reached on October 2. Other members of the expedition are said to have subsequently climbed Teram Kangri I (7464m), II (7407m), and III (7382m). The group also reached the Indira Col at the head of the Siachen. Other Indian climbers have protested that the name Mercury is totally unsuitable for peaks in this region and should not be encouraged.

MOUNTAIN INFO, *High Mountain Sports 235*

The Arganglas Group, exploration and first ascents. During September a joint Indo-American-British expedition explored the previously unvisited Arganglas Group, which lies south of the Sasar Kangri Range. The Arganglas region is home to the Argans, a community comprising the offspring of Yarkandi (or Kashmiri) Muslims who used to frequent the trade routes to Central Asia, and the local Ladakhi women with whom they cohabited.

After a three-day trek across the 3890m Chamba La, British mountaineers Chris Bonington (joint leader) and Jim Lowther, with Americans, Mark Richey and Mark Wilford, and Indians, Satyabrata Dam, Harish Kapadia (joint leader), Divyesh Muni, Cyrus Shroff, Liaison Officer Vrijendra Lingwal, and Sherpas, Samgyal and Wangchuk, reached a 4800m base camp at the foot of the Phunangama Glacier. Subsequently, the expedition attempted five peaks, reached three passes, and explored five glaciers.

The team split into groups with Shroff and Muni along with Samgyal Sherpa climbing a 6360m virgin peak in the Nono Glacier, which they named Abale (Grandfather). Satyabrata Dam, a navy officer from Mumbai, liaison officer Capt. Lingwal and Sherpa Wangchuk climbed another peak, Amale (6312m Grandmother). Bonington and Lowther with Muni and Shroff put their energies into the far more remote Argan Kangri (6789m), the highest peak in the range, but were unable to really get to grips with the mountain due to avalanche-prone conditions.

Dam and Kapadia with three porters explored the Rassa and Yah Glaciers. A camp was first made in the Rassa glacier and from here the pair unsuccessfully attempted Thugu Peak (6158m). They then traversed west to enter the Yah Glacier which is near the shapely peak of Nya Kangri (6480m). The glacier was full of rocky debris and no water was available except near the snout. They camped at the snout and proceeded along the glacier, camping again below its northwestern head. The following day, September 23, the steep pass, Yah La (5770m), was gained but it was not possible to descend the other side toward the Sumur Lungpa as intended. The party retraced their route back to the Arganglas valley. The expedition also reached Konto La (5920m), a col between Karpo Kangri (6540m) and Pk 6640m at the eastern head of the Phunangama Glacier.

The highlight of the trip was the first ascent and subsequently epic descent of Yamandaka (6218m), south of base camp on the southern rim of the Phunangama Glacier. From the day they arrived at base Richey and Wilford had been captivated by an obvious, direct line up the north face of Pk 6218m. The wall was estimated to be about 1,200 meters high and a steep mix of rock and ice. On September 8 the two Marks crossed the Phunangama glacier and set up camp below the face. From the 9th to the 12th the pair climbed over 20 pitches, each of around 60 meters, on technical rock, ice, and mixed ground. All rock climbing was done with crampons in full winter conditions.

The summit was reached on September 13 after a storm. Due to the heavy snowfall their original plans to descend the northeast ridge to the Phunangama glacier seemed excessively dangerous. Instead, they opted for a descent of the south face to the unknown Shingskam Topko valley on the opposite side of the range. Following an epic descent through canyons and waterfalls, they descended to the Nubra, where they met a very relieved porter sent down from base camp to look for them. That day the rest of the expedition was about to organize a helicopter search. Richey and Wilford named the climb Barbarossa after the World War II German/Russian conflict, and the peak was later named Yamandaka after a Buddhist God, who is fearsome but at the same time benevolent. *(Editor's note: A full account of this climb appears early in this journal.)*

This was a happy expedition and the members formed a very well-knit team, demonstrating that international expeditions need not necessarily involve endless squabbles and displays of flag-waving or chest-thumping. If there were regrets it was because, as Jim Lowther said, "We were here for enjoyment, for pleasure, for a challenge, but our very playground (the Siachen) is also a battle arena, where men are fighting, sacrificing their lives."

HARISH KAPADIA, *Honorary Editor, The Himalayan Journal*

LADAKH

Pangong Range, several ascents. A young team of soldiers from the crack 8 Mountain Division of the Indian Army made several ascents in the remote Pangong Range. These peaks lie close to the border with Tibet and are sandwiched between the Military Road southeast of Leh and the huge Pangong Lake (135 kilometers in length) straddling the border to the north. The expedition was led by Lieutenant Colonel Ashok Abbey, an experienced mountaineer and current Principal of the Nehru Institute of Mountaineering in Uttarkashi, Uttaranchal State.

Base camp was established on August 21 at Tatsang Lungpa (4900m), close to the drivable track between Thangtse and Chushul. The team then moved north to make an advanced camp at 5560m. Higher camps were established at various sites to attempt four peaks: Kangju Kangri (6725m), Unnamed Peak (6580m), Kastet Kangri (6461m), and Unnamed Peak (6134m). Details are as follows: Kangju Kangri via the south face on August 30 (summiteers: Lt. Col. A. Abbey, Sub Ram Lal, Hav Shurbir Singh, Nk Shashi Bhusan, L/Nk Manjeet Singh, L/Nk Anoop Singh, and L/Nk Upinder Singh); Unnamed Peak 6580m via the south face and southwest ridge on Sept 2 (summiteers; Lt. Col. A. Abbey, Sub Prem Singh, Hav Baljinder Singh, Nk RK Manahas, L/Nk Bhagat Singh, Hav Gulbar Singh, L/Nk Sudhir Kumar, Nk Vijay Kumar L/Nk Upinder Singh. and L/Nk Rakesh); Kastet Kangri via the southeast face and southwest ridge on September 3 (summiteers; Capt. R. Bhandari, Capt. PS Cheema, Lt. S. Charan, Sub Ram Lal, Nb Sub Gian Chand, L/Nk Manjeet Singh, L/Nk Bhagat Singh, L/Nk Anoop Singh, L/Nk Jagdeep Singh, L/Nk Dhyan Singh, and Rfn Satender Singh); Unnamed Peak 6134m via the northwest face on September 3 (summiteers; Lt. Col A. Abbey, Hav Shurbir Singh, Nk Shashi Bhusan, L/Nk Rakesh and Sepoy P Vellu).

Finally, 18 members, including the leader, crossed the 5630m high Shimdi La and record- ed the first known traverse of the range, finishing at the southern bank of the Pangong Tso. The expedition accomplished its objectives in excellent shape and form, all in a timeframe of 15 days.

LT. COL. ASHOK ABBEY, *Utterkashi, India*

Chaukula, first ascent. On August 13 Chris Mothersdale and Trevor Willis made the first ascent of Chaukula (6529m) by the southeast ridge (Alpine AD). Chaukula is the highest of a group of mountains in the Rupshu area of the Ladakh Himalaya. It lies just north of the Indus River, about halfway between the two lakes Tso Moriri and Pangong Tso. As Rupshu is a border area, it has a strong army presence. Access is therefore strictly controlled and subject to military approval.

The six-person British expedition traveled eastward by road from Leh. The Chaukula group rises steeply above the road beyond Chumatang village, with the peaks hidden by steep ridges. However, where a valley cuts through these barriers, an elegant pointed snow peak can be seen; this is Chaukula itself. The approach on foot was from the southeast, starting at the roadside in Mahe village. A good trail led over the Yaye La to the valley of the Yaye Tso and then through a narrow rocky streambed to the valley of the Skam Tso. BC was located in this valley, with ABC at 5000m near a small spring just below the glacial moraine. From here, a climb through moraine led to the glacier snout and a clear view of the mountain. In four days equip- ment and food were carried via ABC to below the south face of Chaukula. There were no objec- tive dangers such as crevasses or avalanche prone areas on the glacier itself. Observation from the glacier suggested that the rocks bounding the south face on its right (eastern) side would give the best line of ascent. On August 10 a fairly reasonable bivouac spot was found below the snow line on the south face.

The first team, Mothersdale and Willis, made a late (06:30) start from the bivouac on August 13. Conditions were good with no cloud or wind. From the bivouac at 5930m an unroped scram- ble on good rock led to a 40-meter-wide steep snow gully at 6030m. This was crossed with a rope and protection from ice screws. The next section of rock was steeper and looser. At 6200m the rock gave out to a snow slope that steepened from 40 degrees at the bottom to 50 degrees or more near the crest of the ridge. The ridge led in about 30 meters to the summit. Conditions allowed front pointing on the steep section, and Trevor and Chris reached the summit at about 11:00 a.m.

On the 14th the second team, Miriam Denney and Mike Ratty, moved up the bivouac in poor weather. Following an uncomfortable night they were slowed down by cold and limited visibility. Running out of time, they turned back at 6500m.

MIKE RATTY, *United Kingdom*

LAHAUL

Behali Jot North, first ascent. On June 13-15 Norifusa Akakura, Akitoshi Hayakawa, Kaori Iguchi, Shujiro Katsuno, Takao Kurumizawa, Shoji Sakamoto, and Shizuo Takegami from Japan, with three Indians, Pasang and Prakesh Bodh, and LO AK Sharma, made the first recorded ascent of this 6290m peak via the north ridge. Although the topography of the Baihali Jot group is still a little confused, the North Peak appears to have no previous recorded attempts

HARISH KAPADIA, *Honorary Editor, The Himalayan Journal*

Gangstang (6162m), ascents. This well-known peak north of the Chandra River was attempted during August by senior citizens from Japan. Two separate expeditions approached from two different directions. Tsuneo Suziki's team attempted the southwest ridge. They approached from Keylong via Biliang Nala and set up a base camp at 4650m. The leader was a veteran mountaineer, 65 years old, and the other members ranged from 66 to 72, including two ladies over 64 years old. The summit was reached on August 5 and 8 by six members with two Sherpas and four high altitude porters.

The 1999 and 2001 Neverseen Tower attempts took the couloir on the right and climbed one pitch higher. The central rib was climbed to the summit in 1996. *Xavi Llongueras / Orriols*

The second Japanese expedition comprised five senior members between the ages of 50 and 67. Led by Tatsumi Mizumo, they reached the summit via the north face to east ridge. The climbers approached the mountain from Jankar Sumdo and set up a base camp at 4050m. The top was gained on August 5 by four members with three Sherpas and two high-altitude porters.

HARISH KAPADIA, *Honorary Editor, The Himalayan Journal*

Neverseen Tower, attempts in 1999 and 2001. After a four-day trek from Karpat in the Miyar Valley, Fidel Casablancas, Enric Nadal, and I established base camp on September 13, 1999 at 4650m on the moraine of the Tawa Glacier, two hours walk from the Neverseen Tower (ca 5980m). On September 15 we installed a tent at the base of the Tower (ca 5000m) and two days later Fidel and I left this camp at 5:00 a.m. with very heavy backpacks. At 8:00 a.m. we were at the base of the couloir that gives access to the 5450m col south of the Tower. We climbed the couloir in six hours. We climbed the first pitch in the center of the couloir, then crossed to the right to reach the south col in a further four pitches (250m, five pitches, V and 70 degrees). We spent the night on this narrow pass. Next day, September 18, was cloudy and cold. Fidel climbed one pitch on the south face (45m, 6a and A2) but a storm appeared to be approaching. We decided to go down and not leave any fixed ropes. Next day in base camp there was 25cm of snow. We made a good decision.

On September 21 with Enric we climbed an unnamed peak at the end of Tawa glacier (ca 5700m). This was an easy "trekking" peak (60 degrees). On September 23, Fidel and I made another attempt on the Tower but we were tired and not in good condition. Porters had been ordered for the 25th and we left for Manali on that date.

On September 19, 2001 Fidel and I again left Manali for the Miyar Valley. This year the autumn was abnormally cold. We reached our 1999 base camp on the 23rd, and in a further four days had all our equipment at the base of the Tower where we had our camp in 1999. It then snowed for two days. The conditions in the couloir had changed a lot in two years. There was much less snow and the previous belay anchors were three meters above us and impossible to reach. The climbing was harder and we took five days to ascend the couloir, fixing ropes from new belay anchors on the left flank. By October 9 we had the couloir equipped and all our equipment on the small col (5450m). Next day we started climbing but were hit by a storm that sent us back to base camp. After three days of continuous snow the sun began to shine again. On October 14 we climbed directly to the col. We slept there in a hammock but the night was terribly cold: -25°C. Next day Fidel climbed the same pitch as he had first in 1999, but his fingers were very cold and the conditions were bad with snow on the holds. He returned to the col and we spent a second night there. This was also bad and as in the morning we had very cold fingers and toes, we decided to go down. On October 17, we left base camp and the following day reached Manali by public bus. For a report on the first ascent of Neverseen Tower and neighboring peaks, see *AAJ* 1997, pages 274-276.

XAVI LLONGUERAS I ORRIOLS, *Servei General d'Informació de Muntanya, Spain*

Unnamed Peak 6184m, attempt. Situated northeast of Phabrang, this unnamed and unclimbed peak was unsuccessfully attempted during July and August by Yasutada Sawairi's 12-member

Japanese team. The expedition approached from Darcha on the Manali to Leh Military Road and made base camp above Jankar Sumdo. From here they followed the glacier on the right flank and on August 8 achieved a maximum height of ca 5750m. Much bad weather and a constant danger from stonefall are cited as the reasons for failure. In 1999 another Japanese expedition had attempted this peak via the same route.

HARISH KAPADIA, *Honorary Editor, The Himalayan Journal*

Baralacha Peak (6111m), second ascent. This peak close to the Baralacha Pass received a second ascent on September 5 by three members from an Indian team led by Ms. Kalpana Mekherjee. The leader with Taponayan Ghosh and Partha Majumdar reached the summit. The first ascent took place in August 1999 when five Indian mountaineers from Howrah climbed the south ridge, which appears to have been a straightforward ascent over shattered rock, scree, and snow (see *AAJ* 2000).

HARISH KAPADIA, *Honorary Editor, The Himalayan Journal*

Ramjak, attempt. This is a challenging 6318m unclimbed mountain with a sharp icy summit. The peak is located near the Shingo La (ca 5100m), which is crossed on a popular trekking route from Himachal Pradesh to Zanskar. Prior to 2001 there had been at least three attempts on the mountain and one Indian climber had died on its slopes. The first attempt took place in 1994, when a ladies team from Mumbai approached from the west. Another Mumbai team attempted the peak the following year and again in 1996, when Dinesh Shertate died at 5400m due to medical complications.

This year a nine-member expedition organised and sponsored by the Indian Mountaineering Foundation and led by Lt. Col. S. Upadhyay reached the area in early August and trekked along the well-known route from Darcha to Palamo. Base camp was established a little short of Chuminakpo at ca 4620m. After a reconnaissance, Camp 1 (4880m) was set up beside a glacial stream. The next three days were spent exploring a site for Camp 2, which was ultimately established on August 11. On the 12th the climbers reached a rock wall and fixed 400m of rope through a gully. After surmounting the wall and reaching a high point of 5800m, they saw a long ridge running up to the summit. Deterred by the terrain above and the length of ridge still to be climbed, they retreated.

HARISH KAPADIA, *Honorary Editor, The Himalayan Journal*

Unnamed Peak (6248 m), first ascent. This peak lies southeast of Ramjak on the opposite side of the valley and was climbed for the first time on August 15 by Indians, Nitin Gandhi, Paresh Rathod, and Sudhir Raut. These three set up base camp at Chuminakpo (4660m) then continued up valley towards the Shingo La. Moving east, they climbed to a high camp at ca 5410m, from where they ascended steep slopes to a col. The summit was just 200m above them and was gained in poor weather.

HARISH KAPADIA, *Honorary Editor, The Himalayan Journal*

CB 14 (6078m), attempts. During August two expeditions attempted this peak on the South Dakka Glacier. Keiichi Isobe's three-member Japanese team made an attempt on the 28th but failed and subsequently ran out of time. Ermanno Pizzogolio led a 15-member expedition from Italy that planned to attempt the southeast face to northeast ridge. Unfortunately, plagued with continuously bad weather, they were forced to give up.

HARISH KAPADIA, *Honorary Editor, The Himalayan Journal*

Tagne and Sagar, first ascents. A team of young climbers from Imperial College of London made a highly exploratory visit to the fairly recently de-restricted area north of the Kunzum La. The peaks here are non-technical and rather arid, the weather mostly hot and dry. In fact the party reported frequent daytime shade temperatures of 36°C at their base camp during their stay in July. Dan Carrivick, Jon Ellis, Alan Geer, Stephen Jolly, and Andrew Vine approached via the Chandra River and Tokpo Yongma (where a horseman attached to their expedition was killed when he fell in to the river and was swept away). Two first ascents were achieved. On July 20 Tagne (6111m, though sometimes quoted as 6404m) was ascended via the south glacier. The climbers worked up scree to gain a ridge on the south face, from where they reached the upper plateau of the hanging glacier. They then traversed the amphitheater above to gain the west ridge (45 degrees). The crest led past three icy sections (Scottish II) to the summit. The route was comparable with an Alpine AD.

Later, on the 26th, three of the team ascended Sagar (6030m), again at an estimated AD, via the east ridge from a col at the head of the north glacier. The crest had a number of steps at ca 40 degrees and a 100-meter-long icy knife edge. Tagne lies at 32° 35' 44" N and 77° 39' 00" E, while Sagar is situated at 32° 37' 19" N and 77° 38' 04" E.

MOUNTAIN INFO, *High Mountain Sports 235*

SPITI

Chau Chau Kang Nila (6304m), ascent. This popular peak in Spiti was climbed by Dipankar Ghosh's West Bengal expedition, which included three handicapped persons.

HARISH KAPADIA, *Honorary Editor, The Himalayan Journal*

WESTERN GARHWAL

GANGOTRI

Gangotri I (6672m) ascent. Although this high peak south of Gangotri Temple has now seen many ascents, one on September 26 was notable. On that day 12 members of an all-women Indian expedition organized by the Indian Mountaineering Foundation reached the summit via the normal route up the northeast ridge. The team, led by Lata Joshi, started from a base camp in the Rudugaira Kharak and was one of three IMF sponsored expeditions in 2001.

HARISH KAPADIA, *Honorary Editor, The Himalayan Journal*

The first ascent of Manda II (21,548') took took a route on the backside of this view from the east. Arnab Banerjee

Bhrigu Parvat (6041m), ascent. A nine-member Indian expedition led by Dr Anjan Chaudhary approached this peak north of Manda via the Kedar Kharak. The summit was reached on September 2 by Tanmoy Chakraborty and Arun Danti Das.

HARISH KAPADIA, *Honorary Editor, The Himalayan Journal*

Manda I (6511m), ascent. A two-member Korean team attempted this peak via the west face and north ridge, the route taken by the 1981 first ascensionists. Kim Hyoung-Duk and an Indian High Altitude Porter, Laxman, made a final push on September 17. Laxman stopped short of the summit but the Korean continued to the top

HARISH KAPADIA, *Honorary Editor, The Himalayan Journal*

Manda II, second ascent and new route. The climbing history of the Manda group is surprisingly short. Until 2001 Manda II (the highest summit, 6568m) had been climbed only once; from the

The Manda II route from Camp 3 to the summit. Arnab Banerjee

west (Kedar Glacier) in 1982 by an American expedition, which followed the South Ridge from the col between Manda III and II. Manda I (6510m) has seen a few ascents from the west *(Editor's note: Manda III has been climbed once; in 1992 by a predominately British expedition.).* A group of climbers from Junipers (a Calcutta-based climbing club) decided to attempt the peaks from the east. The team comprised Arnab Banerjee, Avijit Das, Arka Ghosh, Kaushik Pal, RK Gambhisana, Thapa (HAP), Dil (HAP), and Dharmi (cook).

We established our base camp on June 9 at 4200m beside the terminal moraine of the Bhrigupanth glacier. After an initial reconnaissance, we realized that Manda II and I would be very difficult to climb by a direct route. Instead, we decided to attempt Manda II and III from the glacier between them. We established Camp 1 at an altitude of 4600m.

Our first major obstacle was a ca 300-meter icefall just above Camp 1. We spent two days serious ice climbing on very dangerous terrain, fixing rope and opening the route to Camp 2. The route was over steep ice faces and broken ice pillars, which were bombarded by rocks falling from high above. We had a few narrow escapes but decided to continue.

The weather closed down as we occupied Camp 2 (5000m), forcing us to take a rest day. After a night of heavy snowfall, the morning dawned clear, so we went ahead with opening the route to Camp 3 (5500m). This route required only one fixed rope on a rock face but demanded tricky navigation through deceptive terrain comprising ice falls and rock fall zones.

From Camp 3 we decided to concentrate on Manda II as it seamed more feasible. Early on the morning of June 21 I started fixing rope below the summit ridge, while the three other members in the summit team followed me. We fixed 360 meters of rope in a tiny ice gully running through sheer rock faces. Then we continued our climb toward the summit, hoping to make the ascent on the same day. Though the weather worsened, we fixed another rope (a total of 760 meters was fixed) just before the main summit and stood on top at around 4: 00 p.m. We celebrated for a while before rushing down to the top camp.

The next day our second team repeated the route to the summit. Climbing down the mountain was another saga. The icefall between Camps 2 and 1 had collapsed, forcing us to re-open the route. Two of us were hit by rock fall but ultimately the team managed to reach base camp without any major casualty. Climbing a new route on a high Himalayan giant is always a very satisfying experience but the joy of exploring rarely visited terrain added more fun.

ARNAB BANERJEE, *India, Junipers.*

Meru North Peak (6450m), attempt. During September and October a three-member Japanese expedition led by Hiroyoshi Manome attempted the northeast face and the north pillar route. They established camps and reached 6050m. Falling stones and objective dangers were experienced. Finally, an avalanche swept away a cache of equipment, which included all their plastic boots, so the team had no option but to retreat.

HARISH KAPADIA, *Honorary Editor, The Himalayan Journal*

Meru Central, spring attempt and successful autumn first ascent. On his second visit to the Gangotri in 2001, Valeri Babanov from Russia made the much sought after first ascent of 6310m Meru Central, commonly referred to as The Shark's Fin. Before his successful ascent in September there had been possibly as many as 15 separate attempts to climb this difficult summit on the sharp crest between Meru South and North. The majority of these attempts had concentrated on the northeast rib, which finishes up the spectacular granite prow of the Shark's Fin and is by far the most compelling line on the peak.

Babanov and his wife Olya arrived at Tapovan Base Camp (4270m) at the end of April. More or less following the line taken on all previous attempts, Babanov climbed the huge snow/ice slope to the right of the initial rocky rib, then beneath the "Black Wall" traversed up left along a ramp to reach the crest. The weather was poor and Babanov reached a high point during mid May of ca 5800m before retreating because of dangerous avalanche conditions. He returned in August and summited solo on September 22 following an easier but loose line to the right of his earlier attempt. Babanov named the route, Shangri La, and graded it Alpine ED F5c/6a A1/A2 M5 and 75-degree ice. He was later awarded the French Piolet d'Or prize for 2001. His full account appears earlier in this *Journal*.

BASED ON REPORTS FROM VALERI BABANOV

Meru South (6660m), east face attempt. On September 17 a six-member Spanish team led by Jordi Corominas established base camp below the south and highest summit of the Meru Group. Advanced base was later established at 4900m and an attempt made on the unclimbed east face/ridge. On October 2 the climbers reached 6100m but were forced down. A second

The first ski descent of Shivling—the "Matterhorn of the Himalaya"—via a line close to the west arête. The rappel was 80 meters long, and the 50-degree slopes below it were sustained. *Emmanuel Ratouis*

attempt, which took place on October 6 and 7, fared slightly better and a height of 6400m was achieved. Serious stone fall prevented them from completing the climb.

HARISH KAPADIA, *Honorary Editor, The Himalayan Journal*

Shivling (6543m), first ski descent. Emmanuel Ratouis led a three-member team, which reached the summit via the west ridge in a 20-hour push from base camp over May 7-8. Ratouis then made the first ski descent of the mountain. Apart from an 80-meter section which he rappelled, he skied all the way, negotiating slopes up to 55 degrees. He took off his skis just 10 minutes walk above base camp. Two other expeditions also summited via the west ridge during the spring.

HARISH KAPADIA, *Honorary Editor, The Himalayan Journal*

Bhagirathi III (6454m), attempt. The four-man German team of Robert Jasper, Walter Hölzler, and Rainer Treppte with cameraman Jochen Schmoll planned to climb the true crest of the southwest pillar, left of the 1982 Barton-Fyffe Route. The climbers established an advanced base during early May in the glacier bay below the west face. They then climbed the left (north) side of the lower crest to place a portaledge camp on the obvious snow patch at around half-height on the pillar. However, bad weather and an early monsoon dogged their efforts and they eventually had to give up in early June after Holzer and Treppte had reached a high point of ca 5800m, just 100 meters or so short of the end of the major rock climbing difficulties.

HARISH KAPADIA, *Honorary Editor, The Himalayan Journal*

Chaukhamba I (7138m), attempts and tragedy. In May a 14-member team from Calcutta led by Brijes Dey attempted the north face of this high mountain, approaching from Badrinath and Mana. They found the huge face very avalanche prone, with many large crevasses barring their way. The attempt was given up. In September another Indian team led by Ujjwal Ganguly also attempted the normal route on the north face. On the 14th four members made a summit attempt from Camp 3 at 6350m. This failed and two members returned down the mountain on the following day when the weather turned bad. Palash Mukherjee and Serabjit Sadhu remained and made a second attempt on the 16th, when the weather improved. However, once again they decided to retreat and began descending at around 10:30 a.m., when the sun had already softened the snow slopes. Within an hour they were engulfed by an avalanche, which was witnessed from Camp 1. Although the Indo-Tibet Border Police sent in helicopters on the 22nd to search for the missing climbers, the two bodies were never located.

HARISH KAPADIA, *Honorary Editor, The Himalayan Journal*

CENTRAL GARHWAL

Shri Parvat, attempt and Bhagat Peak, ascent. Rajesh Gadgil's nine member team from Bombay planned to attempt the second ascent of the beautiful 6175m fluted snow peak, Shri Parvat, which rises from the Deo Dekhni Plateau west of Mana-Badrinath and has not been climbed since its original ascent in 1934 by Eric Shipton and Bill Tilman. Base camp was established at

Nilkanth, 6596m, from the southwest, showing the west ridge route repeated in 2001. *Marko Prezelj* opposite page: Nilkanth from the east.

Khadu Kharak (ca 4400m) alongside the Bhagirathi Kharak Glacier. Subsequently, two more camps were placed at 4950m and 5350m on the Deo Dekhni Plateau. The attempt on Shri Parvat was thwarted due to bad weather but four members earned a consolation prize by making the second ascent of a nearby small peak, Bhagrat (5650m). This was first climbed in 1997 by myself and Ang Nyima Sherpa during an expedition that followed Shipton and Tilman's traverse from the Bhagirathi to the Arwa Valley via the 5700m Shrak La.

HARISH KAPADIA, *Honorary Editor, The Himalayan Journal*

Nilkanth, fourth ascent. The Indian Himalaya offers alpinists unique challenges. Many of these mountain peaks have been discovered slowly due to their infamous reputation and bureaucratic obstacles. The British, who are most connected with this area through their colonial heritage, have held a leading role. Arwa, Changabang, Kishtwar, Rimo, and other interesting objectives have been the result of systematic discovery and exploration of the individual mountain chains. As the main expedition of PZS (Alpine Association of Slovenia) for 2002 (Chomo Lonzo in Tibet) was canceled, my enthusiasm and amazement over the continued new ascents by the British in this part of the world gained new dimensions. In the beginning of September, Matic Jost and I redirected our efforts, energy, and motivation. We decided to approach the Himalaya from India as opposed to expensive Tibet. We first chose Kishtwar but due to the political situation could not get a permit, so we opted instead for Nilkanth.

We obtained the climbing permit for Nilkanth in three short weeks. The minimum term for permit application is three months. The Indian Mountaineering Federation therefore generously showed that, with interest, paper work can be done quickly. We asked the Himalayan Run and Trek agency to help us in the field and it offered very good service at a reasonable price (transport, porters, cook, and food in base camp). However, the climbing permit for a mountain above 6500m and the basic expense for the liaison officer alone amounted to $2,900.

Nilkanth (6596m) had received only three successful ascents before we visited it and several unsuccessful attempts from various directions. According to the available information, the southwest face of the mountain seemed the most interesting for climbing. The third ascent of the mountain was completed from this side via the west ridge in spring 2000 by Martin Moran's commercially organized expedition. We wanted to climb either the south or southwest face, and judging from the only photo we had, we assumed the climbing would be interesting and mixed in character (rock, snow, and ice).

Accompanied by Zare Guzelj, our doctor, we dealt with formalities at the IMF (as the last expedition of the season), reached base camp at 4050m after only three days of walking, and began acclimatizing. The conditions on the mountain contrasted strongly with our expectations based on the only photo we had from this side. There was very little snow. The weather was unstable most of the time–clear in the morning, cloudy in the afternoon (some snow fall). We decided to do the second (and last part) of our acclimatization program on the west ridge, which was of an appropriate height and provided our most probable descent route if we were to climb the southwest face.

We established an advanced base at 5100m below the southwest face and began to climb the west ridge October 13. Conditions were not easy. On the initial slope we encountered many big stones and granite blocks, which were all threatening to move due to lack of snow and ice. The lower part of the ridge turned out to be much more demanding than expected, again due to lack of ice and a thin layer of fresh snow on the rocks. At the beginning we found some unreliable fixed ropes which we didn't use. At about 5600m we arranged an uncomfortable bivouac and continued to climb to the bivouac site. After another uncomfortable night, we descended all the way to base camp. We rappelled nearly 1000 meters, during which falling rock damaged our 70-meter rope so badly that we reached the bottom of the face with only 50 meters remaining.

On October 20, after four days' rest, we left for advanced base in order to attempt the southwest face, our main goal. Due to the high temperature, we were exposed to large quantities of falling ice and rocks while approaching the face. When we arrived at our small tent we were surprised to see that the snow and ice bands, which connected the individual parts of the face, had melted. The logical passages were exposed to falling rocks and water. We carefully considered the possibility of a less risky option across steep sections less exposed to stone fall but decided to descend. Next day the weather confirmed our decision, as the whole face was again covered with a fresh thin blanket of snow. The only alternative was to take an illogical line that involved risky rock climbing (exposed to falling rock and ice), where we would have to use rock shoes, different equipment, and a different strategy.

Despite the rapid organization necessary, the expedition was successful. We made the second ascent of the west ridge in pure alpine style and the fourth overall ascent of Nilkanth. It took us three days to climb and descend a 1500-meter-high route (twice we bivouacked at the same spot). The first climbers (who needed seven days for ascent and descent) estimated the route D+/TD-, with maximum rock difficulties of IV+ (UIAA) and mixed climbing at Scottish II to III (see page 369 of *AAJ* 2001). We more or less agree with the estimate, although given our circumstances and the complex climbing, we felt it more like TD. The conditions necessitated using crampons on plastic boots at all times.

We became acquainted with the Indian Himalaya and its organizational features. Slovenians have not been as active here as in neighboring Nepal, and we are ready to share our experience with anyone who might be interested in this part of the world.

MARKO PREZELJ, *Alpine Association of Slovenia*

The summit ridge (top), crux (middle) and the rock bar pitch on Nilkanth's west ridge route. *Marko Prezelj*

Nilkanth (6596 m), attempts: A seven-member Korean expedition led by Ja Eok Gook originally hoped to attempt Dunagiri, which is on the outer walls of the Nanda Devi Sanctuary. In August they proceeded with full clearance toward this peak but once in the area were then denied permission from the Uttaranchal Forest Authorities. They had to change their objective at the last minute to the unclimbed south face of Nilkanth. Camp II was established but the attempt was called off due to stone fall, avalanches, and crevasses.

The following month Daisuke Narumi's Japanese expedition tried to climb the peak via the north face and upper west ridge from the Satopanth Bank. They tried to overcome a dangerous icefall on the north face but avalanches stopped their progress. They then attempted the west ridge but only reached the col at the start. One member was sick and they finally called off the expedition.

HARISH KAPADIA, *Honorary Editor, The Himalayan Journal*

Kamet (7756m), attempts and ascent. Jerzy Tillak's eight-member Polish expedition attempted the unrepeated west ridge. This team of strong climbers reached 7390m on August 26 having approached the peak from Gamsali and Niti. Camp 4 was placed at 6600m and Camp 5 at 7120m. The Poles encountered very high winds and loose powder snow, which forced them to give up the climb. An Indian expedition comprising senior citizens from retired police and other officers attempted the standard route in the autumn. The 67-year-old leader, Ashwini Kumar, is reported to have died on reaching the lower slopes. Debasashi Kanji's West Bengal team also failed on the same route. However, in early September an Indo-Tibet Border Police expedition was successful. The summiteers included Sange Sherpa, the only man to have climbed Everest from all three sides—south, north, and east (Kangshung).

HARISH KAPADIA, *Honorary Editor, The Himalayan Journal*

EASTERN GARHWAL

Dunagiri, local access problems and an ascent. A Korean expedition had full clearance from Delhi to climb this famous 7066m peak west of Changabang and the Nanda Devi Inner Sanctuary rim. Arriving in the area during August the Uttaranchal Forest Authorities denied them access on the grounds that the peak lay in the prohibited Nanda Devi Sanctuary. After much delay and failed negotiations, the team eventually had to accept Nilkanth instead (see above) but now much time had been lost. The Indian Army expedition that climbed Nanda Devi had no such trouble and were able to make a successful ascent of Dunagiri.

HARISH KAPADIA, *Honorary Editor, The Himalayan Journal*

Kalanka, attempt. We arrived in India on August 24 with permission to visit and climb the remote north side of this 6931m peak during the months of September and October. Although we had official permission from the Indian Mountaineering Foundation for the true north face, once in the region we came up against numerous and lengthy bureaucratic difficulties and delays instigated by the newly formed Uttaranchal State (particularly their Forestry Department). Kalanka lies on the border of the Nanda Devi Sanctuary and is thus a sensitive, environmentally protected mountain. There were some ongoing political power struggles between the federal and state governments in the administration of these lands. The delays cost us about four days in lost time waiting in the village of Joshimath. Given the situation in the region, our agents in New Delhi (Shikhar Travels) did everything they could to facilitate our expedition and succeeded in obtaining a safe passage for our small group. Our base camp was located at 4500m in the same place as the Russian-American 1998 north face of Changabang Expedition BC. Once situated at the foot of the face at our well-stocked advanced base camp (5100m), Jack experienced altitude-related health problems resulting in our only being able to make a detailed reconnaissance of our intended route and the north face. The site of our first planned camp on the face, a small bergshrund above the lower seracs, was at 5660m and stocked with climbing equipment and food. During our stay in the region we experienced exceptionally good weather. We left base camp on October 9 with high hopes of someday returning to our chosen objective. Our base camp cooks from Shikhar Travels, liason officer, and porters could not have been more helpful and friendly.

JACK ROBERTS AND CARLOS BUHLER, AAC

Lampak II (6181m), ascent. All seven members of an Indian expedition led by Swaraj Ghosh made the probable third ascent of this peak between the Siruanch and Kalla Glaciers above the road head at Malari. Base camp was established on August 29 at 4500m and the summit reached via the southeast ridge on September 5. Apart from the leader the other summiteers, all from West Bengal, were Sibrata Banerjee, B. Biswas, Gautam Chatterjee, Anal Das, B. Jetty, and N. P. Rao.

HARISH KAPADIA, *Honorary Editor, The Himalayan Journal*

Siruanch Glacier, Shambhu Ka Qilla, first ascent. On May 16 six members of a British expedition, Roland Arnison, Angela Benham, Chris Drinkwater, Titch Kavanagh, Andy Phillips, and myself (leader) made the first ascent of a previously unnamed peak approximately five kilometers north of Tirsuli on the eastern boundary of the Siruanch Glacier. In doing so we became the first mountaineers, and most probably the first humans, to visit the upper glacier regions below the north side of Tirsuli West. Despite full IMF permission, we were still forced to spend four days in Joshimath before the civil authorities there sanctioned an Inner Line Permit. Then, from the normal road head at Malari (ca 3000m) we spent over a week exploring a suitable route into the Siruanch Gad before eventually setting up base camp on May 2 quite low down in the valley at an area called Chilkuanch (ca 3600m). We were almost certainly the first non-Indian mountaineering group to enter this valley since the 1950 Scottish expedition.

Our expedition had a permit for the then-unclimbed Tirsuli West (7035m). The north side of this peak is a 2500-meter high very broad snow/ice face almost entirely composed of a jumble of seracs, hanging glaciers, and steep rock buttresses. These are capped by large cornices on the long summit ridge. It was soon concluded that an objectively safe line did not exist and we turned our attention to a side glacier to the north, which at its head held an attractive peak on the watershed ridge south of Uja Tirche.

After clearing permission for the climb with our liaison officer, a camp was established at ca 5400m in the upper glacier basin below the south face of the unnamed peak, and a potential line was identified linking a series of couloirs. Six climbers left at 9 p.m. on the 15th, and by dawn the following morning, after relatively straightforward climbing, we were grouped below the steep summit tower. The latter was climbed via a groove system in two pitches, the first being good Scottish 4. The descent went without incident until the last steep snow couloir leading down to the glacier. Here, Angela Benham slipped and fell 300 meters, hitting rocks and sustaining whip-lash injuries to neck and shoulder. We managed to get her back to camp that night and the following morning she was able to walk unladen down to Base. The ca 6160m peak was christened Shambhu Ka Qilla–the Fortress of Shiva—and the 700-meter route on the south face graded an Alpine D+. Photographs taken during the ascent seem to suggest that existing mapping does not accurately reflect the mountain topography in the area, especially with regard to the location of Chalab (6160m), attempted only once from the east (Girthi Ganga), in 1988.

COLIN KNOWLES, *United Kingdom*

Tirsuli West (7035m), attempt. In May a seven-member German team led by Ralf Messbacher attempted the west ridge, reaching ca 6320m, much the same altitude as that achieved on the only previous attempt, in 1995 by an Anglo-New Zealand party. The Germans suffered from generally bad weather whilst they were traversing the several smaller summits that characterize the lower section of this ridge, and were eventually thwarted by avalanches and very loose rock.

HARISH KAPADIA, *Honorary Editor, The Himalayan Journal*

Tirsuli West (7035 m), first ascent. A team from the Nehru Institute of Mountaineering, led by its vice principal, Maj. Kulwant S. Dhami, attempted this virgin peak in June. Located ca 45 km from Jumma, the road head on the Joshimath-Malari road, it was the only remaining unclimbed 7000m+ peak in both the Garhwal and Kumaun Himalaya. NIM is a premier training institute in India and many of its instructors are famed mountaineers, who participate in such ventures.

The team established several camps, the first at the village Dunagiri on June 27, base camp at Bagini on the 28th, Camp 1 on the lateral moraine, and Camp 2 on the Bagini Glacier near the base of the mountain. The team then fixed ca 1300 meters of rope on the rock face of the southwest ridge, and established Camp 3. Climbers then stayed at Camp 2 for five days and fixed more rope, but due to hostile conditions returned to Camp 2 on July 11 and waited for the weather to clear. On July 13 they again reached Camp 3. On the 14th the route was opened to the site of Camp 4 and tents, etc., established the following day. The weather remained bad but the climbers continued to open the route and on the 17th reached the top. The summit was gained at 11:20 a.m. by seven members: the leader, Dhami, SS Bhandari, Deputy Leader Rattan Singh, Amrik Singh, Jagmohan Singh, Karamjit Singh, and Laxman Singh. A total of 3000 meters of rope was fixed. For the first time this virgin mountain unveiled glimpses of its hidden treasures to summiteers from the NIM, who live by the motto of the Institute, "Success lies in Courage."

HARISH KAPADIA, *Honorary Editor, The Himalayan Journal*

Nanda Ghunti, new route. Martin Moran led a six-member British expedition to this 6390m peak. Moran has been a regular visitor to the Garhwal for many years, carrying out significant exploration and making a number of noteworthy ascents. After establishing a camp at 5400m and making a reconnaissance of the mountain, Mike Brennan and the guide, Andy Nisbet, made the first ascent of the south face. The route was completed on June 2 and followed a curving couloir (50-55 degrees) between two pinnacles to reach the upper slopes. These in turn were climbed directly to the summit. The route was awarded an Alpine grade of AD+.

On the same day the rest of the team (Moran with Ian Bapty, Tom Rankin, Des Winterbone, and a local high altitude porter, H Singh), repeated the Normal route up the north ridge. This entailed a long approach from Hom Kund (4650m) over the Ronti Saddle (Ronti is a 6063m peak immediately north of Nanda Ghunti). Most of the route was straightforward, though there was one section of ca 50-degrees. A planned attempt on nearby Trisul was abandoned due to bad weather.

HARISH KAPADIA, *Honorary Editor, The Himalayan Journal*

Nanda Devi Sanctuary, investigative expedition. The president of the Indian Mountaineering Foundation, N Vohra, organized an expedition in June-July 2001 to investigate whether the Sanctuary should be opened to climbers, trekkers, and scientific research (the Sanctuary has been closed since 1983 and even local villagers have been banned entry to their traditional grazing rights). The team was given clearance by the Ministry of Environment and Forest, and the Government of Uttaranchal, a legal requirement as the area has been designated a National Park under an act of Parliament. The IMF expedition studied the area and submitted a 100-page report, which recommended controlled opening of the Sanctuary. This is also the wish of the Uttaranchal State. No decision has yet been taken by the Government, though from a press report it appears that limited access to scientific expeditions may possibly be granted. During their stay in the area three members of the expedition reached the Sunderdhunga Col (5550m) on the southern rim of the Sanctuary, east of Maiktoli (6803m). The only other recorded visit to this col was made by Shipton and Tilman 67 years earlier.

HARISH KAPADIA, HONORARY *Editor, The Himalayan Journal*

Nanda Devi, ascent and environmental clean up. In September a 40-member team from the Garhwal Rifles Regiment successfully climbed the 7816m peak via the Normal Route. This is the third ascent of Nanda Devi since the Inner Sanctuary was officially closed in 1983. All three ascents have come from the Indian Military (Army in 1993, ITBP in 2000, and Army again in 2001). The expedition also collected non-biodegradable garbage left behind by previous expeditions in this 2000-square km bio-reserve. This act was a very significant step in terms of removing environmental pollution from a reserve known for its unique diversity and rich flora and fauna. A total of 83 species of animals and 114 species of plants are found in this biosphere; 14 of the animals on are a list of near extinct species.

Soon after the first forays into the area, a large succession of expeditions left piles of junk and garbage on the mountain slopes. From 1964 onward Nanda Devi experienced the indignity of several hush-hush expeditions attempting to place a nuclear spying device on her summit. Ten years later, the sanctuary was thrown open to mountaineers. The resulting stampede of young Western climbers eager to make their marks on the mountaineering record books led to an environmental disaster. Owing to a short season, forests were hacked to build bridges and provide fodder for animals. Fragile juniper slopes above the tree line were deliberately burnt to provide charcoal for porters accompanying expeditions. Sources are quoted as saying, "In a few decades, the sanctuary, at its worst, resembled a combination of a garbage dump and a badly-maintained public toilet, the animal life reduced to intruding man, the juniper and undergrowth mercilessly destroyed to provide firewood. Ultimately, the sanctuary was declared a national park."

HARISH KAPADIA, *Honorary Editor, The Himalayan Journal*

Nanda Devi, attempt and tragedy. A 16-member team led by Mohammed Mamun Rashid had major plans to climb the 7434m East Peak and traverse to the Main summit. Approaching during the autumn via the usual route from the east, they had set up base camp in the Lwa Gad when a high-altitude supporter, Ang Tendi Sherpa, died. The entire expedition was abandoned. It was felt that the team was possibly not well-prepared for such a serious project.

HARISH KAPADIA, *Honorary Editor, The Himalayan Journal*

KUMAUN

Panch Chuli III, attempt. A 10-member expedition, sponsored by the Indian Mountaineering Foundation and led by Purmal Singh Dharmashaku, claimed to have made the first ascent of 6312m Panch Chuli III from the east, with Tarun Roy from Delhi and three local high altitude porters reaching a point just a few meters below the narrow summit cornice on June 12. They had reportedly climbed via the east face and southeast ridge. However, it now seems that the claim is false. It would appear that the highest point reached was a col on the ridge leading to the main summit. The leader of the expedition has so far only provided a very scanty report and stated that all the summit pictures were subsequently stolen. The Indian Mountaineering Foundation, which organized the expedition, has now agreed that the claim is false and the whole trip remains under a cloud of controversy.

HARISH KAPADIA, *Honorary Editor, The Himalayan Journal*

Panch Chuli IV (6334m), attempt. During May a 12-member team from West Bengal led by Samir Sengupta approached this peak via Sobaba to the east. The climbers established two camps on the mountain (previously climbed only once in 1995) but were prevented from making a summit attempt due to bad weather.

HARISH KAPADIA, *Honorary Editor, The Himalayan Journal*

Nepal

New peaks in 2001. A press release from Kathmandu on April 10 declared that His Majesty's Government would open 15 new peaks within one week and 50 more during the post monsoon season. However, after the spring season was underway the Government announced the opening of just nine peaks with immediate effect. This is the first time any peaks have been opened while a climbing season was in progress. These nine peaks comprised six in the Khumbu and one each in the Manaslu, Annapurna, and Dhaulagiri regions. The peaks listed were: Lhotse Middle (8413m), Peak 38 (Shartse II: 7590m),

Lhotse Middle, 8413m, just opened and already climbed (see full story earlier in the journal). *Yuri Koshelenko*

Hungchi (7136m), Numri (6677m), Teng Kangpoche (6500m), and Nhe Serku (5927m), all in the Khumbu, plus P2 (6251m) in the Manaslu region, Thorang Peak (5751m) in the Annapurna region, and Thapa Peak (6012m) in the Dhaulagiri region.

New Peaks for 2002. The Government of Nepal officially announced the opening of 103 additional peaks to foreign expeditions. The announcement came on Christmas Eve 2001 and took effect from March 1, 2002. Unlike the 10 peaks brought on to the list in 1998 (Visit Nepal Year) for a two-year period only, it is reported these new additions will be permanent. Speaking in Kathmandu, Ganesh Raj Karki, Chief of the Mountaineering Department at the Ministry of Culture, Tourism and Civil Aviation, said, "This would not only help promote Nepal as the prime destination for mountaineering but also help development of the areas around these mountains."

Together with the nine peaks added to the list in spring 2001, mountaineers will now be allowed to climb 263 peaks throughout the Nepal Himalaya. Additionally, the Government has substantially eased the financial and administrative burden on many future expeditions by abolishing the need for a Liaison Officer on peaks below 6500m. This means out of the 263 available peaks, from now on only 89 will require an LO.

For a number of years the Expeditions Commission of the UIAA, in its negotiations with the Nepalese authorities, has continually recommended a complete revision of the now outdated LO system in Nepal and advocated an increase the number of permitted peaks. It submitted a selection of proposed new mountains. Many of these now appear in a new list of open peaks, drawn up from recommendations submitted by a study team from the Central Department of Geography, Tribhuvan University, following request by the Government.

An attempt has been made to group these peaks according to the principle ranges or Himals as defined in the Nepal Himalaya Inventory. These groups have been tabled from east to west. However, as no coordinates have been received at the time of writing, it is likely that some of these entries will be out of sequence, particularly those of the rarely visited Damodar Himal, where two Pokhahans of almost equal height are recorded.

EAST NEPAL

KANGCHENJUNGA REGION

Kangchenjunga Himal
Talung 7349m
Thaple Shikhar (Cross Peak) 6341m
Ramtang Chang 6750m
Chang Himal/Ramtang N
(Wedge Peak) 6750m

Annidesha Himal
Annidesh Chuli 6960m
White Wave 5809m
Merra 6335m
Mojca Peak 6032m

Khumbhakarna Himal
Sobitongje 6670m
Phole 6645m
Kyabura (Khabur) 6332m
Bokta Peak 6143m
Lumba Sumba Peak 5672m
Lumba Samba 5670m

Janak Himal
Lang Chung Kang 6475m
Domekhan (Dome Kang) 7264m
Janak 7090m
Loshar II (Lashar II) 6860m
Loshar I (Lashar I) 6930m
Dazaney (Dzanye Peak) 6710m
Ghhanyala Hies 6779m
Mdm Peak 6270m
Sat Peak 6220m
Chabuk (Tsajirip) 6960m
Pandra 6850m
Syaokang 5960m
Danga 6355m
Sharphu 4 6433m
Sharphu 1 7070m
Sharphu 2 6154m
Sharphu 3 6885m
Sharphu 5 6328m
Sharphu 6 6076m

MAKALU REGION

Mahalangar Himal (Makalu-Barun)
Chago 6893m
Pethangtse 6710m
Kyashar 6770m

CENTRAL NEPAL

KHUMBU REGION

Mahalangur North
Kumbatse (Khumbutse) 6639m
Lintren (Lingtren) 6713m
Machhermo 6273m
Nirekha Peak 6159m
Pharilapcha 6017m
Luza Peak 5726m
Nangpai Gosum 1
(Pasang Lhamu) 7312m
Nangpai Gosum 2 (Cho Aui) 7296m
Nangpai Gosum 3 7110m
Kyazo (Kyajo) Ri 6186m
Palung Ri 7012m
Jobo Ribjang 6666m

Mahalangur South
Abi 6097m
Gorkha Himal? 6092m
Chota –Ri 6934m
Amphu I 6840m
Amphu Gyabjen 5647m
Ombigaichen 6340m
Hunku 6119m
Peak-41 6649m
Peak-43 6779m
Ek Rate Danda 6312m

ROWALING

Rowaling Himal
Pangbuk Ri 6716m
Langmoche Ri 6617m
Tengi Ragi Tau 6948m
Kang Nagchugo (Konyaklemo) 6735m
Bamongo 6400m
Chekigo 6257m
Dingjung Ri 6249m

LANGTANG

Langtang Himal
Yubra Himal 6035m

GANESH REGION

Sringi Himal
Tobsar (Tabsar) Peak 6100m

Ganesh Himal
Ganesh VI 6480m

MANASLU REGION

Peri Himal
Nar Phu 5748m
Himjung (Nemjung?) 7140m
Gyaji Kang 7038m
Panbari 6887m
Tilje 5697m
Ratna Chuli 7128m

Manaslu Himal
Larkya Peak 6010m

EAST MANANG REGION

Annapurna Himal
Chhubohe Peak 5603 m

WEST MANANG REGION

Damodar Himal
Amotsang 6392m
Pokharkan 6346m
Pokharhan 6348m
Gajang 6111m
Chandi Himal? 6096m

MUSTANG REGION

Damodar Himal
Khumjung 6699m
Chhiv Himal 6581m
Jomsom Himal 6581m
Putrung 6466m
Saribung 6346m
Kang Kuru 6320m
Putkhang 6120m
Gauguri 6110m
Arniko Chuli 6039m

DHAULAGIRI REGION

Dhaulagiri Himal
Hongde 6556m

WEST NEPAL

WEST DOLPO REGION

Kanjiroba Himal
Tso Karpo Kang 6556m

HUMLA REGION

Kanti Himal
Kanti 6859m

Chandi Himal
Changwatnang 6125m

SAIPAL REGION

Gurans Himal (Saipal–Raksha Urai)
Korko 6053m
Khiuri Khala 5806m
Dhaulagi (Dhaulagari) 6632m
Rokapi (Nampa South) 6467m
Roma 5407m

API REGION

Gurans Himal (Yokapahar)
Nampa VII (Yokopahar) 6401m
Nampa III 6618m
Nampa II 6700m
Lhayul Peak 6397m

Nepal Himalaya, expedition endorsements cut, Mt. Everest fees lowered, garbage deposits changed.
For several years the American Alpine Club lobbied to remove the endorsement letter required
for expeditions wanting to climb in Nepal. This included high-level meetings in Kathmandu
with the Minister of Culture, Tourism and Civil Aviation, and the Minister of Mountaineering
and Sport.

The AAC received confirmation that on May 2, 2002, His Majesty's Government of Nepal
enacted new "Mountaineering expedition regulation, 2059" (2002), which gets rid of the
endorsement letters for expeditions. The decision to cancel the requirement was first delayed
due to the murder of the King and then by the Maoist insurgency. This makes it much easier
for expeditions. The endorsement process was just another onerous bureaucratic detail that an
expedition had to worry about. Nepal was the last country that required letters of recommendation from an authorized national body.

The Ministry of Tourism came up with these amended mountaineering rules and regulations:

1. Recommendation letters from the climbers' native alpine club are no longer required.

2. The number of climbers who can climb Everest and their new according peak fees are:
    One person: $25,000
    Two people: $40,000
    Three people: $48,000
    Four people: $56,000
    Five people: $60,000
    Six people: $66,000
    Seven people: $70,000

Peak fees, other than Everest, for a team of up to 7 members:
    Above 8000m: $10,000
    Peaks 7,501-8,000m: $4,000
    Peaks 7001-75000m: $3,000
    Peaks 6501-7000m: $2,000
    Peaks less than 6501m: $1,000

3. Garbage deposit (refundable) for Everest and Annapurna region:
    Mt. Everest: $4,000
    All peaks above 8001m: $3,000
    All peaks 7001m to 8000m and Mt. Ama Dablam: $2,000
    Peaks 6501m to 7000m: $1,000
    All peaks below 6500m: $500
    For other regions:
    All peaks above 8000m: $3,000
    All peaks below 8000m: $500

CHARLEY MACE, *AAC Expeditions Committee*

A Nepalese porter wearing clothing on loan from a Himalayan Explorers Connection rental center.
Scott Dimetrosky

Nepal Himalaya, porter assistance efforts. If a snow-covered pass at 4500m is difficult to a Western trekker outfitted with the latest combination of fleece, Gore-Tex, ice axe, crampons, and plastic boots, what is it like for a porter using a bamboo basket, rubber sandals, and cotton trousers? Ill-equipped porters have risked life and limb for the equivalent price of a pint of beer, suffering miserable conditions in the Himalaya, which can result in injury or death. In response, the Himalayan Explorers Connection (HEC), working in partnership with the International Porter Protection Group and Porters' Progress (an initiative of the HEC and a Nepalese registered NGO) has established the HEC Porter Assistance Project. The project seeks to accomplish a number of objectives:

1. To provide independent trekkers and small trekking companies with a convenient and inexpensive means of equipping their porters.
2. To educate the tourist population about acceptable standards of porter treatment.
3. To motivate and empower porters to determine their own means of assistance through offering English language, first aid, and empowerment classes.

Our Kathmandu and Lukla offices (with plans to expand to other Himalayan areas) stockpile water- and wind-resistant jackets and pants, quick-drying synthetic base layers, gloves, socks, hats, sunglasses, and footwear. The equipment donated from manufacturers, ski resorts, and individuals can be borrowed for porters by trekkers and small trekking companies in exchange for a small, refundable deposit. If you would like to donate clothing to the program after a trek in Nepal, drop it off at the HEC Kathmandu office in Thamel, next to the KEEP office on Jyatha (tel: 259 275). To make a similar donation in the USA, contact HEC at ken@hec.org.

The Himalayan Explorers Connection is a non-profit organization with a mission to promote a better understanding of and respect for the environment and cultures of the Himalayan region. The HEC coordinates education, assistance, and cross-cultural experiences for members, volunteers, trekkers, and Himalayan residents. To learn more about this project and other HEC programs please visit our site at www.hec.org or send email to info@hec.org.

SCOTT DIMETROSKY, *Executive Director of HEC, and* KEN STOBER, *Volunteer Development Director and coordinator of programs for the HEC Porter Assistance*

GURANS HIMAL

Api, ascent. This rarely visited 7132m peak was climbed on October 6 and 8 by five members of Ayumi Nozawai's six-man Japanese team. The climbers, all members of the Barbarian Club, established base camp at 4000m in the Api Khola and then repeated the route up the northwest face taken by the original Japanese ascensionists in 1960. Three camps were established and the summiteers were Hirotaka Imamura and Nozawai (on the 6th) and Tomoyuki Furuya, Hiroshi Iwazaki, and Fumihiro Ogiwara (on the 8th). This may be only the second or third ascent of the Original Route (the exact line followed by the successful Korean-Sherpa team in 1991 is unknown).

TAMOTSU NAKAMURA, *Japanese Alpine News*

Raksha Urai, attempt. Hubert Fritzenwaller's five-man Austrian expedition failed at ca 5800m on one of Raksha Urai's unclimbed summits (assumed to be the Rakshi Urai III as mentioned by the British party below). The team gave up on the east face in mid-May.

ELIZABETH HAWLEY

Raksha Urai, attempt. During the post monsoon Phil Amos, Jim de Bank, myself and Simon Woods (all UK) together with Bryan Godfrey (New Zealand), and Graham Rowbotham (Canada) explored part of Far West Nepal with the intention of making the first ascent of Raksha Urai (6593m). The team travelled for three days by bus from Kathmandu to the road head near Deura, then walked for 12 days up the Seti Valley. This area has been rarely visited by Westerners, with only one trekking group and three previous expeditions known. All previous expeditions to Raksha Urai have been turned back by poor conditions low down on the mountain.

Base camp was situated on the east side of the range at 4100m, with easy access to all four of the Raksha Urai peaks. The weather throughout was perfect and progress was relatively rapid for the first week. The team elected to try Raksha Urai III, which had also been singled out by the previous expeditions (who refer to it as Raksha Urai IV) The most likely route of ascent was the east flank and the 900m southeast face.

After a period of acclimatisation and load carrying up to 5400m, Amos, Rowbotham, Woods and I set out for an attempt on the mountain, while de Bank and Godfrey elected to explore the western flank up the Salimor Khola. The latter pair were turned back by an impenetrable gorge on the second day, but it was felt that if a way could be found up the valley, access to the higher peaks would be very good.

On October 8, we four left base camp and climbed to a 5000m advanced base situated at

Raksha Urai III closer up. The slope is 60 degrees, and the high point was 6500m. *Adam Thomas*

the start of the glacier. On the 9th we arrived at Camp 1, where we had previously cached loads. We spent the following day carrying and acclimatising up to a cache at 5800m. On the 11th we all climbed easy ground to a high camp at 5900m, situated on a large serac about 100m up the southeast face. We spent the rest of the day resting and acclimatising. However, a small storm then delayed the summit attempt for a further day. Meanwhile de Bank and Godfrey had returned from their explorations and were coming up to join us, just one day behind.

At 3 a.m. on the 13th the four of us set out for the summit. After climbing for 13 hours up continuous 60-degree ice of varying quality, we hit deep, unconsolidated snow just 50 meters from the summit ridge. There was evidence of an avalanche to our right and as we had not been able to stop on the face for food or liquid, we decided it was best to descend. We estimated that we were less than 150 meters from the summit, reaching a height of 6500m (set by GPS fix).

A difficult night followed. It took nine hours to make the 12 rappels of 60 meters each necessary to descend, using mainly Abalakov Threads and ice screw anchors. Temperatures dropped to –20°C and we had major problems with ice screws freezing up. At 1:00 a.m. on the 14th we were finally greeted at our high camp by de Bank and Godfrey.

Realizing that under the present conditions we were not able to climb the mountain, all six of us retreated to base camp and spent the next week recovering and exploring. During this period we made possibly the first western visit to the Urai Lagna (5200m), a pass on the Tibetan border. We walked out to Chainpur from October 22-30 and flew from there to Kathmandu.

The 1997 German expedition defined the range as having six peaks, which they numbered from south to north as Raksha Urai I to VI. However, we are convinced the peak referred to by the Germans as Raksha Urai I is in fact Dhaulagiri/Dhaulasiri or certainly part of the Dhaulagiri Group, as it is not visible from the main valley and is separated from the other Raksha Urai peaks by a considerable distance. Also, Raksha Urai VI referred to by the Germans is, in our opinion, yet another separate mountain a little north and some way east of the main

Raksha Urai III. The team estimates (via GPS positioning) that they were within 50 meters of the summit ridge and less than 150 meters from the summit when they turned around due to avalanche danger. *Adam Thomas*

range. We therefore suggest the most logical nomenclature for the Raksha Urai Group to be four peaks (I to IV) from south to north, so the Germans' II now becomes I, etc. We also feel that Raksha Urai III, which we attempted, is higher than the quoted 6593m for Raksha Urai and more like 6650m.

All four peaks of Raksha Urai would make for superb high-standard alpinism in a beautiful and remote area. There are also other possibilities in the region, although any trip would necessarily be a long and serious undertaking. More information can be obtained from myself at adamclimb@btinternet.com or from our website at www.virginsummits.org. The expedition won both the Helly Hansen Mountain Adventure and the Lyon Equipment awards in 2001.

ADAM THOMAS, *United Kingdom*

Dhaulagiri, ascents, attempts, and tragedies. On October 12 the Spanish climber, José Antonio 'Pepe' Garces, the leader of a small Spanish-Italian expedition to the Normal Route up the northeast ridge, was killed when he fell to his death from ca 8050m on the summit ridge. His body could not be recovered. On the same day his fellow team member, Silvio Mondinelli, reached the summit. *(Editor's note: 44-year-old Garces was a prolific 8,000m collector and just a few months previously had summited K2. Prior to this he had climbed Everest in 1991, Cho Oyu in 1997, Gasherbrum I and II within one week during 1999, and Manaslu in 2000. He had also reached the Central Summit of Shishapangma.)*

On the much more difficult east face, which has only been climbed by nine people, three Japanese disappeared sometime after October 14. The four-member team first went to the northeast ridge to acclimatise and Hideji Nazuka continued to the summit on his own, reaching the top on the 11th. His fingers became frostbitten and he immediately left the mountain. Forty-six-year-old Nazuka has now climbed nine of the 8,000m peaks, with some of these achieved by outstanding routes, such as the first winter ascent of the southwest face of Everest (1993; his second ascent of Everest), the first ascent of the northwest face of K2 (1990), and the northeast ridge of Kangchenjunga (1991). The remaining three climbers, Masashi Fukumoto, Ryushi Hoshino, and Yukihiko Shinagawa, moved down to the base of the huge east face, which they hoped to climb to an exit on to the northeast ridge at 7500m.

The trio were watched by another Japanese party led by Ryoji Yamada. This party was actually part of the same expedition as Hoshino and friends but Yamada's team had no intention of attempting the east face. Team members saw the east face climbers start up early in the morning of the 12th with three days' food. They later saw them make two bivouacs. Yamada himself watched them on the third day, the 14th, and reported that at 10:00 a.m. they had only reached 6400m or 6500m. "They were moving very slowly, were very tired and not in good condition," he observed. If Hoshino and team-mates had managed to reach the ridge at 7500m as planned, they would probably have been alright, as Yamada had left a camp there for them, stocked with a good supply of food.

Yamada and his party departed base camp on the 16th, leaving only a cook. The latter came back to Kathmandu alone on the 22nd or 23rd and told the trekking agent that the Japanese had not returned. He also added that on the 18th and 19th there had been very heavy snowfall with strong winds around the summit. Yamada was still in Kathmandu when the cook returned and on the 24th he flew by helicopter to Dhaulagiri to search for the missing men. From the air Yamada could see no trace of the climbers nor any signs of avalanching on the face. He concluded that they must have fallen before they reached his ridge camp. Hoshino was 33 and one of the more renowned climbers from Japan with the southwest face of Everest, Cho Oyu, Gasherbrum I and II, and the first ascent of Ultar to his credit.

A third Japanese expedition led by Kiyoshi Ishii was also on the mountain and climbed the northeast ridge. Ishii reported in Kathmandu that two of his members and three Sherpas had reached the summit on October 2, the Sherpas saying that the point reached was the correct summit. However, they, like other climbers before them, were wrong. They had actually reached a false summit. A German woman, Ms. Barbara Hirschbichler, went to the same point at the same time. She said that she had seen a higher point to the west but at the time believed the Japanese team's Sherpas, who said no one went to the other (but true) summit. She therefore did not try to climb it (if she had it would have meant retracing some of her ascent route and then taking a different line, as it is very difficult to climb directly to the main top from the false summit). She was extremely disappointed to learn later that she had been given incorrect information.

ELIZABETH HAWLEY AND TAMOTSU NAKAMURA, *Japanese Alpine News*

Thapa, first official ascent. A French team led by Raphael Guilbert went to Thapa, the least important of the nine new peaks opened by the Nepalese authorities in mid-May. This 6012m peak lies just north of Dhaulagiri I and Tukuche, and is really no more than another bump on a mountain widely known as Dhampus. On October 28 the French made the first officially recognised ascent by its western slopes. From their base camp at 5080m in the Hidden Valley six summiteers took seven hours to make what they reported as an easy walk with a little snow at the top. When they returned to the Hidden Valley, they met several parties of trekkers who intended to climb Thapa. They also learned from their own Sherpas that it is not at all unusual for trekkers to climb it. The French felt they had been fooled into paying the Government a royalty fee of $1,500 for a peak that others go to free of charge.

ELIZABETH HAWLEY

PERI HIMAL

Himlung Himal, second ascent, first ski descent. Our international expedition (French-Swedish-Algerian), which took place from April 15-June 10, comprised amateur climbers from the Grenoble-Oisans section of the French Alpine Club. The summit of Himlung Himal (7126m) had only been reached once before, by a team of Japanese climbers and Nepalese police officers in 1992. Since that time there have only been two other attempts: Germans in 1999 and Spanish in 2000. In common with all these expeditions, our route was also the northwest ridge.

On May 14 Béatrice Poupard, Kouid Beladem, Carole Soubiran, Sirdar Mulal Gurung, and I reached the summit. On May 19, Jean-Marie Gentzbittel, Ariane Chatelet, Eskil Eriksson, Fabrice Pintonato, and Olivier Soudieu also climbed to the top. Eriksson made the first ski descent from the summit.

The ascent of Himlung Himal turned out to be more complicated than we expected. Base camp (4850m) was reached after a nine-day march from Besisahar, leaving the Annapurna Trek at Koto. From there the ascent to Camp I (5400m) could be made in tennis shoes during dry weather, but from Camp I to Camp II (6200m), the glacier was a labyrinth of crevasses and seracs. It was difficult to find the best way. About 150 meters of fixed rope was installed in order to facilitate the negotiation of crevasses and 45-degree slopes. After Camp II, the route followed a long ridge for four or five hours toward the final pyramid. Despite the lack of technical difficulties, the length of this ridge made both the ascent and descent rather strenuous.

After an unsuccessful attempt to reach the summit from Camp II on May 10, Camp III was installed on the ridge about one hour from the start of the final pyramid. The last 800 vertical meters never exceeded 30 degrees and offered no particular technical difficulties, though snow conditions were certainly not perfect (deep snow with some avalanche risk).

Camp II and III were totally dismantled by expedition members, and before leaving base camp two or three porters were hired to bring some equipment down from Camp I. In addition to the mountaineering experience, the team had the pleasure of "discovering" the remote valley of Nar and the village of Phu with its Tibetan culture.

PAUL CAMPION, *French Alpine Club*

MANASLU HIMAL

Manaslu, southeast face to east ridge, first ascent. A large Ukrainian expedition, marking the 10th anniversary of the country's independence in 1991, had as its objectives a new route up the southeast face of Manaslu (8163m) and the first ascent of P2 (6251m a.k.a. Simnag Himal East) immediately south of Manaslu. The expedition, led by Valentyn Symonenko, comprised 15 members, 10 of which were the most skilful climbers in the Ukraine.

Base camp was set up at 4000m and all the equipment transported there by helicopter. We began work on April 8, following the line of a relatively safe spur on the right side of the face to reach the upper east ridge (this spur lies to the right of the previous attempts by Poles, Kazakhs and Ukrainians in past years). From advanced base at 5000m to Camp 5 at 7300m ca 4000m of rope was fixed. Intermediate camps, which were in snow caves, were established at 5500m, 6000m, 6400m, and 6800m. The average angle of the spur was 55 degrees, but there were more difficult sections of 60 degrees to 80 degrees, particularly between Camps 1 and 3 and between Camps 4 and 5. These involved consistently tricky mixed climbing on rock thinly covered with powder snow. Finally, Camp 6 was placed at ca 7500m near the top of the ridge and a little distance below the Pinnacle or East Summit of Manaslu.

On May 19 the summit party climbed the ridge to 7650m but could not climb over the Pinnacle or outflank it on the left due to the very steep terrain and a heavy covering of snow. The following day Vadym Leontyev, Sergiy Kovalov Sergiy Pugachov, and Vladyslav Terzyul climbed around to the right of the Pinnacle and reached the summit plateau at ca 7500m. On May 21 these four stayed in their tents, as the weather was stormy with driving snow and no visibility. Kovalov, Leontyev, and Terzyul left the tent at 6:00 a.m. and reached the summit of Manaslu at 11 a.m. The ascent was made without oxygen and the route as a whole graded Russian 6B. The same day all four climbers descended to 6300m and reached Samagon on the 24th. They were flown back to Kathmandu by helicopter.

MSTYSLAV GORBENKO, *Ukraine*

P2, first ascent. As noted above, one of the aims of the Ukrainian expedition to Manaslu was to make the first ascent of P2 (6251m a.k.a. Simnag Himal East), a minor summit along the east ridge of Ngadi Chuli (7871m a.k.a. Peak 29) immediately south of Manaslu. Getting permission to climb P2 was very difficult, as the peak was only brought on to the permitted list part way through the season. It was necessary for the President of the Ukraine to send a letter to the King of Nepal and for the expedition leader to meet with both the King and Prime Minister of Nepal. We only got the permit at the beginning of May.

Subsequently Mstyslav Gorbenko, Vadim Leontiev, Sergei Pugachov, and Mykhaylo Zagirnyak climbed the northern flanks of P2 above the Pungen Glacier to reach the east ridge at ca 5200m. The main difficulties on this section were deep snow, a big rimaye at 5000m, and an ice slope above. Once on the ridge we cached equipment in a snow cave dug into the south flank in preparation for the final push. The corniced east ridge itself was generally of moderate difficulty but presented two crux sections; a tricky gendarme at around 5800m and, higher, an 80-meter snow-covered rock wall. The climb was awarded an overall grade of 5A on the Russian scale. Three days were spent on the final ascent, with the summit reached at 4 p.m. on May 14.

MSTYSLAV GORBENKO, *Ukraine*

JUGAL HIMAL

Ganchenpo, north face, attempt. Bruno Burr, Oskar Wachter, and I left Kathmandu on May 6 and after a five-day trek through the Langtang Valley established base camp at 4400m in the Nyangtsa Chui Valley. We hoped to climb the north face of Ganchempo (6367m). The monsoon set in early this year, so we changed our strategy and tried to climb the route at night. On May 15 we went up to 5500m, where we placed Camp 1. After seven hours we reached the end of the moraine and were able to have our first view of the hidden glacier below the north face of Ganchenpo. It looked completely different than shown on the map, was full of deep crevasses, and much steeper than we expected. In the time we had available there was no way we would have been able to cross this glacier basin, and as we only carried equipment for one high camp, we retreated. We left base camp on May 20 and started our journey back to Kathmandu. Future parties with designs on the north face should expect to make at least two high camps and allow enough time to cross the glacier basin. *(Editor's note: in the past the north face has received at least three ascents via different lines from unauthorized parties.)*

JÜRGEN SCHÜTZ, *Germany*

KHUMBU HIMAL

Hungchi, attempt. Recently brought on to the permitted list, this 7036m mountain on the Nepal-Tibet watershed south of the Nup La had never received an official attempt before last autumn. Takatsugu Shiro's six-member Japanese party from Osaka attempted the southwest ridge but gave up on October 11 at 6700m.

TAMOTSU NAKAMURA, *Japanese Alpine News*

Kwangde Nup, north buttress direct ascent, Cheap Wine. During the post monsoon Czech climbers, Jan Doudlebsky and Radek Lienerth, completed a new direct finish to the 1989 American route on the North Buttress of Kwangde Nup (6035m). The pair began their climb on October 26 at ca 4800m, reaching the crest of the buttress from the right at 5150m. They completed the route on the 30th, having climbed 37 pitches to the summit. Most of the lower section was III to V+ but in the central section there was one pitch of VI-, two of VI, and one of VII. After climbing the 60-degree snow/ice slope to below the steep headwall of the pillar, where they placed their fourth bivouac, they climbed three big pitches graded VIII/A2, VII+, and VIII-. Two pitches of ice (80 degrees, then 75 degrees) led to more rock, which was climbed in two more pitches of VII- to reach the summit slopes (50 degrees). The ca 1100m route was christened Cheap Wine.

JIRI NOVAK, *Czech Republic*

Kwangde Lho, north face, second ascent of Breashears-Lowe route. After retreating from the right-hand variation on the northwest ridge of Ama Dablam (reported elsewhere), Alasdair Coull and I made the second ascent of the 1982 Breashears-Lowe Route on the north or Hungo Face of Kwangde's highest summit, Kwangde Lho (6187m). The line had been attempted three weeks previously by British climbers, Dave Hollinger and Andy Sharpe, but they had been forced to retreat after 300 meters due to dangerous amounts of powder snow. We found it in much better condition, with all the loose snow having fallen off to leave good névé. As far as we could tell, conditions in the lower runnel were similar to those found on the first ascent; mainly good névé/ice with the seventh and eighth pitches being particularly thin. The average angle was 70-80 degrees.

After bivouacking at the bottom of the face, we managed to climb the whole ca 600-meter runnel on the first day. On the second day we continued to follow the original line, finding mainly straightforward steep snow. However, a couple of pitches were quite exciting due to the sparse protection and unconsolidated nature of the snow. On reaching the middle rock band, we discovered the smear of ice, which provided the crux on the 1982 ascent, to be not properly formed. Instead, we traversed 100 meters to the right and bivouacked below a much fatter parallel band of névé. The following day we climbed through the 80-meter rock barrier at about Scottish IV, exiting on to the upper snowfield. The first half of the snowfield turned out to be perfect névé but the upper half was composed of very steep, unconsolidated runnels.

We managed to find another bivouac site at the top of the snowfield (enough snow for reasonable bivouac ledges was found at all three sites) and in the morning climbed five more pitches of very deep powder to the ridge. We continued up the ridge for two more pitches before contouring to the southwest ridge just below the summit. The route was 1400m high with a crux section of Scottish VI, 5.

As for our descent, the upper rock was rappelled from in situ anchors for 180 meters to reach a snow ridge, which led easily down to a hanging glacier. We had another bivouac here, then spent the next two days descending the original route down to the Lumding Valley and over to the main Dudh Kosi at Ghat. The descent involved very complex route finding. A careful study of Bill O'Connor's Trekking Peaks of Nepal is highly recommended.

SAM CHINNERY, *United Kingdom*

Kwangde Shar, north face, second ascent to the summit, Extra Blue Sky. During the autumn British climbers Jon Bracey and Owen Samuel made the second ascent of Extra Blue Sky to the summit of ca 6100m Kwangde Shar (fourth ascent to its junction with the north east ridge). This route on the north or Hungo Face of Kwangde Shar was climbed in November 1996 by the French, Samuel Beaugey, Christophe Profit, André Rhem, and Jérôme Ruby. Bracey, and Samuel more or less followed the original line to where it begins to slant up left, then followed the route taken in 2000 by British climbers Jules Cartwright and Sam Chinnery through the rock bands and up steep snow to the crest of the northeast ridge. They made three bivouacs on the face and found the climbing to be generally Scottish IV/V ice/mixed except for the crux pitch, a steep thin smear over compact rock (the same as that climbed by Cartwright and Chinnery), which they rated at Scottish VII, 6. On their fourth day they climbed the sustained upper section of the 1978 northeast ridge, surprised to find difficulties up to Scottish VI. After reaching the sharp summit, a further two days were spent making the lengthy descent to the Lumding Valley and back over to the Dudh Kosi.

MOUNTAIN INFO, *High Mountain Sports*

Ama Dablam, northwest ridge, first ascent. A British expedition arrived below the mountain in October and based themselves in the flesh-pots of Pangboche with the aim of attempting the unclimbed northwest ridge of 6812m Ama Dablam. First off the mark were Sam Chinnery and Alasdair Coull, who set their sights of the right hand (southwest) spur descending from Tsuro Ri (a subsidiary summit on the northwest ridge). They approached this in one day (October 27) from Pangboche via the normal Ama Dablam base camp and then northward up a scree gully to an obvious notch at ca 4900m at the start of the main spur. After three days climbing up much disturbingly loose rock, following a line of abandoned fixed rope (thought to be from a previous Russian attempt), they came to a cache of equipment (snow stakes, etc). They climbed two more pitches before deciding to abandon their attempt at ca 5900m due to the poor quality and dangerous nature of the climbing. They rappelled their line of ascent and went back to Pangboche, subsequently turning their attentions to Kwangde (reported elsewhere).

Also setting off on the 27th were Rich Cross and I. We wanted to try to climb directly up the front face of the gable end of Tsuro Ri and continue up the northwest ridge. We camped on the moraine of the Tsuro Glacier at ca 4900m and the next day set off early to climb the initial 300-meter snow/névé slope (ca 50 degrees) that leads to the central weakness in the wall above. The stonefall on this slope was bad but by midday we were belaying at the start of the major climbing. Finding the wall to be steeper, looser, and offering little in the way of ledges, we decided to retreat. There is a fantastic line up this face, but it would almost certainly require big wall tactics (portaledge, haul bag, etc.).

After a short rest period at Pangboche, we decided to attempt the northwest spur of the gable end. Although this is longer, it looked to offer the least technical route to Tsuro Ri and we knew it had been tried many times in the past. We set off at 9:00 a.m. on November 1 with very large rucksacks. We first contoured to the shepherds huts at Ralha and then ascended to the Tsuro Glacier. Crossing the dry glacier, we scrambled up to the lower part of the ridge and then along this for several hours, passing a large gendarme on the left, to arrive at a gravel col (ca 4550m), where we made our first camp. Over the next four days we climbed the ridge to a campsite just below Tsuro Ri (ca 6100m). On this section all the gendarmes were either climbed direct or turned on the north flank, except at two points. The second of these, which occurred at ca 5800m on the last day, involved turning a vertical tower by 20 meters of down-climbing on a snow ramp to reach the upper gable end, then two long mixed pitches of Scottish 6 to regain the crest. Throughout the whole of this section we came across remarkably little in situ gear; just 15 meters of old rope and only two fixed anchors.

The next two days were spent traversing the horizontal section of the ridge. Initially this was snow and ice, but later there were a large number of gendarmes that gave rock and mixed climbing. It was necessary to make one rappel from a particularly large gendarme, which could not be turned. No fixed gear was found here. This section took us to the start of the upper face, which is defended by a very conspicuous serac barrier.

On the eighth day we made a three-pitch traverse rightward below the serac and then climbed back up to its flat plateau top via an ice pitch in a hidden couloir. The next day we climbed good névé runnels, at first trending left, then back right, to join the north ridge about 100 meters below the summit. Throughout this ascent we more or less followed the line of the 1980 Japanese route, which is still festooned with ca 600+ meters of rope and over 30 rock anchors. We camped on the ridge at ca 6700m and the next day, November 10, reached the summit at 9 a.m. In total, our route had involved around 4,000 meters of climbing in generally very settled but cold weather.

JULES CARTWRIGHT, *United Kingdom*

Pumori, west face, new route. A five-man expedition comprising four Swiss and one American split into two groups with three of the team attempting the south ridge and the other two, Swiss guides, Ueli Bühler and Ueli Steck, opting for the west face. After a suitable period of acclimatisation Bühler and Steck crossed the rimaye at the bottom of the 1,400-meter face at 2 a.m. on May 6. They adopted a very lightweight approach, taking one 60-meter rope and virtually no bivouac gear, thereby hoping to make a fast ascent. The pair reported that most of the face was 55-60 degrees with some parts as steep as 80 degrees, while there was a section of mixed climbing at M4. They reached the south ridge at ca 6700m and continued to a bivouac at 6800m. Without gear Bühler and Steck were soon driven out of their bivouac by cold. Climbing again at 2 a.m. on the 7th, they moved quickly up the remaining 350 meters until near disaster struck. While moving together up a 45-degree couloir, Steck set off a windslab avalanche that swept the two climbers back down the face. Fortunately, Bühler was able to stop them both and after getting over the shock they continued upward, reaching the summit at 6 a.m., just in time to see the sunrise. They then descended the east ridge. There were no fixed ropes in place as no one that season had climbed above the east col. Below the col, things became easier as they were able to follow marker wands and use ropes placed by a German expedition. They were finally back in their west face base camp (5200m) at 8:30 p.m., having spent 43 hours on the mountain.

ELIZABETH HAWLEY

Pumori, ascent, attempt, and tragedy. There were two events during the autumn on 7161m Pumori that were noteworthy for entirely different reasons. The good news was the successful ascent by the first Iranian women mountaineers to come on any expedition to the Nepalese Himalaya. The team was led by Zerefeh Rahimzaddeh and comprised 11 members, eight of whom were women. The three men were: an experienced Himalayan climber, Jalal Chesmeh Ghsabani, whom they wanted for his expertise; the team's doctor, whom they needed as they knew of no woman doctor who climbed; and a civil servant who never moved above base camp and got extremely bored, but whom they had to take as their chaperon.

Three of the women successfully reached the summit on October 20 via the Normal Route up the southeast face to the east ridge. The summiteers were Leila Bahrami, Mitra Nazari, and Farhondeh, together with Chesmah Ghsabani and three Sherpas. The Sherpas stopped trying to open the route at two quasi-vertical sections above the col on the east ridge because they thought the women would not be able to manage such difficulty. However, the women insisted, ropes were fixed, and the party of seven went to the top in a 10-hour summit day.

The Iranians had no accidents, but a team of 10 Basque mountaineers was not so lucky. These climbers were also on the Normal Route, but never summited. On October 19 five young alpinists, Iñaki Aiertza (27), Javier Arkauz (22), Benat Arrue (22), Aritz Artieda (23), and César Nieto (23), perished when seracs above them collapsed and the resulting avalanche carried them 600-800 meters down the face. This side of the mountain has a long history of avalanches that have resulted in fatal consequences and for this reason the Iranians never occupied a camp at the top of the southeast face, as the Basques and many other climbers before them had done. The avalanche hit the Basques when they were just 50 meters above their camp, which they had pitched at ca 6200m.

ELIZABETH HAWLEY

Kangtega, east pillar, first ascent, winter ascent. The most interesting climb of the winter 2001-02 season was a new line followed by a trio of Frenchmen on Kangtega, 6779m, a peak in the Everest region southwest of Ama Dablam. Christophe Profit, Olivier Besson, and Andre Rhem made a rapid alpine-style climb of the east pillar to 6400m from a base camp at 5000m on the Hinku Nup Glacier.

Their pillar had never been attempted before, and for the first two days they encountered no very great difficulties. But above their second bivouac at 6,300m, after they had moved another 100 meters to the shoulder, serious problems arose. The pillar ended at the shoulder, and now seracs threatened from above. Straight up from the shoulder were not only dangerous seracs, but also a difficult rock step with mixed rock and ice in some places. They decided to make an easy traverse to the normal route on the southeast face, went to the top from there, and descended the face.

ELIZABETH HAWLEY

Editor's note: Their original intention had been a direct line up the north face to the left of the one climbed by Valeri Babanov. However, conditions were too snowy, so they moved to the unclimbed pillar that marks the left side of the face climbed by another French team in 1998 (AAJ 1999). The three first acclimatized on the Normal Route up the Southeast Face, where they left a camp at 6000m to aid their descent. On the first two days they climbed some delicate mixed ground and steep rock steps with difficulties up to 5+/6a. On the third day they were unable to climb through the big serac barrier below the summit slopes, as the ice was so hard their picks would not penetrate. Instead they made a dangerous traverse left beneath it to gain the southeast ridge. They descended to their pre-placed camp for the night and on the following day climbed up for seven hours to the summit (December 5). It took them just six hours to descend the Normal Route to their base camp.

Everest, pre-monsoon statistics. The largest number of people in any single season reached the summit of Everest during the spring. An astonishing total of 183 went to the top, 101 from the south and 82 from the north. The total far surpassed the previous record of 117 climbers in the spring of 1999. On just one day, May 23, 2001, 47 successfully reached the top via the normal Nepalese route via the South Col, seven more than the previous record set in 1993 of 40 on May 10. It is thought that 50 of the climbers reaching the top during the spring had already summited in previous years, raising the grand total of individual summiteers to 1,114. Counting Sherpas and base camp staff it is estimated that the total number of people operating on the mountain throughout the season was in excess of 1,000, and whereas in 2000 only two ascents were made without oxygen, in spring 2001 the number was nine. To get a more complete picture of the population of the tent villages that sprang up, one must add uncounted dozens of trekkers, who went to base camps and even advanced base camps.

ELIZABETH HAWLEY

Everest, oldest and youngest summiteers. The oldest person ever to reach the summit was a 64-year-old American physician, Sherman ("Sherm") Bull. He was joined at the top by his son, Bradford ("Brad") Bull (33). The pair were only the second father and son team to summit at the same time. Sherman Bull, whose age surpasses by one year the previous oldest summiteer, Toshio Yamamoto, a Japanese climber aged 63 in May 2000, said this had been the fifth time he had gone to Everest. When he finally made it all the way to the top, his success as the oldest summiteer didn't really sink in immediately. However, getting to the top was "a dream come true."

The youngest Everest summiteer was a 16-year-old Nepalese school boy, Temba Tshiri Sherpa, who had unsuccessfully tried to scale it from the Nepalese side in the spring of 2000 and received severely frostbitten fingers, some of which had to be amputated. Now he was back again, this time on the Tibetan side, as his own one-man team but with some help from others on the mountain. Temba later reported he was a bit frightened by the three dead bodies he encountered in one area along the route. He also had difficulty doing things like putting on his harness due to his damaged fingers. However, he had "a great feeling" when he got to the top. Now he plans to concentrate on his studies—he is in ninth grade—rather than to climb again soon, but he could change his mind if someone were to give him "a good chance."

ELIZABETH HAWLEY

Everest, the death of Babu Chiri. Babu Chiri, the incredibly strong and fast mountaineer who was also the most famous Sherpa of recent times, died on April 29 at the age of 35. His most spectacular feats on Everest include staying overnight on the summit without any bottled oxygen for 21 hours in May 1999, and then, after returning to base camp, making another complete ascent later in the same month. The following year he achieved the fastest ever ascent made from base camp to summit on the Nepalese side, when he climbed to the top in just 16 hours and 56 minutes. In May 1995 he became the first person ever to make two ascents of the mountain in the same month. He made 10 ascents of Everest, and if he had been successful in the spring, his total of 11 would have been equalled by only one person, Appa Sherpa.

Babu Chiri was a fine person, a "gentleman" as one frequent American Everest summiteer used to call him. He wanted to build a school for the children of his home village, Taksindu, which has none. His next climbing project was to attempt an incredible traverse of Everest from the Tibetan base camp to the Khumbu base camp, then immediately turn around and reverse the traverse. This was a plan only Babu Chiri would contemplate.

However, this dream died with him when he fell into a crevasse near Camp 2 in the Western Cwm. At around 4 p.m. on April 29 he told others he was going to take some photographs in the vicinity of the camp. When he hadn't returned by 9 p.m., his brother Dawa went out to search for him. Another expedition leader, Willi Benegas, and his head Sherpa, Pemba Gyalzen, joined the search and around midnight found Babu's footprints leading to a crevasse. Due to fresh snow, the crevasse was not readily visible and was only apparent because of the obvious hole caused by someone falling in. While two Sherpas belayed him, Benegas descended around 10 meters into the crevasse, found the body and ascertained Babu was dead. At 6 the following morning the effort to recover the body began and it was brought to the surface three hours later. His death was reported in the media around the world and tributes poured in. King Birendra of Nepal sent a message of condolence to the family. In this statement he declared that Babu's "demise has caused irreparable loss to the nation and to the mountaineering fraternity." The prime minister and other dignitaries paid their respects at the Sherpa Centre in Kathmandu, where Babu's body, covered with flowers and Buddhist ceremonial scarves, had been brought.

ELIZABETH HAWLEY

Everest, first ascent by a blind person. The most remarkable of all the summiteers in the spring was the 32-year-old totally sightless American climber, Erik Weihenmayer. On his return to Kathmandu he said "I spent two and a half months getting there from my arrival at base camp. You work so hard and so long to get there but I just took it day by day. And when I took the last step to the top, it was almost an anticlimax." Weihenmayer was among the 26 successful men and women who reached the summit on May 25, the last day of the season on which anyone reached the top.

A major problem during his climb was the notorious network of crevasses in the Khumbu Icefall. He said it took him a long time to get accustomed to jumping them. He managed to cope because he received guidance from a team-mate who placed Weihenmayer's foot at one edge. Then, in order to judge the distance he had to jump, Weihenmayer probed the other lip with ski poles. Once, he came to a crevasse unexpectedly and in his surprise put a leg down it. His torso landed safely on the far side and he sustained no injury.

A retinal disease made Weihenmayer sightless when he was 13. Before attempting Everest he had considerable climbing experience, which included Aconcagua, McKinley, and El Capitan. Before going into the Everest region, he said in Kathmandu that he was "confident about how I perform in the mountains. The reason I do it is probably the same as that of anyone else. I probably have to put in more effort but for me it is still the same adventure and excitement. I get a lot of pleasure out of the wind and sun on my face and the feeling of rock under my feet; the same kind of pleasure that others get out of the view."

However, there were other climbers on Everest who expected a disaster. One of them callously remarked that he planned to stay near Weihenmayer so that he would be "the first to take a picture of the dead blind guy." However, there was no picture to be taken. Guided by a bell on the rucksack of a team-mate ahead of him and by his own feeling and probing, Weihenmayer, with three team-mates and at least one Sherpa, arrived at the top of the World at 10:05 a.m. on May 25 and descended safely over the next few days.

ELIZABETH HAWLEY

Everest, post monsoon attempts. In stark contrast to the unprecedented hordes of climbers on Everest during the spring, the post monsoon season saw practically no one on the mountain. For the first time since autumn 1970 not a single team came to the Nepalese side of the peak and in Tibet there were only three (see elsewhere).

ELIZABETH HAWLEY

For more on Everest from the north side, see the Tibet reports.

Lhotse Middle, first ascent. The most impressive all of accomplishments in the spring was the first ascent of Lhotse Middle (8413m), which although not exactly a mountain in its own right, stands only 50 meters lower than Makalu and was widely recognised to be the highest unclimbed summit in the world. Various expeditions in recent years had planned to reach it from the west via the main summit of Lhotse, or from the east via Lhotse Shar. Some had tried the south face of the Lhotse-Lhotse Shar ridge. Most of these teams had come from the former Soviet Union but all had failed to make a serious attempt from east or west above the two summits.

In the spring 12 Russian climbers led by Sergei Timofeev took an entirely different approach. First they ascended the Normal Route on Everest as far as the South Col, then they moved along Lhotse's unclimbed north ridge and out on to the previously untouched north or Kangshung face, which is technically in Tibet. Finally, they climbed up to the middle summit's west ridge.

The Nepalese Government had not officially brought Lhotse Shar on to the permitted list when the Russians established Base Camp at the standard Everest site on April 1. As with several previous expeditions attempting the Middle Summit, they were operating under a permit for Lhotse Main and with the help of another expedition comprising just two men, Simone Moro and Denis Urubko, who planned to attempt an Everest-Lhotse traverse (see elsewhere), began to equip the Normal Everest route up to the South Col. By the end of the month they had the route opened and much of the necessary equipment up at Camp 4 on the Col, but still no permit from the Nepalese Government. However, on May 16, two weeks before the proposed end of the expedition, the vice-secretary of the Ministry of Tourism visited Everest Base Camp to hand over personally to the Russians the long awaited permission.

Over the next days Alexey Bolotov, Petr Kuznetsov, Evgeny Vinogradsky, and Timofeev pushed the route across the upper Kangshung Face, fixing more than 1000 meters of rope. On the 22nd they eventually gained the foot of the rock wall below the ridge. The steepness of some of the climbing here was estimated to be at least 65 degrees. Finally, on the 23rd, the Russians climbed a difficult leftward-slanting snow ramp leading to the lower part of the ridge that descends east from Lhotse's Main Summit. They climbed down this ridge to the lowest point and then up the final 70 meters or so of very steep and narrow crest towards the top of Lhotse Middle. The four arrived a little below the top at 3:00 p.m. but felt the snow conditions on the summit cornice were a little too dangerous to climb to the highest point. The final rock step just below the top was a "very difficult 90-degree wall," well led by Bolotov and graded VI.

On the 24th Nikolai Jiline, Yuri Koshelenko, and Gleb Sokolov repeated the ascent, and the following day it was the turn of Vladimir Ianotchkine and Victor Volodin. All summiteers used supplementary oxygen and all except Koshelenko had been to the top of an 8000m peak before. In this respect Vinogradski was the most experienced high altitude climber. He has summited Everest four times, Cho Oyu twice, Lhotse, Lhotse Shar, and was part of the Kangchenjunga traverse expedition. The full story of theis rescue appears earlier in this journal.

ELIZABETH HAWLEY AND YURI KOSHELENKO, *Russia*

Lhotse, rescue. A rather dramatic rescue of a British climber took place on Lhotse's normal west face route. The Briton was 19-year-old Thomas Moores, who was part of an American-led commercially organized expedition. He had reached the summit on May 21 with a Polish climber, Dariusz Zaluski, who was on a different permit. On the descent, close to the base of the couloir, Zaluski saw Moores fall ca 150 meters from an altitude of 8300m

The principal rescuer was Simone Moro, an Italian with another Lhotse permit, who was in his tent at 7950m making preparations for his own summit bid during the next day or so (Moro with the Kazakhstan mountaineer, Denis Urubko, had a permit to link the summits of Everest and Lhotse via the unclimbed north ridge of Lhotse, a much talked about Himalayan objective). At 6 p.m. he heard Zaluski shout about Moores's fall. Later, back in Kathmadu, Moro reported that when he heard Zaluski, he immediately left his tent to rescue the fallen Briton. He said no one in any of the other tents at that camp on Lhotse's west face would join him because they said they would loose their chance at reaching the top. So Moro went up alone. He found Moores at 7 p.m., lying on his back in deep snow, which Moro feared could avalanche at any time. Moores's face was bleeding and he had lost a crampon but had been given more oxygen by Zaluski.

Moro, who has considerable experience on Nepal's great Himalayan peaks, is reported to have hoisted the teenager (who weighed no more than 50 kg) on to his back, though other reports suggest he attached him to his own ice axe, then kicked big steps in the snow to help Moores reach Camp 4, which was situated left of a rock formation on the west face of Lhotse known as The Turtle. Back at Moro's tent, the Italian provided water and first aid, then the following morning organized more oxygen and arranged for a couple of Sherpas from a different expedition to escort Moores down towards the Western Cwm. That day an exhausted Moro realised that he had sacrificed his own summit bid.

Moores was the only member of his expedition to make a summit attempt. The leader, the American, Gary Pfisterer, said later in Kathmandu that he had instructed Moores to spend only one night at the high camp (which had been left behind by a Korean group when they left the mountain) and then to descend. However, the young Briton stayed on for another day and summited without the use of supplementary oxygen. He was later evacuated by helicopter to Kathmandu, where he was found to have internal injuries and was sent on to hospital in Bangkok.

ELIZABETH HAWLEY

The huge south face of Lhotse, attempted in winter by a Japanese party. For route information, see the photograph on the following page. *Photo courtesy of Chunichi Shimbum Ltd.*

Lhotse's south face, showing Russian 1990 summit route, right; Japanese projected route in the lower left; their high point in upper left.

Lhotse, south face, winter attempt. The Japan Alpine Club Tokai Section accomplished a remarkable ascent to open a new route from the west ridge to the west face of K2 in 1997. What would be most appropriate for the next target? It didn't take much time for us to come up with an answer. There was no other choice than the first winter ascent of the formidable South Face of Lhotse which remained as one of the last problems to be tackled among the Himalayan Giants. To take advantage of good and stable weather, the assault needed to be a speedy climb in the shortest possible period. The party was organized with eight members.

In the fall of 2001 we conducted training for acclimatization to high altitude in the Himalaya. Seven members climbed the normal route of Cho Oyu. Six members stood atop on October 9 and 11 in succession. Hideji Nazuka, the strongest member, climbed Dhaulagiri I on October 11 but suffered from serious frostbite that forced him to abandon his participation in the Lhotse climb. Two other members also got sick. Therefore the potential members were reduced to only five climbers

The expedition party departed from Kathmandu on November 9 and established base camp (5200m) at the foot of the overwhelming south face of Lhotse on the 14th. The following is an extract from my diary in which I recorded details of the climb up until the time when we were forced to retreat.

On November 19 we commenced to pave the climbing route of the lower part of the wall. On the 23rd we reached a point of 6400m where CI would have been set up, but as the place was too exposed to the danger of falling rocks and ice, we decided to pitch C1 at 5900m. We had Sherpas who were engaged to carry gear and supplies to C1 till the 28th.

We expected to push our climbing route to a point of 6400m, first following a Himalayan fluted steep slope to the left and then climbing up an ice-snow wall to the right. Here, however, there was also a serious danger of falling rocks. We changed the route to that taken by the Yugoslavians in 1981.

Now winter arrived. On December 1 we set up C1. We negotiated a difficult rock band of about 150m above C1 that led to a snow ridge of distinctive shape. The narrow part between 6400m and 6600m was particularly exposed to the danger of falling rocks. During route preparation work three members suffered bruising. To avoid falling rocks we left C1 at 4 a.m. for route paving. Custom-made down jackets protected us well from the cold. Later on Sherpas carried gear and supplies from C1 to C2, starting from C1 at 1 a.m.

We followed the Yugoslavian route without deviation and set up C2 at 7100m on the 6th. The Himalayan fluted slope was cut and leveled for the camp. On the 8th, the designated "A" party of Ohtani, Hanatani, and two Sherpas extended the route to a point about 30 meters above the snow col of 7350m where the Yugoslavian party positioned their C4. On the 11th, the "B" party of Tanabe, Miyoshi, and two Sherpas overcame the critical part, which is analogous to the "throat" of the south face, and reached a large snow slope. Three sets of wire-ladders that the Yugoslavian party had abandoned still remained on the rock wall en route. The ladders told us how hard they had struggled.

Fine weather had lasted since we had set up BC but on December 15 snow clouds veiled Lhotse's south face for the first time and we had snow fall at BC. Therefore "A" party was ordered to descend from C2 down to BC. It was on the 18th that "B" party resumed route paving upward. As it was bitterly cold at C2, we had to wait for sunshine before moving out of the tent. (The coldest temperatures were below −30°C, estimated.) Such a situation made progress very slow and we could open the route only up to a point of 7600m on the 18th. Ultimately, as a result, 7600m became the highest point we reached; that is just below the Yellow Band crossing the south face. The large slope above the "throat" was incessantly under attack from falling rocks. Tanabe was bruised while descending.

Ferocious winter winds, which were what we had most feared, started to blow on December 19. "B" party set out for route paving against strong winds, but we were unable to proceed. While the winds were getting fiercer on the 20th, we ascended to the "throat," but a terrific gale wouldn't allow us to progress further. Now our members were so exhausted that we knew we no longer had the strength to attempt a further push for the final assault. Without hesitation we decided retreat. We returned to BC on the 22nd.

Our attempt was unsuccessful, but we learned many things on the winter climb. I was convinced that the winter is not a bad season to climb the south face of Lhotse and that a well-organized team of the strongest climbers would possibly scale it in winter in a swift attack of 18 days. We shall return and challenge again in December 2003.

Members: Leader: Osamu Tanabe (40); deputy leader: Masamiki Takine (50); members: Kazuo Tobita (55), Manabu Miyoshi (35), Mikio Suzuki (34), Hisao Ohtani (32), Yasuhiro Hanatani (25). *(Editor's note: Osamu Tanabe participated in the first winter ascent of Everest southwest face in 1991-1993.)*

Sherpas in "A" party: Dawa Tshiri Sherpa, Tshiring Dorge Sherpa. Sherpas in "B" party: Mingma Tshiri Sherpa, Nima Gyalzen Sherpa

Brief climbing chronicle of Lhotse's south face:

1973 spring: Japanese party from Kanagawa reached 7300m.
1975 spring: Italian party led by Ricardo Cassin reached 7500m.
1981 spring: Yugoslavian party reached 8150m.
1984 spring: Czechoslovakian party, first ascent of south face of Lhotse Shar (8398m).
1985 autumn: Polish first reached 8200m.
1987 autumn: Polish second reached 8300m.
1989 spring: International party led by Reinhold Messner reached 7200m.
1989 autumn: Polish third reached 8300m; Jerzy Kukuczka died.
1989 winter: Christof Profit (France) reached 7300m.
1990 spring: Tomo Cesen (Slovenia) possibly made the first ascent, solo (controversial).
1990 autumn: Soviet Union made the second ascent, by a new route.
2001 winter: Japan JAC Tokai reached 7600m.

OSAMU TANABE, *Japan Alpine Club, Tokai Section*

China

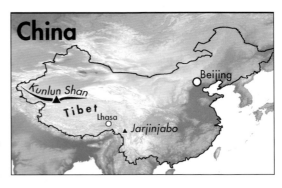

WEST KUN LUN

Seilik Gulam Muztag, first ascent. A Japanese expedition comprising four climbers led by Hiroshi Onishi was successful in making the first ascent of Seilik Gulam Muztag (6691m), formerly known as Kashitashi, completing the route attempted by an expedition in 2000, of which Onishi was a member. The Japanese mountaineers established Base Camp at 3800m on July 31 and a couple of days later Advanced Base at 4500m north west of the peak. Camp 1 was placed at 5170m near the foot of the North Ridge. By the August 11 Camp 3 had been established at 6200m on the ridge, from where several ropes were fixed up steeper snow slopes to the top of a 6400m snow dome, the highest point reached by the 2000 party. At 6:30 a.m. on the 12th all four members left Camp 3 in the dark and reached the top of the dome at 8:00 a.m. Continuing in unstable weather the climbers followed a wide snow ridge split by many small crevasses and then a final knife edge to reach the highest point a little after 3:00 p.m. The weather cleared at this point and the team was able to have fine views of the unclimbed West Peak (6650m) before making their descent.

TAMOTSU NAKAMURA, *Japanese Alpine News*

Yunnan Province

HENGDUAN RANGE

Hengduan Range, Crown Mountain, possible first ascent. During the end of January 2001 I reached the top of a beautiful 5100m peak (according to my altimeter) in the north west of the Yunnan province in China. The peak can be approached from the road from Zhongdian around the last pass before coming down to Deqin. According to Chinese travel books the peak name is The Crown Mountain and it sits opposite of Mt. Baima, northeast of the road facing southwest, and therefore not very snowy on this side. The mountain is made of many small rocky peaks that give it its "crown" name. The highest of them is the one to the northwest. At the 4400m campsite is an old ruin of rock and wood that maybe belongs to yak shepherds or the road builders. We pitched our tents there, and the temperature went to −25° Celsius that night. My partner had mountain sickness for a few days, and so I went up solo and climbed all the peaks from southeast to northwest except the first big one on the southeast, which was probably first ascended by an American who lives in Kunming, Bob Moseley, who confirmed the heights. The start of the climb was easy scramble past rock fall on the ground, the last part involved one or two pitches of 5.7 at the most. A few meters to the northwest there is another lower peak, which seems to have a few rocks one on the other; the approach to the main peak from there seems hard. Therefore I assume my climb was a first ascent. The entire climb down was easier in a 5.5 chimney. The climb takes a few hours. Not far away sits the highest peak in Yunnan, the sacred unclimbed Meili peak, which can be seen from Crown Mountain.

ALON HOD, *Israel*

SICHUAN

Jarjinjabo Range, first ascent of unnamed rock tower. Four Japanese climbers, Eiji Daigo, Yuriko Kowaka, Naoki Ohuchi, and Taizo Yoshida, made the first ascent of an unnamed granite tower in the Jarjinjabo Massif above Zhopu Pasture. This region of West Sichuan lies close to the border (Yangste River) with Tibet and approximately 65 km northeast of Batang on the Sichuan-Tibet Highway. The team established base camp on July 25 at 4050m on the Zhopu Pasture and on the 26th set up an advanced camp at ca 4700m below the tower, after making a non-glaciated approach. On the 27th they fixed the first 100 meters of the south pillar in three pitches and after two days of rain recommenced by climbing 10 pitches and bivouacking. The following day, the 31st, they completed a further three pitches to the summit and descended. The 320-meter-high wall (480 meters of climbing) gave maximum difficulties of 5.10a and A1. Although nearly 70 percent of the route followed good cracks, the team used more aid than expected due to the heavy rain.

TAMOTSU NAKAMURA, *Japanese Alpine News*

Tibet

Gurla Mandata, ascent. Japanese climbers, Masakazu Okunda and Susumu Yamada, together with a high altitude porter, climbed this 7694m peak in Western Tibet via the Original Route up the West Ridge approached from the north. The summit, a.k.a. Naimona'nyi, was reached on September 25.

TAMOTSU NAKAMURA, *Japanese Alpine News*

Yangra Kangri, attempt on a new route. The highest summit in the Ganesh Himal lies on the Nepal-Tibet border and is referred to as Yangra Kangri (in Tibet) or Ganesh I (in Nepal). The 7429m peak was climbed on October 24, 1955 from the Nepalese side by Eric Guachet, Claude Kogan, and Raymond Lambert, but since then nobody else has reached the top. In 1987 a joint expedition between The Himalayan Association of Japan and The Tibet Mountaineering Association succeeded in climbing Labuche Kang (7367m), west of Cho Oyu. In spring 1995, Mr. Cheng Tianliang, the Tibetan leader of that expedition, suggested a 10th anniversary joint expedition, the target being the north side of Yangra Kangri in 1997. As the area around the peak had not yet been opened to foreigners, I lost no time in replying that the HAJ agreed to his suggestion.

I organized a reconnaissance and at the end of September 1996, joined 45 year old Gaya, one of the Tibetan members, in Lhasa. The northern approach planned by us was via Tingri, the north side of Shishapangma, Ma La (5234m) and the Kyirong Zangbo River (the upper stream of the Bhote Kosi River). The route would then proceed southward about 50 km along the river. On September 29 we tried to gather information in Kyirong Prefecture but were given the unhappy news that no road or trail existed on the north side of Yangra Kangri. Although from the maps we found it hard to believe, lack of time forced us to change our route to one that approached from south via the Sanji Glacier. From the prefecture (4127m) to Kyirong

Above: Camp 4 on the ascent of Yangra Kangri. In the background is Mt. Chamar, 7177m, Nepal. *Hideki Sato.* Below: Rama glacier panorama of (left to right) Peak 6192m, Peak 6245m, Peak 6074m. *Kinichi Yamamori*

District (2795m), we had a 75km jeep ride, driving on a road made in the bottom of the river. In a few hours we had moved from desert area to forest. At 10:00 p.m. some local policemen came to us and took our passports away. Next day we visited the border police office, where they told us not to proceed. "Why?" we asked, "we have permission." "The Chinese map is not authentic," they replied. After an hour's discussion, they permitted us to go, saying "We will keep your passport until you come back. Don't take any photographs."

Gaya and I hired four porters and left Kyirong District. We descended southward along the Kyirong Zanbo River, where many laborers were making a roadway. After a five-hour walk we reached a point (2026m) where we had to cross the river via a bamboo basket hung from a single wire rope. Shortly after, we reached Jangzon (2400m), where we stayed the night. Next day we camped early at 3480m close to the river, from where Gaya reached the Lado La (4632m). The entrance to the Sanji Glacier was obscured due to rain, and persistent bad weather meant that we were subsequently prevented from seeing the south face of Yangra Kangri. We had no alternative but to go back, arriving in Kyirong District on October 5.

The reconnaissance had given us an unexpected present. On the way we had noticed a very attractive mountain, Kabang Peak (6717m), from the Ma La, so in the autumn of 1998 I planned a second expedition to look at both this peak and Yangra Kangri. On October 26, after investigating Kabang, we reached Ruka (3050m) on the Kyirong Zangbo River. From there Yosihide Higami and Yasuo Ota ascended the Rama Pu to find the route to the foot of the northeast spur. However, they failed to reach the Pawu Glacier on the north side of Yangra Kangri because it was too hard for only two men to make any progress through marshes and bushes.

Left: Unclimbed Lampa Kangri (6668m) south ridge from Rama Glacier. Right: Yangra Kangri (7429m). The climbing route weaves through seracs on the right to the ridge, then up right on the east ridge. *Kinichi Yamamori (2)*

Our third expedition took place in the autumn of 2001. On September 15 the main party: Kinichi Yamamori (57, leader); Yoshihide Higami (57, deputy leader); Hideki Sato (53, climbing leader); Seiko Mantoku (47); Yasuji Moriyama (51); Yasuo Ota (48); Kunihiko Sato (58), and Masakatsu Tamura (59), left Lhasa and four days later reached Ruka. After finding a suitable route to base camp at 3350m in the forest the other side of the Lama Pu, and building a bridge, we moved our equipment up there on September 24 with the help of 51 local porters. We then established Camp 1 at 4400m beside a lake named Lachang Co. This was close to the start of the northeast spur.

The spur is a branch of the east ridge and itself splits into two branches at ca 6100m. On September 30 we started climbing, aiming for the easterly branch of the spur. It took two hours from Camp 1 to the end of the glacier, after which we climbed a snow face, passing to the right of a rocky tower to reach the foot of the upper face. Camp 2 (5350m) was established below a glass-shaped rock wall.

The route now became difficult. We climbed two pitches on the rock wall then followed a snow ridge, which became very thin and narrow. Above, more ridge led to an icefall. After climbing through the latter, we reached a plateau, where on October 18 we established Camp 3 at 6000m.

From here the route climbed directly up a huge snow face to the east ridge. There were many big steps and crevasses, and shortage of ropes meant that in order to extend the route we had to remove those that had been fixed lower down. On the 24th we sited Camp 4 at 6860m just below the east ridge. Four members stayed there and on the 26th climbed up the east ridge without ropes or pitons (which had all been used below) until they were forced to give up at 6900m.

Although we were unable to succeed in making the second ascent of Yangra Kangri via a new route, we were all satisfied with our expedition, on which a middle-aged team had climbed 2500m at altitude up an ambitious challenge without the help of high altitude porters.

KINICHI YAMAMORI, *The Himalayan Association of Japan*

Mt. Everest, new Mallory and Irvine discoveries, north ridge ascent, rescues. On March 20 our 2001 Mallory and Irvine Research Expedition arrived at Rongbuk Base Camp hoping we could find the camera we believed Andrew Irvine was carrying in 1924. As in 1999, we started early in the season, hopeful for less snow on the upper mountain. Our team of seven professional guides (Dave Hahn, Brent Okita, John Race, Tap Richards, Jake Norton, Andy Politz, and me as leader) was supported by 19 climbing Sherpas, team doctor Lee Meyers and historian Jochen Hemmleb. A group of climbers and trekkers joined us later, accompanied by guides Heidi Eichner, Craig John, Heather Macdonald, and Jason Tanguay. We were several weeks ahead of the many other expedition teams that season, and our climbers and Sherpas fixed the entire modern climbing route and established six camps before others caught up. This included fixing to camp 4/north col (23,200'/7070m), to Camp 5 on the north ridge (25,600'/7800m), to camp 6 (26,900'/8200m) on the North Face, through the Yellow Band, from the base of the first step to the top of the Second Step, the Third Step, and the summit pyramid.

During the last week of April our group conducted two major searches, with a total of seven days spent combing the area between 26,000 and 28,000 feet on the North Face, including a four-day stint at Camp 6 by Richards, Hahn, and Politz. Two days later Okita and Norton climbed the true North Ridge above Camp 5 pioneered by the British, probably for the first time since 1938, searching all the way to the First Step. New discoveries included the British

1922 ABC and Camp 6 sites from 1924 and 1933, as well as the 1960 and 1975 Chinese Camp 6 sites and 1960 Chinese Camp 7. Our first summit bid in early May ended with the successful carry-out rescue from below ABC of two desperately ill Chinese glacial research students unconscious with cerebral edema. A second summit attempt was thwarted by deep snow in the Yellow Band and a third attempt was turned back by bad weather from Camp 5. Finally, on May 19, our non-guided climbers Mike Otis and Terry LaFrance reached the top along with Sherpas Kami, Mingma Ongel, Lhapka Nuru, and Danuru. They climbed the modern north side route from Camp 6, and were the first to the summit in 2001 from either side of Everest.

Our final high altitude search and summit bid saw Hahn, Richards, Tanguay, and Politz give up their summit climb on a perfect day to rescue five climbers stranded overnight near the top and unable to descend: three from Mushroom Rock (28,120'/8570 m) and two from the Third Step (28,500'/8690m). The irony of this did not escape us, as our team had gone looking for evidence of climbers long dead and found instead climbers who were alive, albeit barely. This epic rescue, one of the highest in history, resulted in the AAC's David Sowles award being presented to these four climbers, along with Lobsang and Phurba Sherpa, for their amazing efforts. Our final discovery came not on the slopes of Mt. Everest, but in Beijing, China. In late August 2001, Simonson and Hemmleb interviewed climbers from the 1960 and 1975 Chinese Everest expeditions and came away with previously unrecorded information regarding their climbs and discoveries they had made, including the 1960 sighting of a body in a location completely different from the Mallory site. This could only have been Andrew Irvine. We now conclude that Wang Hongbao sighted the remains of Mallory in 1975. There is still work to be done by future detectives on Everest!

ERIC SIMONSON, *AAC*

Everest, record day and first snowboard descent. May 23 saw the record for the number of climbers reaching the summit in a single day completely smashed. Before last year the record stood at 40, these ascents taking place on the May 10, 1993. On May 23, 2001 47 people from the Nepalese side alone reached the top. When combined with the 42 gaining the summit from the north, this gives a total of 89. Amongst the summiteers from the north that day was the young Frenchman, Marco Siffredi.

The previous night Siffredi had celebrated his 22nd birthday at the 8300m Camp 4 and prior to that had ascended eight times to the North Col (7000m) and several times to Camp 2 (7500m) to aid his acclimatisation. On the 23rd he left Camp 4 at 2:00 a.m. and only four hours and 15 minutes later was sitting on the summit, waiting for his Sherpa, Lobsang Temba, to bring up his snowboard. At 8:00 a.m. he had abandoned his oxygen equipment and was making his first turns on the summit ridge, heading for the Great (Norton) Couloir, the most logical choice for a descent and the scene of previous attempts by skiers such as the great Davo Karnicar from Slovenia.

In the first difficult 150 meters (45 degrees with rocks) one of his bindings broke in the cold. Fortunately, with the help of Lobsang, who was carrying a pair of pliers, he was able to repair it and continue. At 8300m he reached the rock barrier, which he anticipated might require a rappel. However, with so much snow on the mountain after the earlier bad weather, he was able to continue surfing unaided. He descended the couloir (ca 40 degrees) to the seracs near the base, then cut right to reach the North Col. After a rest he surfed the last 600 meters to advanced base on the Rongbuk in a total time of a little over two-and-a-half hours. This was not only the first complete snowboard descent of Everest, but the first complete descent of the Tibetan side of the mountain by either ski or surf.

MOUNTAIN INFO, *High Mountain Sports*

Everest, first descent by paraglider. First to reach the summit on May 22 were Bertrand "Zébulon" Roche and his wife Clair Bernier-Roche. This was the second time for Bertrand on the summit of Everest. In October 1990, when he was 17 years old, he became the youngest non-Nepalese to climb Everest, a record which stills stands to this day. He reached the top with his father, the guide Jean-Noël Roche, the ascent also being the first time a father and son had reached the summit together. Now he is a guide and with his wife owns a paragliding school, where she is an instructor (and also three-times World female champion). They brought their tandem paraglider to the top and when they soared overhead to descend from the summit directly to advanced base at 6400m in just 10 minutes, people below were amazed and fascinated by this spectacular sight. It was the first complete descent of Everest by paraglider.

ELIZABETH HAWLEY

Everest, East (Fantasy) Ridge attempt. The only expedition that did not attempt the standard Everest routes on the north and south side during the spring was a team of 10 Indian climbers and five Nepalese Sherpas led by Santosh Yadav, the first woman to climb Everest twice. This expedition made a brave attempt on the unclimbed east ridge, rising steeply from the middle of the east (Kangshung) face. The only other team to have tried this line was a Japanese expedition in 1991, which abandoned its attempt at 6400m because of the extremely difficult nature of the terrain and the dangerous avalanche potential. Yadav took large quantities of rope and equipment, and before going to the mountain said "I am 100 percent sure about my climbers and my equipment." She could determine these factors but not the constant snow fall. With not a single full day of good weather throughout the expedition period from April 12 to May 24, and white out conditions even at base camp, with frequent avalanches and very few safe sites to establish camps beyond the team's high point of 6900m, the expedition abandoned its attempt and went home, reportedly leaving all the ropes in place. Yadav said she was determined to try this route again.

ELIZABETH HAWLEY

Everest, post monsoon attempts. In complete contrast to the spring, only three expeditions attempted Everest from the north. All were unsuccessful and no one managed to climb higher than 7800m. Two teams were on the standard North Col-north ridge route, including the American double amputee, Ed Hommer. The third expedition was attempting the rarely-climbed east (Kangshung) face. Five climbing members from Hungary under the leadership of David Klein were attempting the 1988 Anglo-American Route. Their maximum altitude was just 6300m, which they reached after more than four weeks on the mountain. They finally abandoned their attempt after many days of heavy snowfall followed by days of dangerous avalanches down the extremely steep face. They would climb a little, snow would fall heavily, they would retreat to a safe camp, wait two days for the avalanches to stop, go back up again and then the same pattern would repeat itself. Luckily none were killed or even seriously injured, though Klein was briefly knocked unconscious by stone fall and two other members were carried inside their tent 250 meters down to the bottom of the face, when an avalanche struck their camp.

ELIZABETH HAWLEY

For information on Everest from the south side, see the Nepal reports.

Shishapangma, southwest face, fast solo ascent and soloing/single-push history. It is easy to lose perspective in the Himalaya. Base camps bulge with expeditions, routes are choked with climbers and the once-pervasive feeling of isolation can be replaced by claustrophobia. On May 23, 2001 I guided clients to the summit of Everest. Eighty nine folks reached the top that day, setting a new record. Although I was among the first 1,100 individuals to summit that peak, it seemed like I was crammed in a very well-refrigerated subway car.

After that experience, I decided to seek solitude in one of the most beautiful places in the Himalaya. On September 9, 2001, I crossed the border into Tibet and headed back to Shishapangma, arriving at base camp in the midst of a stormy day. I had been here before, in October 1999, after climbing Cho Oyu, when on the first morning at base camp an avalanche had roared down the face, claiming the lives of Dave Bridges and Alex Lowe. For the next week high winds and snowstorms had torn at the peak. With little hope of conditions improving, our small expedition had packed up and headed back to Nepal. In 2001 my hope was to climb the Polish-Swiss route, which was in bad shape (and apparently had been for a few years). The three expeditions lining up on the British Route were the only other teams on the face.

I turned my attention to a variation of the British descent route. Carrying a light pack, I began the climb at 10:50 a.m. on September 19. Unroped and 1,000 feet up the icy 60-degree face, I broke an ice axe, shearing the bolt and rendering it useless. Nine rappels later I was on terrain gentle enough to downclimb.

On September 23, I set off again for the summit. The poor conditions I encountered on my first attempt persuaded me to head for the British Route, where I could take advantage of fixed ropes to aid my descent. I left ABC (19,350') at 3:40 p.m. After climbing 7,000 vertical feet on 50- to 70-degree névé, rock, and ice, I reached the main summit at 9 a.m. on the 24th. The descent would prove to be more exciting

The south face of Shishapangma. At least a half-dozen routes ascend most of the visible features. *Chris Warner* than the ascent. A fog bank rolled up to the face, light snow began to fall, and far above the security of the fixed ropes I was caught in a total whiteout. I criss-crossed the 50- to 60-degree couloir seven times before I finally found the ropes, then continued the interminable descent by rappelling for almost 3,500 feet. I returned to my tent at ABC at 10 p.m., 34 hours after beginning the climb.

The southwest face of Shishapangma is quite important within the development of non-stop ascents of 8000m peaks. In 1990 Loretan and Troillet climbed a new route to the central summit in 16 hours. Kurtyka, who was climbing with them, reached the central summit in 22 hours. Kurtyka bivouacked on his descent, while the Swiss returned to the base of the mountain in one push.

In 1993 Wielicki soloed a new route to the right of the British route, reaching the summit in one day. Earlier, he recorded a similar single push ascent on Broad Peak by the Normal route (in 1984 he climbed from base camp to the summit in 16 hours)

Last September Kobi Reichen of Switzerland set off for the summit at mid-day on the 23rd. He stopped at Camp 1 for four to five hours, where he joined two friends to continue up to the summit. They all reached the top about one hour before I did. Reichen and I both climbed via the British route, both having the fastest times yet on that route. I was about 40 minutes quicker, but Kobi was obviously stronger, as he actually moved much faster than I.

As far as I know, this ascent is the first American solo of an 8,000-meter peak. In 1990 George Lowe climbed from Camp 2 to the summit of Dhaulagiri solo. About two days after my ascent of Shishapangma Marty Schmidt soloed the regular route on Cho Oyu in 13 hours (in 1996 Russel Brice from New Zealand soloed Cho Oyu in 11 hours).

In the mid 1980s a handful of climbers brought the single push style from the Alps to the 8000-meter peaks. Since then folks like Wielicki, Troillet, Chamoux, Babu Chirri, and Kammerlander have been literally running up peaks. Does this diminish the accomplishment of the clients I've guided to the summit of Everest? Absolutely not. Each person has their own limits. And each person should exercise their own tolerance for risk. If I didn't go out and run up the southwest Face of Shishapangma, I'd always be wondering what my limits are.

CHRIS WARNER, *AAC*

Nojin Kangsang, probable first ascent of west ridge. On August 15 Aumi Nozawai, Shinichi Miyagawa, and Masao Saito from a six-member Himalayan Association of Japan expedition led by 61-year-old Kunimitsu Sakai, made the probable fourth ascent of 7191m Nojin Kangsang via the west ridge. The team established base camp on July 29 at 4800m on the west flank of the mountain and then placed three camps on the west ridge. The west ridge flanks the north side of the Togolung Glacier and rises directly to the summit.

TAMOTSU NAKAMURA, *Japanese Alpine News*

Nojin Kangsang, attempt from the north. During August 2000 the Japanese climber, Tadakiyo Sakahara, made the first ascent of the East Ridge as reported in *AAJ* 2001. The 56-year-old mountaineer returned in 2001 and set up base camp once again on the eastern side of the peak. He then moved around to the north, where he tried to open a new route. However, although he succeeded in making the first ascent of Gama I (6484m) en route, he was unable to continue on to the summit of Nojin Kangsang.

TAMOTSU NAKAMURA, *Japanese Alpine News*

Looking northwest at the Nonjin Tanglha massif. The left summit is West Peak, 7126m. Central Peak is 7117m. The climbing route ascends directly to the Central Peak from slightly left of center. *Jon Otto*

Nonjin Tanglha Central Peak, ascent. Keith Affleck (UK), Kate Brown (Australia), and Liz Carr, Dan Mazur, and I (all US) traveled overland from Kathmandu to Lhasa. There, we met up with two Tibetan climbing assistants, Nwang and Penba, who were students of the Tibetan Mountaineering Association's High-Altitude Training School. Our objective was the 7177m central peak of Nonjin Tanglha (a.k.a. Nyenchen Tanglha, Nyainqe Tanglha, Nianqing Tanggula: West Peak, 7126m: 91°E, 30°N). The appeal of a 7000m peak in Tibet is that most have never been climbed. Nonjin Tanglha only has a handful of successful summiteers. We would be the first team in two years to attempt the central peak and the only one in spring 2001. If successful, we would be the first climbers from our own countries to summit.

Obscure to most in the West, the Nonjin Tanglha mountain range rolls through the heart of Tibet just north of the Himalaya near the capital, Lhasa. This crown-like cluster of searing summits rises sharply from the shores of heavenly Lake Nam-tso. The local Tibetan herders bestow this monolithic white landmark with its edifying name, "God of the Grasslands."

We established base camp on March 28 at the mouth of Banuco valley (4800m). The rivers were still frozen thick with ice, and vast, desolate rolling hills stretched endlessly. Inevitably, large numbers of herders (children, women, and men) emerged from nowhere, their small compounds of mud houses tucked over ridges just out of view. Tibetans threw paper offerings into the wind at a distant hermitage silhouetted against the dawn sky.

Through several shuttles of gear we set up ABC (5250m) among grazing yaks deep within Banuco valley at the base of a 6000m sheer-walled mini peak that masks the south-southwest face of Central Peak. Finding the route to C1 took several days and, unfortunately, we did not discover the most efficient route until making our descent. The best way is to walk up the valley west of the mini peak, then continue up steep, grassy slopes to a short-lived rocky moraine. From there walk back in an easterly direction up a small ravine to the glacier. C1 (5950m) lies in the saddle between the mini peak and the main face. The entire team was in C1 on April 11

Along the summit ridge of Nonjin Tanglha's Central Peak. *Jon Otto*

having reached this point via a much more arduous traverse of the mini peak.

Most of the team fixed rope to C2 (6500m), from where we thought it would be a straight shot to the summit. Dan and I explored a route we had heard as a possibility but it led into a maze of crevasses. We descended by hugging the left or west side of the slope, skirting along cliffs that dropped for several thousand feet. Time was running out and bad weather arrived (these peaks have an intensely local and volatile weather system due to their proximity to Lake Nam-tso). We hunkered down in our Ozark tents.

On April 15, our last possible summit day, Kate, Liz, Nwang, Penba, Dan, and I headed out in uncertain conditions. Once beyond our previous high-point, Penba and I roped together and took the lead to find the route and place wands, crossing a large flat plateau of wind-blown snow dunes at 6,850m. This ended abruptly at a short 60- to 70-degree snow wall and the last section of fair slope below the summit. The rest of the team popped up at the far end of the plateau. Kate and Nwang continued slowly across the snow dunes while Dan and Liz had to descend. Keith was on the radio. He had left C1 and had only made it half way to ABC when he could not move anymore. A rescue was required. When Dan and Liz reached Keith, he was blue in the face and looked half dead due to dehydration and AMS.

Keith's predicament was not known to the summit climbers, who were waiting in all-encompassing cloud. It soon became obvious that, although it was almost a whiteout, the weather was stable. Penba and I continued upward, reaching the summit with our last wand. Penba became the first Tibetan ever to summit Nonjin Tanglha and I the first American. On our descent we met Kate and Nwang just above the snow wall. Nwang turned around just 30 meters below the summit. Kate had made that heart-wrenching choice all climbers come to face sooner or later: If I make the summit I might not have the energy to go back down. Will I? What now?

I meticulously belayed Kate down, one rope length at a time, as she exhaustedly skirted the edges of cliffs, safely arriving at C2 by midnight. Dan, Liz, and Keith spent the night bivouacked in a storm above ABC. The two Tibetans hastily descended, reaching ABC by nightfall, having cleared a huge pack of gear off the mountain. As we reached base camp the following day our jeeps were waiting to drive us back to Lhasa.

JON OTTO, *AAC*

Editor's Note: The 7126m West Peak was first climbed in 1986 by three members of Mario Kuzunushi's Japanese Expedition via the west ridge. The first ascent of the Central Peak took place in 1989 when Wolfgang Axt and five other Austrians reached the summit via the south-southwest Ridge. This route appears to have been repeated in 1992 by a team from Beijing University. The 2001 ascent is probably the third.

Yarlha Shampo, attempt. This 6635m peak, which lies 80 km southeast of Lhasa at 28° 45' N, 91° 50' E, was attempted for the first time last year. Yoshiki Ito and 17 members of the Yamagata Mountaineering Association met with bad weather (particularly thunderstorms) and were forced to abandon their attempt at 6100m.

TAMOTSU NAKAMURA, *Japanese Alpine News*

The Kangri Garpo Range, showing the Lhagu Glacier from the village of Lhagu. The peaks are unnamed and between 6100m and 6500m high. *John Nankervis*

Kangri Garpo Range, exploration. During October and November 2001, New Zealanders John Wild, Wilf Dickerson, Nick Shearer, Colin Monteath and I (leader), accompanied by trekkers Jos Lang and Betty Monteath went on a recce expedition to the remote and stunningly beautiful Kangri Garpo range, three days' drive southeast of Lhasa largely on the southern Sichuan-Tibet Highway. From the junction at Rawu the last section of the road passes beneath the partially restored monastery of Shugden Gompa and continues to the village of Lhagu. Yaks and ponies

Unnamed peaks in the Kangri Garpo Range. Top: Skiing on the southeastern end of the Lhagu Glacier. The left peak is 6127m and the right peak is 6421m. Bottom: the highest peaks are circa 6500m. *John Nankervis (2)*

were used for transport to a base camp, one day's walk above Lhagu. No high summits were reached. However, what was probably the first traverse of the 30 km long Lhagu glacier to its expansive upper névé was undertaken on skis, an unclimbed subsidiary bump of 5,750 metres was ascended on skis and a legion of 6,000-to 6,600-meter peaks were seen and committed to photographic memory. Colin Monteath was lucky to survive an unroped 20-meter fall into a narrow crevasse high on the Lhagu névé while skiing. Characteristically he continued professional photography from its icy bowels. The group also visited the Ata Kang La area where the Tibetan plateau topples steeply over into the jungles of India. There was clear cold autumn weather for much of the period but unfortunately unsettled spells with wind and light snow came

Lhagu villagers on tent-inspection duty in the Kangri Garpo. *John Nankervis*

at critical periods for climbing. The 250 km long Kangri Garpo range is just north of the Burma and Assam borders and east of the big bend in the Tsangpo river and Namcha Barwa, the farthest outpost of the Himalaya. No major peaks in the range have been climbed. The expedition was supported generously by a Shipton/Tilman grant and a Mount Everest Foundation grant (UK).

JOHN NANKERVIS, *New Zealand Alpine Club*

Editor's note: The Japanese explorer, Tamotsu Nakamura, had trekked through this region of the Kangri Garpo several years previously. In October and November 2001, two elderly Japanese mountaineers from the Silver Turtle Group also visited the Lhagu Glacier. They then moved south and made an extensive reconnaissance of the southeastern part of the range crossing the 4610m Ata Kang La to the Ata Glacier.

Kula Kangri Central and East, first ascents. In spring a joint expedition comprising 11 Japanese (leader, Yoshitsugu Deriha) and eight Tibetans (leader, Tseden Jigmy) made the first ascents of Kula Kangri Central (Kula Kangri II; 7418m) and Kula Kangri East (Kula Kangri III; 7381m), both of which lie along the ridge running east from the Main (7538m) summit. These were wrongly reported in *AAJ* 1998 as having been climbed by a Spanish expedition in May 1997. The Spanish climbed only the main summit, noting the existence of two unclimbed subsidiary summits to the east.

The expedition set up base camp on April 1 in the village of Monda at 4250m, then used 85 horses and donkeys to transport equipment to an advanced base at 5400m. Progressing up the moraines on the west bank of the glacier, the team established Camp 1 at 5900m in the upper cwm below the mountain. A route was opened through a large icefall to reach the ridge connecting the east summit with Karjiang (7221m), and Camp 2 placed at 6350m. One aluminium ladder and 1,500 meters of rope were fixed on this section. The climbers then slanted up the northwestern flank of Kulu Kangri East, fixing another 1,500 meters of rope. By the 30th they

The Karjiang region at the border of Tibet and Bhutan. Top left: Karjiang's west face, 7221m. The attempt did not quite reach the top of the shaded ridge on the right. Top right: Making the first ascent of Kangmi Kangri, 6412m. Bottom left: On the ascent of Taptol Kangri, 6824m. Bottom right: Taptol Kangri's north face. The route follows the sunny snowfields to the upper ridge just left of the skyline cliff band. *Dutch Karjiang Expedition*

had established Camp 3 at ca 7100m on the west side of the east summit, from where two Tibetans and two Japanese reached the previously unclimbed central summit on May 2. Two days later three Tibetans and six Japanese reached the east summit. On May 5 another group left Camp 3 intending to traverse the central summit and continue along the ridge to Kulu Kangri Main. However, due to poor weather and bad visibility they turned back. The following day they made a second attempt and reached the central summit but the weather turned bad again, so they retreated. In total 17 climbers made successful summit bids.

TAMOTSU NAKAMURA, *Japanese Alpine News*

Karjiang attempt, Taptol Kangri and Kangmi Kangri first ascents. During the post monsoon season Rudolf van Aken, Pepijn Bink, Court Haegens, Willem Horstmann, Rein-Jan Koolwijk, and I attempted the first ascent of Karjiang South (7221m), the highest and most impressive summit of the Karjiang Group, situated a few kilometers northeast of Kula Kangri (7554m). We established base camp on September 20 at an altitude of ca 4950m to the north of the group. The only photographs of Karjiang in our possession were from the west but we had one excellent satellite image that promised an encouraging possibility from the northeast. We therefore decided first to go around to the east side.

Advanced base was set up on September 24 and the next day Horstmann and I reached a ca 5800m col, from where we were probably the first human beings to see the impressive northeast face of Karjiang. It looked at least 800 meters in height and even steeper and more difficult than the south face of Chacraraju in Peru. It also looked very dangerous, so we decided to skip an attempt from this side. Before retreating, Haegens made probably the first ascent of Pt 5881m. He was later followed by the rest of the team. Haegens named the peak Rognon of Good Hope. On September 30 Van Aken, Haegens, Horstmann, and I made an attempt on the beautiful Pt 6412m via its west face. Climbing 60-degree ice, we reached a height of ca 6150m, but decided to retreat due to the lateness of the hour.

We then went around to the opposite side of the mountain to make an attempt on the west face of Karjiang. In 1986 a Japanese team climbed the north summit (Karjiang II; 7216m) by its northwest ridge. They called this summit the Central Summit and Karjiang I (7221m) the South Summit. To us Karjiang I looked a lot more than five meters higher than II, especially when seen from the northeast, where Karjiang II looks like a fore-summit.

On October 4 we established another advanced base at 5700m, ca 45 minutes walk below that used by the Japanese expedition, which visited the area in the spring (see above). Unfortunately, it appeared that despite the use of porters, the Japanese had left trash on the way to their advanced base and at the site itself.

The next day Haegens and I fixed 100 meters of static in order to protect a dangerous part in the icefall. It was the only length of rope fixed during the whole expedition and was taken down at the end of the trip. We set up Camp I at ca 6300m close to the bottom of the Karjiang's west face, just below the col between Karjiang and Kula East. After a rest day Van Aken, Haegens, Horstmann, and I made an attempt on the west face. At about 6550m we caused a slab avalanche more than 25 meters wide. It fell 200 meters to the bottom of the face. No one was hurt, but as we expected the whole face to be in the same unstable condition, we withdrew, rappelling the 55- to 60-degree face with the help of snow-anchors and Abalakov threads. The next day we explored the heavily corniced south ridge but concluded it was too dangerous under the present conditions.

Top: Kangmi Kangri. Middle: descending Kula III. Bottom: Karjiang (left) and Kula III (right). *Dutch Karjiang Expedition*

A decision was now made to attempt Kula East (7381m), which looked a far easier proposition. On October 13 we all made a summit attempt from a high camp at 6700m. Low temperatures (-25°C) and a very strong wind (estimated at Force Nine) forced us to retreat from 7110m. Cold temperatures and strong winds proved a problem throughout most of the expedition.

On the 19th Bink, Horstmann, Koolwijk, and I made the first ascent of Pt 6824m, climbing this beautiful pyramid via its north face. The previous day we had spent a long day ascending from base camp via a steep snow ridge to a camp below the face at 6200m. The summit day was again very cold (-24°C). We left camp at 7:45 a.m. The 500-meter-high face was impressive but not particularly difficult (50 degrees with a few short sections of 55 degrees). We arrived on the west ridge at 6700m and from there climbed for another one-and-a-half hours to the summit by a nice snow crest with one steep section at a cornice. The east top, which we reached at 1:37 p.m., proved slightly higher. We graded the route Alpine D and after subsequent discussions with local people, named the peak Taptol Kangri.

In the meantime Van Aken and Haegens put a camp at ca 6100m on the northeast glacier of Karjiang, just below the south-southwest ridge of Pt 6412m. The following day, the 21st, they climbed the narrow snow ridge to the summit (The steep west face was too dangerous because of heavy snowfall the day before). After a large rimaye they climbed a 55-degree ice face to the ridge. Following the crest, they had to climb sections of unstable snow up to 65 degrees on the west flank before reaching the summit at 2:45 p.m. They christened the peak Kangmi Kangri, which means Yeti snow mountain, and also rated the route Alpine D. More information can be found at www.geocities.com/karjiang.

HAROEN SCHIJF, *Nederlandse Klim-en BergsportVereniging (NKBV), the Netherlands*

Tibet, tips on organizing a climbing trip. All peaks over 5,500 meters in Tibet officially require a climbing permit, which be issued by the Chinese Tibetan Mountaineering Association. CTMA is the government organization authorized to oversee mountaineering activities in Tibet. In addition to your climbing permit, CTMA also supplies you with logistical support up to base camp. This includes transportation, liaison officer, lodging and yaks, among others. You pay a fee for all these services in addition to the permit. You cannot simply buy the climbing permit and go to the mountain on your own.

When arranging your climb, your team can apply directly to the CTMA or through an agency that specializes in running climbs to the Himalaya. Dealing directly with the CTMA can be laborious, time consuming, confusing, and often more expensive than going through an agency. These agencies have price contracts with the CTMA, have worked with them for years, and are familiar with the CTMA's exact services, quality of services, and working procedures. Furthermore, an agency can organize every other crucial part of a climb from base camp food, cooks, and equipment to high-altitude climbing assistants (Sherpas), tents, and more—many essential services the CTMA does not even offer.

There are companies that work directly with the CTMA in organizing climbs to the Tibetan Himalaya. A handful are Nepalese agencies based out of Kathmandu. Two North American companies, Himalaya Incorporated (Seattle, WA) and my own BlueSheep Adventures (Bellingham, WA), cater to climbers from around the world. BlueSheep specializes in organizing expeditions to mountains in Tibet and China only. Both companies concentrate on high-quality, inexpensive climbs. They cater to pre-organized teams that only require logistical support to individuals that are looking for a fully supported expedition. They also actively support the use of Tibetans on the mountain as high-altitude climbing assistants, cooks, and porters—work traditionally done by Nepalese Sherpas—as a way to assist poor families in Tibet.

If you work directly with an agency in Asia, consider the Nepalese companies Asian Trekking or Global Expeditions. In Lhasa, a good company that offers trekking, though not climbing services, is Windhorse Adventures; the manager, Jampa, speaks excellent English. Contacts: Jampa_W@hotmail.com or Wha@public.ls.xz.cn; (tel.) + 86-891-6833009; (fax) + 86-891-6836793. Himalaya Incorporated can be reached at: (206) 329-4107; himalayainc@earthlink.net; www.Himalayaclimb.com. My company: Bluesheeptravel.com; 703-593-4799; jotto@bluesheeptravel.com.

You can contact the CTMA directly at East Lingo Rd. #10 Lhasa, Tibet 850000, China; (tel.) + 86-891-6333720; (fax) + 86-891-6336366; (e-mail) ctma@public.ls.xz.cn.

Culturally-oriented maps to most of Tibet can be found at www.tibetmap.com. The Department of Defense 1:500,000-scale TPC H-10A and H-10B maps cover most of Tibet with 1,000-foot contour intervals. Order from: MapLink, (805) 692-6777, www.maplink.com; or Omni Resources, (800) 742-2677, www.omnimap.com.

No matter whom you go through, make sure to verify exactly what is included in the price. Inquire in detail about quality and type of base camp and high-altitude equipment and food; extra potential fees and over-use yak fees; climbing ability, quality, and nationality of the climbing staff (Sherpas), and cooks. You will probably have many other concerns as well. Make sure you get all your questions answered in a satisfactory and clear way.

JON OTTO, AAC, *BlueSheep Adventure*

Southeast Asia

KOREA

Towuangseong Falls, Korean ice climbing overview. For climbers in the Seoul area, the usual place to practice rock-climbing is Insu Peak on Bukhan Mountain. No one is exactly sure when the sport of ice-climbing was introduced to Korea, but long-time members of the Corean Alpine Club first ice-climbed in Cheonbuldong Valley located at Mt. Sorak some time during the early sixties. And to help the program develop, the Corean Alpine Club sent some of its youngest members to study at the Ecole Nationale de Ski et d`Alpinisme in Chamonix, France in the early seventies. After learning the more advanced mountaineering skills and techniques used by Europeans, this new and younger generation of climbers helped the Korean ice-climbing scene get on the right track.

The first Korean protégés of the French alpine school have become the benchmark to which all Korean climbers aspire. They pioneered the way for all Korean climbing enthusiasts by venturing out on Korea's first-ever expeditions to the hard "blue" ice of the Himalayan, Eastern European, and North American ranges. Their experiences, knowledge, and techniques learned and practiced on these and other ranges are what have made it possible for Korea's greatest alpinists to accomplish what they have accomplished today.

Korean ice-climbing does not get into full swing until the latter part of December and lasts into February. Each region has its own area of ice-climbing falls. The waterfalls nearest to Seoul include Gucheon-un Falls in Mt. Bukhan, Hwaeryong-gol Falls at Mt. Dobong, Chun-gong Falls at Mt. Sapae, and Eullyu Falls at Mt. Surak. The one most frequented by climbers in the Seoul area is Gugok Falls at Mt. Bonghwa located in the Gangwon Province. Gugok Falls is most popular because it freezes quicker than any of the falls in the Seoul vicinity due to its location on the cooler and shadier western side of Mt. Bonghwa. Gugok Falls stands 70 meters high with an incline ranging from 60 to 70 degrees, making it an excellent practicing ground for scaling Korea's largest and most famous waterfall, Towuangseong Falls.

Towuangseong Falls, which means "Giant Earth Fortress," is located in Sorak-dong at the entrance to the Mt. Sorak National Park, is the main focus of interest among Korean ice-climbers. It is a Canadian Grade V and is the longest flowing icefall in East Asia. Its formidable height and daring grade present a thrilling opportunity and challenge that cannot be passed up and has become the dream of virtually every Korean ice-climber since the 1970s.

Several ice climbers have lost their lives attempting to reach the top of the falls until Byeong-min Song and Yeong-bae Bak of the Crony Alpine Club finally conquered it in 1977. They spent no less than three days and two nights to successfully complete the 350-meter ascent. But today, with the progress we've made in equipment and technique, the climb, which originally took three days, has been made in as little as an hour by some climbers.

Every winter on January 27, hordes of Korean ice climbers bust loose to show their stuff at the annual Snow Flower Festival in Towuangseong Valley. The record for the fastest solo attempt up the icefall was made in just 50 minutes by Hee-yoon Kang in 1993. The second fastest solo ascent was one hour and twenty minutes by Hak-jae Yoo in 1988. Korea's top three ice climbers today are Hak-jae Yoo, Jeong-seong Gwan, and Yong-gi Kim.

And as I finish writing this now, I can envision the ice-crazed Koreans who migrate each year to Towuangseong Falls. I can hear the whipping and chopping of ice axes, the front-pointing and squeaks of steel on blue ice, and the echoes of falling shrapnel of ice. I can hear the panting, the gritting, and the grunting. I can feel the moist heat of my body's steam struggle to escape through my clothing only to die and evaporate into the freezing air. I can feel the exhilaration of the panic, the challenge, and the accomplishment of each move all wadded up into one ball of satisfaction and thought. And I can imagine how quiet, calm, and peaceful Towuangseong Falls must appear to a very distant onlooker, a calm and cool winter stairway of frozen water connecting the heavens to the earth.

SUNG-DAE CHO (TRANSLATED BY PETER JENSEN-CHOI), *Corean Alpine Club*

Two views of Towuangseong Falls, Korea's premier ice climbing destination. *Jae-sik Son (2)*

LAOS

Paa Daeng Tower, Vang Vieng, new limestone climbs. In November 1999 Kirsten Kremer and I became only the second party to climb in the southeast Asian republic of Laos, when we put up a new route on the overhanging limestone wall of Paa Daeng or The Red Cliff. Paa Daeng is situated in full view of the rapidly expanding village of Vang Vieng, itself ca 150 kilometers north of the capital, Vientiane. We first spent two days cutting a way up third and fourth class vertical jungle terrain, keeping a careful eye on the local cobras and pit vipers, and avoiding a fire ant colony near the top. We reached the base of the main wall and found to our amazement it was a very steep cave, abounding with amazing pocket and tufa features. We had both spent many months climbing the bolted routes in Thailand and always wondered if there was similar terrain in Laos, which could be protected by traditional gear. The rock proved to be the best quality Southeast Asian karst and we committed to a full trad-style route straight out of the cave and up onto the headwall. On the first pitch we found perfect threads through pockets all the way and finally belayed at the top of a large stalactite below the lip of the cave, already 10 meters out from the base of the wall. The following day we began the second pitch, which climbed over the lip of the cave right of the stalactite and onto a slightly overhanging wall of crisp pockets. This pitch was well protected by Tricams, nuts, Camalots, and threads, and ended another eight meters out from the belay, where we placed two bolts. We fixed a rope down to the first belay and descended to town. Judging by the number of cobra skins we saw, bivouacs are not to be recommended.

The third pitch involved vertical razor edges with occasional cracks, fire ants, and some scary snake grass patches. Protection was spaced but adequate. The pitch ended on a fine wind-polished ledge with a large thread. One more pitch led up an amazing overhanging wall of unbelievable-quality red karst with threads readily available. Unfortunately it ended, left of the pointed top of the face, in the most heinous razor-rock vertical jungle imaginable. We descended to clean rock and rappelled the route. Two O'clock Wall is IV+ F6c.

Throughout the last day I had noticed a saffron dot in the sea of green rice below: a monk. The previous climbing party to visit Laos comprised Americans and Japanese, who established a number of sport routes close to the Mekong. The local headman in that area appears to be unhappy about their behavior. Local people have strong beliefs in mountain, cliff, and especially cave spirits, and do not take kindly to people hammering the rock or damaging it by placing bolts. We were careful to pick a venue that avoided offending cave spirits and when we came down that night, the villagers were friendly. We had obviously passed the scrutiny of the monk and had been accepted. The rice harvest was coming and the villagers thought we'd cause bad weather for their harvest by being above the fields and angering the mountain spirits. Moral: always check with your local monk. After that we never had a problem and completed 12 other routes, which were shorter but harder. On our return the following year we were treated like gold. Laos is a place to tread lightly, not only because of the millions of land mines and unexploded bombs. Respect will get you everything. This is a Buddhist/communist country and the people are proud to have survived all their troubles, while trying to find their way in the modern world.

PAUL TURECKI

MALAYSIA

Tioman Island, Dragon's Horns, first ascent. In late August 2000 Nick Tomlin and I spent eight days on Pulau Tioman, an island off the eastern coast of Malaysia, making the first ascent of the impressive Bukit Nekek Semekut, one of two peaks on the island's southern tip known collectively as the Dragon's Horns. Our route, Waking Dream (V 5.9 A2) climbs the prominent 1200-foot south face of the jungle spire, and required four nights on the wall in portaledges. To the best of our knowledge this was the first ascent of the mountain.

The 10-pitch line required the drilling of eight bolts (for belays) and 10 rivets, in addition to the bolts already in place on pitches 1-4 from our previous attempts (1996 and 1998). The rock is relatively

The Dragon's Horns of Tioman Island, Malaysia, formerly virgin. *Scotty Nelson*

good quality granite and our line follows the most obvious weakness on the face. We placed a handful of pins but the route will go clean very easily.

We endured one particularly terrifying lightning storm on the third night but other than that we had excellent weather. Pitch 5 was the crux, where Nick drilled five rivets to reach a thin crack, then used Aliens, hooks, micro nuts, and a very sketchy Tricam placement to lead us onto the lower-angled upper portion of the wall (pitches 3-5 are vertical to slightly overhanging). Pitches 7-10 were climbed in a summit push on the last day and involved mostly free climbing interspersed with some aid. Pitch 9 involved spectacular runout 5.9 face climbing on funky dimples and scoops in a water groove. Pitch 10 involved scampering up 5.5 friction and a bit of "jungle-neering." The top was spectacular, a perfectly flat Bonzai garden with stupendous views of the ocean, the island's interior, and surrounding peaks. We stacked a cairn on the summit boulder and snapped some photos before rappelling to our portaledge at the top of pitch 7 for the night. The following day we continued to the ground.

SCOTTY NELSON

THE LIST

*Introducing "First Ascents and New Routes In The Greater Ranges,"
an annual list compiled by the Expeditions Commission of the
Union Internationale des Associations d'Alpinisme (UIAA).*

JOSS LYNAM

In 1996 the Expeditions Commission of the UIAA decided to try to compile an annual list of First Ascents and New Routes in the Greater Ranges. The aim was twofold: firstly to ensure that mountaineers would have up-to-date information about what had been climbed, secondly to give contact addresses where more information could be obtained. We never guessed what we had let ourselves in for—it was a much bigger task than we had expected. The experienced Commission members present did some calculations on their fingers and decided that at most there would be 100 entries annually. In 1996 we received 65 entries and knew that we were missing more than we'd received. Our most recent list, for 2000, has over 200 entries, and we are pretty sure that we are still missing a few. The number of ascents we've logged is more than the number of entries—an expedition party often climbs more than one peak; this is especially true of Greenland where one entry may cover more than 10 new peaks or new routes.

How have we defined "Greater Ranges"? We look at several factors. Height is obviously one, closeness to centers where climbers live is another, how much of an effort is needed to get to the area a third. We wouldn't want to have to defend our choice with pure logic, but we can try to explain some choices.

- Caucasus omitted: *too well known and mapped*

- Mexico, Rockies of USA and Canada omitted: *too near the US and Canadian mountaineering centers*

- Alaska included: *most climbs are by non-residents*

- Andes included: *most climbs are by non-residents*

- Mali, Kenya, and Madagascar included: *almost entirely climbed by non-residents*

- Antarctica, Greenland, Himalaya, Tien Shan, China-Tibet, Asiatic ex-USSR included: *no justification needed*

What are our sources? We imagined that mountaineers, proud of their exploits would rush to send us information. They didn't. We do get back quite a few of the standard forms of which every UIAA member federation has copies, but often we have to rely on secondary sources, including reports from UIAA federations, research bodies like SGIM, national lists, magazines, and journals. (The *AAJ* has been a particularly good source). The problem with secondary sources is that the information takes longer to reach us and takes longer to process, so that the Annual List for 2000 was only issued in May 2002, and while we are working on the 2001 List, it will hardly be ready before Christmas 2002 (we had hoped that mountaineers planning Greater Ranges climbs would know of the previous years successes). We had originally hoped to include failures as well as successes because they often provide very valuable information for future attempts. So far this is more than we can cope with—but let's hope we'll get there in a few years.

We are now mainly collecting information about new ascents in 2002, but we can still take information about 2001. The List has grown bigger and more complete each year, and I'm sure 2002 will be no exception. We ask all mountaineers to help to make this archive as complete as possible. Report Forms may be obtained from the address below, either as a hard copy or through e-mail.

We are also glad to receive amendments and additions to Lists already issued—each new List includes at the end any new information received about previous years. So, if you know of any mistakes or omissions, please send them to the address below.

Information could be sent through the Expeditions Commission of your National Federation (such as the American Alpine Club), but we would prefer to receive it directly by post, fax, or e-mail. Please send it to:

Joss Lynam
UIAA Expeditions Commission
7 Sorbonne, Ardilea Estate
Dublin 14, Ireland.
Fax: +353-1-2831993
E-mail: jossl@indigo.ie

All the Annual Lists (1996, 97, 98, 99, 2000) are on the UIAA Website: www.uiaa.ch. Look for the Expeditions Commission section. Hard copies of the Annual Lists may be obtained from the address above by sending an A5 (legal-sized) self-addressed envelope and three international postal coupons.

Information comes from many different sources, sometimes hand-written, often with different spellings for the same name. We do our best to provide accurate information but neither the UIAA nor the Expeditions Commission nor any of the officers or members of these bodies nor our sources can be held responsible for the accuracy of the information in this List. Appearance of an entry in this List does NOT mean its correctness has been verified.

I would like to take this opportunity to thank the mountaineers who have sent me information and also (in no particular order) the many other sources which have played a vital role in helping to make the lists complete: Servei General d'Informació de Muntanya, Harish Kapadia, High Mountain Sports (Lindsay Griffin), Risk (Arkadi Klepinin), CISDAE, Japanese Alpine News (Tom Nakamura), American Alpine Journal, Alpine Journal, Elizabeth Hawley, DAV (Prof Dr Welsch and H Dick), PZA (Grzegorz Glazek), FFME.

BOOK REVIEWS

EDITED BY DAVID STEVENSON

Fifty Favorite Climbs: The Ultimate North American Tick List. MARK KROESE. SEATTLE: THE MOUNTAINEERS BOOKS, 2001. 150 COLOR PHOTOS. 224 PAGES. $32.95.

My bet is that within a year *Fifty Favorite Climbs* (henceforth FFC) will be found next to *Fifty Classic Climbs* (FCC) on the bookshelves of most climbers in North America. While FCC was the inspiration for FFC, the two have little in common beyond "Fifty" and "Climbs." Indeed, the contrast is more striking than the comparison, not surprising given the changes in the sport over the 22 years between their respective publications. Only about a fifth of the climbs in FCC were 5.9 or higher (a few, having been freed, were subsequently raised to 5.10), and an ambitious young climber might aspire to repeat all of the routes with the possible exception of Mt. Logan's Hummingbird Ridge. Maybe there are those who contemplate ticking off the list in FFC, but not only will they have to climb at a higher standard (about a fifth of the climbs are 5.12 or 5.13), they will also have to be masters of an increasing range of conditions and techniques, from big walls in alpine conditions to difficult rock climbing with ice tools to the contorting demands of sport climbing. This said, FFC still presents many climbs that today's competent climber could be inspired to attempt, depending on his or her bent.

Instead of updating FCC (as if "classic" could be updated), Kroese sought out fifty of the most accomplished climbers of the last 20 or so years and interviewed them on their favorite climbs. On the one hand, he follows a very strict format for each climber/climb, and on the other he has selected climbers who pursue a wide variety of styles, philosophies, playgrounds, and techniques. The result is a broad picture of the great diversity of the sport as well as specific accounts of the trials and rewards that climbing offers—both panorama and close-up if you will.

As to the format, each unit consists of four pages, starting with a full-page color photo of a climber (usually, but not always, the featured climber) on the climb. The facing page has a small portrait and a brief bio of the climber followed by the history of the climb (if it isn't a first ascent) and an account of the climber's ascent. Not all climbs, by the way, are first ascents or extremely difficult. The variety mentioned above also suggests that many different qualities can make a climb a favorite one ("scared the shit out of me" sometimes seems to be one). The third page continues the account and also has another fairly large photo that shows the route. If need be, the account carries over to the fourth page and is followed by information on first ascent, elevations, difficulty, time required, equipment, special considerations, references, and beta on how to get to the area, the route, the descent, and a detailed topo of the route in case you want to give it a go.

The use of large photos and the beta section necessarily restrict the amount of text, and to my mind this is an advantage. Kroese has decided to write the bio and account of the climb himself, based on extensive interviews, rather than have the climbers do their own. While this may deprive us of the climber's voice, it results in a consistently high quality of writing. In the main, Kroese's prose is remarkably efficient at getting the largest amount of information possible in the space he has allotted himself, and, while he tries to be objective and avoid sweating palm histrionics, he also delights with the occasional turn of phrase or insight or image that makes one smile. The reader might note that in the biography section each of the climbers is presented as something of a superperson, but then upon reading the account of the climb it seems quite likely that he or she really is, at least with respect to climbing.

I suspect that the names of somewhere between 40 and 45 of the climbers will be familiar to most readers. Given the history of the sport, most are men, but eight women grace these pages. Most are American, and all currently reside in the U.S. Jim Donini and Jim Bridwell appear to be the oldest climbers in the collection. Most of the others are seasoned veterans in their 30s or 40s, along with a few young hot shots. A few have highly honed egos, but most come across as desirable rope companions. Are there accomplished, even prestigious climbers who are not included? Might one wonder why X was included but not Y? Of course, but 50 is 50, and if it's my bat it's my rules.

As remarked above, the diversity of the routes is remarkable, from Nabisco Wall in Yosemite (soloed by John Bachar) to Belligerence, a 36 pitch mixed route on Mt. Combatant (Greg Child); from Gorillas in the Mist, modern mixed climbing in the Adirondacks (Jeff Lowe) to Hall of Mirrors on Glacier Point Apron (Johnny Woodward). As might be expected, Alaska and Northern Canada are home to nine of the climbs, the Canadian Rockies and Coast Range to another nine, Yosemite to eight, but then we are treated to areas that have been developed since the days of FCC: Newfoundland, Baffin Island, Red Rocks near Las Vegas, the Needles in the southern Sierra Nevada, Zion, and Canyonlands.

Two climbs especially appealed to my imagination, perhaps because both are imaginative in their conception. One is Ron Kauk's traverse on Middle Cathedral Rock. If solo climbing appeals to you, surely this is your route. Since you are never more than fifteen feet off the ground, if you don't feel up to the 5.12 that day, climb down, walk on a little, resume. If you want a longer climb, do laps. I should interject here that Kroese, and presumably the climbers concerned, take a somewhat relaxed approach to climbing style. One would not go to the Cookie Cliff with an aid rack, but on some of the longer, harder climbs one will find a rating like 5.9 A2, or 5.12b. If the climb is just rated at 5.12d, I guess you know what to expect. As to style, one climber also caught my attention when he was quoted as saying, "The first time I saw the Portrero, I saw about 150 lines I wanted to bolt"—in order to protect subsequent free ascents it turns out. More diversity.

The other climb that fairly shouted (but sotto voce) "what a great day" is Peter Croft's solo traverse of nine summits spaced along an eight-mile ridge in the Evolution Range of the Sierra Nevada. Croft did it in a long day, but the beta suggests two to five days. One could do it with a partner. One could do just three or four summits. It is a wonderful place to be. My pointing out these two routes should not be taken as slighting any of the others. A number of them are notable in their boldness, but then boldness is always notable. A number of them seem quite challenging but also fun. And if you don't want to do a particular climb, there are always the pleasures of reading the account in this book.

JOE FITSCHEN

The Mountains of My Life. Walter Bonatti. TRANSLATED AND EDITED, WITH AN ADDITIONAL CHAPTER, BY ROBERT MARSHALL. NEW YORK: MODERN LIBRARY, 2001. 443 PAGES. $14.95.

Was ever a great climber's life so rich in the bright sunshine of achievement and in the darkness of calumny and paranoia? A shadow fell across the life of the 24-year-old Walter Bonatti, when the accounts of the successful climb of K2 in 1954 elided the crucial support role he'd played at great risk to his life. Alternative reconstructions by different players, miscommunications between the climbers, non-communication in dumb show between them and their Balti porters, cover ups and mendacity by principals in the Italian Alpine Club (Club Alpino Italiano, CAI), all play a part.

The bare bones of this wretched story are as follows. With all other members of the team wasted or in retreat, Bonatti, accompanied by Mahdi, a porter with limited climbing or high altitude experience, carried two crucial tanks of oxygen from Camp 8 to around 26,300 feet, where they had expected to meet and share a tent with the summit team, Compagnoni and Lacedelli. The tent was not at the agreed location, and the summiters made little effort to help Bonatti and Mahdi find them, nor seemed concerned at the danger in which they stood. Unable to reach the higher pair, Bonatti (who'd already spent seven continuous days above 23,000 feet) and the porter bivouacked—this at a time when bivouacs above 8,000 meters were thought to be killers and Herman Buhl's survival of one at the top of Nanga Parbat the previous year deemed a fluke.

Next morning the support pair descended and Compagnoni and Lacedelli retrieved the tanks and summited. All Italy cheered at the achievement, expiating the humiliation of defeat in World War II. But upon returning to base Bonatti was disturbed at the bad vibes coming from Ardito Desio, the leader of the expedition, the summit pair, and the liaison officer.

Bonatti's valor and toughness were barely acknowledged in the final version of the film and the books that followed. On the 10th anniversary of the ascent, the character assassins came out into the open. Compagnoni hand-fed a story to a newspaper alleging that Bonatti 1) attempted to grab the summit for himself and Mahdi, 2) used up a significant part of the oxygen in the tanks that were delivered to the summit pair, and 3) was responsible for Mahdi's terrible frostbite and subsequent amputation of fingers and toes. Bonatti sued for libel and won a judgment, the cash damages going to an orphanage.

The court's ruling did not, however, begin to unravel what had happened on K2, or how these accusations came to be made. On the issue of the oxygen, the court deemed that the accusation was false because the summit pair, and not Bonatti, had the masks and nozzles for the tanks. The mighty CAI refused the enquiry to which Bonatti now felt entitled. His galloping sense of persecution was inflamed by repeated slights and small vilifications. Once the tires of his car were slashed as he gave a slide show. But as he had done from the beginning, Bonatti fought back in print with his version of those events: seeming more of a raving, pathetic figure as time passed and the events dimmed in public memory.

The scene now switches to Melbourne, Australia, to a middle-aged surgeon, Robert Marshall, armchair mountaineer with an interest in Italians first kindled by Fosco Maraini's great classic, *Karakoram.* He learnt literary Italian well enough to try his hand at better translations of Bonatti's first two books, *Le Mie Montagne* (translated in English as *On The Heights,* 1961) and *I Giorni Grandi* 1971 (as *Great Days*). Soon after it was published in Italy in 1985, he also read Bonatti's account of his legal fight in *Processo al K2 (Trial on K2).* He told me in an e-mail, "It was obvious to me that there was a great deal more to the K2 affair than Bonatti had ever guessed."

The real eye-opener was a transcription of Mahdi's deposition, which the court, and Bonatti, had found as crazy and incoherent as had been his ravings and ululations during the night of the bivy. Marshall recognized that Mahdi's representation had an internal coherence and consistency. Provided one understood his assumptions, it explained how the allegation of Bonatti's bid to steal the summit came to pass. In broken English several of the climbers in 1954 had promised Mahdi a shot at the summit bid with little regard to the consequences. In *Le Mie Montagne* Bonatti wrote that he "put the proposal to Mahdi, giving him the impression that he might be able to go on up to the summit with me, Lacedelli and Compagnoni." It was a necessary deception, which, however had a grain of truth to it. Mahdi, who had no idea that a bivouac precluded any attempt on the summit, evidently thought Bonatti was taking him on an end-run around the other pair. The canard got passed onto Desio, who accepted it without questioning Bonatti.

Bonatti was grateful for Marshall's insights. But he was to be even more thankful when in mid-1993 Marshall found the evidence that blew up Compagnoni's version of the events. Browsing through his copy of *Mountain World* 1955, he did a double-take at a photograph he'd seen years earlier without understanding its significance. *Mountain World's* preliminary account of the expedition, authored by Desio, contained a summit picture (never to appear again) in which Compagnoni is seen wearing the oxygen mask and drawing on the tanks that he claimed had emptied two hours earlier and caused him to fling off the mask!

The photograph and Marshall's analysis were published in the Italian mountaineering journal, Alp in June 1994, and the climbing community, which had not been over-excited by the court case, suddenly realized the perfidy. Although its chief witness against Bonatti was exposed as a liar, the CAI remained immovable. So in the official world, where the cynical Italians know everything is fixed, Desio's truth prevails (last year he got a Presidential award for achievements in geology and mountaineering) while in the real world, when Desio died, also last year, at 104, the injustice done to Bonatti featured prominently in the newspaper and magazine obituaries of the old martinet.

But for the 71-year-old Bonatti the story is not over: because the truth so betrayed can never be restored to truth. Robert Marshall tells me that even this book's editors felt that Bonatti in places sounded quite paranoid and insisted that language be toned down, and acerbic attacks on the CAI and Desio cut out. And these are the rescuers of Bonatti's truth! Thus the past persists insidiously and incorrigibly in the present, and full restitution for poor Bonatti is impossible, because the initial conditions that led to the conspiracy cannot be undone. Then, too, there are also loose ends, not the least of which is the character and motives of the summit pair, who are as enshrined in Italy's pantheon of greats as are Hillary and Tensing in the English-speaking world. What did they imagine would they gain from these deceptions? How could they traduce what might have been a great and noble climb?

In any event, the attack had no effect on Bonatti's reputation as a climber, because in the following decade he undertook a chain of exploits that made him a climbing legend: among them are the solo southwest pillar of the Dru, Gasherbrum IV, an epic descent and rescue off the central pillar of Freney, a new route on the north face of the Grande Jorasses, first winter ascent of its Walker Spur, and for a finale the winter solo first ascent of the direct north face of the Matterhorn. In Marshall's vivid translation, these constitute the main and most satisfying part of *The Mountains of My Life,* which also has a few chapters from notable pre-K2 climbs, such as the North faces of Lavaredo in winter.

I've given disproportionate space to *l'affaire K2,* which takes up less than a third of *The Mountains of My Life,* because of the weirdness on K2 and of Marshall's unusual penetration of the wall between the author and reader and the subsequent help he gave Bonatti in finding some restitution and peace of mind.

Another factor in this story is Bonatti's power of attraction in deed and language. His prose is passionate, limpid, and economic. It is romantic, but not excessively colored. And like St. Exupery's writing about flying, Bonatti's accounts seem to be charged with a suppressed Judeo-Christian morality play: as if climbing is above all a test of the spirit, the outward manifestation of a struggle with the demons of human weakness.

The book's penultimate chapter, an account of a solo climb of Mont Blanc's Peuterey Ridge at age 54, shows Bonatti at his most lyrical. This route is a serious and committing climb at any age, yet Bonatti's story has almost no technical details, no stain of physical effort, so dedicated is he to closely tracking his emotions and carefully describing his connections to what he sees and hears. A thousand times I've read that climbing is an inner journey of self-discovery, but most accounts of it are strictly exogenous. With Bonatti no, he has an amazing power to define himself, his quest, and to sweep the reader along. Time and again the prose is like shafts of sunlight breaking through cloud as Bonatti conveys the sublimity and ecstasy of his great trials. Language of such power, in this style, won't ever be written again by a great climber: catch it while you can.

JOHN THACKRAY

Missing in the Minarets: The Search for Walter A. Starr, Jr. WILLIAM ALSUP. FOREWORD BY GLEN DAWSON. YOSEMITE NATIONAL PARK: YOSEMITE ASSOCIATION, 2001. 215 PAGES, NUMEROUS BLACK-AND-WHITE PHOTOGRAPHS. $24.95. NOTE: ALL PROFITS FROM THE YOSEMITE ASSOCIATION GO TO SUPPORT YOSEMITE NATIONAL PARK.

In the summer of 1933, 30-year-old Walter "Pete" Starr, Jr. set off on a solo expedition in California's Sierra Nevada in order to survey the landscape along the new John Muir Trail. In addition to exploration, his purpose was to gather notes for a guidebook he was writing. An experienced mountaineer, Starr was also a lawyer with a San Francisco firm and the scion of a prominent family. When he failed to come out of the mountains at the appointed time, his father became concerned. Several days passed; concern gave way to alarm. A search effort was mounted, involving some of the most famous mountaineers in Sierra history. An intense search over the course of several days in the vicinity of mounts Banner and Ritter as well as on the spectacular Minarets yielded promising clues but no firm results. In the end, the searchers gave up in despair, packed up their camp and filed grimly out of the mountains to home. All of them, that is, except one: the legendary Norman Clyde. When all others had surrendered hope, he alone persevered. What he found in his solitary pursuit became the basis for several generations of stories told around Sierra campfires. Now William Alsup has provided us with a definitive historical account of those fateful August days almost seventy years ago.

Missing in the Minarets is part mountaineering history, part detective story, and part photo album. It is 100 percent engaging reading. Alsup's lucid prose is complemented by the inclusion of numerous well-reproduced photographs, some of which are historical and others documentary images made by the author himself. It would seem that Alsup is ideally suited to write a book like this. As a recognized Sierra historian (author of the excellent *Such a Landscape!*, which recounts William Brewer's 1864 California Survey), a skilled photographer, an enthusiastic mountaineer, and a former San Francisco trial attorney now serving as a federal district judge, he applies his many-sided genius to sorting through a complexity of evidence in order to provide his reader with a clear and compelling account of an important episode in the social history of the Sierra Nevada.

It was no easy task. Most of the people who participated in the events are now dead. There are many gaps in the evidentiary record. What evidence does survive, especially in the form of written records, is often contradictory. Perhaps most challenging of all is the aura of myth that has long surrounded the fate of Starr, a swirl of exaggeration and speculation that makes it difficult for a researcher to separate fact from fiction. Nevertheless, Alsup conducted a painstaking and meticulous investigation, literally leaving no stone unturned (you'll have to read the book to catch this allusion). He sought out the few people still alive who were eyewitnesses; he not only tracked down descendants of the Starr family but also members of a Stockton, California Boy Scout troop who happened to be in the area of Minarets at the same time Starr disappeared. Alsup even got his hands on the film that was found in Starr's camera—the last pictures the man ever took—and printed fresh images, which are published for the first time in this book. Having brought all this new evidence to light, Alsup then applies his keen analytical sensibility to reconstructing a plausible chain of events. The result is a book best described as an exercise in mountaineering forensics. You could say that Alsup has succeeded in putting up a new route on a previously unmapped (or poorly mapped) past.

Accounts of mountaineering accidents serve a curious dual purpose in the climbing community. On the one hand, we say such reading is instructive and indeed essential, because it allows us to learn from other people's often fatal mistakes. On the other hand, we experience a simple, though often unacknowledged, attraction toward the gruesome, the same urge indulged by passing motorists who slow down and gawk at bloody car wrecks. The Germans, with their precise psychological vocabulary, have a word for this feeling: *Schadenfreude*, the joy we take in other people's misery. Much of the continuing interest in Mallory is less attributable to the question of whether or not he made it to the summit than it is to the grisly fascination some people have with the frozen body that lies abject on the upper reaches of the mountain, like a word emptied of its meaning. When you get right down to it, you could say that *Schadenfreude* played no small part in the success of Krakauer's *Into Thin Air*.

In contrast to the fascination with death that characterizes many mountaineering narratives, Missing in the Minarets avoids this emotional dog route and focuses instead on character. The author takes great care to allow the evidence to speak for itself. As a writer, Alsup resists the temptation to identify too closely with his subject matter, and he refrains from entering the narrative himself, except at the very beginning and end, in order to provide the context for the investigation. "I drew on my 25 years as a trial lawyer in sizing up evidence," he explains in the afterward, "as well as my quarter-century of hiking and climbing in the Sierra. In this book I have tried, however, to provide enough of the actual record so that readers can make their own judgments, for, without question, the evidence is sometimes subject to multiple interpretations." As a result, *Missing in the Minarets* becomes a tale of two men, Pete Starr and Norman Clyde, which focuses attention on the philosophical question, What is the nature of a mountaineer?

Pete Starr loved the mountains. He was, on the one hand, "outgoing, the sociable son of a prominent family, a joiner in college and career. On the other, at least in the wild, he preferred the companionship of the landscape itself." He was a man who one time, not having a pencil, signed his name in a mountain register in his own blood. And then there is Norman Clyde, one of the great "characters" in North American mountaineering history, who likewise valued his solitude. For most of his life he was not known to have a regular job and spent his days wandering and climbing in the Range of Light, achieving by far more first ascents than anybody else on record. Even this achievement pales in comparison to his devotion to just being in the mountains. Both these men ought to be compared to the most famous of all Sierra mountaineers, John Muir, who, in writing about his own solitary and dangerous adventures on Mt. Ritter, captured something of the spirit of all those old-time Sierra climbers: "But we little know until tried how much of the uncontrollable there is in us, urging across glaciers and torrents, and up dangerous heights, let the judgment forbid as it may."

The ancient Greek philosopher Heraclitus observed that character is destiny. The exquisitely produced *Missing in the Minarets* demonstrates that, for some characters, destiny lay in the mountains and that this destiny often comes at a dear price. Alsup concludes his book with these admonitory words: "Peter Starr proved how dangerous was the climb; readers definitely should not repeat the act." Wise words. You, however, will likely want to repeat the act of reading this deeply satisfying book.

JOHN P. O'GRADY

The High Himalaya. ART WOLFE. SEATTLE: THE MOUNTAINEERS BOOKS, 2001. 160 PAGES, 140 PHOTOGRAPHS, HARDCOVER. $49.95.

Few contemporary nature photographers are as prolific or talented as Seattle-based Art Wolfe, who spends nine months a year traveling to remote corners of the world in search of stunning images. In just three decades he has produced 45 books and it was only a matter of time before he focused on the Himalaya—perhaps the planet's most magnificent landscape.

Given the impressive number of Himalayan books that have already been published, he faced some very hard acts to follow. As I first flipped through the pages of *High Himalaya*, however, I was pleased to see many signature images that immediately set him apart. I especially liked his strong visual theme of tightly-cropped details, patterns, and textures, a peek at things that is uniquely his own. Some are as intimate as a spray of tiny flowers in the Rongbuk Valley, the ripples in a folded rock, or the snowy slats of a bridge across the Hunza River. Others are grander, ranging from star tracks behind towering mountains to huge fluted snow faces, or hazy ridges receding towards the plains of India. Within these frames he shows us the world as he alone can see it.

In many images Wolfe also demonstrates his mastery of light, shadow and color—as well as the patience to wait until they are perfect. I loved the alpenglow he captured on Masherbrum, Mitre Peak, and many others, and wanted to step right into the "God rays" he saw pouring between the Trango Towers. Also notable were juxtapositions of light and shadow that bring huge depth to some of his images on the Pamir Plateau and one winning shot of Gasherbrum. He knows how to make the most of a swirl of color, or the momentary kiss of warmth into an otherwise frigid environment.

Viewing this book with eyes that have seen more Himalayan pictures than I can remember, I was impressed. It's inspirational to watch how he plays with the light and frames his pictures to maximize curves, jagged edges, repeating shapes, and other compositional elements that make them "Art" (pun intended), not just snapshots. Still, I wish that Wolfe had edited even more tightly toward this distinctive vision.

As with most photography books, *High Himalaya* includes a few pictures that seem to stray from the mix and these puzzled me. There's a yak staring stupidly at the camera in boring mid-day light and a few scenes of various mountains that any trekker might have shot. As well, there are scenes of mountains such as Machhapuchhare or the Trango Towers that break no distinctly new visual ground. But maybe these serve a purpose. By reminding the viewer of the ordinary, they make us appreciate his stronger images all the more.

A more serious critique of *High Himalaya*, however, is the book's inclusion of a text that bears little connection to the images. Aside from Wolfe's own camera notes about each picture—which are fun to read and provide interesting background (as well as the book's only personal story line)—the rest of the words are interviews and short descriptions of the accomplishments of famed mountaineers Reinhold Messner, Ed Viesturs, and Doug Scott, all written by Peter Potterfield. Together with a nicely articulated and very personal introduction by Norbu Tenzing Norgay (Tenzing's son), these echo a common theme that the real rewards of Himalayan mountaineering are encounters with the natural environments and cultures through which alpinists pass in search of their summits. Here, each climber suggests the need to reach out and learn something from local people, and then to give something back.

This is a noble and important message, but it doesn't really fit the pictures. It also leads Wolfe into dangerous ground, inviting comparison not just with landscape photographers—with whom he can hold his own—but also with such brilliant Himalayan cultural photographers as Eric Valli, Roland and Sabrina Michaud or Steve McCurry—with whom he does not. In a few cases he delivers. His best people shots are of Kazakh horsemen galloping together in clouds of dust as they jostle one another for possession of a headless goat. He stopped and really waited to catch them at their best. I also liked the patterns he captured in the exotic yellow hats of Buddhist monks in Kathmandu, the splash of color on the back of a Balti child carrying flowering weeds in Askole, or the rich warm light on the faces of Uygur children in western China.

Over a broader span of pages, however, I was disappointed. The book includes too many listless, unengaged portraits of people staring at the lens, whether they be wrinkled Nepali grandmothers, Hindu "naga babas," gangs of giggling kids, or sultry teenagers sucked closer by a telephoto. It looks as if Wolfe was rushing through his encounters with many of these subjects en route to something more important. Only occasionally does his cultural photography share the same power and attention to detail as his pictures of nature and the mountains—which he, himself, admits to be his forte and greatest love. With a few exceptions, I wish he'd stuck with what he does best.

What really sets a book apart is passion. You can't look at Galen Rowell's *My Tibet*, Eric Valli's *Caravans*, or Steve McCurry's *Monsoon* without feeling a visceral sense of how much they love their subjects. There is no doubt that Wolfe also brims with this for both the art of photography and the wider natural world. In the best pages of *High Himalaya*, that shines clearly through the ink. But as I look more carefully at this somewhat disjointed book, I feel that in Wolfe's exuberance to create powerful mountain images, he hasn't slowed down enough to let the more ethereal Himalaya root deeply in his soul.

GORDON WILTSIE

Enduring Patagonia. GREGORY CROUCH. NEW YORK: RANDOM HOUSE. 224 PAGES, HARDCOVER. $24.95.

Wind, cold wind, rain, snow, waiting, and more wind. These elements define the desolate peaks of Patagonia, mountains of modest altitude, but mountains with subjective dangers always lurking ominously in the background.

Greg Crouch, no stranger to the climbing world, has made his bones as a legitimate climber, and with the release of his new book, *Enduring Patagonia*, he establishes himself as a serious adventure writer. Crouch uses an excellent vocabulary to skillfully paint colorful pictures of this remote, wild area and its people; you can almost feel the golden granite of Fitzroy and Cerro Torre, topped with fragile and perilous rime rising through the clouds. For those with challenged imaginations, 16 pages of beautiful color photos make up for any lack of visualization. Chapter three, "The Nature of Alpinism," masterfully explains the creation of the unique and violent weather of Patagonia, as geographic and meteorological factors collide in an ocean of ice and water.

Crouch's life revolves around climbing. When he is not climbing, he tackles any type of work that will quickly return him to his love/hate affair with Patagonia. Climbing is a visible projection of his philosophy and how it guides his life. It is not about heroics or conquering mountains, but about the fatigue, pain and misery that is endured to achieve not necessarily victory but closure. One quote, "the most remarkable statements of character are often played out in losing efforts and doomed causes," reveals his feeling that often a greater personal victory is found in returning from failure to prevail. Although he pushes the envelope, he has a good sense of his own mortality and knows when to back off and regroup. One contradictory trait that pops up from time to time is his rather blasé approach to supply logistics, starting many climbs with insufficient food, a meager selection of hardware, and once with the wrong size ice boots; to his credit he overcomes these shortages by personal toughness and ingenuity.

The setting of this book is climbing in Patagonia, but the writing rises above the genre of the standard climbing tale. Crouch probes his inner feelings while reminiscing about his personal pantheon of legendary climbers and the human qualities he respects. One begins to feel the inner peace he finds as each climbing goal is achieved. A good ascent can be a summit well won under a blue sky, or it can be the fight of an over-matched boxer, whose victory is the courage to step into the ring and struggle on as long as possible. By a careful mixture of metaphor and simile he lures the reader closer and closer to that scary place that all climbers have visited at one point or another, a mixture of fear, isolation, and doubt that can only be overcome by advancing or accepting the realty of a debilitating retreat. As you read on you feel the fear that gnaws at Crouch and his teammates as they endlessly wait for a break in the weather, a fear he equates to a soldier waiting for D Day. You feel the base camp blues. The terror of sitting out a storm in a tent perched precariously on a lofty ledge, not knowing what is going on in the dark outside, conscious only of the wind tearing at your tent, seeking to hurl you from the side of the mountain. To Crouch, climbing with honor and skill is life itself.

Crouch is rightfully obsessed by the winds of Patagonia, indeed scarcely a page passes without some reference to the wind and anyone coming to this place suffers some degree of anemomania (wind madness). His military training at West Point and Army Ranger School characterize his approach to all obstacles and has well prepared him for the physical and psychological challenges faced in his seven trips to the wilds of Patagonia. Each barrier or crux becomes a frontal assault ending either in victory or retreat, but never defeat. Retreats are resolved as battles to be fought again. It is no accident that on several occasions he uses the word crucible to describe the peaks and valleys, a crucible where the values he so respects are forged.

Climbers and adventure readers will enjoy this book. The technical descriptions are straightforward and detailed enough for the climber, and his thoughtful inclusion of a climbing glossary gives the casual reader a better feel for the climbing sequences.

Thankfully Crouch has avoided the current fad to overuse trendy terminology to the point of rendering most articles incomprehensible to all except the youngest and most hip readers. One thing is made very clear; success in the mountains of Patagonia cannot be bought by well-financed climbing dilettantes. These mountains make themselves accessible only through old school dedication and a long apprenticeship in the alpine trade.

Climbers should read this book, not to learn about climbing, but perhaps to learn more about themselves. Non-climbers should read it to better understand the strange lot that does climb.

JOHN BRAGG

Below Another Sky: A Mountain Adventure in Search of a Lost Father. RICK RIDGEWAY. NEW YORK: OWL BOOKS, 2000. 306 PAGES, PAPERBACK. $15.00.

The book begins in 1980, with the young Rick Ridgeway writing about his surviving an avalanche that killed a close friend: "I need to get this down while it's still fresh." Yet he wisely waited before expanding upon that lead. Twenty years later, *Below Another Sky* was published in New York, where editors cast a wary eye at writers under 40. The conventional wisdom among these publishers is that young writers lack the life experience to perform the so-called "act of literature."

Below Another Sky could not have been written with such lucidity immediately after the avalanche. It is no accident, however, that the best-selling climbing disasters rush cathartically to press from hospital rooms and funerals: Whymper spinning the Matterhorn fall, Herzog agonizing over his Annapurna frostbite, Simpson embellishing his crevasse abandonment, or Krakauer recreating the Everest tragedy. Until Ridgeway's book, there was no climber pulling a *River Runs Through It* and taking a couple of decades to hone their defining tragedy. Don't get me wrong, I've avidly devoured the aforementioned books, but *Below Another Sky* effectively asks if climbing literature is too narcissistic, or lacking in feminine perspective, as if our asexual mountaineers never face the consequences of returning home to any family or community outside the sterile ranges. (In the interest of full disclosure, as a writer, I too may be responsible for this vacuum.) Of course, Ridgeway has also written other expedition books that follow the limitations of traditional form. His *Seven Summits* for instance, became a bestseller eight years before *Into Thin Air*, recounting how wealthy clients were towed up the world's tallest mountain—without a body count. While his other books artfully describe classic moments in mountaineering history, at the appearance of his newest and most inventive book, *Below Another Sky*, the judges for the American Alpine Club unanimously awarded Ridgeway the Literary Award. It is to the reader's advantage that the author waited and contemplated his loss for two decades, so that he could describe a mountaineering disaster with careful hindsight.

So this thoughtful story is rare because it begins—rather than ends—with tragedy, and Ridgeway avoids exploiting Jonathan Wright's death by celebrating his life and focusing on the survivors. Nearly two decades after the accident, Ridgeway takes Wright's daughter, Asia, back to Tibet in order to try and show her her long-dead father. Admittedly, it is an emotional book, which less sensitive literati, equipped with overly sensitive bullshit detectors, might pronounce mawkish. But in my opinion, Ridgeway has taken great verbal risks to unveil some awkward truths. He didn't wait this long to simply weave a tale of sentimentality. By utilizing carefully structured vignettes about past mistakes, Ridgeway's purpose, in the time-honored tradition of a tribal elder, is to pass on wisdom and judgment. Whether he actually told all of these lessons to Asia during their journey is a moot point, because the structure works, while Ridgeway's candidness effectively transports the reader.

For instance, although he openly admires the authenticity of Wright's Buddhist beliefs as quoted in journals and conversations, Ridgeway shows his own skepticism about this sometimes-trendy theology in a hilarious anecdote about a Hollywood Buddhist. Or by freely sharing his and Asia's foibles and doubts, the reader is moved by flesh and blood characters—rather than the understated male prose, the partnership conflicts, or the grieving and one-dimensional caricatures that already dominate this particular disaster genre.

Quietly, without the hoopla of other mountaineering accidents (in 1980, the media wasn't covering deaths on unheard-of peaks such as Minya Konka), Ridgeway has created a durable adventure memoir, a cross between *The Snow Leopard* and *Moments of Doubt*. The story builds like the slow-breaking waves that Ridgeway is fond of surfing, pulling the reader through one anecdote after another, tumbling along with Asia toward the inevitable shore break.

There are also bright nuances about Ridgeway's jail time in South America, his marriage, and his climbing partnership with the luminaries—Yvon Chouinard, Chris Chandler, Ron Fear, John Roskelly—that are at once fascinating and then enlightening for anyone who ever entertained a life of adventure.

As a gifted storyteller, it should come as no surprise that Ridgeway deftly paints the willful Asia, the iconoclastic Yvon, and the sensory aspects of an avalanche ride. To meet Rick Ridgeway is also to know that this book is sincere, because he writes as he talks, softly, describing his fiercely won friends as merely "good buddies" and avoiding, at all costs, the didactic. He is the quintessential filmmaker in this manner, deploying images instead of unnecessary language. In *Below Another Sky* we know where Rick's story will end, with Asia at the grave of her father and his friend, but it's the stops along the way that provide resonance and make this intensely personal book a compelling act of literature.

JONATHAN WATERMAN

Above the Clouds: The Diaries of a High Altitude Mountaineer. ANATOLI BOUKREEV. COLLECTED AND EDITED BY LINDA WYLIE. NEW YORK: ST. MARTIN'S PRESS, 2001. 290 PAGES, 26 PAGES OF COLOR PHOTOGRAPHS. $27.95.

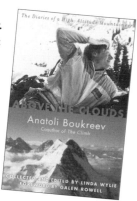

When the American Alpine Club received the first invitation ever from the USSR to climb in the Pamir, in 1974, Anatoli Boukreev was 16 years old—and just beginning his high altitude training in the Tien Shan. He did some first ascents of 5,000 meter peaks even then. What he went on to accomplish would make him a gold medalist many times over if climbing and taking care of others—in and out of the mountains—were an Olympic sport. He managed despite asthma (probably brought on by coal dust), a bout of meningitis, a car accident, a bus accident, and the collapse of the USSR. The latter resulted in the privatization of sports, and thus no more financial support for Russian climbers.

In *Above the Clouds* the reader learns from a collection of Boukreev's journals and articles, edited by his companion Linda Wylie, about the life of an athlete/philosopher raised in Kazakhstan. Through several accounts of his signature climbs between 1990 and 1997, we are given great insight and much more depth on the Russian system of training and the team spirit that prevailed there than is found in his Everest book, *The Climb.*

A lengthy foreword by Galen Rowell, who had been asked to accompany Anatoli on what became his ill-fated Annapurna attempt, provides the reader with good reason to read on, to learn about this man. A sample quote: "Anatoli's fine mind was far more in tune with its body, which it rightly recognized as part of, rather than separate from the natural world…." Having set the stage with comments like this, Rowell also takes some time to put the Everest events of 1996 in perspective.

Linda Wright's 30-page introduction tells us of Anatoli's background—his formative years in the coal town Korkino (which means "the last crust of bread") and later Almaty— both in Kazakhstan—and the Russian style of training: the reliance on team climbing and comradeship.

I had turned down the corners of about 25 pages by the end of the book. When I reviewed what I had marked, I found a consistent reference to his belief that to be in the mountains to the fullest, one needs to train—to "derive pleasure from the process of physical and mental development." I found that he had gone out many times—often alone—from the safety of camp to find or to give aid to comrades late in returning. And then there was his reverence for the mountains: "It is myself that I struggle with in this life, not with the mountains. Their greatness and strength is indisputable, only man is in transit, evolving, growing, and the road that we choose to follow in life depends less on the surrounding world than on our spirit—the internal voice that pushes one to seek new challenges."

The book concludes (except for an epilogue and chronology) with a chapter called "Letters from Annapurna," where Anatoli died in a massive avalanche on December 25, 1997, not long after having been bestowed the American Alpine Club's David Sowles Award for his rescue efforts on Mt. Everest. There are excerpts from a letter to Jim Wickwire and an interview in which he summarizes his quest: "Speaking honestly, I do not feel fear climbing high; rather, my shoulders straighten square like a bird stretching its wings. I enjoy the freedom and the height." And then there is the letter followed by the phone call from from "Tolya" to Linda, along with her personal comments and the final call to her from Simone Moro with the sad news. We feel the closeness and the loss through these few pages.

Climber or not, you should read this account for the simple purity and depth of spirit you will find. And let me not forget to mention the wry humor. There are many surprises in store for you.

JOHN E. (JED) WILLIAMSON

Tenzing Norgay and the Sherpas of Everest. TASHI TENZING, WITH JUDY TENZING. FOREWORDS BY SIR EDMUND HILLARY AND HIS HOLINESS THE DALAI LAMA. CAMDEN, MAINE: RAGGED MOUNTAIN-McGRAW-HILL, 2001. 294 PAGES, MORE THAN 100 BLACK-AND-WHITE PHOTOS. $26.00.

Touching My Father's Soul: A Sherpa's Journey to the Top of Everest. JAMLING TENZING NORGAY WITH BROUGHTON COBURN. INTRODUCTION BY JON KRAKAUER. FOREWORD BY HIS HOLINESS THE DALAI LAMA. SAN FRANCISCO: HARPER COLLINS, 2001. 314 PAGES, COLOR AND BLACK-AND-WHITE PHOTOS. $26.00.

The first to summit Mt. Everest along with Edmund Hillary, Tenzing Norgay has a legacy of achievement that lives on in his son, Jamling Tenzing Norgay, and grandson, Tashi Tenzing. Jamling and Tashi are not father and son, but uncle and nephew, descendants of Tenzing Norgay from his third and first marriages respectively, born within a year of each other in the mid 1960s in Darjeeling, India. Both have climbed Everest, Jamling in 1996 and Tashi 1997, and now each has given us his story. Their books fill great voids in that much-lacking Sherpa perspective in the annals of Himalayan mountaineering.

Tashi Tenzing's book, *Tenzing Norgay and the Sherpas of Everest*, chronicles the history of the Sherpa people and how they came from Tibet to live in the shadow of the mountain they called Chomolungma, the discovery of the worlds highest peak and its subsequent name change by the Royal Geographical Society in London, the halcyon days of British-owned expeditions out of Darjeeling, and the significant role the Sherpas played from the earliest years of exploration in the Himalaya. If in contemplating the conquering of Everest you have ever asked yourself, What about the Sherpas? Then this is the book for you. Tashi has selected a few but memorable Tigers of the Snows, who represent the many Sherpas of selfless courage and devotion, incredible strength and amazing endurance at high altitude. In carrying the loads and making the camps, the Sherpas made possible the exploration of the Himalaya as well as the historical push of Tenzing Norgay and Edmund Hillary to the summit of Everest that day in May 1953.

The greatest attention, of course, is paid to the Sherpa who changed everything for his people. As a young boy growing up in the Khumbu region of Nepal, Tenzing Norgay heard the adventurous stories of Sherpa porters returning home from the early Everest expeditions. In those days, the Buddhist lamas warned the Sherpas against climbing the peaks, and they heeded that warning. But Tenzing yearned not only to join an expedition as a high altitude porter, he dreamt of one day climbing Chomolungma. Details and photos of his early years of expeditions and summits leading up to the 1952 and 1953 attempts on Everest provide tantalizing, foreshadowy glimpses of his successful seventh go, yet nothing in his life prepared Tenzing Norgay for the maelstrom of politics and fame that would meet him when he left the mountain. With good counsel he survived the politics, which faded with time, while the fame followed him throughout his life. Tashi also bravely discusses the burden of great unhappiness that Tenzing Norgay bore in the last years of his life.

The story does not end on a sad note, however. Not only do Tashi and his uncle Jamling go on to summit Everest, Tenzing's extended family and the Sherpa people have produced many great climbers, some of whom are highlighted; Tenzing Norgay and the Sherpas of Everest also includes a chart showing the Sherpas' phenomenal success on Everest: 489 Sherpa/Nepali summits, out of a total of 1,318 summits, through the year 2000. Moreover, thanks in no small part to the Himalayan Trust started by Sir Edmund Hillary, the Sherpa people of the Solu Khumbu region enjoy more schools and hospitals than any other region in the Himalaya, and many have gone on to become professionals in various fields around the world. Nevertheless, Tashi notes that not all progress brings positive change. With the influx of negative outside influences, and the increased commercialization of climbing expeditions, his people face many cultural, ecological, and economic challenges. They are reminded that for inspiration they need go no further than that most famous of Sherpas, Tenzing Norgay, for he, in one amazing lifetime, forged the path the next generations of his people are now navigating.

When you request a divination, you must always be prepared to abide by the answer, Tenzing Norgay once told his son Jamling. The words came back to Jamling Tenzing Norgay in early 1996, after Chatral Rimpoche, a respected Tibetan Buddhist lama, told him that the conditions for the coming season on Everest did not look favorable. But he had already committed to being Climbing Leader of the 1996 Everest IMAX Filming Expedition. Filmmaker David Breashears was counting on him and his story; if he dropped out, Jamling wondered how that would reflect on the expedition and what would happen to his dream, his drive, to climb Everest. Jamling was not a devout Buddhist, yet the divination could not be ignored; his wife urged him to visit her family's lama in Kathmandu, where they hoped for better news. Thus begins Touching My Father's Soul: A Sherpa's Journey to the Top of Everest, and with chapter titles such as "An Ominous Forecast," "Standing Before the Goddess," and "The Wrath of the Goddess," one will soon understand this is not your ordinary expedition narrative.

As we now know, the early divination proved true, and that spring did bring an unfavorable season. The Everest tragedy of 1996 unfolded before the eyes of the IMAX team and the world. Fortunately, the IMAX team returned safe, successful, and with a story to tell. However, the book is not so much about Jamling's eyewitness account of the high-altitude disaster, or how the son of Tenzing Norgay came to be on a 90-foot movie screen, as it is the story of an amazing spiritual journey that started long before Jamling was even born.

Devotees of Tibetan Buddhism, the Sherpa people believe that a female deity called Miyolangsangma is the protector goddess who resides on Mt. Everest. Tenzing Norgay believed that Miyolangsangma guided him safely to the summit of Everest in 1953, and Jamling grew up seeing his father worship the goddess in the chapel in their home in Darjeeling. Before Jamling's mother died, she told Jamling that there was a special bond between their family and the mountain that involved his father's second wife, Ang Lhamu. She told him to find the lama Trulshig Rimpoche, and ask him for the story. Even so, when he sought out Trulshig Rimpoche in 1995, he was unprepared to hear what the lama had to tell him: not only had it been prophesied in the 1930s that a Himalayan Buddhist would be the first person to climb Chomolungma, Jamling was told that there were indications that his stepmother, Ang Lhamu, had been a manifestation, a human embodiment, of the goddess Miyolangsangma. The book masterfully interweaves such moments with little known stories of Tenzing Norgay's early expeditions in the Himalaya, Jamling's own Sherpa perspective on the events on Everest that fateful spring of 1996, and the similar steps that father and son took along the way to the top of the mountain.

Yet the heart of the book lies in something that father and son came to share beyond reaching the summit of Everest. Though Jamling was a nominal Buddhist before his experience on the mountain, when disaster struck and he was confronted with the questions of life and the very real possibility of death, his supplications suddenly felt urgent and sincere. Here is a very personal story of faith that blossomed and grew on the icy slopes, in the powerful arms of the omniscient, bountiful goddess of Everest, Miyolangsangma. In *Touching My Father's Soul* Jamling Tenzing Norgay shares his humble and life-changing experiences of puja, prayer, and patience in his own powerful and provocative witness for Tibetan Buddhism.

LAURIE KALLEVIG

The Dishonorable Dr. Cook: Debunking the Notorious Mount McKinley Hoax. BRADFORD WASHBURN AND PETER CHERICI. SEATTLE: THE MOUNTAINEERS BOOKS, 2001. 192 PAGES, 80 BLACK-AND-WHITE PHOTOS, 8 PAGES DUOTONE INSERT, 6 MAPS, HARDCOVER. $29.95.

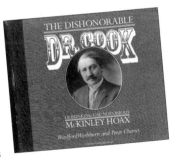

I ask you to read once again Galen Rowell's review of Washburn's *Mountain Photography* from last year's AAJ. There Rowell painted a clear portrait of the character of Washburn, which he saw realized in that beautiful volume. Washburn's newest book with Peter Cherici also represents a wonderful effort from this "single most exacting human being" that Rowell has ever known. In fact, the superb demonstration of scholarship, proper research, attribution, and documentation pales before the passion that gave birth to this completed volume, and all in his 92nd year.

I am very much reminded of Douglas Freshfield and his 50-year scholarly battle to determine which Alpine pass that Hannibal crossed with his elephants. Freshfield began his published comments in the 1870s, stating, "I found that my alpine and geographical sense were both outraged." He continued a lifelong battle with Latin scholars who had limited climbing experience or ability, publishing again in 1914 and continuing to write privately until his death. A holograph letter from 1923 is vibrant with his considerable disgust with the continuing controversy and states that he is not likely to "plunge again" into the controversy in public. It was never far from his mind.

I sense a similar purity of vision and outrage in an alpine and geographical sense from Brad Washburn with regard to Dr. Cook and his claims, especially as published in *To the Top of the Continent*. Most of us who have spent time in the Ruth Gorge and at Mt. McKinley have absolutely no doubt whatsoever that Dr. Cook never came within miles of the summit. The Cook controversy strikes us as an oddity of human behavior that the absurd argument that Cook summited could be taken seriously in this day and age. Yet it is believed by a few, and that fact clearly offends the sensibilities of Washburn. The passion and precision that the Cook Hoax has generated is wonderful to behold, and has produced a book that the Cook Society will find quite painful to read and ponder. A glorious Washburn photograph of the "Fake Peak" (facing page 162) is worth the price of the book alone. There you can barely see a pimple of a protuberance named "Fake Peak" lost among the magnificence of countless other peaks of the Alaska Range all dominated in the background by Mt. McKinley.

Washburn and Cherici provide a solid historical background to Dr. Cook and the Alaska Range. They outline the traditional arguments and evidence, but the greatest value is a complete analysis of the photographic "evidence" as presented in *To the Top of the Continent*. As Dr. Cook kept the negatives of his original photos unpublished during his lifetime, and as they have never been discovered or apparently examined by a competent third party, Washburn went to great efforts to duplicate each of the Cook photos. The narrative of the discovery of each place where each photo was taken is precise in detail and offers an explanation of the particular omission or commission that Cook undertook to maintain his hoax. Even more impressive is Washburn's analysis of the photo equipment used by Cook and then the duplication of photos using similar equipment himself. This approach makes this volume bibliographically significant in and of itself. As technology has progressed to a point where any tyro with very few bucks can fake any photograph today, this book may be the last where actual photos and negatives handled traditionally are used evidentially with certainty. *(Editor's note: the authors relied on the seminal reference, Robert M. Bryce's* Cook & Peary: The Polar Controversy Resolved *[Stackpole Books, 1997] for important factual information. Students of this controversy will want to refer to Mr. Bryce's thorough and insightful account.)*

There is a rich history of travel lies and travel liars, as well as a long list of fakes in publishing. For example, in late 17th and early 18th century in London there was a well-developed industry of publishing 400+ page books concerning purported voyages, all written by people who had never traveled more than 20 miles from St. Paul's Cathedral. A typical example is the following title: *The Voyages, Dangerous Adventures and Imminent Escapes of Captain Richard Falconer. Containing the Laws , Customs, and Manners of the Indians in America, His marrying an Indian Wife, His shipwrecks, and His narrow Escape from the Island of Domenico? Written By Himself, NOW ALIVE. London 1720.*

Capt. Falconer and Dr. Cook shared one significant point in common: they never suspected that any of their readers would make the voyage themselves and then publish their own rebuttal and commentary.

The layout of *The Dishonorable Dr. Cook* is also noteworthy. Whereas *To the Top of the Continent* repeats its title on the top of each page of text in large type, about 300 times, thus reinforcing the impact of the title, Washburn and Cherici reinforce their view at the bottom of the page. The symbolism of the location quite tidily sums up the thesis of each book. Lastly, *The Dishonorable Dr. Cook* is 10 inches wide by 8 and 5/8 inches tall. While the layout might better display the book's photographs, it does not sit comfortably on a shelf, especially next to a copy of *To the Top of the Continent.* The resulting aggravation to any Cook Society bibliophile who finds it necessary to refer to both volumes could be considered an unexpected benefit.

WILLIAM C. LORCH

Exploring the Unknown, Historic Diaries of Bradford Washburn's Alaska/Yukon Expeditions. BRADFORD WASHBURN, EDITED BY LEW FREEDMAN. KENMORE, WASHINGTON: EPICENTER PRESS, 2001. 128 PAGES, SOFTCOVER. $24.95.

This book contains excerpts from the diaries of Bradford Washburn that he wrote during three expeditions to Alaska and the Yukon. They give the reader a day to day glimpse of the struggles of a man and his companions who were scientists, students, and mountaineers exploring unmapped areas of Alaska's great mountains and mountain ranges. Beyond the stunning photographic detail that has made Washburn famous, the trilogy captures his "voice." Those of us who have been privileged to spend any time with him and his wife Barbara, will hear this through the written word. The diaries are descriptive, to the point, and often full of humor.

Washburn was perhaps the first to exploit the use of aircraft to get to places unknown, unseen, and rarely, if ever, traveled. The men from Harvard and Dartmouth who participated in these expeditions assisted Washburn in completing surveys that led to the accurate mapping of the glacial expanses of Mts. Logan, St. Elias, Fairweather, and later Denali. Under his leadership and organizational skill, these men, which include the likes of Barry Bishop and Ad Carter, spent three and four months at a time in remote, uncharted areas, patiently conducting survey activities and making first ascents of many high altitude peaks. They accomplished these feats without modern lightweight equipment, communication, and transportation.

In his time, Washburn was certainly one of a few hard men. *Exploring the Unknown* provides great insight into the personality and skill, both as a mountaineering leader and scientist, of Bradford Washburn, one of the true elders of American mountaineering.

PETER J. PANARESE

Kiss or Kill: Confessions of a Serial Climber. MARK TWIGHT. SEATTLE: THE MOUNTAINEERS BOOKS, 2001. 206 PAGES. $16.95

This book contains a collection of Twight's writings that were published mostly in climbing magazines between 1985 and 2000. As he says in his introduction, this book contains the "author's cuts," not the homogenized fluff offered up by specialty climbing magazine editors who are often unwilling to offend subscribers and advertisers.

When these articles were first published, Twight introduced a controversial new style for mountaineering literature that caught the staid climbing community off guard. His work captured considerable attention at the time because these dramatic stories about attempting difficult alpine routes were told with such an overpowering nihilism that readers were either inspired or revolted. Many climbers were accustomed to and enjoyed reading from existential authors who depicted characters whose actions were the source of their dread and anguish. But for many of these same climbers, reading Mark's climbing stories told with a similar angst elicited a sense of cognitive dissonance. It wasn't surprising that these writings earned him the nickname of "Dr. Doom."

Traditional mountaineering literature often uses climbing metaphors to uplift the reader with stories of courage and daring in the face of adversity. But the stories in this book describe a much darker emotional reaction to the stresses of difficult and committing alpine climbing. It is hard to say if the incongruity between Twight's and many other climber's descriptions of their alpine experiences is a result of differences in personal perspective, or if many of us refuse to acknowledge the inherent contradictions and dangers in climbing.

Viewing many of these stories with a 21st century perspective makes them seem tamer in the way that the 1980s punk music that influenced Twight's writing seems tame when compared to today's new music. Twight makes valid points about honesty—honesty with your emotions, honesty with what you achieved, and honesty with your level of commitment. Although those values remain constant today, time blunts the sharp edges of messages delivered in our youth. Twight is viewed by many as elitist, a stance he readily acknowledges. He claims that this book is a one-time deal; I would like to see more from him in the future to check where time takes his current uncompromising attitudes.

STEVE SWENSON

Extreme Rock & Ice. Garth Hattingh. Seattle: The Mountaineers Books, 2001. 160 PAGES, 200 COLOR PHOTOS, PAPERBACK. $39.95.

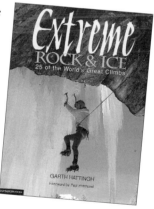

Massively oversized, *Extreme Rock & Ice* is divided into five spectacular sections: Rock Climbs, Ice & Mixed Climbs, Alpine-scale Climbs, Big Wall Climbs, and Big Mountain Climbs. Page after page is filled with excellent photographs. There is hardly a throwaway in the lot, and almost all are spectacular. Even the pictures of the objective itself are well chosen for their clarity. The format is very well conceived, each route consisting of a narrative, map, numerous pictures, objective photo with topo overlaid in red, and the story of the climb. The first two pages of each climb consist of a full-page picture on the left, some text, and a map placing the climb geographically.

Captivating graphic elements such as these make it difficult to focus on the text, yet each climb's narrative tells a story, and that story provides the essence of the adventure. Some, like Twight, House, and Blitz's Alaskan epic "The Gift That Keeps On Giving," have been covered in the climbing press or in other books. Others are likely only known to a much smaller circle, like the controversial ascent of Moby Dick, in Ulamertorssuaq, Greenland. However, the already familiar accounts contain additional details and photographs, so both are well worth perusing.

The word Extreme is greatly overused these days—Extreme Mountain Biking, Extreme Programming, even Extreme Doritos. Is it appropriately attached to this title? Throughout climbing history there have always been climbs and climbers pushing the boundaries of the sport and showing the way for others, but they weren't labeled with anything other than the ratings the first-ascensionists gave them. Some would surely argue that an X, R, or VE rating says it all. Still, these are extremely difficult climbs done by extremely bold climbers. Perhaps a better title would have been "Extremely Dangerous Rock & Ice Climbing By People With An Extremely High Tolerance For Risk," but of course that wouldn't have the cachet, would it?

Are these 25 climbs the most extreme in the world? That's open to debate. I've been right up next to Sea Of Vapors on Mt. Rundle, and it looks like a pretty darn hard climb to me. If Mark Twight's account in his recent book *Kiss or Kill* tells only half of the story, The Gift is about as out-there as you could ask for. And Mark Synnott has told me the story of his and Jared Ogden's epic on Shipton's Spire. It was definitely a tour de force! The Totem Pole in Tasmania, Metanoia on The Eiger, Destivelle Route on Mont Blanc, El Nino on El Cap, Grand Voyage on Great Trango, The Lightning Route on Changabang, The South Face on Lhotse, all these chapters paint pictures of danger and adversity, triumph and tragedy. These and 18 more make for a collection of great stories about challenges met and fears faced.

The stories, historical perspective, route descriptions, climber profiles, and above all the spectacular collection of photographs conspire to make *Extreme Rock & Ice* a book that you will likely come back to again and again. If you are a climber, or even an armchair mountaineer, this is a book of fabulous photographs and captivating accounts you're certain to enjoy.

AL HOSPERS

Arctic Crossing: A Journey Through the Northwest Passage and Inuit Culture. JONATHAN WATERMAN. NEW YORK: ALFRED KNOPF, 2001. 360 PAGES, 85 BLACK-AND-WHITE ILLUSTRATIONS, 8 PAGES COLOR, ENDPAPER MAPS, HARDCOVER. $29.95.

Arctic Crossing chronicles Jon Waterman's 1997-99 adventure traveling under human power (kayak, foot) and other non-motorized forms of locomotion (wind, dogsled) along the northern coast of North America, via a variation of the fabled Northwest Passage. The 2,200-mile odyssey done in six stages over three summers went from Prudhoe Bay, Alaska, to the Gulf of Boothia in the new Canadian province of Nunavut. It was, according to the account (and the accompanying television documentary that Waterman produced), a wildly dramatic and dangerous journey—more committing than any of his demanding mountaineering exploits. He experienced everything from capsizing his kayak several times (deadly in such frigid northern waters) to polar bears chasing him in the open ocean (again, deadly). Huge, daily physical stresses were complemented by the even greater mental challenge of what he'd set out to do and the ever-present question of whether he had the fortitude to complete it.

Waterman's exhaustive research, combined with his unique writing style—in which events are described slowly and with great detail—yields a story with many layers, not unlike a tapestry. Observations of the environment, Waterman's own state of mind, the flora, fauna, weather, and seasons, are interspersed with information on the history of the area and the exploration of the Northwest Passage. Yet, there is a whole lot more to *Arctic Crossing*.

At 45, Waterman has written seven other books about adventure, most of which have been focused on his experiences with Alaskan mountaineering. *Arctic Crossing* offers more because at its core it is an anthropological treatise. By detailing what he knows, then learns, about the Inuit (and that is a considerable amount of information), Waterman paints a wholly consuming portrait of an underdocumented race of people.

When Waterman began his epic, six-stage trip, he assumed he would learn a few things from the Inuit. He saw "The People" as holding the secrets to survival on this far northern land. He was not prepared for the harsh realities he witnessed and heard about during his trips, including the mistreatment of children, women and animals, the sexual abuse, the murders, and all sorts of cultural aberrations. "For example, they can tell you everything about that soap opera," Waterman told me during an interview about *Arctic Crossing*. "But most don't even know their own native language. I had kids ask me 'What is that, that boat that you're paddling?' Their forefathers invented kayaks and they'd never seen or heard of them before."

On the other hand, Waterman also came into contact with a life force that could not be denied. This book tells it all, in riveting detail, capturing the full range of Inuit experience. It is definitely not a romantic wide-eyed portrait of an indigenous culture often considered more innocent than our own. But because it doesn't shrink from describing cultural practices—such as the beating of dogs—that even many Inuits themselves despise, it treats the people as wholly complete beings, and the culture as the complex set of behaviors it really is, rather than the idealized form of life we would prefer it to be.

"Time and time again I'd just be brought up short. I'd be tempted to come to a [negative] conclusion about these people," said Waterman, "and then suddenly they'd do something wonderful like feed me, or offer me help. Which really showed me they had my best interests at heart. I'd show up in a camp, and while they wouldn't ask questions, they were gracious and made me laugh and gave me a place to sleep." Waterman became more than just a student of The People. He became a curiosity, an inspiration, and finally, a friend.

There's no hiding it: I'm a fan of *Arctic Crossing*, and of Waterman's style. He's a careful, considerate writer, with a keen eye for detail and the ability to mix his own story into a picture that is far greater, longer, and deeper.

CAMERON M. BURNS

American Rock: Region, Rock and Culture in American Climbing. DON MELLOR. WOODSTOCK, VERMONT: THE COUNTRYMAN PRESS, 2001. 303 PAGES. $28.

Don Mellor lays it out straight in his introduction to *American Rock:* "This is a book about American rock climbing. It's a celebration of the rich diversity in American climbing experiences, and it's an attempt to stand in the way of the insidious homogenization that is erasing the regional distinctiveness in every facet of American culture, rock climbing included."

From this premise, *American Rock* heads into a wandering 300-page journey that attempts to talk about everything from Robert Underhill's 1931 ascent of Mt. Whitney's East Face to access problems at Hueco Tanks. For the most part, Mellor pulls it off, and the book provides a good look at the history, culture, geology, and eccentricities of almost every major climbing area in the U.S.

While emphasized in the introduction, Mellor's abhorrence with the homogenization that he sees in the sport is not leaned on very much in the body. Neither is any other central theme. Instead, *American Rock* reads like a compendium of essays on the American climbing life in its many facets, leaving readers to form their own conclusions.

The book begins with a quick history of climbing in the U.S. and then moves into a section on climbing media and current trends in the sport. Chapter two is a geology lesson, and it is not until chapter three on page 65 that the book gets into a groove. There, Mellor starts an eight-chapter tour of more than 40 climbing areas from the Shawangunks to Joshua Tree. A wrap-up chapter, "Cherishing the Resources," talks about current threats and issues in American climbing (e.g. the Wilderness Act of 1964, raptor nesting closures).

This bits-and-pieces style produces a book that at times feels disjointed and superficial. With only 300 pages to tackle a monumental subject, *American Rock* is not an encyclopedia on climbing in the U.S., but instead serves as an introduction to its constellation of areas, people, and subcultures.

But it is this same tell-all style that makes the book an overall success. There are a few holes here: almost no coverage of Montana, and minimal attention to Devil's Tower; Mellor may disappoint flatlands climbers like myself by not giving any ink to Midwestern areas such as Devil's Lake. These quibbles aside, the book is thorough, well written, and a first-of-its-kind. It will no doubt expand the consciousness of newbies and serve as a great refresher course for climbing veterans.

STEPHEN REGENOLD

Vertical Margins: Mountaineering and the Landscapes of Neoimperialism. REUBEN ELLIS. MADISON: THE UNIVERSITY OF WISCONSIN PRESS, 2001. 240 PAGES, PAPERBACK. $21.95.

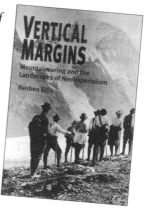

Reuben Ellis' goal is both an admirable and daunting one: "to understand the world we live in," as Ellis paraphrases Edward Said, "we should seek out connections between culture and empire, geography and literature." Ellis explores the interlocking themes of mountaineering, the motivations of those who climb, and the language that they use to describe it. According to the author, climbing cannot be done—or read—in isolation. It must be placed in its appropriate geographical, historical, literary, and political contexts. Thus, mountaineering in the late 19th and early 20th centuries and its literature can only be understood in the context of that time. And, since British and American climbers belonged to nations that were busily expanding their dominions over peoples in the developing world, so, too, were climbers, in a sense, imperialists. Under the guise of scientific exploration, foreign investment, and nationalism, American and British alpinists climbed. Hence, these climbers were not motivated solely by a spiritual need to be in the mountains or a desire for sport. Rather, at the turn of the last century climbers were carrying the banner of their ascendant nations in the "vertical margins" of their respective empires: British climbers in East Africa and the Himalaya, American climbers in that American "sphere of influence," Latin America. However, Ellis tells this interesting, albeit complex, story in a way that likely will alienate the average reader of mountaineering literature. Make no mistake about it, Vertical Margins is, in the best and worst senses, an academic book.

Ellis begins his book by looking at the "blank spaces on the map," when mountains became sites of scientific exploration. Prior to the late 19th century, mountains were seen as places of romance or spirituality, where you might go to test or find faith and mountains and mountaineers were represented in literature as such. In the late 1800s, however, mountains—and the conquest of them—must be seen through the language of empire. No longer were mountains simply depicted in word (and, soon, film) as places of spirituality. Instead, they were places to be investigated scientifically and had significance in the context of the spreading economic, military, and political power of Britain and America.

The second chapter examines the life and climbs of Sir Halford Mackinder, the author of a significant theory of political geography, but also the first man to reach the 17,000-foot peak of Mt. Kenya. As someone who had recently traveled to Kenya in order to follow in Mackinder's footsteps, I can say that I learned precious little new about it. That is because Ellis is more c oncerned with how "Mackinder's narrative [of his climb] engages a broad range of issues revolving around individual ambitions within evolving academic institutions, British colonial politics in East Africa, and racial and cultural difference." You get the picture.

The most interesting chapter was his analysis of Annie Peck Smith's 1911 mountaineering classic, A Search for the Apex of America. A feminist and academic, as well as one of the most prominent climbers of her generation, Smith's book discusses her first ascent of 22,200-foot Huascaran and other exploits in the Peruvian and Bolivian Andes. Ellis, though, focuses upon her mountaineering exploits as they relate to gender dynamics and American foreign investment in the aftermath of the "Roosevelt Corollary," in which (basically) the United States claimed the right to invade any nation in the Western Hemisphere in order to protect its own economic interests.

The final chapter shifts from the writings of climbers to one of the first documentary filmmakers of the alpine world, John Baptist Noel, and his 1927 film, Through Tibet to Everest. Again, Ellis' objective is not to rehash the familiar literature of Everest, but to explore "the evolving documentary film movement, and perhaps Western technology in general, [as it] interacted with the British imperial posture in central Asia in the closing days of the Raj." One of the more interesting aspects of this chapter concerns the super-nationalism of the interwar years, in which people went to suicidal lengths (literally) in order to bag peaks in the names of their respective empires.

Throughout the book, Ellis displays an impressive knowledge of a wide variety of subjects—not simply mountaineering and its literature but also the history of Britain and the United States domestically and internationally. I—a professional academic historian—learned a great deal from reading this book, but I doubt that most of my climbing buddies would have the interest or discipline to slog through it. Ellis makes no attempt to reach a popular audience. As a sidenote, the "dedicatory preface" is a thoroughly enjoyable and well-written short work that hints at Ellis' command of not just academic prose but also intelligent and humorous literary non-fiction.

PETER COLE

The Accidental Adventurer: Memoirs of the First Woman to Climb Mt. McKinley. BARBARA WASHBURN. KENMORE, WASHINGTON: EPICENTER PRESS, 2001. 192 PAGES, PAPERBACK. $19.95.

Rising from the tundra of Alaska to over 20,000 feet in height, the Arctic summit of Denali remains a worthy objective to mountaineers today. So much more so to Barbara Polk Washburn who in 1947 became the first woman to reach the highest point in North America. In *The Accidental Adventurer* she writes:

> "*The view all around was truly the way I imagined heaven to be when I was a little girl.... The wind was gusting to thirty miles an hour and the temperature was twenty degrees below zero.... Before me lay 100,000 square miles of Alaska. Snow covered mountains and terrain stretched to the horizon in a view that left me breathless...There were no windows, no buffers between my body and the cold...I kept telling myself I must keep my head clear and be prepared for the difficulty of the descent. I had to get home to Massachusetts and our three young children.*"

Washburn's previous expeditions to Alaska included the first ascents of Mt. Bertha on her honeymoon and the first ascent of Mt. Hayes. In this engaging memoir, Barbara Washburn modestly states she came along on numerous expeditions to Alaska and around the world to support her husband, the world-renowned explorer Bradford Washburn.

The Accidental Adventurer demonstrates Washburn's own imagination, strength and courage beginning in her teen years. We follow her education at Smith College and in Europe just before World War II, her romance with the handsome young explorer Bradford Washburn and her adventures as mother, wife, teacher, surveyor, mountaineer, and world traveler. We especially admire her steely determination to keep going to achieve her objectives in the face of all obstacles; and her continuing to set an example and raise team morale during the most harrowing circumstances.

In the decades following her ascent of Denali, she helped her husband create maps of the Grand Canyon and do the first aerial mapping of Mt. Everest, went on a photographic safari in Kenya, and made repeated trips to China and Nepal.

In *The Accidental Adventurer* we gain an appreciation for the stamina and verve of this early role model for women climbers. In an era where a woman's place was in the home, she climbed beyond the limitations of gender. Barbara Washburn has led a full and interesting life. Thanks to her and to Lew Freedman of the *Anchorage Daily News* for retelling the stories of her adventures and providing an inspiration for us all.

ARLENE BLUM

IN BRIEF

DENALI: DECEPTION, DEFEAT AND TRIUMPH (Seattle: The Mountaineers Books, 2001; hardbound, $38) collects the works of Frederick Cook, Belmont Browne, and Hudson Stuck—"the stories of the fake, the almost, and the actual first ascent"—together in one volume.

GLORIOUS FAILURES AND COURAGEOUS MISFORTUNE, with forewords by John Harlin III and Mark Synnott respectively (Seattle: The Mountaineers Books, 2001; paperback, $16.95), launch a new anthology series "distinguished by a specific adventuring theme."

THE ALPS, EUROPE'S MOUNTAIN HEART (Ann Harbor: University of Michigan Press; $39.50), by longtime AAC members Nicholas and Nina Shoumatoff, is an "unusual synthesis" of wide ranging scholarship about all aspects of the Alps, unified by the authors' deep understanding of the interdependence between and within the natural and cultural realms.

TOUCH THE TOP OF THE WORLD: A BLIND MAN'S JOURNEY TO CLIMB FARTHER THAN THE EYE CAN SEE (New York: Penguin Putnam; softcover, $14) is Erik Weihenmayer's memoir describing his remarkable climbs, culminating with his successful ascent of Everest.

In Memoriam

Eric Brooks 1902 - 2001

As an old friend and occasional climbing companion of Eric Brooks, and as a fellow member of the Alpine Club of Canada, I would like to offer my remembrance.

Eric started climbing when he met Emmie Milledge, already an enthusiastic climber, in the 1920s, and they climbed together both before and after their marriage in 1935. He and Emmie did many climbs together in the years between the wars, including Mt. Robson, Emmie being the third woman to make that ascent.

Eric joined the Alpine Club of Canada in 1928 and was President from 1941 to 1946, and Honorary President from 1954 to 1965. As such he represented the Alpine Club of Canada at the Centenary of the Alpine Club in London, in 1957. Eric was made an Honorary Member of the Alpine Club, had also been a member of the American Alpine Club since 1943.

During his years as president of the Alpine Club of Canada, Eric organized their annual summer camps. I first met him as a weekend guest at the Consolation Valley camp in 1942. In addition to these regular camps, he was also responsible for a military camp in 1943 for the purpose of training troops in mountaineering techniques. In 1966 he was chair of the selection committee for the Yukon Alpine Centennial Expedition 1967.

After the war (in 1948-49) he spent a year as an exchange teacher at Eastbourne, England, which enabled him to climb in the English Lake District, in Wales, and in the Alps. In his later years he traveled to Britain, to Europe, and to Nepal several times, where as well as trekking he contributed to the building of a school in a remote village, which he visited when over 90. On his 89th birthday, he climbed Snowdon from Bettws-y-coed, and I believe he celebrated his 90th birthday by climbing Scafell!

Not only was he an expert and enthusiastic climber, but also a splendid and unassuming organizer who would take enormous trouble to help others, in the Alpine Club of Canada, in his profession of teaching, and with his private friends, as I can personally attest.

His final decade was marred by progressive blindness, caused by glaucoma, but that did not stop him from continuing to live alone at his home at Madeira Park, on the B.C. coast some 60 miles northwest of Vancouver, until a few weeks before his death. This was made possible for him by frequent visits from his friend Valerie Walker, who came up regularly from Vancouver.

John S.T.Gibson, *AAC, ACC*

Jack Fralick 1919 - 2001

Jack Fralick, a 50-year member of the American Alpine Club, passed away in February, 2001 at the age of 81. Jack served on the Club's Safety Committee, wrote the Committee's fourth annual Safety Report in 1951, and initiated the process of tabulation and statistical analysis of climbing accidents.

Jack also co-founded the Chicago Mountaineering Club in 1940 with Harold and William Plumley, and served as its first president.

He was certainly among the first to build a "rock gym" when in 1962 he nailed plywood sheets to a scaffold using wood scraps for holds to demonstrate climbing skills at a national Boy Scout Exposition in Detroit.

Jack climbed extensively from 1936 to 1969 throughout Wyoming, Colorado, Wisconsin, and Illinois. He had the great fortune to climb with many of the legends of the sport including Petzoldt, Wiessner, Durrance, and the Stettner brothers—superb climbers and life-long friends, who in the 1930s and 40s were pioneering routes and helping to establish the sport of mountaineering in North America. Jack and his friends have several first ascents to their credit including the east face of Monitor Peak in the San Juan Mountains of Colorado. This 1947 climb was at the high end of the difficulty scale for the time in the United States and remained so for several years.

Jack Fralick on the summit of Long's Peak, Colorado, about 1947.

After his active climbing years, Jack's interest in the history of mountaineering remained keen. He was an encyclopedia of facts, dates, and stories about the great climbs, the great tragedies, and the great controversies that occurred as the sport grew. He loved to swap stories and lectured on mountaineering to within three months of his death. Jack published numerous articles on climbing and was often called on by others to edit or contribute to guide books and articles on the sport. He also established a collection of historical equipment, photographs, books, catalogs, and magazines from the early days of American mountaineering at the American Heritage Center at the University of Wyoming.

Jack had a great love for the mountains and had the greatest affection and highest regard for those whom he met there. Mountaineers were among his closest, life-long friends. In preparing this memoriam, it has been very interesting tracking down my dad's old mountain companions, many of whom I only knew through stories told around campfires at Jenny Lake a long time ago.

JOHN FRALICK

MICHAEL S. MARTIN 1940 – 2001

Michael S. Martin drowned September 6, 2001, near the completion of a solo hike up the Upper Black Box Canyon in Utah. He was 61 years old. Mike had recently returned to Denver from a trip to the Tetons and had spent 11 days in the Coast Range of British Columbia in July.

Mike began climbing as a graduate student in mathematics at the University of Washington in Seattle in the early 1960s. He extended his range from the Washington Cascades to the British Columbia Coast Range on trips arranged by Joe and Joan Firey.

Mike Martin at Bluff Lake, 1996. *Mickey Schurr*

You can get a sense of Mike's climbing from his July 2001 trip, his third to the Klattasine area. The first was in 1992, by which time Dave Knudson had been organizing these ventures for several years. Mike, Dave,

Mickey Schurr, and I enjoyed traveling the glaciers and ridges at the eastern end of Klattasine Ridge. We reached some summits previously climbed only by John Clarke and Peter Croft. The Big One, Peak 2468m, soloed by Croft via its beautiful north ridge, eluded us again, as it did in 1992. Mike, Mickey, and I were turned back by the steep and loose south ridge with less than 50 meters to go to the summit, vertically.

Mike would tackle about anything. I know that he savored the memories of the bittersweet moments when we turned back to climb another day almost as much as he did those of the summits. There were many of the latter, some previously unnamed virgin summits among them. Rarer were summits of named but unclimbed peaks, for instance Determination, on whose summit he stood with Dave Knudson, Mickey Schurr, Bruce Watson, and me in August of 1997. From this point we watched the new route we had put on Reliance a few days earlier raked by avalanches. It was at once exhilarating and chastening.

In Canada, Mike climbed many Coast Range classics: Queen Bess, Tiedeman, Cerberus, Geddes, Monarch, Munday, and Waddington among them. His footprints have crisscrossed some of the most beautiful and interesting parts of the Range. We shared successes, failures, and chilly bivouacs in British Columbia and elsewhere. Mike climbed with many other people and in many other places—Colorado, especially, and Europe.

Mike joined the mathematics faculty at the University of Denver after taking his degree at Washington. In July we had discussed the classes he was looking forward to teaching there in fall of 2001. Mike spent several sabbaticals at the Open University in Milton Keynes, England—a base for his European adventures. At Denver, he was advisor to the University's climbing club for a number of years and helped bring others into the sport. He was a member of both the Alpine Club of Canada and the American Alpine Club.

On September 16, 2001, he was warmly remembered by colleagues, students, friends, and family at a memorial held at the University of Denver. He is survived by his sons Neil of Philadelphia, Pennsylvania, and Douglas of Austin, Texas; and by his sisters, Andrea Bachrach of Burlingame, California, and Jane Martin of Berkeley, California.

Whether I was in the mountains or at a desk puzzling over some mathematics, as long as Mike was around, a problem was just an opportunity for mental or physical exercise. He was a splendid comrade. He found the best in things and went ahead strongly and hopefully to the end.

PETER RENZ, AAC

ANTON (AX) NELSON 1918-2001
Ax Nelson passed away in Oakland, California on April 22, 2001 at the age of 83. He was a giant of a man and strong as an ox. By trade he was a carpenter and builder of homes, and by avocation a dedicated humanitarian and a rock climber.

He started climbing at the age of 27 in the San Francisco Bay Area with the Sierra Club shortly after the end of WWII, and quickly graduated to the ranks of those willing and able to take on the most difficult challenges. When he lacked skill he made up for it in strength and determination.

Ax's climbing career spanned only a few years, but two of his ascents left an indelible mark on Yosemite. He was on the team that made the first ascent of the Lost Arrow in 1946 (via a Tyrolean traverse achieved by throwing a rope across the spire) and was the second person to stand on its summit—the first being Jack Arnold and the third Fritz Lippman. Not content with that first ascent, he turned to the last unsolved problem of that era—the Lost Arrow Chimney (see page 24). Since the early 1930s, when technical rock climbers discovered Yosemite Valley, the Lost Arrow became the symbol of the impossible climb. On days when rain prevented climbing, the group that had climbed both the Higher and Lower Cathedral Spires would use binoculars to sweep the 1300 feet of its Chimney and to pick out a possible route.

Ax Nelson (right) with John Salathé after making the first ascent of the Lost Arrow Chimeny, 1947.

Their route consisted of four distinctive sections. The first led to a ledge they named the First Error, the second to a ledge called the Second Error, the third to the notch which was the Third Error, and the fourth from the notch to the summit which was the Last Error. Those puns reflected their conviction that the climb was above their skill level. Despite that, Richard Leonard and David Brower made the first attempt and reached the First Error in 1937. In 1946 a later generation of climbers pushed some 120 feet higher. Still, until Ax Nelson set his sights on this goal in 1947, no one had made a serious attempt at the route.

Ax and John Salathe, spent four days in the Chimney and on the fifth day made the second ascent of the Lost Arrow's spire and the first ascent from the base of its chimney. This feat ushered in the era of Yosemite climbing that knew no limits.

Ax Nelson last climbed in the Valley in 1948 and some years after that he put his humanitarian avocation to work full time. He set off for East Africa to work with the struggling Wameru coffee growers in Tanzania and in his spare time made the first complete traverse of Mt. Kilimanjaro.

I can't complete this without sharing the following anecdote because it is Ax to the nth degree. In the late 1960s, I was at a function in Washington D.C., where I met and talked with someone from the World Bank who had served in Tanzania. I mentioned that Ax Nelson had been there at one time and asked whether he knew of him. He did, he had seen this mad giant of a white man running almost daily through the streets of Dar es Salaam in the heat of the day and, a victim of curiosity, stopped him one day. It was Ax and the Ax that all of us knew.

ROBIN HANSEN, *AAC*

ARTHUR KING PETERS 1919 - 2001

Art Peters, an AAC member since 1964, died peacefully at his home in Bronxville, N.Y. on June 2, 2001 at the age of 81.

A 1940 graduate of Cornell, Arthur served during World War II as an officer in Army counter-intelligence. He later received a Ph.D. in French literature from Columbia University. During the 1970s, while running his own importing business, he taught French at Hunter College during his lunch hour. He was also active as a translator, critic, and author and published five books, including *Jean Cocteau And His*

Arthur Peters in the early 1990s. *Jean Schlemer*

World and *Seven Trails West,* the story of the Lewis and Clark expedition.

Arthur had a long friendship with the late, great French climber, Gaston Rebuffat, and translated a number of his works into English. He introduced Gaston at a memorable New York Section Annual Dinner in 1982.

Arthur climbed extensively in the French Alps, the Shawangunks, and the Tetons where he had a home for many years. He served as the president of the French American Foundation from 1977-83 and received the Chevalier de la Legion d'Honneur from the French Government in 1984.

He leaves a wife, Sarah, three children, six grandchildren and a great many friends here in the New York Section.

PHILIP ERARD, *AAC*

NECROLOGY
Robert C. Black, III, 1914-2001
Robert M. Booher, 1929-2001
Derek "Jay" Bowen, 1968-2001
Tom Dunwiddie, 1951-2001
Monica Eldridge, 1960-2001
Kenneth A. Henderson, 1905-2001
Doris P. Leonard, 1908-2001
Jim McGinnis, 1919-2001
Cicely Nocolai, 1939-2001
Larry Penberthy, 1916-2001
Michelle Potkin, 1956-2001
Ted Roumbanis, 1919-2001
Jack Siegrist, 1963-2001
Francis M. Wheat, 1921-2001

Several of these old friends will be remembered in next year's American Alpine Journal.

CLUB ACTIVITIES

EDITED BY FREDERICK O. JOHNSON

AAC, CASCADE SECTION. The Cascade Section held three events in 2001. The first was the Goran Kropp slideshow on July 13. Organized by Helly Hansen and sponsored by the AAC, this was the amazing story of Goran's bicycle journey from Sweden to Kathmandu and his unassisted solo ascent, without bottled oxygen, of Mt. Everest in 1996. Jim Frush, AAC president, introduced Goran and explained the work the Club does to benefit all climbers.

On November 1 the Section held a benefit for the Central Asia Institute. Jon Krakauer was the keynote speaker along with Greg Mortenson from the CAI. The AAC was one of the sponsors for the event, and the Club's national headquarters donated $1,500. Our Section also donated profits from T-shirt sales to the CAI.

Finally, on November 17, the Section held a reception and slideshow, attracting about 150 members and guests. The free pizza and beer were consumed with gusto! Jim Frush introduced the speaker, Section member Mike Gauthier, Lead Climbing Ranger at Mount Rainier National Park, and told us about of some of the issues the Club has been involved with that are also on Mike's agenda. These include the Denali Park and Rainier Park Management Plans. Mike gave a visually stunning slideshow on Mt. Rainier, which he has climbed 150 times, while discussing current issues about climbing fees, guiding concessions, and rescue services in the Park. He also told the story of his lightweight ascent with fellow Rainier climbing ranger, David Gottlieb, of Alaska's Mt. Foraker via the southeast ridge, taking eight days rather than the planned five.

The Section closely follows the emerging management plans for Olympic and Mount Rainier National Parks. The Olympic Plan is in the first phase of development. The AAC has filed preliminary thoughts about key issues and will monitor and comment on the plan as it develops. Regarding the Rainier Plan, comments and pressure from the AAC and The Mountaineers were effective in removing a proposal to prohibit climbers and backpackers from parking at trailheads and major parking lots. A shuttle system will be developed for the peak season when lots are full. The final plan includes a zoning system designed to protect solitude in more remote areas and to accommodate greater use in current high use areas such as the Muir Snowfield/Disappointment Cleaver route.

On the climbing scene, Bart Paull reported making a 10-hour link-up of the Wine Spires in the Northern Cascades with Kevin Newall. This included ascents of the east face of Chablis Spire (5.6), the south face of Pernod Spire (5.9+), the east face of Chianti Spire (a.k.a. Rebel Yell--5.10), and the north face of Burgundy Spire (5.8). In the fall of 2001 Bart, Rufus Lusk, and Fredrick Wilkinson made the first free ascent of Stryder Wall on Cannon Cliff in New Hampshire, with several new variations. They found wonderful slab climbing and an excellent in-your-face arch pitch with a wild traverse at its end. A few bolts were placed for protection, all by hand and on lead. At 5.11, the climbing is technical and intricate. They named the free version Castles Burning.

Please keep an eye on our Web site, http://cas.alpineclub.org, and e-mail any suggestions or questions about the Section to me at CascadesAAC@hotmail.com.

PETER ACKROYD, *Chair*

THE MOUNTAINEERS. The core climbing programs of The Mountaineers proceed with the same popularity as ever. These programs place high value in having a "stewardship" requirement and promoting a leave-no-trace ethic. Participants have many opportunities to work on projects with numerous federal and state agencies in habitat restoration and trail clearing activities. In addition, Mountaineers climbing programs work closely with other organizations to promote and defend the interests of the climbing community. Some of those endeavors include fixed anchor issues and federally negotiated rulemaking. For these efforts the Access Fund recently recognized The Mountaineers with the "Sharp End Award."

We continue to diversify the overall program in order to address climbing specialties that have emerged. Since the Water Ice program has been very successful, other courses on this model are in the planning stages. The "Climbing Denali" course returned, and a new "Aid/Big Wall" course was offered this year. Web-based electronic sign-up for climb leaders has been of great benefit to members, allowing short-notice climbs to be scheduled and filled successfully. A larger percentage of climbs are scheduled by this means, and the total number of climbs has grown.

The Mountaineers Books was honored to receive a number of awards for books produced in the past year. Two titles won National Outdoor Book Awards for 2001. *Where the Pavement Ends: One Woman's Bicycle Trip Through Mongolia, China and Vietnam*, by Erika Warmbrunn (Winner, Literature category) and *Fifty Favorite Climbs: The Ultimate North American Tick List*, edited by Mark Kroese (Winner, Outdoor Adventure Guidebook category). One of the outdoor world's largest and most prestigious book award programs, the National Outdoor Book Awards (NOBA) is sponsored by the Association of Outdoor Recreation and Education and by Idaho State University to recognize and encourage outstanding writing and publishing about the outdoors.

Three out of five awards presented at the Banff Mountain Book Festival were awarded to Mountaineers Books titles. Over 122 entries from 11 countries were represented in the competition. The awards included: *Fifty Favorite Climbs: The Ultimate North American Tick List*, by Mark Kroese (Mountain Exposition Award); *The High Himalaya*, by Art Wolfe—photography—and Peter Potterfield—text—(Mountain Image Award); and *Kiss or Kill: Confessions of A Serial Climber*, by Mark Twight (Mountain Literature Award).

This past year also marked the publication of two new women's adventure narrative titles appearing in the Barbara Savage "Miles from Nowhere" award series: *Where the Pavement Ends*, by Erika Warmbrunn (a NOBA winner) and *Spirited Waters: Soloing South Through the Inside Passage*, by Jennifer Hahn. The Mountaineers Books also published the first two titles in their anthology series, *Glorious Failures* and *Courage and Misfortune*, which included stories from the world's most experienced and respected climbers, representing some of the finest climbing literature.

The Mountaineers bestows honorary membership on a few individuals who have made significant lifetime contributions to mountaineering. In that capacity the club recently elected Dr. Tom Hornbein an Honorary Member. He is most famous for his first ascent of the west ridge of Mt. Everest with Willi Unsoeld in 1963. The feat was documented in his classic account, *The West Ridge of Everest*. An interest in climbing led Tom to mountain rescue work, which in turn led to medicine. A lifelong professional interest in the physiology of breathing and high altitude adaptation ensued.

DONNA PRICE, *Trustee*

AAC, OREGON SECTION. Throughout the year 2001 the Oregon Section was very active in working on matters of conservation, access, and trail building. With funding from a Lyman Spitzer grant, stairs were built and 210 feet of bouldering landing were prepared at Rocky Butte with a retaining wall and a bark-dust crash pad. Matt Brewster supplied a crane to place railroad ties and provided a portable generator for doweling and cutting. Keith Campbell provided transport for the ties and worked with others cutting, filling, and shoring the landing zone. Doug Hutchinson and Matt put in many hours with the shovels and sledges grooming the 5-foot-wide landing zone to perfection. This project was the direct result of AAC Access Committee incentives. Most satisfying of all were the constant positive, grateful comments by climbers who were using the wall during the construction period. Trail building and maintenance were also done at Broughton's Bluff and at Waterboard Park in Oregon City.

Doug Hutchinson, Richard Bence, and Bob McGown attended multiple meetings of the Madrone Wall Preservation Committee, to which the Section contributed $1,300 from fund raising. Taylor Hunt and Bob McGown led a geological research field trip to the Madrone Wall and Clackamas River Basin climbing areas. Twenty amateur geologists studied the proto-Columbia River, while the local climbers entertained them with their vertical antics. The field trip's intent was to have Portland State University's chapter of the Geological Society of Oregon supplement their study program with the geology of the hidden crags of the Clackamas River Basin. New member Greg Orton has contributed detailed, extensive access information to southwest Oregon climbing areas for his new guide book and Web site of southwest Oregon rock climbs, http://climbsworegon.com.

Several access initiatives have arisen from the Section's initial involvement with the Road 18 Caves EA presented by the U.S.Forest Service. Despite the alliance of Access Fund Conservation Director, Kath Pike (Central Rockies Section), local climbing gyms and climbing clubs, local Section members like Bob Speik and Tom Willard, and a concerted effort at education and information distribution, the Forest Service has adopted a draconian plan that will effectively prohibit climbing in the two lava caves under discussion. There are many excellent routes in the caves of 5.12-5.13 difficulty, presenting a daunting if enchanting prospect. All the climbs are located within about 50 feet of the entrance even to the largest of the caves (40- to 45-foot ceiling height), and given the steepness and sustained nature of the climbing, are not over protected. The Forest Service plan is under appeal, and it is not too late to modify the perception that "sport climbing" has done irreparable harm to caves that have been used for everything from bootlegging to rock concerts and spontaneous keggers for several decades. Since, in part at least, the controversy over the Road 18 Caves arose out of a lack of awareness by climbers that others are sensitive to their activities, the Section has become more active in informing climbers of access issues and providing information about climbing areas where concerns must be respected by climbers.

In conjunction with the Mazama Access Committee, Richard Bence has been creating a database of over 200 climbing areas in Oregon and southern Washington, of which only about a dozen have access issues. This database, available on the Section's Web site, allows members to check for local access issues before climbing in an area. If members find problems with an area, they can report these through forms or e-mail that will update the Web site.

Thanks to the efforts of Jeff Alzner, the Oregon Section conducted an exchange with the Central Rockies Section. Jeff spoke in Fort Collins, Golden, and Boulder, raising funds for the Central Rockies Section with his K2000 and other Himalayan experiences. We then brought

Mike Bearzi to Oregon to present his show on the first free ascent of Cerro Torre. This show was a great success, offering an awe-inspiring look at the legendary peaks of Patagonia from the ice cap. The Section raised nearly $2,500 for the Madrone Wall Preservation Committee and for a new rescue litter for Smith Rock State Park from these presentations Another entertaining evening event for our members featured a program by Andy Selters called *Mountain Spirit.*

There were several dinner gatherings of the Oregon Section during the year. A particularly enjoyable one was an informal planning meeting at Richard Bence's home for all committee members. Tom Thrall hosted a dinner meeting in his hand-hewn Cascadian home deep in Oregon's Coast Range. Tom shared his contributions to the new Sierra Club hiking guide, Neale Creamer told of his adventures in Canada, and John Harlin III gave a slideshow on Baffin Island. Doug Hutchinson and Matt Sullivan gave a talk on various peaks they have climbed and attempted in Canada, including Mt. Robson, in the last two years

Many other events involving the Section ranged from crag gardening projects to Bob Speik's consultations with state committees looking into providing interpretive kiosks at Smith Rock. Tom Bennett has been the source of a steady flow of news and events relating to climbing and climbing personalities visiting the Portland area. Jill Kellogg and Rick Bestwick were elected to the board of directors of Cascades Mountaineers, with Jill's becoming president succeeding Bob Speik.

The Oregon Section is extremely proud of our Web site, http://ors.alpineclub.org/AAC, capably and creatively webmastered by Richard Bence. The Web site has many outstanding images and a wealth of information about Section activities and events, member profiles, general climbing and bouldering information, links, and much more. We encourage all of our members to contribute news of their activities and photos for inclusion on the site. The Web site is part of the Section's concerted effort to be proactive with all climbers in the area, addressing issues of access; providing liason with land managers, public authorities, and other climbing groups in our area; and having events of interest to all climbers in general. The climbing culture in Oregon is rich and diverse, and we wish to be a rallying point for that diversity through the Section's activism and participation in local issues and events.

BOB McGOWN, *Chair*

THE MAZAMAS. The Climbing Committee guides comprehensive mountaineering education from beginning through advanced levels; organizes summer, winter, and rock climbing schedules; selects and trains new climb leaders; and promotes safety in all Mazama mountaineering. In 2001 the 12-person committee, chaired by John Youngman, scheduled 292 climbs led by 72 different leaders.

The Basic Climbing Education Program enlisted 211 students. These included 36 percent women and 72 percent non-Mazama members. In addition to rock and snow training, the groups made several day hikes into difficult terrain and attended indoor lectures and knots and belay practice. The BCEP is a fine-tuned evolution of instruction programs instituted before World War II. It introduces many new members into the Mazamas each year and allows instructors to bond with beginning climbers.

The Intermediate Climbing Program enlisted 37 students under Doug Couch. It instructs seasoned beginners in higher levels of rock and snow climbing and develops and screens future climb leaders. Tight rules by the U.S. Forest Service prevented the ICP from using the Eliot

Glacier on Mt. Hood, the best and most convenient site for glacier rescue practice. White River Glacier is being considered for the 2002 season. The Advanced Rock Program, under Matt Carter, enrolled 20 students. The Rock Review Program involved 45 students on the basalt walls of Rocky Butte in Portland, bolstering knowledge of knots, belaying, rappelling, and fixed line travel. The program maintained a two-to-one ratio of instructors to students. This instruction takes some of the load off the ICP and Advanced Rock Program.

The Advanced Snow and Ice Program, under Steve Heim, began with a week of ice climbing at Ouray, Colorado. The group of eight enjoyed an excellent trip despite ugly weather. Four other sessions were held on Mt. Hood and Mt. Rainier.

The Leadership Training Program enlisted 23 applicants and resulted in the addition of eight new leaders. This included a day seminar at Mount Hood under outside instructors. Plans were made for John Graham, author of *Outdoor Leadership*, to conduct a leadership skills seminar in 2002. John Gooding, Mazama Administrative Assistant, continued to work with the committee on its leadership Web site.

Recipients of Mazama Climbing Awards were: 10 members received the Guardian Peaks Award (Hood, St. Helens, Adams); two the Oregon Cascades Award (Jefferson, Three-Fingered Jack, Washington, Three Sisters); and five the 16 Major Peaks Award (all of the above peaks plus Olympus, Baker, Shuksan, Rainier, Glacier, Stuart, Shasta). Brad French was the sole recipient of the 15-point Leadership Award.

The Outing Committee, chaired by Marty Wilson, fielded a wide variety of trips that included Alpine Lakes Wilderness in the Wenatchee National Forest, Cape Perpetua, Grand Canyon, Hart Mountain Refuge, Maui, Ranch Outing near Bly, Rogue River Trail, Timberline Trail, Tillamook National Forest, Wallowa Ski Outing, and Panama.

The Trail Trips Committee, chaired by Dean Kokko, sponsors the increasingly popular Street Rambles on Tuesday and Thursday evenings in Portland parks and streets. Participants pay a fee of $2 for hikes and $1 for Street Rambles. As in the outing and climbing programs, leaders are required to have first-aid certification.

The Expedition Committee, chaired by Steven A. Warner, granted funds to six expeditions: to Monte Smith and Jerry Eline to support the 2001 Polish Glacier Expedition; Andrew Lewis and Steven A. Warner for attempts on Artesonraju and Huascaran in Peru; Carl Degner, James Brewer, David Byrne, and Ron Fridel for the West Buttress of Mount McKinley; Keith and Charles Daellenbach, John Parsons, and Allen Throop for a ski touring expedition on the Juneau Icefield; Bob Wilson and Eric Hoem for a climbing survey in the Cordillera Blanca in Peru; James Armstrong, Michael DeLaune, Marty Scott, and Shirley Welch for climbing and trekking to Mera Peak and Imje Tse (Island Peak) in Nepal. The Committee hosted Kurt Diemberger with his showing of Summits and Secrets, which proved to be a profitable fundraiser for expedition grants.

At the Mazama Lodge, Todd and Wendy Koebke ended a year as lodge managers, and Lisa Davis moved into the lodge to assume duties in registration, maintenance, and light cooking. Todd Koebke serves as weekend chef.

Doug Wilson succeeded Dr. Christine Mackert as President of The Mazamas. Josh Lockerby was elected vice president; Mary Stadler, membership secretary; David Sauerbrey, recording secretary; Susan Pyle Ericksen, treasurer.

JACK GRAUER, *Historian*

THE ARIZONA MOUNTAINEERING CLUB. The AzMC's membership totaled 518 at year-end 2001. Much of the club's volunteer administrative effort went into reviewing and updating club policies and guidelines, and considering various risk management issues. The club graduated 81 individuals through its Basic Rock School, 56 through its Anchors and Advanced Ropework School, and 31 through its Lead School. A similar number of "assistant instructors" returned to help teach these courses. In addition, over 20 members took Basic Ice Climbing, and 12 joined club-sponsored multi-pitch ice climbing outings.

The basic snow skills class, Glacier Travel and Crevasse Rescue, was again replete with 20 AzMC'ers hanging over imaginary crevasses, but on real snow achors built by student teams. Other special interest offerings in Map and Compass, Wilderness First Aid, and Basic Survival attracted significant participation.

The club continued its tradition of volunteerism with members spending many hours picking up trash in the Queen Creek area and at the Grand Canyon. Volunteers also helped introduce local Hispanic youth organizations to rock climbing.

The club continues to monitor local access issues and has been involved in the forefront of such issues across Arizona. In the near future the City of Scottsdale is expected to open Pinnacle Peak Park, a mainstay in the portfolio of local granite cragging available under the desert sun.

For further information, contact:
Arizona Mountaineering Club
c/o Erik Filsinger, Ph.D., President
10212 E. Charter Oak Drive
Scottsdale, AZ 85260
E-mail: president@azmountaineeringclub.org
Web: http:// www.azmountaineeringclub.org

AAC, CENTRAL ROCKIES SECTION. The principal 2001 activities of the Central Rockies Section are highlighted as follows:

January: The Section donated $300 to the Ice Climbers Festival at Ouray, CO. Members provided support services as belayers. This event has assembled ice climbers from all over the world and introduced many neophytes to the wonderful world of sport-ice climbing in a generally safe environment just a walk from the hotel. Our Section also has assisted with the Chix With Pix program.

March: The Section donated $500 to the Central Asia Institute. This organization helps provide schools for girls and sanitation construction projects for the Balti people of central Pakistan. Greg Mortenson has led the world and climbers to the doorstep of the Balti people in a grand thank-you effort to their porters of so many expeditions.

June: Visiting climber Jeff Alzner from Portland, OR, gave three slide shows in Golden, Boulder, and Fort Collins, CO, as a Section benefit. His program was a retrospective of his 2000 attempt on the north ridge of K2. Along with corporate sponsorship from Polartec and Cody Ice, we hosted the main event at the American Mountaineering Center. It was a big success with money raised to support Section activities throughout the year.

July: The 14th annual International Climber's Festival was held in Lander,WY. This is the fourth year we've attended and supported this summer fun festival. Many AAC members

attended, and the Section staffed a booth. The folks had a chance to meet and greet AAC members and interact with our Club of like-minded climbers.

September: The Section donated $300 to the Longs Peak Reunion, where guides of yesterday and climbers of today gathered to celebrate a long history of climbing on Colorado's Longs Peak. A wonderful series of slide programs was offered in the Estes Park High School auditorium, and a banquet dinner was held at the Aspen Lodge with grand views of the Diamond Face of Longs Peak.

October: The Access Fund has created a national program called Adopt-A-Crag. In support of the program, 20 members, friends, National Park employees, and two of the Club's office staff gathered at Lumpy Ridge in Estes Park to create a new climbers' descent trail off the formidable Sundance Buttress. We shaped 800 vertical feet of alpine trail in the steep east gully. Below the formation, team members also installed 64 timber water-bars to control erosion. We hope this is the first of many partnering projects with the Access Fund.

November: The Section purchased metal signs for the new AAC Hut System. These are being sold to new huts throughout the country. The Section currently has four huts at Ouray and Estes Park, CO, and at Cody and the Teton Climbers Ranch, WY.

December: The Section is working with organizers in Cody, WY, to promote their new Ice Round Up climbers festival. Working with the locals, we hope to enhance their show and public awareness of AAC membership benefits and, most importantly, to have fun climbing.

Annually, funds are expended ($120) to provide our members with an e-mail List Service. This is open for all members to post news, sales, events, shows, projects, outings, current events, or any climbing related issues. The Chairman moderates and filters use to deny any spam or advertising. A Section Web site is also maintained at http://crs.alpineclub.org.

GREG SIEVERS, *Chair*

AAC, NORTH CENTRAL SECTION. Our Section continues to grow after several inactive years without a chair. The Web site was up and running the entire year and has proven to be valuable in spreading information around the Section. Climbers have used the message board to set up trips, communicate problems, and just discuss climbing generally in our area.

A small but dedicated group of seven attended a clean-up day at Blue Mounds State Park in Luverne, MN. We cleaned the area in the morning, climbed in the afternoon, and barbequed in the evening. This park with some notable climbs is at about the geographic center of our Section, and we will continue meeting there in June. Certainly Taylors Falls, the Black Hills, and the North Shore are more popular climbing areas, but Blue Mounds is fair for everyone.

The Taylors Falls area, which is the closest climbing area to the Twin Cities, suffered a major slide, resulting in closure of the Minnesota side. The Wisconsin side remains open. The chairman has been working with the Minnesota Department of Natural Resources in an effort to reopen access to this heavily used area.

A number of Section members attended the annual AAC meeting at Snowbird, UT. While there, taking early time out from skiing one day, we discussed ways to promote our Section's growth. Immediate plans include issuing a Section directory and continuing to upgrade the Web site: http://ncs.alpineclub.org.

SCOTT CHRISTENSEN, *Chairman*

AAC, NEW YORK SECTION. The events of 9/11 here in New York overwhelmed everything else that had transpired before or since in the Section. Virtually everyone knew someone or had friends who were directly affected by the tragedy. Particularly gratifying were the countless letters, phone calls, and e-mails we New Yorkers received from concerned friends from all over the world. September 11 and its aftermath also brought a much needed sense of perspective on the truly important things in life—family and friends—which are sometimes forgotten in the often trivial pursuits of day-to-day existence.

It was with a heightened sense of family, mutual support, and the "fellowship of the rope," as Gaston Rebuffat so aptly called it, that a record 160 members and guests gathered on September 29 for our 22nd Annual Black Tie Dinner. Fortunately our special guest speaker, Erik Weihenmayer, the 32-year-old blind climber who had recently summited Everest, was clearly up to the task of delivering an inspirational, yet witty, presentation that resonated perfectly with the difficult occasion. Erik spoke of not accepting limitations and of the importance of team-work in accomplishing difficult goals. To emphasize the point, he was accompanied by the members of his Everest team, whom he had invited from Colorado to share this special moment with him. Also on the program were two other New Yorkers, Sherman and Brad Bull, who were both part of Erik's team and who also reached the top. At the age of 64 and on his fifth attempt, Sherman set a new age record on the mountain. The Dinner was run as a fundraiser both for the AAC Library and the Twin Towers Fund to benefit needy survivors of the WTC tragedy. Almost $9,000 was raised for both causes, thanks in part to a successful silent auction of climbing equipment, gear, and other valuable items. Finally, we introduced and gently "roasted" 14 new members whom we presented with their membership pins.

In addition, during the year, Section members enjoyed traditional winter and spring climbing outings in the Adirondacks, an organized conditioning hike or two in the Hudson Highlands and Catskills, and a particularly successful "Top Rope" social in the Shawangunks. A crisp October day of 5.7 to 5.11 climbing was followed by a delicious BBQ at Ralph Erenzo's "Bunks in the Gunks" in nearby Gardiner. The event was organized by Jack Reilly.

In early June the Section co-sponsored *Alpinfilm*, the 12th annual New York International Mountain Film Festival. A juried competition with cash prizes for winning films, the festival attracts adventure and climbing films from all over the world and serves as a Spring rendezvous for New York's diverse climbing community. The Rolex Award for best film of the festival went to a French production, *The Great Traverse*, about the attempt of two French explorers to ski unsupported from Siberia to Canada via the North Pole. A pre-theater cocktail party and dinner preceded the event.

Before closing, we wish to express our sincerest condolences to the families of members Walt Noonan, who lost his son in the WTC tragedy, and Larry Huntington, who lost his brother-in-law there as well. Also we mourn the passing of long-time member Art Peters, who passed away in June at the age of 81. Art was a true Renaissance man, climber, and scholar who had authored books as diverse as a biography of Jean Cocteau and *Seven Trails West*, about the Lewis and Clark and other great Western expeditions. Art was a close friend of Gaston Rebuffat, translated his works into English, and introduced him at a memorable NY Section Dinner in 1982. He is survived by his wife, Sally, three children, and six grandchildren.

For current information on New York Section events, do log on to our Web site http://nys.alpineclub.org. Our webmaster, Vaclav (Vic) Benes, is always on the lookout for new stories and photos. So keep them coming!

PHILIP ERARD, *Chair*

AAC, NEW ENGLAND SECTION. The highlight of formal activity was the Section's Sixth Annual Dinner, a black-tie event attended by 93 members and their guests. Everyone, as seems usual, had a good time, and we increased our Henderson Film Fund to $3,000. This is enough funding to start serious planning for archiving and distribution.

John Middendorf from Flagstaff, Arizona, and of big wall Fame, gave an exciting digitally displayed account of big wall climbing around the globe. John was conveniently available at Harvard attending the Graduate School of Design. Hardie Truesdale of the Gunks exhibited many of his beautiful digitally rendered photographs of "The Gunks and Beyond." We auctioned off one photo, and Hardie was happy to have sold several others.

Signed copies of Ed Webster's *Snow in the Kingdom* were available for sale, and a special-expedition-signed edition was auctioned. Phil Erard of New York was the high bidder for what he deemed a real steal. He told us he would take it to his next New York Section Dinner and "auction it there for five times the price—and that's called 'arbitrage,'" he said.

Other items of interest to report for the Section, which increased by 54 members in 2001, included remembering our own Kenneth Henderson, who died at age 96 in September. He was celebrated in Lebanon Center, New Hampshire, on October 13. Representing the AAC were Jed Williamson, Sam Streibert, and Bill Atkinson, who offered remembrances.

Al Hospers of North Conway continues to e-publish and seeks subscribers to his weekly up-country climbing report at www.neclimbs.com. Out West our Rick Merritt, with New York's Bill Guida, reports having climbed Idaho's highest, Mt. Borah (12,662'), by the "Chicken Out" ridge where smoke from wild fires compromised the summit view. Eric Engberg, characteristically, flashed an all-encompassing 10-day California trip with his son Zeb, taking in Lover's Leap, Tuolumne Meadows (Fairview Dome), Yosemite Valley (Royal Arches), Rock Creek, and the Buttermilks near Bishop.

Nancy Savickas, Makoto Takeuchi, and Dick Doucette met Isabel Bey in Switzerland and together explored the Jungfraujoch and climbed many limestone routes in southern Switzerland. I (Bill), with the patient support of Brian Fulton, elevated my old bones to 3000m on the Aiguille du Moine (3412m) from the Couvercle Hut and to the summit of the Aiguille du Tour (3542m), in the Chamonix area.

BILL ATKINSON, CHAIR, AND NANCY SAVICKAS, *Vice Chair*

AAC, ALASKA SECTION. The Alaska Section got a jolt of energy from the AAC Board Meeting in Anchorage in April 2001. I was chosen as the new chair just before the board meeting. During the rest of the year, I worked to renew interest in the Club and its activities. In November a semi-annual meeting was held in Anchorage at the Mexico in Alaska Restaurant, with a larger contingent attending a slide show that followed at the Alaska Rock Gym. During the meeting the positions of vice president, secretary/treasurer, and access coordinator were filled. The Section has scheduled monthly slide shows at Alaska Mountaineering and Hiking in Anchorage to promote the AAC. We now have agreements from five air taxis to provide Club members with 10- to 20-percent discounts on charter services. We are also working more closely with the other local climbing clubs including the Mountaineering Club of Alaska, a local club with over 600 members.

During the AAC board of directors meeting in Anchorage in April, a number of access issues concerning Alaska were discussed. A special committee, to be chaired by Steve Davis, was established specifically for Denali National Park issues. The Backcountry Management Plan and a Rescue Fee Cost Recovery Study were both under review in 2001.

Members were active climbing not only in Alaska, but throughout the world. A number of new routes and first ascents were completed within Alaska. Dave Hart and Paul Berry were part of a multi-national team on Broad Peak (8047m) in the Karakoram in June and July. They reached the summit via the west ridge, and two others reached the fore-summit (8013m) on July 22.

DANNY KOST, *Chair*

MOUNTAINEERING CLUB OF ALASKA. The Mountaineering Club of Alaska had approximately 600 members in 2001. The club held monthly meetings that featured slide shows on Mt. Everest, exploring the Talkeetna Mountains, Wood Tikchik State Park, Mt. Blackburn and Mt. Sanford, Antarctica, climbs in the Tordrillo Mountains, mountain photography, Mt. Foraker, and the first winter ascent of Denali, by Vern Tejas. The club also offered 37 hiking and climbing trips and over 10 different training courses to its members during the past year. The vast majority of club-sponsored trips were in the Chugach, Talkeetna, and Kenai Mountains of south-central Alaska. Through the combined efforts of Steve Parry, Gary Runa, and other volunteer instructors, the club's Training Committee offered instruction in ice climbing, winter camping and survival, glacier travel and crevasse rescue, basic mountaineering, knot-tying, avalanche hazard recognition, telemark skiing, and trip-leader training.

At the request of the Hut Committee, the board acted to address growing concerns over the disposal of human waste at several of the MCA's backcountry huts. The board voted to pursue a grant and to use several member-donations to purchase EPA-approved "Restop" Human Solid

Waste disposal systems manufactured by Innotek, Inc., for our huts in the Chugach Mountains. The Restop system consists of a "bag and bucket" setup that uses special polymers and enzymes to encapsulate and then break down waste within the bag. The systems will be installed at four club huts in the spring and summer of 2002.

The MCA established two new awards in 2001: a President's Award to recognize member contributions to club projects and events in the past calendar year, and a prestigious award named in honor of Vin and Grace Hoeman to recognize persons who have made significant contributions to the exploration, documentation, and promotion of hiking and climbing opportunities in Alaska's mountain ranges.

In terms of community development, the club continued discussions with Chugach State Park regarding the issue of ownership and liability regarding the three mountain huts located along the Eklutna Traverse in the park. Work was completed on the new Serenity Falls Cabin in Chugach State Park– a multi-use public cabin project built by MCA members and volunteers from other local user groups with grant funds solicited by the MCA. Members also continued trail clearing activities on the Gold Mint Trail in partnership with Alaska State Parks, as well as in Sheep Creek Valley of Chugach State Park. Members also assisted the Boy Scouts with their Freeze-a Ree 2001 winter camping event by offering training to groups of scouts on winter survival and winter camping equipment.

Other issues addressed by the club in 2001 included development of a task force to consider growing commercial (guide) use of the club's backcountry huts during the prime climbing seasons. A draft commercial use policy was developed, and the club is clarifying the legal standing of the huts with the State of Alaska in order to devise strategies for addressing growth in occupation of the huts by commercial guides. The club also met with the National Park Service several times to discuss the proposed Denali Rescue Cost Recovery study ordered by Congress as well as the Denali Backcountry Management Plan that is under development.

BILL ROMBERG

AAC, SIERRA NEVADA SECTION. The work of Chairman Steve Schneider, Jane Koski, Tadeusz Gladczenko, Tony Watkin, Paul Romero, and others was reflected in the fact that our section grew to over 900 members by year's end. A brief wrap-up of the year's activities: Traditional Sierra Nevada Ski Weekend, March 24-25; section meeting at Steve Schneider's house, April 11; Owens River Gorge outing April 21-22 near Bishop; Lovers Leap climbing trip July 27-29; Goran Kropp slide show July 11 in San Francisco.

During April through October, new programs were launched in Yosemite: Yosemite Climbers Interpretation program, Camp 4 Coffee Conferences, and Camp 4 Fireside Chats.

George Gluck and his amazing Volunteers in Parks crews finished the new Wilderness Center in Tuolumne Meadows in September. This building is a testament to the dedication and strength of climbers willing to make a positive difference in Yosemite.

Section members Tom Frost, Dick Duane, George Gluck, and Linda McMillan are working to establish a Yosemite Climbers Ranch and Campground on U.S. Forest Service land adjacent to Yosemite National Park. Our preferred site would be about 20 minutes from Yosemite Valley. We are convinced that such a campground would easily serve the missions of the USFS, NPS, and AAC. A formal proposal is now being developed by the Yosemite Committee for discussion with the local Forest Service administrators.

Linda McMillan

CONTRIBUTORS' GUIDELINES

The *American Alpine Journal* records the significant climbing accomplishments of the world in an annual volume. We encourage climbers to submit brief (250-500 words) factual accounts of their climbs and expeditions. While we welcome submissions in a variety of forms, contributors are encouraged to follow certain guidelines when submitting materials. Accounts should be submitted by e-mail whenever possible. Alternatively, submit accounts by regular post on CD, zip, or floppy disk. And provide complete contact information, including e-mail address, postal address, fax, and phone. Please include your club affiliation when submitting accounts.

Deadlines for all accounts are February 1 for the preceding calendar year of January 1 to December 31. For Patagonian climbs, the deadline is extended to February 15. Best is to supply submissions immediately after your climb, or as soon as possible thereafter.

We encourage contributors to submit relevant photographs; we accept both black-and-white and color slides and prints. When submitting an image to show a route line, we ask that you submit the image along with a photo- or laser-copy and draw the lines in on the copy. Please do not draw directly on the photograph. Photos on CDs are also welcome. Scans should be top quality, preferably 300 dpi at a 6-inch by 9-inch scale (15 cm by 23 cm). Smaller scans can only be used for smaller photos in the *AAJ*. With all photos, please caption thoroughly and clearly and include your name and return address.

We prefer original slides and artwork. Duplicates should be reproduction quality. Please send all images via registered mail. The AAC is not responsible for images lost or damaged in the mail. Topos and maps are also encouraged; camera-ready original copies are necessary for quality reproduction.

We do not pay for accounts or lead articles. Those accounts from which we publish a photograph will receive a complimentary copy of the *Journal*. Authors of lead articles and the photographer of the cover photo will receive a one-year complimentary membership to The American Alpine Club.

All *AAJ* submissions are subject to reprinting in other forms by the American Alpine Club, including but not limited to electronic versions of *AAJ* material in the form of CD sets and on our web sites.

Please address all correspondences to:

The American Alpine Journal
710 Tenth Street
Golden, Colorado 80401
Tel.: (303) 384 0110
Fax: (303) 384 0111
E-mail:aaj@americanalpineclub.org
http://www.americanalpineclub.org

INDEX

COMPILED BY JESSICA KANY

C

I

J

P

P2 (Nepal Himalaya) 406
Paa Daeng (Laos) 438
Pahud, Jacques 311-312
Painted Wall (Black Canyon of the Gunnison, Colorado) 215-216
Pakistan Climbs and Expeditions 362-375
Panarese, Peter J. 458
Palcanaju Oeste (Cordillera Blanca, Peru) 301
Palmer, Howard 37, **57**
Pamiagdluk Island (South Greenland) 277-278
Panch Chuli III (Kumaun, India) 394
Pangong Range (Ladakh, India) 378-379
Parkin, Andy 81, 334-337, **336**
Parnell, Ian 88, 100-107, 226, 228
Parrot Beak Peak (Cirque of Unclimbables, Canada) *art.* 116-125, 259
Passu Sar (Pakistan Karakoram) 364
Peak 10,370' (Ruth Gorge, Alaska) 233-236, 234
Peak 11,000+' (Wrangell Mountains, Alaska) 247-248
Peak 11,300' (Ruth Gorge, Alaska) 233-236
Peak 12,360' (Hayes Range, Alaska) 223
Peak 5,376m (Northern Andes, Chile) 328
Peak 6,070m (Northern Andes, Chile) 328
Peak 6,281' (Indian Karakoram) 157
Peak 8,778' (Wrangell Mountains, Alaska) 249
Peak 9,035' (Wrangell Mountains, AK) 247-249
Peak 9,072' (Wrangell Mountains, Alaska) 249
Peak 9,200'+ (Wrangell Mountains, Alaska) 249
Peak 9,400' (Wrangell Mountains, AK) 247-249
Peck, Annie Smith 36
Pecking Order (Parrot Beak Peak, Cirque of Unclimbables) *art.* 116-125, 259
Pennings, Allison 332
Pennings, Michael 207-209, 332
Peri Himal (Nepal) 404-405
Peru Climbs and Expeditions 294-307
Pfingsten, Bridwell 236
Pfingsten, Spencer 236
Phenocryst Spire (Logan Mountains, Can.) 261
Phillips, Evan 250
Pickles, Jason 200-201
Pilling, Bill 255

Pingo Valley (Chile) 333
Pinnacle Peak (Indian Himalaya) 18-19
Poincenot, Aguja 323-327
Porter, Charlie 126-133
Porvaznik, Jan 75
Porzak, Glenn Edward *art.* 64
Potter, Dean 127, 200, 203-204, 321-323
Potter, Layne 212
Prezelj, Marko 82, *art.* 86-99,226, 387-390
Proboscis (Cirque of Unclimbables, Canada) *art.* 116-125, 127, 259-261
Project Mayhem (Mt. Thor, Baffin Island) *art.* 134-143, 258
Pt. 10,002' a.k.a. Mt. Bandaloop (Sierra Nevada, California) 206
Pumori (Nepal Himalaya) 409-410
Puna de Atacama (Northern Andes, Chile) 328
Punta Nunna (Cordillera Blanca, Peru) 303
Purcell Mountains (Canada) 265-267
Puryear, Joseph 199
Putnam, Judge Harrington **56**
Putnam, William Lowell, 47, 52, *art.* **61**
Pyramide de Garcilaso (Cordillera Blanca, Peru) 294-295

Q

Qualizza, Hervé 362-364

R

Raksha Urai (Nepal Himalaya) **401**-403
Ramjak (Lahaul, India) 382
Rayon, Alejandro Perez 292-293
Read, Colin 281
Reclus (Northern Andes, Chile) 328
Red Beard, Mt. (Yentna Glacier, Alaska) 237-238
Red Sea Mountains (Egypt) 347-349
Regenold, Stephen *art.* 461-462
Reeves, Mark 261
Reichardt, Louis 27, *art.* 66
Reichel, Max 205
Reisenhofer, Glenn 77